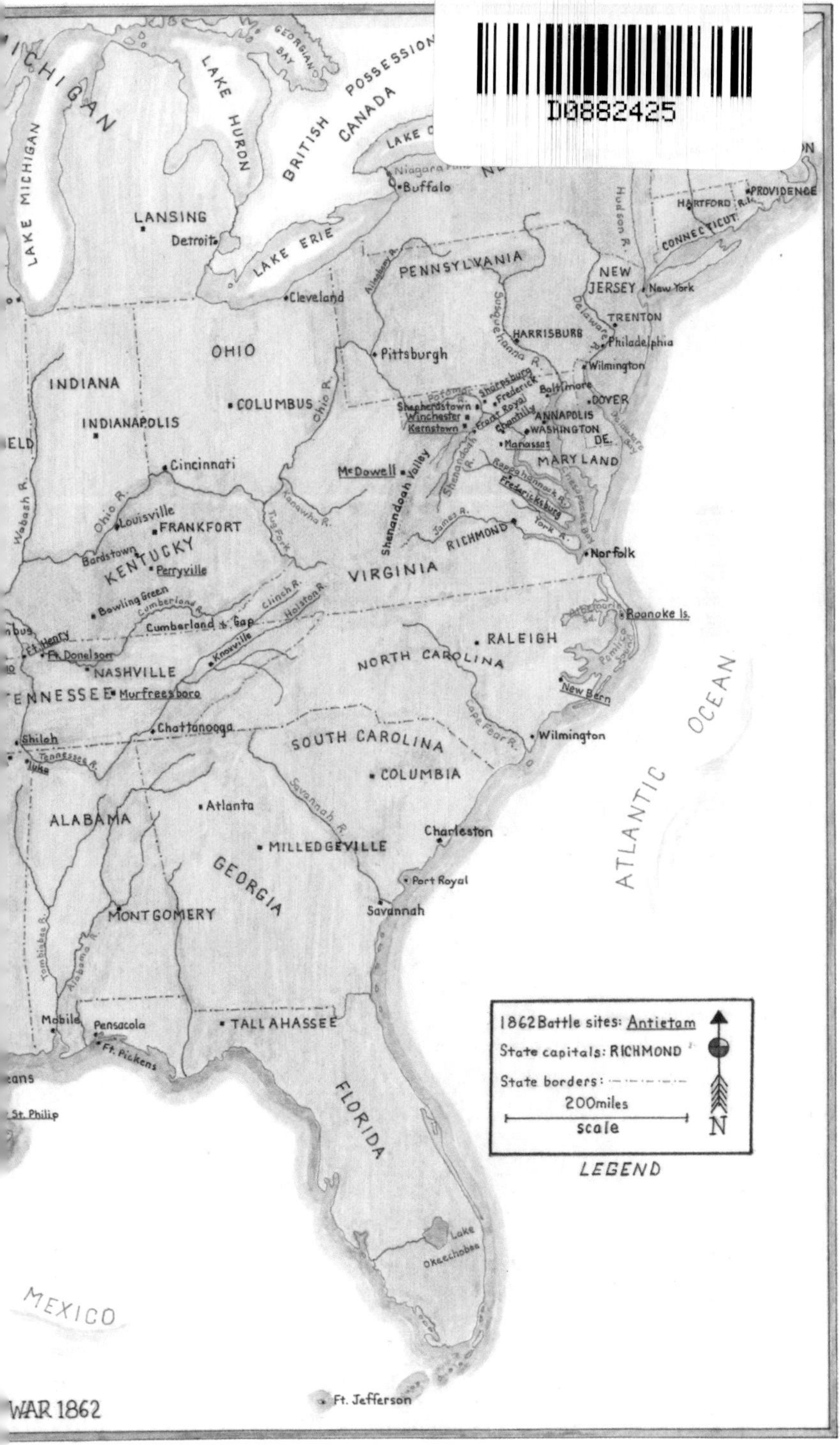

MICHIGAN
LAKE MICHIGAN
LAKE HURON
GEORGIAN BAY
BRITISH POSSESSION
CANADA
LAKE ERIE
Niagara Falls
Buffalo
LANSING
Detroit
PROVIDENCE
HARTFORD
R.I.
CONNECTICUT
Hudson R.
PENNSYLVANIA
NEW JERSEY
New York
TRENTON
Philadelphia
Wilmington
HARRISBURG
Susquehanna R.
Delaware R.
Allegheny R.
Cleveland
Pittsburgh
OHIO
COLUMBUS
Ohio R.
INDIANA
INDIANAPOLIS
Cincinnati
Wabash R.
Louisville
FRANKFORT
Bardstown
KENTUCKY
Perryville
Bowling Green
Cumberland R.
Cumberland Gap
Clinch R.
Holston R.
Knoxville
Ft. Henry
Ft. Donelson
NASHVILLE
TENNESSEE
Murfreesboro
Chattanooga
Shiloh
Iuka
Tennessee R.
Sharpsburg
Frederick
Front Royal
Chantilly
Shepherdstown
Winchester
Kernstown
Baltimore
ANNAPOLIS
WASHINGTON
DOVER
DE.
Manassas
MARYLAND
Delaware Bay
Potomac R.
Shenandoah R.
Rappahannock R.
Fredericksburg
Chesapeake Bay
York R.
James R.
RICHMOND
Norfolk
McDowell
Shenandoah Valley
Kanawha R.
Tug Fork
VIRGINIA
Albemarle Sd.
Roanoke Is.
Pamlico Sound
RALEIGH
NORTH CAROLINA
New Bern
Cape Fear R.
Wilmington
SOUTH CAROLINA
COLUMBIA
Savannah R.
Charleston
Port Royal
Savannah
Atlanta
MILLEDGEVILLE
GEORGIA
ALABAMA
MONTGOMERY
Tombigbee R.
Alabama R.
Mobile
Pensacola
Ft. Pickens
TALLAHASSEE
FLORIDA
Lake Okeechobee
Ft. Jefferson
MEXICO
ATLANTIC OCEAN
St. Philip
1862 Battle sites: Antietam
State capitals: RICHMOND
State borders:
200miles
scale
N
LEGEND
WAR 1862

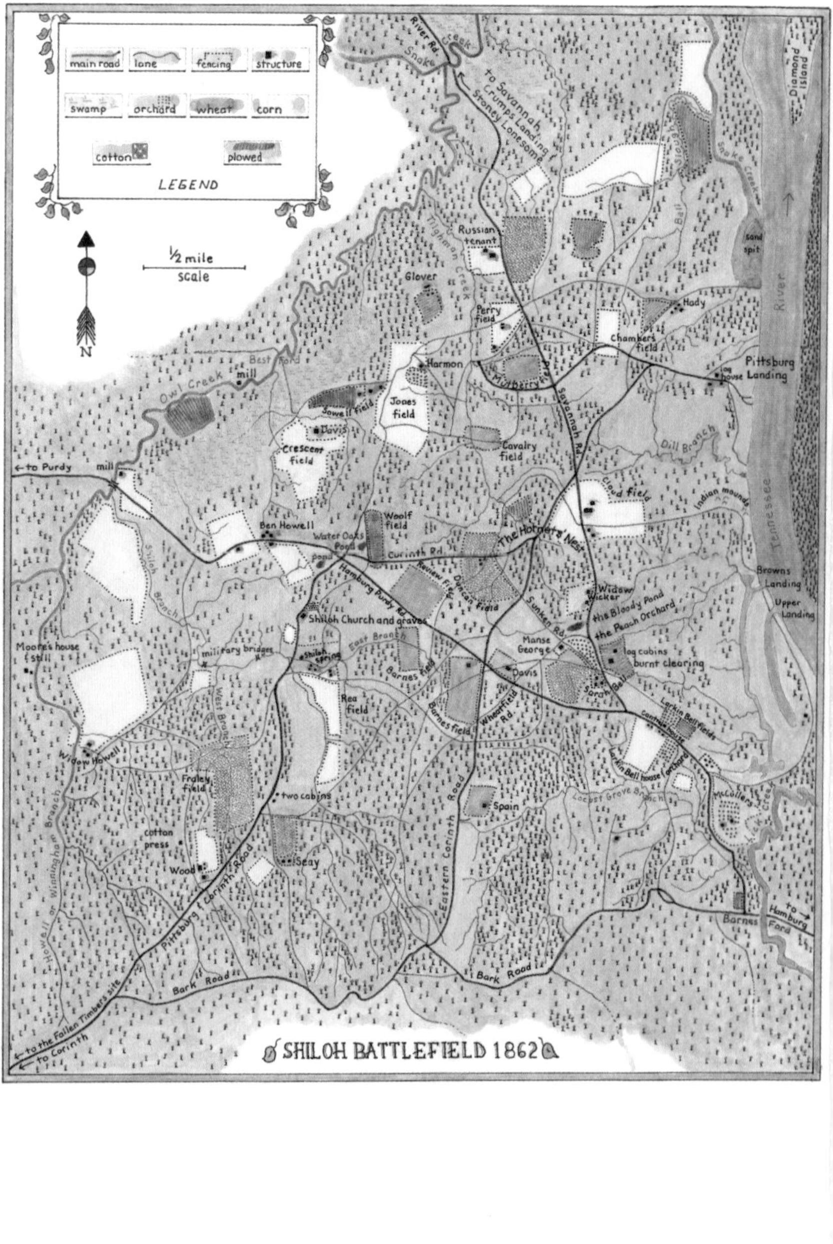
main road
lane
fencing
structure
swamp
orchard
wheat
corn
cotton
plowed
LEGEND
1/2 mile
scale
N
River Rd.
Snake Creek
to Savannah
Crumps Landing
Stoney Lonesome
Diamond Island
Slough
Snake Creek
Sand spit
River
Tennessee
Russian tenant
Glover
Tighman Creek
Perry field
Hady
Chambers field
Pittsburg Landing
log house
Best Ford
Owl Creek
mill
Harmon
Mulberry Rd.
Savannah Rd.
Sowell field
Jones field
Davis
Crescent field
Cavalry field
Dill Branch
Cloud field
Indian mounds
← to Purdy
mill
Ben Howell
Woolf field
Water Oaks Pond
pond
Corinth Rd.
The Hornet's Nest
Shiloh Branch
Hamburg Purdy Rd.
Review field
Duncan field
Sunken Rd.
Widow Bicker
the Bloody Pond
the Peach Orchard
Browns Landing
Upper Landing
Shiloh Church and graves
Moore's house
still
military bridges
Shiloh spring
East Branch
Manse George
log cabins
burnt clearing
Barnes field
Davis
Sarah Bell
West Branch
Rea field
Barnes field
Wheatfield Rd.
Larkin Bell fields
Larkin Bell house | orchard
Widow Howell
Fraley field
two cabins
Spain
Locust Grove Branch
McCullers
Lick Creek
cotton press
Wood
Seay
Eastern Corinth Road
Pittsburg | Corinth Road
Howell or Winningham Branch
Bark Road
Bark Road
Barnes Ford
to Hamburg
← to the Fallen Timbers site
← to Corinth
SHILOH BATTLEFIELD 1862

THE CIVIL WAR

THE SECOND YEAR

THE CIVIL WAR

THE SECOND YEAR TOLD BY THOSE WHO LIVED IT

Stephen W. Sears, editor

THE LIBRARY OF AMERICA

See Note on the Texts on page 798 for acknowledgments.

The paper used in this publication meets the
minimum requirements of the American National Standard for
Information Sciences–Permanence of Paper for Printed
Library Materials, ANSI Z39.48–1984.

Distributed to the trade in the United States
by Penguin Random House Inc.
and in Canada by Penguin Random House Canada Ltd.

Library of Congress Control Number: 2011927424
ISBN 978-1-59853-144-2

Second Printing
The Library of America—221

Manufactured in the United States of America

The Civil War:
The Second Year Told by Those Who Lived It
is published with support from

THE ANDREW W. MELLON FOUNDATION

and

THE NATIONAL ENDOWMENT
FOR THE HUMANITIES

The Civil War: The Second Year Told by Those Who Lived It
is kept in print by a gift from

THE BERKLEY FOUNDATION

to the Guardians of American Letters Fund,
established by The Library of America
to ensure that every volume in the series
will be permanently available.

Contents

Preface

> "Has there ever been another historical crisis of the magnitude of 1861–65 in which so many people were so articulate?"
>
> —Edmund Wilson

THIS Library of America volume is the second in a four-volume series bringing together memorable and significant writing by participants in the American Civil War. Each volume in the series covers approximately one year of the conflict, from the election of Abraham Lincoln in November 1860 to the end of the war in the spring of 1865, and presents a chronological selection of documents from the broadest possible range of authoritative sources—diaries, letters, speeches, military reports, newspaper articles, memoirs, poems, and public papers. Drawing upon an immense and unique body of American writing, the series offers a narrative of the war years that encompasses military and political events and their social and personal reverberations. Created by persons of every class and condition, the writing included here captures the American nation and the American language in the crucial period of their modern formation. Selections have been chosen for their historical significance, their literary quality, and their narrative energy, and are printed from the best available sources. The goal has been to shape a narrative that is both broad and balanced in scope, while at the same time doing justice to the number and diversity of voices and perspectives preserved for us in the writing of the era.

Introduction

PRESIDENT Lincoln began 1862 deeply troubled by the state of the Union, and on January 10 he called a group of advisors and generals to the White House. "The President was greatly disturbed at the state of affairs," wrote one of his listeners, General Irvin McDowell. "Spoke of the exhausted condition of the Treasury; of the loss of public credit; of the Jacobinism in Congress; of the delicate condition of our foreign relations; of the bad news he had received from the West . . . but, more than all, the sickness of General McClellan." The general-in-chief was laid low by typhoid fever, and if something was not done soon, said the President, "the bottom would be out of the whole affair. . . ."

At the other White House, in Richmond, at a cabinet meeting in February, President Davis found the state of the Confederacy equally disturbing. By report, defenses were crumbling east and west, Attorney General Thomas Bragg entered in his diary. "The Pres't said the time had come for diminishing the extent of our lines—that we had not men in the field to hold them and we must fall back." Bragg wondered: "Will the Gov't endure? Can we repel the enemy? Dangers surround us & it commences at our darkest period since the war began."

During the year since the secession of eleven Southern states brought the nation to war with itself, the two presidents had struggled to build, shape, and direct the machinery of war—not a conventional war against a foreign power but a civil war that was by nature peculiarly claustrophobic. Jefferson Davis, for example, felt increasingly hemmed in by enemy incursions wherever he looked.

For Southerners the Union blockade of the Atlantic and Gulf coasts had grown through 1861 from a nuisance to a serious concern, and the Federals' seizure of Port Royal Sound in South Carolina in November gained the blockaders an operational base. Further incursions on both coasts seemed certain in the new year. Confederate efforts in 1861 to wean the border state of Kentucky away from neutrality had resulted in the creation of a thin, largely undermanned defensive line across the state that President Davis discovered he lacked the resources to strengthen. Indeed, Attorney General Bragg's gloomy outlook was brought on by the Yankees breaching this Kentucky line and pressing far up the Tennessee and Cumberland rivers. In the Trans-Mississippi the Rebels' victory at Wilson's Creek in Missouri in August 1861 had not proved decisive enough to secure that border state for the South; certainly the fight would be renewed in 1862, and for Arkansas as well.

Davis's admission that he must draw in his lines applied most immediately to Virginia. The South's stunning victory at Manassas in July 1861, and a second, lesser victory at Ball's Bluff on the upper Potomac in October, had raised hopes for maintaining the Potomac as the Confederacy's northern frontier. The new year dashed such hopes. Keeping Joseph E. Johnston's army at Manassas was no longer tenable in the face of the huge Yankee buildup of forces at Washington. Johnston must fall back to a safer posting. The Confederacy started 1862 on the defensive everywhere.

Lincoln might not feel hemmed in by enemy armies as was Davis, but still he was much constricted by an array of forces, domestic and foreign. His catalog of complaints that January 10 was real. As 1861 turned to 1862, the Union war machine was stalled, making it difficult for the Treasury to find money and credit to support it. The Congress that convened in December was dominated by radical Republicans—to some they raised echoes of the Jacobins of the French Revolution—who challenged the administration's war policies, a challenge given teeth by the investigative Joint Committee on the Conduct of the War. Relations with Great Britain had been badly strained in November when two Confederate envoys were taken off the British steamer *Trent* by U.S.S. *San Jacinto*. The envoys had since been released, but the administration still worried about possible European intervention in the conflict. Lincoln's mention of bad news from the West referred to the continuing reluctance of his generals in the western theater to start moving.

One of the President's more challenging problems was General George B. McClellan. McClellan—dubbed the Young Napoleon by the press—had arrived with fanfare to pick up the pieces after the debacle at Manassas and to resuscitate the

Army of the Potomac. On November 1 McClellan was named general-in-chief of all the Union's armies, replacing Winfield Scott. By the turn of the year, however, McClellan had worn out his welcome through his policy of stubborn inactivity. Confederate cannon closed commerce on the Potomac below Washington, and communications on the upper Potomac were interrupted, leaving the capital to suffer a humiliating partial blockade. McClellan's sole remedial effort ended badly at Ball's Bluff. The typhoid that rendered him hors de combat for some three weeks at the turn of the year brought these problems to a head. Lincoln remarked, according to McDowell, "if General McClellan did not want to use the army, he would like to '*borrow it*,' provided he could see how it could be made to do something."

The Civil War expanded with explosive force in 1862. The rebellion became a war, and by year's end the war became a revolution against slavery. These selections by witnesses to this second year of conflict—their diaries, journals, letters, addresses, essays, memoirs, battle reports, proclamations, newspaper accounts—pick up and develop threads from 1861 and open a number of new ones. The year begins in military stalemate, marks major Union gains in a rush of action, then finds Confederate resistance stiffening. By summer the tide turns, and autumn brings joint Confederate offensives east and west. These invasions crest and fall back. Two Union winter offensives, east and west, end the year as it began, in a military stalemate.

These multiple campaigns took a toll beyond what anyone in that day could have imagined. The tally of the two days at Shiloh on April 6–7 reached 23,700, twice the number of casualties in all the fighting since Fort Sumter. The cost of the Seven Days on the Virginia Peninsula at the end of June came to 36,000. Antietam in Maryland on September 17 was the bloodiest single day of the entire war. The battlefields of 1862 counted at least 208,000 dead, wounded, and captured/missing.

The men who did the fighting on these unprecedented American battlefields have their say in these pages. For many these were the most momentous, unforgettable days of their lives, and whether in letters and diaries or later memoirs, they strove to capture what it had been like. The women who nursed the myriad wounded wanted the world to know their truth as well.

This second year of war marked the first extended test of battlefield commands. Generals rise, flourish, and (some of them) fade away. For the Union, in the western theater, U.S. Grant, William T. Sherman, and William S. Rosecrans show the most gains and the most promise. But their theater commander, Henry W. Halleck, stalls the western war machine. John Pope has his day on the Mississippi; brought east, he comes a cropper in the second battle at Manassas. Don Carlos Buell has *his* day at Perryville in Kentucky, fritters away the victory, and is replaced. In taking New Orleans, Flag Officer David Farragut demonstrates the Union's command of the sea. For the Confederacy, Albert Sidney Johnston seeks at Shiloh to counter Grant's initiative and dies in the attempt. In the autumn Braxton Bragg raises Southern hopes with a drive into Kentucky, then falters and falls back. The western Confederacy ends 1862 where it began, on the defensive, and with that much less to defend.

In the eastern theater, generalship traces a different course. Beginning in April McClellan presses his "grand campaign" on the Peninsula right to the gates of Richmond. His opponent, Joseph E. Johnston, falls wounded on May 31, and afterward remarks, "The shot that struck me down is the very best that has been fired for the Southern cause yet." So it proves. Robert E. Lee takes Johnston's place and alters the course of the war. In less than three months, Lee drives McClellan away from Richmond, whips Pope at Second Manassas, and in September carries the war across the Potomac into Maryland. His invasion is checked by McClellan at Antietam. But McClellan, like Buell in the West, continues to suffer from "the slows" (in Lincoln's phrase) and in due course he too is dismissed. His replacement, Ambrose Burnside, fares ill at Lee's hands at Fredericksburg in December. At year's end only Robert E. Lee is left standing in the eastern theater.

Another, truly revolutionary theme develops in parallel to this landscape of battle in 1862—Abraham Lincoln's sometimes tortuous path to emancipation. Slaves in uncounted numbers cast their votes for emancipation in escaping to Union lines, gaining the status of contraband of war. Congressional confiscation, colonization, plans for compensated emancipation—all have their day before the Emancipation Proclamation is finally promulgated. In his State of the Union message on December 1, Lincoln explains what is at stake for the nation: "In *giving* freedom to the *slave*, we *assure* freedom to the *free*—honorable alike in what we give, and what we preserve. We shall nobly save, or meanly lose, the last best, hope of earth."

Stephen W. Sears

Frederick Douglass: What Shall Be Done with the Slaves If Emancipated?

January 1862

From the beginning of hostilities in April 1861, Frederick Douglass had advocated enlisting black soldiers and had criticized the Lincoln administration for not making the destruction of slavery an essential aim of the war. On January 14, 1862, Douglass warned a Philadelphia audience, "We have attempted to maintain our Union in utter defiance of the moral chemistry of the universe," explaining, "We have sought to bind the chains of slavery on the limbs of the black man, without thinking that at last we should find the other end of that hateful chain about our own necks." That same month, in his journal *Douglass' Monthly*, the nation's leading black abolitionist looked ahead to a time without chains.

It is curious to observe, at this juncture, when the existence of slavery is threatened by an aroused nation, when national necessity is combining with an enlightened sense of justice to put away the huge abomination forever, that the enemies of human liberty are resorting to all the old and ten thousand times refuted objections to emancipation with which they confronted the abolition movement twenty-five years ago. Like the one stated above, these pro-slavery objections have their power mainly in the slavery-engendered prejudice, which every where pervades the country. Like all other great transgressions of the law of eternal rectitude, slavery thus produces an element in the popular and depraved moral sentiment favorable to its own existence. These objections are often urged with a show of sincere solicitude for the welfare of the slaves themselves. It is said, what will you do with them? they can't take care of themselves; they would all come to the North; they would not work; they would become a burden upon the State, and a blot upon society; they'd cut their masters' throats; they would cheapen labor, and crowd out the poor white laborer from employment; their former masters would not employ them, and they would necessarily become vagrants, paupers and criminals, overrunning all our alms houses, jails and prisons. The laboring classes among the whites would come in bitter conflict with them in all the avenues of labor, and regarding them as occupying places and filling positions which should be occupied and filled by white men; a fierce war of races would be the inevitable consequence, and the black race would, of course, (being the weaker,) be exterminated. In view of this frightful, though happily somewhat contradictory picture, the question is asked, and pressed with a great show of earnestness at this momentous crisis of our nation's history, What shall be done with the four million slaves if they are emancipated?

This question has been answered, and can be answered in many ways. Primarily, it is a question less for man than for God —less for human intellect than for the laws of nature to solve. It assumes that nature has erred; that the law of liberty is a mistake; that freedom, though a natural want of the human soul, can only be enjoyed at the expense of human welfare, and that men are better off in slavery than they would or could be in freedom; that slavery is the natural order of human relations, and that liberty is an experiment. What shall be done with them?

Our answer is, do nothing with them; mind your business, and let them mind theirs. Your *doing* with them is their greatest misfortune. They have been undone by your doings, and all they now ask, and really have need of at your hands, is just to let them alone. They suffer by every interference, and succeed best by being let alone. The Negro should have been let alone in Africa—let alone when the pirates and robbers offered him for sale in our Christian slave markets—(more cruel and inhuman than the Mohammedan slave markets)—let alone by courts, judges, politicians, legislators and slave-drivers—let alone altogether, and assured that they were thus to be let alone forever, and that they must now make their own way in the world, just the same as any and every other variety of the human family. As colored men, we only ask to be allowed to *do* with ourselves, subject only to the same great laws for the welfare of human society which apply to other men, Jews, Gentiles, Barbarian, Sythian. Let us stand upon our own legs, work with our own hands, and eat bread in the sweat of our own brows. When you, our white fellow-countrymen, have attempted to do anything for us, it has generally been to deprive us of some right, power or privilege which you yourself would die before you would submit to have taken from you. When the planters of the West Indies used to attempt to puzzle the pure-minded Wilberforce with the question, How shall we get rid of slavery? his simple answer was, "quit stealing." In like manner, we answer those who are perpetually puzzling their brains with questions as to what shall be done with the Negro, "let him alone and mind your own business." If you see him plowing in the open field, leveling the forest, at work with a spade, a rake, a hoe, a pick-axe, or a bill—let him alone; he has a right to work. If you see him on his way to school, with spelling book, geography and arithmetic in his hands—let him alone. Don't shut the door in his face, nor bolt your gates against him; he has a right to learn—let him alone. Don't pass laws to degrade him. If he has a ballot in his hand, and is on his way to the ballot-box to deposit his vote for the man whom he thinks will most justly and wisely administer the Government which has the power of life and death over him, as well as others—let him *alone*; his right of choice as much deserves respect and protection as your own. If you see him on his way to the church, exercising religious liberty in accordance with this or that religious persuasion—let him alone.—Don't meddle with him, nor trouble yourselves with any questions as to what shall be done with him.

The great majority of human duties are of this negative character. If men were born in need of crutches, instead of having legs, the fact would be otherwise. We should then be in need of help, and would require outside aid; but according to the wiser and better arrangement of nature, our duty is done better by not hindering than by helping our fellow-men; or, in other words, the best way to help them is just to let them help themselves.

We would not for one moment check the outgrowth of any benevolent concern for the future welfare of the colored race in America or elsewhere; but in the name of reason and religion, we earnestly plead for justice before all else. Benevolence with justice is harmonious and beautiful; but benevolence without justice is a mockery. Let the American people, who have thus far only kept the colored race staggering between partial philanthropy and cruel force, be induced to try what virtue there is in justice. First pure, then peaceable—first just, then generous.—The sum of the black man's misfortunes and calamities are just here: He is everywhere treated as an exception to all the general rules which should operate in the relations of other men. He is literally scourged beyond the beneficent range of truth and justice.—With all the purifying and liberalizing power of the Christian religion, teaching, as it does, meekness, gentleness, brotherly kindness, those who profess it have not yet even approached the position of treating the black man as an equal man and a brother. The few who have thus far risen to this requirement, both of reason and religion, are stigmatized as fanatics and enthusiasts.

What shall be done with the Negro if emancipated? Deal justly with him. He is a human being, capable of judging between good and evil, right and wrong, liberty and slavery, and is as much a subject of law as any other man; therefore, deal justly with him. He is, like other men, sensible of the motives of reward and punishment. Give him wages for his work, and let hunger pinch him if he don't work. He knows the difference between fullness and famine, plenty and scarcity. "But will he work?" Why should he not? He is used to it. His hands are already hardened by toil, and he has no dreams of ever getting a living by any other means than by hard work. But would you turn them all loose? Certainly! We are no better than our Creator. He has turned them loose, and why should not we?

But would you let them all stay here?—Why not? What better is *here* than *there*? Will they occupy more room as freemen than as slaves? Is the presence of a black freeman less agreeable than that of a black slave? Is an object of our injustice and cruelty a more ungrateful sight than one of your justice and benevolence? You have borne the one more than two hundred years—can't you bear the other long enough to try the experiment? "But would it be safe?" No good reason can be given why it would not be. There is much more reason for apprehension from slavery than from freedom. Slavery provokes and justifies incendiarism, murder, robbery, assassination, and all manner of violence.—But why not let them go off by themselves? That is a matter we would leave exclusively to themselves. Besides, when you, the American people, shall once do justice to the enslaved colored people, you will not want to get rid of them. Take away the motive which slavery supplies for getting rid of the free black people of the South, and there is not a single State, from Maryland to Texas, which would desire to be rid of its black people. Even with the obvious disadvantage to slavery, which such contact is, there is scarcely a slave State which could be carried for the unqualified expulsion of the free colored people. Efforts at such expulsion have been made in Maryland, Virginia and South Carolina, and all have failed, just because the black man as a freeman is a useful member of society. To drive him away, and thus deprive the South of his labor, would be as absurd and monstrous as for a man to cut off his right arm, the better to enable himself to work.

There is one cheering aspect of this revival of the old and threadbare objections to emancipation—it implies at least the presence of danger to the slave system. When slavery was assailed twenty-five years ago, the whole land took the alarm, and every species of argument and subterfuge was resorted to by the defenders of slavery. The mental activity was amazing; all sorts of excuses, political, economical, social, theological and ethnological, were coined into barricades against the advancing march of anti-slavery sentiment. The same activity now shows itself, but has added nothing new to the argument for slavery or against emancipation.—When the accursed slave system shall once be abolished, and the Negro, long cast out from the human family, and governed like a beast of burden, shall be gathered under the divine government of justice, liberty and humanity, men will be ashamed to remember that they were ever deluded by the flimsy nonsense which they have allowed themselves to urge against the freedom of the long enslaved millions of our land. That day is not far off.

"O hasten it in mercy, gracious Heaven!"

John Boston to Elizabeth Boston

John Boston wrote to his wife in Owensville, Maryland, from Upton's Hill in Arlington, Virginia. It is not known if Elizabeth Boston ever received his letter, which soon came into the possession of a committee of the Maryland House of Delegates that was attempting to have fugitive slaves excluded from Union army camps. When the committee wrote to Secretary of War Edwin M. Stanton in March 1862 asking that fugitive slaves be expelled from army camps, it received a reply from Assistant Secretary Peter H. Watson stating that "the alleged harboring" of slaves would receive Stanton's attention "as soon as he is relieved from more important and pressing duties."

Upton Hill January the 12 1862

My Dear Wife it is with grate joy I take this time to let you know Whare I am i am now in Safety in the 14th Regiment of Brooklyn this Day i can Adress you thank god as a free man I had a little truble in giting away But as the lord led the Children of Isrel to the land of Canon So he led me to a land Whare fredom Will rain in spite Of earth and hell Dear you must make your Self content i am free from al the Slavers Lash and as you have chose the Wise plan Of Serving the lord i hope you Will pray Much and i Will try by the help of god To Serv him With all my hart I am With a very nice man and have All that hart Can Wish But My Dear I Cant express my grate desire that i Have to See you i trust the time Will Come When We Shal meet again And if We dont met on earth We Will Meet in heven Whare Jesas ranes Dear Elizabeth tell Mrs Ownees That i trust that She Will Continue Her kindness to you and that god Will Bless her on earth and Save her In grate eternity My Acomplements To Mrs Owens and her Children may They Prosper through life I never Shall forgit her kindness to me Dear Wife i must Close rest yourself Contented i am free i Want you to rite To me Soon as you Can Without Delay Direct your letter to the 14th Reigment New york State malitia Uptons Hill Virginea In Care of Mr Cranford Comary   Write my Dear Soon As you C   Your Affectionate Husban   Kiss Daniel For me

John Boston

Give my love to Father and Mother

"VIGOROUS PROSECUTION OF THE WAR": WASHINGTON, D.C., JANUARY 1862

Salmon P. Chase: Journal, January 6, 1862

In the wake of the Union defeat at Ball's Bluff, Virginia, in October 1861, Congress established the investigative Joint Committee on the Conduct of the War on December 10. The seven-member committee, made up of three senators and four representatives, was dominated by Radical Republicans, including Ohio's Senator Benjamin F. Wade, its chairman. In early January 1862 Major General George B. McClellan, general-in-chief of the Union armies and commander of the Army of the Potomac, fell seriously ill with typhoid fever, leaving the war machine stalled. With a Confederate army camped at Manassas, twenty-five miles southwest of Washington, and Confederate artillery blockading the Potomac River below the city, bellicose committee members initiated a meeting with President Lincoln and his cabinet. As reported by Secretary of the Treasury Salmon P. Chase, they called for a new Army of the Potomac commander, the Radicals' favorite, Irvin McDowell.

MONDAY JANUARY 6TH. Received a note from McClellan's Aid, saying that the General had read the despatch sent him last night, and would take immediate measures to protect the Road; that reinforcements would be immediately sent to Hancock; and that Genl. Banks had been ordered to support Lander.

In fulfillment of engagement with the President of the American Bank Note Company, went to Ulke's, who took a number of Photographs.

Cabinet Meeting held at night to confer with the Joint Committee of the two Houses of Congress on the Conduct of the War. The members of the Committee, especially Messrs. Chandler, Wade, Johnson, Odell and Covode, were very earnest in urging the vigorous prosecution of the War, and in recommending the appointment of Genl. McDowell as Major-General, to command the Army of the Potomac.

A great deal of discussion took place. I expressed my own

views, saying that, in my judgment, Genl. McClellan was the best man for the place he held known to me—that, I believed, if his sickness had not prevented he would by this time have satisfied every body in the country of his efficiency and capacity—that I thought, however, that he tasked himself too severely—that no physical or mental vigor could sustain the strains he imposed on himself, Often on the saddle nearly all day and transacting business at his rooms nearly all night—that, in my judgment, he ought to confer freely with his ablest and most experienced Generals, deriving from them the benefits which their counsels, whether accepted or rejected, would certainly impart, and communicating to them full intelligence of his own plans of action, so that, in the event of sickness or accident to himself, the movements of the army need not necessarily be interrupted or delayed. I added that, in my own opinion, no one person could discharge fitly the special duties of Commander of the Army of the Potomac, and the general duties of Commanding General of the Armies of the United States; and that Genl. McClellan, in undertaking to discharge both, had undertaken what he could not perform.

Much else was said by various gentlemen, and the discussion was concluded by the announcement by the President that he would call on Genl. McClellan, and ascertain his views in respect to the division of the commands.

Abraham Lincoln to Don Carlos Buell and Henry W. Halleck

With General McClellan ill, Lincoln in his role as commander-in-chief sought action from his generals in the western theater. He urged Don Carlos Buell, commander of the Department of the Ohio, to advance into Tennessee, and asked Henry W. Halleck, commander of the Department of Missouri, to support Buell with an attack on the Confederate position at Columbus, Kentucky. When Halleck replied that he was in no condition to support Buell ("I am satisfied that the authorities in Washington do not appreciate the difficulties with which we have to contend here," he wrote), the President endorsed Halleck's response: "It is exceedingly discouraging. As everywhere else, nothing can be done." Lincoln then wrote both his generals with his thoughts on the larger strategic picture, making reference to the Bull Run campaign of July 1861.

COPY—one also sent to Gen. Halleck.

Brig. Genl. Buell. Executive Mansion,
My dear Sir: Washington, Jan. 13, 1862.

Your despatch of yesterday is received, in which you say "I have received your letter and Gen. McClellan's; and will, at once devote all my efforts to your views, and his." In the midst of my many cares, I have not seen, or asked to see, Gen. McClellan's letter to you. For my own views, I have not offered, and do not now offer them as orders; and while I am glad to have them respectfully considered, I would blame you to follow them contrary to your own clear judgment—unless I should put them in the form of orders. As to Gen. McClellan's views, you understand your duty in regard to them better than I do. With this preliminary, I state my general idea of this war to be that we have the *greater* numbers, and the enemy has the *greater* facility of concentrating forces upon points of collision; that we must fail, unless we can find some way of making *our* advantage an over-match for *his*; and that this can only be done by menacing him with superior forces at *different* points, at the *same* time; so that we can safely attack, one, or both, if he makes no change; and if he *weakens* one to *strengthen* the other, forbear to attack the strengthened one, but seize, and hold the weakened one, gaining so much. To illustrate, suppose last summer, when Winchester ran away to re-inforce Mannassas, we had forborne to attack Mannassas, but had seized and held Winchester. I mention this to illustrate, and not to criticise. I did not lose confidence in McDowell, and I think less harshly of Patterson than some others seem to. In application of the general rule I am suggesting, every particular case will have its modifying circumstances, among which the most constantly present, and most difficult to meet, will be the want of perfect knowledge of the enemies' movements. This had it's part in the Bull-Run case; but worse, in that case, was the expiration of the terms of the three months men. Applying the principle to your case, my idea is that Halleck shall menace Columbus, and "down river" generally; while you menace Bowling-Green, and East Tennessee. If the enemy shall concentrate at Bowling-Green, do not retire from his front; yet do not fight him there, either, but seize Columbus and East Tennessee, one or both, left exposed by the concentration at Bowling Green. It is matter of no small anxiety to me and one which I am sure you will not over-look, that the East Tennessee line, is so long, and over so bad a road. Yours very truly

A. LINCOLN.

Abraham Lincoln: President's General War Order No. 1 and President's Special War Order No. 1

Lincoln's efforts to start the Union war effort moving became more specific with these two orders, both of which set Washington's birthday as a target date. Special War Order No. 1, directed at General McClellan and the Army of the Potomac, was intended to execute the President's plan for turning the Confederates' position at Manassas by threatening their communications.

President's General War Order No. 1

Executive Mansion,
Washington, January 27, 1862.

President's general
War Order No. 1

Ordered that the 22nd. day of February 1862, be the day for a general movement of the Land and Naval forces of the United States against the insurgent forces.

That especially—

The Army at & about, Fortress Monroe.
The Army of the Potomac.
The Army of Western Virginia
The Army near Munfordville, Ky.
The Army and Flotilla at Cairo.
And a Naval force in the Gulf of Mexico, be ready for a movement on that day.

That all other forces, both Land and Naval, with their respective commanders, obey existing orders, for the time, and be ready to obey additional orders when duly given.

That the Heads of Departments, and especially the Secretaries of War and of the Navy, with all their subordinates; and the General-in-Chief, with all other commanders and subordinates, of Land and Naval forces, will severally be held to their strict and full responsibilities, for the prompt execution of this order. ABRAHAM LINCOLN

Draft of Order sent to Army & Navy Departments respectively this day. A. LINCOLN

Jan. 27. 1862.

The Secretary of War will enter this Order in his Department, and execute it to the best of his ability. A. LINCOLN
Jan. 27, 1862.

President's Special War Order No. 1

Executive Mansion
Washington January 31, 1862

Presidents special War Order, No. 1.

Ordered that all the disposable force of the Army of the Potomac, after providing safely for the defense of Washington, be formed into an expedition, for the immediate object of siezing and occupying a point upon the Rail Road South Westward of what is known of Manassas Junction, all details to be in the discretion of the general-in-chief, and the expedition to move before, or on, the 22nd. day of February next.

ABRAHAM LINCOLN

A CAMPAIGN AGAINST RICHMOND: FEBRUARY 1862

George B. McClellan to Edwin M. Stanton

Upon receiving Special War Order No. 1, General McClellan secured Lincoln's permission "to submit in writing my objections to his plan and my reasons for preferring my own." McClellan's plan, addressed to the new secretary of war, Edwin M. Stanton, proposed to strike at the Confederate capital by way of the lower Chesapeake Bay and the Virginia Peninsula. Although his proposal was dated January 31, 1862, McClellan actually submitted it to Stanton on February 3. McClellan's plan, in modified form, would in due course be accepted, reluctantly, by the President.

Hon E M Stanton
Secty of War — Head Quarters of the Army
Sir: — Washington January 31st 1862

I ask you indulgence for the following paper, rendered necessary by circumstances.

I assumed command of the troops in the vicinity of Washington on Saturday July 27 1861, 6 days after the battle of Bull Run.

I found no army to command, a mere collection of regiments cowering on the banks of the Potomac, some perfectly raw, others dispirited by their recent defeat.

Nothing of any consequence had then been done to secure the southern approaches to the Capital by means of defensive works; nothing whatever had been undertaken to defend the avenues to the city on the northern side of the Potomac.

The troops were not only undisciplined, undrilled & dispirited—they were not even placed in military positions—the city was almost in a condition to have been taken by a dash of a single regiment of cavalry.

Without one day's delay I undertook the difficult task assigned to me—the task the Hon Secty knows was given to me without my solicitation or foreknowledge. How far I have accomplished it will best be shown by the past & present. The

Capital is secure against attack—the extensive fortifications erected by the labor of our troops enable a small garrison to hold it against a numerous army; the enemy have been held in check; the State of Maryland is securely in our possession; the detached counties of Virginia are again within the pale of our laws, & all apprehension of trouble in Delaware is at an end; the enemy are confined to the positions they occupied before 21 July;—more than all this, I have now under my command a well drilled & reliable Army to which the destinies of the country may be confidently committed. This Army is young, & untried in battle, but it is animated by the highest spirit, & is capable of great deeds. That so much has been accomplished, & such an Army created in so short a time from nothing will hereafter be regarded as one of the highest glories of the Administration & the nation.

Many weeks, I may say many months, ago this Army of the Potomac was fully in condition to repel any attack;—but there is a vast difference between that & the efficiency required to enable troops to attack successfully an Army elated by victory, and entrenched in a position long since selected, studied, & fortified. In the earliest papers I submitted to the Presdt I asked for an effective movable force far exceeding the aggregate now on the banks of the Potomac—I have not the force I asked for. Even when in a subordinate position I always looked beyond the operations of the Army of the Potomac; I was never satisfied in my own mind with a barren victory, but looked to combined & decisive operations.

When I was placed in command of the Armies of the U.S. I immediately turned my attention to the whole field of operations—regarding the Army of the Potomac as only *one*, while the most important, of the masses under my command.

I confess that I did not then appreciate the absence of a general plan which had before existed, nor did I know that utter disorganization & want of preparation pervaded the western armies. I took it for granted that they were nearly, if not quite, in condition to move towards the fulfillment of my plans—I acknowledge that I made a great mistake.

I sent at once, with the approval of the Executive, officers I considered competent to command in Kentucky & Missouri—their instructions looked to prompt movements. I soon found that the labor of creation & organization had to be performed there—transportation, arms, clothing, artillery, discipline—all were wanting; these things required time to procure them; the Generals in command have done their work most creditably—but we are still delayed. I had hoped that a general advance could be made during the good weather of December—I was mistaken.

My wish was to gain possession of the Eastern Tennessee Railroads as a preliminary movement,—then to follow it up immediately by an attack on Nashville & Richmond as nearly at the same time as possible.

I have ever regarded our true policy as being that of fully preparing ourselves & then seeking for the most decisive results;—I do not wish to waste life in useless battles, but prefer to strike at the heart.

Two bases of operations seem to present themselves for the advance of the Army of the Potomac.—

I. That of Washington—its present position—involving a direct attack upon the enemy's entrenched positions at Centreville, Manassas etc, or else a movement to turn one or both flanks of those positions, or a combination of the two plans.

The relative force of the two Armies will not justify an attack on both flanks.

An attack on his left flank alone involves a long line of wagon communication & cannot prevent him from collecting for the decisive battle all the detachments now on his extreme right & left.

Should we attack his right by the line of the Occoquan & a crossing of the Potomac below the Occoquan & near his batteries, we could perhaps prevent the junction of the enemy's extreme right with his centre (we *might* destroy the former), we would remove the obstructions to the navigation of the Potomac, reduce the length of wagon transportation by establishing new depots at the nearest points of the Potomac, & strike more directly his main railway communication.

The fords of the Occoquan below the mouth of Bull Run are watched by the rebels, batteries are said to be placed on the heights in rear (concealed by the woods), & the arrangement of his troops is such that he can oppose some considerable resistance to a passage of the stream. Information has just been received to the effect that the enemy are entrenching a line of heights extending from the vicinity of Sangster's (Union Mills?) towards Evansport. Early in Jany. Sprigg's ford was occupied by Genl Rhodes with 3600 men & 8 guns; there are strong reasons for believing that Davis' Ford is occupied.

These circumstances indicate, or prove, that the enemy anticipate the movement in question & are prepared to resist it.

Assuming for the present that this operation is determined upon, it may be well to examine briefly its probable progress.

In the present state of affairs our columns (for the movement of so large a force must be made in several columns, at least 5 or 6) can reach the Accotinck without danger; during the march thence to the Occoquan our right flank becomes exposed to an attack from Fairfax Station, Sangster's & Union Mills;—this danger must be met by occupying in some force either the two first named places, or, better, the point of junction of the roads leading thence to the village of Occoquan—this occupation must be continued so long as we continue to draw supplies by the roads from this city, or until a battle is won.

The crossing of the Occoquan should be made at all the fords from Wolf's Run to the mouth, the points of crossing not being necessarily confined to the fords themselves.

Should the enemy occupy this line in force we must, with what assistance the flotilla can afford, endeavor to force the passage near the mouth, thus forcing the enemy to abandon the whole line or be taken in flank himself.

Having gained the line of the Occoquan, it would be necesary to throw a column by the shortest route to Dumfries, partly to force the enemy to abandon his batteries on the Potomac, partly to cover our left flank against an attack from the direction of Acquia, & lastly to establish our communication with the river by the best roads, & thus give us new depots.

The enemy would by this time have occupied the line of the Occoquan above Bulls Run, holding Brentsville in force & perhaps extending his lines somewhat further to the S.W.

Our next step would be to prevent the enemy from crossing the Occoquan between Bull Run & Broad Run, to fall upon our right flank while moving on Brentsville; this might be effected by occupying Baconrace Church & the cross roads near the mouth of Bull Run, or still more effectually by moving to the fords themselves & preventing him from debouching on our side. These operations would probably be resisted, & would require some time to effect them. As nearly at the same time as possible we should gain the fords necessary to our purposes above Broad Run.

Having secured our right flank it would become necessary to carry Brentsville at any cost, for we could not leave it between our right flank & main body. The final movement on the Railroad must be determined by circumstances existing at the time.

This brief sketch brings out in bold relief the great advantage possessed by the enemy in the strong central position he occupies, with roads diverging in every direction, & a strong line of defence enabling him to remain on the defensive with a small force on one flank, while he concentrates everything on the other for a decisive action. Should we place a portion of our force in front of Centreville while the rest crosses the Occoquan we commit the error of dividing our Army by a very difficult obstacle & by a distance too great to enable the two portions to support each other, should either be attacked by the masses of the enemy while the other is held in check.

I should perhaps have dwelled more decidedly on the fact that the force left near Sangster's must be allowed to remain somewhere on that side of the Occoquan, until the decisive battle is over, to cover our retreat in the event of disaster, unless it should be decided to select & entrench a new base somewhere near Dumfries—a proceeding involving much time.

After the passage of the Occoquan by the main Army, this covering force could be drawn in to a more central & less exposed position, say Brimstone Hill or nearer the Occoquan.

In this latitude the weather will for a considerable period be very uncertain, & a movement commenced in force on roads in tolerably firm condition will be liable, almost certain, to be much delayed by rains & snow. It will therefore be next to impossible to surprise the enemy, or take him at a disadvantage by rapid manoeuvres;—our slow progress will enable him to divine our purposes & take his measures accordingly.

The probability is, from the best information we possess,

that he has improved the roads leading to his lines of defence, while we must work as we advance.

Bearing in mind what has been said, & the present unprecedented & impassable condition of the roads, it will be evident that no precise period can be fixed upon for the movement on this line, nor can its duration be closely calculated; it seems certain that many weeks *may* elapse before it is possible to commence the march.

Assuming the success of this operation & the defeat of the enemy as certain, the question at once arises as to the importance of the results gained.

I think these results would be confined to the possession of the field of battle, the evacuation of the line of the upper Potomac by the enemy, & the moral effect of the victory—important results it is true, but not decisive of the war, nor securing the destruction of the enemy's main Army; for he could fall back upon other positions, & fight us again & again, should the condition of his troops permit.

If he is in no condition to fight us again out of range of the entrenchments at Richmond we would find it a very difficult & tedious matter to follow him up there—for he would destroy the railroad bridges & otherwise impede our progress through a region where the roads are as bad as they well can be; & we would probably find ourselves forced at last to change the entire theatre of war, or to seek a shorter land route to Richmond with a smaller available force & at an expenditure of much more time than were we to adopt the short line at once.

We would also have forced the enemy to concentrate his forces & perfect his defensive measures at the very points where it is desirable to strike him where least prepared.

II. The second base of operations available for the Army of the Potomac is that of the lower Chesapeake Bay, which affords the shortest possible land routes to Richmond, & strikes directly at the heart of the enemy's power in the East.

The roads in that region are passable at all seasons of the year.

The country now alluded to is much more favorable for offensive operations than that in front of Washington (which is *very* unfavorable)—much more level—more cleared land—the woods less dense—soil more sandy—the spring some two or three weeks earlier.

A movement in force on that line obliges the enemy to abandon his entrenched position at Manassas, in order to hasten to cover Richmond & Norfolk.

He *must* do this, for should he permit us to occupy Richmond his destruction can be averted only by entirely defeating us in a battle in which he must be the assailant.

This movement if successful gives us the Capital, the communications, the supplies of the rebels; Norfolk would fall; all the waters of the Chesapeake would be ours; all Virginia would be in our power; & the enemy forced to abandon Tennessee & North Carolina.

The alternatives presented to the enemy would be to beat us in a position selected by ourselves; disperse;—or pass beneath the Caudine Forks. Should we be beaten in a battle, we have a perfectly secure retreat down the Peninsula upon Fort Monroe, with our flanks perfectly secured by the fleet. During the whole movement our left flank is covered by the water, our right is secure for the reason that the enemy is too distant to reach us in time—he can only oppose us in front; we bring our fleet into full play.

After a successful battle our position would be—Burnside forming our left, Norfolk held securely, our centre connecting Burnside with Buell, both by Raleigh & Lynchburg, Buell in Eastern Tennessee & Northern Alabama, Halleck at Nashville & Memphis.

The next movement would be to connect with Sherman on the left, by reducing Wilmington & Charleston; to advance our centre into South Carolina & Georgia; to push Buell either towards Montgomery, or to unite with the main army in Georgia; to throw Halleck southward to meet the Naval Expedition at New Orleans.

We should then be in a condition to reduce at our leisure all the southern seaports; to occupy all the avenues of communication; to use the great outlet of the Mississippi; to reestablish our Govt & arms in Arkansas, Louisiana & Texas; to force the slaves to labor for our subsistence instead of that of the rebels; —to bid defiance to all foreign interference.

Such is the object I have ever had in view; this is the general plan which I have hoped to accomplish. For many long months I have labored to prepare the Army of the Potomac to play its part in the programme; from the day when I was placed in command of all our armies, I have exerted myself to place all the other armies in such a condition that they too could perform their allotted duties. Should it be determined to operate from the lower Chesapeake, the point of landing which promises the most brilliant results is Urbana on the lower Rappahannock.

This point is easily reached by vessels of heavy draught, it is neither occupied nor observed by the enemy; it is but one long march from West Point, the key to that region, & thence but two marches to Richmond.

A rapid movement from Urbana would probably cut off Magruder in the *Peninsula*, & enable us to occupy Richmond before it could be strongly reinforced. Should we fail in that we could, with the cooperation of the Navy, cross the James & throw ourselves in rear of Richmond, thus forcing the enemy to come out & attack us—for his position would be untenable, with us on the southern bank of the river.

Should circumstances render it not advisable to land at Urbana we can use Mob Jack Bay,—or—the worst coming to the worst—we can take Fort Monroe as a base, & operate with complete security, altho' with less celerity & brilliancy of results, up the Peninsula.

To reach whatever point may be selected as the base, a large amount of cheap water transportation must be collected—consisting mainly of canal boats, barges, wood boats, schooners etc towed by small steamers—all of a very different character from those required for all previous expeditions. This can certainly be accomplished within 30 days from the time the order is given.

I propose, as the best possible plan that can, in my judgment, be adopted, to select Urbana as the landing place of the first detachments. To transport by water four (4) Divisions of Infantry, with their batteries, the Regular Infty, a few wagons, one bridge train & a few squadrons of Cavalry—making the vicinity of Hooker's position the place of embarkation for as many as possible. To move the Regular Cavalry, & Reserve Artillery, the remaining bridge trains, & wagons to a point somewhere near Cape Lookout, then ferry them over the river by means of North River ferry boats, march them over to the Rappahannock (covering the movement by an Infantry force placed near Heathsville), cross the Rappahannock in a similar way.

The expense & difficulty of the movement will thus be much diminished (a saving of transportation of about 10,000 horses!), & the result none the less certain.

The concentration of the Cavalry etc in the lower counties of Maryland can be effected without exciting suspicion, & the movement made without delay from that cause.

This movement, if adopted, will not at all expose the city of Washington to danger.

The total force to be thrown upon the new line would be (according to circumstances) from 110,000 to 140,000. I hope to use the latter number, by bringing fresh troops into Washington, & still leaving it quite safe.

I fully realize that, in all projects offered, time is probably the most valuable consideration—it is my decided opinion that in that point of view the 2nd plan should be adopted. It is possible, nay highly probable, that the weather & state of the roads may be such as to delay the direct movement from Washington, with its unsatisfactory results & great risks, far beyond the time required to complete the second plan. *In the first case*, we can fix no definite time for an advance—the roads have gone from bad to worse—nothing like their present condition has ever been known here before—they are impassable at present, we are entirely at the mercy of the weather. In the second plan, we can calculate almost to a day, & with but little regard to the season.

If at the expense of 30 days delay we can gain a decisive victory which will probably end the war, it is far cheaper than to gain a battle tomorrow that produces no final results, & may require years of warfare & expenditure to follow up.

Such, I think, is precisely the difference between the two plans discussed in this long letter. A battle gained at Manassas will result merely in the possession of the field of combat—at best we can follow it up but slowly, unless we do what I now propose, viz:—change the line of operations.

On the Manassas line the rebels can, if well enough disciplined (& we have every reason to suppose that to be the case) dispute our advance, over bad roads, from position to position.

When we have gained the battle, if we do gain it, the question will at once arise—"What are we to do next?"—

It is by no means certain that we can beat them at Manassas.

On the other line I regard success as certain by all the chances of war.

We demoralize the enemy, by forcing him to abandon his prepared position for one which we have chosen, in which all is in our favor, & where success must produce immense results. My judgment as a General is clearly in favor of this project.

Nothing is *certain* in war—but all the chances are in favor of this movement.

So much am I in favor of the southern line of operations, that I would prefer the move from Fort Monroe as a base, as a certain, tho' less brilliant movement than that from Urbana, to an attack on Manassas.

I know that his Excellency the President, you & I all agree in our wishes—& that our desire is to bring this war to as prompt a close as the means in our possession will permit. I believe that the mass of the people have entire confidence in us—I am sure of it—let us then look only to the great result to be accomplished, & disregard everything else.

In conclusion I would respectfully, but firmly, advise that I may be authorized to undertake at once the movement by Urbana.

I believe that it can be carried into execution so nearly simultaneously with the final advance of Buell & Halleck that the columns will support each other.

I will stake my life, my reputation on the result—more than that, I will stake upon it the success of our cause.

I hope but little from the attack on Manassas;—my judgment is against it. Foreign complications may entirely change the state of affairs, & render very different plans necessary. In that event I will be ready to submit them.

I am very respectfully your obedient servant
Geo B McClellan
Maj Genl Comdg USA

Julia Ward Howe: The Battle Hymn of the Republic; from Reminiscences, 1819–1899

February 1862

Julia Ward Howe, a poet and the coeditor of the Boston abolitionist newspaper *The Commonwealth*, published "The Battle Hymn of the Republic" in the *Atlantic Monthly* for February 1862. The poem was written during a visit she made to Washington, D.C., in late 1861 with her husband, the social reformer Samuel Gridley Howe, and the Republican governor of Massachusetts, John A. Andrew. Howe later recalled the circumstances of its composition in her 1899 memoir. The music of the song "John Brown's Body" was that of the hymn "Say, brothers, will you meet us?," while its words were collectively composed by the members of a Massachusetts militia battalion in the spring of 1861. Despite its stirring sentiments, the "Battle Hymn" did not replace the singing of the "John Brown" lyrics among all Union soldiers, many of whom were partial to its line "They will hang Jeff. Davis to a tree!"

BATTLE HYMN OF THE REPUBLIC.

MINE eyes have seen the glory of the coming of the Lord:
He is trampling out the vintage where the grapes of wrath are stored;
He hath loosed the fateful lightning of His terrible swift sword:
His truth is marching on.

I have seen Him in the watch-fires of a hundred circling camps;
They have builded Him an altar in the evening dews and damps;
I can read His righteous sentence by the dim and flaring lamps:
His day is marching on.

I have read a fiery gospel writ in burnished rows of steel:
"As ye deal with my contemners, so with you my grace shall deal;
Let the Hero, born of woman, crush the serpent with his heel,
Since God is marching on."

He has sounded forth the trumpet that shall never call retreat;
He is sifting out the hearts of men before His judgment-seat:
Oh, be swift, my soul, to answer Him! be jubilant, my feet!
Our God is marching on.

In the beauty of the lilies Christ was born across the sea,
With a glory in his bosom that transfigures you and me:
As he died to make men holy, let us die to make men free,
While God is marching on.

I distinctly remember that a feeling of discouragement came over me as I drew near the city of Washington at the time already mentioned. I thought of the women of my acquaintance whose sons or husbands were fighting our great battle; the women themselves serving in the hospitals, or busying themselves with the work of the Sanitary Commission. My husband, as already said, was beyond the age of military service, my eldest son but a stripling; my youngest was a child of not more than two years. I could not leave my nursery to follow the march of our armies, neither had I the practical deftness which the preparing and packing of sanitary stores demanded. Something seemed to say to me, "You would be glad to serve, but you cannot help any one; you have nothing to give, and there is nothing for you to do." Yet, because of my sincere desire, a word was given me to say, which did strengthen the hearts of those who fought in the field and of those who languished in the prison.

We were invited, one day, to attend a review of troops at

some distance from the town. While we were engaged in watching the manœuvres, a sudden movement of the enemy necessitated immediate action. The review was discontinued, and we saw a detachment of soldiers gallop to the assistance of a small body of our men who were in imminent danger of being surrounded and cut off from retreat. The regiments remaining on the field were ordered to march to their cantonments. We returned to the city very slowly, of necessity, for the troops nearly filled the road. My dear minister was in the carriage with me, as were several other friends. To beguile the rather tedious drive, we sang from time to time snatches of the army songs so popular at that time, concluding, I think, with

"John Brown's body lies a-mouldering in the ground;
His soul is marching on."

The soldiers seemed to like this, and answered back, "Good for you!" Mr. Clarke said, "Mrs. Howe, why do you not write some good words for that stirring tune?" I replied that I had often wished to do this, but had not as yet found in my mind any leading toward it.

I went to bed that night as usual, and slept, according to my wont, quite soundly. I awoke in the gray of the morning twilight; and as I lay waiting for the dawn, the long lines of the desired poem began to twine themselves in my mind. Having thought out all the stanzas, I said to myself, "I must get up and write these verses down, lest I fall asleep again and forget them." So, with a sudden effort, I sprang out of bed, and found in the dimness an old stump of a pen which I remembered to have used the day before. I scrawled the verses almost without looking at the paper. I had learned to do this when, on previous occasions, attacks of versification had visited me in the night, and I feared to have recourse to a light lest I should wake the baby, who slept near me. I was always obliged to decipher my scrawl before another night should intervene, as it was only legible while the matter was fresh in my mind. At this time, having completed my writing, I returned to bed and fell asleep, saying to myself, "I like this better than most things that I have written."

The poem, which was soon after published in the "Atlantic Monthly," was somewhat praised on its appearance, but the vicissitudes of the war so engrossed public attention that small heed was taken of literary matters. I knew, and was content to know, that the poem soon found its way to the camps, as I heard from time to time of its being sung in chorus by the soldiers.

A GENERAL IS ARRESTED:
WASHINGTON, D.C., FEBRUARY 1862

The New York Times: An Important Arrest; The Ball's Bluff Disaster— Gen. McClellan and Gen. Stone

February 11, 1862; April 12, 1863

On October 21, 1861, several Union regiments crossed the Potomac upriver from Washington in a failed attempt to dislodge Confederate troops from Leesburg, Virginia. The battle of Ball's Bluff cost the Union more than 900 men killed, wounded, and missing; among the dead was Colonel Edward D. Baker, a serving Republican senator from Oregon and a friend of President Lincoln. In investigating the defeat, the Joint Committee on the Conduct of the War heard testimony—all of it hearsay and much of it perjured—impugning not the competence but the loyalty to Brigadier General Charles P. Stone, Union commander in the battle. In reporting Stone's arrest, the *Times* correspondent based his story on leaks of supposedly secret testimony supplied him by the committee. The damning testimony against Stone by "officers and men under his command" was in fact a conspiracy, engineered by soldiers whom Stone had charged with "misbehavior before the enemy." Secretary of War Stanton ordered Stone's arrest, and he was held in military prisons, without trial or even charges, for more than six months. He was only released in August 1862. When the committee's Ball's Bluff testimony was published a year later, a *Times* editorial took a new stance on the Stone case. A vindictive Stanton denied Stone important commands and dogged his footsteps until he resigned his commission in 1864.

AN IMPORTANT ARREST.

Gen. Stone Charged with Treason, and Confined in Fort Lafayette.

NATURE OF THE CHARGES AGAINST HIM.

Misbehavior at the Battle of Ball's Bluff—Complicity with the Enemy, and Treachery.

WASHINGTON, Monday, Feb. 10.

Gen. STONE was arrested on Sunday morning, at 2 o'clock, by order of the War Department, by a guard under the immediate command of Brig.-Gen. SYKES, of the Provost-Marshal's force, and sent to Fort Lafayette by the afternoon train. The charge against him is understood to be *treasonable complicity with the rebels* in the affair at Ball's Bluff and subsequently. He was lately before the Joint Committee on the Conduct of the War, to answer charges made against him in reference to this, and also to some other later and equally suspicious actions; and it is owing to the revelations made by himself and others before the Committee that he has been deprived of his command and committed to prison.

The following is the substance of the charges under which he was arrested:

1. For misbehavior at the battle of Ball's Bluff.

2. For holding correspondence with the enemy before and since the battle of Ball's Bluff, and receiving visits from rebel officers in his camp.

3. For treacherously suffering the enemy to build a fort or strong work, since the battle of Ball's Bluff, under his guns, without molestation.

4. For a treacherous design to expose his force to capture and destruction by the enemy, under pretence of orders for a movement from the Commanding-General, which had not been given.

A Court-martial will be speedily ordered.

The arrest excites great commotion in public circles here; and certain military functionaries are also greatly perturbed about it. It is rumored that still other arrests will be made immediately. Secretary STANTON has the spirit, the courage, and the determination, to strangle treason, or complicity with treason, wherever and in whomsoever it is discovered.

It is notable that STONE'S strongest friends here are Secessionists and Semi-Secessionists of both sexes, and his strongest enemies, or rather those who make the most serious charges against him, are the officers and men under his command. The searching investigation that has been made into his case was owing, in great measure, to the influence brought to bear from a source whence it would seem none could come—his own men. Political influence or personal rivalry have had nothing whatever to do with the case.

Gen. STONE'S antecedents are good, bad and dubious. He is a native of Massachusetts, a graduate and afterwards a Professor of Ethics in West Point, served in the Ordnance Corps, was a Lieutenant in command of a battery at the siege of Vera Cruz, was brevetted for gallant conduct at Molino del Rey, and served on the entire line of operations from Vera Cruz to the City of Mexico, under the eye of Gen. SCOTT, who has always expressed the highest confidence in his loyalty and military skill. In 1856 he resigned from the army and went into civil life. He became interested in certain land speculations (known as the Stone-Isham Purchase) in the States of Northern Mexico, Sonora and Chihuahua, but charges of fraud, if not of fillibustering, were made against him by the Mexican officials, and, while engaged with a strong party in surveying his pretended purchase, he was driven from Mexico by the authorities. He tried to raise a sufficient force to hold the land against the Mexicans; but failing, he came here in the early part of the Buchanan *regime*, to try and get the Government to send troops to the Mexican frontier, or otherwise make a demonstration in his favor. It was believed here that he had made, or was going to make, a good deal of money from this Mexican speculation, but not much was known about his operations. It was while staying here, and still engaged in this, as well as other jobs, that the rebellion broke out. On the first of last year, upon the recommendation of Gen. SCOTT, he was appointed to organize the militia of the District of Columbia; and while Washington was yet trembling in fear of the advent of the rebels, his action seemed both loyal and efficient. In May he was appointed

Colonel of the Fourteenth Infantry, and shortly after was made a Brigadier-General, and placed in command of a column under Gen. BANKS, on the Upper Potomac. It was while in this position, and in his command, that the horrible tragedy of Ball's Bluff was enacted. It has been attempted by some to place the responsibility for this affair on the shoulders of the gallant BAKER; but he can no more be held responsible than any of the private soldiers who, like himself, were slaughtered. The rebel General who commanded on that occasion, it will be remembered, attempted to exculpate STONE by giving publicity to certain orders and documents found on the battle-field, but, unfortunately, he did not publish *all* the documents he found. When Senator SUMNER recently referred to STONE in Congress, in connection with this affair, STONE sent the Senator an insulting letter, which has never been published, but in which, it is said, he tried to drag the Senator into a duel. It certainly seems impossible to explain certain circumstances connected with that murderous affair on the Upper Potomac on any other ground than that of treasonable complicity with the rebels in some high quarter.

Col. GORMAN, of the Minnesota First, has been put in temporary command of STONE's column. He at once proceeded to shell the rebels away from an earthwork they were throwing up on the opposite side of the Potomac, at Edwards' Ferry; he arrested a known rebel spy, whom Gen. STONE had defended, and took other active measures against the rebels in the vicinity of his command. Some of the parties formerly near to Gen. STONE have also been placed under surveillance.

The facts in STONE's career and his military action for the last six months certainly require explanation, particularly as regards the Ball's Bluff affair, (the facts in which are so familiar to the public,) and also in reference to still later and very suspicious communications with the enemy across the river. His case, it is believed, will speedily pass under the jurisdiction of a military tribunal.

The facts brought to light in Gen. STONE's case, and the necessary action consequent upon their discovery, have greatly affected Gen. MCCLELLAN, both in body and spirit. Visitors who called upon him on Monday learned that he was confined to his room, with his physician in attendance, and were consequently excluded.

February 11, 1862

THE BALL'S BLUFF DISASTER— GEN. McCLELLAN AND GEN. STONE.

No event in the history of the war has so shocked the public mind as the needless exposure of 1,700 of our soldiers to the murderous onslaught of 4,000 of the enemy at Ball's Bluff, in October of the first year. Nor has any event remained in so much obscurity. All that the people have known of it is that "somebody blundered." But who it was, and why he has never been brought to account, has been a standing puzzle from that day to the present. The dealings with Gen. STONE only complicated the enigma. If he was the man in fault, why should he have been retained in the same command for three months afterward without rebuke, or any diminution of trust? When, afterward, he was so suddenly arrested, why was he suffered to lie in Fort Lafayette nearly a year without trial, or the slightest opportunity of meeting the charges against him? Why was he finally so suddenly released? And why, ever since, has he in vain sought a Court-martial or a Court of Inquiry? These questions have exercised the public mind not a little, but to no purpose. The whole chapter, from beginning to end, has been as impenetrable as the veil of Isis. There was *something* behind, but that was all that could be made out.

The Report of the Committee on the Conduct of the War, as published by us on Friday, has done much toward dispelling the mystery. On some interesting points it is not conclusive, because of conflict of testimony; but it pretty effectually clears up the matters of chief concern. The Committee observe the same impartial course in their report of this affair as in their other reports—confining themselves strictly to a digest of the evidence, avoiding both deductions and comments. But the evidence on the principal points is so specific that it must make the same impression on all fair minds.

It is made apparent that *the prime cause of the disastrous movement was a misconception on the part of Gen. Stone, produced by the default of Gen. McClellan.* The day before the battle (Sunday) Gen. STONE was informed by telegraph from Gen. McCLELLAN in Washington, that a large force under Gen. McCALL was at Drainsville, was at that time "sending out heavy reconnoissances in all directions from that point." Gen. STONE was directed in this telegram "to keep a good lookout upon Leesburgh, to see if this movement has the effect to drive them (the rebels) away;" and it was added, "perhaps a slight demonstration on your part would have the effect to move them." Gen. STONE on the same day started a second reconnoitering party toward Leesburgh, and immediately telegraphed the fact to Gen. McCLELLAN. To that telegram no reply was made; and Gen. STONE was left in entire ignorance of the fact that Gen. McCALL's force was ordered by Gen. McCLELLAN *back* from Drainsville on Monday morning. That fact did not become known to him until Monday night, *after* the battle. The consequence was that Gen. STONE supposed, on the morning of the battle—and had reason to suppose—that Leesburgh was to be threatened on the other side by Gen. McCALL's regiments. It was this error, for which he was not responsible, that made the movement across the river, with such insufficient means for retreat, an act of ruinous rashness, instead of being, what it would have been otherwise, a perfectly safe and highly serviceable operation, in full pursuance of the original orders.

It is also made quite apparent that the *movement was approved by McClellan* both at the time and afterward. According to the evidence, Gen. STONE apprised him on the day of the battle that the crossing had been made—received from him a congratulatory dispatch in return, and was directed by him after the battle to hold Edwards' Ferry and "all the ground you now have on the Virginia shore," by intrenching, if necessary, with a promise of reinforcements. This testimony, in conjunction with the fact that Gen. STONE was retained in his full command for three months afterward, would seem to forbid all doubt that he was considered at headquarters to have been not at all in fault.

Again, it is shown that *the primary responsibility of Gen. Stone's arrest and long confinement without trial belongs to Gen. McClellan.* He himself admits, in his own testimony, that Gen.

STONE was arrested and consigned to Fort Lafayette at his instance. Previous to his arrest Gen. STONE was summoned before the War Committee to testify in regard to the Ball's Bluff affair, but his testimony was very indefinite and unsatisfactory. It now appears, from evidence given by him before the Committee six weeks ago, that his reserve at the first examination was owing to instructions which he had received at Gen. McCLELLAN's headquarters on the same morning, that "officers giving testimony before the Committee should not state, *without his authority*, anything regarding his plans, his orders for the movements of troops, or his orders concerning the position of troops;" and that this was understood to apply to past orders and transactions as well as future. No authority to make such disclosures was ever accorded by Gen. McCLELLAN. In consequence, Gen. STONE could not vindicate himself before the Committee. He was sent directly afterwards to Fort Lafayette. His urgent appeal for a military trial, and those of his friends to the same end, were unheeded throughout his incarceration of eleven months; and, to the very last day of Gen. McCLELLAN's command, he could get no hearing whatever. We consider the War Department to have been greatly to blame for consenting to this thing. It did so, as was announced at the time, on the ground that the trial could not be had without detriment to the campaigns then in progress, and Gen. McCLELLAN may have so represented; but this ought not to have been regarded. The complete investigation should have been promptly made, whatever Gen. McCLELLAN might have thought of it, or however he might have suffered from it. As it is, Gen. STONE has sustained a most flagrant wrong—a wrong which will probably stand as the very worst blot on the National side in the history of the war.

We await with great interest the publication of the entire evidence taken by the Committee relative to the Ball's Bluff calamity, and the subsequent treatment of Gen. STONE. If it shall in any respect present Gen. McCLELLAN in a less unfavorable light, we shall note the fact with pleasure.

April 12, 1863

ATTACK ON FORT DONELSON:
TENNESSEE, FEBRUARY 1862

Lew Wallace: from An Autobiography

It was in the western theater that the Union war machine finally moved. In September 1861 Brigadier General Ulysses S. Grant took command of the Union forces at Cairo, Illinois, at the junction of the Mississippi and Ohio. During the winter he and Flag Officer Andrew H. Foote, commanding the gunboat flotilla based at Cairo, made plans to gain control of the Tennessee and Cumberland rivers, which led into the heart of the Confederacy. Early in February Grant opened the campaign, his targets Forts Henry and Donelson, guarding the two rivers just below the Kentucky-Tennessee border. On February 6 Flag Officer Foote's gunboats bombarded Fort Henry, on the Tennessee, into surrender. Fort Donelson, on the Cumberland, proved a harder nut to crack. On February 15 the Confederates punched a hole in Grant's investing lines. Union division commander Wallace, author of the celebrated novel *Ben-Hur*, described the fighting in his 1906 autobiography.

I HAD long since learned that proud men in the throes of ill-fortune dislike to have the idle and curious make spectacles of them; especially do they hate condolence; wherefore I refrained from going to take a look at the first division reorganizing in my rear. It seemed to me a good time to attend to my own business.

However, as the town clocks in cities of the country endowed with such luxuries were getting ready to strike three, an officer rode up from the rear, and hearing him ask for me, I went to him.

"Are you General Wallace?" he asked.

"I am—at your service."

"Well," he said, "I am—"

Just then a round shot from the fort, aimed lower than usual, passed, it really seemed, not more than a yard above us. We both "ducked" to it, and when I raised my head almost from my horse's neck the stranger was doing himself the same service. We looked at each other, and it was impossible not to laugh.

"I don't know," he said, jocularly, "in what school you were taught to bow, but that one was well done."

"Yes," I retorted, "mine was nearly as low as yours."

To which he added, "They were both behind time"; meaning that they were given after the ball had passed.

Then he took up his fractured remark.

"I was about to say I am General McClernand."

Now I had known General John A. McClernand by reputation as a Democratic politician. His speeches in Congress had been frequent and creditable. My predilections were all on his side, and I ran him over with interest. His face was agreeable, though weather-beaten and unshaven. The snow light gave his eyes a severe squint. His head was covered with one of the abominable regulation wool hats hooked up at one side. Besides being thin and slightly under average height, he was at further disadvantage by sitting too far back in his saddle, and stooping. We shook hands, and he was giving me the details of his battle of the morning, when General Grant joined us, mounted, and attended by a single orderly. I noticed papers in General Grant's right hand which had the appearance of telegrams, and that he seemed irritated and bothered trying to keep some active feeling down. Of course McClernand and I saluted, and gave him instant attention.

From the hollow in front of my position a dropping fire kept ascending.

"Pickets?" General Grant asked.

"My pickets," I replied.

"They will get over that afterwhile," he remarked; then, seriously: "Foote must go to Cairo, taking his iron-clads, some of which are seriously damaged. We will have to await his return; meantime, our line must be retired out of range from the fort."

He stopped. The idea was detestable to him—bitterly so, and, seeing it, I asked to make a suggestion.

He turned to me with a questioning look.

"We have nobody on the right now," I said, "and the road to Clarksville is open. If we retire the line at all, it will be giving the enemy an opportunity to get away to-night with all he has."

Grant's face, already congested with cold, reddened perceptibly, and his lower jaw set upon the other. Without a word, he looked at McClernand, who began to explain. Grant interrupted him.

"Gentlemen," he said, "that road must be recovered before night." Gripping the papers in his hand—I heard them crinkle—he continued: "I will go to Smith now. At the sound of your fire, he will support you with an attack on his side."

Thereupon he turned his horse and rode off at an ordinary trot, while following him with my eyes, wondering at the simplicity of the words in a matter involving so much, I saw Colonel Morgan L. Smith coming up the road beyond him at the head of some troops, and guessed who they were.

General McClernand then spoke. "The road ought to be recovered—Grant is right about that. But, Wallace, you know I am not ready to undertake it."

The significance of the remark was plain. The road in question ran through the position his division had occupied in the morning; and feeling now that General Grant had really been addressing him, General McClernand was asking me to take the proposed task off his hands. I thought rapidly—of my division, by Cruft's return intact, and reinforced—of the Eleventh Indiana and the Eighth Missouri so opportunely arrived—of Colonel Morgan L. Smith—of the order holding me strictly to the defensive now released.

"Did you send to General Charles F. Smith for assistance?" I asked McClernand.

"Yes."

"Well, I see some troops coming, ordered probably to report to you; if they are, and you will direct the officer commanding to report to me, I will try recovery of the road."

At McClernand's request one of my aides—Ross, I think—rode at speed to meet Colonel Morgan L. Smith. Returning, he said, "It is Colonel Smith from General Charles F. Smith, ordered to report to General McClernand."

"Go back, then," said McClernand, "and tell the colonel that I request him to report to General Wallace."

Whereupon I said: "It is getting late, and what is done must be before night. If you will excuse me, I will go at it."

"Certainly," McClernand replied, adding, "I have two or three regiments in order under Colonel Ross, of my division, whom you may find useful."

"All right; send them on."

And as General McClernand left me, I sent to Colonel Smith directing him to halt his regiments behind the battery; with my staff, I then set out to see as much as possible of the ground to be recovered, and decide how best to arrange the attack. My horse objected to the dead men still lying in the road; but getting past them, the hill dipped down into a hollow of width and depth. At the left there was a field; all else appeared thinly covered with scattered trees. The pickets in the hollow were maintaining a lively fusillade, so I turned into the field. I could then see the road ran off diagonally to the right. A bluff rose in front of me partially denuded, and on top of it Confederate soldiers were visible walking about and blanketed. Off to the left the bluff flattened as it went. In that direction I also saw a flag not the stars and stripes, and guessed that the fort lay in studied contraction under it. I saw, too, a little branch winding through the hollow, and thought of my poor horse, then two days without water. The men keeping the thither height caught sight of my party, and interrupted me in the study of their position. Their bullets fell all around us. One cut a lock out of the mane of a horse of one of my orderlies. But I had what we came for, and got away, nobody hurt.

Upon my rejoining them at the battery, the old regiments (Eighth and Eleventh) cheered me; whereat the fort opened, firing harmlessly at the sound. The Eleventh, from their stacked arms, crowded around John—"Old Bailey," they called him—and filling a capful of crumbled crackers, some of them fed him what he would eat. They would have given him drink from their canteens had there been a vessel at hand to hold the water.

While that went on, I got my orders off. Cruft was told, by messenger, to take his brigade down into the hollow, and form line at the foot of the hill held by the Confederates, his left resting on the Wynne's Ferry road. When in position he was to notify me.

Smith was informed of what I have called the bluff, and told that it was to be his point of attack—that he was to conduct the main attack, supported by Cruft on his right and by Ross on the left, and that he was to make the ascent in column of regiments.

Thayer I directed to keep his present position, holding his brigade in reserve with the battery.

By-and-by Colonel Ross—he of Illinois—came up, bringing the Seventeenth and Forty-ninth Illinois regiments that had behaved with distinction in Colonel Morrison's misassault of the 14th. To him I explained that his position would be on the left of the main attack as a support.

I also gave notice to Smith and Ross that I would personally put them in position.

When these preliminaries were disposed of, I looked at the sun and judged that there were at least two hours left me for the operation.

While waiting to hear from Cruft, I chaffed with the old regiments. Of the Eighth Missouri I wanted to know at what hotel they had put up for the night.

"At the Lindell, of course," one of them responded.

"How were the accommodations?"

"Cold, but cheap."

This excited a great laugh.

Halting in front of the Eleventh, I said: "You fellows have been swearing for a long time that I would never get you into a fight. It's here now. What have you to say?"

A spokesman answered: "We're ready. *Let her rip!*"

Very un-Napoleonic, but very American.

Then heavy firing arose out of the hollow, and soon afterwards a man galloped up the hill to tell me that Colonel Cruft was in position, his left on the road.

"It is time to move," I said to Smith.

"Wait until I light a fresh cigar."

That done, and Colonel Ross told to follow, we set off down the road. Hardly had Smith, with whom I was riding, got halfway across the hollow, going straight for the bluff, when a fire ran along the top of it and bullets zipped angrily through the trees, showering us with leaves and twigs. To reply would have required a halt. At the foot of the ascent I left my Missouri friend, saying, "Try the Zouave on them, colonel, and remember to deploy McGinnis when you are nearly up."

Colonel Ross, to whom I rode next, had deployed his command. Going with him until clear of Smith's ground, I asked, "You understand your part, colonel?"

"Yes," he said, "it is to take care of the left of the main attack."

It took me but a moment to get to Cruft, who was exchanging a ragged fire with the enemy above him.

"Colonel Smith is next you on the left," I said to him. "Keep a little behind his line, and when you have cleared the hill, swing left towards the fort, pivoting on him."

I hurried then to the open field spoken of; and by the time I reached it, selected a stand-point for general oversight, and adjusted my field-glass, the advance had become general where Ross and Cruft were ascending slowly, inch by inch, the musketry had risen in measure, and the trees stood half veiled in a smoke momentarily deepening.

Presently my glass settled on Colonel Morgan L. Smith and the climb in his front, which I judged of three hundred short steps. In the patches of snow on the bluffy breast I also noticed some clumps of shrubs and a few trees, and here and there what appeared to be outcropping of rock. The disadvantages were obvious; yet, counting them as odds in the scale of chances, they were not enough to shake my confidence in the outcome, for there were advantages to be taken into the account—among them the Zouave training of both the regiments, meaning that they were nimble on their hands and knees far beyond the ordinary infantrymen, that they could load on their backs and fire with precision on their bellies, and were instinctively observant of order in the midst of disorder. Indeed, *purpose* with them answered all the ends of alignment elbow to elbow.

While making these observations my attention was drawn off by musketry blent with the pounding of artillery in the distance over at the left. It was General Charles F. Smith's supporting attack as promised by General Grant. Then it came to me suddenly that the crisis of the great adventure was on the army, and that as it went the victory would go. A feverish anxiety struck me. My tongue and throat grew dry and parched. I have the feeling now even as I write, such power have incidents at times to stamp themselves on memory.

Returning then to Colonel Smith, I saw skirmishers spring out and cover the front of his column. To my astonishment I also saw the man himself on horseback behind his foremost regiment, bent on riding up the hill—a perilous feat under the most favorable circumstances.*

I would like to describe the ascension of the height by the regiments under Smith, but cannot, for, take it all in all, it was the most extraordinary feat of arms I ever beheld. In the way of suggestion merely, the firing from the top was marked by lulls and furious outbursts. In the outbursts the assailants fell to their hands and knees, and took to crawling, while in the lulls—occasioned by smoke settling so thickly in front of the defenders that they were bothered in taking aim—yards of space were gained by rushes. And these were the spectacles impossible of description. To get an idea of them the reader must think of nearly two thousand vigorous men simultaneously squirming or dashing up the breast of a steep hill slippery with frost, in appearance so many black gnomes burrowing in a cloud of flying leaves and dirty snow. As they climbed on the alignment with which they started became loose and looser until half-way up it seemed utterly lost. There was no firing, of course, except by the skirmishers, and no cheering, not a voice save of officers in exhortation. Occasionally we heard Smith or McGinnis, but most frequently the enemy flinging taunts on the laborers below. "Hi, hi, there, you damned Yanks! Why don't you come up? What are you waiting for?"

They were nearing the top, probably a third of the distance remaining, when the Eleventh, in loose array as it was, rushed by the left flank out of column. They stumbled, and slipped, and fell down, but presently brought up, and faced front, having uncovered the Eighth. To get into line with the latter cost but a moment. About the same time I saw the skirmishers drop and roll out of sight, leaving the line of fire unobstructed. A furious outbreak from the enemy and both regiments sank

*I asked Colonel Smith afterwards what he meant by riding. He gave me a characteristic reply. "I thought the sight of me would encourage the boys." In further illustration of the man under fire, a bullet cut his cigar off close to his lips. "Here," he shouted, "one of you fellows bring me a match." The match was brought, and, lighting a fresh cigar, he spurred on and up.

down, and on their bellies half buried in snow delivered their first ragged volley. The next I saw of them they were advancing on their hands and knees. That they would win was no longer a question.

I gave a glance in Cruft's direction and another to Ross. Both were well up in their sections of attack. Just then some one near by broke into a laugh, and called out, "Look there!"

"Where?" I asked, not relishing the diversion.

A party of surgeon's assistants, six or eight in number, seeing us in the field, and thinking it a safe place, started to come across. A shower of bullets overtook them, and when my eyes reached them they were snuggling in the snow behind the kits they carried. And when I remembered how thin the kits were, nothing but oil-cloth, and not more resistant of a minié-ball than tissue-paper, I excused the laugh by joining in it.

Another look towards Cruft, another to Ross, then a brief study of Smith's forlorn hope, by that time nearly to its goal, and I took action.

Regaining the road, I hastened into the hollow, and when about half-way across it noticed a slackening of the enemy's fire; then, hardly a minute elapsing, it ceased entirely. The meaning was unmistakable. We had won! Calling Kneffler, I told him to go to General McClernand and tell him we were on the hill, and that he would oblige me if his artillery did not fire in our direction.

In these moves my horse had answered me readily but with his head down—a thing that had not happened before. The other horses of the company were worse off. There was need for me up on the height, but we stopped by the little brook and broke through the ice. While the poor brutes were drinking greedily, Colonel Webster came to me.

"General Grant sends me," he said, "to tell you to retire your command out of range of the fort and throw up light intrenchments. He thinks it best to wait for reinforcements."

I gave a thought to the position just recovered, with loss unknown, and asked the colonel, "Does the general know that we have retaken the road lost in the morning?"

"I think not," he replied.

"Oh, well! Give him my compliments, colonel, and tell him *I have received the order.*"

Webster gave me a sharp look and left me. I had resolved to disobey the direction, and he saw it, and justified me without saying so—as did General Grant subsequently.

THE SUN was just going down when, with my staff, I rode on to the height just won. To my eager search for what of war and combat it had to offer there was at first nothing which one may not find in any neglected woods pasture; only the air was heavy with the sulphurous smell of powder burned and burning, and through the thin assemblage of trees there went an advancing line of men stretching right and left out of sight. My first point was to catch that line.

The enemy had not waited the coming up of the Yanks. His main body had retired towards his works, and the three commands, Cruft's, Ross's, and Smith's, with just enough resistance before them to keep their blood up, were pushing forward at a pace calling for energetic action if they were to be brought to a halt. That done, however, the three were closed on the centre; then, skirmishers being thrown to the front, we advanced slowly and cautiously.

It was not long until we came on the aftermath of General McClernand's morning struggle. Dead men, not all of them ours, were lying in their beds of blood-stained snow exactly as they had fallen. And the wounded were there also. These, fast as come upon, were given drink and covered with blankets, but left to be picked up later on; and there was no distinction shown between the blue and the gray. The wonder was to find any of them alive.

While following the line I saw a man sitting against a stump in a position natural as life. Besides the Confederate homespun of which his clothes were made, he sported a coon-skin cap with the tail of the animal for plume. His eyes were wide open and there was a broad grin on his face. I would have sworn the look and grin were at me, and, stopping, I spoke to an orderly.

"Find out what that fellow means by grinning that way. If he answers decently, help him."

The orderly dismounted and shook the man, then said, "Why he's dead, sir."

"That can't be. See where he's hit."

The cap when taken off brought away with it a mass that sickened us. A small bullet—from a revolver, probably—had gone through the inner corner of his eye leaving no visible wound, but the whole back of the head was blown off and the skull entirely emptied.

On a little farther we rode over the body of a Confederate lying on his back spread-eagle fashion. A gun clutched in his hand arrested me.

"Get that gun," I said, and one of my men jumped down for it.

It is in my study now, a handsomely mounted, muzzle-loading, old-style squirrel rifle. Sometimes I take it out to try at a mark, when, as a souvenir, it strikes me with one drawback—touching it is to revive the memory of its owner looking up at the sky from his sheet of crimson snow; and that he brought the piece to the field with him intending to kill Yankees as he was in the habit of killing long-tailed rodents does not always suffice to allay the shiver it excites.

It is to be remembered that, in common with my whole command, I was profoundly ignorant of the topography of the locality. That we were moving in the direction of the fort I knew rather as a surmise than a fact. The skirmishers kept up their fire; otherwise the silence impressed me as suspicious. Once I heard the report of a great gun in the distance, and shortly a shell of half-bushel proportions went with a locomotive's scream through the tree-tops; whereupon we knew ourselves in the line of fire from the gun-boats in the river. Disagreeable—yes, vastly so—but there was no help for it. Right after—indeed, as if the unearthly scream of the big shell had been an accepted signal—the holders of the fort awoke, and set their guns to work—how many I had no means of judging.

Through the woods then there sped a peculiar short-stop whistling; nor was there need of one of greater experience in battle to tell us that we were objects of search by cannister and possibly grape-shot. Fragments of the limbs above us rattled down, and occasionally—the thing of greatest impression upon me—a sharp resound, like the cracking of green timber in a zero night, rang through the woods; and that we also instinctively knew to be bullets of iron embedding themselves in some near-by tree-trunks.

Now, as I have no wish to take credit not strictly my due, the effect of this visitation startled me—thc more so as it came in the nature of a surprise. I asked myself, however, "Where are we going?" And as the answer did not come readily, I made haste to order another halt.

It happened that my position at the moment was behind Cruft's brigade in what I took to be the road to Charlotte, also the object of anxious solicitude. Making way through the halted line, the situation revealed itself. There, not farther than three hundred yards, a low embankment stretched off on both sides, and behind it, in the background, rose an elaborate earthen pile which a drooping flag on a tall, white staff told me was Fort Donelson proper. Some field-pieces behind the low intrenchment were doing the firing, supported by men lying in the ditch. The heads of these bobbed up and down; and every time one of them bobbed up it was to let loose a streak of brilliant flame, with a keen report and a rising curl of smoke as close attendants. In front of the outwork far extending were our skirmishers behind stumps and logs, and in every depression affording cover, and they, too, were shooting. The interval of separation between the enemies ranged from eighty yards to a hundred and fifty.

The scene was stirring; but it must not be thought it held me long—far from it. While I looked, a sense of responsibility touched me with a distinct shock. What next?

Two things were possible; to continue on or go back out of range. The first meant an assault, and I doubted my authority to go so far. It seemed a step within the province of the commander. Perhaps he was not ready to order it. To be successful, moreover, there was need of support, otherwise the whole garrison could be concentrated against me. So, resolving the skirmishers as they were into a grand guard, Colonel Morgan L. Smith in charge, I retired the line five or six hundred yards.

There was nothing for us then but another night in bivouac without fires, and nothing to eat but crackers; literally suffering from the pinch of hunger added to misery from the pinch of cold. Yet I did not hear a murmur. This, I think, because there was not a soldier there so ignorant as not to know the necessity of keeping a tight grip upon our position.

With the advent of darkness the gun practice ceased, and later even the pickets quit annoying one another. Then silence, and a February night, with stars of pitiless serenity, and a wind not to be better described than as a marrow-searcher.

FORT DONELSON SURRENDERS:
TENNESSEE, FEBRUARY 1862

John Kennerly Farris to Mary Farris

The repulse of the Confederate counterattack on February 15 caused Brigadier General Simon B. Buckner, the commander of the Fort Donelson garrison, to ask Grant for surrender terms, eliciting the soon-to-be-famous reply: "No terms except an unconditional and immediate surrender can be accepted. I propose to move immediately upon your works." Buckner and 12,000 Confederates surrendered on February 16, giving the North its first great victory of the war. The fall of Fort Henry allowed Union gunboats to steam up the Tennessee as far as Muscle Shoals in northern Alabama, while the surrender of Fort Donelson gave Grant control of the Cumberland River and forced the Confederate evacuation of Nashville. Among the Southerners who surrendered at Fort Donelson was John Kennerly Farris, a physician serving with the 41st Tennessee Infantry. He wrote to his wife in the fall of 1862 after being freed in a prisoner exchange. Farris's mention of "Forest Cavalry" near the end of his narrative refers to Lieutenant Colonel Nathan Bedford Forrest, who refused to surrender and slipped away with his men to fight many another day.

Camp Cold Water near Holly Springs, Misisissippi
Friday, October 31, 1862

Well Mary,

I have several times thought I would give you a brief history of my time at Ft. Donnelson and how I hapened to get there.

Thursday, Feb. 13th, 1862. I was in the City of Nashville with some 16 or 20 of our Regt. when I heard the fight had begun at Ft. Donnelson and, knowing our Regt. was there, I was very anxious to be with them—so I went to Lieut. Wilhoit who was in command of the detachment of our Regt., and I believe the detachment of all the Regts. which belonged to Gen. Buckners command, and asked him for an order to rejoin the Regt. He told me he could not give me one without laying himself liable as I was the only Physician with him, or under his command.

This troubled me a good deal and I became anxious to be

with them, and studied about an hour how I would manage to get to the Regt. and the propriety of leaving without an order. Suddenly an idea struck me that I might get an order from the Commander of the Post at Nashville, who I allowed would out rank Lieut. Wilhoit and make me safe in leaving. By enquiring for his quarters, I found him without any difficulty and told him how I was situated there and, further, that I had sent all the sick under my charge to the Hospittle and was there idle and thought my services might be demanded at Ft. Donnelson and I desired to go there. Without returning a word he wrote me a pass down there and told me to take the first boat. I immediately returned to my quarters, took my napsack from my trunk, with a suit of clothes, went down to the River and got abord of a little job boat preparing to leave for Ft. Donnelson.

This was 8 o'clock a.m. The boat was soon ready to start, but was found to be fast upon a pile of iron which the water had covered. They worked to get it off untill two o'clock, apparently to no effect. I grew tired, got off the boat and gave out going, for I was suffering considerably with Rheumatic pains in my shoulders and concluded that I might be more in the way than otherwise. I strolled over town untill nearly sunset when I again concluded that I would go down to the Ft. anyway if I could get off. So I went down to the River again and found the boat off the iron and about ready to start. I got abord, and in a very short time the boat began its move but unfortunately washed down against an old boat which was under repair and lodged against it.

There we remained untill 8 o'clock p.m. when we got clear and started down the River. The little thing was so crowded with passengers that her cabin would not hold over one-fourth of us. So the remainder had to take passage on her decks where we had liked to have frozen during the night; could get neither supper or breakfast Friday morning. Friday about 1 o'clock p.m. we got down to Clarksville. There I got off the uncomfortable little job Boat and got on the *Reunion*, a nice and comfortable boat. We there learned that they were still fighting at Dover. This made all apparently anxious to get on down.

We did not stay there long but went on down the River. When we got in some ten or twelve miles of Dover, we stoped and took on wood enough to pile all round on lower deck to protect the hands from the balls of the enemy, as we did not know but what the boat would be shot into. About dark we landed at Dover. Everything was quiet. The two contending forces were as still as though they had been friends almost. About 10 o'clock in the night I found our Regt. and found the boys nearly worn out with fasting, fatigue and cold. They had not a tent and scarcly a fire. Some were lying on the snow wrapt in their blankets asleep. Some were sitting round a few coals of fire, and some at one thing and some another.

I was very hungry, and asked them for something to eat, as I had eaten but a snack since Thursday morning. They told me they had nothing, nor had had in some time. But one of the boys had a little parched coffee in his pocket, which he gave to me and which I pounded in a tin cup the best I could with an old chunk, and borrowed a coffee pot and made it full of coffee for five of us, who had constructed a little fire barely sufficient to boil a coffee pot of water. We drank the coffee, which seemed to do us a good deal of good, though it was barely fit to drink and would not at all been used under ordinary circumstances.

We five sit around the same little fire untill 3 o'clock a.m. of Saturday talking of the previous and expected fight. All through the night we could once and a while hear the pickets shooting at each other, and some very close to us. At 3 o'clock the Officers came round and gave orders for the men to get in line, for it was thought we might be attacked in a short time. Notwithstanding the ground was covered with snow and the weather very cold, I felt pretty lively and was anxious for the coming conflict, though I knew and told the boys that day would not close without some as hard fightin as had been done dureing the war. Just at day break the Regt. was ordered forward. It was generally known that we were going round on our left wing and engage the enemy, and I never felt more contented in my life.

During the night everything had been quite still, with the exception of an occasional fire by the pickets, and so remained untill we had gone near a half a mile, and by which time the sun had just begun to show itself, peeping as it were over the hills and mountains of the east. At that time we were moving on in line, I keeping with the file closers and watching the appearance of the boys particularly, which I was enabled to do as I had my gun to carry. We struck the foot of a large hill, marched rather across the point, but to my great surprise, just as we got barely on top of the hill, the enemy discovered us & turned loose at us with a cannon—the first that I had ever heard fire in battle. The boys all dropped to the ground, and I followed suit, but we rose in an instant and were ordered to double quick. The ball passed immediate over us.

When I got up, I felt considerably confused & must acknowledge a little fear. The first thing in my mind was that I had got myself voluntarily into a devil of a snap, but at the same moment I thought of you and Sammy & determined not to disgrace you & him if my head was shot off. So I braced myself up & marched strate forward as resolute as death itself, but not without feeling somewhat uncomfortable. I looked at every man in the Regt. to see how they looked. None looked like they were scared, & I argued to myself that it did not look reasonable that God Almighty had so constituted me as to make me more of a coward than any of the Regt.

We had not double quicked over fifty yards untill they cut loose again with a shell. The boys, being used to them, droped to the ground again, and at the same moment I accidently sliped down, hurting my knee on the frozen ground slightly. The shell passed immediately over me, and I think would have cut me into had I not been on the ground. It burst in about 20 yards of us but done us no harm. I rose instantly, and the first thing said to myself, "Well, I will not get hurt today, for providence has saved my life, and God is on my side." We went down the hill at a double quick then followed a hollow something like a quarter or half a mile, the enemy not molesting us. At length we struck the foot of another high hill, at which place a good many of us droped our napsacks and left them on account of fatigue.

It was a good piece to the top, and about half way up a battery had stalled, and the enemy was pouring it to them with ball and shell rapidly. We marched up to it and stoped for it to get out of the way, some of our men assisting in pushing it. At this moment Gen. Floyd rode up and ordered us onward. Our Col. told him we were waiting for the Artillery to get out of the way. He said wait for nothing, but go ahead. We started, the enemy giving us grape, canister and shell heavily. At that point I got used to the things and feared them no more.

We moved on to the top of the Hill, or almost, and was ordered to lie down in a little hollow to the right of the road just behind one of our batterys, which was playing upon the enemy. But was soon ordered to recross the road and lie on the breast of the hill at the termination of a large hollow in the rear of the battery and to the right—also in rear of the 14th Misp. Regt., and a short distance behind them, who were and had been for some time fighting like fury. The enemy endeavored to shell us out of the Hollow, but failed in doing so as their shells passed generally over us. They tried us with grape and canister, but with no effect. We lay there untill eleven o'clock with the exception of 3 companys, which had been ordered off to drive the sharp shooters from some of our batterys and defend them.

Gen. Floyd and our Brigade Surgeon took their position just behind us. About 11 o'clock there came a man running down to us and asked for a Physician to go up to the 14th Misp. Regt. The cries of the wounded at this time was horrorable. The roar of the cannon and the noise of the musketry was deafening. The Brigade surgeon ordered me to go to them. I rose and started as fast as I could to them, having to cross a heavy cannon fire before I reached them, and immediately after crossing that I was in range of the musket balls, which fell all around me and passed over my head so thick that it looked like I could have held up my hat and caught it full.

The Mississippi boys fell fast, but fought like men. I went to work on them, as best I could, and had at length to tear up my havorsack for bandages. I found a fellow with two wounds in the breast and saw he was bleeding from an artery. I carried him down in the hollow to get assistance in dressing his wounds. The brigade surgeon assisted me and ordered me to accompany him to the hospittal and told me to report myself to the medicle director, which I did.

The boats by this time had arrived (I suppose it was 11 1/2 o'clock) to take off the wounded. I was ordered to service in a hospittal, which was in a vacated Hotel, but about the time I got warm, Dr. Clopton sent for me to assist him in the Hospittal he had charge of, which was just across the road. I went over and went to work, but did not work long untill the Yankeys turned loose at the Hospittals and struck ours with several grape loads and passed two cannon balls through.

We went to work to raise the flags higher, and I suppose brought them into notice in about an hour and a half. At about half after one J. K. Buckner was brought in. Poor fellow. I was so sorry for him. I got Dr. Clopton to dress his wound immediately and started him to the boat, telling him never to stop untill he got home. Clopton, myself and another Physician, with occasional help from others, worked on untill 8 o'clock in the night, at which time we got through with all that were sent to our hospittal and got most of them on the boats. The fighting stoped when darkness forbid farther action.

We got our instruments cleaned & sit down to rest at 9 o'clock, & I do not think I was ever tireder in my life. Several Physicians & officers came in, & we talked over some of what we had seen. I told them that we who lived would all be prisoners of war by 3 hours by sun Sunday morning. I felt very much like it. I had seen all day that the enemy had 4 or 5 to one & had us surrounded. I thought we would fight next morning, but knew we would be overpowered. At ten o clock p.m. we lay down on the floor to take a nap for the first in a long time.

At 3 o'clock some fellow came and told us that our forces were going to retreat and ordered us to have the remainder of our wounded put upon the boat and then make our escape if we could and, if not, to surrender as prisoners of war, and we would soon be released. As the order came from the surgeon General, we went to work and after a while got most of them off. I kept asking every one that I would see comeing from our Regt. what had gone with it. At length a gentleman told me that it had cut its way through and was retreating. I ran in and told Dr. Clopton the same and told him I thought we had better go also. So we bundled up and started down to the boats to try to get abord, but could not get nigh them for the guards.

Dr. Clopton asked me what we could do. It was near daylight. I told him we must foot it up the River bank. He did not believe it practable. I insisted on trying; so we put out only taking one blanket. I suppose we went a half mile when we saw, as it was getting a little light, 5 men comeing meeting us, and who we took to be Yankeys. "There," said he, "look yander. What shall we do?" Says I, "March strait forward, for if we run, they will shoot us." We met them. They asked us where we were going. We told them, "Into the Country a little piece". Said they, "The enemy is just before us out here, and you cannot get out." We found that they were our men, who been trying just what we were going to try. It was then proposed that we cross the River on some logs and agreed to, but before we could find any, daylight came upon us, & to our surprise no Regt. but Forest Cavalry had gone, & the white flags were visable upon our works. So we were all prisoners.

Henry Walke: The Western Flotilla at Fort Donelson, Island Number Ten, Fort Pillow and Memphis

Henry Walke entered the navy in 1827 and served in the Mexican War. In 1862 he commanded the gunboat *Carondelet* at Fort Donelson and later fought in a series of battles on the Mississippi at Island No. Ten (so named because it was the tenth island in the river south of its junction with the Ohio), April 4–7; at Fort Pillow, Tennessee, May 10; and at Memphis, June 6, 1862. He described the campaign in a postwar article written for the *Century* magazine series *Battles and Leaders of the Civil War.*

On the 7th of February, the day after the capture of Fort Henry, I received on board the *Carondelet* Colonels Webster, Rawlins, and McPherson, with a company of troops, and under instructions from General Grant proceeded up the Tennessee River, and completed the destruction of the bridge of the Memphis and Bowling Green Railroad.

On returning from that expedition General Grant requested me to hasten to Fort Donelson with the *Carondelet*, *Tyler*, and *Lexington*, and announce my arrival by firing signal guns. The object of this movement was to take possession of the river as soon as possible, to engage the enemy's attention by making formidable demonstrations before the fort, and to prevent it from being reënforced. On February 10th the *Carondelet* alone (towed by the transport *Alps*) proceeded up the Cumberland River, and on the 12th arrived a few miles below the fort.

Fort Donelson occupied one of the best defensive positions on the river. It was built on a bold bluff about 120 feet in height, on the west side of the river, where it makes a slight bend to the eastward. It had 3 batteries, mounting in all 15 guns: the lower, about twenty feet above the water; the second, about fifty feet above the water; the third, on the summit.

When the *Carondelet*, her tow being cast off, came in sight of the fort and proceeded up to within long range of the batteries, not a living creature could be seen. The hills and woods on the west side of the river hid part of the enemy's formidable defenses, which were lightly covered with snow; but the black rows of heavy guns, pointing down on us, reminded me of the dismal-looking sepulchers cut in the rocky cliffs near Jerusalem, but far more repulsive. At 12:50 P.M., to unmask the silent enemy, and to announce my arrival to General Grant, I ordered the bow-guns to be fired at the fort. Only one shell fell short. There was no response except the echo from the hills. The fort appeared to have been evacuated. After firing ten shells into it, the *Carondelet* dropped down the river about three miles and anchored. But the sound of her guns aroused our soldiers on the southern side of the fort into action; one report says that when they heard the guns of the *avant-courrier* of the fleet, they gave cheer upon cheer, and rather than permit the sailors to get ahead of them again, they engaged in skirmishes with the enemy, and began the battle of the three days following. On the *Carondelet* we were isolated and beset with dangers from the enemy's lurking sharp-shooters.

On the 13th a dispatch was received from General Grant, informing me that he had arrived the day before, and had succeeded in getting his army in position, almost entirely investing the enemy's works. "Most of our batteries," he said, "are established, and the remainder soon will be. If you will advance with your gun-boat at 10 o'clock in the morning, we will be ready to take advantage of any diversion in our favor."

I immediately complied with these instructions, and at 9:05, with the *Carondelet* alone and under cover of a heavily wooded point, fired 139 70-pound and 64-pound shells at the fort. We received in return the fire of all the enemy's guns that could be brought to bear on the *Carondelet*, which sustained but little damage, except from two shots. One, a 128-pound solid, at 11:30 struck the corner of our port broadside casemate, passed through it, and in its progress toward the center of our boilers glanced over the temporary barricade in front of the boilers. It then passed over the steam-drum, struck the beams of the upper deck, carried away the railing around the engine-room and burst the steam-heater, and, glancing back into the engine-room, "seemed to bound after the men," as one of the engineers said, "like a wild beast pursuing its prey." I have preserved this ball as a souvenir of the fight at Fort Donelson. When it burst through the side of the *Carondelet*, it knocked down and wounded a dozen men, seven of them severely. An immense quantity of splinters was blown through the vessel. Some of them, as fine as needles, shot through the clothes of the men like arrows. Several of the wounded were so much excited by the suddenness of the event and the sufferings of their comrades, that they were not aware that they themselves had been struck until they felt the blood running into their shoes. Upon receiving this shot we ceased firing for a while.

After dinner we sent the wounded on board the *Alps*, repaired damages, and, not expecting any assistance, at 12:15 we resumed, in accordance with General Grant's request, and bombarded the fort until dusk, when nearly all our 10-inch and 15-inch shells were expended. The firing from the shore having ceased, we retired.

At 11:30 on the night of the 13th Flag-Officer Foote arrived below Fort Donelson with the iron-clads *St. Louis*, *Louisville*, and *Pittsburgh*, and the wooden gun-boats *Tyler* and *Conestoga*. On the 14th all the hard materials in the vessels, such as chains, lumber, and bags of coal, were laid on the upper decks to protect them from the plunging shots of the enemy. At 3 o'clock in the afternoon our fleet advanced to attack the fort, the *Louisville* being on the west side of the river, the *St. Louis* (flag-steamer) next, then the *Pittsburgh* and *Carondelet* on the east side of the river. The wooden gun-boats were about a thousand yards in the rear. When we started in line abreast at a moderate speed, the *Louisville* and *Pittsburgh*, not keeping up to their positions, were hailed from the flag-steamer to "steam up." At 3:30, when about a mile and a half from the fort, two shots were fired at us, both falling short. When within a mile of the fort the *St. Louis* opened fire, and the other iron-clads followed, slowly and deliberately at first, but more rapidly as the fleet advanced. The flag-officer hailed the *Carondelet*, and ordered us not to fire so fast. Some of our shells went over the fort, and almost into our camp beyond. As we drew nearer, the enemy's fire greatly increased in force and effect. But, the officers and crew of the *Carondelet* having recently been long under fire, and having become practiced in fighting, her gunners were as cool and composed as old veterans. We heard the deafening crack of the bursting shells, the crash of the solid shot, and the whizzing of fragments of shell and wood as they sped through the vessel. Soon a 128-pounder struck our anchor, smashed it into flying bolts, and bounded over the vessel, taking away a part of our smoke-stack; then another cut away the iron boat-davits as if they were pipe-stems, whereupon the boat dropped into the water. Another ripped up the iron plating and glanced over; another went through the plating and lodged in the heavy casemate; another struck the pilot-house, knocked the plating to pieces, and sent fragments of iron and splinters into the pilots, one of whom fell mortally wounded, and was taken below; another shot took away the remaining boat-davits and the boat with them; and still they came, harder and faster, taking flag-staffs and smoke-stacks, and tearing off the side armor as lightning tears the bark from a tree. Our men fought desperately, but, under the excitement of the occasion, loaded too hastily, and the port rifled gun exploded. One of the crew, in his account of the explosion soon after it occurred, said: "I was serving the gun with shell. When it exploded it knocked us all down, killing none, but wounding over a dozen men and spreading dismay and confusion among us. For about two minutes I was stunned, and at least five minutes elapsed before I could tell what was the matter. When I found out that I was more scared than hurt, although suffering from the gunpowder which I had inhaled, I looked forward and saw our gun lying on the deck, split in three pieces. Then the cry ran through the boat that we were on fire, and my duty as pumpman called me to the pumps. While I was there, two shots entered our bow-ports and killed four men and wounded several others. They were borne past me, three with their heads off. The sight almost sickened me, and I turned my head away. Our master's mate came soon after and ordered us to our quarters at the gun. I told him the gun had burst, and that we had caught fire on the upper deck from the enemy's shell. He then said: 'Never mind the fire; go to your quarters.' Then I took a station at the starboard tackle of another rifled bow-gun and remained there until the close of the fight." The carpenter and his men extinguished the flames.

When within four hundred yards of the fort, and while the

Confederates were running from their lower battery, our pilot-house was struck again and another pilot wounded, our wheel was broken, and shells from the rear boats were bursting over us. All four of our boats were shot away and dragging in the water. On looking out to bring our broadside guns to bear, we saw that the other gun-boats were rapidly falling back out of line. The *Pittsburgh* in her haste to turn struck the stern of the *Carondelet*, and broke our starboard rudder, so that we were obliged to go ahead to clear the *Pittsburgh* and the point of rocks below. The pilot of the *St. Louis* was killed, and the pilot of the *Louisville* was wounded. Both vessels had their wheel-ropes shot away, and the men were prevented from steering the *Louisville* with the tiller-ropes at the stern by the shells from the rear boats bursting over them. The *St. Louis* and *Louisville*, becoming unmanageable, were compelled to drop out of battle, and the *Pittsburgh* followed; all had suffered severely from the enemy's fire. Flag-Officer Foote was wounded while standing by the pilot of the *St. Louis* when he was killed. We were then about 350 yards from the fort.

There was no alternative for the *Carondelet* in that narrow stream but to keep her head to the enemy and fire into the fort with her two bow-guns, to prevent it, if possible, from returning her fire effectively. The enemy saw that she was in a manner left to his mercy, and concentrated the fire of all his batteries upon her. In return, the *Carondelet's* guns were well served to the last shot. Our new acting gunner, John Hall, was just the man for the occasion. He came forward, offered his services, and with my sanction took charge of the starboard-bow rifled gun. He instructed the men to obey his warnings and follow his motions, and he told them that when he saw a shot coming he would call out "Down" and stoop behind the breech of the gun as he did so; at the same instant the men were to stand away from the bow-ports. Nearly every shot from the fort struck the bows of the *Carondelet*. Most of them were fired on the ricochet level, and could be plainly seen skipping on the water before they struck. The enemy's object was to sink the gun-boat by striking her just below the water-line. They soon succeeded in planting two 32-pound shots in her bow, between wind and water, which made her leak badly, but her compartments kept her from sinking until we could plug up the shot-holes. Three shots struck the starboard casemating; four struck the port casemating forward of the rifle-gun; one struck on the starboard side, between the water-line and plank-sheer, cutting through the planking; six shots struck the pilot-house, shattering one section into pieces and cutting through the iron casing. The smoke-stacks were riddled.

Our gunners kept up a constant firing while we were falling back; and the warning words, "Look out!" "Down!" were often heard, and heeded by nearly all the gun-crews. On one occasion, while the men were at the muzzle of the middle bow-gun, loading it, the warning came just in time for them to jump aside as a 32-pounder struck the lower sill, and glancing up struck the upper sill, then, falling on the inner edge of the lower sill, bounded on deck and spun around like a top, but hurt no one. It was very evident that if the men who were loading had not obeyed the order to drop, several of them would have been killed. So I repeated the instructions and warned the men at the guns and the crew generally to bow or stand off from the ports when a shot was seen coming. But some of the young men, from a spirit of bravado or from a belief in the doctrine of fatalism, disregarded the instructions, saying it was useless to attempt to dodge a cannon-ball, and they would trust to luck. The warning words, "Look out!" "Down!" were again soon heard; down went the gunner and his men, as the whizzing shot glanced on the gun, taking off the gunner's cap and the heads of two of the young men who trusted to luck, and in defiance of the order were standing up or passing behind him. This shot killed another man also, who was at the last gun of the starboard side, and disabled the gun. It came in with a hissing sound; three sharp spats and a heavy bang told the sad fate of three brave comrades. Before the decks were well sanded, there was so much blood on them that our men could not work the guns without slipping.

We kept firing at the enemy so long as he was within range, to prevent him from seeing us through the smoke.

The *Carondelet* was the first in and the last out of the fight, and was more damaged than any of the other gun-boats, as the boat-carpenters who repaired them subsequently informed me. She was much longer under fire than any other vessel of the flotilla; and, according to the report of the Secretary of the Navy, her loss in killed and wounded was nearly twice as great as that of all the other gun-boats together. She fired more shot and shell into Fort Donelson than any other gun-boat, and was struck fifty-four times. These facts are given because a disposition was shown by correspondents and naval historians to ignore the services of the *Carondelet* on this and other occasions.

In the action of the 14th all of the armored vessels were fought with the greatest energy, skill, and courage, until disabled by the enemy's heavy shot. In his official report of the battle the flag-officer said: "The officers and men in this hotly contested but unequal fight behaved with the greatest gallantry and determination."*

Although the gun-boats were repulsed in this action, the

*From the report of Captain B. G. Bidwell, "the only officer connected with the heavy batteries of Fort Donelson who was fortunate enough to escape," we take this account of the engagement:

"All was quiet until the evening of the 14th (Friday), when 4 boats came around the point, arranged themselves in line of battle, and advanced slowly, but steadily, up the river to within 200 yards of our battery, and halted, when a most incessant fire was kept up for some time. We were ordered to hold our fire until they got within range of our 32-pounders. We remained perfectly silent, while they came over about one and a half miles, pouring a heavy fire of shot and shell upon us all the time. Two more boats came around the point and threw shell at us. Our gunners were inexperienced and knew very little of the firing of heavy guns. They, however, did some excellent shooting. The rifled gun was disabled by the ramming of a cartridge while the wire was in the vent, it being left in there by a careless gunner,—being bent, it could not be got out,—but the two center boats were both disabled, the left-center (I think) by a ricochet shot entering one of the port-holes, which are tolerably large. The right-center boat was very soon injured by a ball striking her on top, and also a direct shot in the port hole, when she fell back, the two flank boats closing in behind them and protecting them from our fire in retreat. I think these two were not seriously injured. They must have fired near two thousand shot and shell at us. Our Columbiad fired about 27 times, the rifled gun very few times, and the 32-pounders about 45 or 50 rounds each. A great many of our balls took effect, being well aimed. I am confident the efficiency of the gun-boat is in the gun it carries rather than in the boat itself. We can whip them always if our men will only stand to their guns. Not a man of all ours was hurt, notwithstanding they threw grape at us. Their fire was more destructive to our works at 2 miles than at 200 yards. They over-fired us from that distance."

demoralizing effect of their cannonade, and of the heavy and well-sustained fire of the *Carondelet* on the day before, must have been very great, and contributed in no small degree to the successful operations of the army on the following day.

After the battle I called upon the flag-officer, and found him suffering from his wounds. He asked me if I could have run past the fort, something I should not have ventured upon without permission.

The 15th was employed in the burial of our slain comrades. I read the Episcopal service on board the *Carondelet*, under our flag at half-mast; and the sailors bore their late companions to a lonely field within the shadows of the hills. When they were about to lower the first coffin, a Roman Catholic priest appeared, and his services being accepted, he read the prayers for the dead. As the last service was ended, the sound of the battle being waged by General Grant, like the rumbling of distant thunder, was the only requiem for our departed shipmates.

On Sunday, the 16th, at dawn, Fort Donelson surrendered and the gun-boats steamed up to Dover. After religious services the *Carondelet* proceeded back to Cairo, and arrived there on the morning of the 17th, in such a dense fog that she passed below the town unnoticed, and had great difficulty in finding the landing. There had been a report that the enemy was coming from Columbus to attack Cairo during the absence of its defenders; and while the *Carondelet* was cautiously feeling her way back and blowing her whistle, some people imagined she was a Confederate gun-boat about to land, and made hasty preparations to leave the place. Our announcement of the victory at Fort Donelson changed their dejection into joy and exultation. On the following morning an order congratulating the officers and men of the *Carondelet* was received from Flag-Officer Foote.

A few days later the *Carondelet* was taken up on the ways at Mound City, Illinois,—six or seven miles above Cairo on the Ohio River,—for repairs; and a crowd of carpenters worked on her night and day. After the repairs were completed, she was ordered to make the experiment of backing up-stream, which proved a laughable failure. She would sheer from one side of the river to the other, and with two anchors astern she could not be held steady enough to fight her bow-guns down-stream. She dragged both anchors alternately, until they came together, and the experiment failed completely.

On the morning of the 23d the flag-officer made a reconnoissance to Columbus, Kentucky, with four gun-boats and two mortar-boats, accompanied by the wooden gun-boat *Conestoga*, convoying five transports. The fortifications looked more formidable than ever. The enemy fired two guns, and sent up a transport with the pretext, it was said, of effecting an exchange of prisoners. But at that time, as we learned afterward from a credible source, the evacuation of the fort (which General Grant's successes at Forts Henry and Donelson had made necessary) was going on, and the last raft and barge loads of all the movable munitions of war were descending the river, which, with a large quantity previously taken away, could and would have been captured by our fleet if we had received this information in time. On the 4th of March another reconnoissance in force was made with all the gun-boats and four mortar-boats, and the fortress had still a formidable, life-like appearance, though it had been evacuated two days before.

On the 5th of March, while we were descending the Mississippi in a dense fog, the flag-steamer leading, the Confederate gun-boat *Grampus*, or *Dare-devil Jack*, the sauciest little vessel on the river, suddenly appeared across our track and "close aboard." She stopped her engines and struck her colors, and we all thought she was ours at last. But when the captain of the *Grampus* saw how slowly we moved, and as no gun was fired to bring him to, he started off with astonishing speed and was out of danger before the flag-steamer could fire a gun. She ran before us yawing and flirting about, and blowing her alarm-whistle so as to announce our approach to the enemy who had now retired to Island Number Ten, a strong position sixty miles below Columbus (and of the latitude of Forts Henry and Donelson), where General Beauregard, who was now in general command of our opponents, had determined to contest the possession of the river.

On March 15th the flotilla and transports continued on their way to Island Number Ten, arriving in its vicinity about nine in the morning. The strong and muddy current of the river had overflowed its banks and carried away every movable thing.

Houses, trees, fences, and wrecks of all kinds were being swept rapidly down-stream. The twists and turns of the river near Island Number Ten are certainly remarkable. Within a radius of eight miles from the island it crosses the boundary line of Kentucky and Tennessee three times, running on almost every point of the compass. We were greatly surprised when we arrived above Island Number Ten and saw on the bluffs a chain of forts extending for four miles along the crescent-formed shore, with the white tents of the enemy in the rear. And there lay the island in the lower corner of the crescent, with the side fronting the Missouri shore lined with heavy ordnance, so trained that with the artillery on the opposite shore almost every point on the river between the island and the Missouri bank could be reached at once by all the enemy's batteries.

On the 17th an attack was made on the upper battery by all the iron-clads and mortar-boats. The *Benton* (flag-steamer), lashed between the *Cincinnati* and *St. Louis*, was on the east side of the river; the *Mound City*, *Carondelet*, and *Pittsburgh* were on the west side; the last, however, changed her position to the east side of the river before the firing began. We opened fire on the upper fort at 1:20, and by order of the flag-officer fired one gun a minute. The enemy replied promptly, and some of his shot struck the *Benton*, but, owing to the distance from which they were fired, did but little damage. We silenced all the guns in the upper fort except one. During the action one of the rifled guns of the *St. Louis* exploded, killing and wounding several of the gunners,—another proof of the truth of the saying that the guns furnished the Western flotilla were less destructive to the enemy than to ourselves.

From March 17th to April 4th but little progress was made in the reduction of the Confederate works—the gun-boats firing a few shot now and then at long range, but doing little damage. The mortar-boats, however, were daily throwing 13-inch bombs, and so effectively at times that the Confederates were driven from their batteries and compelled to seek refuge in caves and other places of safety. But it was very evident that the great object of the expedition—the reduction of the works and the capture of the Confederate forces—could not be effected by the gun-boats alone, owing to their mode of structure and to the disadvantage under which they were fought in the strong and rapid current of the Mississippi. This was the opinion not only of naval officers, but also of General Pope and other army officers.

On the 23d of March the monotony of the long and tedious investment was unfortunately varied in a very singular manner. The *Carondelet* being moored nearest the enemy's upper fort, under several large cottonwood trees, in order to protect the mortar-boats, suddenly, and without warning, two of the largest of the trees fell across her deck, mortally wounding one of the crew and severely wounding another, and doing great damage to the vessel. This was twelve days before I ran the gauntlet at Island Number Ten with the *Carondelet*.

To understand fully the importance of that adventure, some explanation of the military situation at and below Island Number Ten seems necessary. After the evacuation of New Madrid, which General Pope had forced by blockading the river twelve miles below, at Point Pleasant, the Confederate forces occupied their fortified positions on Island Number Ten and the eastern shore of the Mississippi, where they were cut off by impassable swamps on the land side. They were in a *cul-de-sac*, and the only way open for them to obtain supplies or to effect a retreat was by the river south of Island Number Ten. General Pope, with an army of twenty thousand men, was on the western side of the river below the island. Perceiving the defect in the enemy's position, he proceeded with great promptness and ability to take advantage of it. It was his intention to cross the river and attack the enemy from below, but he could not do this without the aid of a gun-boat to silence the enemy's batteries opposite Point Pleasant and protect his army in crossing. He wrote repeatedly to Flag-Officer Foote, urging him to send down a gun-boat past the enemy's batteries on Island Number Ten, and in one of his letters expressed the belief that a boat could pass down at night under cover of the darkness. But the flag-officer invariably declined, saying in one of his letters to General Pope that the attempt "would result in the sacrifice of the boat, her officers and men, which sacrifice I would not be justified in making."

During this correspondence the bombardment still went on, but was attended with such poor results that it became a subject of ridicule among the officers of Pope's army, one of whom

(Colonel Gilmore, of Chillicothe, Ohio) is reported to have said that often when they met, and inquiry was made respecting the operations of the flotilla, the answer would generally be: "Oh! it is still bombarding the State of Tennessee at long range." And a Confederate officer said that no casualties resulted and no damage was sustained at Island Number Ten from the fire of the gun-boats.

On March 20th Flag-Officer Foote consulted his commanding officers, through Commander Stembel, as to the practicability of taking a gun-boat past the enemy's forts to New Madrid, and all except myself were opposed to the enterprise, believing with Foote that the attempt to pass the batteries would result in the almost certain destruction of the boat. I did not think so, but believed with General Pope that, under the cover of darkness and other favorable circumstances, a gun-boat might be run past the enemy's batteries, formidable as they were with nearly fifty guns. And although fully aware of the hazardous nature of the enterprise, I knew that the aid of a gun-boat was absolutely necessary to enable General Pope to succeed in his operations against the enemy, and thought the importance of this success would justifiy the risk of running the gauntlet of the batteries on Island Number Ten and on the left bank. The army officers were becoming impatient, and it was well known that the Confederates had a number of small gun-boats below, and were engaged in building several large and powerful vessels, of which the renowned *Arkansas* was one. And there was good reason to apprehend that these gun-boats would ascend the river and pass or silence Pope's batteries, and relieve the Confederate forces on Island Number Ten and the eastern shore of the Mississippi. That Pope and Foote apprehended this, appears from the correspondence between them.

The flag-officer now called a formal council of war of all his commanding officers. It was held on board the flag-steamer, on the 28th or 29th of March, and all except myself concurred in the opinion formerly expressed that the attempt to pass the batteries was too hazardous and ought not to be made. When I was asked to give my views, I favored the undertaking, and advised compliance with the requests of General Pope. When asked if I was willing to make the attempt with the *Carondelet*, I replied in the affirmative. Foote accepted my advice, and expressed himself as greatly relieved from a heavy responsibility, as he had determined to send none but volunteers on an expedition which he regarded as perilous and of very doubtful success.

Having received written orders from the flag-officer, under date of March 30th, I at once began to prepare the *Carondelet* for the ordeal. All the loose material at hand was collected, and on the 4th of April the decks were covered with it, to protect them against plunging shot. Hawsers and chain cables were placed around the pilot-house and other vulnerable parts of the vessel, and every precaution was adopted to prevent disaster. A coal-barge laden with hay and coal was lashed to the part of the port side on which there was no iron plating, to protect the magazine. It was truly said that the *Carondelet* at that time resembled a farmer's wagon prepared for market. The engineers led the escape-steam, through the pipes aft, into the wheel-house, to avoid the puffing sound it made when blown through the smoke-stacks.

All the necessary preparations having been made, I informed the flag-officer of my intention to run the gauntlet that night, and received his approval. Colonel N. B. Buford, who commanded the land forces temporarily with the flotilla, assisted me in preparing for the trip, and on the night of the 4th brought on board Captain Hottenstein, of the 42d Illinois, and twenty-three sharp-shooters of his command, who volunteered their services, which were gratefully accepted. Colonel Buford remained on board until the last moment, to encourage us. I informed the officers and crew of the character of the undertaking, and all expressed a readiness to make the venture. In order to resist boarding parties, in case of being disabled, the sailors were well armed, and pistols, cutlasses, muskets, boarding-pikes, and hand-grenades were within reach. Hose was attached to the boilers for throwing scalding water over any who might attempt to board. If it should be found impossible to save the vessel, it was designed to sink rather than burn her. During the afternoon there was a promise of a clear, moonlight night, and it was determined to wait until the moon was down, and then to make the attempt, whatever the chances. Having gone so far, we could not abandon the project without an effect on the men almost as bad as failure.

At 10 o'clock the moon had gone down, and the sky, the earth, and the river were alike hidden in the black shadow of a thunder-storm, which had now spread itself over all the heavens. As the time seemed favorable, I ordered the first master to cast off. Dark clouds now rose rapidly over us and enveloped us in almost total darkness, except when the sky was lighted up by the welcome flashes of vivid lightning, to show us the perilous way we were to take. Now and then the dim outline of the landscape could be seen, and the forest bending under the roaring storm that came rushing up the river.

With our bow pointing to the island, we passed the lowest point of land without being observed, it appears, by the enemy. All speed was given to the vessel to drive her through the tempest. The flashes of lightning continued with frightful brilliancy, and "almost every second," wrote a correspondent, "every brace, post, and outline could be seen with startling distinctness, enshrouded by a bluish white glare of light, and then her form for the next minute would become merged in the intense darkness." When opposite Battery No. 2, on the mainland,* the smoke-stacks blazed up, but the fire was soon subdued. It was caused by the soot becoming dry, as the escape-steam, which usually kept the stacks wet, had been sent into the wheel-house, as already mentioned, to prevent noise. With such vivid lightning as prevailed during the whole passage, there was no prospect of escaping the vigilance of the enemy, but there was good reason to hope that he would be unable to point his guns accurately. Again the smoke-stacks took fire, and were soon put out; and then the roar of the enemy's guns began, and from Batteries Nos. 2, 3, and 4 on the mainland came the continued crack and scream of their rifle-shells, which

*During the dark and stormy night of April 1st Colonel George W. Roberts, of the 42d Illinois Regiment, executed a brilliant exploit. Forty picked men, in five barges, with muffled oars, left for Battery No. 1. They proceeded in silence, and were unobserved until within a few rods of the fort, when a flash of lightning discovered them to the sentries, who fired. Our men, who did not reply, were soon climbing up the slippery bank, and in three minutes more the six guns were spiked, Colonel Roberts himself spiking a huge 80-pounder pivot-gun. Some of these guns had been previously dismounted by our fleet, and were now rendered doubly useless.—H. W.

seemed to unite with the electric batteries of the clouds to annihilate us.

While nearing the island or some shoal point, during a few minutes of total darkness, we were startled by the order, "Hard a-port!" from our brave and skillful pilot, First Master William R. Hoel. We almost grazed the island, and it appears were not observed through the storm until we were close in, and the enemy, having no time to point his guns, fired at random. In fact, we ran so near that the enemy did not, probably could not, depress his guns sufficiently. While close under the lee of the island and during a lull in the storm and in the firing, one of our pilots heard a Confederate officer shout, "Elevate your guns!" It is probable that the muzzles of those guns had been depressed to keep the rain out, and that the officers ordered the guns elevated just in time to save us from the direct fire of the enemy's heaviest fort; and this, no doubt, was the cause of our remarkable escape.

Having passed the principal batteries, we were greatly relieved from suspense, patiently endured, however, by the officers and crew. But there was another formidable obstacle in the way—a floating battery, which was the great "war elephant" of the Confederates, built to blockade the Mississippi permanently. As we passed her she fired six or eight shots at us, but without effect. One ball struck the coal-barge, and one was found in a bale of hay; we found also one or two musket-bullets. We arrived at New Madrid about midnight with no one hurt, and were most joyfully received by our army. At the suggestion of Paymaster Nixon, all hands "spliced the main brace."

On Sunday, the 6th, after prayers and thanksgiving, the *Carondelet* with General Gordon Granger, Colonel J. L. Kirby Smith of the 43d Ohio, and Captain Louis H. Marshall of General Pope's staff on board, made a reconnoissance twenty miles down, nearly to Tiptonville, the enemy's forts firing on her all the way down. We returned their fire, and dropped a few shells into their camps beyond. On the way back, we captured and spiked the guns of a battery of one 32-pounder and one 24-pounder, in about twenty-five minutes, opposite Point Pleasant. Before we landed to spike the guns, a tall Confederate soldier, with cool and deliberate courage, posted himself behind a large cottonwood tree, and repeatedly fired upon us, until our Illinois sharp-shooters got to work on him from behind the hammock nettings. He had two rifles, which he soon dropped, fleeing into the woods with his head down. The next day he was captured and brought into camp at Tiptonville, with the tip of his nose shot off. After the capture of this battery, the enemy prepared to evacuate his positions on Island Number Ten and the adjacent shores, and thus, as one of the historians of the civil war says, the *Carondelet* struck the blow that secured that victory.

Returning to New Madrid, we were instructed by General Pope to attack the enemy's batteries of six 64-pounders which protected his rear; and besides, another gun-boat was expected. The *Pittsburgh* (Lieutenant-Commander Thompson) ran the gauntlet without injury, during a thunder-storm, at 2 in the morning of April 7th, and arrived at 5 o'clock; but she was not ready for service, and the *Carondelet* attacked the principal batteries at Watson's Landing alone and had nearly silenced them when the *Pittsburgh* came up astern and fired nearly over the *Carondelet's* upper deck, after she and the Confederates had ceased firing. I reported to General Pope that we had cleared the opposite shores of the enemy, and were ready to cover the crossing of the river and the landing of the army. Seeing themselves cut off, the garrison at Island Number Ten surrendered to Foote on the 7th of April, the day of the Confederate repulse at Shiloh. The other Confederates retreating before Pope's advance, were nearly all overtaken and captured at 4 o'clock on the morning of the 8th; and about the same time the cavalry under Colonel W. L. Elliott took possession of the enemy's deserted works on the Tennessee shore.

The result of General Pope's operations in connection with the services of the *Carondelet* below Island Number Ten was the capture of three generals (including General W. W. Mackall, who ten days before the surrender had succeeded General John P. McCown in the command at Madrid Bend), over 5000 men, 20 pieces of heavy artillery, 7000 stand of arms, and a large quantity of ammunition and provisions, without the loss of a man on our side.

On the 12th the *Benton* (flag-steamer), with the *Cincinnati*, *Mound City*, *Cairo*, and *St. Louis*, passed Tiptonville and signaled the *Carondelet* and *Pittsburgh* to follow. Five Confederate gun-boats came up the next day and offered battle; but after the exchange of a few shots at long range they retired down the river. We followed them all the way to Craighead's Point, where they were under cover of their fortifications at Fort Pillow. I was not aware at the time that we were chasing the squadron of my esteemed shipmate of the U. S. Frigates *Cumberland* and *Merrimac*, Colonel John W. Dunnington, who afterward fought so bravely at Arkansas Post.

On the 14th General Pope's army landed about six miles above Craighead's Point, near Osceola, under the protection of the gun-boats. While he was preparing to attack Fort Pillow, Foote sent his executive officer twice to me on the *Carondelet* to inquire whether I would undertake, with my vessel and two or three other gun-boats, to pass below the fort to coöperate with General Pope, to which inquiries I replied that I was ready at any time to make the attempt. But Pope and his army (with the exception of 1500 men) were ordered away, and the expedition against Fort Pillow was abandoned. Between the 14th of April and the 10th of May two or three of the mortar-boats were towed down the river and moored near Craighead's Point, with a gun-boat to protect them. They were employed in throwing 13-inch bombs across the point into Fort Pillow, two miles distant. The enemy returned our bombardment with vigor, but not with much accuracy or effect. Several of their bombs fell near the gun-boats when we were three miles from the fort.

The Confederate fleet called the "River Defense" having been reënforced, they determined upon capturing the mortar-boats or giving us battle. On the 8th three of their vessels came to the point from which the mortar-boats had thrown their bombs, but, finding none, returned. Foote had given special orders to keep up steam and be ready for battle any moment, day or night. There was so much illness at that time in the flotilla that about a third of the officers and men were under medical treatment, and a great many were unfit for duty. On the 9th of May, at his own request, our distinguished commander-in-chief, Foote, was relieved from his arduous duties. He had become very much enfeebled from the wounds received at Fort Donelson and from illness. He carried with him the sympathy and regrets of all his command. He was succeeded by Flag-Officer Charles Henry Davis, a most excellent officer.

This paper would not be complete without some account of the naval battles fought by the flotilla immediately after the retirement of Flag-Officer Foote, under whose supervision and amid the greatest embarrassments it had been built, organized, and equipped. On the morning of the 10th of May a mortar-boat was towed down the river, as usual, at 5 A. M., to bombard Fort Pillow. The *Cincinnati* soon followed to protect her. At 6:35 eight Confederate rams came up the river at full speed. The *Carondelet* at once prepared for action, and slipped her hawser to the "bare end," ready for orders to "go ahead." No officer was on the deck of the *Benton* (flag-steamer) except the pilot, Mr. Birch, who informed the flag-officer of the situation, and passed the order to the *Carondelet* and *Pittsburgh* to proceed without waiting for the flag-steamer. General signal was also made to the fleet to get under way, but it was not visible on account of the light fog.

The *Carondelet* started immediately after the first verbal order; the others, for want of steam or some other cause, were not ready, except the *Mound City*, which put off soon after we were fairly on our way to the rescue of the *Cincinnati*. We had proceeded about a mile before our other gun-boats left their moorings. The rams were advancing rapidly, and we steered for the leading vessel, *General Bragg*, a brig-rigged, side-wheel steam ram, far in advance of the others, and apparently intent on striking the *Cincinnati*. When about three-quarters of a mile from the *General Bragg*, the *Carondelet* and *Mound City* fired on her with their bow-guns, until she struck the *Cincinnati* on the starboard quarter, making a great hole in the shell-room, through which the water poured with resistless force. The *Cincinnati* then retreated up the river and the *General Bragg* drifted down, evidently disabled. The *General Price*, following the example of her consort, also rammed the *Cincinnati*. We fired our bow-guns into the *General Price*, and she backed off, disabled also. The *Cincinnati* was again struck by one of the enemy's rams, the *General Sumter*. Having pushed on with all speed to the rescue of the *Cincinnati*, the *Carondelet* passed her in a sinking condition, and, rounding to, we fired our bow and starboard broadside guns into the retreating

General Bragg and the advancing rams, *General Jeff. Thompson*, *General Beauregard*, and *General Lovell*. Heading up-stream, close to a shoal, the *Carondelet* brought her port broadside guns to bear on the *Sumter* and *Price*, which were dropping down-stream. At this crisis the *Van Dorn* and *Little Rebel* had run above the *Carondelet*; the *Bragg*, *Jeff. Thompson*, *Beauregard*, and *Lovell* were below her. The last three, coming up, fired into the *Carondelet*; she returned their fire with her stern-guns; and, while in this position, I ordered the port rifled 50-pounder Dahlgren gun to be leveled and fired at the center of the *Sumter*. The shot struck the vessel just forward of her wheel-house, and the steam instantly poured out from her ports and all parts of her casemates, and we saw her men running out of them and falling or lying down on her deck. None of our gun-boats had yet come to the assistance of the *Carondelet*. The *Benton* and *Pittsburgh* had probably gone to aid the *Cincinnati*, and the *St. Louis* to relieve the *Mound City*, which had been badly rammed by the *Van Dorn*. The smoke at this time was so dense that we could hardly distinguish the gun-boats above us. The upper deck of the *Carondelet* was swept with grape-shot and fragments of broken shell; some of the latter were picked up by one of the sharp-shooters, who told me they were obliged to lie down under shelter to save themselves from the grape and other shot of the *Pittsburgh* above us, and from the shot and broken shell of the enemy below us. Why some of our gun-boats did not fire into the *Van Dorn* and *Little Rebel* while they were above the *Carondelet*, and prevent their escape, if possible, I never could make out.

As the smoke rose we saw that the enemy was retreating rapidly and in great confusion. The *Carondelet* dropped down to within half a mile above Craighead's Point, and kept up a continual fire upon their vessels, which were very much huddled together. When they were nearly, if not quite, beyond gunshot, the *Benton*, having raised sufficient steam, came down and passed the *Carondelet*; but the Confederates were under the protection of Fort Pillow before the *Benton* could reach them. Our fleet returned to Plum Point, except the *Carondelet*, which dropped her anchor on the battle-field, two miles or more below the point, and remained there two days on voluntary guard duty. This engagement was sharp, but not decisive.

From the first to the last shot fired by the *Carondelet*, one hour and ten minutes elapsed. After the battle, long-range firing was kept up until the evacuation of Fort Pillow.

On the 25th seven of Colonel Ellet's rams arrived,—a useful acquisition to our fleet. During the afternoon of June 4th heavy clouds of smoke were observed rising from Fort Pillow, followed by explosions, which continued through the night; the last of which, much greater than the others, lit up the heavens and the Chickasaw bluffs with a brilliant light, and convinced us that this was the parting salute of the Confederates before leaving for the lower Mississippi. At dawn next morning the fleet was all astir to take possession of Fort Pillow, the flag-steamer leading. We found the casemates, magazines, and breastworks blown to atoms.

On our way to Memphis the enemy's steamer *Sovereign* was intercepted by one of our tugs. She was run ashore by her crew, who attempted to blow her up, but were foiled in their purpose by a boy of sixteen whom the enemy had pressed into service, who, after the abandonment of the vessel, took the extra weights from the safety-valves, opened the fire-doors and flue-caps, and put water on the fires, and, having procured a sheet, signaled the tug, which came up and took possession. It may be proper to say that on our way down the river we respected private property, and did not assail or molest any except those who were in arms against us.

The morning of the 6th of June we fought the battle of Memphis, which lasted one hour and ten minutes. It was begun by an attack upon our fleet by the enemy, whose vessels were in double line of battle opposite the city. We were then at a distance of a mile and a half or two miles above the city. Their fire continued for a quarter of an hour, when the attack was promptly met by two of our ram squadron, the *Queen of the West* (Colonel Charles Ellet) leading, and the *Monarch* (Lieutenant-Colonel A. W. Ellet, younger brother of the leader). These vessels fearlessly dashed ahead of our gun-boats, ran for the enemy's fleet, and at the first plunge succeeded in sinking one vessel and disabling another. The astonished Confederates received them gallantly and effectively. The *Queen of the West* and *Monarch* were followed in line of battle by the gun-boats, under the lead of Flag-Officer Davis, and all of them opened fire, which was continued from the time we got within good range until the end of the battle—two or three tugs keeping all the while a safe distance astern. The *Queen of the West* was a quarter of a mile in advance of the *Monarch*, and after having rammed one of the enemy's fleet, she was badly rammed by the *Beauregard*, which then, in company with the *General Price*, made a dash at the *Monarch* as she approached them. The *Beauregard*, however, missed the *Monarch* and struck the *General Price* instead on her port side, cutting her down to the water-line, tearing off her wheel instantly, and placing her *hors de combat*. The *Monarch* then rammed the *Beauregard*, which had been several times raked fore and aft by the shot and shell of our iron-clads, and she quickly sank in the river opposite Memphis. The *General Lovell*, after having been badly rammed by the *Queen of the West*, was struck by our shot and shell, and, at about the same time and place as the *Beauregard*, sank to the bottom so suddenly as to take a considerable number of her officers and crew down with her, the others being saved by small boats and our tugs. The *Price*, *Little Rebel* (with a shot-hole through her steam-chest), and our *Queen of the West*, all disabled, were run on the Arkansas shore opposite Memphis; and the *Monarch* afterward ran into the *Little Rebel* just as our fleet was passing her in pursuit of the remainder of the enemy's fleet, then retreating rapidly down the river. The *Jeff. Thompson*, below the point and opposite President's Island, was the next boat disabled by our shot. She was run ashore, burned, and blown up. The Confederate ram *Sumter* was also disabled by our shell and captured. The *Bragg* soon after shared the same fate and was run ashore, where her officers abandoned her and disappeared in the forests of Arkansas. All the Confederate rams which had been run on the Arkansas shore were captured. The *Van Dorn*, having a start, alone escaped down the river. The rams *Monarch* and *Switzerland* were dispatched in pursuit of her and a few transports, but returned without overtaking them, although they captured another steamer.

The scene at this battle was rendered most sublime by the desperate nature of the engagement and the momentous consequences that followed very speedily after the first attack. Thousands of people crowded the high bluffs overlooking the river. The roar of the cannon and shell shook the houses on shore on either side for many miles. First wild yells, shrieks, and clamors, then loud, despairing murmurs, filled the affrighted city. The screaming, plunging shell crashed into the boats, blowing some of them and their crews into fragments, and the rams rushed upon each other like wild beasts in deadly conflict. Blinding smoke hovered about the scene of all this confusion and horror; and, as the battle progressed and the Confederate fleet was destroyed, all the cheering voices on shore were silenced. When the last hope of the Confederates gave way, the lamentations which went up from the spectators were like cries of anguish.

Boats were put off from our vessels to save as many lives as possible. No serious injury was received by any one on board the United States fleet. Colonel Ellet received a pistol-shot in the leg; a shot struck the *Carondelet* in the bow, broke up her anchor and anchor-stock, and fragments were scattered over her deck among her officers and crew, wounding slightly Acting-Master Gibson and two or three others who were standing at the time on the forward deck with me. The heavy timber which was suspended at the water-line, to protect the boats from the Confederate rams, greatly impeded our progress, and it was therefore cut adrift from the *Carondelet* when that vessel was in chase of the *Bragg* and *Sumter*. The latter had just landed a number of her officers and crew, some of whom were emerging from the bushes along the bank of the river, unaware of the *Carondelet's* proximity, when I hailed them through a trumpet, and ordered them to stop or be shot. They obeyed immediately, and by my orders were taken on board a tug and delivered on the *Benton*.

General Jeff. Thompson, noted in partisan or border warfare, having signally failed with those rams at Fort Pillow, now resigned them to their fate. It was said that he stood by his horse watching the struggle, and seeing at last his rams all gone, captured, sunk, or burned, he exclaimed, philosophically, "They are gone, and I am going," mounted his horse, and disappeared.

An enormous amount of property was captured by our squadron; and, in addition to the Confederate fleet, we captured at Memphis six large Mississippi steamers, each marked

"C. S. A." We also seized a large quantity of cotton in steamers and on shore, and the property at the Confederate Navy Yard, and caused the destruction of the *Tennessee*, a large steam-ram, on the stocks, which was to have been a sister ship to the renowned *Arkansas*. About one hundred Confederates were killed and wounded and one hundred and fifty captured. Chief of all results of the work of the flotilla was the opening of the Mississippi River once for all from Cairo to Memphis, and the complete possession of Western Tennessee by the Union forces.

CONFEDERATE STRATEGY: FEBRUARY 1862

Braxton Bragg to Judah P. Benjamin

By mid-February it was evident that the Confederacy's strategy of defending an extended perimeter in the western theater was failing, due especially to the Union's dominance on the western rivers. Braxton Bragg, a West Point graduate who had fought in the Seminole and Mexican wars, was a noted artillery officer in the prewar army who became a Confederate general in 1861. Bragg was commanding troops along the eastern Gulf coast when he suggested a new strategy of concentration in this letter to Confederate Secretary of War Judah P. Benjamin.

HDQRS. DEPARTMENT ALABAMA AND WEST FLORIDA,
Mobile, Ala., February 15, 1862.

Hon. J. P. BENJAMIN,
Secretary of War, Richmond, Va.:

SIR: You will excuse me, at this time of great danger to our cause, for presuming to depart from my usual course and to offer a few suggestions on our future military policy.

1. Our means and resources are too much scattered. The protection of persons and property, as such, should be abandoned, and all our means applied to the Government and the cause. Important strategic points only should be held. All means not necessary to secure these should be concentrated for a heavy blow upon the enemy where we can best assail him. Kentucky is now that point. On the Gulf we should only hold New Orleans, Mobile, and Pensacola; all other points, the whole of Texas and Florida, should be abandoned, and our means there made available for other service. A small loss of property would result from their occupation by the enemy; but our military strength would not be lessened thereby, whilst the enemy would be weakened by dispersion. We could then beat him in detail, instead of the reverse. The same remark applies to our Atlantic seaboard. In Missouri the same rule can be applied to a great extent. Deploring the misfortunes of that

gallant people, I can but think their relief must reach them through Kentucky.

2. The want of success with our artillery everywhere is deplorable; but I believe it can be explained and remedied. This arm requires knowledge, which nothing but study and experience combined can give. Unfortunately, many of our higher officers and a larger proportion of our men consider there is no duty to be done in this contest but to fight. Gallant to a fault, they ignore preparation, and exhaust their energies and time in clamoring for this fight. Calamitous results teach them too late the unfortunate error.

The enemy's light-draught gunboats require of us different defenses for our assailable points. An old-fashioned artillery will not answer. We must have long range guns to reach them, and they must be properly mounted, supplied, and served. Our 8 and 10 inch shell guns have my preference. The rifle gun I consider yet an experiment, not a success, except the light field piece—bronze; still I use them as an auxiliary. Whenever the enemy has brought his shell guns against our lighter metal, we have had to yield. But at Pensacola we crippled and drove off two of his largest and heaviest armed ships with only two 8-inch guns in an open sand battery, served, it is true, by brave men, thoroughly instructed and directed by a competent artillery officer.

We must then oppose the enemy's heavy metal by the same, and put competent men to mount, supply, and serve our own guns. If we have not the guns, it is better to yield the positions than to sacrifice our men and means in a futile attempt at defense. And when you have the guns, it is equally futile if they are handled by incompetent troops. From reports which reach us, it would appear that at least half our guns are rendered useless after the first hour, from different accidents, not attributable to the enemy, but to a want of knowledge, skill, or attention on our own part.

We have the right men, and the crisis upon us demands they should be in the right places. Our little army at Pensacola could furnish you hundreds of instructors competent to build batteries, mount guns, and teach the use of them. Our commanders are learning by bitter experience the necessity of teaching their troops; but a want of instructors is sadly felt.

Pardon me if I have been too free in the expression of my feelings and opinions, and attribute any error to an overzeal in the great cause we all have at heart.

I am, sir, very respectfully, your obedient servant,

BRAXTON BRAGG,
Major-General, Commanding.

John B. Jones: Diary, February 8–28, 1862

John B. Jones, editor of the *Southern Monitor*, a weekly journal he published in Philadelphia, fled to Richmond shortly before the outbreak of the war and took a job as clerk in the Confederate War Department. That post gave him early notice of a disheartening series of Confederate reverses in February 1862. Jones attended the inauguration of Jefferson Davis on February 22. In his address, Davis was both candid and defiant. "After a series of successes and victories, which covered our arms with glory, we have recently met with serious disasters," he said. "But in the heart of a people resolved to be free these disasters tend but to stimulate to increased resistance."

FEBRUARY 8–20TH.—Such astounding events have occurred since the 8th instant, such an excitement has prevailed, and so incessant have been my duties, that I have not kept a regular journal. I give a running account of them.

Roanoke has fallen before superior numbers, although we had 15,000 idle troops at Norfolk within hearing of the battle. The government would not interfere, and Gen. Huger refused to allow the use of a few thousand of his troops.

But Gen. Wise is safe; Providence willed that he should escape the "man-trap." When the enemy were about to open fire on his headquarters at Nag's Head, knowing him to be prostrated with illness (for the island had then been surrendered after a heroic defense), Lieutenants Bagly and Wise bore the general away in a blanket to a distance of ten or fifteen miles. The Yankees would have gladly exchanged all their prisoners for Gen. Wise, who is ever a terror to the North.

Capt. O. Jenning Wise fell, while gallantly cheering his men, in the heat of the battle. A thousand of the enemy fell before a few hundred of our brave soldiers. We lost some 2500 men, for there was no alternative but to surrender.

Capt. Wise told the Yankee officers, who persisted in forcing themselves in his presence during his dying moments, that the South could never be subjugated. They might exterminate us, but every man, woman, and child would prefer death to abject subjugation. And he died with a sweet smile on his lip, eliciting the profound respect of his most embittered enemies.

The enemy paroled our men taken on the island; and we recovered the remains of the heroic Capt. Wise. His funeral here was most impressive, and saddened the countenances of thousands who witnessed the pageant. None of the members of the government were present; but the ladies threw flowers and evergreens upon his bier. He is dead—but history will do him justice; and his example will inspire others with the spirit of true heroism.

And President Tyler is no more on earth. He died after a very brief illness. There was a grand funeral, Mr. Hunter and others delivering orations. They came to me, supposing I had written one of the several biographies of the deceased which have appeared during the last twenty years. But I had written none—and none published were worthy of the subject. I could only refer them to the bound volumes of the MADISONIAN in the State library for his messages and other State papers. The originals are among my papers in the hands of the enemy. His history is yet to be written—and it will be read centuries hence.

Fort Henry has fallen. Would that were all! The catalogue of disasters I feared and foretold, under the policy adopted by the War Department, may be a long and a terrible one.

The mission of the spies to East Tennessee is now apparent. Three of the enemy's gun-boats have ascended the Tennessee River to the very head of navigation, while the women and children on its banks could do nothing more than gaze in mute despair. No batteries, no men were there. The absence of these is what the traitors, running from here to Washington, have been reporting to the enemy. Their boats would no more have ventured up that river without the previous exploration of spies, than Mr. Lincoln would dare to penetrate a cavern without torch-bearers, in which the rattle of venomous snakes could be heard. They have ascended to Florence, and may get footing in Alabama and Mississippi!

And Fort Donelson has been attacked by an immensely superior force. We have 15,000 men there to resist, perhaps, 75,000! Was ever such management known before? Who is responsible for it? If Donelson falls, what becomes of the ten or twelve thousand men at Bowling Green?

FEBRUARY 21ST.—All our garrison in Fort Henry, with Gen. Tilghman, surrendered. I think we had only 1500 men there. Guns, ammunition, and stores, all gone.

No news from Donelson—and that is *bad* news. Benjamin says he has no definite information. But prisoners taken say the enemy have been reinforced, and are hurling 80,000 against our 15,000.

FEBRUARY 22D.—Such a day! The heavens weep incessantly. Capitol Square is black with umbrellas; and a shelter has been erected for the President to stand under.

I walked up to the monument and heard the Inaugural read by the President. He read it well, and seemed self-poised in the midst of disasters, which he acknowledged had befallen us. And he admitted that there had been errors in our war policy. We had attempted operations on too extensive a scale, thus diffusing our powers which should have been concentrated. I like these candid confessions. They augur a different policy hereafter, and we may hope for better results in the future. We must all stand up for our country.

Mr. Hunter has resigned, and taken his place in the Senate.

FEBRUARY 23D.—At last we have the astounding tidings that Donelson has fallen, and Buckner, and 9,000 men, arms, stores, everything are in the possession of the enemy! Did the President know it yesterday? Or did the Secretary keep it back till the new government (permanent) was launched into existence? Wherefore? The Southern *people* cannot be daunted by calamity!

Last night it was still raining—and it rained all night. It was a lugubrious reception at the President's mansion. But the President himself was calm, and Mrs. Davis seemed in spirits. For a long time I feared the bad weather would keep the people away; and the thought struck me when I entered, that if there were a Lincoln spy present, we should have more ridicule in the Yankee presses on the paucity of numbers attending the reception. But the crowd came at last, and filled the ample rooms. The permanent government had its birth in storm, but it may yet flourish in sunshine. For my own part, however, I think a provisional government of few men, should have been adopted "for the war."

FEBRUARY 24TH.—Gen. Sydney Johnston has evacuated Bowling Green with his *ten* or *twelve* thousand men! Where is his mighty army now? It never did exist!

FEBRUARY 25TH.—And Nashville must fall—although no one seems to anticipate such calamity. We must run the career of disasters allotted us, and await the turning of the tide.

FEBRUARY 26TH.—Congress, in secret session, has authorized the declaration of martial law in this city, and at some few other places. This might be well under other circumstances; but it will not be well if the old general in command should be clothed with powers which he has no qualifications to wield advantageously. The facile old man will do *anything* the Secretary advises.

Our army is to fall back from Manassas! The Rappahannock is not to be our line of *defense*. Of course the enemy will soon strike at Richmond from some direction. I have given great offense to some of our people by saying the policy of permitting men to go North at will, will bring the enemy to the gates of the city in ninety days. Several have told me that the prediction has been marked in the Secretary's tablets, and that I am marked for destruction if it be not verified. I reply that I would rather be destroyed than that it should be fulfilled.

FEBRUARY 27TH.—Columbus is to be evacuated. Beauregard sees that it is untenable with Forts Henry and Donelson in possession of the enemy. He will not be caught in such a trap as that. But he is erecting a battery at Island No. 10 that will give the Yankees trouble. I hope it may stay the catalogue of disasters.

FEBRUARY 28TH.—These calamities may be a wholesome chastening for us. We shall now go to work and raise troops enough to defend the country. Congress will certainly pass the Conscription Act recommended by the President.

RICHMOND, VIRGINIA, FEBRUARY 1862

Jefferson Davis: Message to the Confederate Congress

The Confederate Provisional Congress adjourned on February 17, 1862, and was succeeded the next day by the First Confederate Congress, which had been elected in November 1861. Three days after being inaugurated for a full six-year term as president, Jefferson Davis submitted a written message to the new Congress on "the State of the Confederacy."

Richmond, February 25, 1862

IN OBEDIENCE to the Constitutional provision requiring the President from time to time to give to the Congress information of the State of the Confederacy, and recommend to their consideration such measures as he shall judge necessary and expedient, I have to communicate that since my message at the last session of the Provisional Congress, events have demonstrated that the Government had attempted more than it had power successfully to achieve.

Hence, in the effort to protect by our arms the whole of the territory of the Confederate States, Sea-board and inland, we have been so exposed as recently to encounter serious disasters. When the Confederacy was formed, the States composing it were, by the peculiar character of their pursuits and a misplaced confidence in their former associates, to a great extent destitute of the means for the prosecution of the war on so gigantic a scale as that which it has attained. The workshops and artisans were mainly to be found in the Northern States, and one of the first duties which devolved upon this Government was to establish the necessary manufactories, and in the meantime, to obtain by purchase from abroad, as far as practicable whatever was required for the public defence. No effort has been spared to effect both these ends, and though the results have not equalled our hopes, it is believed that an impartial judgment will, upon full investigation, award to the various departments of the Government credit for having done all which human power and foresight enabled them to accomplish. The valor and devotion of the people have not only sustained the efforts of the Government, but have gone far to supply its deficiencies.

The active state of military preparation among the nations of Europe in April last, the date when our agents first went abroad, interposed unavoidable delays in the procurement of arms, and the want of a navy has greatly impeded our efforts to import military supplies of all sorts.

I have hoped for several days to receive official reports in relation to our discomfiture at Roanoke Island, and the fall of Fort Donelson. They have not yet reached me, and I am, therefore, unable to communicate to you such information of those events and the consequences resulting from them, as would enable me to make recommendations founded upon the changed condition which they have produced. Enough is known of the surrender at Roanoke Island to make us feel that it was deeply humiliating, however imperfect may have been the preparations for defence. The hope is still entertained that our reported losses at Fort Donelson have been greatly exaggerated, inasmuch as I am not only unwilling but unable to believe that a large army of our people have surrendered without a desperate effort to cut their way through investing forces, whatever may have been their numbers, and to endeavor to make a junction with other divisions of the Army. But in the absence, of that exact information which can only be afforded by official reports, it would be premature to pass judgment, and my own is reserved, as I trust yours will be, until that information is received. In the meantime, Strenuous efforts have been made to throw forward reenforcements to the Armies at the positions threatened, and I cannot doubt that the bitter disappointments we have borne, by nerving the people to still greater exertions, will speedily secure results more accordant with our just expectation, and as favorable to our cause as those which marked the earlier periods of the War.

The reports of the Secretaries of War and the Navy will exhibit the mass of resources for the conduct of the War which we have been enabled to accumulate notwithstanding the very serious difficulties against which we have contended.

They afford the cheering hope that our resources, limited as they were at the beginning of the contest, will, during its progress, become developed to such an extent as fully to meet our future wants.

The policy of enlistment for short terms against which I have steadily contended from the commencement of the war has, in my judgment, contributed in no immaterial degree to the recent reverses which we have suffered, and even now renders it difficult to furnish you an accurate statement of the Army. When the War first broke out many of our people could with difficulty be persuaded that it would be long or serious. It was not deemed possible that anything so insane as a persistent attempt to subjugate these States could be made—still less that the delusion would so far prevail as to give to the war the vast proportions which it has assumed. The people, incredulous of a long War, were naturally averse to long enlistments, and the early legislation of Congress rendered it impracticable to obtain Volunteers for a greater period than twelve months. Now that it has become probable that the war will be continued through a series of years, our high-spirited and gallant soldiers, while generally re-enlisting, are, from the fact of having entered the service for a short term, compelled in many instances to go home to make the necessary arrangements for their families during their prolonged absence.

The quotas of new regiments for the war, called for from the different States, are in rapid progress of organization. The whole body of new levies and re-enlisted men will probably be ready in the ranks within the next thirty days. But, in the meantime, it is exceedingly difficult to give an accurate statement of the number of our forces in the field. They may, in general terms, be stated at 400 regiments of infantry, with a proportionate force of Cavalry and artillery, the details of which will be shown by the report of the Secretary of War. I deem it proper to advert to the fact that the process of furloughs and re-enlistment in progress for the last month had so far disorganized and weakened our forces as to impair our ability for successful defence; but I heartily congratulate you that this evil, which I had foreseen and was powerless to prevent, may now be said to be substantially at an end, and that we shall not again during the war be exposed to seeing our strength diminished by this fruitful cause of disaster—short enlistments.

The people of the Confederate States being principally engaged in agricultural pursuits, were unprovided at the commencement of hostilities with ships, ship-yards, materials for shipbuilding, or skilled mechanics and seamen in sufficient numbers to make the prompt creation of a navy a practicable task even if the required appropriations had been made for the purpose. Notwithstanding our very limited resources, however, the report of the Secretary will exhibit to you a satisfactory progress in preparation, and a certainty of early completion of vessels of a number and class on which we may confidently rely for contesting the vaunted control of the enemy over our waters.

The financial system devised by the wisdom of your predecessors has proved adequate to supplying all the wants of the Government notwithstanding the unexpected and very large increase of expenditures resulting from the great augmentation in the necessary means of defence. The report of the Secretary of the Treasury will exhibit the gratifying fact that we have no floating debt; that the credit of the Government is unimpaired, and that the total expenditure of the Government for the year has been in round numbers one hundred and seventy millions of dollars; less than one-third of the sum wasted by the enemy in his vain effort to conquer us—less than the value of a single article of export—the cotton crop of the year.

The report of the Post Master General will show the condition of that department to be steadily improving—its revenues increasing, and already affording the assurance that it will be selfsustaining at the date required by the Constitution while affording ample mail facilities for the people.

In the Department of Justice, which includes the Patent Office and Public Printing, some legislative provisions will be required, which will be specifically stated in the report of the head of that Department. I invite the attention of Congress to the duty of organizing a Supreme Court of the Confederate States; in accordance with the mandate of the Constitution.

I refer you to my message communicated to the Provisional Congress in November last for such further information touching the condition of public affairs as it might be useful to lay before you; the short interval which has since elapsed not having produced any material changes in that condition other than those to which reference has already been made.

In conclusion, I cordially welcome Representatives who, recently chosen by the people, are fully imbued with their views and feelings, and can so ably advise me as to the needful provisions for the public service. I assure you of my hearty cooperation in all your efforts for the common welfare of the country

JEFFERSON DAVIS

"THE BOLDEST FEAT": MARYLAND, MARCH 1862

George E. Stephens to the Weekly Anglo-African

The son of free blacks who fled to Philadelphia from Virginia after the Nat Turner slave rebellion, George E. Stephens was an abolitionist who worked before the war as a cabinetmaker, upholsterer, and sailor. In October 1861 he became a correspondent for the New York *Weekly Anglo-African*, an influential black newspaper, while serving as a cook and personal servant to Lieutenant Colonel Benjamin Tilghman of the 26th Pennsylvania Infantry Regiment. Stephens spent the winter of 1861–62 along the lower Potomac in Charles County, Maryland, reporting on army camp life and the interactions among soldiers, slaves, and slaveholders. His letter of March 2 appeared in the *Anglo-African* on March 15, 1862.

Head Quarters, Hooker's Division,
Near Budd's Ferry, Md.,
March 2d, 1862.

Mr. Editor.—We have had high winds for the last two or three days, interspersed of course with rain, but if the rain would cease these driving March winds would soon dry up the roads, and the grand army of the Potomac would be able to walk dry shod over into the unhappy land of Canaan, (Dixie's land.)

The rumor has reached us that Gen. Banks has been defeated, and his forces completely routed on the upper Potomac.

Professor Lowe has been unable to make his usual daily balloon reconnaissance on account of the high wind. The wind blew so violently on Tuesday last that he was compelled to disinflate his balloon, but will reinflate it as soon as the winds subside.

We are reliably informed that the rebels immediately in front of us have received large reinforcements; they evidently anticipate an attack.

Brigadier General Naglee, of Pennsylvania, arrived in camp on the 17th ult., and took command of 1st Brigade, in place of

Col. Cowdin, of the 1st Massachusetts regiment, who returns to his command.

Captain Page who has commanded at Liverpool Point, where the contrabands are employed unloading vessels, etc., and where the army supplies are stored, relates that two of these contrabands undertook and accomplished the boldest feat of the war, thus furnishing us with another irrefutable evidence of the courage, daring and skill of the negro, when brought face to face with danger; the strength and permanence of his affections, which is the noblest evidence, too, of a pure, perfect and elevated nature. These men belong to the party Col. Graham brought off when he made his inroad into Virginia. The captain says that one of them came to him and asked permission to recross the river to rescue his wife, declaring that he was almost certain that he could bring her off safely. The captain thought the fellow mad, but he plead so earnestly that he gave him permission, and gave notice of the fact to the commander of the flotilla, to prevent his being fired upon by the gun boats. He left Liverpool Point on a dark night, in a small skiff with muffled oars. His wife lived some six or seven miles up the Occoquan Bay. He reached her, brought her off safe, gathered much valuable information of the strength and position of the enemy, and returned the following night to Liverpool Point with his companion, safe and unharmed. This man is a true type of the negro; jet black, erect and athletic. The other man, a type of the mixed blood, seeing the triumph of his comrade, asked and received permission to secure his wife, and not having as far to go, brought her off triumphantly and returned the same evening that he went upon his errand. When it is remembered that the rebels are very vigilant on account of the expected attack of our forces, and that the beach is lined with sentinels from Martha's Point to Occoquan Bay, whose bivouac fires can be seen every night with common glasses, and also that if they had been detected nothing but instant death would have been meted out to them, we must accord these two of the most daring ventures and successful exploits of the war. If these men and their brethren were allowed to become active instead of passive co-operators with the Union forces, how long would treason be able to so impudently defy the federal powers?

Here is an item I give you for the special benefit of your fair readers. The more susceptible of the sterner sex may also gather whatever satisfaction this little story of love, struggle and triumph, may give. One of the most painful of the revolting sights one sees when sojourning in this land of slavery, is the universal prostitution by their masters of beautiful slave women. There are scarcely any farms or plantations in the south that can boast of no pretty women. They are prized, petted, bartered and sold according to the nature and extent of their charms. Beauties rivaling those of the Caucasian are sold in the slave marts of the U.S. No matter how loathsome to her the purchaser of her charms may be, the hard remorseless necessities of her position compel her to yield. Mary Thomas, a beautiful negress, the slave of a man by the name of Henry Eglon, living near Newport, belonged to this class. Her master had already engaged her to an old lecherous scoundrel. She fell violently in love with an Anglo-African in one of the companies. Longing to be free, and to escape that living martyrdom, the life which her master had marked out for her, and also unite her destiny with that of her lover, she made a bold stroke for life, love and liberty. She did not clothe herself in male apparel, like many of the paler heroines and amazons have done, but maintained a distinction of sex. She had not gone far before Ferrel, a slave master near Port Tobacco, arrested her and locked her up in the jail at that place. Her lover broke the jail open and released her. She had not been released five minutes before Johnny Shackelford, a noted slave hunter, re-arrested her; but the girl fought him bravely. Her lover and the soldiers could not quietly look on such a contest as this; they came to the rescue, and just barely left life in the hunter. And why should she not triumph? Did not she turn her back on slavery and ruin, while the path which she proposed to tread was illuminated with the bright hope of salvation, liberty and love? I rejoice to say that Mary Thomas to-day is free!

There is nothing more galling to a black man than the iteration and reiteration of the foul misrepresentations which the advocate of man-stealing, man-torturing, and man-slaughtering slavery urge against him. There never has been a time in the history of this country, when there was such a scarcity of material to build these heartless lies on. They may oppose us and deny us rights, but our friends and ourselves will soon settle the contest of ideas; but when our enemies add "insult to injury" it incites in us the desire to cut their throats or give them a taste of the horrors of the system they so much love. Although the Government has spurned the loyalty of the negro more pointedly and peremptorily than it has the treason of these slaveholding dogs and their Northern tools and accomplices, they have, as by some unseen power, become active and prominent in this great civil contest, and have impressed the indelible truth upon the minds of the thinking portion of this nation that he is a dreadful power for evil or a grand and noble one for good.

Rum Point and Liverpool Point, as I have often before remarked, are the points where the supplies are landed. Before the contrabands were brought here, details from the various regiments were made to unload the vessels and to store the provisions; these details generally numbered about a hundred men—a whole company. The soldiers were not allowed for this special duty any extra compensation; so the result was, that they skulked out of as much work as they could, upon the principle that it is far more agreeable and much more reasonable to play for nothing than to work for nothing. They were certain to get their $13 per month, and this poor pay and poorer fare formed no incentive to hard manual labor. Since the 30 or 40 muscular blacks have arrived at Liverpool Point it is made the principle depot for stores and Rum Point is made the passenger depot; and these 30 or 40 men do more in the same space of time than a hundred white men—thus reversing the order of things. The black man under the incentives of Free labor, pay, and freedom, goes blithely and gaily to his task; while the white man under the repulsiveness of forced labor and no pay, lounges about and skulks sulkily away. They are also temperate and cleanly; are comfortably housed, clothed and fed by the Government, wives, children, and all; and are to receive ten cents a day pay, which is small—but when the housing, clothing and feeding of a man and his family are considered, his pay is nearly as good as the enlisted soldier; it can all be saved up by them, and will make a small start for them when they shall be released by the authorities.

G.E.S.

Orpheus C. Kerr: from The Orpheus C. Kerr Papers

The never-changing bulletin "All Quiet on the Potomac," issued by the seemingly immovable Army of the Potomac through the winter of 1861–62, inspired the satirist Robert Henry Newell, writing in the guise of his commentator Orpheus C. Kerr (i.e. "office seeker") to construct a fable. Newell's dispatches, published in the *New York Sunday Mercury*, had many admirers, including President Lincoln, and were published in three wartime volumes under the rubric *The Orpheus C. Kerr Papers.*

WASHINGTON, D. C., March 3d, 1862.

I KNOW a man, my boy, who was driven to lunacy by reliable war news. He was in the prime of life when the war broke out, and took such an interest in the struggle that it soon became nearly equal to the interest on his debts. With all the enthusiasm of vegetable youth he subscribed for all the papers, and commenced to read the reliable war news. In this way he learned that all was quiet on the Potomac, and immediately went to congratulate his friends, and purchase six American flags. On the following morning he wrapt himself in the banner of his country and learned from all the papers that all was quiet on the Potomac. His joy at once became intense; he hoisted a flag on the lightning-rod of his domicil, purchased a national pocket-handkerchief, bought six hand-organs that played the Star-Spangled Banner, and drank nothing but gunpowder tea. In the next six months, however, there was a great change in our military affairs; the backbone of the rebellion was broken, the sound of the thunder came from all parts of the sky, and fifty-three excellent family journals informed the enthusiast that all was quiet on the Potomac. He now became fairly mad with bliss, and volunteered to sit up with a young lady whose brother was a soldier. On the following morning he commenced to read Bancroft's History of the United States, with Hardee's Tactics appended, only pausing long enough to learn from the daily papers that all was quiet on the Potomac. Thus, in a fairy dream of delicious joy, passed the greater part of this devoted patriot's life; and even as his hair turned gray, and his form began to bend with old age, his eye flashed in eternal youth over the still reliable war news. At length there came a great change in the military career of the Republic; the rebellion received its death-wound, and Washington's Birthday boomed upon the United States of America. It was the morning of that glorious day, and the venerable patriot was tottering about the room with his cane, when his great-grandchild, a lad of twenty-five, came thundering into the room with forty-three daily papers under his arm.

"Old man!" says he, in a transport, "there's great news."

"Boy, boy!" says the aged patriot, "do not trifle with me. Can it be that—"

"Bet your life—"

"Is it then a fact that—"

"Yes—"

"Am I to believe that—"

"ALL IS QUIET ON THE POTOMAC!"

It was too much for the venerable Brutus; he clutched at the air, spun once on his left heel, sang a stave of John Brown's body, and stood transfixed with ecstacy.

"Thank Heving," says he, "for sparing me to see this day!"

After which he became hopelessly insane, my boy, and raved so awfully about all our great generals turning into mud-larks that his afflicted family had to send him to the asylum.

This veracious and touching biography will show you how dangerous to public health is reliable war news, and convince you that the Secretary's order to the press is only a proper in-sanitary measure.

I am all the more resigned to it, my boy, because it affects me so little that I am even able to give you a strictly reliable account of a great movement that lately took place.

I went down to Accomac early in the week, my boy, having heard that Captain Villiam Brown and the Conic Section of the Mackerel Brigade were about to march upon Fort Muggins, where Jeff Davis, Beauregard, Mason, Slidell, Yancey, and the whole rebel Congress were believed to be intrenched. Mounted on my gothic steed Pegasus, who only blew down once in the whole journey, I repaired to Villiam's department, and was taking notes of the advance, upon a sheet of paper spread on the ground, when the commander of Accomac approached me, and says he:

"What are you doing, my bantam?"

"I'm taking notes," says I, "for a journal which has such an immense circulation among our gallant troops that when they begin to read it in the camps, it looks, from a distance, as though there had just been a heavy snow-storm.'

"Ah!" says Villiam, thoughtfully, "newspapers and snow-storms are somewhat alike; for both make black appear white. But," said Villiam philosophically, "the snow is the more moral; for you can't lie in that with safety, as you can in a newspaper. In the language of General Grant at Donelson," says Villiam, sternly: "I propose to move upon your works immediately."

And with that he planted one of his boots right in the middle of my paper.

"Read that ere Napoleonic dockyment," says Villiam, handing me a scroll. It was as follows:

EDICK.

Having noticed that the press of the United States of America is making a ass of itself, by giving information to the enemy concerning the best methods of carrying on the strategy of war, I do hereby assume control of all special correspondents, forbidding them to transact anything but private business; neither they, nor their wives, nor their children, to the third and fourth generation.

I. It is ordered, that all advice from editors to the War Department, to the general commanding, or the generals commanding the armies in the field, be absolutely forbidden; as such advice is calculated to make the United States of America a idiot.

II. Any newspaper publishing any news whatever, however obtained, shall be excluded from all railroads and steamboats, in order that country journals, which receive the same news during the following year, may not be injured in cirkylation.

III. This control of special correspondents does not include the correspondent of the London Times, who wouldn't be believed if he published all the news of the next Christian era. By order of

VILLIAM BROWN, Eskevire,
Captain Conic Section Mackerel Brigade.

I had remounted Pegasus while reading this able State paper, my boy, and had just finished it, when a nervous member of the advance-guard accidentally touched off a cannon, whose report was almost immediately answered by one from the dense fog before us.

"Ha!" says Captain Villiam Brown, suddenly leaping from his steed, and creeping under it—to examine if the saddle-girth was all right—"the fort is right before us in the fog, and the rebels are awake. Let the Orange County Company advance with their howitzers, and fire to the north-east."

The Orange County Company, my boy, instantly wheeled their howitzers into position, and sent some pounds of grape toward the meridian, the roar of their weapons of death being instantaneously answered by a thundering crash in the fog.

Company 3, Regiment 5, Mackerel Brigade, now went forward six yards at double-quick, and poured in a rattling volley of musketry, dodging fearlessly when exactly the same kind of a volley was heard in the fog, and wishing that they might have a few rebels for supper.

"Ha!" says Captain Villiam Brown, when he noticed that nobody seemed to be killed yet; "Providence is on our side, and this here unnatural rebellion is squelched. Let the Anatomical Cavalry charge into the fog, and demand the surrender of Fort Muggins," continued Villiam, compressing his lips with mad valor, "while I repair to that tree back there, and see if there is not a fiendish secessionist lurking behind it."

The Anatomical Cavalry immediately dismounted from their horses, which were too old to be used in a charge, and gallantly entered the fog, with their sabres between their teeth, and their hands in their pockets—it being a part of their tactics to catch a rebel before cutting his head off.

In the meantime, my boy, the Orange County howitzers and the Mackerel muskets were hurling a continuous fire into the clouds, stirring up the angels, and loosening the smaller planets. Sturdily answered the rebels from the fog-begirt fort; but not one of our men had yet fallen.

Captain Villiam Brown was just coming down from the top of a very tall tree, whither he had gone to search for masked batteries, when the fog commenced lifting, and disclosed the Anatomical Cavalry returning at double-quick.

Instantly our fire ceased, and so did that of the rebels.

"Does the fort surrender to the United States of America?" says Villiam, to the captain of the Anatomicals.

The gallant dragoon, sighed, and says he:

"I used my magnifying glass, but could find no fort."

At this moment, my boy, a sharp sunbeam cleft the fog as a sword does a vail, and the mist rolled away from the scene in two volumes, disclosing to our view a fine cabbage-patch, with a dense wood beyond.

Villiam deliberately raised a bottle to his face, and gazed through it upon the unexpected prospect.

"Ha!" says he sadly, "the garrison has cut its way through the fog and escaped, but Fort Muggins is ours! Let the flag of our Union be planted on the ramparts," says Villiam, with much perspiration, "and I will immediately issue a proclamation to the people of the United States of America."

Believing that Villiam was somewhat too hasty in his conclusions, my boy, I ventured to insinuate that what he had taken for a fort in the fog, was really nothing but a cabbage inclosure, and that the escaped rebels were purely imaginary.

"Imaginary!" says Villiam, hastily placing his canteen in his pocket. "Why, didn't you hear the roar of their artillery?"

"Do you see that thick wood yonder?" says I.

Says he, "It is visible to the undressed eye."

"Well," says I, "what you took for the sound of rebel firing, was only the echo of your own firing in that wood."

Villiam pondered for a few moments, my boy, like one who was considering the propriety of saying nothing in as few words as possible, and then looked angularly at me, and says he:

"My proclamation to the press will cover all this, and the news of this here engagement will keep until the war is over. Ah!" says Villiam, "I wouldn't have the news of this affair published on any account; for if the Government thought I was trying to cabbage in my Department, it would make me Minister to Russia immediately."

As the Conic Section of the Mackerel Brigade returned slowly to head-quarters, my boy, I thought to myself: How often does man, after making something his particular forte, discover at last that it is only a cabbage-patch, and hardly large enough at that for a big hog like himself!

Yours, philanthropically,
ORPHEUS C. KERR.

BATTLE OF ELKHORN TAVERN:
ARKANSAS, MARCH 1862

Dabney H. Maury: Recollections of the Elkhorn Campaign

Following their victory at Wilson's Creek in southwestern Missouri in August 1861, the Confederates were pushed back into northwestern Arkansas by Brigadier General Samuel R. Curtis. A counterstroke by Major General Earl Van Dorn, Confederate commander in the Trans-Mississippi, led to the battle of Elkhorn Tavern (or Pea Ridge) on March 7–8, 1862. With 14,000 Confederate and 10,000 Union troops engaged, it was the war's largest battle west of the Mississippi. The Union lost 1,384 men killed, wounded, or missing, while Confederate casualties may have totaled 2,000. Colonel Dabney H. Maury, a West Point graduate, served on Van Dorn's staff and offered a Confederate view of the fighting in an article published by the Southern Historical Society in 1876. The Northern victory at Elkhorn Tavern kept Missouri in the Union and disrupted Confederate plans for the Trans-Mississippi.

MONTGOMERY WHITE SULPHUR SPRINGS, VA.,
June 10th, 1876.

Colonel WM. PRESTON JOHNSTON:

My dear Colonel—In compliance with your request, I will endeavor to write you some recollections of the campaign of Elkhorn. As I am not able to refer to any documents, I can only give you my recollections; and I hope, therefore, that any one who can correct my mistakes of omission will do so, for after a lapse of so long a time, passed in events of such absorbing interest as those of our great war, one's memory loses many facts.

In January, 1862, General Earl Van Dorn was appointed commander of the Trans-Mississippi Department, then a part of the great territorial command of your father, General Sydney Johnston. I was ordered from the Potomac to go with Van Dorn as chief of the staff of his Trans-Mississippi district.

In February we reached Jacksonport, Arkansas, on the White

river, and soon after moved up to Pocahontas, in the northeastern part of Arkansas, and began to organize an expedition against Saint Louis. Van Dorn's plan was to carry Saint Louis by a *coup de main*, and then to throw his forces into Illinois and transfer the war into the enemy's country.

We had been busily occupied in preparing for this operation, when, late in February, Colonel Clay Taylor arrived at headquarters with dispatches from General Price, then in Boston mountains in northwest Arkansas. General Price related that after his victory at Springfield, or Oakhill, he had been forced by the reinforced enemy to retreat through Missouri down into Arkansas; that General McCulloch, commanding the Texans, was near him in Boston mountain; that the enemy, under Generals Curtis and Siegel, were lying only two marches distant, not over 18,000 strong, and might be overcome by a vigorous, combined attack of all the forces of McCulloch and Price,—but that points of difference of opinion and precedence of rank had arisen between them, in consequence of which no co-operation could be efficiently conducted; and he prayed that Van Dorn, as their common superior, would come at once to Boston mountains, combine the forces of the discordant generals, and lead them to attack the enemy's army.

As our designed operations upon Saint Louis depended mainly upon these commands of Price and McCulloch for success, Van Dorn at once set out for Boston mountains, where he knew he would find a battle ready for him, and, should victory crown him, the success of his Saint Louis expedition would be assured.

We took a steamer for Jacksonport, whence on February 23d, we mounted our horses and started upon our ride across the State to Van Buren. Our party consisted of Van Dorn, myself, Lieutenant Sullivan, who was nephew and aid-de-camp to General Van Dorn, my negro boy Jem, and a guide—a stupid, hulking fellow, who did us more harm than service. Leaving Jacksonport in the morning, we rode twelve miles to the spacious and hospitable farm house of a planter named Bryan, I think. I shall be sorry if I have not given his name, for he was very intelligent and very hospitable, and with him and the kind mistress of his house and her daughters, we found the most cordial and comfortable entertainment we ever met with beyond the Mississippi, and in the trials and disappointments which soon after befell us, we often reverted to that night as a "green spot" in our Arkansas experience.

Next morning, February 24th, we set out after a most abundant breakfast, on our ride across the State of Arkansas. Van Dorn on his black mare, a powerful, hardy thoroughbred, led off in a trot which, for the ensuing five days, carried us along at about fifty miles a day.

He wore a very beautiful Turkish cimeter, the gift of a friend. It was the only article of personal belonging in which I ever knew him to evince especial pleasure. When about five miles from the house he missed his sabre from its sheath. Sullivan insisted on riding back to look for it, while we pursued our way in that relentless trot. Something was said about the "bad omen," which jarred on my feelings and was remembered. Sullivan soon rejoined us with the sword, which he found lying in the road a mile or so behind us.

On the second day, February 25th, we crossed Black river. The stream was narrow, but rapid and deep to the banks. The ferryboat was a long "dug out."

Van Dorn entered first, taking with him Jem, and at the moment of leaving the shore the guide also stepped into the boat and capsized it. Van Dorn, being at the further end, was thrown well out into the stream—encumbered with his heavy cavalry cloak, boots, spurs and sabre; but he struck strongly out for the shore, with a countenance as smiling as ever a schoolboy wore in a summer bath.

Seeing he was all right, I directed my interest and efforts to Jem, who, though a stout swimmer and not excessively encumbered by raiment, seemed to realise all the gravity of his position. His round eyes were distended to their utmost, and he blew the water out at every stroke with the snort of a porpoise, and was the picture of a negro who knew he was swimming for his life. I stood ready with my sash to throw out to him, but he soon struck bottom at the very shore, and scrambled out. The day was very bleak; and after crossing over the river we halted for two hours in a very comfortless house, where Van Dorn made an ineffectual effort to dry his clothes, which resulted in the severest attack of chill and fever I ever saw. It clung to him throughout the campaign, and except when in the presence of the enemy, made him quake as Cassius tells us Cæsar did.

I revert to this whole march as peculiarly devoid of interest or pleasure. The country was monotonous and unpicturesque, while some of the people were ignorant of the causes and objects of the war and unsympathetic with us; but there were many honorable exceptions to this, and every night of our five days' trip we received hospitable entertainment in the house of an Arkansas planter; and every night we each slept in a feather bed, which closed about us like a poultice and drew out all the soreness of the sore bones and the saddle-galls which our fifty miles' ride had left with us. After a lifetime of experience in the cavalry service, I then discovered in a feather bed the only panacea for a jaded horseman's ills.

Although I had not made a day's march in the saddle for months prior to our trip across Arkansas, and although every day we trotted from fifty to fifty-five miles, on leaving our feather beds at dawn for our saddles, we found all the stiffness and soreness had been drawn out of us, and we were as fresh and nimble as if we were just setting out.

The United States War Department ought to know about this, and all the cavalry ought to sleep in feather beds: no man can get good rest on the bare ground. And "post traders" would make great profit in feathers if the constituted authorities would only adopt them.

We rode into Van Buren on the evening of February 28th, and next morning, March 1st, left Van Buren for Price's camp in Boston mountains, distant about thirty miles.

The weather was bitter cold, and all day we rode over an ascending mountain road until dark, when we came to the little farm house in which the leader of the Missourians had made his headquarters.

I was much impressed by the grand proportions and the stately air of the man who up to that time had been the foremost figure of the war beyond the Mississippi.

General Price was one of the handsomest men I have ever seen. He was over six feet two inches in stature, of massive proportions, but easy and graceful in his carriage and his gestures; his hands and feet were remarkably small and well shaped; his hair and whiskers, which he wore in the old English fashion, were silver white; his face was ruddy and very benignant, yet firm in its expression; his profile was finely chiseled, and bespoke manhood of the highest type; his voice was clear and ringing, and his accentuation singularly distinct. A braver or a kinder heart beat in no man's bosom; he was wise in counsel and bold in action, and never spared his own blood on any battle field. No man had greater influence over his troops; and as he sat his superb charger with the ease and lightness of one accustomed all his days to "ride a thoroughbred horse," it was impossible to find a more magnificent specimen of manhood in its prime, than Sterling Price presented to the brave Missourians, who loved him with a fervor not less than we Virginians felt for Lee.

On this our first meeting, General Price showed us the hospitality traditional of his native State (Virginia). He took Van Dorn to share his chamber, and sent a staff officer to conduct Sullivan and me to the bivouac of his staff, where we found sumptuous entertainment.

Never before or since have I enjoyed such luxurious accommodations in camp as were at my service that wintry night, in the camp of Price's staff in the Boston mountains.

We were conducted to a beautiful little meadow, where the staff and the band (all through the war he carried with him a fine band) had cast their lines in one of the pleasantest places I have ever been in during campaign. The General's following was very numerous, and it seemed to me they were as thoroughly good fellows as I ever met. We were entertained at a glorious supper and soon after were conducted to our tent. It was a very large wall tent, the central portion of which was occupied by a bed of blankets and buffalo robes near a foot deep. In front of the tent, a huge fire of logs had been burning for more than an hour, heating the ground and the air of the tent, the doors of which were thrown wide open to receive the genial warmth.

We were soon enjoying, in a wearied soldier's slumber, all of these judicious arrangements, and awoke next morning in prime condition for anything before us.

And first came a breakfast, the peer of the supper, and the last breakfast of that quality I ever saw. I can never forget—for it was the first and the last time I enjoyed that dish—the *kidneys stewed in sherry!* which, late in the course of that breakfast, were served to me as a sort of *chasse* by a generous young Missouri colonel, who had brought to that rough field of war this memento of the more refined culinary accomplishments he had acquired in Saint Louis.

The breakfast dispatched, we mounted our horses and were soon on our way over the mountain ridge which divided Price's camp from that of the Texans under General McCulloch.

McCulloch's little army was bivouacked several miles distant from the Missourians. We found the noted Texan ranger occupying a small farm house on the mountain side—comfortless and bare enough it was.

In person, in manner and in character, McCulloch presented a strong contrast with Price. He was near six feet tall, was spare and wirey, and somewhat inclined to a stoop in his shoulders. His deep set gray eyes were shaded by rather heavy eyebrows, which gave an expression of almost suspicious scrutiny to his countenance. In manner, he was undemonstrative, reticent, and, to us, even cautious. He was calm and anxious in view of the enterprise we had undertaken; but avowed his confidence in it, and co-operated heartily for its success.

His whole conduct during these operations impressed us very favorably as to his capacity for war, and but for his untimely death, he would have played an important part in our struggle.

His staff was limited to five or six earnest, working men, and all about him bespoke the stern seriousness of soldiers trained to arms. Frank Armstrong, Lindsay Lomax, Edward Dillon, —— Kimmell, were members of his staff, whom I found with him, all of whom served often and long with me in the stirring events of the great contest we had embarked in.

A full conference with McCulloch, whose remarkable knowledge of roads and country were much relied upon in the operations of that campaign, enabled Van Dorn to organize the corps of Price and of McCulloch into an army of about 16,000 men, and to march at dawn of March 1st to attack the enemy in the valley of Sugar creek at the "Elkhorn tavern."

The night had been bitter cold. We had slept in a sort of barn or stable, and had only a little coffee and hard bread to eat. The snow was falling fast as we rode to the head of the column: and we did not feel very bright, until we were struck with the splendid appearance of a large regiment we were passing. It halted as we came upon its flank, faced to the front and presented arms, and as General Van Dorn reached its centre, three rousing cheers rang out upon the morning air, and made us feel we were with soldiers. It was the ever glorious Third Louisiana which thus cheered us.

That day we crossed over Boston mountain, and encamped near Fayetteville. Our cavalry, under McIntosh, was sent forward to make a demonstration.

Next morning, March 2d, we passed through Fayetteville, and camped for the night at Fulton springs, a few miles this side of Bentonville.

Van Dorn knew the enemy was occupying three detached camps, and the design was to strike the main body at Elkhorn before the divisions of Siegel or of Carr could join it.

He ordered the army to march at 3 A. M. of the third, hoping to reach Bentonville before Siegel, with his 7,000 men, could pass that point and join Curtis in Sugar creek canon. But the enemy was up before we could get the troops to move; and on the march, they would delay at the crossing of every stream (and they were numerous), till they could pass by single file over a log dry shod. And thus it was, that when the head of our column debouched from the timber out upon the open prairie, three miles from Bentonville, we had the mortification to see the head of Siegel's column already entering that village, and marching so rapidly through it, on the Sugar Creek road, that we were unable to intercept or delay his movements.

Even yet McIntosh, with his mounted men, might have thrown himself across his (Siegel's) road, dismounted and formed line in his front, and thus delayed him till we could close in behind and cause his surrender. But his impetuous valor induced him to attempt a sort of charge upon Siegel's veteran infantry, with his wild men on wilder horses. Siegel met the attack with a volley or two, which scattered McIntosh's horsemen in every direction, and then resumed his rapid march.

We pressed on in pursuit, but the road led along a narrow canon shut in by steep rocks and hills, and we could only *follow* Siegel, who, whenever he passed a favorable point, placed a battery in position to check the head of our column as we reached it. Long before dark he had closed up upon Curtis' army, and we halted for the night beyond cannon range.

Our march had been along the main Telegraph road from Bentonville to Springfield, on which, in our front, lay the enemy's army, Van Dorn had learned from McCulloch of a road by which we might turn off to the left from the Telegraph road, make a detour of eight miles, and come into the Telegraph road again in the enemy's rear. We therefore halted, as if for the night, just at the junction of this road; and as soon as it was full dark, the army was moved out upon this road to the left, leaving a force of 1,000 men to cover the movement, and occupy the enemy.

We found the route very bad, and it had been much obstructed by the enemy; so that our march was slow, and it was 8 A. M. when we debouched into the main Telegraph road, about two miles north of Elkhorn tavern and quite in rear of the enemy. We occupied the only route by which he could retire to Missouri.

The game seemed now to be in our own hands; but never was a well conceived plan more completely defeated in its execution than ours was by the remarkable mischances which befell us that day—all of which were plainly traceable to our own want of discipline.

When Price's corps advanced along the Telegraph road, we found only some skirmishers and a battery to oppose us, the whole Federal army having concentrated towards its front, where we were supposed to be; but very soon Curtis discovered he had a heavy force in his rear, and made such quick and efficient changes to meet us that we had plenty to do; but we bore the enemy steadily back, and were pretty warmly engaged, when McCulloch sent to request that instead of closing up and joining in our attack, he should strike the enemy from where he then was. Van Dorn assented, and soon both armies were warmly engaged, McCulloch's position being some three miles distant from ours, and his attack being made upon the enemy's defences in the front.

By two o'clock, Price had forced the enemy back along his whole line, and Van Dorn sent orders to McCulloch to press the enemy vigorously in his front, and he would close in upon him with all his (Price's) force, and end the battle.

Just at this moment a staff officer, Colonel Edward Dillon, galloped up, with disaster on his face. Riding close up to Van Dorn, he said, in a low tone, "McCulloch is killed, McIntosh is killed, Hebert is killed, and the attack on the front has ceased."

The General set his lips, ordered every thing to be urged to the attack, and that the troops of McCulloch's corps should be at once moved up to join us.

Meantime the enemy, finding himself no longer pressed in front, transferred heavy reinforcements to meet us. About sunset we discovered that a new line of battle had been formed 300 yards in our front, in the edge of the timber. The fences had been cleared, so as to form breastworks of the rails, before we knew of this attack, and had the enemy charged us then, we would have been probably beaten.

But he gave us fifteen minutes, in which time Van Dorn brought up some guns in a position to enfilade his line, and quickly dismounted all of the cavalry within reach, to extend our line upon the left, and then we all charged with a yell, and the enemy, delivering a brief fire, broke and fled, and our whole line pursued him quite into his wagon trains.

It was not yet dark, we had every thing on the move, and Van Dorn was urging up all available troops to join in the continued pressure of the enemy, when he found General Price had already stopped the pursuit and ordered the troops to fall back to take up a position for the night.

We made our headquarters for the night at the Elkhorn tavern, where the enemy's had been in the morning.

Price's corps had been hotly engaged from 10 A. M. till after sunset, and had been constantly victorious. We had now won the field, but we had lost very heavily. Generals Slack, McCulloch, McIntosh and Hebert were killed, while General Price and many others were wounded, and our losses told upon us. The ammunition of the troops in action was exhausted, and to our dismay, when the reserve train of ammunition was sought for, it could not be found. The prudent and intelligent ordnance officer in charge of it had sent it off beyond Bentonville, about fifteen miles, and the enemy lay between!

McCulloch's corps was much disorganized, and when it was found there was no fresh supply of ammunition for Price's troops, all idea of resuming the attack next morning was abandoned. Van Dorn decided to await attack on the ground he had won, and meantime to put his wagon trains upon a road towards Van Buren, and to make the best dispositions for a defensive movement in the morning. Our line was formed about 1,200 yards from the Elkhorn tavern, south of it, and was under command of General Henry Little, one of the best and bravest of the Missourians. With him was the brigade of Colonel Rives and Little's own brigade. All of these were staunch troops, veterans of many battles. He had also Bledsoe's battery, Wade's battery, McDonald's battery and the battery of the gallant young Churchill Clarke, already the Pelham of that army. A cannon shot carried off his head that morning while he was working his guns.

This line was held most gallantly till 10 o'clock, when, the trains and the artillery and most of the army being on the road, we withdrew it and ordered it to cover our march. The gallant fellows faced about with cheers, believing they were only changing front to fight in some other position. The enemy was too much crippled to follow, and we marched back to Van Buren.

The battle of Elkhorn was then ended, and many a noble soldier had fallen, but of all who fell that day, I remember none who was more regretted than Colonel Rives. His very presence and manner bespoke a man of lofty nature, worthy of all the love and admiration in which he was held throughout that army. Only a few minutes before he fell he rode out of the line to give some explanation in person to Van Dorn of the condition of affairs, and as he concluded his brief interview, and turned his horse to gallop back to his place, we exclaimed, "What a noble looking fellow he is." Ten minutes after an aid-de-camp reported, "Colonel Rives is down, sir."

The battle of Elkhorn illustrates the danger of co-operative attack. Had Van Dorn adhered to his original plan and fallen on the enemy's rear with all the forces of Price and McCulloch, the disasters of the day would have been averted. We may fairly conclude that it was lost through want of discipline and cohesion in our army. Had we marched at the hour appointed in the order on the morning of the 4th, we would have cut off

Siegel at Bentonville; even had we moved as rapidly as infantry should march, we must have met him there.

The remarkable fatality which befell McCulloch and McIntosh was fairly attributable to the same indiscipline. McCulloch was killed by a sharpshooter while riding alone to reconnoitre the ground in front of his army—where he ought not to have been.

McIntosh, being thus left in command of that wing, yielded to a gallant impulse and placed himself at the head of a regiment of Texas horse, which was moving to charge a Federal battery. He was one of the few killed in the charge, and was entirely out of his proper place when he fell.

The battle might yet have gone in our favor had it been pressed half an hour longer on the evening of the 5th. The cessation of our attack then was a fatal error.

And finally, the inexcusable incompetency of the ordnance officer who sent our ordnance train beyond reach, so that we could not resume the offensive on the morning of the 6th, completed the mischances which caused a well planned, bold and bravely fought battle to go against the Confederate arms, and left no other results than a loss to the enemy in killed and wounded, a few prisoners and two light batteries, which we took with us back to Van Buren, and the moral effect with which our unexpected attack had impressed him by the boldness and energy of our enterprise, so that he did not venture upon any aggressive movement against us.

WASHINGTON, D.C., MARCH 1862

Abraham Lincoln: Message to Congress on Compensated Emancipation; Abraham Lincoln to James A. McDougall

In his annual message of December 3, 1861, President Lincoln recommended that Congress financially support states that adopted measures for gradual emancipation and that it provide for the colonization of freed slaves outside of the United States. Four months later, Lincoln renewed his call for gradual and compensated emancipation in the hopes of ending slavery in the border states of Delaware, Maryland, Kentucky, and Missouri. His letter to Senator James A. McDougall was intended to counter objections to the plan's cost, but the California Democrat opposed it as an unconstitutional use of federal funds. Although Congress passed the resolution Lincoln sought, the border states refused to act and no enabling legislation was introduced.

March 6, 1862

Fellow-citizens of the Senate, and House of Representatives,

I recommend the adoption of a Joint Resolution by your honorable bodies which shall be substantially as follows:

"Resolved that the United States ought to co-operate with any state which may adopt gradual abolishment of slavery, giving to such state pecuniary aid, to be used by such state in it's discretion, to compensate for the inconveniences public and private, produced by such change of system."

If the proposition contained in the resolution does not meet the approval of Congress and the country, there is the end; but if it does command such approval, I deem it of importance that the states and people immediately interested, should be at once distinctly notified of the fact, so that they may begin to consider whether to accept or reject it. The federal government would find it's highest interest in such a measure, as one of the most efficient means of self-preservation. The leaders of the existing insurrection entertain the hope that this government will ultimately be forced to acknowledge the independence of some part of the disaffected region, and that all the slave states North of such part will then say "the Union, for which we have struggled, being already gone, we now choose to go with the Southern section." To deprive them of this hope, substantially ends the rebellion; and the initiation of emancipation completely deprives them of it, as to all the states initiating it. The point is not that *all* the states tolerating slavery would very soon, if at all, initiate emancipation; but that, while the offer is equally made to all, the more Northern shall, by such initiation, make it certain to the more Southern, that in no event, will the former ever join the latter, in their proposed confederacy. I say "initiation" because, in my judgment, gradual, and not sudden emancipation, is better for all. In the mere financial, or pecuniary view, any member of Congress, with the census-tables and Treasury-reports before him, can readily see for himself how very soon the current expenditures of this war would purchase, at fair valuation, all the slaves in any named State. Such a proposition, on the part of the general government, sets up no claim of a right, by federal authority, to interfere with slavery within state limits, referring, as it does, the absolute control of the subject, in each case, to the state and it's people, immediately interested. It is proposed as a matter of perfectly free choice with them.

In the annual message last December, I thought fit to say "The Union must be preserved; and hence all indispensable means must be employed." I said this, not hastily, but deliberately. War has been made, and continues to be, an indispensable means to this end. A practical re-acknowledgement of the national authority would render the war unnecessary, and it would at once cease. If, however, resistance continues, the war must also continue; and it is impossible to foresee all the incidents, which may attend and all the ruin which may follow it. Such as may seem indispensable, or may obviously promise great efficiency towards ending the struggle, must and will come.

The proposition now made, though an offer only, I hope it may be esteemed no offence to ask whether the pecuniary consideration tendered would not be of more value to the States and private persons concerned, than are the institution, and property in it, in the present aspect of affairs.

While it is true that the adoption of the proposed resolution would be merely initiatory, and not within itself a practical measure, it is recommended in the hope that it would soon lead to important practical results. In full view of my great responsibility to my God, and to my country, I earnestly beg the attention of Congress and the people to the subject.

ABRAHAM LINCOLN
March 6. 1862.

Hon. James A. McDougal
U.S. Senate

Executive Mansion
Washington, March 14, 1862

My dear Sir: As to the expensiveness of the plan of gradual emancipation with compensation, proposed in the late Message, please allow me one or two brief suggestions.

Less than one half-day's cost of this war would pay for all the slaves in Delaware at four hundred dollars per head:

Thus, all the slaves in Delaware, by the Census of 1860, are	1798
	400
Cost of the slaves, ...	$ 719,200.
One day's cost of the war	"2,000,000.

Again, less than eighty seven days cost of this war would, at the same price, pay for all in Delaware, Maryland, District of Columbia, Kentucky, and Missouri.

Thus, slaves in Delaware	1798
" " Maryland	87,188
" " Dis. of Col.	3,181
" " Kentucky	225,490
" " Missouri	114,965
	432,622
	400
Cost of the slaves	$173,048,800
Eightyseven days' cost of the war	"174,000,000.

Do you doubt that taking the initiatory steps on the part of those states and this District, would shorten the war more than eighty-seven days, and thus be an actual saving of expense?

A word as to the *time* and *manner* of incurring the expence. Suppose, for instance, a State devises and adopts a system by which the institution absolutely ceases therein by a named day —say January 1st. 1882. Then, let the sum to be paid to such state by the United States, be ascertained by taking from the Census of 1860, the number of slaves within the state, and multiplying that number by four hundred—the United States to pay such sum to the state in twenty equal annual instalments, in six per cent. bonds of the United States.

The sum thus given, as to *time* and *manner*, I think would not be half as onerous, as would be an equal sum, raised *now*, for the indefinite prossecution of the war; but of this you can judge as well as I.

I inclose a Census-table for your convenience. Yours very truly

A. LINCOLN

Catesby ap Roger Jones: from "Services of the 'Virginia' (Merrimac)"

The outbreak of war found the steam frigate U.S.S. *Merrimack* laid up at the Norfolk navy yard for engine repairs. Scuttled and burned by the Federals when they evacuated the yard, she was raised and rebuilt as the ironclad ram C.S.S. *Virginia*. In an article written for the *Southern Historical Society Papers* in 1883, Catesby ap Roger Jones, *Virginia*'s executive officer, describes the two-day battle with the Union squadron at Hampton Roads on March 8–9. Franklin Buchanan, *Virginia*'s commander, was wounded on March 8 by a sharpshooter ashore, and Jones commanded against U.S.S. *Monitor* in the historic duel of the ironclads the next day.

THE ATTACK was postponed to Saturday, March 8th. The weather was favorable. We left the navy yard at 11 A. M., against the last half of the flood tide, steamed down the river past our batteries, through the obstructions, across Hampton Roads, to the mouth of James river, where off Newports News lay at anchor the frigates Cumberland and Congress, protected by strong batteries and gunboats. The action commenced about 3 P. M. by our firing the bow-gun* at the Cumberland, less than a mile distant. A powerful fire was immediately concentrated upon us from all the batteries afloat and ashore. The frigates Minnesota, Roanoke and St. Lawrence with other vessels, were seen coming from Old Point. We fired at the Congress on passing, but continued to head directly for the Cumberland, which vessel we had determined to run into, and in less than fifteen minutes from the firing of the first gun we rammed her just forward of the starboard fore chains. There were heavy spars about her bows, probably to ward off torpedoes, through which we had to break before reaching the side

*It killed and wounded ten men at the after pivot gun of the Cumberland. The second shot from the same gun killed and wounded twelve men at her forward pivot gun. Lieutenant Charles C. Simms pointed and fired the gun.

of the ship. The noise of the crashing timbers was distinctly heard above the din of battle. There was no sign of the hole above water. It must have been large, as the ship soon commenced to careen. The shock to us on striking was slight. We immediately backed the engines. The blow was not repeated. We here lost the prow, and had the stem slightly twisted. The Cumberland* fought her guns gallantly as long as they were above water. She went down bravely, with her colors flying. One of her shells struck the still of the bow-port and exploded; the fragments killed two and wounded a number. Our after nine-inch gun was loaded and ready for firing, when its muzzle was struck by a shell, which broke it off and fired the gun. Another gun also had its muzzle shot off; it was broken so short that at each subsequent discharge its port was set on fire. The damage to the armor was slight. Their fire appeared to have been aimed at our ports. Had it been concentrated at the water-line we would have been seriously hurt, if not sunk. Owing to the ebb tide and our great draft we could not close with the Congress without first going up stream and then turning, which was a tedious operation, besides subjecting us twice to the full fire of the batteries, some of which we silenced.

We were accompanied from the yard by the gunboats Beaufort, Lieutenant-Commander W. H. Parker, and Raleigh, Lieutenant-Commander J. W. Alexander. As soon as the firing was heard up James river, the Patrick Henry, Commander John R Tucker, Jamestown, Lieutenant Commander J. N. Barney, and the gunboat Teaser, Lieutenant-Commander W. A. Webb, under command of Captain John R. Tucker, stood down the river, joining us about four o'clock. All these vessels were gallantly fought and handled, and rendered valuable and effective service.

The prisoners from the Congress stated that when on board that ship it was seen that we were standing up the river, that three cheers were given under the impression that we had quit the fight. They were soon undeceived. When they saw us

*She was a sailing frigate of 1,726 tons, mounting two ten-inch pivots and twenty-two nine-inch guns. Her crew numbered 376; her loss in killed and wounded was 121.

heading down stream, fearing the fate of the Cumberland, they slipped their cables, made sail, and ran ashore bows on. We took a position off her quarter, about two cables' length distant, and opened a deliberate fire. Very few of her guns bore on us, and they were soon disabled. The other batteries continued to play on us, as did the Minnesota, then aground about one and one-half miles off. The St. Lawrence also opened on us shortly after. There was great havoc on board the Congress. She was several times on fire. Her gallant commander, Lieutenant Joseph B. Smith,* was struck in the breast by the fragment of a shell and instantly killed. The carnage was frightful. Nothing remained but to strike their colors, which they did. They hoisted the white flag, half-masted, at the main and at the spanker gaff. The Beaufort and Raleigh were ordered to burn her. They went alongside and secured several of her officers and some twenty of her men as prisoners. The officers urgently asked permission to assist their wounded out of the ship. It was granted. They did not return. A sharp fire of musketry from the shore killed some of the prisoners and forced the tugs to leave. A boat was sent from the Virginia to burn her, covered by the Teaser. A fire was opened on them from the shore, and also from the Congress, with both of her white flags flying, wounding Lieutenant Minor and others. We replied to this outrage upon the usages of civilized warfare by reopening on the Congress with hot shot and incendiary shell. Her crew escaped by boats, as did that of the Cumberland. Canister and grape would have prevented it; but in neither case was any attempt made to stop them, though it has been otherwise stated, possibly from our firing on the shore or at the Congress.

We remained near the Congress to prevent her recapture. Had she been retaken, it might have been said that the Flag-Officer permitted it, knowing that his brother† was an officer of that vessel.

A distant and unsatisfactory fire was at times had at the Min-

*His sword was sent by flag of truce to his father, Admiral Joseph Smith.

†One of the sad attendants of civil war—divided families—was here illustrated. The Flag-Officer's brother was Paymaster of the Congress. The First and Second Lieutenants had each a brother in the United States army. The father of the Fourth Lieutenant was also in the United States army. The father of one of the Midshipmen was in the United States navy.

nesota. The gunboats also engaged her. We fired canister and grape occasionally in reply to musketry from the shore, which had become annoying.

About this time the Flag Officer was badly wounded by a rifle-ball, and had to be carried below. His bold daring and intrepid conduct won the admiration of all on board. The Executive and Ordnance officer, Lieutenant Catesby Ap R. Jones, succeeded to the command.

The action continued until dusk, when we were forced to seek an anchorage. The Congress was riddled and on fire. A transport steamer was blown up. A schooner was sunk and another captured. We had to leave without making a serious attack on the Minnesota, though we fired at her as we passed on the other side of the Middle Ground, and also at the St. Lawrence.* The latter frigate fired at us by broadsides, not a bad plan for small calibres against iron-clads, if concentrated. It was too dark to aim well. We anchored off our batteries at Sewell Point. The squadron followed.

The Congress† continued to burn; "she illuminated the heavens, and varied the scene by the firing of her own guns and the flight of her balls through the air," until shortly after midnight, "when her magazine exploded, and a column of burning matter appeared high in the air, to be followed by the stillness of death," [extract from report of General Mansfield, U. S. A.] One of the pilots chanced about 11 P. M. to be looking in the direction of the Congress, when there passed a strange looking craft, brought out in bold relief by the brilliant light of the burning ship, which he at once proclaimed to be the Ericsson. We were therefore not surprised in the morning to see the Monitor at anchor near the Minnesota. The latter ship was still aground. Some delay occurred from sending our wounded out of the ship; we had but one serviceable boat left. Admiral Buchanan was landed at Sewell Point.

At eight A. M. we got under way, as did the Patrick Henry, Jamestown and Teaser. We stood towards the Minnesota and opened fire on her. The pilots were to have placed us

*A sailing frigate of fifty guns and 1,726 tons.

†A sailing frigate of 1,867 tons, mounting fifty guns. She had a crew of 434, of whom there were 120 killed and missing.

half-a-mile from her, but we were not at any time nearer than a mile. The Monitor* commenced firing when about a third of a mile distant. We soon approached, and were often within a ship's length; once while passing we fired a broadside at her only a few yards distant. She and her turret appeared to be under perfect control. Her light draft enabled her to move about us at pleasure. She once took position for a short time where we could not bring a gun to bear on her. Another of her movements caused us great anxiety; she made for our rudder and propeller, both of which could have been easily disabled. We could only see her guns when they were discharged; immediately afterward the turret revolved rapidly, and the guns were not again seen until they were again fired. We wondered how proper aim could be taken in the very short time the guns were in sight. The Virginia, however, was a large target, and generally so near that the Monitor's shot did not often miss. It did not appear to us that our shell had any effect upon the Monitor. We had no solid shot. Musketry was fired at the lookout holes. In spite of all the care of our pilots we ran ashore, where we remained over fifteen minutes. The Patrick Henry and Jamestown, with great risk to themselves, started to our assistance. The Monitor and Minnesota were in full play on us. A small rifle-gun on board the Minnesota, or on the steamer alongside of her, was fired with remarkable precision.

When we saw that our fire made no impression on the Monitor, we determined to run into her if possible. We found it a very difficult feat to do. Our great length and draft, in a comparatively narrow channel, with but little water to spare, made us sluggish in our movements, and hard to steer and turn. When the opportunity presented all steam was put on; there was not, however, sufficient time to gather full headway before striking. The blow was given with the broad wooden stem, the iron prow having been lost the day before. The Monitor received the blow in such a manner as to weaken its effect, and the damage was to her trifling. Shortly after an

*She was 173 feet long and 41 feet wide. She had a revolving circular iron turret eight inches thick, nine feet high and twenty feet inside diameter, in which were two eleven-inch guns. Her draft was ten feet.

alarming leak in the bows was reported. It, however, did not long continue.

Whilst contending with the Monitor, we received the fire of the Minnesota,* which we never failed to return whenever our guns could be brought to bear. We set her on fire and did her serious injury, though much less than we then supposed. Generally the distance was too great for effective firing. We blew up a steamer alongside of her.

The fight had continued over three hours. To us the Monitor appeared unharmed. We were therefore surprised to see her run off into shoal water where our great draft would not permit us to follow, and where our shell could not reach her. The loss of our prow and anchor, and consumption of coal, water, &c., had lightened us so that the lower part of the forward end of the shield was awash.

We for some time awaited the return of the Monitor to the Roads. After consultation it was decided that we should proceed to the navy-yard, in order that the vessel should be brought down in the water and completed. The pilots said if we did not then leave that we could not pass the bar until noon of the next day. We therefore at 12 M. quit the Roads and stood for Norfolk. Had there been any sign of the Monitor's willingness to renew the contest we would have remained to fight her. We left her in the shoal water to which she had withdrawn, and which she did not leave until after we had crossed the bar on our way to Norfolk.

The official report says: "Our loss is two killed and nineteen wounded. The stem is twisted and the ship leaks; we have lost the prow, starboard anchor, and all the boats; the armor is somewhat damaged, the steam-pipe and smoke-stack both riddled, the muzzles of two of the guns shot away. It was not easy to keep a flag flying; the flag-staffs were repeatedly shot away; the colors were hoisted to the smoke-stack, and several times cut down from it." None were killed or wounded in the fight with the Monitor. The only damage she did was to the

*She was a screw steam frigate of 3,200 tons, mounting forty-three guns of eight, nine and ten-inch calbre. She fired 145 ten-inch, 349 nine-inch, and 35 eight-inch shot and shell, and 5,567 pounds of powder. Her draft was about the same as the Virginia.

armor. She fired forty-one shots. We were enabled to receive most of them obliquely. The effect of a shot striking obliquely on the shield was to break all the iron, and sometimes to displace several feet of the outside course; the wooden backing would not be broken through. When a shot struck directly at right angles, the wood would also be broken through, but not displaced. Generally the shot were much scattered; in three instances two or more struck near the same place, in each case causing more of the iron to be displaced, and the wood to bulge inside. A few struck near the water-line. The shield was never pierced; though it was evident that two shots striking in the same place would have made a large hole through everything.

A VISIT TO WASHINGTON AND VIRGINIA: MARCH 1862

Nathaniel Hawthorne: from "Chiefly About War-Matters"

"There is no remoteness of life and thought, no hermetically sealed seclusion, except, possibly, that of the grave, into which the disturbing influences of this war do not penetrate," Nathaniel Hawthorne observed at the beginning of "Chiefly About War-Matters," an essay describing the celebrated writer's March visit to Washington and Virginia that was published in the *Atlantic Monthly* for July 1862. Hawthorne deleted the passage recalling his meeting with Lincoln after *Atlantic* editor James T. Fields objected to his description of the President's "awkwardness & general uncouth aspect." (The suppressed section is restored here, and the differences between Hawthorne's original version and the 1862 magazine text are described in the endnotes in this volume.) The argumentative footnotes supposedly by editor Fields are actually by Hawthorne. His mention in the first paragraph of the President's "private grief" refers to the death of Willie Lincoln, age eleven, who died on February 20.

Of course, there was one other personage, in the class of statesmen, whom I should have been truly mortified to leave Washington without seeing; since (temporarily, at least, and by force of circumstances) he was the man of men. But a private grief had built up a barrier about him, impeding the customary free intercourse of Americans with their chief-magistrate; so that I might have come away without a glimpse of his very remarkable physiognomy, save for a semi-official opportunity of which I was glad to take advantage. The fact is, we were invited to annex ourselves, as supernumeraries, to a deputation that was about to wait upon the President, from a Massachusetts whip-factory, with a present of a splendid whip.

Our immediate party consisted only of four or five, (including Major Ben Perley Poore, with his note-book and pencil,) but we were joined by several other persons, who seemed to have been lounging about the precincts of the White House, under the spacious porch, or within the hall, and who swarmed in with us to take the chances of a presentation. Nine o'clock had been appointed as the time for receiving the deputation, and we were punctual to the moment, but not so the President, who sent us word that he was eating his breakfast, and would come as soon as he could. His appetite, we were glad to think, must have been a pretty fair one; for we waited about half-an-hour, in one of the ante-chambers, and then were ushered into a reception-room, in one corner of which sat the Secretaries of War and of the Treasury, expecting, like ourselves, the termination of the presidential breakfast. During this interval, there were several new additions to our groupe, one or two of whom were in a working-garb; so that we formed a very miscellaneous collection of people, mostly unknown to each other, and without any common sponsor, but all with an equal right to look our head-servant in the face. By-and-by, there was a little stir on the staircase and in the passage-way; and in lounged a tall, loose-jointed figure, of an exaggerated Yankee port and demeanor, whom, (as being about the homeliest man I ever saw, yet by no means repulsive or disagreeable,) it was impossible not to recognize as Uncle Abe.

Unquestionably, Western man though he be, and Kentuckian by birth, President Lincoln is the essential representative of all Yankees, and the veritable specimen, physically, of what the world seems determined to regard as our characteristic qualities. It is the strangest, and yet the fittest thing in the jumble of human vicissitudes, that he, out of so many millions, unlooked-for, unselected by any intelligible process that could be based upon his genuine qualities, unknown to those who chose him, and unsuspected of what endowments may adapt him for his tremendous responsibility, should have found the way open for him to fling his lank personality into the chair of state—where, I presume, it was his first impulse to throw his legs on the council-table, and tell the cabinet-ministers a story. There is no describing his lengthy awkwardness, nor the uncouthness of his movement; and yet it seemed as if I had been in the habit of seeing him daily, and had shaken hands with him a thousand times in some village-street; so true was he to the aspect of the pattern American, though with a certain extravagance which, possibly, I exaggerated still further by the delighted eagerness with which I took it in. If put to guess his calling and livelihood, I should have taken him for a country-schoolmaster, as soon as anything else. He was dressed in a rusty black frock-coat and pantaloons, unbrushed, and worn so faithfully that the suit had adapted itself to the curves and angularities of his figure, and had grown to be an outer skin of the man. He had shabby slippers on his feet. His hair was black, still unmixed with gray, stiff, somewhat bushy, and had apparently been acquainted with neither brush nor comb, that morning, after the disarrangement of the pillow; and as to a night-cap, Uncle Abe probably knows nothing of such effeminacies. His complexion is dark and sallow, betokening, I fear, an insalubrious atmosphere around the White House; he has thick black eyebrows and an impending brow; his nose is large, and the lines about his mouth are very strongly defined.

The whole physiognomy is as coarse a one as you would meet anywhere in the length and breadth of the States; but, withal, it is redeemed, illuminated, softened, and brightened, by a kindly though serious look out of his eyes, and an expression of homely sagacity, that seems weighted with rich results of village-experience. A great deal of native sense; no bookish cultivation, no refinement; honest at heart, and thoroughly so, and yet, in some sort, sly—at least, endowed with a sort of tact and wisdom that are akin to craft, and would impel him, I think, to take an antagonist in flank, rather than to make a bull-run at him right in front. But, on the whole, I liked this sallow, queer, sagacious visage, with the homely human sympathies that warmed it; and, for my small share in the matter, would as lief have Uncle Abe for a ruler as any man whom it would have been practicable to put in his place.

Immediately on his entrance, the President accosted our Member of Congress, who had us in charge, and, with a comical twist of his face, made some jocular remark about the length of his breakfast. He then greeted us all round, not waiting for an introduction, but shaking and squeezing everybody's hand with the utmost cordiality, whether the individual's name was announced to him or not. His manner towards us was wholly without pretence, but yet had a kind of natural dignity, quite sufficient to keep the forwardest of us from clapping him on the shoulder and asking for a story. A mutual acquaintance being established, our leader took the whip out of its case, and began to read the address of presentation. The whip was an exceedingly long one, its handle wrought in ivory, (by some artist in the Massachusetts state-prison, I believe,) and ornamented with a medallion of the President, and other equally beautiful devices; and along its whole length, there was a succession of golden bands and ferules. The address was shorter than the whip, but equally well made, consisting chiefly of an explanatory description of these artistic designs, and closing with a hint that the gift was a suggestive and emblematic one, and that the President would recognize the use to which such an instrument should be put.

This suggestion gave Uncle Abe rather a delicate task in his reply, because, slight as the matter seemed, it apparently called for some declaration, or intimation, or faint foreshadowing of policy in reference to the conduct of the war, and the final treatment of the rebels. But the President's Yankee aptness and not-to-be-caughtness stood him in good stead, and he jerked or wriggled himself out of the dilemma with an uncouth dexterity that was entirely in character; although, without his gesticulation of eye and mouth—and especially the flourish of the whip, with which he imagined himself touching up a pair of fat horses—I doubt whether his words would be worth recording, even if I could remember them. The gist of the reply was, that he accepted the whip as an emblem of peace, not punishment; and this great affair over, we retired out of the presence in high good humor, only regretting that we could not have seen the President sit down and fold up his legs, (which is said to be a most extraordinary spectacle,) or have heard him tell one of those delectable stories for which he is so celebrated. A good many of them are afloat upon the common talk of Washington, and are certainly the aptest, pithiest, and funniest little things imaginable; though, to be sure, they smack of the frontier freedom, and would not always bear repetition in a drawing-room, or on the immaculate page of the Atlantic.

Good Heavens, what liberties have I been taking with one of the potentates of the earth, and the man on whose conduct more important consequencies depend, than on that of any other historical personage of the century! But with whom is an American citizen entitled to take a liberty, if not with his own chief-magistrate? However, lest the above allusions to President Lincoln's little peculiarities (already well-known to the country and to the world) should be mis-interpreted, I deem it proper to say a word or two, in regard to him, of unfeigned respect and measurable confidence. He is evidently a man of keen faculties, and, what is still more to the purpose, of powerful character. As to his integrity, the people have that intuition of it which is never deceived. Before he actually entered upon his great office, and for a considerable time afterwards, there is no reason to suppose that he adequately estimated the gigantic task about to be imposed on him, or, at least, had any distinct idea how it was to be managed; and, I presume, there may have been more than one veteran politician who proposed to himself to take the power out of President Lincoln's hands into his own, leaving our honest friend only the public responsibility for the good or ill-success of the career. The extremely imperfect developement of his statesmanly qualities, at that period, may have justified such designs. But the President is teachable by events, and has now spent a year in a very arduous course of education; he has a flexible mind, capable of much expansion, and convertible towards far loftier studies and activities than those of his early life; and, if he came to Washington as a backwoods humorist, he has already transformed himself into as good a statesman (to speak moderately) as his prime-minister.*

Among other excursions to camps and places of interest in the neighborhood of Washington, we went, one day, to Alexandria. It is a little port on the Potomac, with one or two shabby wharves and docks, resembling those of a fishing vil-

*We hesitated to admit the above sketch, and shall probably regret our decision in its favor. It appears to have been written in a benign spirit, and perhaps conveys a not inaccurate impression of its august subject; but it lacks *reverence*, and it pains us to see a gentleman of ripe age, and who has spent years under the corrective influence of foreign institutions, falling into the characteristic and most ominous fault of Young America.

lage in New England, and the respectable old brick town rising gently behind. In peaceful times, it no doubt bore an aspect of decorous quietude and dulness; but it was now thronged with the Northern soldiery, whose stir and bustle contrasted strikingly with the many closed warehouses, the absence of citizens from their customary haunts, and the lack of any symptom of healthy activity; while army-wagons trundled heavily over the pavements, and sentinels paced the sidewalks, and mounted dragoons dashed to-and-fro on military errands. I tried to imagine how very disagreeable the presence of a Southern army would be, in a sober town of Massachusetts; and the thought considerably lessened my wonder at the cold and shy regards that are cast upon our troops, the gloom, the sullen demeanor, the declared or scarcely hidden sympathy with rebellion, which are so frequent here. It is a strange thing in human life, that the greatest errors both of men and women often spring from their sweetest and most generous qualities; and so, undoubtedly, thousands of warm-hearted, sympathetic, and impulsive persons have joined the rebels, not from any real zeal for the cause, but because, between two conflicting loyalties, they chose that which necessarily lay nearest the heart. There never existed any other government, against which treason was so easy, and could defend itself by such plausible arguments, as against that of the United States. The anomaly of two allegiances (of which that of the State comes nearest home to a man's feelings, and includes the altar and the hearth, while the General Government claims his devotion only to an airy mode of law, and has no symbol but a flag) is exceedingly mischievous in this point of view; for it has converted crowds of honest people into traitors, who seem to themselves not merely innocent, but patriotic, and who die for a bad cause with as quiet a conscience as if it were the best. In the vast extent of our country—too vast, by far, to be taken into one small human heart—we inevitably limit to our own State, or, at farthest, to our own Section, that sentiment of physical love for the soil which renders an Englishman, for example, so intensely sensitive to the dignity and well-being of his little island, that one hostile foot, treading anywhere upon it, would make a bruise on each individual breast. If a man loves his own State, therefore, and is content to be ruined with her, let us shoot him if we can, but allow him an honorable burial in the soil he fights for.*

In Alexandria, we visited the tavern in which Colonel Ellsworth was killed, and saw the spot where he fell, and the stairs below, whence Jackson fired the fatal shot, and where he himself was slain a moment afterwards; so that the assassin and his victim must have met on the threshold of the spirit-world, and perhaps came to a better understanding before they had taken many steps on the other side. Ellsworth was too generous to bear an immortal grudge for a deed like that, done in hot blood, and by no skulking enemy. The memorial-hunters have completely cut away the original woodwork around the spot, with their pocket-knives; and the staircase, balustrade, and floor, as well as the adjacent doors and door-frames, have recently been renewed; the walls, moreover, are covered with new paper-hangings, the former having been torn off in tatters; and thus it becomes something like a metaphysical question whether the place of the murder actually exists.

Driving out of Alexandria, we stopt on the edge of the city to inspect an old slave-pen, which is one of the lions of the place, but a very poor one; and a little farther on, we came to a brick church where Washington used sometimes to attend service—a pre-revolutionary edifice, with ivy growing over its walls, though not very luxuriantly. Reaching the open country, we saw forts and camps on all sides; some of the tents being placed immediately on the ground, while others were raised over a basement of logs, laid lengthwise, like those of a log-hut, or driven vertically into the soil in a circle; thus forming a solid wall, the chinks closed up with Virginia mud, and above it the pyramidal shelter of the tent. Here were in progress all the occupations, and all the idleness, of the soldier in the tented field; some were cooking the company-rations in pots hung over fires in the open air; some played at ball, or developed their muscular power by gymnastic exercise; some read newspapers; some smoked cigars or pipes; and many were cleaning their arms and accoutrements, the more carefully, perhaps,

*We do not thoroughly comprehend the author's drift in the foregoing paragraph, but are inclined to think its tone reprehensible, and its tendency impolitic in the present stage of our national difficulties.

because their division was to be reviewed by the Commander-in-Chief, that afternoon. Others sat on the ground, while their comrades cut their hair; it being a soldierly fashion (and for excellent reasons) to crop it within an inch of the skull. Others, finally, lay asleep in breast-high tents, with their legs protruding into the open air.

We paid a visit to Fort Ellsworth, and from its ramparts (which have been heaped up out of the muddy soil, within the last few months, and will require still a year or two to make them verdant) we had a beautiful view of the Potomac, a truly majestic river, and the surrounding country. The fortifications, so numerous in all this region, and now so unsightly with their bare, precipitous sides, will remain as historic monuments, grass-grown and picturesque memorials of an epoch of terror and suffering; they will serve to make our country dearer and more interesting to us, and afford fit soil for poetry to root itself in; for this is a plant which thrives best in spots where blood has been spilt long ago, and grows in abundant clusters in old ditches, such as the moat around Fort Ellsworth will be, a century hence. It may seem to be paying dear for what many will reckon but a worthless weed; but the more historical associations we can link with our localities, the richer will be the daily life that feeds upon the past, and the more valuable the things that have been long established; so that our children will be less prodigal than their fathers, in sacrificing good institutions to passionate impulses and impracticable theories. This herb of grace, let us hope, may be found in the old footprints of the war.

Even in an aesthetic point of view, however, the war has done a great deal of enduring mischief by causing the devastation of great tracts of woodland scenery, in which this part of Virginia would appear to have been very rich. Around all the encampments, and everywhere along the road, we saw the bare sites of what had evidently been tracts of hard-wood forest, indicated by the unsightly stumps of well-grown trees, not smoothly felled by regular axe-men, but hacked, haggled, and unevenly amputated, as by a sword or other miserable tool in an unskilful hand. Fifty years will not repair this desolation. An army destroys everything before and around it, even to the very grass; for the sites of the encampments are converted into barren esplanades, like those of the squares in French cities, where not a blade of grass is allowed to grow. As to other symptoms of devastation and obstruction, such as deserted houses, unfenced fields, and a general aspect of nakedness and ruin, I know not how much may be due to a normal lack of neatness in the rural life of Virginia, which puts a squalid face even upon a prosperous state of things; but undoubtedly the war must have spoilt what was good, and made the bad a great deal worse. The carcasses of horses were scattered along the wayside. One very pregnant token of a social system thoroughly disturbed was presented by a party of Contrabands, escaping out of the mysterious depths of Secessia; and its strangeness consisted in the leisurely delay with which they trudged forward, as dreading no pursuer, and encountering nobody to turn them back.

They were unlike the specimens of their race whom we are accustomed to see at the North, and, in my judgment, were far more agreeable. So rudely were they attired—as if their garb had grown upon them spontaneously—so picturesquely natural in manners, and wearing such a crust of primeval simplicity, (which is quite polished away from the northern black man,) that they seemed a kind of creature by themselves, not altogether human, but perhaps quite as good, and akin to the fauns and rustic deities of olden times. I wonder whether I shall excite anybody's wrath by saying this? It is no great matter. At all events, I felt most kindly towards these poor fugitives, but knew not precisely what to wish in their behalf, nor in the least how to help them. For the sake of the manhood which is latent in them, I would not have turned them back, but I should have felt almost as reluctant, on their own account, to hasten them forward to the stranger's land; and, I think, my prevalent idea was, that, whoever may be benefitted by the results of this war, it will not be the present generation of negroes, the childhood of whose race is now gone forever, and who must henceforth fight a hard battle with the world, on very unequal terms. On behalf of my own race, I am glad, and can only hope that an inscrutable Providence means good to both parties.

There is an historical circumstance, known to few, that connects the children of the Puritans with these Africans of Virginia, in a very singular way. They are our brethren, as being lineal descendants from the May Flower, the fated womb of which, in her first voyage, sent forth a brood of Pilgrims upon Plymouth Rock, and, in a subsequent one, spawned Slaves upon the southern soil;—a monstrous birth, but with which we have an instinctive sense of kindred, and so are stirred by an irresistible impulse to attempt their rescue, even at the cost of blood and ruin. The character of our sacred ship, I fear, may suffer a little by this revelation; but we must let her white progeny offset her dark one—and two such portents never sprang from an identical source before!

While we drove onward, a young officer on horseback looked earnestly into the carriage, and recognized some faces that he had seen before; so he rode along by our side, and we pestered him with queries and observations, to which he responded more civilly than they deserved. He was on General McClellan's staff, and a gallant cavalier, high-booted, with a revolver in his belt, and mounted on a noble horse, which trotted hard and high without disturbing the rider in his accustomed seat. His face had a healthy hue of exposure and an expression of careless hardihood; and, as I looked at him, it seemed to me that the war had brought good fortune to the youth of this epoch, if to none beside; since they now make it their daily business to ride a horse and handle a sword, instead of lounging listlessly through the duties, occupations, pleasures —all tedious alike—to which the artificial state of society limits a peaceful generation. The atmosphere of the camp and the smoke of the battle-field are morally invigorating; the hardy virtues flourish in them, the nonsense dies like a wilted weed. The enervating effects of centuries of civilization vanish at once, and leave these young men to enjoy a life of hardship, and the exhilarating sense of danger—to kill men blamelessly, or to be killed gloriously—and to be happy in following out their native instincts of destruction, precisely in the spirit of Homer's heroes, only with some considerable change of mode. One touch of nature makes not only the whole world, but all time akin. Set men face to face, with weapons in their hands, and they are as ready to slaughter one another, now, after playing at peace and good-will for so many years, as in the rudest ages, that never heard of peace-societies, and thought no wine so delicious as what they quaffed from an enemy's skull! Indeed, if the report of a Congressional committee be reliable, that old-fashioned kind of goblet has again come into use, at the expense of our northern head-pieces—a costly drinking-cup to him that furnishes it. Heaven forgive me for seeming to jest upon such a subject;—only, it is so odd, when we measure our advances from barbarism, and find ourselves just here!*

We now approached General McClellan's head-quarters, which, at that time, were established at Fairfax Seminary. The edifice was situated on a gentle elevation, amid very agreeable scenery, and, at a distance, looked like a gentleman's seat. Preparations were going forward for reviewing a division of ten or twelve thousand men, the various regiments composing which had begun to array themselves on an extensive plain, where, methought, there was a more convenient place for a battle than is usually found, in this broken and difficult country. Two thousand cavalry made a portion of the troops to be reviewed. By-and-by, we saw a pretty numerous troop of mounted officers, who were congregated on a distant part of the plain, and whom we finally ascertained to be the Commander-in-Chief's staff, with McClellan himself at their head. Our party managed to establish itself in a position conveniently close to the General, to whom, moreover, we had the honor of an introduction; and he bowed, on his horseback, with a good deal of dignity and martial courtesy, but no airs, nor fuss, nor pretension, beyond what his character and rank inevitably gave him.

Now, at that juncture, and, in fact, up to the present moment, there was, and is, a most fierce and bitter outcry, and detraction loud and low, against General McClellan, accusing him of sloth, imbecility, cowardice, treasonable purposes, and, in short, utterly denying his ability as a soldier, and questioning his integrity as a man. Nor was this to be wondered at; for when, before, in all history, do we find a general in command of half-a-million of men, and in presence of an enemy inferior in numbers and no better disciplined than his own troops, leaving it still debateable, after the better part of a year, whether

*We hardly expected this outbreak in favor of War, from the Peaceable Man; but the justice of our cause makes us all soldiers at heart, however quiet in our outward life. We have heard of twenty Quakers in a single company of a Pennsylvania regiment.

he was a soldier or no? The question would seem to answer itself in the very asking. Nevertheless, being most profoundly ignorant of the art of war, like the majority of the General's critics, and, on the other hand, having some considerable impressibility by men's characters, I was glad of the opportunity to look him in the face, and to feel whatever influence might reach me from his sphere. So I stared at him, as the phrase goes, with all the eyes I had; and the reader shall have the benefit of what I saw—to which he is the more welcome, because, in writing this article, I feel disposed to be singularly frank, and can scarcely restrain myself from telling truths, the utterance of which I should get slender thanks for.

The General was dressed in a simple, dark-blue uniform, without epaulets, booted to the knee, and with a cloth cap upon his head; and, at first sight, you might have taken him for a corporal of dragoons, of particularly neat and soldierlike aspect, and in the prime of his age and strength. He is only of middling stature, but his build is very compact and sturdy, with broad shoulders and a look of great physical vigor, which, in fact, he is said to possess; he and Beauregard having been rivals in that particular, and both distinguished above other men. His complexion is dark and sanguine, with dark hair. He has a strong, bold, soldierly face, full of decision; a Roman nose, by no means a thin prominence, but very thick and firm; and if he follows it, (which I should think likely,) it may be pretty confidently trusted to guide him aright. His profile would make a more effective likeness than the full face, which, however, is much better in the real man than in any photograph that I have seen. His forehead is not remarkably large, but comes forward at the eyebrows; it is not the brow nor countenance of a prominently intellectual man, (not a natural student, I mean, or abstract thinker,) but of one whose office it is to handle things practically and to bring about tangible results. His face looked capable of being very stern, but wore, in its repose, when I saw it, an aspect pleasant and dignified; it is not, in its character, an American face, nor an English one. The man, on whom he fixes his eye, is conscious of him. In his natural disposition, he seems calm and self-possessed, sustaining his great responsibilities cheerfully, without shrinking or weariness, or spasmodic effort, or damage to his health, but all with quiet, deep-drawn breaths; just as his broad shoulders would bear up a heavy burthen without aching beneath it.

After we had had sufficient time to peruse the man, (so far as it could be done with one pair of very attentive eyes,) the General rode off, followed by his cavalcade, and was lost to sight among the troops. They received him with loud shouts, by the eager uproar of which—now near, now in the centre, now on the outskirts of the division, and now sweeping back towards us in a great volume of sound—we could trace his progress through the ranks. If he is a coward, or a traitor, or a humbug, or anything less than a brave, true, and able man, that mass of intelligent soldiers, whose lives and honor he had in charge, were utterly deceived, and so was this present writer; for they believed in him, and so did I; and, had I stood in the ranks, I should have shouted with the lustiest of them. Of course, I may be mistaken; my opinion, on such a point, is worth nothing, although my impression may be worth a little more; neither do I consider the General's antecedents as bearing very decided testimony to his practical soldiership. A thorough knowledge of the science of war seems to be conceded to him; he is allowed to be a good military critic; but all this is possible, without his possessing any positive qualities of a great general, just as a literary critic may show the profoundest acquaintance with the principles of epic poetry, without being able to produce a single stanza of an epic poem. Nevertheless, I shall not give up my faith in General McClellan's soldiership until he is defeated, nor in his courage and integrity even then.*

THE WATERS around Fortress Monroe were thronged with a gallant array of ships of war and transports, wearing the Union

*Apparently with the idea of balancing his gracious treatment of the Commander-in-chief, the author had here inserted some idle sarcasms about other officers whom he happened to see at the review; one of whom (a distinguished general,) he says, "sat his horse like a meal-bag, and was the stupidest looking man he ever saw." Such license is not creditable to the Peaceable Man, and we do him a kindness in crossing out the passage.

flag—"Old Glory"—as I hear it called in these days. A little withdrawn from our national fleet lay two French frigates, and, in another direction, an English sloop, under that banner which always makes itself visible, like a red portent in the air, wherever there is strife. In pursuance of our official duty, (which had no ascertainable limits,) we went on board the flag-ship, and were shown over every part of her, and down into her depths, inspecting her gallant crew, her powerful armament, her mighty engines, and her furnaces, where the fires are always kept burning, as well at midnight as at noon, so that it would require only five minutes to put the vessel under full steam. This vigilance has been felt necessary, ever since the Merrimac made that terrible dash from Norfolk. Splendid as she is, however, and provided with all but the very latest improvements in naval armament, the Minnesota belongs to a class of vessels that will be built no more, nor ever fight another battle; being as much a thing of the past as any of the ships of Queen Elizabeth's time, which grappled with the galleons of the Spanish Armada.

On her quarter-deck, an elderly flag-officer was pacing to-and-fro, with a self-conscious dignity to which a touch of the gout or rheumatism perhaps contributed a little additional stiffness. He seemed to be a gallant gentleman, but of the old, slow, and pompous school of naval worthies, who have grown up amid rules, forms, and etiquette, which were adopted full-blown from the British navy into ours, and are somewhat too cumbrous for the quick spirit of to-day. This order of nautical heroes will probably go down, along with the ships in which they fought valorously, and strutted most intolerably. How can an Admiral condescend to go to sea in an iron pot? What space and elbow-room can be found for quarter-deck dignity in the cramped look-out of the Monitor, or even in the twenty feet diameter of her cheese-box? All the pomp and splendor of naval warfare are gone by. Henceforth, there must come up a race of engine-men and smoke-blackened cannoniers, who will hammer away at their enemies under the direction of a single pair of eyes; and even heroism—so deadly a gripe is science laying on our noble possibilities—will become a quality of very minor importance, when its possessor cannot break through the iron crust of his own armament and give the world a glimpse of it.

At no great distance from the Minnesota, lay the strangest-looking craft I ever saw. It was a platform of iron, so nearly on a level with the water that the swash of the waves broke over it, under the impulse of a very moderate breeze; and on this platform was raised a circular structure, likewise of iron, and rather broad and capacious, but of no great height. It could not be called a vessel at all; it was a machine, and I have seen one of somewhat similar appearance employed in cleaning out the docks; or, for lack of a better similitude, it looked like a gigantic rat-trap. It was ugly, questionable, suspicious, evidently mischievous; nay, I will allow myself to call it devilish; for this was the new war-fiend, destined, along with others of the same breed, to annihilate whole navies and batter down old supremacies. The wooden walls of Old England cease to exist, and a whole history of naval renown reaches its period, now that the Monitor comes smoking into view; while the billows dash over what seems her deck, and storms bury even her turret in green water, as she burrows and snorts along, oftener under the surface than above. The singularity of the object has betrayed me into a more ambitious vein of description than I often indulge; and, after all, I might as well have contented myself with simply saying that she looked very queer.

Going on board, we were surprised at the extent and convenience of her interior accommodations. There is a spacious ward-room, nine or ten feet in height, besides a private cabin for the commander, and sleeping accommodations on an ample scale; the whole well-lighted and ventilated, though beneath the surface of the water. Forward, or aft, (for it is impossible to tell stem from stern,) the crew are relatively quite as well provided for as the officers. It was like finding a palace, with all its conveniences, under the sea. The inaccessibility, the apparent impregnability, of this submerged iron fortress are most satisfactory; the officers and crew get down through a little hole in the deck, hermetically seal themselves, and go below; and until they see fit to re-appear, there would seem to be no power given to man, whereby they can be brought to light. A storm of cannon-shot damages them no more than a handful of dried peas. We saw the shot-marks made by the great artillery of the Merrimac on the outer casing of the iron tower; they were about the breadth and depth of shallow saucers, almost imperceptible dents; with no corresponding bulge on the interior surface. In fact, the thing looked altogether too safe; though it may not prove quite an agreeable predicament to be thus boxed up in impenetrable iron, with the possibility, one would imagine, of being sent to the bottom of the sea, and, even there, not drowned, but stifled. Nothing, however, can exceed the confidence of the officers in this new craft. It was pleasant to see their benign exultation in her powers of mischief, and the delight with which they exhibited the circumvolutory movement of the tower, the quick thrusting forth of the immense guns to deliver their ponderous missiles, and then the immediate recoil, and the security behind the closed port-holes. Yet even this will not long be the last and most terrible improvement in the science of war. Already we hear of vessels, the armament of which is to act entirely beneath the surface of the water; so that, with no other external symptoms than a great bubbling and foaming, and gush of smoke, and belch of smothered thunder out of the yesty waves, there shall be a deadly fight going on below; and, by-and-by, a sucking whirlpool, as one of the ships goes down.

The Monitor was certainly an object of great interest; but on our way to Newport News, whither we next went, we saw a spectacle that affected us with far profounder emotion. It was the sight of the few sticks that are left of the frigate Congress, stranded near the shore, and still more, the masts of the Cumberland rising midway out of the water, with a tattered rag of a pennant fluttering from one of them. The invisible hull of the latter ship seems to be careened over, so that the three masts stand slantwise; the rigging looks quite uninjured, except that a few ropes dangle loosely from the yards. The flag (which never was struck, thank Heaven!) is entirely hidden under the waters of the bay, but is still doubtless waving in its old place, although it floats to-and-fro with the swell and reflux of the tide, instead of rustling on the breeze. A remnant of the dead crew still man the sunken ship, and sometimes a drowned body floats up to the surface.

That was a noble fight. When was ever a better word spoken

than that of Commodore Smith, the father of the commander of the Congress, when he heard that his son's ship was surrendered?—"Then Joe's dead!" said he; and so it proved. Nor can any warrior be more certain of enduring renown than the gallant Morris, who fought so well the final battle of the old system of naval warfare, and won glory for his country and himself out of inevitable disaster and defeat. That last gun from the Cumberland, when her deck was half-submerged, sounded the requiem of many sinking ships. Then went down all the navies of Europe, and our own, Old Ironsides and all, and Trafalgar and a thousand other fights became only a memory, never to be acted over again; and thus our brave countrymen come last in the long procession of heroic sailors that includes Blake and Nelson, and so many Mariners of England, and other mariners as brave as they, whose renown is our native inheritance. There will be other battles, but no more such tests of seamanship and manhood as the battles of the past; and, moreover, the millennium is certainly approaching, because human strife is to be transferred from the heart and personality of man into cunning contrivances of machinery, which, by-and-by, will fight out our wars with only the clank and smash of iron, strewing the field with broken engines, but damaging nobody's little finger except by accident. Such is obviously the tendency of modern improvement. But, in the meanwhile, so long as manhood retains any part of its pristine value, no country can afford to let gallantry like that of Morris and his crew, any more than that of the brave Worden, pass unhonored and unrewarded. If the Government do nothing, let the people take the matter into their own hands, and cities give him swords, gold boxes, festivals of triumph, and, if he needs it, heaps of gold. Let poets brood upon the theme, and make themselves sensible how much of the past and future is contained within its compass, till its spirit shall flash forth in the lightning of a song!

THE "GRAND CAMPAIGN" OPENS: VIRGINIA, MARCH 1862

George B. McClellan to the Army of the Potomac and to Samuel L. M. Barlow

On March 8 Joseph E. Johnston's Confederate army at Manassas began withdrawing southward behind the Rappahannock River. This forced McClellan to shift the starting point of his "grand campaign" against Richmond from Urbanna on the Rappahannock to Fort Monroe, at the tip of the Virginia Peninsula. The first troops embarked on March 17. In the close of his address to the army, McClellan drew on an address of Napoleon's to his army during the Italian campaign. With McClellan taking the field with the Army of the Potomac, Lincoln removed him from the general-in-chief's post without appointing a successor. The general told his confidant Samuel L. M. Barlow, a New York lawyer and Democratic political leader, that Lincoln was his strongest friend, but in fact the President was then virtually his only friend in the administration.

SOLDIERS OF THE ARMY OF THE POTOMAC! Headquarters Army of the Potomac, *Fairfax Court House, Va., March 14, 1862.*

For a long time I have kept you inactive, but not without a purpose: you were to be disciplined, armed and instructed; the formidable artillery you now have, had to be created; other armies were to move and accomplish certain results. I have held you back that you might give the death-blow to the rebellion that has distracted our once happy country. The patience you have shown, and your confidence in your General, are worth a dozen victories. These preliminary results are now accomplished. I feel that the patient labors of many months have produced their fruit; the Army of the Potomac is now a real Army,—magnificent in material, admirable in discipline and instruction, excellently equipped and armed;—your commanders are all that I could wish. The moment for action has arrived, and I know that I can trust in you to save our country. As I ride through your ranks, I see in your faces the sure presage of victory; I feel that you will do whatever I ask of you. The period of inaction has passed. I will bring you now face to face with the rebels, and only pray that God may defend the right. In whatever direction you may move, however strange my actions may appear to you, ever bear in mind that my fate is linked with yours, and that all I do is to bring you, where I know you wish to be,—on the decisive battlefield. It is my business to place you there. I am to watch over you as a parent over his children; and you know that your General loves you from the depths of his heart. It shall be my care, as it has ever been, to gain success with the least possible loss; but I know that, if it is necessary, you will willingly follow me to our graves, for our righteous cause. God smiles upon us, victory attends us, yet I would not have you think that our aim is to be attained without a manly struggle. I will not disguise it from you: you have brave foes to encounter, foemen well worthy of the steel that you will use so well. I shall demand of you great, heroic exertions, rapid and long marches, desperate combats, privations, perhaps. We will share all these together; and when this sad war is over we will all return to our homes, and feel that we can ask no higher honor than the proud consciousness that we belonged to the ARMY OF THE POTOMAC.

GEO. B. MCCLELLAN
Major General Commanding

My dear Barlow Washington March 16 1862

I am here for a few hours only, my Hd Qtrs being on the other side of the river.

I came back last night from Fairfax C.H.—en route for the decisive battle. My movements gave us Manassas with the loss of one life—a gallant cavalry officer—history will, when I am in my grave, record it as the brightest passage of my life that I accomplished so much at so small a cost. It will appear in the future that my advance from Harper's Ferry, & the preparation for turning their right flank have induced them to give up what Halleck & the newspapers would call "the rebel stronghold of the East."

I shall soon leave here on the wing for Richmond—which you may be sure I will take. The Army is in magnificent spirits, & I think are half glad that I now belong to them alone.

Mrs McC joins me in kindest regards to Mrs B & yourself. Do not mind the abolitionists—all I ask of the papers is that they should defend me from the most malicious attacks—tho' to speak frankly I do not care to pay much attention to my enemies.

My wife received your note & desires her thanks for it.

The President is all right—he is my strongest friend.

In haste sincerely yours
Geo B McClellan

S L M Barlow Esq

BRITAIN AND THE IRONCLADS: LONDON, APRIL 1862

Charles Francis Adams to Charles Francis Adams Jr.

Charles Francis Adams, the son of John Quincy Adams and grandson of John Adams, had served as U.S. minister to Great Britain since May 1861. He wrote to his son, a lieutenant with the 1st Massachusetts Cavalry stationed at Port Royal, South Carolina, to remark on how the reverberations of the *Virginia-Monitor* battle on March 9 had quieted the British lion.

London, April 4, 1862

THE LATE military successes have given us a season of repose. People are changing their notions of the power of the country to meet such a trial, which is attended with quite favorable consequences to us in our position. Our diplomacy is almost in a state of profound calm. Even the favorite idea of a division into two states is less put forward than it was. Yet the interest with which the struggle is witnessed grows deeper and deeper. The battle between the Merrimack and our vessels has been the main talk of the town ever since the news came, in Parliament, in the clubs, in the city, among the military and naval people. The impression is that it dates the commencement of a new era in warfare, and that Great Britain must consent to begin over again. I think the effect is to diminish the confidence in the result of hostilities with us. In December we were told that we should be swept from the ocean in a moment, and all our ports would be taken. They do not talk so now. So far as this may have an effect to secure peace on both sides it is good. . . .

We are much encouraged now by the series of successes gained, and far more by the marked indications of exhaustion and discouragement in the south. They must be suffering in every way. Never did people pay such a penalty for their madness. And the worst is yet to come. For emancipation is on its way with slow but certain pace. Well for them if it do not take them unaware.

"HIS BIG HEART SHOT AWAY": MASSACHUSETTS, MARCH 1862

Emily Dickinson to Louise and Frances Norcross

Late March 1862

On March 14, in battle at New Berne, the Union army enlarged its foothold on the North Carolina coast. Lieutenant Colonel William S. Clark, 21st Massachusetts Infantry, wrote in his official report that while leading an attack "the noblest of us all, my brave, efficient, faithful adjutant, First Lieut. F.A. Stearns, Company I, fell mortally wounded. . . ." They brought the body of Frazar Stearns back home to Amherst, where his father was president of the college there, for services and burial. Emily Dickinson was watching.

Dear Children,

You have done more for me—'tis least that I can do, to tell you of brave Frazer—"killed at Newbern," darlings. His big heart shot away by a "minie ball."

I had read of those—I didn't think that Frazer would carry one to Eden with him. Just as he fell, in his soldier's cap, with his sword at his side, Frazer rode through Amherst. Classmates to the right of him, and classmates to the left of him, to guard his narrow face! He fell by the side of Professor Clark, his superior officer—lived ten minutes in a soldier's arms, asked twice for water—murmured just, "My God!" and passed! Sanderson, his classmate, made a box of boards in the night, put the brave boy in, covered with a blanket, rowed six miles to reach the boat,—so poor Frazer came. They tell that Colonel Clark cried like a little child when he missed his pet, and could hardly resume his post. They loved each other very much. Nobody here could look on Frazer—not even his father. The doctors would not allow it.

The bed on which he came was enclosed in a large casket shut entirely, and covered from head to foot with the sweetest flowers. He went to sleep from the village church. Crowds came to tell him goodnight, choirs sang to him, pastors told how brave he was—early-soldier heart. And the family bowed their heads, as the reeds the wind shakes.

So our part in Frazer is done, but you must come next summer, and we will mind ourselves of this young crusader—too brave that he could fear to die. We will play his tunes—maybe he can hear them; we will try to comfort his broken-hearted Ella, who, as the clergyman said, "gave him peculiar confidence." . . . Austin is stunned completely. Let us love better, children, it's most that's left to do.

Love from
Emily.

Frederick Douglass: The War and How to End It

March 25, 1862

In the winter and spring of 1862 abolitionist orators such as William Lloyd Garrison, Wendell Phillips, and Frederick Douglass lectured to audiences increasingly receptive to their call for an immediate end to slavery. Douglass delivered this address in Rochester, New York, where he had made his home since 1848, and printed the text in the April *Douglass' Monthly.*

I STAND here to-night to advocate in my humble way, the unrestricted and complete Emancipation of every slave in the United States, whether claimed by loyal or disloyal masters. This is the lesson of the hour.

Through the certain operation of the *changeless laws of the universe*, Emancipation, which has long been a great and solemn national duty, pressing heavily on the national conscience has at last become a great and all commanding national necessity.

I choose not to insist upon these comprehensive propositions as a colored man to-night nor as one having special reasons for hating slavery, although, upon these grounds I might well base a claim to be heard, but my ground is taken as an American citizen, feeling with all others a deep and living interest in the welfare of the whole country.

In the tremendous conflict through which we are passing, all events steadily conspire, to make the cause of the slave and the cause of the country identical. He who to-day fights for Emancipation, fights for his country and free Institutions, and he who fights for slavery, fights against his country and in favor of a slaveholding oligarchy.

This was always so, though only abolitionists perceived the fact. The difference between them and others is this: They got an earlier glimpse at the black heart of slavery—than others did. They saw in times of seeming peace, for the peace we have had, was only seeming—what we can only see in times of open war. They saw that a nation like ours, containing two such opposite forces as liberty and slavery, could not enjoy permanent peace, and they said so and got mobbed for saying so. But let that pass.

Before I proceed to discuss the subject announced for my lecture this evening, allow me to make a few remarks on the mighty events which have marked and are marking the progress of the war. It requires a large share of wisdom and coolness, to properly weigh and measure the great facts which have already passed into history; but it requires a much larger share of these qualities, to enable man to discriminate between, and to determine the proper relations and bearings of the great living facts, transpiring before our eyes.

The obvious reason is this: important events often succeed each other so rapidly, and take the place of each other so quickly, that it becomes almost impossible to give to any one of them, that measure of reflection, which is necessary to form an intelligent judgement.

We are an intelligent people, apt scholars, but I think that few of us fully appreciate the solemn events that are now passing before our eyes.

It is known that we are at war, at war among ourselves, civil war the worst of all wars, but the real scope and significance of this war is but imperfectly understood by millions of the American people.

The very air is filled with conflicting statements in respect to the cause of this war, and naturally enough, it is also filled with contradictory theories as to the manner of restoring the country to peace.

I shall not stay here to discuss the long train of events, and the certain action of social forces which have finally culminated in this rebellion. The limits of the occasion will not permit any such lengthy discussion. The most that I can do, is to point out a few of the leading features of the contest, and enforce the lesson which I think they plainly teach and the path of duty they mark out for our feet.

The first enquiry which concerned the loyal north upon the

sudden outburst of this stupendous rebellion, naturally related to the strength of the rebels, and the amount of force and skill required for their speedy suppression. Even at this vital point we blundered. We misconceived the real state of the case, and misread the facts then passing before us. We were quite incredulous of the tremendous strength and vigor of the foe against whom we were called upon to battle.

We are a charitable people, and in excess of charity were disposed to put the very best construction upon the strange behavior of our southern brethren. We admitted that South Carolina might secede. It was like her to do so. She had talked extravagantly about going out of the union, and she must do something extravagant and startling to save a show of consistency. Georgia too, we thought might possibly go out, but we were quite sure that these twin rebel States, would stand alone in their infamy, and that they would soon tire of their isolation, repent of their folly, and come back to the union. Traitors fled the Cabinet, the House and the Senate, and hastened away to fan the flames of treason at home. Still we doubted that any thing very serious would come of it. We treated it as a bubble on the wave, a nine day's wonder. Calm and thoughtful men ourselves, we relied on the sober second thought of others. Even a shot at one of our ships, an insult offered to our flag, caused only a momentary feeling of indignation and resentment, such as a mother might feel toward a naughty child who had thrown away his bread and stamped defiance at her authority. It was not until Beauregard opened his slave built batteries upon the starving garrison in Charleston harbor, that the confiding North, like a sleeping lion, was roused from his lair, and shook his thundering mane in wrath. We were slow to wake, but we did awake. Still we were scarcely conscious of the skill, power and resources of the enemy. We still hoped that wiser and better counsels would ultimately prevail. We could not believe but that a powerful union sentiment still existed at the South, and that a strong reaction would yet take place there in favor of the union. To the very last we continued to believe in the border States. We could not believe that those States would plunge madly into the bloody vortex of rebellion. It required the assaults of a blood thirsty mob spilling the blood of loyal soldiers to convince us of Baltimore treason.

I need not tell you, how in all this study of passing events, we have been grossly mistaken. Every hope based upon the sanity, loyalty, and good disposition of the South has been woefully disappointed. While armies were forming, and the most formidable preparations were making, we continued to dream of peace, and even after the war was fairly begun, we thought to put down the rebellion by a show of force rather than by an exercise of force. We showed our teeth but did not wish to use them. We preferred to fight with dollars rather than daggers. The fewer battles the better was the motto, popular at Washington, and peace in sixty days trembled along the wires. We now see what we could not at first comprehend. We are astonished at the strength and vigor of the foe. Treason had shot its poisonous roots deeper, and has spread them farther than our calculations had allowed for. Now I have a reason for calling attention to this unwillingness on our part to know the worst. It has already caused much trouble, and I have reason to apprehend that it will cause us much more. We need warnings a thousand times repeated. A hint to the wise is enough for the wise, and although we are wise and can take a hint, the trouble is we don't heed it unless it comes in the shape of a rifled cannon ball battering against the walls of our forts, or an iron clad ram, sinking our navy and threatening our whole Atlantic Coast. Let me under score this point of weakness and as I think blindness on our part for it still lingers with us.

Even now, you need not go far to find newspapers clinging still to the delusion that there is a strong union sentiment at the South. While the rebels are waging a barbarous war, of unparalleled ferocity, marshalling the savage Indian to the slaughter of your sons, and poisoning the wells in their retreats, we are still speaking of them as our erring brothers, to be won back to the union by fondling, rather than fighting. This has been our great error. We failed to comprehend the vital force of the rebellion. First, because we were dazzled and bewildered by the wild rapidity of the strange events, which burst upon us, and secondly because of our habitual leniency to the South and to slaveholders grimly confronting us at the outset.

I have said that the first question was how to whip the rebels. That was the bitter problem. We were sadly unprepared to fight.

Treason had become the warp and woof of the army and navy. Floyd had stolen all the arms, and Cobb had stolen all the money. The nation was at the mercy of the merciless. How to procure arms, and brave men to use them, was naturally first in order. Like the rod of Moses it swallowed all others. It even hushed the voice of abolitionists and wheeled them into line with its imperative demands.

It was the great physical question. Men of muscle understood it as well as men of mind. But now there is another and a mightier question destined to try men's souls more severely than the first.

For not that which is spiritual is first, but that which is natural; after that, that which is spiritual. The physical part of this tremendous conflict is at last in a hopeful way. The great armies of the North are in motion. Baltimore is at the mercy of McHenry, Western Virginia clings to the union, Kentucky is no longer neutral, Missouri has gone to Arkansas. North Carolina is invaded, Florida has followed the fortunes of Bragg, and Tennessee is under Foote.

Brave hearts and strong hands, have met and disposed of the first question. I knew they would from the first. The slaveholding rebels have fought, and have fought well, and will do so again. They are proud, brave and desperate, but proud, brave and desperate as they are, I tell no secret when I say, they can run as well as fight.

General McClellan in his recent address to his army—takes pains to compliment these traitors. He is "sad" at the thought of striking them. The traitors themselves show no such weakness. The language of their Generals is altogether of another character. There is no epithet too vile for them, by which to characterize our army. But McClellan, is careful to tell us that the Southern army is composed of foemen worthy of our steel. I do not like this. It looks bad. Instead of being foemen worthy of our steel, they are rebels and traitors worthy of our hemp.

I do not wonder that all the haters of Impartial Liberty at the North are especially devoted to this "sad" reluctant General, who instead of portraying the baseness of the traitors takes pains to compliment them. It is seriously doubted if he will ever try his steel upon them. Thus far he has entirely failed to do any thing of the sort. But, whether McClellan ever overtakes the rebels or not, the army of the Potomac has moved, and brave men sweep both the Eastern and Western border of the rebellion. So that I look upon the first question, the question as to how to break down the military power of the rebels as in good hands and the public mind is happily relieved at that point.

But now a higher and more important problem presses for consideration. It is a problem for statesmen rather than Generals. Soldiers can capture a State, but statesmen must govern a State. It is sometimes hard to pull down a house but it is always harder to build one up.

This is the question now to be decided, having broken down the rebel power in the seceded States, how shall we extend the Constitution and the Union over them? We know how to make war, we know how to conquer, but the question is do we know how to make peace? We can whip the South, but can we make the South loyal? Baltimore is in our hands, but her parlors and drawing rooms are full of Traitors. The army is at Nashville but the people have fled. General Sherman writes loving epistles to erring rebels, but no one will carry them to the rebels, nor will the rebels touch them. The fact is the South hates the north. It hates the Union. The feeling is genuine and all-pervading. Whence comes this hate? This is an imperative inquiry for statesmen, who would place the peace of this government on an immovable foundation. You are of the same race, the same language, the same sacred historic memories. Why do they hate you? Certainly not because you have been in any manner ungenerous or unjust to them. Why do they hate you? Is it because they are naturally worse than other men? Not at all. I hold that the slaveholder is just as good as his slave system will allow him to be. If I were a slaveholder, and was determined to remain such, I would equal the worst, both in cruelty to the slave and in hatred to the north. I should hate the declaration of Independence, hate the Constitution, hate the Golden rule, hate free schools, free speech, free press, and every other form of freedom. Because in them all, I should see an enemy to my claim of property in man. I should see that the whole North is a point blank and killing condemnation of all my pretensions. The real root of bitterness, that which has generated this intense Southern hate toward the North, is Slavery. Here is the stone of stumbling and the rock of offence. Once I felt it necessary to argue this point. The time for such argument has past. Slavery stands confessed as the grand cause of the war. It has drilled every rebel soldier, loaded, primed, aimed and fired every rebel cannon since the war began. No other interest, commercial, manufacturing or political, could have wrought such a social earthquake amongst us. It has within itself that which begets a character in all around it favorable to its own continuance. It makes slaves of the negroes, vassals of the poor whites and tyrants of the masters. Pride, injustice, ingratitude, lust of dominion, cruelty, scorn, and contempt are the qualities of this rebellion, and slavery breeds them all. The tyrant wants no law above his own will, no associates but men of his own stamp of baseness. He is willing to administer the laws when he can bend them to his will, but he will break them when he can no longer bend them. Where labor is performed under the lash, justice will be administered under the bowie knife. The south is in this respect just what slavery has made her. She has been breeding thieves, rebels and traitors, and this stupendous conflict is the result. She could not do otherwise and cherish slavery in the midst of her.

Now the great question is what shall be the conditions of peace? What shall be done with slavery? We have gradually drifted to this vital question. Slavery is the pivot on which turns all the machinery of this tremendous war, and upon it will depend the character of the future of our peace or want of it.

It is really wonderful how we have been led along towards this grand issue, and how all efforts to evade, postpone, and prevent its coming, have been mocked and defied by the stupendous sweep of events.

It was oracularly given out from Washington many months ago, that whether this rebellion should succeed or fail, the status of no man in the country would be changed by the result. You know what that meant. Europe knew what that meant. It was an assurance given to the world in general, and the slaveholding states in particular, that no harm should come to slavery in the prosecution of the war for the Union. It was a last bid for a compromise with the rebels. But despite of diplomatic disclaimers, despite border State influence, despite the earlier proclamation of the President himself, the grand question of

Emancipation now compels attention and the most thoughtful consideration of men in high places of the nation.

By the events of this war, Washington has become to the nation what Syracuse was to the State of New York after the rescue of Jerry, the grand centre for abolition meetings. A new Congress has assembled there.

Dr. Cheever, Ralph Waldo Emerson, Gerrit Smith, Wendell Phillips, William Goodell and William Lloyd Garrison may now utter in safety their opinions on slavery in the national capital. Meanwhile Congress has a bill before it for the abolition of slavery in the District of Columbia. Kill slavery at the heart of the nation, and it will certainly die at the extremities. Down with it there, and it is the brick knocked down at the end of the row by which the whole line is prostrate.

More and better, the infernal business of slave catching by our army in Missouri and on the Potomac, is at last peremptorily forbidden under penalty of dismissal from the service. This looks small, but is not so. It is a giant stride toward the grand result.

I thank all the powers of earth and sky, that I am permitted to be a witness to this day's events. That slavery could always live and flourish in this country I have always known to be a foul and guilty heresy. That the vile system must eventually go down I have never doubted, even in the darkest days of my life in slavery. But that I should live to see the President of the United States deliberately advocating Emancipation was more than I ever ventured to hope.

It is true that the President lays down his propositions with many qualifications some of which to my thinking, are unnecessary, unjust and wholly unwise. There are spots on the Sun. A blind man can see where the President's heart is. I read the spaces as well as the lines of that message, I see in them a brave man trying against great odds, to do right. An honest patriot endeavoring to save his country in its day of peril. It is the first utterance, and first utterances are not according to Carlyle the most articulate and perfect. Time and practice will improve the President as they improve other men. He is tall and strong but he is not done growing, he grows as the nation grows. He has managed to say one good word, and to say it so distinctly that all the world may hear. He has dared to say that the highest interest of the country will be promoted by the abolition of slavery. And this, bear in mind, is not said in the bitterness of defeat, but when every morning brought news of glorious victories over the slaveholding rebels. The message comes at the call of no desperation. The time selected for sending it to Congress and the nation must be read with the document itself in order to appreciate its true significance.

Right upon the heels of the message comes the appointment of John C. Frémont, a man whose name thrills the young heart of America with every sentiment of honor, patriotism, and bravery. John C. Frémont carries his department in his name. He goes to free the mountains of rebels and traitors and the good wishes of all but traitors will go with him. Here is a new chapter of the war:

Frémont's proclamation, was revised and modified by the President; Frémont was removed from his post when in the act of striking the foe. Calumny did its worst upon Frémont. But he was brave and calm, with Jessie by his side he could not well be otherwise, and though strong himself without that pride of American women to support him, he must have fallen. I saw them as they passed eastward, after the chief had fallen. One glance at the young General and his noble wife told me that Frémont would rise again. He has risen. The rebels will hear it. His war horse is already pawing on all their mountains! But what shall be the conditions of peace? How shall the Union be reconstructed? To my mind complete Emancipation is the only basis of permanent peace. Any other basis will place us just at the point from which we started. To leave slavery standing in the rebel States, is to leave the eggs of treason in the nest from whence we shall have to meet a larger brood of traitors, and rebels at another time; it is to transmit to posterity the question that ought to be settled to-day. Leave slavery where it is, and you leave the same generator of hate towards the north which has already cost us rivers of blood and millions of treasure. Leave slavery in the south and it will be as dangerous for a Northern man to travel in the south, as for a man to enter a powder magazine with fire. Despots are suspicious, and every slaveholder is an unmitigated despot, a natural foe to every form of freedom. Leave slavery in the south, and you will fill the north with a full fledged breed of servile panderers to slavery, baser than all their predecessors.

Leave slavery where it is and you will hereafter, as heretofore, see in politics a divided, fettered, north, and an united south. You will see the statesmen of the country facing both ways, speaking two languages, assenting to the principles of freedom in the north, and bowing to the malign spirit and practices of slavery at the South. You will see all the pro-slavery elements of the country attracted to the south, giving that section ascendancy again in the counsels of the nation and making them masters of the destinies of the Republic. Restore slavery to its old status in the Union and the same elements of demoralization which have plunged this country into this tremendous war will begin again to dig the grave of free Institutions.

It is the boast of the South that her Institutions are peculiar and homogeneous, and so they are. Her statesmen have had the wit to see that contact with the free North must either make the North like herself, or that she herself must become like the North. They are right. The South must put off the yoke of slavery or the North must prepare her neck for that yoke, provided the union is restored. There is a middle path—We have pursued that middle path. It is *compromise* and by it we have reached the point of civil war with all its horrid consequences. The question is shall we start anew in the same old path?

Who wants a repetition of the same event thro' which we are passing? Who wants to see the nation taxed to keep a standing army in the South to maintain respect for the Federal Government and protect the rights of citizens of the United States? To such a man I say, leave slavery still dominant at the South and you shall have all your wants supplied.

On the other hand abolish slavery and the now disjointed nation like kindred drops would speedily mingle into one. Abolish slavery and the last hinderance to a solid nationality is abolished. Abolish slavery and you give conscience a chance to grow, and you will win the respect and admiration of mankind. Abolish slavery and you put an end to all sectional politics founded upon conflicting sectional interests, and imparting strife and bitterness to all our general elections, and to the debates on the floor of Congress. Abolish slavery and the citizens of each state will be regarded and treated as equal citizens of the United States, and may travel unchallenged and unmolested in all the states of the Union. Abolish slavery and you put an end to sectional religion and morals, and establish free speech and liberty of conscience throughout your common country. Abolish slavery and rational, law abiding Liberty will fill the whole land with peace, joy, and permanent safety now and forever.

"BUT YOU MUST ACT": WASHINGTON, D.C., APRIL 1862

Abraham Lincoln to George B. McClellan

Departing Washington for Fort Monroe with his army, General McClellan told his wife, "I feel very glad to get away from that sink of iniquity. . . ." In his contempt he left behind a careless, poorly drawn plan for protecting the capital, with the result that Lincoln retained Irvin McDowell's army corps for its defense. On meeting the first Confederate resistance on the Peninsula, at Yorktown, McClellan determined on a siege, and initiated what became the leitmotif of his campaign—the constant (and delusional) complaint that he was greatly outnumbered. In his letter the President sought to reason with the general.

Major General McClellan. Washington,
My dear Sir. April 9. 1862

Your despatches complaining that you are not properly sustained, while they do not offend me, do pain me very much.

Blencker's Division was withdrawn from you before you left here; and you knew the pressure under which I did it, and, as I thought, acquiesced in it—certainly not without reluctance.

After you left, I ascertained that less than twenty thousand unorganized men, without a single field battery, were all you designed to be left for the defence of Washington, and Manassas Junction; and part of this even, was to go to Gen. Hooker's old position. Gen. Banks' corps, once designed for Manassas Junction, was diverted, and tied up on the line of Winchester and Strausburg, and could not leave it without again exposing the upper Potomac, and the Baltimore and Ohio Railroad. This presented, (or would present, when McDowell and Sumner should be gone) a great temptation to the enemy to turn back from the Rappahanock, and sack Washington. My explicit order that Washington should, by the judgment of *all* the commanders of Army corps, be left entirely secure, had been neglected. It was precisely this that drove me to detain McDowell.

I do not forget that I was satisfied with your arrangement to leave Banks at Mannassas Junction; but when that arrangement was broken up, and *nothing* was substituted for it, of course I was not satisfied. I was constrained to substitute something for it myself. And now allow me to ask "Do you really think I should permit the line from Richmond, *via* Mannassas Junction, to this city to be entirely open, except what resistance could be presented by less than twenty thousand unorganized troops?" This is a question which the country will not allow me to evade.

There is a curious mystery about the *number* of the troops now with you. When I telegraphed you on the 6th. saying you had over a hundred thousand with you, I had just obtained from the Secretary of War, a statement, taken as he said, from your own returns, making 108,000 then with you, and *en route* to you. You now say you will have but 85,000, when all *en route* to you shall have reached you. How can the discrepancy of 23,000 be accounted for?

As to Gen. Wool's command, I understand it is doing for you precisely what a like number of your own would have to do, if that command was away.

I suppose the whole force which has gone forward for you, is with you by this time; and if so, I think it is the precise time for you to strike a blow. By delay the enemy will relatively gain upon you—that is, he will gain faster, by *fortifications* and *re-inforcements*, than you can by re-inforcements alone.

And, once more let me tell you, it is indispensable to *you* that you strike a blow. *I* am powerless to help this. You will do me the justice to remember I always insisted, that going down the Bay in search of a field, instead of fighting at or near Mannassas, was only shifting, and not surmounting, a difficulty—that we would find the same enemy, and the same, or equal, intrenchments, at either place. The country will not fail to note—is now noting—that the present hesitation to move upon an intrenched enemy, is but the story of Manassas repeated.

I beg to assure you that I have never written you, or spoken to you, in greater kindness of feeling than now, nor with a fuller purpose to sustain you, so far as in my most anxious judgment, I consistently can. *But you must act.* Yours very truly

A. LINCOLN

BATTLE OF SHILOH: TENNESSEE, APRIL 1862

Ulysses S. Grant to Commanding Officer, Advance Forces; to Julia Dent Grant; to Nathaniel H. McLean; to Jesse Root Grant; and to Elihu B. Washburne

With their perimeter defense in tatters, the Confederate commanders in the West, Albert Sidney Johnston and Pierre G. T. Beauregard, turned to concentration, gathering about 40,000 men at Corinth, in northern Mississippi, to try to counter Grant's southward advance along the Tennessee River. Grant's army of 40,000, camped at Pittsburg Landing on the Tennessee, was unprepared for the sudden Confederate attack on April 6; the two-day battle took the name of a country church called Shiloh. This set of Grant's correspondence charts the course of the action and the aftermath. He wrote first to a commander in Don Carlos Buell's army, on the march to join him. In writing to his wife, Grant considerably overcounts the enemy forces. His official report details the arrival of reinforcements that enabled him to counterattack on April 7. In writing his father, Grant defends himself against press reports that he was taken by surprise at Shiloh. Jesse Grant sent the letter to the *Cincinnati Commercial*, which printed it on May 2 as coming from "a personal friend of Gen. Grant." Grant sought further support from his confidant Congressman Elihu B. Washburne, who on May 2 defended the general in a speech to the House.

Pittsburg, April 6th 1862

COMD.G OFFICER
ADVANCE FORCES NEAR PITTSBURG, TEN.
GEN.

The attack on my forces has been very spirited from early this morning. The appearance of fresh troops on the field now would have a powerful effect both by inspiring our men and disheartining the enemy. If you will get upon the field leaving all your baggage on the East bank of the river it will be a move to our advantage and possibly save the day to us.

The rebel forces is estimated at over 100.000 men.

My Hd Qrs. will be in the log building on top of the hill where you will be furnished a staff officer to guide you to your place on the field.

Respectfully &c
U. S. GRANT
Maj. Gen.

Pittsburg, Ten. April 8th 1862

DEAR JULIA,

Again another terrible battle has occured in which our arms have been victorious. For the number engaged and the tenacity with which both parties held on for two days, during an incessent fire of musketry and artillery, it has no equal on this continent. The best troops of the rebels were engaged to the number of 162 regiments as stated by a deserter from their camp, and their ablest generals. Beaurigard commanded in person aided by A. S. Johnson, Bragg, Breckenridge and hosts of other generals of less note but possibly of quite as much merit. Gen. Johnson was killed and Bragg wounded. The loss on both sides was heavy probably not less than 20,000 killed and wounded altogether. The greatest loss was sustained by the enemy. They suffered immensly by demoralization also many of their men leaving the field who will not again be of value on the field.

I got through all safe having but one shot which struck my sword but did not touch me.

I am detaining a steamer to carry this and must cut it short.

Give my love to all at home. Kiss the children for me. The same for yourself.

Good night dear Julia.

ULYS.

Head Quarters Disct of West Tenn
Pittsburgh April 9th 1862

CAPT N H McLEAN
A A GENL DEPT OF THE MISSISSIPPI
SAINT LOUIS. MO.
CAPT

It becomes my duty again to report another battle fought between two great armies, one contending for the maintainance of the best Government ever devised the other for its destruction. It is pleasant to record the success of the army contending for the former principle.

On Sunday morning our pickets were attacked and driven in by the enemy. Immediately the five Divisions stationed at this place were drawn up in line of battle ready to meet them. The battle soon waxed warm on the left and center, varying at times to all parts of the line.

The most continuous firing of musketry and artillery ever heard on this Continent was kept up until night fall, the enemy having forced the entire line to fall back nearly half way from their Camps to the Landing. At a late hour in the afternoon a desperate effort was made by the enemy to turn our left and get possession of the Landing, transports &c. This point was guarded by the Gun boats Tyler and Lexington, Capt's Gwinn & Shirk U S N commanding Four 20 pounder Parrott guns and a battery of rifled guns. As there is a deep and impassable ravine for artillery or Cavalry and very difficult for Infantry at this point. No troops were stationed here except the neccessary Artillerists and a small Infantry force for their support Just at this moment the advance of Maj Genl Buells Column (a part of the Division under Genl Nelson) arrived, the two Generals named both being present. An advance was immediately made upon the point of attack and the enemy soon driven back.

In this repulse much is due to the presence of the Gun boats Tyler and Lexington and their able Commanders Capt Gwinn and Shirk.

During the night the Divisions under Genl Crittenden and McCook arrived. Genl Lew Wallace, at Crumps Landing six miles below, was ordered at an early hour in the morning to hold his Division in readiness to be moved in any direction to which it might be ordered. At about 11 oClock the order was delivered to move it up to Pittsburgh, but owing to its being led by a circuitous route did not arrive in time to take part in Sundays action.

During the night all was quiet, and feeling that a great moral advantage would be gained by becoming the attacking party, an advance was ordered as soon as day dawned. The result was a gradual repulse of the enemy at all parts of the line from morning until probably 5 oClock in the afternoon when it became evident the enemy was retreating. Before the close of the action the advance of Genl T J Woods Division arrived in time to take part in the action.

My force was too much fatigued from two days hard fighting and exposure in the open air to a drenching rain during the intervening night to pursue immediately.

Night closed in cloudy and with heavy rain making the roads impracticable for artillery by the next morning. Genl Sherman however followed the enemy finding that the main part of the army had retreated in good order.

Hospitals of the enemies wounded were found all along the road as far as pursuit was made. Dead bodies of the enemy and many graves were also found.

I enclose herewith report of Genl Sherman which will explain more fully the result of this pursuit.

Of the part taken by each seperate Command I cannot take special notice in this report, but will do so more fully when reports of Division Commanders are handed in.

Genl Buell, coming on the Field with a distinct army, long under his command, and which did such efficient service, commanded by himself in person on the field, will be much better able to notice those of his command who particularly distinguished themselves than I possibly can.

I feel it a duty however to a gallant and able officer Brig Genl W T Sherman to make special mention. He not only was with his Command during the entire of the two days action, but displayed great judgment and skill in the management of his men. Altho severely wounded in the hand the first day, his place was never vacant. He was again wounded and had three horses killed under him. In making this mention of a gallant officer no disparagement is intended to the other Division Commanders Major Generals John A McClernand and Lew Wallace, and Brig Generals S A Hurlbut, B M. Prentiss and W H L Wallace, all of whom maintained their places with credit to themselves and the cause Genl Prentiss was taken prisoner in the first days action, and Genl W H L Wallace severely, probably mortally wounded. His Ass Adj Genl Capt William McMichael is missing, probably taken prisoner.

My personal Staff are all deserving of particular mention, they having been engaged during the entire two days in conveying orders to every part of the field. It consists of Col J D Webster, Chief of Staff, Lt Col J B McPherson Chief Engineer, assisted by Lieuts W L B Jenney and William Kossack, Capt J A Rawlins A A Genl Capts W S Hillyer, W R Rowley and C B Lagow aides-de-Camp Col G. G. Pride Volunteer aide and Capt J P Hawkins Chief Commissary who accompanied me upon the field.

The Medical Department under the direction of Surgeon Hewitt Medical Director, showed great energy in providing for the wounded and in getting them from the field regardless of danger.

Col Webster was placed in special charge of all the artillery and was constantly upon the field. He displayed, as always heretofore, both skill and bravery. At least in one instance he was the means of placing an entire Regiment in a position of doing most valuable service, and where it would not have been but for his exertions.

Lt Col McPherson attached to my staff as Chief Engineer deserves more than a passing notice for his activity and courage. All the grounds beyond our Camps for miles have been reconnoitred by him, and plats carefully prepared under his supervision, give accurate information of the nature of approaches to our lines. During the two days battle he was constantly in the saddle leading troops as they arrived to points where their services were required. During the engagement he had one horse shot under him.

The Country will have to mourn the loss of many brave men who fell at the battle of Pittsburgh, or Chilo more properly. The exact loss in killed and wounded will be known in a day or two. At present I can only give it approximately at 1500 killed and 3500 wounded.

The loss of Artillery was great, many pieces being disabled

by the enemies shots and some loosing all their horses and many men. There was probably not less than two hundred horses killed.

The loss of the enemy in killed and left upon the field was greater than ours. In wounded the estimate cannot be made as many of them must have been sent back to Corinth and other points.

The enemy suffered terribly from demorilization and desertion. A flag of Truce was sent in to day from Genl Beaurigard. I enclose herewith a copy of the Correspondence.

I am. Very Respectfully
Your Obt Servt
U. S. Grant
Major General Comdg

Pittsburg Landing, Tenn., April 26, 1862.

I will go on, and do my duty to the very best of my ability, without praise, and do all I can to bring this war to a speedy close. I am not an aspirant for any thing at the close of the war.

There is one thing I feel well assured of; that is, that I have the confidence of every brave man in my command. Those who showed the white feather will do all in their power to attract attention from themselves. I had perhaps a dozen officers arrested for cowardice in the first day's fight at this place. These men are necessarily my enemies.

As to the talk about a surprise here, nothing could be more false. If the enemy had sent us word when and where they would attack us, we could not have been better prepared. Skirmishing had been going on for two days between our reconnoitering parties and the enemy's advance. I did not believe, however, that they intended to make a determined attack, but simply that they were making a reconnoisance in force.

My headquarters were in Savannah, though I usually spent the day here. Troops were constantly arriving to be assigned to brigades and divisions, all ordered to report at Savannah, making it necessary to keep an office and some one there. I was also looking for Buell to arrive, and it was important that I should have every arrangement complete for his speedy transit to this side of the river.

U. S. GRANT.

Camp Near Corinth, Miss.
May 14th 1862

HON. E. B. WASHBURN,
DEAR SIR:

The great number of attacks made upon me by the press of the country is my apology for not writing to you oftener, not desiring to give any contradiction to them myself.—You have interested yourself so much as my friend that should I say anything it would probably be made use of in my behalf. I would scorn being my own defender against such attacks except through the record which has been kept of all my official acts and which can be examined at Washington at any time.

To say that I have not been distressed at these attacks upon me would be false, for I have a father, mother, wife & children who read them and are distressed by them and I necessarily share with them in it. Then too all subject to my orders read these charges and it is calculated to weaken their confidance in me and weaken my ability to render efficient service in our present cause. One thing I will assure you of however; I can not be driven from rendering the best service within my ability to suppress the present rebellion, and when it is over retiring to the same quiet it, the rebellion, found me enjoying.

Notoriety has no charms for me and could I render the same services that I hope it has been my fortune to render our just cause, without being known in the matter, it would be infinately prefferable to me.

Those people who expect a field of battle to be maintained, for a whole day, with about 30,000 troops, most of them entirely raw, against 70,000, as was the case at Pittsburg Landing, whilst waiting for reinforcements to come up, without loss of life, know little of War. To have left the field of Pittsburg for the enemy to occupy until our force was sufficient to have gained a bloodless victory would have been to left the Tennessee to become a second Potomac.—There was nothing left for me but to occupy the West bank of the Tennessee and to hold it at all hazards. It would have set this war back six months to have failed and would have caused the necessity of raising, as it were, a new Army.

Looking back at the past I cannot see for the life of me any important point that could be corrected.—Many persons who have visited the different fields of battle may have gone away displeased because they were not permitted to carry off horses, fire arms, or other valuables as trophies. But they are no patriots who would base their enmity on such grounds. Such I assure you are the grounds of many bitter words that have been said against me by persons who at this day would not know me by sight yet profess to speak from a personal acquaintance.

I am sorry to write such a letter, infinately sorry that there should be grounds for it. My own justification does not demand it, but you, a friend, are entitled to know my feelings.

As a friend I would be pleased to give you a record, weekly at furthest, of all that transpires in that portion of the army that I am, or may be, connected with, but not to make public use of.

I am very truly Yours
U. S. GRANT.

"WE CAUGHT THE FIRST THUNDER": TENNESSEE, APRIL 1862

William T. Sherman to Ellen Ewing Sherman

Brigadier General William T. Sherman had taken command of a division under Grant in March. Shermans' division caught the brunt of the Confederates' initial attack at Shiloh on Sunday, April 6, and he was more candid than Grant in admitting that it came as a surprise, and how unprepared were the Union forces. The "old Louisiana cadet" prisoner whom he mentions was from the Louisiana Seminary and Military Academy, where Sherman was superintendent before the war.

Camp Shiloh, Apl. 11, 1862

Dearest Ellen,

Well we have had a big battle where they Shot real bullets and I am safe, except a buckshot wound in the hand and a bruised shoulder from a spent ball—The first horse I rode was one I captured from the Enemy soon after I got here, a beautiful sorrel race mare that was as fleet as a deer, and very easy in her movements to which I had become much attached—She was first wounded and then shot dead under me. This occurred Sunday when the firing on both sides was terrific and I had no time to save saddle, holsters or valise. I took the horse of my aid McCoy till it was shot, when I took my Doctors horse and that was shot—My Camp was in advance of all others and we caught the first thunder, and they captured all our tents and two horses of mine hitched to the trees near my tent were Killed. So I am completely unhorsed—The first man killed in the Battle was my orderly close by my side a young handsome faithful soldier who carried his Carbine ever ready to defend me his name was Holliday and the Shot that killed him was meant for me. After the Battle was over I had him brought to my camp and buried by a tree Scarred with balls and its top carried off by a Cannon ball. These about embrace all the personal events connected with myself—My troops were very raw and Some Regiments broke at the first fire. Others behaved better, and I managed to keep enough all the time to form a Command and was the first to get back to our front Line. The Battle on Sunday was very severe. They drove back our left flank on the River, but I held the Right flank out about a mile & half, giving room for Reinforcements to come in from Crumps landing to our North, and for Buells army to land—Beauregard, Bragg Johnston, Breckinridge and all their Big men were here, with their best soldiers and after the Battle was over I found among the prisoners an old Louisiana Cadet named Barrow who sent for me and told me all about the others, many of whom were here and Knew they were fighting me. I gave him a pair of socks, drawers & Shirt and treated him very kindly. I wont attempt to give an account of the Battle, but they Say that I accomplished some important results, and Gen. Grant makes special mention of me in his Report which he shew me. I have worked hard to Keep down but somehow I am forced into prominence and might as well submit. One thing pleased me well—On Sunday we caught thunder and were beaten back—Buell arrived very opportunely and came out to see me—the place of operations was agreed on, and his fresh Kentucky troops to advance boldly out direct from the Steamboat landing to Shiloh my Head Qrs.—I was on the Right and to advance when he got abreast of me—This was done, and I edged to the Road, and reached it about 500 yards from here, just where the hardest fighting was, and then met the same Kentucky troops I had at Muldrough hill. They all recognized me and such shouting you never heard. I asked to pass their Ranks and they gave me the lead. I have since visited their Camps and never before received such marks of favor—Johns Brigade is also here, indeed we must now have 75,000 men. Figures begin to approximate my standard—Halleck is coming with reinforcements. We have been attacked & beaten off our enemy. Now we must attack him. This would occur at once, but it has been raining so that our Roads are almost impassable. The Enemy expected to crush us before Buell got here. The scenes on this field would have cured anybody of war. Mangled bodies, dead, dying, in every conceivable shape, without heads, legs; and horses! I think we have buried 2000 since the fight our own & the Enemy, and the wounded fill houses, tents, steamboats and Every conceivable place. My division had about 8000 men—at least half ran away, and out of the remaining half, I have 302 soldiers 16 officers killed and over 1200 wounded. All I can say this was a Battle, and you will receive so many graphic accounts that my picture would be tame. I Know you will read all accounts—cut out paragraphs with my name for Willy's future Study—all Slurs you will hide away, and gradually convince yourself that I am a soldier as famous as Gen. Greene. I still feel the horrid nature of this war, and the piles of dead Gentlemen & wounded & maimed makes me more anxious than ever for some hope of an End but I know such a thing cannot be for a long long time. Indeed I never expect it or to survive it. You ask for money—I have none, and now am without horse saddle bridle, bed, or anything—The Rebels, Breckinridge had my Camp and cleaned me out. You must learn to live without money, as that is going to be a scarce commodity—plant a garden & raise your own vegetables—[ ]

"THEY RAN IN EVERY DIRECTION": TENNESSEE, APRIL 1862

George W. Dawson to Laura Amanda Dawson

Captain Dawson's 1st Missouri Infantry, in John C. Breckinridge's Reserve Corps, pressed the Federal left on the first day of Shiloh. The fighting Dawson describes for his wife, at the so-called Sunken Road, was some of the fiercest of the battle, and at day's end his regiment had pushed close enough to the Tennessee to draw the fire of the Union gunboats. Shiloh cost the Union 13,000 men killed, wounded, or missing, while Confederate casualties totaled about 10,700.

Memphis, Tenn.
April 26th

My dear sweet Wife,

I wrote you a short note by Mart Dunklin but for fear you didn't get it I send you this by Mr. Robbins. You are no doubt uneasy and anxious to hear what had become of me and others. Well I will give you a kind of history. After I left you I came to Memphis and from thence I went to Murfeestown, Tenn. where I found the Reg. & in a day or so we marched & continued to do so till we arrived ten miles this side of Huntsville, Ala. Here we took Rail for 20 miles and then footed it again to Corinth, Miss. Having marched through 1/4 of Ky. all of Tenn. part of Alabama and 30 miles into Miss. you may be assured that we were some what leg weary. We arrived at Corinth Some time before the fight at Shiloh. So you might guess that we had a hand in the fight—and I must say that it was no tea party—but a hard fought Battle. Yet when ever we pressed the Yanks they gave way and we again charged them but that they ran in every direction. We were held in reserve till about 10 oclock Sunday Morning. We were then ordered forward at the double quick step for 2 1/2 miles and as soon as formed into line the Feds opened on us—at the first fire 3 of my men were wounded slightly but one of them Jim Henley has since died of Lock Jaw.

We immediately charged them and put them to rout, we then changed our direction and soon found another Brigade which poured a heavy fire on us which we returned in good stile. Our Col. Rich was shot off of his horse. Lt. Carrington was badly wounded. Capt. Sprague was here killed. We received reinforcements and charged them when they threw down their guns and scampered off like cowardly dogs. We continued to press them and run them down the river bank immediately to their gun boats if which had not been there we would have captured the last one of them. They shelled us from the Gun Boats for over 1 hour. I never heard such thunder and such shower of shell and C. Yet, these did not damage except to kill one or two men—Night coming one we drew off to one of their Camps where we found every thing a solider could want to which we helped our selves. We ate their grub, and slept in their cots as quietly as if we had no enemy in 100 miles. But they Continued to throw Shell at us all night and shell all burst beyond us—passing over our camp. Monday Morning the Feds having been reinforced with 40,000 men renewed the fight—about sun up. We commenced drawing off our forces before we were Attacked. Our Brigade fought them all day Monday in covering the retreat of our army—which was done in the very best of order Lieut. Joseph T. Hargett was killed Monday. I had 43 men when I went into the fight and on coming out had 21 having lost in killed and wounded 22. Yet most of the wounded are slightly so. The other companies of our Reg. did not suffer so much. I had forgotten to tell you I had been Elected Capt. Cam Riley having been elected Lt. Col. He had Command of our Reg. during the fight and acted bravely.

We are expecting a fight at Corinth which will be the biggest fight that will be on record in the next 100 years. I am satisfied that they will out number us but when we have them out of reach of their Gun Boats we will whip them worse that at Shiloh. The fate of our cause rests on us here. I know we have right on our side God is also with us and we must succeed will do it. War is dangerous and one cannot tell after coming out of one hard fought battle whether there is a chance to get out of the second, but I will hope for the best, knowing that if I am killed that I die fighting for My Country and my rights, also that I have your prayers constantly ascending to Heaven. Just hope you and my dear children if I am not allowed to see you again you must bear up and don't get unhappy I yet may see you again Oh what a pleasure is the thought. If you & children are only with me I could be happy but I am lonely & sad.

I have sold some of my land to Robbins so you may sign the deed. I will invest the money in Texas. Where I only wish you were.

Bob, Will Hunter, Wm. Post, Wm. Watkins and T. I. F. all were uninjured Cam Pinnell died of his wounds. Thos. Emory was slightly wounded—All are improving. Many will be able to go into the next fight.

I wish you to write me a long letter giving a detailed account of every thing that has taken place since I left, also how you are getting along and what prospect you have for something to eat this Summer and Winter. I feel very anxious to hear—and if there is any chance I want you to come down to Memphis and I will try to get you to Texas.

My love to all—but especially to you my sweet wife. Kiss our dear children a thousand times for me. Remember me to my friends if I have any. Hoping to hear from you soon I remain your devoted husband.

Geo. W. Dawson

Excuse mistakes the gas is so high up that I can't see.

Herman Melville: Shiloh

Herman Melville remembered the "dying foemen" in a poem that first appeared in *Battle-Pieces and Aspects of the War*, published in August 1866. In his preface to the book, Melville wrote that with "few exceptions, the Pieces in this volume originated in an impulse imparted by the fall of Richmond," suggesting that most of the poems were written after April 1865.

Shiloh

A Requiem

(APRIL, 1862)

Skimming lightly, wheeling still,
  The swallows fly low
Over the field in clouded days,
  The forest-field of Shiloh—
Over the field where April rain
Solaced the parched ones stretched in pain
Through the pause of night
That followed the Sunday fight
  Around the church of Shiloh—
The church so lone, the log-built one,
That echoed to many a parting groan
    And natural prayer
  Of dying foemen mingled there—
Foemen at morn, but friends at eve—
  Fame or country least their care:
(What like a bullet can undeceive!)
  But now they lie low,
While over them the swallows skim,
  And all is hushed at Shiloh.

RICHMOND, VIRGINIA, APRIL 1862

Confederate Conscription Acts

With one-year enlistments in the Confederate army expiring in the spring of 1862, Jefferson Davis saw conscription as the only answer to impending chaos. To Congress on March 28 he proposed that all men between eighteen and thirty-five "should pay their debt of military service to the country, that the burdens should not fall exclusively on the most ardent and patriotic." Congress approved his proposal on April 16, and equally important, extended current enlistments to three years or the duration of the war. Substitutes might be hired, and, under further legislation adopted on April 21, exemptions were made for a variety of occupations. In September 1862 the age of eligibility for conscription was raised to forty-five, and the following month exemptions were extended to cover one white male from every plantation with twenty or more slaves. The Confederate conscription act was the first draft law in American history, and became highly controversial. It was denounced as illegitimate because the Confederate Constitution had not explicitly authorized conscription, while the "twenty slaves" provision was attacked for favoring the rich; its enforcement would provoke widespread evasion and resistance throughout the South, especially in upland regions.

An Act to further provide for the public defence.

In view of the exigencies of the country, and the absolute necessity of keeping in the service our gallant army, and of placing in the field a large additional force to meet the advancing columns of the enemy now invading our soil: Therefore

The Congress of the Confederate States of America do enact, That the President be, and he is hereby authorized to call out and place in the military service of the Confederate States, for three years, unless the war shall have been sooner ended, all white men who are residents of the Confederate States, between the ages of eighteen and thirty-five years at the time the call or calls may be made, who are not legally exempted from military service. All of the persons aforesaid who are now in the armies of the Confederacy, and whose term of service will expire before the end of the war, shall be continued in the service for three years from the date of their original enlistment. unless the war shall have been sooner ended: *Provided, however*, That all such companies, squadrons, battalions, and regiments, whose term of original enlistment was for twelve months, shall have the right, within forty days, on a day to be fixed by the Commander of the Brigade, to re-organize said companies, battalions, and regiments, by electing all their officers, which they had a right heretofore to elect, who shall be commissioned by the President: *Provided, further*, That furloughs not exceeding sixty days, with transportation home and back, shall be granted to all those retained in the service by the provisions of this Act beyond the period of their original enlistment, and who have not heretofore received furloughs under the provisions of an Act entitled "An Act providing for the granting of bounty and furloughs to privates and non-commissioned officers in the Provisional Army," approved eleventh December, eighteen hundred and sixty-one, said furloughs to be granted at such times and in such numbers as the Secretary of War may deem most compatible with the public interest: and *Provided, further*, That in lieu of a furlough the commutation value in money of the transportation herein above granted, shall be paid to each private, musician, or non-commissioned officer who may elect to receive it, at such time as the furlough would otherwise be granted: *Provided, further*, That all persons under the age of eighteen years or over the age of thirty-five years, who are now enrolled in the military service of the Confederate States, in the regiments, squadrons, battalions, and companies hereafter to be re-organized, shall be required to remain in their respective companies, squadrons, battalions and regiments for ninety days, unless their places can be sooner supplied by other recruits not now in the service, who are between the ages of eighteen and thirty-five years; and all laws and parts of laws providing for the re-enlistment of volunteers and the organization thereof into companies, squadrons, battalions, or regiments, shall be and the same are hereby repealed.

SEC. 2. *Be it further enacted*, That such companies, squadrons, battalions, or regiments organized, or in process of organization by authority from the Secretary of War, as may be within thirty days from the passage of this Act, so far completed as to have the whole number of men requisite for organization actually enrolled, not embracing in said organizations any persons now in service, shall be mustered into the service of the Confederate States as part of the land forces of the same, to be received in that arm of the service in which they are authorized to organize, and shall elect their company, battalion, and regimental officers.

SEC. 3. *Be it further enacted*, That for the enrollment of all persons comprehended within the provisions of this Act, who are not already in service in the armies of the Confederate States, it shall be lawful for the President, with the consent of the Governors of the respective States, to employ State officers, and on failure to obtain such consent, he shall employ Confederate officers, charged with the duty of making such enrollment in accordance with rules and regulations to be prescribed by him.

SEC. 4. *Be it further enacted*, That persons enrolled under the provisions of the preceding Section, shall be assigned by the Secretary of War, to the different companies now in the service, until each company is filled to its maximum number, and the persons so enrolled shall be assigned to companies from the States from which they respectively come.

SEC. 5. *Be it further enacted*, That all Seamen and ordinary Seamen in the land forces of the Confederate States, enrolled under the provisions of this Act, may, on application of the Secretary of the Navy, be transferred from the land forces to the Naval service.

SEC. 6. *Be it further enacted*, That in all cases where a State may not have in the army a number of Regiments, Battalions, Squadrons or Companies, sufficient to absorb the number of persons subject to military service under this Act, belonging to such State, then the residue or excess thereof, shall be kept as a reserve, under such regulations as may be established by the Secretary of War, and that at stated periods of not greater than three months, details, determined by lot, shall be made from said reserve, so that each company shall, as nearly as practicable, be kept full: *Provided*, That the persons held in reserve may remain at home until called into service by the President: *Provided, also*, That during their stay at home, they shall not receive pay: *Provided, further*, That the persons comprehended in this Act, shall not be subject to the Rules and Articles of War, until mustered into the actual service of the Confederate States; except that said persons, when enrolled and liable to duty, if they shall wilfully refuse to obey said call, each of them shall be held to be a deserter, and punished as such, under said Articles: *Provided, further*, That whenever, in the opinion of the President, the exigencies of the public service may require it, he shall be authorized to call into actual service the entire reserve, or so much as may be necessary, not previously assigned to different companies in service under provision of section four of this Act; said reserve shall be organized under such rules as the Secretary of War may adopt: *Provided*, The company, battalion and regimental officers shall be elected by the troops composing the same: *Provided*, The troops raised in any one State shall not be combined in regimental, battalion, squadron or company organization with troops raised in any other States.

SEC. 7. *Be it further enacted*, That all soldiers now serving in the army or mustered in the military service of the Confederate States, or enrolled in said service under the authorizations heretofore issued by the Secretary of War, and who are continued in the service by virtue of this Act, who have not received the bounty of fifty dollars allowed by existing laws, shall be entitled to receive said bounty.

SEC. 8. *Be it further enacted*, That each man who may hereafter be mustered into service, and who shall arm himself with a musket, shot-gun, rifle or carbine, accepted as an efficient weapon, shall be paid the value thereof, to be ascertained by the mustering officer under such regulations as may be prescribed by the Secretary of War, if he is willing to sell the same, and if he is not, then he shall be entitled to receive one dollar a month for the use of said received and approved musket, rifle, shot-gun or carbine.

SEC. 9. *Be it further enacted*, That persons not liable for duty may be received as substitutes for those who are, under such regulations as may be prescribed by the Secretary of War.

SEC. 10. *Be it further enacted*, That all vacancies shall be filled by the President from the company, battalion, squadron or regiment in which such vacancies shall occur, by promotion according to seniority, except in case of disability or other incompetency: *Provided, however*, That the President may, when in his opinion, it may be proper, fill such vacancy or vacancies by the promotion of any officer or officers, or private or privates from such company, battalion, squadron or regiment who shall have been distinguished in the service by exhibition of valor and skill; and that whenever a vacancy shall occur in the lowest grade of the commissioned officers of a company, said vacancy shall be filled by election: *Provided*, That all appointments made by the President shall be by and with the advice and consent of the Senate.

SEC. 11. *Be it further enacted*, That the provisions of the first section of this Act, relating to the election of officers, shall apply to those regiments, battalions, and squadrons which are composed of twelve months and war companies combined in the same organization, without regard to the manner in which the officers thereof were originally appointed.

SEC. 12. *Be it further enacted*, That each company of infantry shall consist of one hundred and twenty-five, rank and file; each company of field artillery of one hundred and fifty, rank and file; each of cavalry, of eighty, rank and file.

SEC. 13. *Be it further enacted*, That all persons, subject to enrollment, who are not now in the service, under the provisions of this Act, shall be permitted, previous to such enrollment, to volunteer in companies now in the service.

APPROVED April 16, 1862.

An Act to exempt certain persons from enrollment for service in the Armies of the Confederate States.

The Congress of the Confederate States of America do enact, That all persons who shall be held to be unfit for military services under rules to be prescribed by the Secretary of War; all in the service or employ of the Confederate States; all judicial and executive officers of Confederate or State Governments; the members of both Houses of the Congress and of the Legislatures of the several States and their respective officers; all clerks of the officers of the State and Confederate Governments allowed by law; all engaged in carrying the mails; all ferrymen on post routes; all pilots and persons engaged in the marine service and in actual service on river and railroad routes of transportation; telegraphic operators, and ministers of religion in the regular discharge of ministerial duties; all engaged in working iron mines, furnaces and foundries; all journeymen printers actually employed in printing newspapers; all presidents and professors of colleges and academies, and all teachers having as many as twenty scholars; superintendents of the public hospitals, lunatic asylums and the regular nurses and attendants therein, and the teachers employed in the institution for the deaf and dumb, and blind; in each apothecary store now established and doing business, one apothecary in good standing who is a practical druggist; superintendents and operatives in wool and cotton factories, who may be exempted by the Secretary of War;—shall be and are hereby exempted from military service in the armies of the Confederate States.

APPROVED April 21, 1862.

ABOLISHING SLAVERY IN THE DISTRICT OF COLUMBIA: APRIL 1862

Abraham Lincoln: Message to Congress

In April Congress abolished slavery in the District of Columbia, providing compensation of up to $300 per slave and appropriating $100,000 for the voluntary colonization of freed slaves outside the United States. The bill received unanimous Republican support, but was opposed by a majority of Democrats and border state unionists. Signed into law by President Lincoln, who privately favored gradual emancipation in the District, the measure freed some 3,200 people. (Congress passed the supplemental legislation Lincoln asked for on July 12.) On June 19 Lincoln would sign a bill abolishing slavery in the federal territories, without compensation or provision for colonization.

April 16, 1862

Fellow citizens of the Senate, and House of Representatives.

The Act entitled "An Act for the release of certain persons held to service, or labor in the District of Columbia" has this day been approved, and signed.

I have never doubted the constitutional authority of congress to abolish slavery in this District; and I have ever desired to see the national capital freed from the institution in some satisfactory way. Hence there has never been, in my mind, any question upon the subject, except the one of expediency, arising in view of all the circumstances. If there be matters within and about this act, which might have taken a course or shape, more satisfactory to my judgment, I do not attempt to specify them. I am gratified that the two principles of compensation, and colonization, are both recognized, and practically applied in the act.

In the matter of compensation, it is provided that claims may be presented within ninety days from the passage of the act "but not thereafter"; and there is no saving for minors, femes-covert, insane, or absent persons. I presume this is an omission by mere over-sight, and I recommend that it be supplied by an amendatory or supplemental act.

ABRAHAM LINCOLN

April 16. 1862.

RUNNING THE GAUNTLET:
LOUISIANA, APRIL 1862

John Russell Bartlett: The "Brooklyn" at the Passage of the Forts

On the night of April 23–24, 1862, Flag Officer David G. Farragut signaled his battle fleet to force the passage between Forts Jackson and St. Philip, which guarded the Mississippi about seventy miles below New Orleans. Four days earlier, two daring gunboat captains had made a breach in the hulks and chains barricading the river just wide enough for Farragut's warships to pass through one at a time and challenge the forts. John Russell Bartlett, then a midshipman aboard the sloop of war *Brooklyn*, described the fighting in *Battles and Leaders of the Civil War.*

From February 2d to March 7th, 1862, the United States steamer *Brooklyn*, Captain Thomas T. Craven, was engaged in blockading Pass à l'Outre, one of the mouths of the Mississippi River. It is impossible to describe the monotony of the life on board ship during this period. Most of the time there was a dense fog, so thick that we could not see the length of the ship. The fog collected in the rigging, and there was a constant dripping from aloft like rain, which kept the decks wet and made things generally uncomfortable. No news was received from the North, and our waiting and watching seemed endless. We had our routine of drill each day, but nothing to talk about. Our only excitement was the lookout at the maintopgallant cross-tree, who was above the fog-bank, shouting "Smoke h-oo!" It was a great relief to shout through the deck-trumpet, "Where away?" but the answer was always the same, —"Up the river, sir!" Days and weeks went by, and the smoke came no nearer. Once only, on February 24th, it came out of the river, and we had an exciting chase of a blockade-runner, following her for miles, with an officer aloft conning the ship by the smoke seen above the fog; we captured the chase, which proved to be the steamer *Magnolia* with 1200 bales of cotton.

At last the spell was broken, for on the 7th of March the *Hartford* and *Pensacola* arrived with Captain D. G. Farragut, then flag-officer commanding the West Gulf Blockading Squadron, and we learned that we were going to open the Mississippi River.

I had never met Farragut, but had heard of him from officers who were with him in the *Brooklyn* on her previous cruise. He had been represented as a man of most determined will and character—a man who would assume any responsibility to accomplish necessary ends. I saw a great deal of him at the Head of the Passes and after we passed the forts. Often, when I came on board the *Hartford* with a message from the captain of the *Brooklyn*, Farragut sent me somewhere to carry an order or to do certain duty. I was much impressed with his energy and activity and his promptness of decision and action. He had a winning smile and a most charming manner and was jovial and talkative. He prided himself on his agility, and I remember his telling me once that he always turned a handspring on his birthday, and should not consider that he was getting old until he was unable to do it. The officers who had the good fortune to be immediately associated with him seemed to worship him. He had determination and dash in execution, but in planning and organizing he appeared to want method. He showed me one day an old envelope containing memoranda, and said that that was all the record or books that he kept. He had, however, the good fortune to have on his staff two of the best organizers and administrators of detail in the service,—Captains Henry H. Bell at New Orleans and Percival Drayton at Mobile.

On the 15th of March we began to congregate at the Head of the Passes, and at this time the energy and activity of the flag-officer made themselves felt. We lay here several weeks preparing our ships for the coming action, drilling the crews, firing at targets, and getting in provisions and coal. Farragut was about the fleet from early dawn until dark, and if any officers or men had not spontaneous enthusiasm he certainly infused it into them. I have been on the morning watch, from 4 to 8, when he would row alongside the ship at 6 o'clock, either hailing to ask how we were getting along, or, perhaps, climbing over the side to see for himself. One of the preparations that we made at the Head of the Passes was to hang the chain-cables along each side, abreast of the engine and boilers. A jack-stay, or iron rod, was fastened by means of eye-bolts to the ship's side about eight feet above the water, and one of the chain-cables in bights was suspended to it and fastened with spun yarn. The links of the cable were of iron an inch and a half in diameter, and each strand, or bight, was lapped over the next, the links fitting between each other so that it made an almost continuous coat of mail. It extended about two feet below the water-line. Around the steam-drum, which rose five feet above the berth-deck, sand-bags were piled, and the sick-bay, in the bow, was filled solid with hawsers and rigging, taken from the hold, which had been cleared to form a hospital for the surgeon. Everything was arranged for the convenience of the surgeon in attending the wounded. At the main hatch a cot-frame was rigged and slung from two davits so that the wounded men could be lowered to the berth-deck and thence carried to the surgeon in the forehold. A howitzer was placed in the foretop and one in the maintop. A large kedge-anchor was hung to the main brace bumkin on each quarter, with a hawser attached, to be used whenever it became necessary to turn the ship suddenly.

There was considerable delay in getting the larger vessels over the bar and in filling up with ammunition and coal. At last, on April 16th, Farragut steamed up with the fleet and anchored just below the point where Porter's mortar-vessels, or, as the sailors used to call them, the "bummers," had taken their position and had made ready to open fire upon the forts. Admiral Porter has described in this work the part taken by these vessels in the opening of the lower Mississippi. I can vouch for the accuracy of their aim, for I used to sit on the cross-trees all day, when not on duty, seeing the shells fall into the fort and witnessing the havoc they made in it.

We had plenty of occupation while anchored below the forts, and as an accompaniment one of the mortars was fired every half minute all day. It was trying work for the poor fellows on the mortar-schooners, for when their mortar was fired, all of them were obliged to go aft and stand on tiptoe with open mouths to receive the concussion. The powder blackened everything, and the men looked like negroes. At intervals fire-rafts came down. The first one caused much alarm, and we prepared to slip our cable and get out of the way. The rafts were immense flat-boats with wood piled loosely twenty feet high and saturated with tar and resin, and the flame from them would rise a hundred feet into the air. They certainly looked dangerous, but they were set adrift only one at a time and otherwise were so badly managed that in a little while they merely served to amuse us. The fleet lay under the point on the right bank, and the rafts would tend to the left bank with the strength of the current, and so pass harmlessly by or ground on the bank. Others caught in the obstructions and failed to come down. Sometimes boats from the ships were sent to help tow them away. If there had been any one man to direct the enemy's operations, and so secure concert of action, we should have fared badly; for half a dozen rafts chained together and pushed into position by their gun-boats would have made havoc with the fleet. One night five rafts were sent down, one of which had been towed over to the right bank and came almost directly into the fleet; the *Westfield* made for it and pushed it out into the stream; but it came so near that even with hose playing on the side and rigging the *Brooklyn's* paint was badly blistered.

The forts kept up a continual fire from their rifle-guns, and now and then a shell would pass uncomfortably near the ship. To keep down this fire as much as possible, and thus protect the mortar-vessels, one of the smaller sloops or two of the gun-boats were kept under way. They would steam up to the west bank under cover of the trees and suddenly shoot out into the stream and open fire with their 11-inch pivots, and then drift down-stream. As they were always in rapid motion, it was difficult for the gunners in the forts to hit them; still, a number of men were wounded.*

On the 23d, after five days of continual firing, Commander Porter informed the flag-officer that his men were worn out from want of sleep and rest, and that his ammunition was

*There were none killed in the sloops or gun-boats in the bombardment preceding the battle. Twenty-four men were wounded, including one on board the schooner *Norfolk Packet.* Two deaths are reported April 18th–24th, one of them on board the mortar-schooner *Arletta*, and one by a fall from the mast-head on board the *Katahdin.*—J. R. B.

nearly expended. The obstructions, which had formed an apparently impassable barrier, had now been overcome. The opening of a passage through the hulks was one of the most daring feats of the war, and here again the want of concert among the independent floating commands of the enemy led him to neglect the protection of what was really his main reliance for defense. The only cause for delay was now removed. Councils of war were held on board the *Hartford* every day during the bombardment, and the plan of running by the forts was fully discussed. Some of the captains thought it suicidal and believed that the whole fleet would be annihilated; others, that perhaps one or two vessels might get by, but they would be sunk by the rams. All this time Farragut maintained that it must and should be done, even if half the ships were lost. A final council was called on the afternoon of the 23d, and it was decided to attempt the passage that night.*

The present article is intended merely as a personal narrative of the passage of the forts as seen from the deck of the *Brooklyn*. This vessel was a flush-deck sloop-of-war, carrying 22 9-inch guns, 1 80-pounder Dahlgren rifle, and 1 30-pounder Parrott rifle. A small poop-deck extended about fifteen feet from the taffrail, and under this were the steering-wheel and binnacles. I was a midshipman on board doing lieutenant's duty, having charge of a regular watch and in command of a division of guns. My division consisted of 4 guns (2 guns' crews) at the after end of the ship. The guns were numbered in pairs 10 and 11. The No. 11 gun on the starboard side was shifted over to the port side under the poop-deck, and both the No. 11 guns were manned by the marines. It was expected that our principal work would be with our port battery directed against Fort Jackson on the right bank. My two crews manned the No. 10

*In July, 1861, I was on board the steam frigate *Mississippi* when she made a visit to the Southwest Pass, and having been sent to the *Powhatan*, commanded by Lieutenant D. D. Porter, near by, I walked up and down the quarter-deck with the commanding officer. He was very much exasperated that the department at Washington delayed sending vessels of proper draught to enter the river, and said that if he had half a dozen good vessels he would undertake to run by the forts and capture New Orleans. Admiral Porter has already recounted in this work the prominent part that he took in the opening of the Mississippi, and I therefore omit further reference to it.—J. R. B.

gun on each side, and also prepared to man the 30-pounder on the poop if occasion should require. On each side of the poop there was a ladder to the main deck. While steaming up to the hulks and until it was necessary for me to be at my guns, I stood on the port ladder with my head above the rail, where I could watch our approach to the forts, and I mounted this ladder several times to see what was going on as we advanced.

On the poop were Captain Craven, Midshipman John Anderson, who had volunteered a few days before from the *Montgomery*, which did not take part in the action, Captain's Clerk J. G. Swift, afterward a graduate of West Point and a lieutenant in the army, and two quartermasters. There was a small piece of ratline stuff carried around the poop, about waist-high. Captain Craven stood at the forward edge of the poop with his hands on this line, and did not move during the whole passage. I had the good fortune during the war to serve with many brave commanders, but I have never met in the service, or out of it, a man of such consummate coolness, such perfect apparent indifference to danger as Admiral Craven. As I write, I hear the sad news of his death.

At 2 o'clock on the morning of the 24th two red lights were hoisted at the peak of the flag-ship as a signal to get under way. All hands had been on deck since midnight to see that everything about the deck and guns was ready for action, and when the decks were wet down and sanded, it really began to look as if we were going to have some pretty hot business on our hands. The anchor was hove up with as little noise as possible, and at half-past 2 we steamed off, following the *Hartford* toward the entrance to the opening which had been made in the obstructions. The Confederates opened fire about 3 o'clock, when the advance division came in sight and range of the forts, and as we passed ahead of the mortar-vessels we also came in range; but the forts were so far ahead that we could not bring our broadside guns to bear. For twenty minutes we stood silent beside the guns, with the shot and shell from Forts St. Philip and Jackson passing over us and bursting everywhere in the air. As we came to the obstruction the water-battery on the Fort Jackson side opened a most destructive fire, and here the *Brooklyn* received her first shot. We gave the water-battery a broadside of grape. With our own smoke and the smoke from the vessels immediately ahead, it was impossible to direct the ship, so that we missed the opening between the hulks and brought up on the chain. We dropped back and tried again; this time the chain broke, but we swung alongside of one of the hulks, and the stream-anchor, hanging on the starboard quarter, caught, tore along the hulk, and then parted its lashings. The cable secured us just where the Confederates had the range of their guns, but somebody ran up with an axe and cut the hawser, and we began to steam up the river.* A few moments later there was a sudden jar, and the engines stopped. The propeller had no doubt struck some hard object, but no one knew the cause of the stoppage; and as Craven called out, "Stand by the starboard anchor," and a fatal pause under the enemy's fire seemed imminent, a thrill of alarm ran through the ship. The alarm was groundless, however, as no injury was done, and presently the engines started again, and the ship moved on.

There were many fire-rafts, and these and the flashing of the guns and bursting shells made it almost as light as day, but the smoke from the passing fleet was so thick that at times one could see nothing ten feet from the ship. While entangled with the rafts, the *Brooklyn* was hulled a number of times; one shot from Fort Jackson struck the rail just at the break of the poop and went nearly across, plowing out the deck in its course. Another struck Barney Sands, the signal quartermaster, and cut his body almost in two. The first lieutenant, Lowry, coming along at the time, inquired who it was, and understanding the response to be "Bartlett," instead of "Barney," he passed the word that he had sent down "all that was left of poor Bartlett." As he came on deck and was about in all parts of the ship during the fight, he gave the men news of the progress of the fight and of the casualties, and for once I was completely out of existence.

The ship was now clear of the hulks and steamed up the river, throwing shells and shrapnel into Fort Jackson as fast as

*I went on the poop to help clear the hawser, and looked around for my classmate Anderson. He must have been knocked overboard by a shot when we first came to the obstructions. The anchor on the port quarter was broken off close to the stock at this point by a shot from Fort Jackson.—J. R. B.

the guns could be loaded and fired. When just abreast of the fort a shot struck the side of the port of No. 9 gun on the port side, and at the same time a shell burst directly over the gun. The first captain's head was cut off and nine of the gun's crew were wounded. I was standing amidships between the two No. 10 guns, and was struck on the back by the splinters and thrown to the deck. I was on my feet in a moment and turned to my port gun. There were only two men standing at it, the first loader and the first sponger, who were leaning against the side of the ship: the others were all flat on deck, one of them directly in the rear of the gun. The gun had just been loaded, and I pulled this man to one side, clear of the recoil, and fired the gun. It was a time when every one felt that he must do something. After the discharge of the gun the men on the deck got up and came to their places. None of them were seriously hurt. The captain of the gun found a piece of shell inside his cap, which did not even scratch his head; another piece went through my coat-sleeve.

Just after passing Fort Jackson we saw a bright glare on the starboard quarter, and a moment after Captain Craven said, in his deep bass voice, "One bell!" (to slow down), and then, "Two bells!" (to stop her). I went up the poop ladder, and there in plain sight on the left bank, just below Fort St. Philip, was the *Hartford*, with a fire-raft alongside and with flames running up the rigging on the tarred rope to the mast-head. The tug *Mosher* was near by, but I did not see the ram *Manassas*. It was evidently Craven's intention when he saw Farragut's trouble to go to his rescue. As the engine stopped, the *Brooklyn* dropped down, her head swinging to starboard, until she was on a line between Fort Jackson and the *Hartford*. The fort immediately opened fire on the *Brooklyn* with renewed energy, and she would have been blown out of the water had not the enemy aimed too high and sent the shot through the rigging, boats, and hammock-nettings, many of them just clearing the rail. The port battery was manned, and shell and shrapnel were fired as fast as the guns could be loaded. The *Brooklyn* remained under the fire of Fort Jackson until Craven saw Farragut free from the fire-raft, and then she steamed ahead. This was one of the coolest and bravest acts that I saw during the war, but it was not mentioned in any official report or newspaper account at the time. In fact, the *Brooklyn's* passage of the forts was hardly noticed by the newspaper correspondents, as Craven had old-fashioned ideas and would allow no reporters on board. I am glad, even at this late date, that I can put on record this act of heroism.

As the *Hartford* lay aground with the fire-raft alongside, her crew were at their work, and I saw the flag-officer distinctly on the port side of the poop looking toward us. From this point the *Brooklyn* steamed ahead, toward Fort St. Philip, and passed close to the fort, firing grape from the starboard battery. When she first came abreast of the fort there was a long blaze of musketry from the parapet, but it soon stopped when she got to work.* We were at this time less than one hundred feet from the bank, and the *Hartford* had passed ahead. The barbette guns of the fort not being depressed sufficiently, we received no damage while passing, but we were so close that the powder scorched the faces and clothes of the men. A bullet entered the port of No. 1 gun and struck Lieutenant James O'Kane, who had charge of the first division, in the leg. He fell to the deck, but would not allow himself to be carried below until he had himself fired two of the broadside guns into Fort St. Philip. But the most uncomfortable position on board the ship, during this part of the engagement, was that of the quartermaster, Thomas Hollins, who stood in the starboard main chains, heaving the lead and calling out the soundings. The outside of the ship near him was completely peppered with bullets, and the flames from the enemy's guns seemed almost to reach him; still he stood coolly at his post, and when abreast of the fort he was heard calling out, "Only thirteen feet, sir."

As we passed clear of Fort St. Philip, Captain Craven gave orders to load the starboard battery with solid shot. He had seen the iron-clad *Louisiana*, moored just above the fort. She gave us one or two shots, but when we came directly abeam of her, she closed her port shutters and received our broadside.

*I was afterward in charge of a boat from the *Brooklyn* which landed the paroled Confederate prisoners at New Orleans, and they said that the grape came like rain, but that the worst of all were the "infernal lamp-posts" that we fired; that the fort was full of them. These were the stands that held the grape—cylinders attached to a cast-iron base, around which the grape-shot are secured.—J. R. B.

We could hear our shot strike against her iron sides. We gave but one broadside and then sheered out into the river. A 9-inch shell, fired by the *Louisiana*, struck the *Brooklyn* about a foot above the water-line, on the starboard side of the cutwater, near the wood ends, forced its way for three feet through the dead-wood and timbers, and remained there. At New Orleans this shot was cut out, and it was found that in their hurry the gunners had neglected to remove the lead patch from the fuse, so that the shell did not explode. Had it done so it would have blown the whole bow off, and the *Brooklyn* would have gone to the bottom.

As we swung out into the current and steamed up the river, we began to see the vessels ahead fighting with the Confederate gun-boats, and a few moments later the cry came aft, "A steamer coming down on our port bow." We could see two smoke-stacks and the black smoke from them. I took a look from the poop ladder, and saw a good-sized river steamer coming down on us, crowded with men on her forward deck, as if ready to board. The order had already been given, "Stand by to repel boarders," and to load with shrapnel; the fuses were cut to burn one second. As she approached, Craven gave the vessel a sheer to starboard, and we began with No. 1 gun, the guns aft following in quick succession, the shells bursting almost immediately as they left the guns. There was a rush of steam, shrieks from the people on board the steamer, and, when it came time for my No. 10 gun to fire, the steamer was lost in the smoke. This was the only one of the river flotilla which we encountered or fired into. Just after our engagement with this steamer, a column of black smoke, which came from the dreaded *Manassas*, was seen on the starboard side, and the cry was passed along by men who were looking out of the ports, "The ram, the ram!" Craven called out, "Give her four bells! Put your helm hard-a-starboard!" Then I saw the smoke-stacks of the *Manassas* and the flash from her gun, and the next moment I was nearly thrown on the deck by the concussion, caused by her striking us just amidships. The ram was going full speed but against the current, and, with our helm to starboard, the blow was not at right angles to our keel, though nearly so. I ran to the No. 10 port, the gun being in, and looked out, and saw her almost directly alongside. A man came out of her little hatch aft, and ran forward along the port side of the deck, as far as the smoke-stacks, placed his hand against one, and looked to see what damage the ram had done. I saw him turn, fall over, and tumble into the water, but did not know at the moment what caused his sudden disappearance, until I asked the quartermaster, who was leadsman in the chains, if he had seen him fall.

"Why, yes, sir," said he, "I saw him fall overboard,—in fact, I helped him; for I hit him alongside of the head with my hand-lead."

No guns were fired at the ram from the starboard battery; all the crews a moment before had been at the port guns. As the *Manassas* drifted by I ran up on the poop, calling the gun's crew with me, to see if I could hit her with the 30-pounder Parrott, but we were unable to depress it sufficiently, at its high elevation, to bring it to bear before she was lost to sight in the smoke. The shot which she had fired came through the chain and planking, above the berth-deck, through a pile of rigging placed against the ship's side, and just entered the sand-bags placed to protect the steam-drum.

A few moments after this incident a vessel passed on our starboard side, not ten feet from us, and I could see through the port the men loading a pivot gun. She was directly abreast of No. 10 gun and I took the lock-string to fire, when a cry came from on board the vessel, "Don't fire, it is the *Iroquois!*" At the same moment, Lieutenant Lowry also shouted from near the mainmast, "Don't fire!" Seeing the black smoke pouring from her stack, and noticing that it was abaft the mainmast, I called to Captain Craven, "It can't be the *Iroquois!* It is not one of our vessels, for her smoke-stack is abaft her mainmast!" Captain Craven, however, repeated the order, "Don't fire!" and I obeyed. I was sure it was one of the Confederate gun-boats, but it was my duty to obey orders, and thus the Confederate gun-boat *McRae* escaped being sunk by the *Brooklyn*; for the gun had been depressed, and a 9-inch shell would have gone through her deck and out below the water-line.

Just after leaving Fort St. Philip a shot came in on the starboard quarter and went across the deck, taking off a marine's head and wounding three other men. Lieutenant Lowry came along about this time, and I heard him report to Captain Craven that Lieutenant O'Kane had been wounded. Craven directed him to put me in charge of the First Division, to which Lowry answered:

"I sent poor Bartlett down below half an hour ago cut in two."

"Oh, no, you did not," said Craven; "he is on deck close to you."

Lowry turned and was as much surprised as if he had seen a ghost, and told me to run forward and take charge of the First Division. There had been terrible havoc here. The powder-man of the pivot gun had been struck by a shell, which exploded and blew him literally to atoms, and parts of his body were scattered all over the forecastle. The gun was disabled, a primer having broken off in the vent; but there was nothing to fire at, as all the vessels that we passed had been run on the bank and either set on fire or deserted. It was now almost daylight, and we could see the crews of the deserted boats running for cover to the woods a little way back. Shortly after, the *Brooklyn* came up with the other vessels and anchored near a point where there had been an encampment of troops. They only remained long enough to land and bury the dead. The commanding officers assembled on board the *Hartford* to offer their congratulations to the flag-officer.

About the time that the *Brooklyn* arrived at quarantine the *Manassas* was seen steaming up the river, and Farragut made signal to the *Mississippi* to attack her. She ran down toward her, but the *Manassas* sheered toward the left bank and ran her nose ashore. When the *Mississippi* opened fire upon her, the crew poured out of the little hatch aft, ran along the deck, and jumped on shore and over the levee into the swamp beyond.

The fleet steamed up the river during the afternoon of the 24th until dark, and then came to anchor. Nothing of importance occurred during the passage. Soon after midnight a great blaze of light was seen up the river, and fearing fire-rafts, all the vessels got under way, and remained so until daylight, when they proceeded up the river toward New Orleans. At 6 o'clock we passed a large vessel loaded with cotton on fire, and at 7:30 passed two more in the same condition. Arrived at Chalmette, four miles below the city, we found that batteries had been erected on both banks, armed with field-pieces. A few broadsides made the troops leave their guns and disperse into the country. The *Brooklyn* fired 21 shells from the 80-pound Dahlgren into the battery on the left bank and a couple of broadsides into that on the right.

The fleet steamed on to the city, passing close to the levees, which were swarming with people. They were simply a howling mob. The Confederate flags were flying about the city, and we passed so close—not more than two hundred feet from the bank—that the people called out abusive names and shouted at us in derision. In the French quarter there was apparently some disturbance, and a body of troops was seen firing a volley into the crowd. As the ship arrived abreast of the Custom-house and anchored off Canal street, a pouring rain came down, but even this did not seem to reduce the crowd. Soon after we had anchored, burning steamers, barges, and other vessels loaded with cotton came drifting down on fire. Among the burning vessels was the Confederate iron-clad *Mississippi*. It seemed the purpose of the mob to destroy everything. During the night the city was set on fire in a dozen different places, and there was a continual ringing of fire-alarm bells.

The next day we steamed up the river, as obstructions and batteries had been reported above the city. All the fortifications were deserted, but an immense raft was found lying along the left bank. This was made of four logs lashed together side by side, with a heavy chain extending their whole length. It had been the intention of the Confederates to stretch this boom across the river to prevent Foote and his flotilla from reaching New Orleans. The barrier looked formidable as it lay under the river-bank, but when the Confederates had finished their work they could not get the raft across the river on account of the current. They made the lower end fast to the bank, and with three steamboats took the upper end and endeavored to reach the opposite bank, but the huge structure was more than they could manage, and the current swept it down the river with such force that it broke, drifted from the steamers, and swung around against the bank and so proved a failure.*

On the day after the passage of the forts, it was noticed that

*The river, when we arrived at New Orleans, was higher than it ever had been known to be before, and the levees had been added to, to prevent the

the *Brooklyn* leaked more than usual, but not enough to give any alarm, as the steam-pumps were able to keep her free, and in the course of a few days the leak diminished. It was not until the coal in the starboard bunker had been used up and the side of the ship was uncovered that we realized what a blow she had received from the *Manassas*. On the outside the chain had been driven its depth into the planking, and on the inside, for a length of five feet or more, the planking was splintered and crushed in. The only thing that prevented the prow of the *Manassas* from sinking us was the fact that the bunker was full of coal.

The wound gave no trouble so long as we remained in the river, as the mud held in suspension in the river water filled up all the interstices between the fibers of the wood. When we went out to sea and rolled about a little, and the ship began to work, it was found that she leaked very badly, and she was obliged to go to Pensacola, heave down, and bolt on a large patch of plank to cover the spot where the ram had struck.

---

water from overflowing. As we found it, the water was within a few inches of the top of the levee.—J. R. B.

NOTE.—Since writing the above article, I have compared it carefully with letters I wrote to my father from New Orleans. In some instances I do not agree with the official reports in the sequence of events, but I hold to my own account. Craven says he encountered the *Manassas* a few minutes after passing the obstructions. I place this event well above the forts, and this is corroborated by Captain Warley of the *Manassas*. Farragut, in his official report, does not state exactly where he encountered the fire-raft, but says: "The fire was extinguished. In the meantime our battery was never silent, but poured its missiles of death into Fort St. Philip, opposite to which we had got by this time." I place the *Hartford* at this time just below the fort, or abreast of the lower flanking battery, as the iron-clad *Louisiana* was moored to the bank immediately above. When the *Manassas* rammed the *Brooklyn* she had two smoke-stacks, but she lost one before she drifted down the river.—J. R. B.

THE FALL OF NEW ORLEANS: LOUISIANA, APRIL 1862

George Hamilton Perkins to Susan G. Perkins

Twenty-five-year-old Lieutenant George Hamilton Perkins piloted the gunboat *Cayuga* in the passage of Forts Jackson and St. Philip and afterwards accompanied Captain Theodorus Bailey, Farragut's second in command, to accept the surrender of New Orleans. Their walk to City Hall was witnessed by the writer George Washington Cable, then aged seventeen. "Two officers of the United States Navy were walking abreast, unguarded and alone, looking not to right or left, never frowning, never flinching, while the mob screamed in their ears, shook cocked pistols in their faces, cursed and crowded and gnashed upon them," Cable wrote in 1885. "It was one of the bravest deeds I ever saw done." On April 28 the bypassed Forts Jackson and St. Philip surrendered, and troops led by Major General Benjamin F. Butler occupied the city on May 1 as the Union gained control of both ends of the Mississippi River.

NEW ORLEANS, April 27, 1862.

We arrived here two days ago, after what was 'the most desperate fight and greatest naval achievement on record,' so every one says. Wednesday night, April 23, we were ordered to lead the way, and be ready to run by the forts at two o'clock in the morning; and at two o'clock precisely the signal was made from the Hartford to 'get underweigh.'

Captain Harrison paid me the compliment of letting me pilot the vessel, and though it was a starlight night we were not discovered until we were well under the forts; then they opened a tremendous fire on us. I was very anxious, for the steering of the vessel being under my charge gave me really the whole management of her. The Cayuga received the first fire, and the air was filled with shells and explosions which almost blinded me as I stood on the forecastle trying to see my way, for I had never been up the river before. I soon saw that the guns of the forts were all aimed for the mid-stream, so I steered close under the walls of Fort St. Philip, and although our masts and rigging got badly shot through, our hull was but little damaged.

After passing the last battery and thinking we were clear, I looked back for some of our vessels, and my heart jumped up into my mouth, when I found I could not see a *single one.* I thought they all must have been sunk by the forts. Then looking ahead I saw eleven of the enemy's gunboats coming down upon us, and it seemed as if we were '*gone*' sure. Three of these made a dash to board us, but a heavy charge from our eleven-inch gun settled the Gov. Moore, which was one of them. A ram, the Manasses, in attempting to butt us, just missed our stern, and we soon settled the third fellow's 'hash.' Just then some of our gunboats, which had passed the forts, came up, and then all sorts of things happened. There was the wildest excitement all round. The Varuna fired a broadside into *us*, instead of the enemy. Another of our gunboats attacked one of the Cayuga's prizes,—I shouted out, 'Don't fire into that ship, she has surrendered!' Three of the enemy's ships had surrendered to us before any of our vessels appeared, but when they did come up we all pitched in, and settled the eleven rebel vessels, in about twenty minutes. Our short fight with the Gov. Moore—it used to be the Morgan—was very exciting. We were alongside of each other, and had both fired our guns, and it all depended on which should get reloaded first. The large forward gun on the Gov. Moore was a ten-inch shell, ours an eleven-inch, and we were so near, they were almost muzzle to muzzle.

Ours was fired first, and Beverly Kennon, the Captain of the Gov. Moore, is now a prisoner on board the Cayuga. He tells me our shot was the one that ruined him,—disabled his vessel, capsized his gun, and killed thirteen of the gun's crew. Beverly Kennon used to be an officer in our navy.

The Cayuga still led the way up the river, and at daylight we discovered a regiment of infantry encamped on shore. As we were very close in, I shouted to them to come on board and deliver up their arms, or we would blow them all to pieces. It seemed rather odd for a regiment on shore to be surrendering to a ship! They hauled down their colors, and the Colonel and command came on board and gave themselves up as prisoners of war. The regiment was called the Chalmette Regiment, and has been quite a famous one. The officers we released on parole and allowed them to retain their side-arms, all except one Captain, who I discovered was from New Hampshire. His name is Hickory, and he came from Portsmouth. I took his sword away from him and have kept it.

The next thing that happened was the sinking of the Varuna, which had been disabled by one of the enemy's vessels running into her. Soon after this the Commodore came up in the Hartford and ordered us all to anchor and take a little rest before attacking New Orleans, which was now within twenty miles.

By this time our ship had received forty-two shots in masts and hull, and six of our men had been wounded; one of the boys had to have one of his legs cut off. All this time, night and day, firerafts and ships loaded with burning cotton had been coming down the river and surrounded us everywhere. Besides these, the bombardment was continuous and perfectly awful. I do not believe there ever was anything like it before, and I never expect to see such a sight again. The river and shore were one blaze, and the sounds and explosions were terrific. Nothing I could say would give you any idea of these last twenty-four hours!

The next morning, April 25, we all got underweigh again, the Cayuga still leading, and at about nine o'clock New Orleans hove in sight. We called all hands and gave three cheers and a tiger!

There were two more fortifications still between us and New Orleans, called the Chalmette Batteries, but Captain Bailey thought they could not be of much account, and that we had best push on. When we arrived in sight of these batteries, no flag floated over them, and there was not a man to be seen—nothing but the guns, which seemed abandoned. In fact, though, there were a lot of treacherous rascals concealed in these batteries, and when we had come close enough to make them feel sure they could sink us, they opened a heavy fire. We gave them back as well as we could, but they were too much for one gunboat; so, after getting hit fourteen times, and the shot and shell striking all about us, we decided not to advance any further until some of the ships came up. Soon we had the Hartford on one side and the Pensacola on the other, and then the rebel battery was silenced very quick.

After this, there were no further obstacles between us and the city, and the fleet were soon anchored before it. The Commodore ordered Captain Bailey to go on shore, and demand its surrender, and he asked me to go with him. We took just a boat and a boat's crew, with a flag of truce, and started off. When we reached the wharf there were no officials to be seen; no one received us, although the whole city was watching our movements, and the levee was crowded in spite of a heavy rainstorm. Among the crowd were many women and children, and the women were shaking rebel flags, and being rude and noisy.

They were all shouting and hooting as we stepped on shore, but at last a man, who, I think, was a German, offered to show us the way to the council-room, where we should find the mayor of the city.

As we advanced, the mob followed us in a very excited state. They gave three cheers for Jeff Davis and Beauregard, and three groans for Lincoln. Then they began to throw things at us, and shout, 'Hang them!' 'Hang them!' We both thought we were in a *bad fix*, but there was nothing for us to do, but just go on.

We reached the city hall, though, in safety, and there we found the mayor and council. They seemed in a very solemn state of mind, though I must say, from what they said, they did not impress me as having much *mind* about anything, and certainly not much sense. The mayor said *he* had nothing to do with the city, as it was under martial law, and we were obliged to wait till General Lovell could arrive.

In about half an hour this gentleman appeared. He was very pompous in his manner and silly and airy in his remarks. He had about fifteen thousand troops under his command, and said he would 'never surrender,' but would withdraw his troops from the city as soon as possible, when the city would fall into the hands of the mayor and he could do as he pleased with it.

The mob outside had by this time become perfectly infuriated. They kicked at the doors and swore they would have us out and hang us! Of course Captain Bailey and I *felt perfectly at our ease all this while!* Indeed, every person about us, who had any sense of responsibility, was frightened for our safety. As soon as the mob found out that General Lovell was not going to surrender, they swore they would have us out anyway;

but Pierre Soule and some others went out and made speeches to them, and kept them on one side of the building, while we went out the other, and were driven to the wharf in a close carriage. Finally we got on board ship all right; but of all the blackguarding I ever heard in my life that mob gave us the worst.

The mayor told the flag-officer this morning that the city was in the hands of the mob, and was at our mercy, and that he might blow it up or do with it as he chose. They still fly the state flag on the custom-house, and as we have not yet any forces with which to land and make an attack, we can do nothing at present, unless we blow up the city.

I do not know where General Butler is. So far, only fourteen of our fleet have passed the forts out of all the ships that started. None of us know what has become of them, and the forts have not yet surrendered. Until then, there can be no going up and down the river.

This morning we have been ordered to take Captain Bailey down to a bayou, where he will pass out in a boat, and taking a ship below will proceed home, as bearer of despatches.

We expect to make another attack on the forts to-morrow or next day, if General Butler arrives with the troops. The Southerners say our victory was one of the greatest ever known. They never dreamed of our being able to pass the forts; and if the attempt had been made in the daytime, our fleet must surely all have been sunk. We may be in a bad fix now, if the forts do not fall, and it is not safe for any one to leave our ships and go anywhere in a boat. The mob rule in the city, and they are perfectly reckless. We are still feeling the effects of the excitement which the attack caused. Nothing is settled, and there is danger and risk about every movement.

I have written this letter at railroad speed. I am all right so far, as regards my health. We expect another good fight to-morrow or next day, when we go back to take the forts.

I hope you are all well at home, and you must excuse this letter, for it seems as though I could not stop to form words. Should I ever see you again I can tell it all so much better. I cannot say yet how many men have been lost on our side, but I think the number is quite small.

Charles S. Wainwright: Diary, May 5, 1862

General McClellan required a month to get his siege guns posted to bombard the Yorktown lines. At the last moment, Joseph E. Johnston evacuated the position and withdrew up the Peninsula. On May 5, at Williamsburg, the Confederates fought a rear-guard action against the pursuing Union forces. Major Charles S. Wainwright, commanding the artillery in Joseph Hooker's division, records his first time under fire.

BATTLE OF WILLAMSBURG, MAY 5, 1862, MONDAY. By three o'clock we were again stirring. Leaving orders for Bramhall and Smith to push on so soon as horses and men were fed, I rode on and routed up Osborn and Webber. The men were tired and wet, for it had begun to rain at two o'clock and was now pouring; cold too, the chill striking into one's very bones. The crossroad from the church was very muddy, and when we got into the Warwick Court House road it was so terribly cut up that it was with difficulty we could get along. Starting out the men, and moving the four or five miles, which seemed twenty, I made it after seven o'clock when I got up to where General Hooker had halted the infantry. He said that he was only waiting for me to come up in order to attack, and where would I put my batteries? As of course I had to look about me a little, the General rode up the road with me; but so soon as we emerged from the woods the rebs opened on us so sharp that we got off our horses, and proceeded out on foot and alone.

The rain was coming down in torrents, making all objects at any distance very indistinct. The road by which we had come up lay through a heavy wood for half a mile or more behind us; some hundred yards inside this wood it made a thorough cut of say thirty yards in length, the bank being six to eight feet high on either side. On both sides of the road the rebs had felled a large amount of the timber as it debouches into the plain in front of Williamsburg. Directly up the road, about eight hundred yards from where we stood at the outer edge of the felled timber, was a large redoubt from which they were firing quite lively. To the right and left of this one we could see a number of other earthworks in the distance; on our left there seemed to be a field battery behind the crest of a knoll (have since found that it was in a small redoubt built in a hollow so that the top of the parapet was about on a level with the top of the crest). On our side of the plain I could see nothing but woods on either hand with a heavy slashing of felled trees in front. The road was the only way to get on to the plain, and that would be ugly enough for some five hundred yards; the rebel redoubt, Fort Magruder, having a raging fire down it. Still I thought the open plain the proper place, and told the General so; but he said he could not support the batteries out there, his pickets only being at the outer edge of the slashing. On our left the slashing extended up the road about three hundred yards farther than it did on the right, a large triangular field having been lately cleared there, and planted in corn last year. Not being able to go out on to the plain, I told the General that the only place left one was this fallow lot; but I might get a couple of guns in the road. "Get them in then as quick as you can," were his orders.

Going back to the edge of the woods, where Captain Webber had halted his battery, I directed him to put his first piece out at the farthest corner of the slashing in the road; his second also in the road but some twenty yards to the rear, a slight bend in the road here placing them thus in echelon; and the other two sections in the newly cleared field to the right of the road: leaving his caissons in the wood. He at once moved out himself with the first section, while I directed the posting of the other two. Gaps in the fence were pulled down, and after a great deal of trouble from bad drivers and balky horses I got them all in. Almost before the first piece had turned into the field, Lieutenant Eakin fell at my feet terribly wounded in the shoulder. We were both of us on foot, he standing about four feet in front of me. A shell struck the road half a dozen yards from us and burst as it fell, a piece of it entering his left shoulder just below the collar bone; he fell against me, and at once called out that he was a dead man. I got a couple of men to carry him off, but had full occupation myself driving the horses of the guns up to the pulling point. At last, I had all four guns posted; when looking around what was my horror, on seeing that nearly all the limber had cleared off under shelter of the woods, and that there was not more than one or two men near each gun. This was an awful beginning for one's first battle, and knowing what a wretched battery this was, I reproached myself with having so far yielded to Webber's claims as senior officer as to have given him the advance instead of Bramhall.

Rushing back to the road, where the men had hid themselves behind the large felled trees, I met Webber, without his hat, covered with mud and almost wild. "Major," says he, "Lieutenant Pike and two men have been hit and I cannot get the others up to their guns." Though we slammed at them with our sabres, and poked them out with the point, it was no good; drive two or three to a gun, and by the time you got some more up the first had hid again. Never in my life was I so mortified, never so excited, never so mad. It had at any rate the good effect of making me forget my own danger, and the place was an awful hot one there in the road. There was a certain amount of excuse for the men. Their captain had just joined them; their other officers knew nothing; two of them were shot down at once, as also a couple of the men, and one horse of the leading gun killed; it was a very hot place for men to have their first experience in; and they were a wretched lot of men. Some of them did stick to their guns, but not enough to work them, and the drivers had carried the limbers way to the rear. The first piece had three men keep to it, who got off two or three shots; a wheel horse of their limber being killed, the drivers could not run away with it, so they ran off without it.

General Hooker meantime, it seems, was anxiously waiting for the battery to open. Seeing how things stood, for he was not far to the rear, he sent Captain Dickenson, his adjutant-general, to me to say that he would give me a company of infantry to work the guns. Looking at it coolly now, I have no doubt it was only meant, in good part, to get me out of my trouble; but then it appeared as a slur on the artillery, almost an insult, and made me very mad. "Thank the General," said I, "but I have artillery men that can and will man those guns." Running back to my horse, I rode to Osborn's battery, just in the rear of Webber's caissons; shouted to the men that General

Hooker wanted to send infantry to fight our guns; called upon them for the honour of the First New York Artillery to save me, their own major, from such a disgrace; in short made them a speech, the first speech of my life; and closed by asking who would volunteer to serve the guns of an abandoned regular battery. The men were mounted on the chests, sergeants and officers at their posts. I have no doubt all heard me, for I was very much excited, and don't know now what I said; but almost before I had done, Sergeant Horn of the first or second piece, whom I had often had occasion to praise on drill, standing up in his stirrups, replied, "Every one of us, Sir." The men jumped from the boxes, officers dismounted, detachments were regularly formed, and marched to the abandoned pieces as if on drill. A more beautiful thing it was impossible to see, not a man flinching; the infantry on the roadside gave them three cheers, and wasn't I a proud man?—proud of the First New York Artillery.

Fire once opened, the enemy's shots were not nearly so sure and it became comparatively safe to be about there. It was just about eight o'clock when we opened fire; half an hour later Bramhall came up, and I at once moved his battery into the fallow lot, to the right of Webber's. One of his pieces had been left behind stuck in the mud, and though it came up later in the day, was not put in position. Webber's men kept coming back as they got over their fright, but there were not over five of them to a gun at any time during the day. The rain made all objects at any distance very indistinct. At no time could we see any large body of the enemy; our work was simply to silence and keep silent their artillery. They seemed to have three guns in Fort Magruder and three or more in the sunken redoubt. Occasionally a shot would come from a third work still farther to their right, but their works to our right did not trouble us at all during the day. In an hour we had silenced them totally, at least for a time, and held up our own fire. . . .

Half an hour, perhaps, after we had ceased firing, long rolls of musketry were heard at this point to the left. Every moment I expected to see our men rush into the open, but after a time we found the firing to recede into the woods, as if our men were being beaten instead of gaining ground; so I turned my four left pieces to the left, and opened on the corner of the woods. Infantry officers tell me that shell fell directly in the rebel column, and burst with great effect. It was now my turn to get it hot and heavy from all three of the rebel batteries; the redoubt away to our left opening very strong, which forced me to throw Bramhall's right far forward in echelon. How long this fight lasted I do not know, but it seemed to me all day. At last, however, we got their fire under, and shortly afterward, all being quiet, I spoke to General Hooker about dispositions for the night, thinking it must be near sundown. He thought too it was late, and we were both astonished when Captain Dickenson told us it was twenty minutes passed eleven!—the day not half through. It seemed a good week since I got up.

This time they left us quiet for an hour or more, so that one had a little time to look around. I proposed to General Hooker to get my two twelve-pounder howitzers around to where the infantry were, so as to fire down the ravine by which the enemy's columns came up, if possible, but he said there was no road by which he could get them there that he knew of. Since then I have been sorry that I did not go to look for myself, as there was a small wood road, I find, which led in that direction. General Hooker stayed all the time just where the road came out of the wood, and did not go over to the place where our infantry were engaged at all. On passing around among my guns, I found that two of Bramhall's pieces were disabled by shot wedging in the bore. One of them we replaced with his sixth piece which had been stuck on the road coming up; the other shot, I believe, they got home after a time. One of Webber's howitzers had cracked so badly as to render it unsafe, and was hauled off. This left us ten guns in position, but my men had got the range, and worked admirably. . . .

During this lull General Hooker sent word to Sumner on our right that he was holding the enemy here, and begging him to attack. Captain Benson commanding, "M" of the Second Artillery took the message, passing out on the open ground in front of the wood. He got back safely, and brought his saddle in, but left his horse dead on the plain. Many of our officers said they could hear firing to our right, quite early in the day; though I did not hear any myself. It seems it was Hancock's attack. Had old Sumner followed him up with the whole of Smith's division as he asked, and as Smith himself wanted to do, there is not a doubt in my mind that Williamsburg could have been carried, the heavy losses in our division saved, and probably very many prisoners, and a good part of their train captured. I hear that Wheeler with "E" Company of our regiment was in with Hancock, and that the latter did grandly.

About twelve-thirty o'clock the enemy made a second charge on our infantry, driving them back some distance into the wood at one time; their artillery fired but little, and I could render but little aid for fear of firing into our own men. General Hooker was a good deal worried at one time, and much excited. Taylor's brigade was sent over to reinforce the others, and drove the rebs back again. Whenever there would be a regular succession of volleys the General would rub his hands, and exclaim "That's Dwight, that's Dwight." This fight was doubtless a hard one, but when it was over everything settled down and remained so quiet that I began to hope it was over for the day.

My own men were very tired, some of them completely broken down; they were all unaccustomed to fighting and doubtless worked harder than was necessary. Finally we were getting short of men at some of the guns, so many being required on account of their sinking and the badness of the ground; and as everything was so quiet I asked the General's permission to ride back and look up Smith who had not yet made his appearance, though he had no farther to come than Bramhall and should have started at the same time. Some three hundred to four hundred yards back in the woods I passed our field hospitals where the wounded were receiving their first dressing, and then sent back in ambulances about a mile or so to where the main hospital was established in and around a fine large house occupied by the overseer of "Buck" Allen, who has large plantations around here. Our little Doctor Goddard remained all day at the front, and gave his first care to our wounded almost among the guns where they fell. The road was now awful; my horse sank to his knees at almost every step. Ammunition and hospital waggons were stuck all along. . . . When we got to within a mile of the front, I heard heavy firing for the first time since I had gone back. Pushing on as fast as I could alone, just as I reached the hospital I met the first of a string of ambulances, waggons, and other vehicles, just breaking into a run; the men too were starting, hospital attendants and such like. In fact, the commencement of a stampede. The road was so narrow at this point that but one waggon could pass at a time. One of my limbers was first; all were yelling and hollering to their horses and to those in front to get on. Drawing my sabre, I rode right at the lead driver of the limber, and brought that up short, so stopping the whole concern. The firing at the front was diminishing, and the stampede died out in a few minutes. Just then Chauncey McKeever came galloping back, waving his sword and swearing like a demon, "Shoot the cowards!" In a few minutes a couple of squadrons of cavalry, who had been sent around by a road to our left came back. McKeever insisted they should fire on the waggoners, though I told him that the fright was all over. The man seemed crazy, so fearing the officer in command of the cavalry might be as great a fool as himself and fire, I pushed on to the front out of the way.

There I found a sad change for the worse had taken place during my absence. The enemy, reinforced it is said by Longstreet's whole division, which had come back from six miles beyond Williamsburg, had attacked at the old point, and driven our men entirely back to the road. Colonel Starr had withdrawn his regiment from the slashing on the left of my guns, and gone to help our infantry. The enemy pushed on over the felled timber to our left, and through the woods behind it, until they had possession of the road in rear of the batteries. All was up then at once with the guns, there being no exit, at least that we knew of, for horses; and had there been they could not possibly have hauled the pieces out of the soft ground of the field. Bramhall turned his guns at once towards them and fired canister until they were directly on him, when he withdrew his men over the slashing in his rear into the wood, and so across to the other road where General Sumner was, and reported to him, getting most undeservedly cursed for his pains. Our infantry had fought nobly, Dwight's regiment especially. It lay in the slashing, and held their ground until all their ammunition was gone, Dwight and Farnum both wounded, and the rebs all but surrounding them.

By the time I got up the fighting was over. We had lost possession of all the slashing on the left of the road, but held the woods for some distance in that direction. General Heintzelman was there in consultation with Hooker. Osborn had got a dozen or so of his men together, and manned one piece which he had planted in the road just in front of the little thorough cut. So soon as Smith came up, to hurry whom I sent Lieutenant Ames back, I put two of his Parrotts and his section of six-pounders in position on . . . a little knoll, and comparatively open; they had perfect command of the road but nothing more. We did not have to wait many minutes. It was perhaps half an hour after the other guns were captured when the rebs charged in column down the road; my five pieces were all loaded with canister, but I held fire until the head of the column was well down to within about 150 yards of us, and two whole regiments were plainly in view. Three rounds to a gun then blew the whole thing away, except small parties which got into the slashing on the left of the road, and picked off my cannoneers so badly that after trying two or three rounds of canister on them I was obliged to let the men cover themselves behind the trees. Finding no infantry at all near my guns to reply to these fellows, I went back to General Hooker, and asked him to send some, which he promised to do. After waiting ten minutes or so, and finding that the rascals were working up nearer and nearer to me all the time, I again went back and found General Grover, to whom I made the same request, and from whom I received the same promise. Still no supports came. Four of Smith's men had been hit, and I began to be anxious lest another attack should be made, as I could find no infantry within 100 yards to my rear. Going a third time, I found the head of Kearny's column just come up. To Kearny I put my request. This time, instantly he turned to the First Company of a Michigan regiment: "Captain, you will take your company, and put them wherever Major Wainwright here says"—which was done as promptly as it was ordered, and I saw no more of my friends in the slashing. . . .

Shortly before sunset the whole of our division was withdrawn, Kearny's taking our place, and Thompson's battery of the Second Artillery relieving Smith's on the knoll, which with Osborn's I moved back to an open field about three-fourths of a mile to the rear where we bivouacked for the night.

Thus ended my first fight. In looking back to it, I cannot

but first of all be grateful to Providence that I escaped unhurt. For a good part of ten hours I was exposed to more or less artillery and musketry fire; when we ran the gauntlet with Kearny, and when the canister was fired over our heads, it was almost a miracle that I was not hit. Besides this, I was kicked over by one of "H" Company's horses while trying to force them into the field, his hoof striking me just below the stomach, and throwing me halfway across the road; an inch higher or lower would have ruined me for life if it did not prove fatal. Quite early in the day a minie ball carried off my left stirrup, slitting the wooden side of its whole breadth, but not even cutting the shoe. My good bay was equally fortunate, escaping unhurt, a mere shaving of one hoof only being cut off.

Of my officers, Bramhall and his lieutenants were all that I could have asked of them, cool, quiet, attending closely to their business and taking good care of their men. When they were not actually firing, the large stumps left in the field afforded excellent cover; and to the fact that their officers required them to use this cover, it must be attributed, together with the softness of the ground, which swallowed up the enemy's shot as it were, and the fact that the large part of their fuses were not cut at all, that there was not a single man hit in this battery. Osborn was slow (as I expected), but did capital service. He astonished me, when in the evening I told him to move to the rear, by replying in his drawling way, "Major, I shan't go until I get that gun out." The gun he spoke of was one that lay buried in the mud on the side of the road, just in front of the knoll in a small hollow where at the time the rebel shot and shell were falling so fast, that I told him he might leave it till morning, as there was no fear of Kearny being driven back. He did get the gun, though with the loss of a man; and I learned that there was a good deal more grit in him than I thought. . . .

I saw but two or three cases among the men of the volunteer batteries of any inclination to shirk, while the very admirable behaviour of Sergeant Horn, and of Sergeant Doran with his Irishmen, almost wiped out the disgrace the men of "H" Company brought on themselves at the beginning of the fight. One of these men I found afterward with a musket he had picked up hunting around for cartridges and fighting it out on his own account.

The total loss in our division was 1,576 out of not more than 8,000 actually engaged. I have heard of but one field officer killed, Major L. M. Morris, of the Eighth New Jersey. Seven out of nine captains in this regiment, I hear, were killed or wounded. My own loss was four killed, and twenty wounded, one mortally. It is wonderful that it should have been so small. One man also is missing, but may turn up. At night I was much worried as I did not know what had become of Bramhall's men or Webber's either.

Wet to the skin and very tired, I lay down at night with the officers of Osborn's battery under a paulin, but could not sleep much for the cold, and for thinking. I had often asked myself how I should feel in my first fight, and expected to be a good deal frightened, though I knew pride would keep one up to the mark. The sight of blood often making me feel faint, I was more afraid of the effect the sight of dead and wounded would have on me than of anything else. Whatever may have been the cause, whether it was having so much to do, or whether it was excitement, or both together. I know not, but I cannot recall having felt the least personal fear while under fire. After I got back to the rear after Smith, there was some reluctance to go to the front again, a sort of nervous lassitude, but the instant I heard the heavy firing this was over. The excitement too was different from what I expected; I certainly never was more conscious nor did my mind ever see things more coolly or reason clearer. As to seeing men shot, dead or dying, I had no feeling but one of perfect indifference. When Lieutenant Eakin fell against me, and cried out that he was "a dead man," I had no more feeling for him, than if he had tripped over a stump and fallen; nor do I think it would have been different had he been my brother.

As to my official acts, I see but two that I wish had been different. First, that I did not go over myself on to the ground where our infantry were, and see whether it were not possible to get my howitzers around there; and second, that I should have gone to the rear for Smith's battery. To be sure, it is very doubtful whether he would have got up at all had I not gone; neither can I see that anything more could have been done or saved had I remained; but the guns were lost during my absence, and I confess it, I am a little ashamed to have been to the rear at that time.

General Hooker was in the road just to the rear of my batteries, and under fire all day, as brave as brave could be beyond a doubt. But he seemed to know little of the ground where his infantry were fighting; and I must say did not impress me at all favourably as to his powers as a general. His great idea was to go ahead quick until you ran against the enemy, and then fight him; the spirit of Heintzelman's order of the night before, "not to let Sumner get into Williamsburg first," seemed to be his main rule of action. Kearny on the other hand was calm and deliberate, and would not put a man into position until he had examined his ground, and knew what he had to do. Old Heintzelman did not get there until about one P.M. or later; he may have done a great deal without my knowing it. . . .

Soon after the enemy's second attack, which took all our troops to drive back, say by 12:30 o'clock, General Hooker sent to Heintzelman and Sumner for reinforcements. None came until Kearny arrived, he says at two o'clock; I feel very sure it was nearly if not quite four o'clock. He came up all the way from Yorktown. General Sumner had the whole of Keyes's corps, three divisions, only a mile or two to our right. . . . As early as ten o'clock in the morning Hancock with his brigade attacked the extreme left of the enemy, drove them back, and shortly afterward got possession of one of their works, when he sent back word to General Smith, his division commander, that if he would give him another brigade he could push around to the rear of Williamsburg. Smith at once ordered up the whole division, but was stopped by Sumner who would not let Hancock go any farther; and lay there all day with his 30,000 doing nothing. It is very hard to understand such things. I know there is an awful amount of jealousy among our leading generals, but hardly think it can go so far; at the same time, it is equally hard to suppose they are actual fools.

John B. Jones: Diary, May 14–19, 1862

Johnston resumed his retreat after Williamsburg, with McClellan following slowly up the Peninsula until his army was within sight of Richmond. Norfolk was abandoned and the C.S.S. *Virginia* blown up to prevent her capture, opening the James to the Union navy. Confederate War Department clerk Jones speculated on the fate of the capital.

MAY 14TH—Our army has fallen back to within four miles of Richmond. Much anxiety is felt for the fate of the city. Is there no turning point in this long lane of downward progress? Truly it may be said, our affairs at this moment are in a critical condition. I trust in God, and the chivalry and patriotism of the South *in the field.*

The enemy's fleet of gun-boats are ascending James River, and the obstructions are not completed. We have but one or two casemated guns in battery, but we have brave men there.

MAY 15TH.—The enemy's gun-boats, Monitor, Galena, etc. are at Drewry's Bluff, eight miles below the city, shelling our batteries, and our batteries are bravely shelling them. The President rode down to the vicinity this morning, and observed the firing.

The guns are heard distinctly in the city, and yet there is no consternation manifested by the people. If the enemy pass the obstructions, the city will be, it is true, very much at their mercy. They may shell us out of it, and this may occur any hour. South of the city the enemy have no forces, and we can find refuge there. I suppose the government would go to Lynchburg. I shall remain with the army, *and see that the tobacco be burnt, at all hazards, according to law.* I have seen some of our generals, and am convinced that the Baltimore rabble, and those that direct them, will be suppressed, or exterminated, if they attempt to throw impediments in the way of our soldiers in the work of destroying the tobacco, as enjoined by Congress.

Our marksmen will keep up an incessant fire into the portholes of the gun-boats; and if it be at all practicable, we will board them. So hope is by no means extinct. But it is apprehended, if the enemy gets within shelling distance of the city, there will be an attack along our lines by McClellan. We must beat him there, as we could never save our guns, stores, etc. retreating across the river. And we *will* beat him, for we have 80,000 men, and more are coming.

Joyful tidings! the gun-boats have been repulsed! A heavy shot from one of our batteries ranged through the Galena from stem to stern, making frightful slaughter, and disabling the ship; and the whole fleet turned about and steamed down the river! We have not lost a dozen men. We breathe freely; and the government will lose no time in completing the obstructions and strengthening the batteries.

MAY 16TH.—McClellan is intrenching—that is, at least, significant of a respite, and of apprehension of attack.

MAY 17TH.—Gen. Lee has admonished Major Griswold on the too free granting of passports. Will it do any good?

MAY 18TH.—All quiet to-day except the huzzas as fresh troops arrive.

MAY 19TH.—We await the issue before Richmond. It is still believed by many that it is the intention of the government and the generals to evacuate the city. If the enemy were to appear in force on the south side, and another force were to march on us from Fredricksburg, we should be inevitably taken, in the event of the loss of a battle—an event I don't anticipate. Army, government, and all, might, it is true, be involved in a common ruin. Wrote as strong a letter as I could to the President, stating what I have every reason to believe would be the consequences of the abandonment of Richmond. There would be demoralization and even insubordination in the army. Better die here! With the exception of the business portion of the city, the enemy could not destroy a great many houses by bombardment. But if defeated and driven back, our troops would make a heroic defense in the streets, in the walled grave-yards, and from the windows. Better electrify the world by such scenes of heroism, than surrender the capital and endanger the cause. I besought him by every consideration, not to abandon Richmond to the enemy short of the last extremity.

The legislature has also passed resolutions calling upon the C. S. Government to defend Richmond at all hazards, relieving the Confederate authorities, in advance, of all responsibility for any damage sustained.

This will have its effect. It would be pusillanimous to retire now.

But every preparation had been made to abandon it. The archives had been sent to Columbia, S. C., and to Lynchburg. The tracks over the bridges had been covered with plank, to facilitate the passage of artillery. Mr. Randolph had told his page, and cousin, "you must go with my wife into the country, for to-morrow the enemy will be here." Trunks were packed in readiness—for what? Not one would have been taken on the cars! The Secretary of the Treasury had a special locomotive and cars, constantly with steam up, in readiness to fly with the treasure.

Nevertheless, many of the *old* secessionists have resolved not to leave their homes, for there were no other homes for them to fly to. They say they will never take the oath of allegiance to the despised government of the North, but suffer whatever penalties may be imposed on them. There is a sullen, but generally a calm expression of inflexible determination on the countenances of the people, men, women, and children. But there is no consternation; we have learned to contemplate death with composure. It would be at least an effectual escape from dishonor; and Northern domination is dishonor.

"A BLACK REGIMENT": CANADA, MAY 1862

Garland H. White to Edwin M. Stanton

A minister and personal servant of Senator Robert Toombs of Georgia, Garland H. White escaped from slavery before the Civil War and fled to Canada. Although White received no answer to this letter to the secretary of war, he would later canvass "the intire north & west urging my people to inlist" and in 1864 became the chaplain of the 28th U.S. Colored Infantry, a regiment White helped recruit in Indiana.

London Canada West May 7th 1862

dear sir. please indulg me the liberty of writing you afew lines upon a subject of grave importance to your & my country It is true I am now stoping in canada for awhile but it is not my home—& before I proceen further I must inform you of your humble correspondent. My name is G. H. White formerly the Servant of Robert Toombs of Georgia. Mr Wm H Seward knows something about me I am now a minister, & am called upon By my peopel to tender to your *Hon* thir willingness to serve as soldiers in the southern parts during the summer season or longer if required. our offer is not for speculation or self interest but for our love for the north & the government at large, & at the same time we pray god that the triumph of the north & restoration of peace if I may call it will prove an eternal overthrow of the institution of slavery which is the cause of all our trouble if you desire to see me let me hear at an early day. I am certain of raising a good no. in the west & in the north. I am aquainted all thro the south for I traveled with Senator Toombs all over it nearly. I am quite willing to spend my life in preaching against sin & fighting against the same. Mr Seward & many other of both white & colored know me in Washington please let me hear from your Hon soon your most humble servant

Garland H. White

please excuse my bad writing as I never went to School a day in my left. I learnd what little I know by the hardest. yet I feel that the simplist instroment used in the right direction sometimes accomplishs much good. I pray you in gods name to consider the condition of your humble speaker in the distant. A man who are free from all the calumities of your land. yet when he thinks of his sufferring countrymen he can but feel that good might make him instromental in your hands to the accomplishments of some humble good. as simple as this request may seeme to you yet it might prove one of the greatest acts of your life. an act which might redown to your honor to the remotest generation— I want to see my friends at port royal & other places in the South. I now close by saying I hope to hear from you as soon as possible. I shall not be happy till I hear from you on this very important subject & not then if I am denied— So now my chance to do good as I think rest altogether with you. now may the good lord help you to make a faverorabl desition heaven bless you & your dear family is the prayer & your most obedient sirvant G. H. White minister of the gospel London Canada West

A Black regiment headed by the Revd Garland. H. White offers their services in protection of the southern forts during the sickly season

Abraham Lincoln: Proclamation Revoking General Hunter's Emancipation Order

In March 1862 David Hunter, a general known for his antislavery views, became the commander of the Union-held enclaves along the South Carolina and Georgia coasts. Hunter issued his emancipation order on May 9 without informing the administration, which learned about it from newspaper reports. When Secretary of the Treasury Chase urged Lincoln not to revoke the order, the President replied: "No commanding general shall do such a thing, on *my* responsibility, without consulting me." Lincoln used his proclamation revoking the order to renew his call for gradual compensated emancipation, while asserting that as commander-in-chief he had the power to free slaves if it became "a necessity indispensable to the maintenance of the government."

May 19, 1862

By the President of The United States of America.
A Proclamation.

Whereas there appears in the public prints, what purports to be a proclamation, of Major General Hunter, in the words and figures following, towit:

Headquarters Department of the South,
Hilton Head, S.C., May 9, 1862.

General Orders No. 11.—The three States of Georgia, Florida and South Carolina, comprising the military department of the south, having deliberately declared themselves no longer under the protection of the United States of America, and having taken up arms against the said United States, it becomes a military necessity to declare them under martial law. This was accordingly done on the 25th day of April, 1862. Slavery and martial law in a free country are altogether incompatible; the persons in these three States—Georgia, Florida and South Carolina—heretofore held as slaves, are therefore declared forever free.

DAVID HUNTER,
(Official) Major General Commanding.
ED. W. SMITH, Acting Assistant Adjutant General.

And whereas the same is producing some excitement, and misunderstanding: therefore

I, Abraham Lincoln, president of the United States, proclaim and declare, that the government of the United States, had no knowledge, information, or belief, of an intention on the part of General Hunter to issue such a proclamation; nor has it yet, any authentic information that the document is genuine. And further, that neither General Hunter, nor any other commander, or person, has been authorized by the Government of the United States, to make proclamations declaring the slaves of any State free; and that the supposed proclamation, now in question, whether genuine or false, is altogether void, so far as respects such declaration.

I further make known that whether it be competent for me, as Commander-in-Chief of the Army and Navy, to declare the Slaves of any state or states, free, and whether at any time, in any case, it shall have become a necessity indispensable to the maintainance of the government, to exercise such supposed power, are questions which, under my responsibility, I reserve to myself, and which I can not feel justified in leaving to the decision of commanders in the field. These are totally different questions from those of police regulations in armies and camps.

On the sixth day of March last, by a special message, I recommended to Congress the adoption of a joint resolution to be substantially as follows:

> *Resolved*, That the United States ought to co-operate with any State which may adopt a gradual abolishment of slavery, giving to such State pecuniary aid, to be used by such State in its discretion to compensate for the inconveniences, public and private, produced by such change of system.

The resolution, in the language above quoted, was adopted by large majorities in both branches of Congress, and now stands an authentic, definite, and solemn proposal of the nation to the States and people most immediately interested in the subject matter. To the people of those states I now earnestly appeal. I do not argue. I beseech you to make the arguments for yourselves. You can not if you would, be blind to the signs of the times. I beg of you a calm and enlarged consideration of them, ranging, if it may be, far above personal and partizan politics. This proposal makes common cause for a common object, casting no reproaches upon any. It acts not the pharisee. The change it contemplates would come gently as the dews of heaven, not rending or wrecking anything. Will you not embrace it? So much good has not been done, by one effort, in all past time, as, in the providence of God, it is now your high previlege to do. May the vast future not have to lament that you have neglected it.

In witness whereof, I have hereunto set my hand, and caused the seal of the United States to be affixed.

Done at the City of Washington this nineteenth day of May, in the year of our Lord one thousand eight hundred and sixty-two, and of the Independence of the United States the eighty-sixth. ABRAHAM LINCOLN.

By the President:

WILLIAM H. SEWARD, Secretary of State.

MEETING STONEWALL JACKSON: VIRGINIA, MAY 1862

Richard Taylor: from Destruction and Reconstruction

Thomas J. Jackson—forever "Stonewall" after his stand at Bull Run in July 1861— initiated a bold campaign in the Shenandoah Valley in the spring of 1862 to distract the Union command and prevent reinforcements from reaching McClellan on the Peninsula. In an 1879 memoir, General Richard Taylor, son of former President Zachary Taylor, recounts joining Jackson with his Louisiana brigade and the action at Front Royal, on May 23, that started the Union flight from the Valley. Taylor affirms that the much-heralded spy Belle Boyd told Stonewall nothing he did not already know.

AT NIGHTFALL of the second day in this camp, an order came from General Jackson to join him at Newmarket, twenty odd miles north; and it was stated that my division commander, Ewell, had been apprised of the order. Our position was near a pike leading south of west to Harrisonburg, whence, to gain Newmarket, the great Valley pike ran due north. All roads near our camp had been examined and sketched, and among them was a road running northwest over the southern foot-hills of Massanutten, and joining the Valley pike some distance to the north of Harrisonburg. It was called the Keazletown road, from a little German village on the flank of Massanutten; and as it was the hypothenuse of the triangle, and reported good except at two points, I decided to take it. That night a pioneer party was sent forward to light fires and repair the road for artillery and trains. Early dawn saw us in motion, with lovely weather, a fairish road, and men in high health and spirits.

Later in the day a mounted officer was dispatched to report our approach and select a camp, which proved to be beyond Jackson's forces, then lying in the fields on both sides of the pike. Over three thousand strong, neat in fresh clothing of gray with white gaiters, bands playing at the head of their regiments, not a straggler, but every man in his place, stepping jauntily as on parade, though it had marched twenty miles and more, in open column with arms at "right shoulder shift," and rays of the declining sun flaming on polished bayonets, the brigade moved down the broad, smooth pike, and wheeled on to its camping ground. Jackson's men, by thousands, had gathered on either side of the road to see us pass. Indeed, it was a martial sight, and no man with a spark of sacred fire in his heart but would have striven hard to prove worthy of such a command.

After attending to necessary camp details, I sought Jackson, whom I had never met. And here it may be remarked that he then by no means held the place in public estimation which he subsequently attained. His Manassas reputation was much impaired by operations in the Valley, to which he had been sent after that action. The winter march on Romney had resulted in little except to freeze and discontent his troops; which discontent was shared and expressed by the authorities at Richmond, and Jackson resigned. The influence of Colonel Alek Boteler, seconded by that of the Governor of Virginia, induced him to withdraw the resignation. At Kernstown, three miles south of Winchester, he was roughly handled by the Federal General Shields, and only saved from serious disaster by the failure of that officer to push his advantage, though Shields was usually energetic.

The mounted officer who had been sent on in advance pointed out a figure perched on the topmost rail of a fence overlooking the road and field, and said it was Jackson. Approaching, I saluted and declared my name and rank, then waited for a response. Before this came I had time to see a pair of cavalry boots covering feet of gigantic size, a mangy cap with visor drawn low, a heavy, dark beard, and weary eyes—eyes I afterward saw filled with intense but never brilliant light. A low, gentle voice inquired the road and distance marched that day. "Keazletown road, six and twenty miles." "You seem to have no stragglers." "Never allow straggling." "You must teach my people; they straggle badly." A bow in reply. Just then my creoles started their band and a waltz. After a contemplative suck at a lemon, "Thoughtless fellows for serious work" came forth. I expressed a hope that the work would not be less well done because of the gayety. A return to the lemon gave me the opportunity to retire. Where Jackson got his lemons "no fellow could find out," but he was rarely without one. To have lived twelve miles from that fruit would have disturbed him as much as it did the witty Dean.

Quite late that night General Jackson came to my camp fire, where he stayed some hours. He said we would move at dawn, asked a few questions about the marching of my men, which seemed to have impressed him, and then remained silent. If silence be golden, he was a "bonanza." He sucked lemons, ate hard-tack, and drank water, and praying and fighting appeared to be his idea of the "whole duty of man."

In the gray of the morning, as I was forming my column on the pike, Jackson appeared and gave the route—north—which, from the situation of its camp, put my brigade in advance of the army. After moving a short distance in this direction, the head of the column was turned to the east and took the road over Massanutten gap to Luray. Scarce a word was spoken on the march, as Jackson rode with me. From time to time a courier would gallop up, report, and return toward Luray. An ungraceful horseman, mounted on a sorry chestnut with a shambling gait, his huge feet with outturned toes thrust into his stirrups, and such parts of his countenance as the low visor of his shocking cap failed to conceal wearing a wooden look, our new commander was not prepossessing. That night we crossed the east branch of the Shenandoah by a bridge, and camped on the stream, near Luray. Here, after three long marches, we were but a short distance below Conrad's store, a point we had let several days before. I began to think that Jackson was an unconscious poet, and, as an ardent lover of nature, desired to give strangers an opportunity to admire the beauties of his Valley. It seemed hard lines to be wandering like sentimental travelers about the country, instead of gaining "kudos" on the Peninsula.

Off the next morning, my command still in advance, and Jackson riding with me. The road led north between the east bank of the river and the western base of the Blue Ridge. Rain had fallen and softened it, so as to delay the wagon trains in rear. Past midday we reached a wood extending from the mountain to the river, when a mounted officer from the rear called Jackson's attention, who rode back with him. A moment later, there rushed out of the wood to meet us a young, rather well-looking woman, afterward widely known as Belle Boyd. Breathless with speed and agitation, some time elapsed before she found her voice. Then, with much volubility, she said we were near Front Royal, beyond the wood; that the town was filled with Federals, whose camp was on the west side of the river, where they had guns in position to cover the wagon bridge, but none bearing on the railway bridge below the former; that they believed Jackson to be west of Massanutten, near Harrisonburg; that General Banks, the Federal commander, was at Winchester, twenty miles northwest of Front Royal, where he was slowly concentrating his widely scattered forces to meet Jackson's advance, which was expected some days later. All this she told with the precision of a staff officer making a report, and it was true to the letter. Jackson was possessed of these facts before he left Newmarket, and based his movements upon them; but, as he never told anything, it was news to me, and gave me an idea of the strategic value of Massanutten—pointed out, indeed, by Washington before the Revolution. There also dawned on me quite another view of our leader than the one from which I had been regarding him for two days past.

Convinced of the correctness of the woman's statements, I hurried forward at "a double," hoping to surprise the enemy's idlers in the town, or swarm over the wagon bridge with them and secure it. Doubtless this was rash, but I felt immensely "cocky" about my brigade, and believed that it would prove equal to any demand. Before we had cleared the wood Jackson came galloping from the rear, followed by a company of horse. He ordered me to deploy my leading regiment as skirmishers on both sides of the road and continue the advance, then passed on. We speedily came in sight of Front Royal, but the enemy had taken the alarm, and his men were scurrying over the bridge to their camp, where troops could be seen forming. The situation of the village is surpassingly beautiful. It lies near the east bank of the Shenandoah, which just below unites all its waters, and looks directly on the northern peaks of Massanutten. The Blue Ridge, with Manassas Gap, through which passes the railway, overhangs it on the east; distant Alleghany bounds the horizon to the west; and down the Shenandoah, the eye ranges over a fertile, well-farmed country. Two bridges spanned the river—a wagon bridge above, a railway bridge some yards lower. A good pike led to Winchester, twenty miles, and another followed the river north, whence many cross-roads united with the Valley pike near Winchester. The river, swollen by rain, was deep and turbulent, with a strong current. The Federals were posted on the west bank, here somewhat higher than the opposite, and a short distance above the junction of waters, with batteries bearing more especially on the upper bridge.

Under instructions, my brigade was drawn up in line, a little retired from the river, but overlooking it—the Federals and their guns in full view. So far, not a shot had been fired. I rode down to the river's brink to get a better look at the enemy through a field-glass, when my horse, heated by the march, stepped into the water to drink. Instantly a brisk fire was opened on me, bullets striking all around and raising a little shower-bath. Like many a foolish fellow, I found it easier to get into than out of a difficulty. I had not yet led my command into action, and, remembering that one must "strut" one's little part to the best advantage, sat my horse with all the composure I could muster. A provident camel, on the eve of a desert journey, would not have laid in a greater supply of water than did my thoughtless beast. At last he raised his head, looked placidly around, turned, and walked up the bank.

This little incident was not without value, for my men welcomed me with a cheer; upon which, as if in response, the enemy's guns opened, and, having the range, inflicted some loss on my line. We had no guns up to reply, and, in advance as has been mentioned, had outmarched the troops behind us. Motionless as a statue, Jackson sat his horse some few yards away, and seemed lost in thought. Perhaps the circumstances mentioned some pages back had obscured his star; but if so, a few short hours swept away the cloud, and it blazed, Sirius-like, over the land. I approached him with the suggestion that the railway bridge might be passed by stepping on the cross-ties, as the enemy's guns bore less directly on it than on the upper bridge. He nodded approval. The 8th regiment was on the right of my line, near at hand; and dismounting, Colonel Kelly led it across under a sharp musketry fire. Several men fell to disappear in the dark water beneath; but the movement continued with great rapidity, considering the difficulty of walking on ties, and Kelly with his leading files gained the opposite shore. Thereupon the enemy fired combustibles previously placed near the center of the wagon bridge. The loss of this structure would have seriously delayed us, as the railway bridge was not floored, and I looked at Jackson, who, near by, was watching Kelly's progress. Again he nodded, and my command rushed at the bridge. Concealed by the cloud of smoke, the suddenness of the movement saved us from much loss; but it was rather a near thing. My horse and clothing were scorched, and many men burned their hands severely while throwing brands into the river. We were soon over, and the enemy in full flight to Winchester, with loss of camp, guns, and prisoners. Just as I emerged from flames and smoke, Jackson was by my side. How he got there was a mystery, as the bridge was thronged with my men going at full speed; but smoke and fire had decidedly freshened up his costume.

"THE PROGRESS OF EVENTS": WASHINGTON, D.C., MAY 1862

Elizabeth Blair Lee to Samuel Phillips Lee

Elizabeth Blair Lee filled letters to her naval officer husband, serving under Farragut on the Mississippi, with military and domestic news gleaned in part from her well-connected family: father Francis Preston Blair, a longtime Washington political figure and counselor to President Lincoln; brother Montgomery, Lincoln's postmaster general; and brother Frank, Missouri congressman and chairman of the House Committee on Military Affairs. Among her topics were the widespread effects of Jackson's Valley campaign, and the Union navy's attack on Fort Darling, or Drewry's Bluff, on the James River.

Silver Spring May 26, 1862

Dear Phil I tried to see Capt Fox yesterday to ascertain how get this to Capt Davis but as I failed to see him Minna brought me word today to send it Cairo— so here goes a few lines to meet & welcome you to Memphis whither yr last letter say will be yr destination & many is the anxious hour has it cost me for I had hoped the Iron Navy would *do up* all that part of the work—

We are all very well I am entirely over my attack (Mother says on New Orleans) & have got hearty & sunburnt in my garden over my rejoicings & thanksgivings at your wonderful deliverance from "all of yr enemies— I will never cease to be thankful for so great a mercy miraculous it appears to me the more I think of what you encountered I lived in terror for weeks about the Forts— but it never occurred to me that they had any naval force of import above them— & I thought the Mortars would demolish them— but alas they were comparatively useless Maigre Fox & Comre Porter I was proud of your good temper & patriotic desire to have all things done well & peaceably in the Squadron but it cost me some jealous pangs Ill confess—

I wish I could send you some glad tidings & just at this moment— but by a Cabal (a most pertinacious one) against

McClellan Banks was deprived of all his troops but 6,000 & they were sent to McDowell to get him into Richmond via Fredricksburg before McClellan but as Genl fatty did not manage it & McClellan is now in sight of the Steeples of Richmond McDowell is ordered to rescue Banks after he is disgraced by a most disgraceful rout Frémont to was whipped at Franklin by Jackson & then Banks which fact is suppressed by Stanton who is utterly abolitionized & was no doubt the promptor of Hunter's proclamation so say Army people in the City— & Now he is telegraphing all creation & evidently trying to affright the world by his own scare which is described as dreadful— He wanted sink stone ships & block up the Potomac from the Merrimac— but Old Welles put his foot & commission on the proceeding & stopped & the other day when Rogers was repulsed at Fort Darling they say Stanton was all affright but Old Grey beard assured them he was not discouraged & would not be if he lost all of our ships in the James River— I must say I like this calmness— it contrasts handsomely with this fuzzy tricky lawyer's jerks— Who is pretty much divided between his intrigues & jobbing & devotions to the White house where he is ever so prostrate that one can scarce approach old Abe" with giving him a shove to get at him— He and Chase now hunt in couples & both have mounted the Extreme Abolition lacky

I am sorry our friend P King too in his tremors about reelection has joined Wendall Phillips— but our friend Doolittle is still a Republican & so is 9 tenths of the party still loyal to that platform & the Constitution of their Country & to white men rather than the black one— Our fat friend has not been to see us this spring nor to see Frank— but we have been steady in our attentions & will continue them— in spite of his Frémont proclivities for which I say we all ought to be the last to make points upon as to the feelings of other people—

Frank & his family are now staying here with us— & Blair revels in so many juvenile companions & it is refreshing to see them playing with new mown hay on the lawn which never looked as beautiful before & I must add I think the children too were a fine looking set— so sturdy & rosy & joyous the Donkey Cart hauls off the hay & they rake & put it in & it is a lovely hay making to my partial eyes I went to Johns yesterday after church— I did not see who was too vain to let me see his swollen face which gives the poor fellow some pain he took cold when down in the Country a few days since Nelly was jubilant over Banks & Frémonts defeat tho she is very prudent in her talk to everybody but John & me— I have prayed her not to talk to her boys & she has quit it—

I had a long letter from Fanny She is in better health & spirits I sent you a long letter from her to Ship Island— They are all prospering again with the return of trade from Nashville where they are sending bread & meat for cotton & tobacco— in large quantities but secesh does all it can to conceal this revival of trade— they want the money but refuse to see the sources of their prosperity— May God enlighten them is my constant prayer when I think of southern people & the delirious frenzy now upon so many of them—

All of our kindred and friends are well & the papers will post you better than I can as to the progress of events Our whole well doing now seems to hang on the results at Corinth & Richmond— Some think here that the Battle of New Orleans has stopped the Intervention project England hates our progress especially that of the Navy & will hurt whenever she can without ruin to herself & Louis Napoleon only holds off because he hopes the growing enmity between us & England will move to his benefit or that of his Dynasty The people over the waters suffer more from this war than our northern people do who bear its whole expense in every sense & this *strength* is alarming— to all the crowned Heads Goodbye Ill write another Extra soon I send my regular bulletins to Ship Island still Blair sleeps or would join me in love & kisses Yr devoted Lizzie

"NO SIMILAR INSTANCE OF INFAMY":
LOUISIANA, MAY 1862

Thomas O. Moore: To the People of Louisiana

When the Union soldiers occupying New Orleans were treated with blatant contempt by many of the female inhabitants—from her French Quarter balcony one woman emptied her chamber pot on the head of Flag Officer Farragut—their commander, Major General Benjamin F. Butler, issued General Order No. 28. Butler's "Women's Order" threatened to treat such contempt as the action of "a woman of the town plying her avocation" and subject to arrest (Butler later wrote that his "order executed itself" and no arrests were made). Louisiana's outraged governor, Thomas O. Moore, issued this proclamation in response.

PROCLAMATION.

EXECUTIVE OFFICE,
Opelousas, La., May 24, 1862.

To the People of Louisiana:

The general commanding the troops of the United States now holding possession of New Orleans issued the following order on the 15th instant:

> As the officers and soldiers of the United States have been subject to repeated insults from the women (calling themselves ladies) of New Orleans, in return for the most scrupulous non-interference and courtesy on our part, it is ordered that hereafter, when any female shall, by word, gesture, or movement, insult or show contempt for any officer or soldier of the United States, she shall be regarded and held liable to be treated as a woman of the town plying her avocation.
> By command of Major-General Butler.

The annals of warfare between civilized nations afford no similar instance of infamy to this order. It is thus proclaimed to the world that the exhibition of any disgust or repulsiveness by the women of New Orleans to the hated invaders of their home and the slayers of their fathers, brothers, and husbands shall constitute a justification to a brutal soldiery for the indulgence of their lust. The commanding general, from his headquarters, announces to his insolent followers that they are at liberty to treat as women of the town the wives, the mothers, the daughters of our citizens, if by word, gesture, or movement any contempt is indicated for their persons or insult offered to their presence. Of the nature of the movement and the meaning of the look these vagabond refuse of the Northern States are to be the judges.

What else than contempt and abhorrence can the women of New Orleans feel or exhibit for these officers and soldiers of the United States? The spontaneous impulse of their hearts must appear involuntary upon their countenances and thus constitute the crime for which the general of those soldiers adjudges the punishment of rape and brutalized passion.

History records instances of cities sacked and inhuman atrocities committed upon the women of a conquered town, but in no instance in modern times, at least without the brutal ravishers suffering condign punishment from the hands of their own commanders. It was reserved for a Federal general to invite his soldiers to the perpetration of outrages at the mention of which the blood recoils in horror—to quicken the impulses of their sensual instincts by the suggestion of transparent excuses for their gratification, and to add to an infamy already well merited these crowning titles of a panderer to lust and a desecrator of virtue.

Maddened by the noble loyalty of our people to the Government of their affections, and at their disgust and execration of their invaders; stung into obliviousness of the world's censure by the grand offering made of our property upon the altar of our liberties; his passions inflamed by the sight of burning cotton illumining the river upon whose waters floats the powerful fleet that effected the downfall of our chief city; disappointed, chafed, and chagrined that our people, unlike his own, do not measure liberty, truth, or honor by a pecuniary standard, he sees the fruits of a victory he did not help to win eluding his grasp, and nothing left upon which to gloat his vengeance but unarmed men and helpless women.

Louisianians! will you suffer such foul conduct of your oppressors to pass unpunished? Will you permit such indignities to remain unavenged? A mind so debased as to be capable of conceiving the alternative presented in this order must be fruitful of inventions wherewith to pollute humanity. Shameless enough to allow their publication in the city, by the countenance of such atrocities they will be multiplied in the country. Its inhabitants must arm and strike, or the insolent victors will offer this outrage to your wives, your sisters, and your daughters. Possessed of New Orleans by means of his superior naval force, he cannot penetrate the interior if you resolve to prevent it. It does not require a force of imposing magnitude to impede his progress. Companies of experienced woodsmen in every exposed locality, with their trusty rifles and shot-guns, will harass his invading columns, deprive him of his pilots, and assure him he is in the country of an enemy. At proper points larger forces will be collected, but every man can be a soldier to guard the approaches to his home. Organize, then, quickly and efficiently. If your enemy attempt to proceed into the interior let his pathway be marked by his blood. It is your homes that you have to defend. It is the jewel of your hearths—the chastity of your women—you have to guard. Let that thought animate your breasts, nerve your arms, quicken your energies, and inspire your resolution. Strike home to the heart of your foe the blow that rids your country of his presence. If need be let his blood moisten your own grave. It will rise up before your children as a perpetual memento of a race whom it will teach to hate now and evermore.

THOS. O. MOORE.

Lord Palmerston to Charles Francis Adams
Benjamin Moran: Journal, June 25, 1862

Butler's order provoked outrage not only in the Confederacy but in Great Britain as well. Two days after he wrote to envoy Adams, Lord Palmerston told the House of Commons that "an Englishman must blush to think that such an act has been committed by one belonging to the Anglo-Saxon race." Benjamin Moran, a secretary at the American legation, recorded Adams's response to the prime minister.

Confidential. BROCKET, 11 June, 1862.

MY DEAR SIR,—I cannot refrain from taking the liberty of saying to you that it is difficult if not impossible to express adequately the disgust which must be excited in the mind of every honorable man by the general order of General Butler given in the inclosed extract from yesterday's *Times.* Even when a town is taken by assault it is the practice of the Commander of the conquering army to protect to his utmost the inhabitants and especially the female part of them, and I will venture to say that no example can be found in the history of civilized nations till the publication of this order, of a general guilty in cold blood of so infamous an act as deliberately to hand over the female inhabitants of a conquered city to the unbridled license of an unrestrained soldiery.

If the Federal Government chuses to be served by men capable of such revolting outrages, they must submit to abide by the deserved opinion which mankind will form of their conduct. My dear Sir, Yours faithfully,

PALMERSTON.

C. F. Adams Esqr.

(Address: Private. His Excelcy Chas. F. Adams Esqr.
Palmerston.)

Wednesday, June 25, 1862. A serious correspondence has just taken place between Lord Palmerston and Mr. Adams which is destined to become historical. His Lordship with that impudence that only an Englishman can be guilty of wrote a private and confidential note to Mr. Adams on the 11th Inst., about Gen'l Butler's late order at New Orleans in which he said he could not "express adequately the disgust which must be excited in the mind of every honorable man" at that regulation "of a General guilty of so infamous an act as to deliberately hand over the female inhabitants of a conquered city to the unbridled license of an unrestrained soldiery."

Mr. Adams replied on the 12th refusing to recognise the note, unless he was assured it was official, and expressing surprise at such an unusual proceeding on the part of the Prime Minister, instead of the Minister of Foreign Affairs,—with whom Foreign Ministers carry on their correspondence on matters connected with the duties of their Mission.

To this Ld. Palmerston rejoined on the 15th by saying his note was official.

In the interview Mr. Adams saw Lord Russell and stated the case to him. He was much offended, & said Ld. Palmerston had exceeded the bounds of good behavior—a thing he had often done of late, and had no business to write such a note.

Mr. Adams renewed the subject on the 16th and after commenting on the nature of his Lordship's letter, said that "the Government he represented would visit with just indignation upon its servants abroad their tame submission to receive under the seal of privacy any indignity which it might be the disposition of the servants of any sovereign however exalted, to offer to it in that form."

Palmerston with his usual insolence answered this in a sophistical strain on the 19th, & on the 20th Mr. Adams closed the affair by a note in which he said he would decline while here to receive such communications from him. This severe reprimand had its intended effect, and his Lordship has remained silent under it.

The incident placed Mr. Adams in a very critical position, and for a few days we considered things so serious as to strongly anticipate a sudden rupture of all intercourse. Fortunately, Mr. Adams' decision saved such a result.

A more impudent proceeding than that of Palmerston in this case cannot be discovered in the whole range of political life. Knowing the brutality of his own officers and soldiers he readily imagined ours of the same stamp, and insolently presumed to lecture Mr. Adams on a thing which was not his business. His ill-manners were properly rebuked. American soldiers, he will find out, are not beasts, altho' English soldiers are; and he will also learn that it is only a debased mind that would construe Gen'l Butler's order as he has done. He has defined it according to English practice. That is all.

This proceeding of Lord Palmerston is one of the most remarkable, and probably without a parallel in Diplomatic history. Mr. Adams was placed in a most awkward predicament & managed the affair with great skill. When the story shall be made public, it will create great astonishment in certain quarters. Had not Palmerston taken the course he did, it was Mr. Adams' intention to have published the correspondence privately and sent it to his colleagues so that they might know what they might at some time or other expect from his Lordship should he remain in office.

BATTLE OF FAIR OAKS: VIRGINIA, MAY–JUNE 1862

Henry Ropes to William Ropes

McClellan's army, as it closed on Richmond, straddled the Chickahominy River, and on May 31–June 1 Joseph E. Johnston struck at the isolated Union left wing south of the river. The brigade of Lieutenant Henry Ropes, 20th Massachusetts Infantry, part of Edwin Sumner's Second Corps, was hurried across the flooding Chickahominy to counter the attack. The battle of Fair Oaks (or Seven Pines) cost the Confederates 6,134 men, killed, wounded, or missing; the Union 5,031; and the fighting ended about where it began. Among the seriously wounded was Johnston, and on June 1 Jefferson Davis replaced him with General Robert E. Lee.

Camp near Fair Oaks Station Va.
1 P.M. Tuesday June 3d 1862.

My dear Father.

I take the first opportunity to inform you of my safety, that a Kind Providence has mercifully preserved me in battle, and above all that I was enabled to do my duty there.

On Saturday last, May 31st, we had not the slightest idea of danger being near till about noon when very heavy firing broke out from the woods West of us and at one time approached very near. We were ordered under arms, but I had no particular expectation of a battle, for we have been often called out in the same way before. The firing ceased, and we heard a report that Casey had been repulsed, but we did not know what to believe. At about 4 O'cl. orders came to fall in with one day's rations and we marched from Camp, and crossed the Chickahominy on the log bridge built by the Mich. Regimt. We came out on a low meadow where our Artillery was stuck in the mud. The 19th Mass. was on picket behind us, the Tammany we left here, and the 7th Mich. and we pushed on alone. After passing the meadow we ascended a small hill and found the country dry and hilly in front. Soon we halted, loaded and primed and then marched on again. In a few moments we heard guns ahead, and we pushed on rapidly, crossed a stream knee deep and took the double quick, for musketry and artillery were now heard in front, rapidly increasing. We drove forward out of breath and very hot, saw the smoke rising over the trees, and soon the road turned from along the edge of the woods, and we saw at the farther end of a large field our Artillery firing with the greatest rapidity, the Infantry forming, all hid in smoke. We again took the double quick step and ran through deep mud and pools of water toward the battle. The whole field in the rear of the line of firing was covered with dead; and wounded men were coming in in great numbers, some walking, some limping, some carried on stretchers and blankets, many with shattered limbs exposed and dripping with blood. In a moment we entered the fire. The noise was terrific, the balls whistled by us and the Shells exploded over us and by our side; the whole scene dark with smoke and lit up by the streams of fire from our battery and from our Infantry in line on each side. We were carried to the left and formed in line, and then marched by the left flank and advanced to the front and opened fire. Our men behaved with the greatest steadiness and stood up and fired and did exactly what they were told. The necessary confusion was very great, and it was as much as all the Officers could do to give the commands and see to the men. We changed position 2 or 3 times under a hot fire. Donnelly and Chase of my company fell not 2 feet from me. The shell and balls seemed all round us, and yet few seemed to fall. We kept up this heavy firing for some time, when the enemy came out of the woods in front and made a grand attack on the battery. They were met by grape and canister and a tremendous fire of the Infantry. They faltered and fell back. Some Regiment charged on them: the whole Rebel line was now in front of us, and Genl. Sumner ordered our whole line to advance. We rushed on with tremendous cheers, the whole together at a charge. The Rebels did not wait for the bayonets but broke and fled. Our Regiment came over a newly ploughed field and sank to the knee. We drove them to the edge of the woods and opened a tremendous fire for a few moments, and then

June 4th 12M. 1862.

I was forced to stop suddenly yesterday for our Company went to occupy a house and yard in advance of our Regiment, and I expected to finish there, but the enemy appeared unexpectedly and opened fire on us and wounded 2 men of Company H, and I was fully occupied till this morning. I will continue my letter where I left it off.

We fired into the woods and then charged and drove them before us. We were then ordered back, and by the left flank and again charged the Rebels in a field on the left where they had rallied. We drove them and halted in the middle of the field and give a few final volleys. It was then dark. We staid there that night. Ground covered with their killed and wounded. We took many prisoners. I will write more fully when I have more time.

On Sunday they attacked us tremendously. We were not in the heat of it and only lost one man.

Fighting more or less all the time till now. No signs of the Rebels today. All Officers well and unhurt. Colonel well, but very busy. He desires me to ask you to send word to his family. I am on picket to-day. The Regiment will probably soon be relieved. Our total loss 30. My Company suffered most in the battle.

Love to Mother and all.

Your affectionate Son
Henry.

A MILITARY ASSESSMENT: VIRGINIA, JUNE 1862

Robert E. Lee to Jefferson Davis

General Lee served as unofficial chief of staff to President Davis for three months before taking command of the Army of Northern Virginia, and as he writes here, he continued supporting Stonewall Jackson's campaign in the Shenandoah. As he organized and reinforced his army, Lee planned his "diversion" against McClellan—this time an assault on the Union right wing north of the Chickahominy River.

Confidential

Hd. Qrs: Near Richmond 5 June '62

After much reflection I think if it was possible to reinforce Jackson strongly it would change the character of the war. This can only be done by the troops in Georgia, S.C. & N.C. Jackson could in that event cross Maryland into Penna. It would call all the enemy from our Southern coast & liberate those states— If these states will give up their troops I think it can be done. McClellan will make this a battle of Posts. He will take position from position, under cover of his heavy guns, & we cannot get at him without storming his works, which with our new troops is extremely hazardous. You witnessed the experiment Saturday. It will require 100,000 men to resist the regular siege of Richmond, which perhaps would only prolong not save it— I am preparing a line that I can hold with part of our forces in front, while with the rest I will endeavour to make a diversion to bring McClellan out. He sticks under his batteries & is working day & night— He is obliged to adhere to the R. R. unless he can reach James river to provision his Army. I am endeavouring to block his progress on the R. R. & have written up to see if I can get made an iron battery on trucks with a heavy gun, to sweep the country in our front. The enemy cannot move his heavy guns except on the R. R. You have seen nothing like the roads in the Chick—bottom. Our people are opposed to work. Our troops, officers, community & press. All ridicule & resist it. It is the very means by which McClellan has

& is advancing. Why should we leave to him the whole advantage of labour. Combined with valour fortitude & boldness, of which we have our fair proportion, it should lead us to success. What carried the Roman soldiers into all countries, but this happy combination. The evidences of their labour last to this day. There is nothing so military as labour, & nothing so important to an army as to save the lives of its soldiers—

I enclose a letter I have recd from Genl D. H. Hill, for your own perusal. Please return it to me. I have taken means to arrest stragglers—I hope he is mistaken about his Brigadiers—I fear not in Rains case. Of Featherston I know nothing. I thought you ought to know it. Our position requires you should know everything & you must excuse my troubling you— The firing in our front has ceased. I believe it was the enemys shell practice. Col Long &c went down early this morg. to keep me advised, but as I hear nothing from them, I assume it is unimportant very respt & truly

R E Lee

ARMING FREED SLAVES: SOUTH CAROLINA, JUNE 1862

David Hunter to Edwin M. Stanton

At the same time as he issued his emancipation order in May 1862, General Hunter began organizing a regiment of freed slaves. He wrote to the secretary of war after his actions were challenged by Kentucky congressman Charles A. Wickliffe, a vehement opponent of arming blacks. Denied War Department sanction, Hunter disbanded his slave regiments, but his efforts, and similar efforts by General John W. Phelps on the Gulf coast, marked a first step toward recruiting blacks for the army.

Port Royal So Ca June 23rd 1862

Sir: I have the honor to acknowledge the receipt of a communication from the Adjutant General of the Army, dated June 13th 1862, requesting me to furnish you with information necessary to answer certain resolutions introduced in the House of Representatives, June 9th 1862, on motion of the Hon. Mr. Wickliffe of Kentucky,—their substance being to inquire;

1st Whether I had organized or was organizing a regiment of "Fugitive Slaves" in this Department.

2nd Whether any authority had been given to me from the War Department for such organization;—and

3rd Whether I had been furnished by order of the War Department with clothing, uniforms, arms, equipments and so forth for such a force?

Only having received the letter covering these inquiries at a late hour on Saturday night, I urge forward my answer in time for the Steamer sailing today (Monday),—this haste preventing me from entering as minutely as I could wish upon many points of detail such as the paramount importance of the subject calls for. But in view of the near termination of the present session of Congress, and the wide-spread interest which must have been awakened by Mr Wickliffe's Resolutions, I prefer sending even this imperfect answer to waiting the period necessary for the collection of fuller and more comprehensive data.

To the First Question therefore I reply that no regiment of "Fugitive Slaves" has been, or is being organized in this Department. There is, however, a fine regiment of persons whose late masters are "Fugitive Rebels,"—men who everywhere fly before the appearance of the National Flag, leaving their servants behind them to shift as best they can for themselves.—So far, indeed, are the loyal persons composing this regiment from seeking to avoid the presence of their late owners, that they are now, one and all, working with remarkable industry to place themselves in a position to go in full and effective pursuit of their fugacious and traitorous proprietors.

To the Second Question, I have the honor to answer that the instructions given to Brig. Gen. T. W. Sherman by the Hon. Simon Cameron, late Secretary of War, and turned over to me by succession for my guidance,—do distinctly authorize me to employ all loyal persons offering their services in defence of the Union and for the suppression of this Rebellion in any manner I might see fit, or that the circumstances might call for. There is no restriction as to the character or color of the persons to be employed, or the nature of the employment, whether civil or military, in which their services should be used. I conclude, therefore that I have been authorized to enlist "Fugitive Slaves" as soldiers, could any such be found in this Department.— No such characters, however, have yet appeared within view of our most advanced pickets,—the loyal slaves everywhere remaining on their plantations to welcome us, aid us, and supply us with food, labor and information.— It is the masters who have in every instance been the "Fugitives", running away from loyal slaves as well as loyal soldiers, and whom we have only partially been able to see,—chiefly their heads over ramparts, or, rifle in hand, dodging behind trees,— in the extreme distance.— In the absence of any "Fugitive Master Law", the deserted Slaves would be wholly without remedy, had not the crime of Treason given them the right to pursue, capture and bring back those persons of whose protection they have been thus suddenly bereft.

To the Third Interrogatory, it is my painful duty to reply that I never have received any Specific authority for issues of clothing, uniforms, arms, equipments and so forth to the troops in question,—my general instructions from Mr Cameron to employ them in any manner I might find necessary, and the military exigencies of the Department and the country, being my only, but in my judgment, sufficient justification. Neither have I had any Specific authority for supplying these persons with shovels, spades and pick axes when employing them as laborers, nor with boats and oars when using them as lightermen,—but these are not points included in Mr. Wickliffe's Resolution.— To me it seemed that liberty to employ men in any particular capacity implied with it liberty, also, to supply them with the necessary tools; and acting upon this faith, I have clothed, equipped and armed the only loyal regiment yet raised in South Carolina.

I must say, in vindication of my own conduct, that had it not been for the many other diversified and imperative claims on my time and attention, a much more satisfactory result might have been hoped for; and that in place of only one, as at present, at least five or six well-drilled, brave and thoroughly acclimated regiments should by this time have been added to the loyal forces of the Union.

The experiment of arming the Blacks, so far as I have made it, has been a complete and even marvellous success. They are sober, docile, attentive and enthusiastic, displaying great natural capacities for acquiring the duties of the soldier. They are eager beyond all things to take the field and be led into action; and it is the unanimous opinion of the officers who have had charge of them, that in the peculiarities of this climate and Country they will prove invaluable auxiliaries,—fully equal to the similar regiments so long and successfully used by the British Authorities in the West India Islands.

In conclusion I would say it is my hope,—there appearing no possibility of other reinforcements owing to the exigencies of the Campaign in the Peninsula,—to have organized by the end of next Fall, and to be able to present to the Government, from forty eight to fifty thousand of these hardy and devoted soldiers.— Trusting that this letter may form part of your answer to Mr Wickliffe's Resolutions, I have the honor to be, most respectfully, Your Very Obedt Servt.

FEAR OF THE "YANKEES": LOUISIANA, JUNE–JULY 1862

Kate Stone: Journal, June 29–July 5, 1862

Brokenburn, a cotton plantation some thirty miles northwest of Vicksburg, Mississippi, in what is now Madison Parish, Louisiana, was home to twenty-one-year-old Kate Stone, who recorded the impressment of slave labor for an early Union effort to bypass the Vicksburg citadel. The rumors she mentions in her July 5 entry refer to the Seven Days' Battles at Richmond.

June 29: Brother Walter brought a letter from My Brother to Mamma. It was sent by Tom Manlove, who is at home on sick leave. In the letter he is despondent and homesick and very anxious about us all now that the enemy is at our very doors. He says that it will kill him to remain idle in Virginia when we are in such danger and that he must come back to see about us and fight with the Mississippi army. He seems so desperate. We fear he will do something rash and get into trouble. He cannot realize that we are safe enough for the present.

We hear today that the Yankees are impressing all the Negro men on the river places and putting them to work on a ditch which they are cutting across the point opposite Vicksburg above DeSoto. They hope to turn the river through there and to leave Vicksburg high and dry, ruining that town and enabling the gunboats to pass down the river without running the gauntlet of the batteries at Vicksburg. They have lately come up as far as Omega, four miles from us, taking the men from Mr. Noland's place down. We hear several have been shot attempting to escape. We were satisfied there would soon be outrages committed on private property. Mamma had all the men on the place called up, and she told them if the Yankees came on the place each Negro must take care of himself and run away and hide. We think they will.

From a late paper we see that Butler is putting his foot down more firmly every day. A late proclamation orders every man in the city to take the oath of allegiance. There will be the most severe penalties in case of refusal. Butler had Mr. Mumford, a gentleman of New Orleans, shot for tearing down the first flag hoisted in New Orleans over the mint. The most infamous order and murder of which only Butler is capable. Is the soul of Nero reincarnated in the form of Butler? Why can he not fall of the scourge of New Orleans, yellow fever?

Gen. Breckinridge started to Vicksburg yesterday in a carriage, and he runs great risk of being captured, as they have pickets across the point. Several of our soldiers have been taken trying to make their way across there. Brother Walter slipped through just in time.

The drought was broken last night by a good rain and the planters are feeling better. This insures a good corn crop and it was beginning to suffer. It is so essential to make good food crops this year. When we heard the cool drops splashing on the roof, "We thanked God and took fresh courage." Such a lovely morning. It is a pleasure to breathe the soft, cool air and look out over the glad, green fields, flashing and waving in the early sunlight.

Mamma had a chill and was in bed all day. How I dread to see her start again having fevers.

Martha, one of Courtney's twins, will die, they think tonight. The poor little creature has suffered a long time.

Mr. Catlin, Mrs. Bledsoe, and my pet aversion, Dr. Slicer, are amusing themselves during all this time of threatened ruin and disaster by getting up fish frys and picnics, aided and abetted by all that set back there calling themselves second-class—and they have named themselves truly.

Sister sent Douglas's hat over to him. Joe Carson's is nearly done, but only Mamma can finish it and she is sick.

June 30: The excitement is very great. The Yankees have taken the Negroes off all the places below Omega, the Negroes generally going most willingly, being promised their freedom by the vandals. The officers coolly go on the places, take the plantation books, and call off the names of all the men they want, carrying them off from their masters without a word of apology. They laugh at the idea of payment and say of course they will never send them back. A good many planters are leaving the river and many are sending their Negroes to the back country. We hope to have ours in a place of greater safety by tomorrow.

Dr. Nutt and Mr. Mallett are said to be already on their way to Texas with the best of their hands. Jimmy and Joe went to the Bend and Richmond today. They saw Julia and Mary Gustine, who sent me word that I was a great coward to run away. Mary had talked to a squad of Yankee soldiers for awhile and found them anything but agreeable.

All on this place, Negroes and whites, are much wrought up. Of course the Negroes do not want to go, and our fear is when the Yankees come and find them gone they will burn the buildings in revenge. They are capable of any horror. We look forward to their raid with great dread. Mrs. Savage sent for her silver today. We have been keeping it since the gunboats came. They will all leave in two days for Bayou Macon. Would like to see them before they get off.

Mamma has been in bed all day. Sister is suffering with a large rising on her leg and Brother Walter from a severe cold. He is spitting blood, all yesterday and today, and tomorrow is compelled to go on a long trip. We have been arranging everything for an early start.

July 5: Another Fourth of July has gone by without any festivities, not even a dinner for the Negroes, but they have holiday. The Yankees told Mr. McRae, while they were holding him prisoner, that they would celebrate the day by a furious attack on Vicksburg. But we have heard few guns since the third. That day we heard them very distinctly, almost a continuous roar. It was said both mortar fleets were firing on Vicksburg. We have not heard the result.

The Yankees are gathering in the Negroes on the river as fast as possible. They have taken all the men able to work from Lake Providence to Pecan Grove and from Omega to Baton Rouge. They are hourly expected at Pecan Grove. Robert is with us to be out of the way when they do come. He is nearly well. The Negroes are eager to go, leaving wife and children and all for freedom promised them, but we hear they are being worked to death on the canal with no shelter at night and not much to eat.

There has been no attempt at resistance. Some of the plantations have been deserted by the owners, some of them burned by the Yankee bands, and some of them not molested. It depends on the temper of the officer in charge. If he feels malicious, he burns the premises. If a good-natured enemy, he takes what he wants and leaves the buildings standing. Most of them are malicious. Mamma will have the Negro men taken to the back country tomorrow, if she can get them to go. Generally when told to run away from the soldiers, they go right to them and I cannot say I blame them.

Mamma has been sick in bed since Sunday and is not yet able to be up all day. We sent for Dr. Devine first, and he gave her a dose of podophyllin that completely exhausted her, since she always suffers dreadfully with nausea, and that nearly killed her. So we sent for Dr. Dancy, and she is improving, but slowly.

Brother Walter went out to Monroe, eighty miles, and got back yesterday. He succeeded in buying enough molasses to last the place the year and some little necessaries at enormous prices. The trading boats are coming down the river again with groceries at ridiculously low prices, but of course no patriot could think of buying from them. Mamma was able to sell her surplus corn and that helped her on wonderfully. She had such quantities of it. And we certainly will have eatables this year, judging from the looks of the great fields of corn, peas, and potatoes. Not much cotton planted.

Mamma so longed for ice while she was ill, but it was impossible to get it, while those wretches on the gunboats could even have ice cream if they wished it.

People going and coming all the week. Mrs. Carson kindly brought Mamma a substitute for lemonade and some crackers. She was out twice.

It is hard for sick people to live on cornbread. We fortunately have a little flour, sent Mamma by Mr. Hardison as a specimen of some home-grown wheat. Joe has been out several times. The last time I was just finishing his hat. I gave it to him and it fitted beautifully. He was so pleased with the gift that it repaid me for the yards of plaiting. Joe is the only "stay-at-home" I would give anything to, but I know so well it is not his fault. Mr. Hornwasher came out with Mrs. Carson, his black eyes sparkling and dancing even more than usual. He still speaks of joining the army.

We hear rumors of a great battle in Virginia and the utter discomfiture of McClellan with Gen. Lee attacking him in front and Stonewall Jackson with 2,800 men in the rear. That was a "stonewall" McClellan found hard to climb. My Brother and Uncle Bo must both have been in the fight, but we have had no news from them for such a long time. It is heart-sickening.

THE SEVEN DAYS BEGIN: VIRGINIA, JUNE 1862

Edward Porter Alexander: *from* Fighting for the Confederacy

In less than a month Lee raised the Army of Northern Virginia to its greatest strength of the war—100,000 men, nearly equal to the Federal army—and determined to break McClellan's impending siege of Richmond. Lieutenant Colonel Edward Porter Alexander, Lee's ordnance chief, records in his personal reminiscences the lead-up to the Seven Days (June 25–July 1) and the fighting on the first three days, through the battle of Gaines's Mill. His memoir, drafted in 1897–99, was published in 1989 as *Fighting for the Confederacy: The Personal Recollections of General Edward Porter Alexander*, edited by Gary W. Gallagher. In his draft Alexander sometimes referred to maps, reports, and figures he intended to add to his manuscript; some of this material is presented in the endnotes to this volume.

THIS BRINGS us to the Seven Days fighting about Richmond. I will give a little map & will outline briefly the principal events & can then in a very small space outline my personal experiences during their occurrence.

Early in June, Gen. Stonewall Jackson, whose reputation up to this time had simply been that of a desperate & stubborn fighter (having only fought so far in the battle of Bull Run), suddenly broke loose up in the Valley of Virginia & not only astonished the weak minds of the enemy almost into paralysis, but dazzled the eyes of military men all over the world by an aggressive campaign which I believe to be unsurpassed in all military history for brilliancy & daring. It seems indeed to me to be only approached by Napoleon's best Italian campaigns. I write away from all books of reference & cannot therefore go into any details, but in general terms what he did was about as follows.

There were two Federal armies out after him in the Valley, one coming up the Valley from the north & one over the mountains from the south west, both superior to him in numbers. Meanwhile, too, McDowell with about 40,000 was at Fredericksburg about 100 miles to his east. But McD. was out not for Jackson, but for Richmond & to co-operate with McClellan against Lee. And he was just about to move too when Jackson began his performances by bouncing upon the army in front of him in the Valley—under Banks I believe—& giving it a complete defeat at Strasburg on _____ & chasing it down the Valley nearly or quite to the Potomac River. This alarmed the Federals for Washington & McDowell was stopped from his proposed advance to Richmond & was ordered to send a strong body of troops to get behind Jackson & unite with the force advancing from the southwest under Frémont. But Jackson hurried back from the Potomac so rapidly as to get between these converging enemies & to defeat each of them separately & to drive each of them back. These battles took place on Jun. 8 & 9th.

Gen. Lee now conceived the plan of bringing Jackson down from the Valley swiftly & secretly & having him surprise & fall upon the Federal right flank. This was posted at Ellison's Mill on Beaver Dam Creek in the same beautiful position—absolutely impregnable to a front attack—which we engineers had selected for our own left-flank had we taken line of battle north of the Chickahominy. Thence the Federal line ran down the Chick. to below the Nine Mile or New Bridge Road, crossing where it crossed & ran over past Seven Pines.

Gen. Lee issued a regular battle order setting forth his whole plan in detail & I cannot explain it better than by simply copying the official copy of it which I received as chief of ordnance. This order & the map will make all clear.

Meanwhile also elaborate efforts were made to deceive the enemy by making him think that our game was to reinforce Jackson strongly up in the Valley, & have him make a vigorous attack on Washington itself. For this purpose Whiting's division (2 brigades, his own & Hood's) was withdrawn from our lines, & sent by rail up to Jackson. Also Lawton's big brigade, arriving from Savannah, was also railroaded up to Jackson. But all was so planned that by railroad & by marching, they would all be back, & all of Jackson's original men with them, concentrated at Ashland on the evening of Wednesday, Jun. 25th. There the battle order took them in hand at 3 A.M. on June 26th,

& started them to march around the enemy's flank at Beaver Dam & to cross the creek above it & to take the enemy in rear, while A. P. & D. H. Hill crossing by Meadow Bridge & Mechanicsville roads threatened its front.

And now I shall have to tell, as my narrative proceeds, of how upon several occasions in the progress of the fighting during the next six days, Gen. Lee's best hopes & plans were upset & miscarried, & how he was prevented from completely destroying & capturing McClellan's whole army & all its stores & artillery by the incredible slackness, & delay & hanging back, which characterized Gen. Jackson's performance of his part of the work.

But little has been said about it in the press. As compared with Longstreet's alleged shortcomings at Gettysburg nothing at all. Gen. Fitzhugh Lee, in his life of Gen. Lee, devotes pages to the latter, & does not remotely refer to the former. But to suppress it robs Gen. Lee of the credit of what seems to me perhaps his greatest achievement. As it was, within a month of taking command he scattered all the tremendous forces concentrated for his destruction & practically deposed McClellan, the "Young Napoleon" of the Federals. But think of the moral effect on the country, & the world had he captured this entire army of 100,000 men with all its stores & arms & artillery. And this he would indoubtedly have done had the Gen. Jackson of those six days been the same Gen. Jackson who had marched & fought in the Valley but a few weeks before, or the same who upon every other battlefield afterward—Cedar Mountain, Second Manassas, Harpers Ferry, Sharpsburg, & Fredericksburg, to his lamented death at Chancellorsville in May '63—made a reputation unequalled in military annals. And just to think—it was practically all done within less than 12 months.

We of Gen. Lee's staff knew at the time that he was deeply, bitterly disappointed, but he made no official report of it & glossed all over as much as possible in his own reports. Indeed, I never thoroughly understood the matter until long after, when all the official reports were published, & I read Gen. Jackson's own statements of times & things, & those of the officers under him & compared them with what I knew of the whole situation.

The question naturally arises, what was the matter with him?

Although the public has heard little of the matter, it has by no means entirely escaped comment and I will give presently some of the things which have been said by Gen. D. H. Hill, his brother in law, & others of his friends.

For myself I think that the one defect in Gen. Jackson's character as a soldier was his religious belief. He believed, with absolute faith, in a personal God, watching all human events with a jealous eye to His own glory—ready to reward those people who made it their chief care, & to punish those who forgot about it. And he specially believed that a particular day had been set aside every week for the praise of this God, & that a personal account was strictly kept with every man as to how he kept this day & that those who disregarded it need expect no favors, but that those who sacrificed all other considerations, however recklessly, to honoring Him by its observance, would be rewarded conspicuously. And I see in Gen. Jackson's whole conduct during the Seven Days a sort of faith that he had God on his side & could trust to Him for victory without overexerting himself & his men.

The only quotation I have at hand concerning Gen. Jackson's conduct during the fighting is from Gen. D. H. Hill, who was Gen. Jackson's brother-in-law & was in his command at the time. In an account of the movements on June 30th & July 1st ending with the Battle of Malvern Hill, published in the Century War Book, Gen. H. says—speaking of the affair at White Oak Swamp on June 30th (which will be more fully explained later):

Our cavalry returned by the lower ford & pronounced it perfectly practicable for infantry. But Jackson did not advance. Why was this? It was the critical day for both commanders, but especially for McClellan. With consummate skill he had crossed his vast train of 5,000 wagons & his immense parks of artillery safely over White Oak Swamp, but he was more exposed now than at any time in his flank march. Three columns of attack were converging upon him, and a strong corps was pressing upon his rear. Escape seemed impossible for him, but he did escape. . . . Gen. Lee through no fault in his plans was to see his splendid prize slip through his hands. Longstreet & A. P. Hill struck the enemy at Frazier's Farm (or Glendale) at 3 P.M., and, both being always ready for a fight, immediately attacked. Magruder, who followed them down the Darbytown Road was ordered to the assistance of Gen. Holmes on the New Market Road, who was not then engaged, & their two divisions took no part in the action. Huger, on the Charles City Road, came upon Franklin's left flank but made no attack. . . . So there were five divisions within sound of the firing, & within supporting distance, but not one of them moved. . . . Maj. Dabney in his life of Jackson thus comments on the inaction of that officer: "On this occasion it would appear, if the vast interests dependent upon Gen. Jackson's co-operation with the proposed attack upon the centre were considered, that he came short of the efficiency in action for which he was everywhere else noted." After showing how the crossing of White Oak might have been effected, Dabney adds: "The list of casualties would have been larger than that presented on the 30th, of one cannoneer wounded, but how much shorter would have been the bloody list filled up the next day at Malvern Hill. This temporary eclipse of Jackson's genius was probably to be explained by physical causes. The labor of the previous days, the sleeplessness, the wear of gigantic cares with the drenching of the comfortless night, had sunk the elasticity of his will, & the quickness of his invention for the nonce below their wonted tension."

And Gen. Hill adds his own solution of the mystery as follows: "I think that an important factor in this inaction was Jackson's pity for his own corps, worn out by long & exhausting marches, & reduced in numbers by its numerous sanguinary battles. He thought that the garrison of Richmond ought now to bear the brunt of the fighting."

This seems to be to me a most remarkable excuse to be tendered by a friend. It was indeed whispered about in the army afterward that Gen. Jackson had said that he did not intend that his corps should do all the fighting, but it was regarded as a slander. I don't think Major Dabney's excuse that his inaction was due to physical exhaustion will at all bear analysis. For three successive nights & two entire days, since the battle of Gaines's Mill, he had been in camp near that battlefield. He had especially done nothing all day Sunday—although every hour then was precious. My own solution of the matter is that he thought that God could & would easily make up for any little shortcomings of his own & give us the victory anyhow.

But in this connection I will quote only one sentence more from Gen. D. H. Hill: "Had all our troops been at Frazer's Farm there would have been no Malvern Hill." And perhaps it is as well to put here also, what Gen. Franklin said about it—who was opposite Jackson on the 30th at White Oak Swamp. It is also from the Century War Book.

And now I can go back to my narrative & outline of the principal events which is to be completed before taking up the story of my small individual experiences.

Gen. Jackson started down to Richmond for a personal conference with Gen. Lee on the approaching event, by rail on Saturday, June 21. The train was due to arrive in Richmond about daylight Sunday morning & the conference might easily have been held on Sunday. But Gen. J. was unwilling to travel on Sunday, at least when such momentous events were in hand. So before midnight he left the train at Louisa C.H., spent the rest of the night with a friend, attended church, two or three times the next day, Sunday, & then, after 12 o'clock Sunday night, mounted his horse & rode the balance of the way to Richmond, about 60 miles—I have not at hand the details of the hour of his arrival, the time of the conference & the time of his return to his command, but all were from 24 to 48 hours later than they need have been, & Gen. Jackson had more over the personal fatigue of a very trying horseback ride of ____ miles. But I believe neither Prest. Davis or Gen. Lee disapproved, & I have no doubt that Gen. Jackson thought that such a conspicuous respect for the Sabbath at such a time would do more to give us a victory than all that his whole army could accomplish without special Divine aid. Wednesday night found himself & his whole command concentrated at Ashland.

He was ordered to march for the enemy's flank at 3 A.M. on Thursday but the official reports which mention the hour of starting all concur that it was after sunrise. The distance he had to go to the enemy's flank was about ____ miles, & early that morning the whole of Gen. Lee's army on the south of the Chickahominy was alert & listening for Jackson's guns & ready to take their respective parts as laid down in the order of battle already given. I remember seeing Mr. Davis & his staff on the hills overlooking the Chickahominy, near the Mechanicsville Road, where Gen. Lee had made his temporary head qrs., & my recollection is that he came as early, at 10 or eleven o'clock, & was on or about the ground all day. For hour after hour passed & nothing was heard of Jackson. At last about 3 P.M., when it was plain that the day was almost gone, our extreme left flank, A. P. Hill's division, crossed the Chick. at Meadow Bridge & started the ball without him, hoping he would still turn up by the time the fight became hot. Hill, on crossing, moved down stream & soon cleared off the small Federal forces about Mechanicsville & opened that road, when D. H. Hill brought over a part of his division & joined him.

They found themselves confronted by the Federal right flank under Fitz John Porter, behind Beaver Dam Creek, near Ellison's Mill. It was the very position told of selected by the engineers & myself for our own flank, had we fought on that side of the river, & they had fortified it with infantry breast works, & pits for guns, & by cutting down all timber in range to give unobstructed fire. The valley of the creek was rendered impassable by the fallen trees & brush, & by the creek on one side of it, & the mill race on the slope of the eastern bank, just in front of the enemy's line. Briefly there was no cover in front within musket range, say 400 yards, & the enemy's line could not be reached by an assaulting force, & his men were quite well sheltered from fire. But there were our people in front of it, & the day was drawing to a close & our major generals were all brash to do something. And the full strength of the position, particularly the inaccessible feature of it, was not apparent to the eye until one had entirely crossed the plain swept by their fire & gotten actually up to the valley of the creek. A. P. Hill's men, advancing confidently were at first allowed by the enemy to approach quite closely, when a sudden & tremendous fire of infantry & artillery at short range drove them back with some loss. We then brought up artillery, & a very severe duel ensued between, perhaps, fifty guns about equally divided between the two sides & there was also some heavy musketry, but at rather long range. A. P. Hill seems now to have recognised the strength of the position—at least he did not again force his infantry close upon it.

But somehow it happened that two regts. of Ripley's brigade of D. H. Hill's division were ordered to charge it. It was a tragic illustration of the absurdities which often happen upon battlefields. Fitz John Porter had about 25,000 men sheltered

& inaccessible & about 1,500 are launched into his fire & told to charge him home. The regiments sent were big green regiments never before under fire but full of the spirit & prestige given to our whole army by our former successes.

Had those green regiments been given anything to do which was within the bounds of possibility it seems reasonable to believe that they would have done it, & in doing it acquired a self confidence which would have made them ever afterward as near invincible as soldiers can get to be. For their charge was indeed a glorious one. Across the level meadows which stretched from Mechanicsville to the edge of the rather deep & narrow Beaver Dam valley, where even every occasional scattered shade tree had been previously cut down by the enemy to give a free field of fire, they swept without a break through all the fire the enemy could throw. And when they finally reached the rather steep descent into the valley, with its swamp & felled timber & creek & race—all within 200 yards of Fitz John Porter's intrenched 20,000—they knew too little of war to turn back but plunged on down & into the entanglement.

There is no wonder that, as the Federal officer wrote, their dead laid "like flies in a bowl of sugar." The following details from the official reports will assist in forming a correct idea of the affair.

Where was General Jackson with his 20,000 men? The official reports show that he went quietly into camp before sundown at Pole Green Church with the noise of the musketry & artillery at Beaver Dam only 3 miles away ringing in his ears. He had marched only 14 miles over good roads & had no opposition except that a single squadron of Federal cavalry had opposed his crossing of Totopotomoy Creek for a little while & then made their escape without loss. A further advance that afternoon of 3 1/2 miles would have completely cut off the retreat of Fitz John Porter's whole corps. Not until the next morning did Fitz John retire safely bag & baggage to the position behind Powhite Creek not far from Gaines's Mill 3 miles below. Comfortably the next morning Gen. Jackson made the 3 1/2 mile march, which closed the trap Gen. Lee had designed for the capture of Porter, & then turning to his right advanced towards where Porter had been the night before. Presently seeing some skirmishers approaching he fired on them with artillery. They were the advance of A. P. Hill's men who had discovered the enemy's retreat & were following. Jackson's fire took the arm off of Capt. Heise of Columbia, S.C., a gentleman I knew well in after years.

Gen. Lee now had 3 divisions, A. P. Hill, D. H. Hill, & Longstreet, across the Chick. & united with Jackson, having his own & Ewell's divisions & the two brigades of Hood & Whiting united under the latter, say 5 1/4 or 6 divisions—& about 50,000 men.

The enemy had excellent engineers & had found a new position nearly as strong as Beaver Dam. I will quote from Gen. Fitz John Porter in the Century War Book:

> The position selected was east of Powhite Creek, about 6 miles from Beaver Dam Creek. The line of battle was semicircular, the extremities being in the Valley of the Chickahominy while the intermediate portion occupied the high grounds along the bank of the creek, & curved around past McGehee's to Elder Swamp. Part of the front was covered by the ravine of the creek. The east bank was lined with trees & underbrush which afforded concealment & protection to our troops, & artillery. . . . Our new line of battle was well selected & strong though long & requiring either more troops to man it than I had, or too great a thinning of my line by the use of the reserves. The east bank of the creek, from the valley of the Chick. to its swampy sources, was elevated sloping & timbered. The bed of the stream was nearly dry, & its west bank gave excellent protection to the first line of infantry, posted under it, to receive the enemy descending the cleared field sloping to it. The swampy grounds along the sources of the creek were open to our view in front for hundreds of yards, & were swept by the fire of infantry & artillery. The roads from Gaines's Mill, & Old Cold Harbor, along which the enemy were compelled to advance, were swept by artillery posted on commanding ground.

In this strong position Porter had about 30,000 men & 75 guns. Slocum reinforced Porter at 4 P.M. with 10,000 & French & Meagher after sundown with 4,000.

Lee's forces crowded the available roads & their advance was slow, but about noon, A. P. Hill got into action with a small advanced force of the enemy at Gaines's Mill, & drove it back upon the main body—& before two o'clock we were up against the enemy's line, A. P. Hill on our right, with Longstreet behind him, Jackson on our left, & all the rest in reserve and in between.

Strong as was Porter's position we had men good enough & enough of them to have beaten him on the very first charge, had one grand simultaneous effort been made. But somehow, God only knows how, every body else seemed to stand still & let A. P. Hill's division, from 2 o'clock until near or quite four, wreck itself in splendid, but vain & bloody, isolated assaults.

But I will again let our adversary, Fitz John Porter tell about it. (He was my old instructor in cavalry drill & tactics at West Point & was one of the best soldiers in all the Federal army.) He first says (in the same article already quoted) about Jackson's strange inactivity opposite his right flank, "The advance column of these troops came a little earlier than those under Longstreet & A. P. Hill, *but were more cautious, and for some hours not so aggressive*" (the italics are mine). Not only was a great deal of useless blood shed caused by the loss of those hours, but the precious daylight was lost, necessary to gather the fruits of victory when finally won. And this is his description of A. P. Hill's fight:

> Soon after 2 P.M., A. P. Hill's force, between us & New Cold Harbor again began to show an aggressive disposition, independent of its own troops on its flanks, by advancing from under cover of the woods, in lines well formed & extending, as the contest progressed from in front of Martin's battery to Morell's left. Dashing across the intervening plains, floundering in the swamps, & struggling against the tangled brushwood, brigade after brigade seemed almost to melt away before the concentrated fire of our artillery & infantry; yet others pressed on, followed by supports as dashing & as brave as their predecessors, despite their heavy losses, & the disheartening effect of having to clamber over many of their disabled & dead, & to meet their surviving comrades rushing back in great disorder from the deadly contest. For nearly two hours the battle raged, extending more or less along the whole line to our extreme right. The fierce firing of artillery & infantry, the crash of the shot, the bursting of shells & the whizzing of bullets, heard above the war of artillery & the volleys of musketry, all combined was something fearful.
>
> Regiments quickly replenished their exhausted ammunition by borrowing from more bountifully supplied & generous companions.

Some withdrew, temporarily, for ammunition, & fresh regiments took their places, ready to repulse, sometimes to pursue, their desperate enemy for the purpose of retaking ground from which we had been pressed, & which it was necessary to occupy in order to hold our position.

It was only after A. P. Hill's division was worn out to a frazzle, and when Fitz John Porter had received a reinforcement of a fresh division under Slocum, that the rest of the Confederate divisions began to be put in, & even then attacks were disjointed & partial until near about sundown, when at last Gen. Lee had gradually gotten every thing in, & when a charge by Hood's Texas Brigade finally carried one of the strongest parts of the enemy's line. This break was promptly followed by others at many places, & the bloody victory was ours. But the lateness of the hour, & two fresh brigades sent to him across the Chick., enabled Porter to make an excellent retreat & with wonderfully little loss.

Had Jackson attacked when he first arrived, or during A. P. Hill's attack, we would have had an easy victory—comparatively, & would have captured most of Porter's command. Gen. D. H. Hill wrote in the Century article before quoted, "Porter's weak point at Gaines's Mill was his right flank. A thorough examination of the ground would have disclosed that, & had Jackson's command gone in on the left of the road running by the McGehee house, Porter's whole position would have been turned & the line of retreat cut off."

Had our army been as well organised at this time as it became afterward, & as seasoned to battle, the morning after the battle—Sat., June 28—would doubtless have brought us active movements for new dispositions. For though the enemy had successfully withdrawn his defeated men & guns to the south side of the Chick., we had his whole army cut off from their base of supplies, at the White House on the Pamunkey River, & it was plain that they would have to move, & that immediately. It was a question whether they would go to the James River near City Point, where their fleet & supplies could meet them; or whether they would seek to recross the Chick. lower down & go back to the York.

Ewell's division & Stuart's cavalry were sent down the Chick. on the north side to reconnoitre & see what they were doing.

They were abandoning & burning what they could not move & it was clear that they had adopted the first mentioned alternative. The other divisions all laid in camp or bivouac all of the 28th, recovering from the wear & tear of the battle, caring for wounded, & burying dead of both sides.

BATTLE OF GAINES'S MILL:
VIRGINIA, JUNE 1862

Charles A. Page:
from Letters of a War Correspondent

Correspondent Charles A. Page's account of the battle of Gaines's Mill (June 27) appeared in the *New-York Daily Tribune* on July 4. While Fitz John Porter's Fifth Corps fought for its life north of the Chickahominy, McClellan held his four other army corps south of the river, facing Richmond, expecting to be attacked by Confederate forces he imagined to be 200,000 strong.

SAVAGE'S STATION, Saturday, June 28, 1862.

THE EVENTS of the last two days, recounted in detail, with full lists of the casualties, would require a triple sheet of the "Tribune." Set forth with the ordinary discursiveness of army correspondents, McClellan might push forward to Richmond or be pushed back to Yorktown, before the task were completed by one pen. I shrink from even so much as I mark out for this letter. At no time in the history of the campaign have events so tread upon each other, and at this hour they seem to thicken in a whirl of the immediate future. God grant that these last two days of June, which loom up so portentous, may hasten our advent into Richmond more than the last forty-eight hours seem to have done!

Day before yesterday Porter's corps was strongly attacked in his position at the extreme right, near Mechanicsville, at a late hour in the afternoon. Not being on the ground, I am unable to give a detailed account; but the general features are given me by the brigade commanders.

McCall's Division bore the brunt of the encounter, though Morrell was severely engaged. Our superiority in artillery compensated in a measure for their superiority in numbers.

During long hours of the declining day and through half the night, anxious thousands of brave hearts who fight under Hooker and Keyes and Heintzelman and Sumner listened to that tremendous cannonading, and wondered how it fared with their brethren in arms.

Every attack was magnificently repelled, every inch of ground retained. Our loss was 300 to 400. It was the opinion of our generals that the position could have been maintained yesterday, but authentic information having reached General McClellan that the enemy had been re-enforced by Stonewall Jackson, our whole force was ordered to the Chickahominy, and the movement commenced during the night. The Eighth Illinois Cavalry, Colonel Farnsworth, formed the vigilant rear-guard. The enemy followed closely, took numbers of prisoners, including Company K, of the Pennsylvania Bucktails, and forced our quartermasters to burn at least $100,000 worth of stores. Captain Hooker, one of the best officers of the Eighth Illinois, was mortally wounded and left on the field. But the concentration of forces designed was effected with less loss than was doubtless expected when the order was given. Early in the forenoon of yesterday the pursued columns had taken position on the east bank of the Chickahominy and awaited the pursuers. They had not to wait long.

At this juncture your correspondent reached the field, and henceforth the narrative is that of an eye-witness.

The battle was fought in dense woods. Our forces were posted on the south side of a belt of forest on a line nearly two miles long, the general course of which was nearly parallel with the Chickahominy. The woods vary in depth from forty to one hundred rods; a small stream flows the entire length, and the ascent on either side is quite sharp. Cultivated fields cover the brow and crest of the hills on either side, and in the right rear of our position extend half a mile to the bottom-land of the Chickahominy. On the left the fringe of woods reaches to this bottom-land. At eleven A. M., when I reached the field, our pickets occupied the top of the hill across the ravine along its whole winding length. They reported a battery of the enemy at Gaines House, a mile north in his left rear, and numbers of Rebels in distinct view. This battery soon exchanged shots with guns on our right. Half an hour later they saluted our left with an occasional shell from a position so far westerly as to enfilade our line. Meanwhile an occasional report from a sharpshooter's rifle warned of the enemy's approach. The fire of our batteries on the right gradually grew more rapid, but the day wore away until it was three P. M., and there had been few casualties. *Would the enemy make a serious demonstration?* A volley from one company of a regiment on the left, directed at as many of the enemy who appeared on the crest of the opposite hill, causing them to hurry back, did not answer the question conclusively, for it was followed by dead silence. Twenty minutes later the answer came, and it was unmistakable—it was a tornado of musketry.

Butterfield's Brigade was on our extreme left, Martindale's at his right, Griffin's next, and at our extreme right Sykes' Division of regulars. McCall's Division formed the second line, and were held in reserve.

The ball opened with the centre, but only a moment, and the tornado swept right and left as if one current of electricity had discharged every man's musket. Our men disappeared, sending back cheerful shouts as they rushed into that dense wood where now corpses are thick as the trees. A spatter of Rebel lead lifted little puffs of dust on the hill from which, with straining eyes, I in vain sought to penetrate those dark recesses. A dull, heavy undercurrent of murmur as of the swarming of bees, the sharp ring of a random Minie overhead, the incessant roar of musketry, and now the wounded and the dead being borne out of those jaws of death tell how fierce is the fight. There are cheers and yells, for our men *cheer*, while they, like other savages, *yell.* But we drive them. As yet their superior numbers, enabling them to oppose always with fresh troops, do not tell. The fire slackens from left to right.

A tawny sergeant, whose moustache would vie with a Turkish pasha's tails—I see the fierce light in his eyes now—inquires of me where he shall carry the wounded man he bears on his back, and says, "The sinners are skedaddling!"

The battle had now raged three-fourths of an hour; Slocum's Division, which had already marched to the Chickahominy, was ordered up and McCall had not been engaged. The situation appeared promising. But only a small portion of the enemy's force had been beaten, and he was not disposed to cry quits. For the next hour the terrific firing would break out now at one point, anon at another, indicating that fresh columns were being continually pushed against our decimated lines. During this time every man of McCall's Pennsylvania Reserve was brought into action. Some time earlier his regiments had rushed at double-quick to the supporting positions assigned them, and had thrown themselves flat upon the ground till the order should come, "Up and at them!" At intervals, as some point in the line seemed weak, they went sternly into that wooded valley and shadow of death. Up to this time not a regiment had behaved unseemly. When relieved by new men, to be sure, they would straggle out like a dispersing mob, but they did not fail to "fall in" on the hill at the order. Sometimes a wounded man would be surrounded by a suspicious number of friends, but the skulkers bore no proportion to the true men.

Still at this hour, between half-past five and six, the situation was not hopeful. Beat back as many Rebel regiments as you would, fresh ones were poured into their places. The evidence is conclusive that no repelled assault—and there were a score of such—was renewed by the same column. Our coolest officers began to perceive that the enemy's force was overwhelming—probably 75,000, and 25,000 larger than had been anticipated or provided for.

At this time, Slocum's Division (late Franklin's) was brought into action. There were no more reserves, save cavalry. Every available regiment was fighting or had become exhausted in strength and in cartridges.

I saw Slocum's men go into the fight, and they did it handsomely, the brigades being conducted to their positions amid a murderous fire, by Lieut. Fred. Mead of his staff, who, sick for a month, left his couch for the battle-field. But I confess, from this time on, so great was the confusion that I know nothing circumstantial of the movements and fighting of the several brigades and regiments of any of the divisions, notwithstanding I was coaxed some distance into the woods by Mr. Crountze of "The World," who seemed bent on securing a place among the martyrs.

My note-book says that, at six o'clock, the enemy commenced a determined attack on our extreme left, evidently with a design of flanking us. It was an awful firing that resounded from that smoke-clouded valley,—not heavier than some in the earlier part of the engagement, but more steady and determined. I am told that some men on the other side and farther up the river saw more than a dozen Rebel regiments march in at that point, and, remaining only a few minutes, file out a little distance up the ravine. It was only by overbearing exhausted men with fresh ones that the enemy succeeded in turning that flank, as at length he did succeed, only too well. And he accomplished it in three-quarters of an hour. At the expiration of that time our officers judiciously ordered their men to fall back; the order was not obeyed so judiciously, for they ran back broken, disordered, routed. Simultaneously the wounded and skulkers about the buildings used as hospitals caught a panic, whether from a few riderless horses plunging madly across the field, or from instantaneously scenting the rout, does not appear. A motley mob started pell-mell for the bridges. They were overtaken by many just from the woods, and it seemed as if Bull Run were to be repeated.

As the infantry betook themselves from the point of attack, some twenty guns, fortunately posted in the morning for such an emergency, and which had not yet made a sign, opened a terrific fire of canister at short range. The enemy recoiled. The bridge of Lodi was not half so terrible. Until night set in, until the Valley of the Chickahominy was canopied with sulphur, until their ammunition was exhausted—and many of them went upon the field with over two-hundred rounds—did those guns hold the raging enemy at bay.

Meanwhile, the panic extended. Scores of gallant officers endeavored to rally and re-form the stragglers, but in vain, while many officers forgot the pride of their shoulder-straps and the honor of their manhood, and herded with sneaks and cowards. O that I had known the names of those officers I saw, the brave and the cowardly, that here, now, I might reward and punish by directing upon each individual the respect or the contempt of a whole people!

That scene was not one to be forgotten. Scores of riderless, terrified horses dashing in every direction; thick-flying bullets singing by, admonishing of danger; every minute a man struck down; wagons and ambulances and cannon blockading the way; wounded men limping and groaning and bleeding amid the throng; officers and civilians denouncing and reasoning and entreating, and being insensibly borne along with the mass; the sublime cannonading; the clouds of battle-smoke, and the sun just disappearing, large and blood-red—I cannot picture it, but I see it, and always shall.

Among those most earnest in withstaying the frightened host was ex-Governor Wood of Illinois. A large, handsome old man, with a flowing white beard and the voice of a Stentor. I should not have been astonished had those poor, bewildered men taken him for some old patriarch risen from the dead and calling to them; *had* one risen from the dead they would not have heeded him. I thought, too, of the old regicide who left his concealment to head the simple Puritan villagers against the savages, and then vanished as quickly, leaving his appearance as the tradition of a heavenly visitant.

About this time a new battery and two fresh regiments of Meagher's Brigade were brought up, headed by that officer. The mob parted, and they passed rapidly through, cheering as they went. The answering cheers were sickly.

I do not wish to be harsh with these men. Many of them had fought and marched all the previous day and night. The day was excessively hot. The men were exhausted. I do not think they left the field with an average of two cartridges to the man. If there was a single regiment that did not go into the battle with spirit and maintain it with credit, I do not know it. Besides, he must be a brave and a strong man who whips three of equal training. This much in extenuation. Add to it the statement of several generals that men never fought better. Still, I cannot refrain from expressing the one thought that possessed me at the time,—the fact that 10,000 men were in full retreat.

Some time after the main body had passed on, when that stream had become decently small, in company with Governor Wood, I rode to find the Illinois Cavalry, and came upon them stretched across the plain halting every unwounded man. They had cooped up several thousands, but the task of re-forming them was found impossible by even such officers as their Colonel and Major Clendenning, and they were at length permitted to continue rearward.

I crossed the Chickahominy at eleven P. M., at which time comparative order had been restored. The enemy were in possession of our hospitals and the battle-field, but we still showed a determined front. It was not known by the brigadier-generals whether we should try to hold the position the next day, or cross the river during the night.

At six o'clock this morning I rode to the bridge, with the intention of re-crossing, but was some distance off when I heard the explosion that destroyed it, the force having passed over mainly after midnight. It is impossible at this day to estimate our loss. But few of the dead were brought from the field, and not one-half the wounded. Hundreds of the latter were brought as far as the river, but could not be brought over before the destruction of the bridges. Basing my opinion on the number who were brought over (about 800), and the proportion that number must bear to the remainder, I estimate, the entire wounded at 3500 and the killed at 800. How many prisoners and what amount of stores are lost, it is even still more difficult to estimate. I judge but few stores and several thousand prisoners. The loss in officers is particularly severe.

AN ACCUSATION OF BETRAYAL:
VIRGINIA, JUNE 1862

George B. McClellan to Edwin M. Stanton

Even before the Gaines's Mill defeat, General McClellan determined to give up his campaign and retreat across the Peninsula to the James River and the protection of the navy's gunboats. This telegram to the secretary of war reveals his greatly distorted view of events. The concluding paragraph so shocked the head of the War Department telegraph office that he deleted it before delivering the telegram to Stanton.

Savage Station June 28 12.20 am

I now know the full history of the day. On this side of the river—the right bank—we repulsed several very strong attacks. On the left bank our men did all that men could do, all that soldiers could accomplish—but they were overwhelmed by vastly superior numbers even after I brought my last reserves into action. The loss on both sides is terrible—I believe it will prove to be the most desperate battle of the war. The sad remnants of my men behave as men—those battalions who fought most bravely & suffered most are still in the best order. My regulars were superb & I count upon what are left to turn another battle in company with their gallant comrades of the Volunteers. Had I (20,000) twenty thousand or even (10,000) ten thousand fresh troops to use tomorrow I could take Richmond, but I have not a man in reserve & shall be glad to cover my retreat & save the material & personnel of the Army.

If we have lost the day we have yet preserved our honor & no one need blush for the Army of the Potomac. I have lost this battle because my force was too small. I again repeat that I am not responsible for this & I say it with the earnestness of a General who feels in his heart the loss of every brave man who has been needlessly sacrificed today. I still hope to retrieve our fortunes, but to do this the Govt must view the matter in the same earnest light that I do—you must send me very large reinforcements, & send them at once.

I shall draw back to this side of the Chickahominy & think I can withdraw all our material. Please understand that in this battle we have lost nothing but men & those the best we have.

In addition to what I have already said I only wish to say to the Presdt that I think he is wrong, in regarding me as ungenerous when I said that my force was too weak. I merely reiterated a truth which today has been too plainly proved. I should have gained this battle with (10,000) ten thousand fresh men. If at this instant I could dispose of (10,000) ten thousand fresh men I could gain the victory tomorrow.

I know that a few thousand men more would have changed this battle from a defeat to a victory—as it is the Govt must not & cannot hold me responsible for the result.

I feel too earnestly tonight—I have seen too many dead & wounded comrades to feel otherwise than that the Govt has not sustained this Army. If you do not do so now the game is lost.

If I save this Army now I tell you plainly that I owe no thanks to you or any other persons in Washington—you have done your best to sacrifice this Army.

G B McClellan

Hon E M Stanton

June 28, 1862

"THE PRESENT CONDITION OF THE WAR": WASHINGTON, D.C., JUNE 1862

Abraham Lincoln to William H. Seward

Secretary of State Seward took this letter with him to New York for a conference with Northern governors, intending to craft a call for new troops. Seward reversed the usual process and persuaded the governors to "respectfully request" of Lincoln "that you at once call upon the several States for such number of men as may be required. . . ." Seward backdated the request to June 28 to avoid any note of panic over McClellan's failings on the Peninsula. Lincoln hastened to "comply" with the governors' call, setting the figure at 300,000. The evacuation of Corinth in northern Mississippi that the President mentions saw the Confederates' western army evade the clutches of General Halleck's hugely superior force.

Hon. W. H. Seward — Executive Mansion
My dear Sir — June 28. 1862.

My view of the present condition of the War is about as follows:

The evacuation of Corinth, and our delay by the flood in the Chicahominy, has enabled the enemy to concentrate too much force in Richmond for McClellan to successfully attack. In fact there soon will be no substantial rebel force any where else. But if we send all the force from here to McClellan, the enemy will, before we can know of it, send a force from Richmond and take Washington. Or, if a large part of the Western Army be brought here to McClellan, they will let us have Richmond, and retake Tennessee, Kentucky, Missouri &c. What should be done is to hold what we have in the West, open the Mississippi, and, take Chatanooga & East Tennessee, without more—a reasonable force should, in every event, be kept about Washington for it's protection. Then let the country give us a hundred thousand new troops in the shortest possible time, which added to McClellan, directly or indirectly, will take Richmond, without endangering any other place which we now hold—and will substantially end the war. I expect to maintain this contest until successful, or till I die, or am conquered, or my term expires, or Congress or the country forsakes me; and I would publicly appeal to the country for this new force, were it not that I fear a general panic and stampede would follow—so hard is it to have a thing understood as it really is. I think the new force should be all, or nearly all infantry, principally because such can be raised most cheaply and quickly. Yours very truly

A. LINCOLN

THE UNION RETREAT:
VIRGINIA, JUNE–JULY 1862

Charles B. Haydon: Journal, June 25–July 1, 1862

Lieutenant Charles B. Haydon, 2nd Michigan, served in Philip Kearny's division, Army of the Potomac. His journal describes his experiences in the Seven Days. He witnessed the first battle, on June 25 at Oak Grove, a stunted Union advance. Lee's offensive at Mechanicsville and Gaines's Mill north of the Chickahominy was only heard by Haydon. In the retreat across the Peninsula the bitterest fighting he experienced was at Glendale on June 30, where Lee very nearly cut the Potomac army in half. Haydon was not engaged but under fire at the conclusion of the Seven Days, at Malvern Hill on the James. Despite the Union victory at Malvern Hill, McClellan continued his retreat to Harrison's Landing, farther down the James. The Seven Days' Battles cost the Confederates 20,204 men killed, wounded, or missing, while Union losses totaled 15,855.

JUNE 25, 1862 Was a clear cool day. Our Regt. & the 3d Mich. started for picket at 7 A.M. There was a pretty general movement of the troops in our Div. and in Hooker's. It is understood that certain parts of the line are to be advanced. Our left is stationary but a line of skirmishers is thrown forward extending toward the right across our picket front & Hooker's & perhaps farther. The skirmishers advance slowly a short distance when a fire is opened on Hooker's line. It gradually increased to heavy volleys & continued till about 11 A.M. when our men having gained the desired ground ceased to advance.

Everything was quiet till abt 2 P.M. when the enemy opened with field pieces & the musketry was soon after briskly renewed. The musketry soon slackened & the field pieces were reported as taken & retaken by bayonet charges. Four pieces were brought out into the edge of the woods & fired slowly till near night. The trees & bushes rendered them of little service. Abt 5 P.M. the Rebs raised a great shout & charged the battery. Our men lying concealed cut them terribly as they advanced. They gave way unable to stand the fire. For near half an hour there was a continuous & very heavy infantry fire. Several charges were made. The clear, ringing Union cheers & the sharp wild yells of the rebels were every few minutes heard with great distinctness. All we know is that the desired ground was without very great loss gained & held. The battle extended up to the right of our line but our Regt. was not engaged.

JUNE 26 Was a very quiet day till abt 3 P.M. when far to the right was heard the heavy but indistinct roar of musketry. The cannon opened soon after. From that time till 8 P.M. there was the heaviest cannonade I have yet heard. It was continued with great regularity and at the rate of 25 to 40 shots per minute. At dark far along the line toward the right great cheering was heard. It passed rapidly along to our camp. News soon came to us of a great battle & victory at Mechanicsville. The camps were wild with enthusiasm. Our joy was not less lively but we could not give vent to it in the same manner. I got most awfully wet & muddy going up & down the line carrying orders & cautioning the men to unusual vigilance lest the enemy should on some other part of the line attempt to redeem their fortunes. Save the heavy rumble of artillery & baggage wagons along our own lines the stillness of the night was hardly disturbed by a sound.

JUNE 27 We came off picket at 10 A.M. We were called to the rifle pits at one & remained till sundown. The firing on the right was renewed at daylight. It continued till 10 A.M., a part of the time with great rapidity. Towards night there was firing far to the north & much farther to the rear than was agreeable. Troops were seen soon after moving at double quick back along the R.R. This at once suggested that something was wrong but our men were so tired & sleepy that they paid little attention. They seemed to feel a sort of sullen, dogged determination to fight to the last where they were & not to move for anybody. A few more days & nights like the past few & they would as soon die as live. Soon after dark we were called out again & remained till after 10. The picket line is nearly broken up. The 63d Pa. ran like sheep as soon as they were fired on.

JUNE 28 We were called to the rifle pits at 2 1/2 A.M. and remained till 7 when we went in for breakfast but returned immediately after. Before daylight there was fighting far to the right. We could see the explosion of the shells but could not hear the guns. For several reasons I think it best to bring this book (a pocket memorandum) to a close. I cannot send it away & I do not wish it to fall into the hands of the rebels. It is possible it may if it remains with me.

Things just now are checkered. The right wing has fallen back & we are ready for a move of some kind. I dont know what it may be. If a retreat we are the rear guard. If this should be the last news from me good bye all at home. May God bless & prosper you. Arthur will use what money I leave to complete his education. We all realize our situation but everyone is calm, cheerful & determined. We carry 150 rounds of ammunition & intend that the enemy shall have reason to remember Kearney's Div. If I fall it will be in vain for you to attempt to recover my body. Having spoken of the dark side I may say that we by no means acknowledge that we are not to be victorious. I have still great hope of success in the coming battles. I half believe that this retreat is not forced. If it be we are still powerful to hold our own in a new position.

Arthur: my boy, if I should not see you again be of good cheer & console yourself with the thought that I died in a good cause. I would like right well to see you, Father, Eliza & all for a few minutes but it will make little difference in the end. But I have already said too much. We mean to send you news of the greatest victory of the war or at least to make like work for those who shall follow us. All the baggage has been sent away & the road is clear. The most perfect quiet prevails. The men are most of them talking in calm, subdued tones indicative of settled purpose. A few are slowly & silently walking to & fro communing with themselves. The weather is very hot. Ever since the battle of Williamsburgh I have seen some indications of what may happen.

There are many N.Y. & Penn. troops in our army. I have little confidence in them. If they were from Michigan, God bless the state, or from any of the western or New England states there would not be a shadow of doubt as to their conduct. If they run as is quite possible, we may be overwhelmed by numbers in spite of all exertions.

What tries my heart the worst is the disaster to the country if we are beaten. It is awful. Do not however despair. They will lose at least as many men as we & ours will be easier replaced. Wage the war to the last desolate acre of the accursed South. We are sure to conquer in the end. This defeat if it be one can be repaired in 30 days. If they are victorious they cannot live if we hold our ground in other places. I hope soon to see clear day through the clouds & uncertainty which now surround us. I intend to relate the events of this war beneath the shade of the glorious maples where we have passed so many happy hours.

Father: be the result what it may I thank you for having always been to me the kindest & best of parents. Eliza: placed as you were in a peculiar and difficult position as regards me you have always been more than I could have asked. Give my good wishes to all my old acquaintances. Arthur, I advise you to make your education liberal if health will permit but by all means look to that as your help will be needed at home before the other children are old enough to assist. I wish I could see the little ones. I feel a lively interest in them although we are still unacquainted. I have written thus because we all believe that our situation is one of uncommon danger.

JUNE 29 I was kept up all night by a multitude of orders. The tents were struck at 10 P.M. There was a light rain towards morning. We have destroyed everything we cannot carry. At 6 A.M. we moved off by the left flank to our left & rear halting near a sawmill. The rest of the brigade here passed us & went on further to the rear.

Everything is very quiet. There has been no firing since yesterday noon. When everything had passed we retired beyond the second line of rifle pits. We then deployed 5 Co's. across our front abt 1/4 mile off & halted till one P.M. We then fell back abt 3/4 of a mile. At this time Richardson's Div. was sharply engaged near the Williamsburgh road.

At 3 P.M. we retire still farther. The rest of the brigade has gone on & we are only waiting for our skirmishers. Hooker's Div. occupy the road. We have peremptory orders to join the brigade & attempt to pass them. We have to open right & left & a battery passes at full run. We continue retreating through the woods & bushes on each side & some confusion arises. The road becomes narrower & the confusion increases. Some other

Regts. try to crowd through & they make matters still worse. Our Regt. & most of the others are cool & perfectly manageable. The confusion is due entirely to want of efficiency on the part of the officers. The column should at once be halted till order is restored. More artillery passes. A Regt. at double quick cuts ours in two between the 3d & 4th Co's. Three Co's. continue on & 7 Co's. are thrown off to the left on another road. We went abt 1/2 mile when finding that matters were becoming worse the 38th N.Y. and our 3 Co's. filed out of the road & halted till the others passed. When the road is clear we move on again. Gen. Kearney orders us to go slowly as our 3 Co's. are "the rear guard of all God's Creation." This was an encouraging prospect for us with a total of 100 men.

We reach the swamp at Jordan's ford, are ordered to cross, to go to the Charles City road & hold it agt all comers. We cross the first ford, then a second one abt 60 rods wide with water 2 1/2 feet deep. We proceed abt a mile when a Co. of the 3d Maine encounter the enemy. We are deployed through the woods to support them. The force of the enemy is small & soon gives way.

Finding that they were in force nearby Gen. Kearney ordered us to fall back across the fords. Our Co's. were left to cover the retreat. I had hardly any expectation of escaping. The enemy moved down rapidly but our men were soon out of the way & we retired in line with a loss of only 3 men, on the extreme left of the line, who were taken by a party who tried to cut us off from the ford. Several smart volleys & a number of shells followed us but did no harm. We crossed the fords in good time, leaving other troops to guard them & made for another ford 3 miles lower down.

It was now dark. We marched rapidly & notwithstanding their prayers & entreaties we were compelled to leave by the roadside some wounded men of the 3d Maine who had been brought across both fords. We reached the ford abt 9 P.M. & learned that Hooker's Div. & the balance of our Regt. had crossed an hour & a half before. We considered ourselves fortunate to have got thus far though we were apprehensive that we should find the Rebs at the other end of the ford. We plunged in, crossed safely & marched till 11 P.M. The night was very dark

& we did not dare to proceed farther. Nearly choking for want of water we lay down & rested or slept for 3 hours. We were disturbed once by a loose horse which came galloping over us & once by picket firing.

JUNE 30 We were up at 2 A.M. We moved forward a mile & found the rest of the Regt. We move on 1/2 mile farther & halted in a fine open field to rest. We here made coffee, the first we had had in 24 hours. It refreshed us very much. We have nothing but hard crackers to eat. At noon the enemy appeared. We marched 1 1/2 miles at double quick & then formed our line. Our brigade was formed in columns in the woods & remained there an hour.

There is heavy cannonading on our right. We move back 1/2 mile farther. Musketry opens on our left, in front & soon after on our right. We advance to the front where a low, rude breastwork of logs, rails, stones, turf, anything to stop bullets had been hastily thrown up. Two batteries are in position. We are in the edge of woods, before us is an open field 60 rods wide in the wood on the other side of which is the enemy. The 20th Ind. were already at the work & there was no room for us. We move back abt 10 rods & lie flat down waiting for our turn.

The Rebs charge three times in heavy columns determined to break the line. The batteries double shotted with canister played on them at short range, some of the time not more than 10 rods, for an hour & a half. They were at the same time enveloped by the fire of the infantry. I never before saw such slaughter. The head of the column seemed to sink into the ground. Beyond a certain point they could not come. Four Regts. from behind the work kept up an incessant fire which was replied to by the enemy with equal rapidity.

Things remain thus till sundown when the batteries run out of ammunition. We relieve the 20th at the pits & the fire is carried on with renewed vigor. The enemy display a courage & determination known only to Americans. Darkness comes & the full moon shines forth in all its beauty but its mild, peaceful light only serves to render our aim more certain. For an hour after dark there is a steady succession of flashes which are almost blinding. The enemy cease firing. We give tremendous cheers. They send us a terrible volley which we return. Both parties then give three cheers & the day's work is done.

The Rebs were busy till 2 oclock carrying off their wounded. The wounded of 21 different Regts. lay on the field before us, as we learned from the Rebs themselves. Their cries & groans loaded the air, some calling for comrades, some for water, some praying to be killed & others swearing because they were not carried off the field. Our men lay close & the loss in our Regt. is light. The enemy sometimes in looking after their wounded came within a few feet of our picket line but we did not trouble them.

JULY 1, 1862 Gen. Richardson by hard fighting opened the road on which we are to retreat. While we held the enemy in front the army nearly all retreated. At 2 A.M. we withdraw as quietly as possible & commence our retreat. Our dead & all the wounded who could not walk had to be left. It was sad indeed the way the poor fellows begged to be taken along. It could not be done. The most of them will die. The Rebs cannot even take care of their own wounded. Our Regt. was separated by some runaway teams & troops coming in on another road got between the parts.

At sunrise we came to a large, open, undulating field in sight of James River. It was as beautiful a country as my eyes ever beheld. The cultivated field interspersed with belts & clusters of timber & dotted with delightful residences extended several miles. The hills were quite high but the slopes gradual & free from abruptness. Wheat was in the shock, oats were ready for the harvest & corn was abt waist high. All were of most luxuriant growth. The clusters of buildings are almost like villages.

All parts of the field are favorable for Cav. & Arty. There was hard fighting on a part of it yesterday. The country was laid waste, the fences burned, the harvested grain was used by the soldiers for beds & the unharvested was trodden into the ground. The field was covered with troops. I spent two hours in ineffectual search after our lost Co's. They rejoined us soon after I returned. Here we hoped for a little rest but it was not more than an hour before we had to fall in.

We made a circuit of about 2 miles then halted & our brigade was drawn up in a column by battalions on the back side of a gently sloping hill on the crest of which were two batteries. We had been here but a short time when the enemy appeared on the crest of another hill abt a mile off. The inclination of the ground was so slight that our brigade as well as the supports of their batteries could be seen from several points. Both parties opened with shot, shell & shrapnel. We had nothing to do but lie on the ground in the burning sun & take things just as they came.

Their shots were not wild. Almost the first shot (12 lbs. solid) struck among the N.Y. 1st as they lay on the ground killing two & wounding another. One of them was thrown more than 5 ft. into the air. A shell burst in the ground not 4 ft. from Benson's head. One struck abt 10 ft. short of me in the ground & exploded nearly burying me in sand & stubble. I caught a ball from a shrapnel shell before it stopped rolling. Two others struck within reach of me. Three men of our Co. were wounded by one shot. Most of their shell burst abt 150 feet in the air & the fragments scattered over a great space. The wounded were carried to the rear in considerable numbers. The loss of the brigade is 85.

The scene was exciting but I was so exhausted that despite the noise & the bullets I went to sleep. I know not how long I should have slept if the order "Fall in" had not aroused me. The 2d moved off to support another battery. I felt weak & quite used up. When I tried to lead off at double quick I reeled & came near falling. I certainly should have fallen if we had gone far. Presently the fire slackened in our locality. There is a long line of artillery on this range of hills. On a higher one in our rear are a line of heavier pieces which fire over us. From the river in rear of us the gunboats fire by signals over all with 200 lb. shells.

The firing towards night was very heavy, musketry brisk & frequent charges. Our loss is moderate, that of the enemy very severe. With another hour of daylight I believe we could utterly rout them. The cannonading was kept up till long after dark. I went onto a hill in front & saw 50 pieces of artillery playing into a piece of woods where the Rebs had taken shelter. This day's fighting has been the grandest I ever saw. It reminded me of the pictures of great battles in Europe. If our army had been fresh I should have liked all to have been risked on a battle on this field.

WOUNDED AT GLENDALE:
VIRGINIA, JUNE–JULY 1862

Asa D. Smith: Narrative of the Seven Days' Battles

Corporal Smith of the 16th Massachusetts Infantry served in Joseph Hooker's division during the Seven Days. His narrative begins on June 29 as the Army of the Potomac retreated toward the James River. Seriously wounded at Glendale on June 30, Smith eventually reached a hospital at the Naval Academy at Annapolis where he began his recovery. "I guess you can't bite cartridges, nor eat hardtack," said his doctor, who recommended Smith for a discharge that was granted on July 25, 1862.

WE WERE awakened at an early hour, and strange sights met our eyes. We had been told that everything on the right was favorable to our arms, and had no reason to disbelieve it. On this morning the first thing I noticed was that the tents of the officers were cut into ribbons, then that the Quartermaster's stores had been fired. Great piles of bread and meat were on the fire, men were busy banging the stocks of rifles against the trees and throwing the barrels into fires to ruin them. Barrels of sugar and whiskey were being emptied into pools of brackish water, in fact everything was being destroyed that could not be carried. There was an immense amount of property destroyed. We were ordered to tear our overcoats into four pieces and leave them. Then to sling knapsacks and fill our cartridge boxes, haversacks were replenished, and a hearty breakfast eaten.

As soon as possible we were marched into the entrenchments, where we found double the number of troops that usually manned them. I soon discovered that all the artillery had been withdrawn, not a piece being in sight.

It was strange to see the different ideas the men had as to what had happened; so great had been their faith in "Little Mac" that it was almost impossible for some of them to believe it could mean anything but a rapid pursuit of a retreating enemy. We actually thought we had been victorious on the right and were going to move forward. As for myself, as soon as I perceived the destruction going on around me, I felt that things were going wrong, and that it could only mean a withdrawal of our lines.

One thing was noticeable, that no one seemed at all disheartened or worried, everyone said, "We'll make them skedaddle yet." Everyone seemed to think that it was only a temporary affair, and that we might whip them during the movements that were to take place, and that we were fully able to do it.

It was a bit foggy for a while so that one could not see a great distance; but as it came daylight the fog cleared away, and far to the right and left the same conditions appeared.

We were commanded to make no noise, and in a short time the troops began to withdraw, toward the Chickahominy. After falling back some distance, the brigade left the road and filed into a field on the left. As we marched I saw that there were many guns in position on the edge of the wood on our right, and large numbers of men behind them.

Soon we were brought to a front in a place where timber had been cut but not carried away, there being several trees lying on the ground. We were ordered to lie down in position, the brigade being formed left in front, bringing the 16th in the front line.

The ground in our front rose gradually for a short distance, and a railroad cut ran nearly at right angles with our line. On the edge of the cut were three batteries of artillery (eighteen pieces) so placed as to nearly enfilade it, and we were to support them.

About the time we got into position, we heard the rebel yell as they came upon our abandoned works, and knew that they would soon be upon us. Soon artillery and musketry fire began up the line of the railroad, nearer to Richmond, and very quickly came toward us; and shell began to come in our direction. We remained here under this fire for about an hour and a half, and did not see a rebel soldier, as the infantry in the neighborhood were trying to advance down the cut, thus being entirely out of our sight.

The infantry fire became quite heavy, and remained so for at least an hour. Quite a number of unexploded shell and shrapnel came over, but only one did any damage. I saw this one coming straight for us, but it was a little high and struck in the lines of the Pennsylvania 26th, killing a man. As he was lying on the ground it tore off one arm, one leg, and the foot from the remaining leg. The victim gave one shriek and died in a few moments.

After a time the firing ceased, and we were marched to the rear at a lively pace.

The roads were crowded with troops of all arms, making it hard work to move; but we were pushed unmercifully. After some time we reached Savage Station on the railroad, and found troops marching through the village toward the James River. Every road was full, and all were hustling lively.

Great quantities of supplies were being destroyed here, one large warehouse being filled with clothing. All were burned.

On we went toward White Oak Swamp, through the narrow roads, through a growth of tall pine which shut out the breeze, while the sun's rays beat upon us fiercely. The air was full of dust, so that it was impossible to tell the color of anyone's hair or of his uniform. The pace was hurried, and we found ourselves getting short of water and becoming exhausted.

I staggered in the ranks, but did not fall out as did many. At last when it seemed as if I could go but little farther, I was refreshed by a swallow of vinegar kindly given me by a comrade, and struggled along until we reached the swamp, where in company with hundreds of others I got down upon my hands and knees and drank from the rut in the road, where men, horses, mules, guns, etc., had been passing all day.

No time was given us to fill canteens, and we pushed on through the swamp and over White Oak Creek, not coming to a halt till sunset, when we bivouacked in a field on the right of the road, the opposite side being occupied by the 11th U.S. Infantry. Orders were issued to lie behind the stacks, and without tents, just unrolling a blanket, and holding ourselves in readiness to march at two minutes' notice. As soon as relieved, I started after water for my tentmates as well as myself; taking canteens and dippers while they made ready to get supper, gathering wood, etc.

After going some distance I found a well near a house, but was unable to get water as the Headquarters Cavalry Escort had control of it, and no one else could get near it. Hearing of a brook at some distance ahead in a piece of woods I pushed on, and found it; but also found several hundred soldiers washing their feet in it. I followed their example; and after filling my canteens and dippers returned to the regiment just in season to find out that we should have to content ourselves with hardtack and cold water, as General Grover came along and ordered all fires out, saying that they would cause us to be shelled out within a half hour. (As I look back upon this day I do not see how we could have gone through it with so few stragglers. It was a terrible march.)

We lay all night behind the stacks, ready to move at a moment's notice, and at daylight June 30 were aroused and ordered to get breakfast. So I skirmished around and traded some sugar for coffee, and we soon had hot coffee and hardtack for a meal. Shortly after eating, we were ordered to fall in, and were sent through the fields to where the Charles City road was crossed by one leading down from Richmond, and found the road filled with wagons headed for the James River, which were hurrying along as fast as possible. They were in single file, and no wagon was allowed to pass another. If anything broke about wagon or harness, the mules were detached from the wagon and it was pulled out of the line and burned, together with its contents. This procession was passing nearly all day.

The brigade was posted across the Richmond Road, and the division extended to the left with the 1st Division (General Philip Kearny's) beyond that, while the 2nd Corps (General Edwin V. Sumner) joined us on the right. It did not appear that the officers feared an attack here, nevertheless about noon the line was advanced a short distance toward Richmond and posted on higher ground, the 16th being in the advanced line of the division. It was understood that the Pennsylvania Reserves (Generals George G. Meade and George A. McCall) were in our front, and this was probably the reason for not expecting attack. General Hooker and staff rode up an eminence in our rear, and after looking about, the General said, "This would be a good place for a battery; but I guess we won't need it today."

Here we stacked arms, and proceeded to make ourselves as comfortable as possible. There had been considerable fighting about two miles to the right of our position, where Stonewall Jackson was trying to cross White Oak Swamp, and shortly after this the firing grew very heavy in that direction.

In the course of an hour or two, skirmishing commenced in front of McCall, followed very quickly by heavy firing of both artillery and infantry. In a little while it appeared to be nearer, and we were called to arms. We were formed behind a worm fence on a side hill, and in a few minutes a battery came galloping up and took the position previously noted by General Hooker.

Before long the Pennsylvanians began to approach us at a run, and attempted to break to the rear. We gathered in all that we could and reformed them (or part of them) in our rear. Very soon the enemy's artillery opened and quickly got the range, the shells bursting in the air just in front so as to send the pieces directly among us. This continued for some time while the advance forces were being driven. Without any warning there came a sudden, sharp crack followed closely by others, and the screeching of shell from the battery in the rear. The guns were so near that it seemed as though our ear drums would burst; but in a few moments we became somewhat accustomed to the sounds, and minded them very little.

The enemy's shell flew thick and fast, and there were some close calls. One piece came down and grazed the side of my left shoe, partly burying itself in the ground. As I stooped and got hold of it, the Captain saw it, and said, "A miss is as good as a mile, Corporal," and I felt the same way about it.

About this time the enemy got into long rifle range, and began firing. From their position in the bush they could see us, while themselves hidden. The Colonel, wishing to hold his fire and keep the men steady, began to practice them in the manual of arms. (Some years after the war, I heard General Hooker tell the Massachusetts House of Representatives of this, saying that "he had never seen it better done on parade.") The enemy began to climb the rising ground toward our position, and the

Colonel ordered that no man fire until he gave the command, when the front rank was to fire, then the rear rank, after which we were "to load and fire at will."

The men were at the highest pitch of excitement, but so well disciplined were they that this order was obeyed to the letter. Then the men began to cheer (the gray trousers could now be seen below the cloud of smoke, as they steadily approached), when the Colonel said, "Remember the State you come from," whereupon the adjutant called for "three cheers for the old Bay State," which were given with a will.

General Hooker approached the front and said, "Give them hell, boys," and the fight was on.

The ground on the side hill in front was clear of trees for some little distance; but on the right of the road in front of the 2nd Corps the woods came well up to the line. On our left front was an orchard of apple trees (apparently), and sharpshooters were concealed amid the branches and had kept up a steady fire from the first.

The Johnnies climbed the hill with a rush, causing the line to waver for a moment, then it closed up and gave them a murderous fire.

Just as the shock came, I turned my head to the right to speak a word of defiance in the ear of Corporal William E. Eldridge, and before it was turned square to the front something hit me. It felt as though an immense timber had struck me end first, with great force. It was not painful; but seemed to partly daze me. I did not fall, but dropped my rifle and put my hand to my chin, and found that it felt as though torn to pieces. Lieutenant Meserve saw me and told me to go to the rear as soon as possible. From the direction that the ball came, I am of the opinion that it was fired by one of the sharpshooters in the trees.

I started for the 3rd Corps field hospital, which was established in the Willis Church, a small building on the Quaker Road (so called) leading to Malvern Hill. It was but a short distance in the rear, and the nearest way was through the wood and was marked by small hospital flags at intervals. On my way I found two or three small, coarse towels which evidently had been thrown away by some soldier, and used them to try to staunch the hemorrhage, which was quite severe.

On arriving at the field hospital station, I found several surgeons busily at work, with men wounded in apparently about every conceivable manner. The operating tables were made from the seats of the church, placed upon empty beef or pork barrels.

I got a seat beside a young rebel who was shot in one foot and waited for a time, but as nobody came to my assistance I went outside and found D. Harris Clark of Co. B, who was on detail and was an old acquaintance. He found a young New York surgeon and prevailed upon him to attend to my case. Upon his coming (as I could not talk) I made him understand that I wished to know if I would recover, upon which he shook his head and said, "Doubtful." And, after a short interval, "I have seen men recover who were hurt as badly as you are."

This was not very encouraging; but somehow hope was strong and I made up my mind to try for it.

The surgeon took a bandage and, passing it under my chin, pinned the ends together on the top of my head, and said, "This is all I can do for you now." Then he ordered Clark to take my equipment off and get a board and lay me upon it alongside the church, which he did, using my cartridge box and haversack for a pillow.

I lay on the side nearest the field of battle, and so near that very often the bullets would strike the building, but I was not struck.

The fight lasted some two or three hours, during which time I remained in this position, and later got up and sat on a plank placed between two trees near the road.

During the evening the surgeon and assistant surgeon of the regiment (Drs. Jewett and Whiston) found me and looked me over as best they could under the circumstances, and Dr. Jewett told me that he would operate in the morning, saying, "Keep up your courage; we'll make quite a man out of you." I suppose he did not mean to intimate that I previously had not been one. At any rate, it gave me more hope. Then he told Clark to take me into the little schoolhouse where I could sleep on the floor with other wounded.

Then the surgeons started off, and in a moment Dr. Whiston came back and put his fingers into my mouth; then he called Dr. Jewett, saying, "Doctor, his jaw is dislocated on the left side." Dr. Jewett came back, examined it again, and reduced the dislocation. After the dr's. departure, Clark took me to the schoolhouse where I found a great many wounded, among others Lieutenant Colonel Meacham of the regiment.

I lay upon the floor, suffering severely for want of water, and feeling very faint. Someone called Lieutenant Colonel Meacham's attention to me, when he handed me a small flask containing brandy and told me to take a little, but be sparing as it was all he had. After a time I got easier and must have fallen into a doze, from which I was awakened about 2 o'clock A.M. by hearing a call, "Get up and skedaddle; the Johnnies will be here in half an hour."

I got out and met Dr. Jewett, who ordered Comrade Clark and another man to carry me on a stretcher. This they attempted to do; but soon found it was impossible, as the narrow road was filled with columns of infantry and artillery, marching side by side and being pushed to the utmost by their officers.

I got up on my feet, and seeing a Massachusetts regiment (15th) passing I got among the color guard and attempted to keep up with them. As I was very weak I must have bothered them some, and one of them told me to get out, upon which the color sergeant rebuked him, telling him that "he might be wounded some time," and told me to "stay with them as long as I wished."

In the early forenoon we came to open ground, and in front was rising ground, a long slope, with buildings at the top: the now well-known Malvern Hill. On the right as you faced it was a deep ravine through which ran a small stream (Turkey Creek). This hill was about three miles from the James River.

When we came in sight, our forces were marching in every direction about it and forming lines of battle as fast as possible. Under ordinary circumstances it would have been a spectacle well worth seeing. But I was in a terrible condition, and left the 15th regiment and started up the hill by the road toward the river. When I had gotten about one third of the distance, the lieutenant in charge of a battery just swung into position across the road saw me; he came and advised me to get away as soon as possible, as there would be a fight there. So I trudged along, hungry and thirsty, with no canteen or dipper, unable to eat if

I had food and barely able to swallow any drink, if I had been possessed of any.

The day was very warm and my progress was necessarily slow, as I had to stop for rest at short intervals. Quite a number of ambulances passed me; but I was not allowed to occupy one of them.

After some time the fleet in the river opened fire through the creek so as to protect our left flank, and threw a great many 11-inch shells over my head. These shells were known to the soldiers as "dutch ovens," and sometimes were called "blacksmith's shops."

Some time in the afternoon I met Sergeant Matthias Brigham of my company, who was a townsman of mine. He was in charge of a squad of eight men who had been to the river with a wagon train. In the squad were two men of the company (Privates Geo. W. Risley and Perrin H. Benton) and I walked up to them, but none of them knew me. Taking off my forage cap, I showed them the number of the regiment and letter of the company, upon which one of them said, "My God! It's Smith."

After a moment's consultation, these two asked the sergeant if they could go with me to the river, and he said that they were very tired and he was afraid they would not be able to get up with the regiment before night; but they pleaded and he consented, and we started on with one of them on each side holding me up.

After a while we reached a boat landing near a large house, which I was told was Aiken's. The grounds were fenced, so that it was impossible to get to the river, as a guard was set.

My companions inquired for a surgeon, and presently a young man appeared, but did nothing for me, as he was one of a lot of young surgeons sent down to assist in the emergency, and had no instruments as yet, nor any supplies. He thought that it would not be long before some one could attend to me.

As they could do no more and the sound told us that a battle was raging, they left for the front after expressing great sympathy for me. After proceeding a short distance, Benton retraced his steps and offered me his blanket and tin cup. I tried to persuade him to keep them, as I knew that I was unable to carry them, but he threw them down at my feet and departed, with tears streaming down his cheeks.

I remained here for a short time, when I heard that there were a large number of sick and wounded in a ravine some distance above, so I started and was fortunate enough to be directed to the place.

I found there some 1,500 (so I was told), mostly from the 3rd Corps, and began to look about for help. Finally I found Captain James Mason of Co. B, whom I had known before the war. He interested himself, and soon brought Brigadier Surgeon Richard Salter to see me.

Dr. Salter said that he could do nothing for me, telling the captain that I could not live 48 hours. The captain urged him, when he said that he was upon the sick list himself, and was not able for duty; that he had no anesthetics and no instruments with the exception of a small pocket case, and but few bandages, which he felt that he ought to keep as he might save someone's life with them, while they would do me no good.

The captain then asked him as a *personal favor* to do what he could, saying that he had known me before my enlistment; upon which the doctor said he did not think I could survive the operation; but as the captain was persistent the doctor asked me if I thought I could stand it, and knowing that it was my only chance, nodded my head as I was unable to talk.

He then told me to sit down on the ground with my back against a tree, and ordered Sergeant Hugh Boyd of Co. I and another man who (years after) I learned was John Seates of Co. G, Mass. 1st Infantry, to hold my hands and head. My moustache had become matted with blood and was with difficulty cut away, and then before examining the wound he began to dissect out the small pieces of bone, stopping occasionally to ask me if I could "stand it." Although it was terrible to bear, I nodded my head and he went on. After finishing the cutting, he began sewing up the wound in the chin and the holes through my cheeks, after which he moistened a piece of sponge with turpentine and inserted it in the lower part of the wound, which was left open for drainage.

When he had finished, he counted the pieces of bone and said there were eighteen; then after looking at me for a short time he said, "Young man, you have got more nerve than any man I ever saw." He then wanted to know if there was anything in the way of nourishment to be had, and one of the soldiers replied that he had a little honey that I might have, whereupon they stirred some into a little warm water and tried to have me partake of it; but I could not, as it immediately set me to coughing so that I could not swallow anything.

Finally they found a little beef tea (so-called) and I got a very little of it down, the most of it having gone through the opening left for drainage. The surgeon then called for a knapsack, and on one being procured he caused it to be filled with straw, and placed me face down with my forehead resting upon it. Then saying he would dress the wound in the morning, he departed.

Later it began to rain and conditions became very bad, the ground getting muddy, and it being very dark one was liable to be trod upon by others.

Being very much exhausted, I finally got asleep, but was suddenly awakened by a stampede of a large number of mules, who ran over and among us. Fortunately I was not hurt, and had dozed off again when the experience of the previous night was repeated as a squadron of lancers ("Turkey drivers") rode up and ordered us to "skedaddle," as the Johnnies were coming.

Once more I roused myself and started downstream (as we had been directed). It was a very dark night, and the road was narrow, with a column of infantry filling one side of it and artillery the other. The bushes that grew at the side of the road were pushed aside by the passing soldiers, and as they came back into position kept hitting my face, so that I was compelled to take to the fields for the greater part of this distance, which I was told was seven miles. The greater portion of the way it was uncultivated land, some wood; but there were quite a number of large wheat fields through which I made my way; being a great deal of the time halfway to my knees in mud.

Toward daylight the weather cleared, and shortly after sunrise I came upon the bivouac of a regiment of Connecticut infantry who were preparing their breakfast. Some of them took pity upon me and invited me to partake with them; but they had nothing that I could eat, so they gave me what hot coffee I could swallow (which wasn't much) and wished me good luck; and I went on to the river at what I found was Harrison's Landing.

I found a large, square, brick house with outbuildings, overlooking the river, and a long, pile wharf extending to deep water. The river was full of men-of-war, and vessels of every description with supplies for man and beast.

Troops were bivouacked in the mud all about, and were coming in rapidly. After looking about a little, I made my way to the house, as being the place most likely to be used by surgeons. I found two at work in what had been the best room, and wounded men in large numbers anxiously awaiting their turn.

I got into the hall and sat upon the front stairs for a long time, until some officer (if I recollect rightly) took me into the room and told me to sit upon the floor in one corner, so that I should sooner be taken care of.

I passed a terrible day, hungry, thirsty, and faint, watching the surgeons work without anesthetics, and at times seeing a display of brutality by one of them.

I earnestly hoped that I should not fall into his hands, and fortunately I did not. I was not reached until about 4 P.M., when my wound was thoroughly cleaned, and a new piece of sponge moistened with turpentine inserted, a new bandage applied, and a cloth fastened so as to fall over the mouth and keep the flies from it. After this I went to the unfinished attic, where I found several wounded men lying on the floor.

I found a large dictionary, and taking it for a pillow lay down in front of one of the large chimneys, and hoped to get some sleep. After a little time Rev. Arthur B. Fuller, chaplain of the regiment (known by the boys as Glass-eye, owing to some peculiarity of the eyes) appeared, with a kettle of (what he called) beef tea, and inquired if there were any 16th Mass. men there. One of my company was the other side of the chimney and answered. The chaplain gave him some of the tea, whereupon others asked for it, and were told that he had but little and must give it to the wounded of his own regiment. As I could not talk and my companion did not think about me, the chaplain started to go downstairs, so I gave my comrade a pull and made signs that I wished for some, so he called the "Holy Joe" back and I was given a tin cupful; but owing to the conditions of the wound I could swallow but little.

Shortly after, I heard someone say that a boatload of wounded were to go down to the river that night, and knowing that unless I got to a hospital very soon there would be no chance for me, I roused up and went outdoors, where I found some surgeons with four hundred badly wounded men just ready to start for the boat landing.

I immediately attempted to fall in, but was prevented by a surgeon who said the number was already made up; but after looking at me for a moment said, "Follow us down, perhaps we can find room for you." Upon reaching the landing I found a large crowd on the same errand as myself, and was much disappointed; but waited until the four hundred had been taken in boats to a steamer lying in the river. When the last of them were in the boat, the surgeon (who stood at the top of the stairs) looked in my direction and made motions with his hands at the same time saying, "Let that man with the cloth over his face come here." I immediately went forward, and upon my arriving he lifted the cloth that hung over my mouth and chin and said, "Get right into the boat."

"OUR BELEAGUERED CITY": VIRGINIA, JUNE 1862

Judith W. McGuire: Diary, June 27–30, 1862

Judith W. McGuire and her husband, John, had fled their home in Alexandria, Virginia, in 1861 when the Yankees came. In her diary she narrated the scene in Richmond during the Seven Days, beginning with the battle at Mechanicsville. Her journal was published in 1867 as *Diary of a Southern Refugee, During the War*, with the author identified as "A Lady of Virginia."

June 27th.—Yesterday was a day of intense excitement in the city and its surroundings. Early in the morning it was whispered about that some great movement was on foot. Large numbers of troops were seen under arms, evidently waiting for orders to march against the enemy. A. P. Hill's Division occupied the range of hills near "Strawberry Hill," the cherished home of my childhood, overlooking the old "Meadow Bridges." About three o'clock the order *to move*, so long expected, was given. The Division marched steadily and rapidly to the attack —the Fortieth Regiment, under command of my relative, Colonel J. M. Brockenbrough, in which are so many of our dear boys, leading the advance. The enemy's pickets were just across the river, and the men supposed they were in heavy force of infantry and artillery, and that the passage of the bridge would be hazardous in the extreme; yet their courage did not falter. The gallant Fortieth, followed by Pegram's Battery, rushed across the bridge at double-quick, and with exultant shouts drove the enemy's pickets from their posts. The enemy was driven rapidly down the river to Mechanicsville, where the battle raged long and fiercely. At nine o'clock all was quiet; the bloody struggle over for the day. Our victory is said to be glorious, but not complete. The fighting is even now renewed, for I hear the firing of heavy artillery. Last night our streets were thronged until a late hour to catch the last accounts from couriers and spectators returning from the field. A bulletin from the Assistant Surgeon of the Fortieth, sent to his anxious father, assured me of the safety of some of those most dear to me; but the sickening sight of the ambulances bringing in the wounded met my eye at every turn. The President, and many others, were on the surrounding hills during the fight, deeply interested spectators. The calmness of the people during the progress of the battle was marvellous. The balloons of the enemy hovering over the battle-field could be distinctly seen from the outskirts of the city, and the sound of musketry as distinctly heard. All were anxious, but none alarmed for the safety of the city. From the firing of the first gun till the close of the battle every spot favourable for observation was crowded. The tops of the Exchange, the Ballard House, the Capitol, and almost every other tall house were covered with human beings; and after nightfall the commanding hills from the President's house to the Alms-House were covered, like a vast amphitheatre, with men, women and children, witnessing the grand display of fireworks—beautiful, yet awful—and sending death amid those whom our hearts hold so dear. I am told (for I did not witness it) that it was a scene of unsurpassed magnificence. The brilliant light of bombs bursting in the air and passing to the ground, the innumerable lesser lights, emitted by thousands and thousands of muskets, together with the roar of artillery and the rattling of small-arms, constituted a scene terrifically grand and imposing. What spell has bound our people? Is their trust in God, and in the valour of our troops, so great that they are unmoved by these terrible demonstrations of our powerful foe? It would seem so, for when the battle was over the crowd dispersed and retired to their respective homes with the seeming tranquility of persons who had been witnessing a panorama of transactions in a far-off country, in which they felt no personal interest; though they knew that their countrymen slept on their arms, only awaiting the dawn to renew the deadly conflict, on the success of which depended not only the fate of our capital, but of that splendid army, containing the material on which our happiness depends. Ah! many full, sorrowful hearts were at home, breathing out prayers for our success; or else were busy in the hospitals, administering to the wounded. Those on the hill-sides and house-tops were too nervous and anxious to stay at home—not that they were apprehensive for the city, but for the fate of those who were defending it, and their feeling was too deep for expression. The same feeling, perhaps, which makes me write so much this morning. But I must go to other duties.

Ten o'Clock at Night.—Another day of great excitement in our beleaguered city. From early dawn the cannon has been roaring around us. Our success has been glorious! The citizens—gentlemen as well as ladies—have been fully occupied in the hospitals. Kent, Paine & Co. have thrown open their spacious building for the use of the wounded. General C., of Texas, volunteer aid to General Hood, came in from the field covered with dust, and slightly wounded; he represents the fight as terrible beyond example. The carnage is frightful. General Jackson has joined General Lee, and nearly the whole army on both sides were engaged. The enemy had retired before our troops to their strong works near Gaines's Mill. Brigade after brigade of our brave men were hurled against them, and repulsed in disorder. General Lee was heard to say to General Jackson, "The fighting is desperate; can our men stand it?" Jackson replied, "General, I know our boys—they will never give back." In a short time a large part of our force was brought up in one grand attack, and then the enemy was utterly routed. General C. represents the valour of Hood and his brigade in the liveliest colours, and attributes the grand success at the close of the day greatly to their extraordinary gallantry. The works were the strongest ever seen in this country, and General C. says that the armies of the world could not have driven our men from them.

Another bulletin from the young surgeon of the Fortieth. That noble regiment has lost heavily—several of the "Potomac Rifles" among the slain—sons of old friends and acquaintances. Edward Brockenbrough, dreadfully wounded, has been brought in, and is tenderly nursed. Our own boys are mercifully spared. Visions of the battle-field have haunted me all day. Our loved ones, whether friends or strangers—all Southern soldiers are dear to us—lying dead and dying; the wounded in the hot sun, the dead being hastily buried. McClellan is said to be retreating. "Praise the Lord, O my soul!"

28*th.*—The casualties among our friends, so far, not very numerous. My dear Raleigh T. Colston is here, slightly wounded; he hopes to return to his command in a few days. Colonel Allen, of the Second Virginia, killed. Major Jones, of the same regiment, desperately wounded. Wood McDonald killed. But what touches me most nearly is the death of my young friend, Clarence Warwick, of this city. Dearly have I loved that warm-hearted, high-minded, brave boy, since his early childhood. To-night I have been indulging sad memories of his earnest manner and affectionate tones, from his boyhood up; and now what must be the shock to his father and brothers, and to those tender sisters, when to-morrow the telegraph shall tell them of their loss! His cousin, Lieutenant-Colonel Warwick, is desperately wounded. Oh, I pray that his life may be spared to his poor father and mother! He is so brave and skilful an officer that we cannot spare him, and how can they? The booming of cannon still heard distinctly, but the sound is more distant.

June 30.—McClellan certainly retreating. We begin to breathe more freely; but he fights as he goes. Oh, that he may be surrounded before he gets to his gun-boats! Rumours are flying about that he is surrounded; but we do not believe it—only hope that he may be before he reaches the river. The city is sad, because of the dead and dying, but our hearts are filled with gratitude and love. The end is not yet—oh that it were!

"DEATH HELD A CARNIVAL": VIRGINIA, JUNE–JULY 1862

Sallie Brock: from Richmond During the War

A tutor in prewar Virginia, Sallie Brock spent the war years in Richmond. She described the Seven Days in her memoir, published anonymously "by a Richmond Lady" in 1867.

RICHMOND suffered heavily in the loss of citizens in these battles. There was scarcely a family that had not some one of its numbers in the field. Mothers nervously watched for any who might bring to them news of their boys. Sisters and friends grew pale when a horseman rode up to their doors, and could scarcely nerve themselves to listen to the tidings he brought. Young wives clasped their children to their bosoms, and in agony imagined themselves widows and their little ones orphans. Thoughtful husbands, and sons, and brothers, and lovers, dispatched messengers to report their condition whenever they could, but, alas! the worst fears of many were realized.

Conspicuous amongst the dead of Richmond was the young Colonel of the Fourth Texas regiment. He had won honorable distinction in Italy, under Garibaldi. News arrived of his instant death on the field, and his heart-broken family sat up to receive his body until after the hour of midnight; but when it arrived, and "he lives" was told his mother, the reaction of joy almost deprived her of being. She could not realize it. The revulsion was too great. He spent a few days of mortal agony, and then a sad, mournful procession of heart-broken friends and relatives, and the riderless horse of the young warrior, announced, ah! how sadly, that Richmond's gallant son, Colonel Bradfute Warwick, had fallen!

A horseman rode up to the door of one of our houses on —— street, and cried out to the anxious mother: "Your son, madam, is safe, but Captain —— is killed!" On the opposite side, on the portico of her dwelling, a fair young girl, the betrothed of Captain ——, was said to have been sitting at the moment, and thus heard the terrible announcement!

Every family received the bodies of the wounded or dead of their friends, and every house was a house of mourning or a private hospital.

The clouds were lifted, and the skies brightened upon political prospects, but death held a carnival in our city. The weather was excessively hot. It was midsummer, gangrene and erysipelas attacked the wounded, and those who might have been cured of their wounds were cut down by these diseases.

Our hospitals were loathsome with the bloated, disfigured countenances of the victims of disease, rather than from ghastly wounds. Sickening odors filled the atmosphere, and soldiers' funerals were passing at every moment. Frequently they would be attended by only one or two of the convalescent patients of the hospitals, and sometimes the unknown dead would be borne to the grave, with only the driver of the hearse or cart to attend it.*

The mournful strains of the "Dead March," and the sounds of the muffled drum, betokened an officer *en route* for "the city of the dead," but these honors could not be accorded the poor fellows from the ranks. There were too many of them passing away—the means for costly funerals were not within

*One of the grave-diggers at a soldiers' cemetery said to the writer, when speaking of this time, (at a subsequent period,) "We could not dig graves fast enough to bury the soldiers. They were sometimes brought and put out of the hearse or cart, beside an open grave, and we were compelled to bury them in turn. Frequently we were obliged to leave them over night, when, sometimes, the bodies would swell, and burst the coffins in which they were placed, so slightly were they made. Our work was a horrible one! The odor was stifling. On one occasion, one of our grave-diggers contracted disease from a dead body, which he buried, that came to him in this terrible condition, and he died from it in less than twenty-four hours. After that we were almost afraid to continue our business, but then the soldiers must be buried, poor fellows!"

We listened to this horrible account as we stood on the hillside, and saw the hillocks innumerable, that marked the graves of our soldiers. A little girl, who visited the cemetery, on returning to the city said:—"Why, grandma, the soldiers' graves are as thick as potatoe-hills!" And she saw only a moiety of the many which crowded the hillsides around our city, for this was an extension of Hollywood cemetery only. There were several cemeteries especially laid out for the soldiers, and they were soon all filled with the mounds that marked the soldier dead.

our reach—yet were not our hearts less saddened by the less imposing cortege that was borne along with the private nor by the rude coffin in the cart, slowly wending its way unattended by friends, to the soldiers' cemetery. Mothers and sisters, and dear friends came from all parts of the South, to nurse and comfort dear ones in our hospitals, and some, alas! arrived to find a husband, brother, or son already dead or dying, and had the sad companionship of the dead back to their homes.

A RICHMOND HOSPITAL: VIRGINIA, JUNE–JULY 1862

Sara Agnes Pryor: from Reminiscences of Peace and War

When the Seven Days began Sara Agnes Pryor was nursing her fever-stricken husband Roger, a former U.S. and Confederate congressman now serving as a brigadier general in Lee's army. While her husband rejoined his brigade, Pryor volunteered as a nurse in Richmond, an experience she recalled in a 1904 memoir.

KENT & PAINE'S warehouse was a large, airy building, which had, I understood, been offered by the proprietors for a hospital immediately after the battle of Seven Pines. McClellan's advance upon Richmond had heavily taxed the capacity of the hospitals already established.

When I reached the warehouse, early on the morning after the fight at Mechanicsville, I found cots on the lower floor already occupied, and other cots in process of preparation. An aisle between the rows of narrow beds stretched to the rear of the building. Broad stairs led to a story above, where other cots were being laid.

The volunteer matron was a beautiful Baltimore woman, Mrs. Wilson. When I was presented to her as a candidate for admission, her serene eyes rested doubtfully upon me for a moment. She hesitated. Finally she said: "The work is very exacting. There are so few of us that our nurses must do anything and everything—make beds, wait upon anybody, and often a half a dozen at a time."

"I will engage to do all that," I declared, and she permitted me to go to a desk at the farther end of the room and enter my name.

As I passed by the rows of occupied cots, I saw a nurse kneeling beside one of them, holding a pan for a surgeon. The red stump of an amputated arm was held over it. The next thing I knew I was myself lying on a cot, and a spray of cold water was falling over my face. I had fainted. Opening my eyes, I found the matron standing beside me.

"You see it is as I thought. You are unfit for this work. One of the nurses will conduct you home."

The nurse's assistance was declined, however. I had given trouble enough for one day, and had only interrupted those who were really worth something.

A night's vigil had been poor preparation for hospital work. I resolved I would conquer my culpable weakness. It was all very well,—these heroics in which I indulged, these paroxysms of patriotism, this adoration of the defenders of my fireside. The defender in the field had naught to hope from me in case he should be wounded in my defence.

I took myself well in hand. Why had I fainted? I thought it was because of the sickening, dead odor in the hospital, mingled with that of acids and disinfectants. Of course this would always be there—and worse, as wounded men filled the rooms. I provided myself with sal volatile and spirits of camphor,—we wore pockets in our gowns in those days,—and thus armed I presented myself again to Mrs. Wilson.

She was as kind as she was refined and intelligent. "I will give you a place near the door," she said, "and you must run out into the air at the first hint of faintness. You will get over it, see if you don't."

Ambulances began to come in and unload at the door. I soon had occupation enough, and a few drops of camphor on my handkerchief tided me over the worst. The wounded men crowded in and sat patiently waiting their turn. One fine little fellow of fifteen unrolled a handkerchief from his wrist to show me his wound. "There's a bullet in there," he said proudly. "I'm going to have it cut out, and then go right back to the fight. Isn't it lucky it's my left hand?"

As the day wore on I became more and more absorbed in my work. I had, too, the stimulus of a reproof from Miss Deborah Couch, a brisk, efficient middle-aged lady, who asked no quarter and gave none. She was standing beside me a moment, with a bright tin pan filled with pure water, into which I foolishly dipped a finger to see if it were warm; to learn if I would be expected to provide warm water when I should be called upon to assist the surgeon.

"This water, Madam, was prepared for a raw wound," said Miss Deborah, sternly. "I must now make the surgeon wait until I get more."

Miss Deborah, in advance of her time, was a germ theorist. *My* touch evidently was contaminating.

As she charged down the aisle with a pan of water in her hand, everybody made way. She had known of my "fine-lady faintness," as she termed it, and I could see she despised me for it. She had volunteered, as all the nurses had, and she meant business. She had no patience with nonsense, and truly she was worth more than all the rest of us.

"Where can I get a little ice?" I one day ventured of Miss Deborah.

"Find it," she rejoined, as she rapidly passed on; but find it I never did. Ice was an unknown luxury until brought to us later from private houses.

But I found myself thoroughly reinstated—with surgeons, matron, and Miss Deborah—when I appeared a few days later, accompanied by a man bearing a basket of clean, well-rolled bandages, with promise of more to come. The Petersburg women had gone to work with a will upon my table-cloths, sheets, and dimity counterpanes—and even the chintz furniture covers. My springlike green and white chintz bandages appeared on many a manly arm and leg. My fine linen underwear and napkins were cut, by the sewing circle at the Spotswood, according to the surgeon's directions, into lengths two inches wide, then folded two inches, doubling back and forth in a smaller fold each time, until they formed pointed wedges for compresses.

Such was the sudden and overwhelming demand for such things, that but for my own and similar donations of household linen, the wounded men would have suffered. The war had come upon us suddenly. Many of our ports were already closed, and we had no stores laid up for such an emergency.

The bloody battle of Gaines's Mill soon followed—then Frazier's Farm, within the week, and at once the hospital was filled to overflowing. Every night a courier brought me tidings of my husband. When I saw him at the door my heart would die within me! One morning John came in for certain supplies. After being reassured as to his master's safety, I asked, "Did he have a comfortable night, John?"

"He sholy did! Marse Roger cert'nly was comfortable las' night. He slep' on de field 'twixt two daid horses!"

The women who worked in Kent & Paine's hospital never seemed to weary. After a while the wise matron assigned us hours, and we went on duty with the regularity of trained nurses. My hours were from seven to seven during the day, with the promise of night service should I be needed. Efficient, kindly colored women assisted us. Their motherly manner soothed the prostrate soldier, whom they always addressed as "son."

Many fine young fellows lost their lives for want of prompt attention. They never murmured. They would give way to those who seemed to be more seriously wounded than themselves, and the latter would recover, while from the slighter wounds gangrene would supervene from delay. Very few men ever walked away from that hospital. They died, or friends found quarters for them in the homes in Richmond. None complained! Unless a poor man grew delirious, he never groaned. There was an atmosphere of gentle kindness, a suppression of emotion for the sake of others.

Every morning the Richmond ladies brought for our patients such luxuries as could be procured in that scarce time. The city was in peril, and distant farmers feared to bring in their fruits and vegetables. One day a patient-looking middle-aged man said to me, "What would I not give for a bowl of chicken broth like that my mother used to give me when I was a sick boy!" I perceived one of the angelic matrons of Richmond at a distance, stooping over the cots, and found my way to her and said: "Dear Mrs. Maben, have you a chicken? And could you send some broth to No. 39?" She promised, and I returned with her promise to the poor wounded fellow. He shook his head. "To-morrow will be too late," he said.

I had forgotten the circumstance next day, but at noon I happened to look toward cot No. 39, and there was Mrs. Maben herself. She had brought the chicken broth in a pretty china bowl, with napkin and silver spoon, and was feeding my doubting Thomas, to his great satisfaction.

It was at this hospital, I have reason to believe, that the little story originated, which was deemed good enough to be claimed by other hospitals, of the young girl who approached a sick man with a pan of water in her hand and a towel over her arm.

"Mayn't I wash your face?" said the girl, timidly.

"Well, lady, you may if you want to," said the man, wearily. "It has been washed fourteen times this morning! It can stand another time, I reckon."

I discovered that I had not succeeded, despite many efforts, in winning Miss Deborah. I learned that she was affronted because I had not shared my offerings of jelly and fruit with her, for her special patients. Whenever I ventured to ask a loan from her, of a pan or a glass for water or the little things of which we never had enough, she would reply, "I must keep them for the nurses who understand reciprocity. Reciprocity is a rule *some* persons never seem to comprehend." When this was hammered into my slow perception, I rose to the occasion. I turned over the entire contents of a basket the landlord of the Spotswood had given me to Miss Deborah, and she made my path straight before me ever afterward.

At the end of a week the matron had promoted me! Instead of carving the fat bacon, to be dispensed with corn bread, for the hospital dinner, or standing between two rough men to keep away the flies, or fetching water, or spreading sheets on cots, I was assigned to regular duty with one patient.

The first of these proved to be young Colonel Coppens, of my husband's brigade. I could comfort him very little, for he was wounded past recovery. I spoke little French, and could only try to keep him, as far as possible, from annoyance. To my great relief, place was found for him in a private family. There he soon died—the gallant fellow I had admired on his horse a few months before.

Then I was placed beside the cot of Mr. (or Captain) Boyd of Mecklenburg, and was admonished by the matron not to leave him alone. He was the most patient sufferer in the world, gentle, courteous, always considerate, never complaining. I observed he often closed his eyes and sighed. "Are you in pain, Captain?" "No, no," he would say gently. One day, when I returned from my "rest," I found the matron sitting beside him. Tears were running down her cheeks. She motioned me to take her place, and then added, "No, no, I will not leave him."

The Captain's eyes were closed, and he sighed wearily at intervals. Presently he whispered slowly:—

> "There everlasting spring abides,"

then sighed, and seemed to sleep for a moment.

The matron felt his pulse and raised a warning hand. The sick man's whisper went on:—

> "Bright fields beyond the swelling flood
> Stand—dressed—in living green."

The surgeon stood at the foot of the cot and shook his head. The nurses gathered around with tearful eyes. Presently in clear tones:—

> "Not Jordan's stream—nor death's cold flood
> Shall fright us—from—the shore,"

and in a moment more the Christian soldier had crossed the river and lain down to rest under the trees.

Each of the battles of those seven days brought a harvest of wounded to our hospital. I used to veil myself closely as I walked to and from my hotel, that I might shut out the dreadful sights in the street,—the squads of prisoners, and, worst of all, the open wagons in which the dead were piled. Once I *did* see one of these dreadful wagons! In it a stiff arm was raised, and shook as it was driven down the street, as though the dead owner appealed to Heaven for vengeance; a horrible sight never to be forgotten.

DEBATING BLACK SOLDIERS: WASHINGTON, D.C., JULY 1862

Whitelaw Reid: General Hunter's Negro Soldiers

Although General Hunter's "experiment" of turning slaves into soldiers did not immediately bear results, his letter on the subject (see Hunter to Stanton, June 23, 1862, in this volume) reached the House of Representatives, where Kentucky conservatives Wickliffe and Mallory opposed printing the letter for the record. The resulting debate was reported in a dispatch by Reid, the Washington correspondent for the *Cincinnati Gazette*. Wickliffe's mention of the "late disaster in South Carolina" referred to the Union defeat at Secessionville at Charleston Harbor on June 16. On August 25 Stanton took a step forward on the matter of black soldiers, authorizing Brigadier General Rufus Saxton, superintendent of contrabands on the South Carolina coast, to enlist "volunteers of African descent." Stanton's order led to the organization of the 1st South Carolina Volunteers in October.

1862, July 6

Gen. David Hunter's letter about his Negro soldiers brought up a lively debate in the House Saturday, in which some very conservative men said some very ultra things, that must prove sadly 'firing for the Southern heart.' Charles A. Wickliffe wanted to reconsider the vote by which Hunter's letter was ordered printed and couldn't contain himself on the insult Hunter had offered to local people. He charged officers of the Government and of the army with having undertaken without law, against order, and in violation of every principle of humanity, to assume the power of enlisting slaves to serve against their masters. General Hunter's letter was in manner and terms unbecoming a General. He held Secretary Stanton responsible for Hunter's conduct and sneeringly said Hunter had better been seeing to his business when the late disaster in South Carolina took place than tinkering with Negroes. Robert Mallory made the usual Kentucky speech against arming the blacks. He ridiculed the idea of making them soldiers; said a single cannon shot would put ten thousand of them to flight; and closed by declaring that arming them was barbarous, inhuman and contrary to the practice of all civilized nations, and that it was most as bad as putting the tomahawk into the hands of the savage. This stirred up Thaddeus Stevens, who inquired, how does it come that they are so dangerous to their masters, when a single cannon shot will put ten thousand to flight? Or how is it they have not courage enough to make soldiers when you call them as savage and dangerous as Indians? But the gentleman was mistaken in his facts. Common history, he repeated, proved them false. It had been the general practise of civilized nations to employ slaves for military purposes, whenever and wherever needed. Owen Lovejoy here begged leave to interrupt, and read from common school history about Jackson's arming slaves in the War of 1812 and his promise to give freedom to all who served. He then read Jackson's General Order, thanking the Negroes for their gallant success, saying that he had not been unaware of their good qualities as soldiers, but that they had far surpassed his highest expectations and reassuring them of emancipation as a reward for their conduct. Lovejoy concluded his demonstration on the Negro-frightened gentlemen by reference to another history, showing that one fourth of the men who helped with Perry's victory on the lakes were Negroes. The effect of all this was sensational. Men who had been denouncing Hunter couldn't have been more astonished if one of Hunter's own bombshells from Port Royal had been dropped among them.

Charles B. Sedgewick heightened the effect by reading an elaborate statement of the New York State Librarian, showing that nearly every civilized Nation had, sometime or other, employed Negroes as soldiers and always with success, and winding up with the example of Brazil, the largest slaveholding empire of the world, using regiments of slaves at this very day as among the best soldiers they have. Alexander S. Diven begged to trespass on Stevens' time, just to say that he had long been profoundly convinced that Congress failed in its imperative duty, just so long as it failed to provide for enlisting Negro troops to serve in unhealthy regions to which they had become acclimated, and he now had a bill to that end prepared and was ready to offer it at the first opportunity. That, resumed Mr.

Stevens, is precisely what I would have done long ago, only I wasn't a conservative, and so they'd have called it an Abolition scheme. Stevens then went on with unusual earnestness and force, to urge the necessity for using Negroes to save white men. He declared that all over his State, households were everywhere desolated today because we hadn't troops enough, and now they wanted to call on them for more, to be sent into unwholesome climates, where exposure was certain death to any white man, and asserting that while such a policy was pursued, the suppression of the rebellion was hopeless. The effect of the discussion was seen when at the close of Stevens' speech, the House laid Wickliffe's motion on the table by a vote of 74 to 29.

There will be no more sneering at Hunter's letter or his Negro brigade.

"CIVIL AND MILITARY POLICY": VIRGINIA, JULY 1862

George B. McClellan to Abraham Lincoln

The President visited the Army of the Potomac at Harrison's Landing on July 8 to gauge its morale and its prospects, and McClellan took advantage of the opportunity to hand him this letter. McClellan had actually drafted the letter a week or so before the Seven Days, when he was confident of taking Richmond and anticipated resuming the general-in-chief post and advising on war policy. Now, anticipating possible martyrdom on the battlefield, he offered it as a sort of last military will and testament. Lincoln, sharing McClellan's letter with Congressman Frank Blair on the return journey to Washington, remarked that the general's advisory reminded him of a story, the one about "the man who got on a horse, and the horse stuck his hind foot into a stirrup. The man said, 'If you're going to get on I'll get off.'"

(Confidential) Head Quarters, Army of the Potomac
Mr President Camp near Harrison's Landing, Va. July 7th 1862

You have been fully informed, that the Rebel army is in our front, with the purpose of overwhelming us by attacking our positions or reducing us by blocking our river communications. I can not but regard our condition as critical and I earnestly desire, in view of possible contingencies, to lay before your Excellency, for your private consideration, my general views concerning the existing state of the rebellion; although they do not strictly relate to the situation of this Army or strictly come within the scope of my official duties. These views amount to convictions and are deeply impressed upon my mind and heart.

Our cause must never be abandoned; it is the cause of free institutions and self government. The Constitution and the Union must be preserved, whatever may be the cost in time, treasure and blood. If secession is successful, other dissolutions are clearly to be seen in the future. Let neither military disaster, political faction or foreign war shake your settled purpose to enforce the equal operation of the laws of the United States upon the people of every state.

The time has come when the Government must determine upon a civil and military policy, covering the whole ground of our national trouble. The responsibility of determining, declaring and supporting such civil and military policy and of directing the whole course of national affairs in regard to the rebellion, must now be assumed and exercised by you or our cause will be lost. The Constitution gives you power sufficient even for the present terrible exigency.

This rebellion has assumed the character of a War; as such it should be regarded; and it should be conducted upon the highest principles known to Christian Civilization. It should not be a War looking to the subjugation of the people of any state, in any event. It should not be, at all, a War upon population; but against armed forces and political organizations. Neither confiscation of property, political executions of persons, territorial organization of states or forcible abolition of slavery should be contemplated for a moment. In prosecuting the War, all private property and unarmed persons should be strictly protected; subject only to the necessities of military operations. All private property taken for military use should be paid or receipted for; pillage and waste should be treated as high crimes; all unnecessary trespass sternly prohibited; and offensive demeanor by the military towards citizens promptly rebuked. Military arrests should not be tolerated, except in places where active hostilities exist; and oaths not required by enactments—Constitutionally made—should be neither demanded nor received. Military government should be confined to the preservation of public order and the protection of political rights.

Military power should not be allowed to interfere with the relations of servitude, either by supporting or impairing the authority of the master; except for repressing disorder as in other cases. Slaves contraband under the Act of Congress, seeking military protection, should receive it. The right of the Government to appropriate permanently to its own service claims to slave labor should be asserted and the right of the owner to compensation therefor should be recognized. This principle might be extended upon grounds of military necessity and security to all the slaves within a particular state; thus working manumission in such state—and in Missouri, perhaps in Western Virginia also and possibly even in Maryland the expediency of such a military measure is only a question of time. A system of policy thus constitutional and conservative, and pervaded by the influences of Christianity and freedom, would receive the support of almost all truly loyal men, would deeply impress the rebel masses and all foreign nations, and it might be humbly hoped that it would commend itself to the favor of the Almighty. Unless the principles governing the further conduct of our struggle shall be made known and approved, the effort to obtain requisite forces will be almost hopeless. A declaration of radical views, especially upon slavery, will rapidly disintegrate our present Armies.

The policy of the Government must be supported by concentrations of military power. The national forces should not be dispersed in expeditions, posts of occupation and numerous Armies; but should be mainly collected into masses and brought to bear upon the Armies of the Confederate States; those Armies thoroughly defeated, the political structure which they support would soon cease to exist.

In carrying out any system of policy which you may form, you will require a Commander in Chief of the Army; one who possesses your confidence, understands your views and who is competent to execute your orders by directing the military forces of the Nation to the accomplishment of the objects by you proposed. I do not ask that place for myself. I am willing to serve you in such position as you may assign me and I will do so as faithfully as ever subordinate served superior.

I may be on the brink of eternity and as I hope forgiveness from my maker I have written this letter with sincerity towards you and from love for my country.

Very respectfully your obdt svt
Geo B McClellan
Maj Genl Comdg

His Excellency A Lincoln
Presdt U.S.

BUILDING A CONFEDERATE CRUISER:
ENGLAND, JULY 1862

Thomas H. Dudley and J. Price Edwards: An Exchange

Dudley, the American consul at Liverpool, battled with British authorities over the building of Confederate warships in Great Britain's shipyards, which Dudley charged was in violation of the neutrality laws. His adversary was the Confederate naval agent James D. Bulloch. The vessel that is the subject of this correspondence was labeled by her Laird shipbuilders as "steamer No. 290." To Dudley's frustration, No. 290 set sail from Liverpool on July 29 without hindrance from customs agent Edwards. She took her armament in the Azores and was christened the soon-to-be-notorious C.S.S. *Alabama*.

UNITED STATES CONSULATE,
Liverpool, July 9, 1862.

SIR: In accordance with a suggestion of Earl Russell, in a communication to Mr. Adams, the American minister in London, I beg to lay before you the information and circumstances which have come to my knowledge relative to the gunboat being fitted out by Messrs. Laird, at Birkenhead, for the confederates of the southern United States of America, and intended to be used as a privateer against the United States.

On my arrival and taking charge of the consulate at Liverpool, in November last, my attention was called by the acting consul, and by other persons, to two gunboats being or to be fitted out for the so-called confederate government—the Oreto, fitted out by William C. Miller and Sons and Messrs. Fawcett Preston and Co., and the one now in question. Subsequent events fully proved the suspicion, with regard to the Oreto, to be well founded. She cleared from Liverpool in March last for Palermo and Jamaica, but sailed direct for Nassau, where she now is receiving her armament as a privateer for the so-called confederate government. And my attention was called repeatedly to the gunboat building by Mr. Laird by various persons, who stated that she was also for a confederate privateer, and was being built by Messrs. Laird for that express purpose. In May last two officers of the southern privateer Sumter, named Caddy and Beaufort, passed through Liverpool on their way to Havana or Nassau; while here, stated that there was a gunboat building by Mr. Laird, at Birkenhead, for the southern confederacy, and not long after that a foreman, employed about the vessel in Messrs. Lairds' yard, stated that she was the sister of the Oreto, and intended for the same service; and, when pressed for an explanation, further stated that she was to be a privateer for the southern government in the United States.

When the vessel was first tried, Mr. Wellsman, one of the firm of Fraser, Trenholm and Co., (who are well known as agents for the confederate government) Andrew and Thomas Byrne, and other persons, well known as having been for months actively engaged in sending munitions of war for said government, were present, and have accompanied her on her various trials, as they had accompanied the Oreto on her trial trip and on her departure. In April last the southern screw steamer Annie Childs, which had run the blockade out of Charleston, and the name of which was changed at this port to the Julia Usher, was laden with munitions of war, consisting of a large quantity of powder, rifled cannon, &c., by Messrs. Fraser, Trenholm and Co., for the southern confederacy, and left Liverpool to run the blockade under the command of a Captain Hammer, and having on board several of the crew of the privateer Sumter, to which I have before referred. For some unknown reason this vessel came back, and is now here. Since her return a youth named Robinson, who had gone in her as a passenger, has stated that the gunboat building at Laird's for the southern confederacy was a subject of frequent conversation among the officers while she (Julia Usher) was out, she was all the time spoken of as a confederate vessel, and that Captain Bullock was to command her. That the money for her was advanced by Fraser, Trenholm and Co. That she was not to make any attempt to run the blockade, but would go at once as a privateer. That she was to mount eleven guns. That if the Julia Usher were not going, the six men from the Sumter who were on board the Julia Usher were to join the gunboat. This youth, being a native of New Orleans, was extremely anxious to get taken on board the gunboat, and wished the persons he made the communication to, to assist him and see Captain Bullock on his behalf. He has, I understand, been removed to a school in London. With reference to his statement, I may observe that Captain Hammer referred to is a South Carolinian; has been many years in Fraser, Trenholm and Co.'s employ; is greatly trusted by them, and is also intimate with Captain Bullock, so that he would be likely to be well informed on the subject; and as he had no notion at that time of returning to Liverpool, he would have no hesitation in speaking of the matter to his officers and the persons from the Sumter. I may also state, the Captain Bullock referred to is in Liverpool; that he is an officer of the confederate navy; that he was sent over here for the express purpose of fitting out privateers and sending over munitions of war; that he transacts his business at the office of Fraser, Trenholm and Co.; that he has been all the time in communication with Fawcett, Preston and Co., who fitted out the Oreto, and with Lairds, who are fitting out this vessel; that he goes almost daily on board the gunboat, and seems to be recognized as in authority.

A Mr. Blair, of Paradise street, in this town, who furnished the cabins of the Laird gunboat, has also stated that all the fittings and furniture were selected by Captain Bullock, and were subject to his approval, although paid for by Mr. Laird.

The information on which I have formed an undoubting conviction that this vessel is being fitted out for the so-called confederate government, and is intended to cruise against the commerce of the United States, has come to me from a variety of sources, and I have detailed it to you as far as practicable.

I have given you the names of the persons making the statements; but as the information, in most cases, is given to me by persons out of friendly feeling to the United States and in strict confidence, I cannot state the names of my informants; but what I have stated is of such a character, that little inquiry will confirm its truth. Everything about the vessel shows her to be a war vessel; she has well-constructed magazines; she has a number of canisters of a peculiar and expensive construction, for containing powder; she has already platforms screwed to her decks for the reception of swivel guns. Indeed, the fact she is a war vessel is not denied by Messrs. Laird, but they say she is for the Spanish government. This they stated on the 3d April last, when General Burgoyne visited their yard, and was shown over it and the vessels being built there by Messrs. John Laird, jun., and Henry H. Laird, as was fully reported in the papers at the time. Seeing the statement, and having been already informed from so many respectable sources that she was for the so-called confederate government, I at once wrote to the minister in London to ascertain from the Spanish embassy whether the statement was true. The reply was a positive assurance that she was not for the Spanish government. I am therefore authorized in saying that what was stated on that occasion, as well as statements since made, that she is for the Spanish government, are untrue.

I am satisfied, beyond a doubt, that she is for a confederate war vessel.

If you desire any personal explanation or information, I shall be happy to attend you whenever you may request it.

Very respectfully, I am your obedient servant,

THOMAS H. DUDLEY, *Consul.*

J. Price Edwards, Esq.,
Collector of Customs, Liverpool.

Custom-House,
Liverpool, July 10, 1862.

Sir: I beg to acknowledge the receipt of your communication of yesterday's date, (received this morning,) and to acquaint you that I shall immediately submit the same for the consideration and direction of the board of customs, under whom I have the honor to serve. I may observe, however, that I am respectfully of opinion that the statement made by you is not such as could be acted upon by the officers of this revenue, unless legally substantiated by evidence.

I have the honor to be, sir, your obedient servant,

J. PRICE EDWARDS, *Collector.*

Consul for the United States of America.

CUSTOM-HOUSE,
Liverpool, July 16, 1862.

SIR: With reference to my letter of the 10th instant, acknowledging your communication of the 9th, relative to the vessel built by Messrs. Laird, of Birkenhead, I have to acquaint you, that I am directed by the commissioners of her Majesty's customs to apprise you that their solicitor informs them that the details given by you in regard to the said vessel are not sufficient, in a legal point of view, to justify me in taking upon myself the responsibility of the detention of this ship.

I have the honor to be, sir, your most obedient servant,
J. PRICE EDWARDS, *Collector.*

T. H. DUDLEY, Esq., *&c., &c.*

WASHINGTON, D.C., JULY 1862

Abraham Lincoln: Appeal to Border State Representatives for Compensated Emancipation

The President, in a renewed bid to gain support for compensated emancipation, convened a gathering of border state representatives and senators from Delaware, Maryland, Kentucky, Missouri, Tennessee, and the pending state of West Virginia and read them this appeal. Their response, signed by a majority (twenty out of twenty-eight), rejected the plan on such varied grounds as too costly, unconstitutional, inspiriting to the rebellion, and threatening "rights of property." On July 14 Lincoln sent a draft bill for compensated emancipation to Congress, where it failed of action before adjournment.

July 12, 1862

GENTLEMEN. After the adjournment of Congress, now very near, I shall have no opportunity of seeing you for several months. Believing that you of the border-states hold more power for good than any other equal number of members, I feel it a duty which I can not justifiably waive, to make this appeal to you. I intend no reproach or complaint when I assure you that in my opinion, if you all had voted for the resolution in the gradual emancipation message of last March, the war would now be substantially ended. And the plan therein proposed is yet one of the most potent, and swift means of ending it. Let the states which are in rebellion see, definitely and certainly, that, in no event, will the states you represent ever join their proposed Confederacy, and they can not, much longer maintain the contest. But you can not divest them of their hope to ultimately have you with them so long as you show a determination to perpetuate the institution within your own states. Beat them at elections, as you have overwhelmingly done, and, nothing daunted, they still claim you as their own. You and I know what the lever of their power is. Break that lever before their faces, and they can shake you no more forever.

Most of you have treated me with kindness and consideration; and I trust you will not now think I improperly touch what is exclusively your own, when, for the sake of the whole country I ask "Can you, for your states, do better than to take the course I urge?" Discarding *punctillio*, and maxims adapted to more manageable times, and looking only to the unprecedentedly stern facts of our case, can you do better in any possible event? You prefer that the constitutional relation of the states to the nation shall be practically restored, without disturbance of the institution; and if this were done, my whole duty, in this respect, under the constitution, and my oath of office, would be performed. But it is not done, and we are trying to accomplish it by war. The incidents of the war can not be avoided. If the war continue long, as it must, if the object be not sooner attained, the institution in your states will be extinguished by mere friction and abrasion—by the mere incidents of the war. It will be gone, and you will have nothing valuable in lieu of it. Much of it's value is gone already. How much better for you, and for your people, to take the step which, at once, shortens the war, and secures substantial compensation for that which is sure to be wholly lost in any other event. How much better to thus save the money which else we sink forever in the war. How much better to do it while we can, lest the war ere long render us pecuniarily unable to do it. How much better for you, as seller, and the nation as buyer, to sell out, and buy out, that without which the war could never have been, than to sink both the thing to be sold, and the price of it, in cutting one another's throats.

I do not speak of emancipation *at once*, but of a *decision* at once to emancipate *gradually*. Room in South America for colonization, can be obtained cheaply, and in abundance; and when numbers shall be large enough to be company and encouragement for one another, the freed people will not be so reluctant to go.

I am pressed with a difficulty not yet mentioned—one which threatens division among those who, united are none too strong. An instance of it is known to you. Gen. Hunter is an honest man. He was, and I hope, still is, my friend. I valued him none the less for his agreeing with me in the general wish that all men everywhere, could be free. He proclaimed all men free within certain states, and I repudiated the proclamation. He expected more good, and less harm from the measure, than I could believe would follow. Yet in repudiating it, I gave dissatisfaction, if not offence, to many whose support the country can not afford to lose. And this is not the end of it. The pressure, in this direction, is still upon me, and is increasing. By conceding what I now ask, you can relieve me, and much more, can relieve the country, in this important point. Upon these considerations I have again begged your attention to the message of March last. Before leaving the Capital, consider and discuss it among yourselves. You are patriots and statesmen; and, as such, I pray you, consider this proposition; and, at the least, commend it to the consideration of your states and people. As you would perpetuate popular government for the best people in the world, I beseech you that you do in no wise omit this. Our common country is in great peril, demanding the loftiest views, and boldest action to bring it speedy relief. Once relieved, it's form of government is saved to the world; it's beloved history, and cherished memories, are vindicated; and it's happy future fully assured, and rendered inconceivably grand. To you, more than to any others, the previlege is given, to assure that happiness, and swell that grandeur, and to link your own names therewith forever.

WASHINGTON, D.C., JULY 1862

Second Confiscation Act

On August 6, 1861, Congress passed the First Confiscation Act, authorizing the seizure of slaves used to militarily support the rebellion. After months of contentious debate, Congress adopted a second confiscation measure in July 1862 authorizing the seizure of slaves and other property from persons found by federal courts to be inciting or aiding rebellion. Lincoln found parts of the act legally dubious and prepared a veto message, but when Congress passed a resolution addressing many of his concerns, he signed the act and returned it along with his intended veto message. Although the Second Confiscation Act was seldom enforced, its passage demonstrated the increasing willingness of Congress to act against slavery.

An act to suppress insurrection, to punish treason and rebellion, to seize and confiscate the property of rebels, and for other purposes.

Be it enacted by the Senate and House of Representatives of the United States of America in Congress assembled, That every person who shall hereafter commit the crime of treason against the United States, and shall be adjudged guilty thereof, shall suffer death, and all his slaves, if any, shall be declared and made free; or, at the discretion of the court, he shall be imprisoned for not less than five years and fined not less than $10,000, and all his slaves, if any, shall be declared and made free; said fine shall be levied and collected on any or all of the property, real and personal, excluding slaves, of which the said person so convicted was the owner at the time of committing the said crime, any sale or conveyance to the contrary notwithstanding.

SEC. 2. *And be it further enacted*, That if any person shall hereafter incite, set on foot, assist, or engage in any rebellion or insurrection against the authority of the United States, or the laws thereof, or shall give aid or comfort thereto, or shall engage in, or give aid and comfort to, any such existing rebellion or insurrection, and be convicted thereof, such person shall be punished by imprisonment for a period not exceeding ten years, or by a fine not exceeding ten thousand dollars, and by the liberation of all his slaves, if any he have; or by both of said punishments, at the discretion of the court.

SEC. 3. *And be it further enacted*, That every person guilty of either of the offenses described in this act shall be forever incapable and disqualified to hold any office under the United States.

SEC. 4. *And be it further enacted*, That this act shall not be construed in any way to affect or alter the prosecution, conviction, or punishment of any person or persons guilty of treason against the United States before the passage of this act, unless such person is convicted under this act.

SEC. 5. *And be it further enacted*, That, to insure the speedy termination of the present rebellion, it shall be the duty of the President of the United States to cause the seizure of all the estate and property, money, stocks, credits, and effects of the persons hereinafter named in this section, and to apply and use the same and the proceeds thereof for the support of the Army of the United States—that is to say:

First. Of any person hereafter acting as an officer of the army or navy of the rebels in arms against the Government of the United States.

Secondly. Of any person hereafter acting as President, Vice-President, member of Congress, judge of any court, cabinet officer, foreign minister, commissioner or consul of the so-called Confederate States of America.

Thirdly. Of any person acting as Governor of a State, member of a convention or Legislature, or judge of any court of any of the so-called Confederate States of America.

Fourthly. Of any person who, having held an office of honor, trust, or profit in the United States, shall hereafter hold an office in the so-called Confederate States of America.

Fifthly. Of any person hereafter holding any office or agency under the government of the so-called Confederate States of America, or under any of the several States of the said Confederacy, or the laws thereof, whether such office or agency be national, state, or municipal in its name or character: *Provided*, That the persons thirdly, fourthly, and fifthly above described shall have accepted their appointment or election since the date of the pretended ordinance of secession of the State, or shall have taken an oath of allegiance to, or to support the Constitution of, the so-called Confederate States.

Sixthly. Of any person who, owning property in any loyal State or Territory of the United States, or in the District of Columbia, shall hereafter assist and give aid and comfort to such rebellion; and all sales, transfers, or conveyances of any such property shall be null and void; and it shall be a sufficient bar to any suit brought by such person for the possession or the use of such property, or any of it, to allege and prove that he is one of the persons described in this section.

SEC. 6. *And be it further enacted*, That if any person within any State or Territory of the United States, other than those named, as aforesaid, after the passage of this act, being engaged in armed rebellion against the Government of the United States, or aiding or abetting such rebellion, shall not, within sixty days after public warning and proclamation duly given and made by the President of the United States, cease to aid, countenance, and abet such rebellion, and return to his allegiance to the United States, all the estate and property, money, stocks, and credits of such person shall be liable to seizure, as aforesaid, and it shall be the duty of the President to seize and use them as aforesaid or the proceeds thereof. And all sales, transfers, or conveyances of any such property after the expiration of the said sixty days from the date of such warning and proclamation shall be null and void; and it shall be a sufficient bar to any suit brought by such person for the possession or the use of such property, or any of it, to allege and prove that he is one of the persons described in this section.

SEC. 7. *And be it further enacted*, That to secure the condemnation and sale of any of such property, after the same shall have been seized, so that it may be made available for the purpose aforesaid, proceedings in rem shall be instituted in the name of the United States in any district court thereof, or in any Territorial court or in the United States district court for the District of Columbia, within which the property above described, or any part thereof, may be found, or into which the same, if movable, may first be brought, which proceedings shall conform as nearly as may be to proceedings in admiralty or revenue cases; and if said property, whether real or personal, shall be found to have belonged to a person engaged in rebellion, or who has given aid or comfort thereto, the same shall be condemned as enemies' property and become the property of the United States, and may be disposed of as the court shall decree, and the proceeds thereof paid into the Treasury of the United States for the purposes aforesaid.

SEC. 8. *And be it further enacted*, That the several courts aforesaid shall have power to make such orders, establish such forms of decree and sale, and direct such deeds and conveyances to be executed and delivered by the marshals thereof where real estate shall be the subject of sale, as shall fitly and efficiently effect the purposes of this act, and vest in the purchasers of such property good and valid titles thereto. And the said courts shall have power to allow such fees and charges of their officers as shall be reasonable and proper in the premises.

SEC. 9. *And be it further enacted*, That all slaves of persons who shall hereafter be engaged in rebellion against the Government of the United States, or who shall in any way give aid or comfort thereto, escaping from such persons and taking refuge within the lines of the Army; and all slaves captured from such persons or deserted by them and coming under the control of the Government of the United States, and all slaves of such persons found *on* or being within any place occupied by rebel forces and afterward occupied by the forces of the United States shall be deemed captives of war, and shall be forever free of their servitude, and not again held as slaves.

SEC. 10. *And be it further enacted*, That no slave escaping into any State, Territory, or the District of Columbia, from any other State, shall be delivered up, or in any way impeded or hindered of his liberty, except for crime, or some offense against the laws, unless the person claiming said fugitive shall first make oath that the person to whom the labor or service of such fugitive is alleged to be due is his lawful owner, and has not borne arms against the United States in the present rebellion, nor in any way given aid and comfort thereto; and no person engaged in the military or naval service of the United States shall, under any pretense whatever, assume to decide on the validity of the claim of any person to the service or labor of any other person, or surrender up any such person to the claimant, on pain of being dismissed from the service.

SEC. 11. *And be it further enacted*, That the President of the United States is authorized to employ as many persons of African descent as he may deem necessary and proper for the suppression of this rebellion, and for this purpose he may organize and use them in such manner as he may judge best for the public welfare.

SEC. 12. *And be it further enacted*, That the President of the United States is hereby authorized to make provision for the transportation, colonization, and settlement, in some tropical country beyond the limits of the United States, of such persons of the African race, made free by the provisions of this act, as may be willing to emigrate, having first obtained the consent of the government of said country to their protection and settlement within the same, with all the rights and privileges of freemen.

SEC. 13. *And be it further enacted*, That the President is hereby authorized, at any time hereafter, by proclamation, to extend to persons who may have participated in the existing rebellion in any State or part thereof, pardon and amnesty, with such exceptions and at such time and on such conditions as he may deem expedient for the public welfare.

SEC. 14. *And be it further enacted*, That the courts of the United States shall have full power to institute proceedings, make orders and decrees, issue process, and do all other things necessary to carry this act into effect.

APPROVED July 17, 1862.

JOINT RESOLUTION explanatory of "An act to suppress insurrection, to punish treason and rebellion, to seize and confiscate the property of rebels, and for other purposes."

Resolved by the Senate and House of Representatives of the United States of America in Congress assembled, That the provisions of the third clause of the fifth section of "An act to suppress insurrection, to punish treason and rebellion, to seize and confiscate the property of rebels, and for other purposes," shall be so construed as not to apply to any act or acts done prior to the passage thereof, nor to include any member of a State Legislature or judge of any State court who has not, in accepting or entering upon his office, taken an oath to support the constitution of the so-called "Confederate States of America;" nor shall any punishment or proceedings under said act be so construed as to work a forfeiture of the real estate of the offender beyond his natural life.

APPROVED July 17, 1862.

"SUCCESS AND GLORY":
WASHINGTON, D.C., JULY 1862

John Pope: Address to the Army of Virginia

General Pope was a career soldier who had gained notice for capturing Island No. 10 and New Madrid, Missouri, during the Union operations to open the Mississippi. He had then commanded the Army of Mississippi under Henry Halleck in the nearly bloodless advance on Corinth. Pope issued this address thinking to overcome what he took to be a spiritless and defeatist attitude among the troops of his new command, the Army of Virginia, assembled from the various units that had chased after Stonewall Jackson in the Shenandoah Valley.

HEADQUARTERS ARMY OF VIRGINIA,
Washington, D. C., July 14, 1862.

To the Officers and Soldiers of the Army of Virginia:

By special assignment of the President of the United States I have assumed the command of this army. I have spent two weeks in learning your whereabouts, your condition, and your wants, in preparing you for active operations, and in placing you in positions from which you can act promptly and to the purpose. These labors are nearly completed, and I am about to join you in the field.

Let us understand each other. I have come to you from the West, where we have always seen the backs of our enemies; from an army whose business it has been to seek the adversary and to beat him when he was found; whose policy has been attack and not defense. In but one instance has the enemy been able to place our Western armies in defensive attitude. I presume that I have been called here to pursue the same system and to lead you against the enemy. It is my purpose to do so, and that speedily. I am sure you long for an opportunity to win the distinction you are capable of achieving. That opportunity I shall endeavor to give you. Meantime I desire you to dismiss from your minds certain phrases, which I am sorry to find so much in vogue amongst you. I hear constantly of "taking strong positions and holding them," of "lines of retreat," and of "bases of supplies." Let us discard such ideas. The strongest position a soldier should desire to occupy is one from which he can most easily advance against the enemy. Let us study the probable lines of retreat of our opponents, and leave our own to take care of themselves. Let us look before us, and not behind. Success and glory are in the advance, disaster and shame lurk in the rear. Let us act on this understanding, and it is safe to predict that your banners shall be inscribed with many a glorious deed and that your names will be dear to your countrymen forever.

JNO. POPE,
Major-General, Commanding.

A CHANGE IN POLICY:
WASHINGTON, D.C., JULY 1862

John Pope: General Orders Nos. 5, 7, 11

These general orders, issued "By command of General Pope," marked a hardening of attitudes toward Southern civilians in the war zone. They were prepared at Secretary of War Stanton's direction and approved by the President, but their notoriety clung to Pope. The more draconian measures were not carried out, but the order "to subsist upon the country" was widely followed. "The lawless acts of many of our soldiers are worthy of worse than death," complained an Army of Virginia officer. "The villains urge as authority, 'Gen Pope's order.'" Robert E. Lee, when he saw the orders, termed Pope a "miscreant" and told Stonewall Jackson, "I want Pope to be suppressed."

GENERAL ORDERS, No. 5. } HEADQUARTERS ARMY OF VIRGINIA,
Washington, July 18, 1862.

Hereafter, as far as practicable, the troops of this command will subsist upon the country in which their operations are carried on. In all cases supplies for this purpose will be taken by the officers to whose department they properly belong under the orders of the commanding officer of the troops for whose use they are intended. Vouchers will be given to the owners, stating on their face that they will be payable at the conclusion of the war, upon sufficient testimony being furnished that such owners have been loyal citizens of the United States since the date of the vouchers. Whenever it is known that supplies can be furnished in any district of the country where the troops are to operate the use of trains for carrying subsistence will be dispensed with as far as possible.

By command of Major-General Pope:

GEO. D. RUGGLES,
Colonel, Assistant Adjutant-General, and Chief of Staff.

GENERAL ORDERS, No. 7. HEADQUARTERS ARMY OF VIRGINIA, *Washington, July* 20, 1862.

The people of the valley of the Shenandoah and throughout the region of operations of this army living along the lines of railroad and telegraph and along the routes of travel in rear of the United States forces are notified that they will be held responsible for any injury done to the track, line, or road, or for any attacks upon trains or straggling soldiers by bands of guerrillas in their neighborhood. No privileges and immunities of warfare apply to lawless bands of individuals not forming part of the organized forces of the enemy nor wearing the garb of soldiers, who, seeking and obtaining safety on pretext of being peaceful citizens, steal out in rear of the army, attack and murder straggling soldiers, molest trains of supplies, destroy railroads, telegraph lines, and bridges, and commit outrages disgraceful to civilized people and revolting to humanity. Evil-disposed persons in rear of our armies who do not themselves engage directly in these lawless acts encourage them by refusing to interfere or to give any information by which such acts can be prevented or the perpetrators punished.

Safety of life and property of all persons living in rear of our advancing armies depends upon the maintenance of peace and quiet among themselves and upon the unmolested movements through their midst of all pertaining to the military service. They are to understand distinctly that this security of travel is their only warrant of personal safety.

It is therefore ordered that wherever a railroad, wagon road, or telegraph is injured by parties of guerrillas the citizens living within 5 miles of the spot shall be turned out in mass to repair the damage, and shall, beside, pay to the United States in money or in property, to be levied by military force, the full amount of the pay and subsistence of the whole force necessary to coerce the performance of the work during the time occupied in completing it.

If a soldier or legitimate follower of the army be fired upon from any house the house shall be razed to the ground, and the inhabitants sent prisoners to the headquarters of this army. If such an outrage occur at any place distant from settlements, the people within 5 miles around shall be held accountable and made to pay an indemnity sufficient for the case.

Any persons detected in such outrages, either during the act or at any time afterward, shall be shot, without awaiting civil process. No such acts can influence the result of this war, and they can only lead to heavy afflictions to the population to no purpose.

It is therefore enjoined upon all persons, both for the security of their property and the safety of their own persons, that they act vigorously and cordially together to prevent the perpetration of such outrages.

Whilst it is the wish of the general commanding this army that all peaceably disposed persons who remain at their homes and pursue their accustomed avocations shall be subjected to no improper burden of war, yet their own safety must of necessity depend upon the strict preservation of peace and order among themselves; and they are to understand that nothing will deter him from enforcing promptly and to the full extent every provision of this order.

By command of Major-General Pope:

GEO. D. RUGGLES,
Colonel, Assistant Adjutant-General, and Chief-of-Staff.

GENERAL ORDERS, No. 11. } HEADQUARTERS ARMY OF VIRGINIA, *Washington, July* 23, 1862.

Commanders of army corps, divisions, brigades, and detached commands will proceed immediately to arrest all disloyal male citizens within their lines or within their reach in rear of their respective stations.

Such as are willing to take the oath of allegiance to the United States and will furnish sufficient security for its observance shall be permitted to remain at their homes and pursue in good faith their accustomed avocations. Those who refuse shall be conducted South beyond the extreme pickets of this army, and be notified that if found again anywhere within our lines or at any point in rear they will be considered spies, and subjected to the extreme rigor of military law.

If any person, having taken the oath of allegiance as above specified, be found to have violated it, he shall be shot, and his property seized and applied to the public use.

All communication with any person whatever living within the lines of the enemy is positively prohibited, except through the military authorities and in the manner specified by military law; and any person concerned in writing or in carrying letters or messages in any other way will be considered and treated as a spy within the lines of the United States Army.

By command of Major-General Pope:

GEO. D. RUGGLES,
Colonel, Assistant Adjutant-General, and Chief of Staff.

THE "IDOL" OF THE ARMY: VIRGINIA, JULY 1862

Fitz John Porter to Joseph C. G. Kennedy

General Porter, Fifth Corps, Army of the Potomac, had commanded in three of the battles in the Seven Days. He was McClellan's closest confidant and purveyor of his views. He wrote to Kennedy, head of the Census Office, thinking him to be influential in the capital. Much to Porter's later discomfort, Kennedy sent the letter to Secretary of State Seward as an example of the "undisguised opinions of men whose convictions are worthy of consideration," and from Seward the letter made its way to Lincoln, Stanton, and even John Pope.

Westover Landing, James River.
July 17" '62

My dear Sir,

Your kind and complimentary letter was recieved last evening. However just & correct my opinions, or of whatever value, I beg of you never to dissiminate them as mine. Where they should have influence they will be unheeded, where they would be received they exist. I have no desire to appear before the public except in my record as military man: in my efforts to crush & speedily this rebellion.

I regret to see that Genl Pope has not improved since his youth and has now written himself down, what the military world has long known, an ass. His address to his troops will make him ridiculous in the eyes of military men abroad as well as at home, and will reflect no credit on Mr. Lincoln who has just promoted him. If the theory he proclaims is practised you may look for disaster.

You say you have reason to believe that an army of 175000 men will soon be ready to march on Richmond. How is it to march? Are fresh, raw troops, to be united with the (acknowledged by him) demoralized troops of Genl Pope, and put in motion from the direction of Washington, Manassas, Warrenton &c? That army will not reach Richmond unless this one clears the way, or it (the former) goes there as prisoners. Or are the troops sufficient to swell this army to 175000 men to be sent to the 75000 now here of well disciplined, well drilled, well officered, veteran troops—who in three days if properly supported can be knocking at the gates of Richmond? Our obstacles lie just in front of that city: The other army has them in every mile of its advance as well as at Richmond, and that very one which Pope scouts—care of communications or attention to the rear—is no trifling one. If opposed Pope's army will be the guard merely for an enormous wagon train—and will not move as a body on an average 20 miles in two weeks. This army sees no reinforcements coming to it, though all feel if there are truly patriotic men of sense at home having influence, they must know that if the ranks of the regiments now in the field were filled up one man would be worth five to service if in new regiments. The confederates know this and have thrown their conscripts into the ranks where they fight like the disciplined troops by their sides. Many lessons in military matters may be taken from them. One is decision, energy, determination and unity in its administration—and in having a policy. I hear the men talk of what they design when they go home. I tell you, the voice is a warning one, and I hear it from the western army, and bodes no good to the present administration, party or to the radicals. I have heard them say among themselves (and officers say it) that the President promised help, but they will put no faith in him, till they see evidences strong as holy writ. They have believed in him as "honest"—but with honesty is expected firmness and decision, and professions alone will not avail. These murmurs bode no good. Our army will soon be getting restless. It is recuperating rapidly, and becoming equipped again, and if we had even 20000 more men Richmond would be looking for us. We must and soon will take the offensive, and we hope for success, but heart must be given our men by support from home. If we could see two or three regiments arriving daily our officers & men would not be afflicted with any other nostalgia than of their home, Richmond.

I have heard that General McClellan has lost favor at Washington: a report which I hope is unfounded and that General Halleck is to be called to Washington as General-in-Chief. I regret both if true. There is no more able commander than McClellan—and no one in whom the army has more confidence. Every army has its idol, and McClellan is the idol of this, and I should deeply regret for the sake of our country anything being done to supercede him. There is no one here in whom the army has more confidence. He is no politician but moves along with the spirit of a true soldier to use to the best advantage the means placed at his disposal to break down this rebellion. But enough of this. All I hope & pray & work for is, a speedy termination of the war by a restoration of union feeling: but many, many lives have to be lost.

The members of my staff are all well and desire remembrance to yourself and family. Butterfield has gone home sick, will return soon if well enough. Excuse this hasty and disconnected letter, written during an hundred interruptions and accept for yourself & family the best & warmest wishes of

Yours faithfully
F.J. Porter

J.C.G. Kennedy
Washington, D.C.

AN APPEAL FOR NEGOTIATION:
RHODE ISLAND, JULY 1862

August Belmont to Thurlow Weed

Belmont, the noted financier and national chairman of the Democratic Party, wrote to influential Republican Weed, editor of the *Albany Evening Journal*, in expectation that his letter would find its way to the President, as indeed it did; it is preserved in Lincoln's papers. Belmont's views represented the conservative "War Democrat" wing of his party—supporting the war against secession, but seeking some negotiated path to bring the rebellious states back into a Union "as it was." Lincoln wrote Belmont on July 31, not in direct reply but clearly aware of his views: "Those enemies must understand that they cannot experiment for ten years trying to destroy the government, and if they fail still come back into the Union unhurt."

Copy

New-port. R. I. July 20. 1862.

My dear Mr. Weed.

I have made several attempts to see you during your fleeting visits to New-York, but have not been so fortunate as to find you in.—.

Our National affairs are in a most critical position, more so than they have been at any time since the beginning of this unfortunate war.—.

What frightens me more than the disasters in the field is the apathy and distrust which I grieve to say I meet at every step even from men of standing and hitherto of undoubted loyalty to the Union—

You know my own feelings & convictions on the subject of our national troubles, & I am sure I can speak to you in all candor without the fear of having my thoughts misconstrued, though you may perhaps not share my views.—

My firm conviction is that any other solution to our present difficulties than a reconstruction of but one Government over all the states of our Confederacy would entail upon us & our children an inheritance of the most fearful consequences which must end in the utter disintegration & ruin of the whole country.—.

There are only two modes by which to prevent such a calamity, which is certainly at this moment more threatening than it has ever been before.—.

The one is by an energetic & unrelenting prosecution of the war to crush the rebellion, the other would be to negociate with the leaders of the Rebellion, (to which it would be madness to withold the character of a gigantic revolution) and to see whether it may not yet be possible to reestablish a federal Union—

Both alternatives present difficulties of the gravest nature & which they did not possess in the same degree at the beginning of the contest—

Our army has been decimated by disease & the casualities of war.

I am informed from reliable sources, that McClellan has barely 70.000 men all told & Pope's army, including the corps of McDowell Sigel & Banks is said to number barely 40.000—men. What can we expect to do with such a force against Richmond, which is defended by an enemy having probably double that number under arms, flushed with recent successes, commanded by generals at least equal to our's, directed by *one master spirit* & occupying a central position, in a country hostile to us?—

It is true the President has called out 300/m men, but it would be a *fatal delusion* to beleive, that this number would be sufficient to crush the enemy, even if it was sure that under the present system of volunteers the men would come forward.—. I think I make a liberal estimate, if I put the figure of the federal armies, all told at 400.000 effective men & this number will be reduced to 300/m before the new levies can be brought into the field.—.

When we stopped recruiting in the midst of our successes we dealt a fatal blow to our army, and it is really a wonder to me that our Commanding generals consented to submit to such a measure which crippled them when an overwhelming force became necessary to finish up the good work;— It was a policy hardly less suicidal than if we had stopped sending supplies & amunition to our men in the field. Where we would have found last winter 10 men eager to enlist, anxious to share in our triumphs we will hardly now find one, so deep are the gloom and distrust which have taken hold of our people.—. It would be worse than folly, to shut our eyes to this fact.—. I think ours is the first instance in history where a Government shut off its supplies of men in the midst of a gigantic war.

Look at England her enlistments in the Crimean war, lasted until the very day of the conclusion of peace.—.

There is now only one way to remedy our fatal error, that is for the President to establish a system of conscription by which instead of 300/m *at least 500.000 men are to be called under arms.*—

A straight forward proclamation of the President, setting forth the necessities of the case & appealing to the patriotism of the people will give more confidence than all the ill concealed attempts at palliating our desperate condition.—.

Instead of levying new regiments commanded by inexperienced officers of their own choosing & who for a year to come would barely add anything to our efficiency in the field, the new recruits ought to be collected at camps of instruction in healthy localities East & West, where under the direction of *West point graduates* they should be drilled and disiplined.—.

From thence as fast as they are fit for active duty, they should be forwarded to the army, to be incorporated in the old regiments *without reference to states & only where they are most needed.* This is the only way to create for this war an efficient *United States Army* & will strike a severe blow, to that most fatal of heresies (*States right & States pride*) which lies at the bottom of all our misfortunes. Besides that such a mode would be infinitely more enconomical, and the raw recruits mixed with our old Soldiers, would be of course much more reliable & steady before the enemy's fire, than in seperate regiments, commanded by officers just as inexperienced as themselves.

Simultaneously with these measures which ought to be taken, with the utmost vigor & despatch, we must infuse more life and energie in our naval department. The fact is we have made the great mistake to undertake a war on a gigantic scale by land where our oponnents are at least nearly as strong as we are, instead of throwing our best resources & energies upon that mode of warfare where we had the enemy at our mercy.—.

Had we at the very outset of the rebellion ordered 50 Iron Gunboats, even at the cost of 1 Million of Dollars a piece, we should before last January have been in possession of every southern port. With 200000 men we could have held by land, the line of the Potomac, Missouri & Tennessee and thus hemmed in we would have brought the south to terms, just as Russia had to sue for peace after the fall of Sebastapool.—

I think it is still in our power to accomplish this, though the task has become more difficult since Charleston, Savanah & Mobile have been so strongly fortified during the last six months. No time money & efforts ought to be spared, to build at *least 20* more large iron steamships with which to take & hold every important city on the rebel coast from North Carolina to Texas. If authority for all these measures is not vested in the President, he ought at once to call an extra session of Congress.

I have thus far given you my views of the steps which I consider indispensible if the sword is to be the arbiter of our future destiny, but is there no other way of saving our country, from all the horror & calamities, which even a successful war must entail upon us?

It may appear almost hopeless to attempt to bring the south back to the Union by negociation. Men & women alike in that distracted portion of our country have become frantic & exasperated by the teachings of unprincipled leaders and the miseries of cival war.—. Still I cannot bring myself to the beleif that the door to a reconciliation between the two sections is irrevocably & for ever shut.

The losses & sufferings which have befallen us, have been felt tenfold in the revolted states, and the thinking men of the south must see that a continuation of the war must end, in the utter destruction of their property & institutions.

The frightful carnage of many a battlefield must have convinced each section of the bravery of its opponents and how much better it will be to have them as friends than foes.—.

While I am convinced that the President would be willing to

see the South in the lawful possession of all its constitutional rights. —

—I have not lost all hope, that with these rights guaranteed a reunion of the two sections could not be accomplished. In any event it seems to me that an attempt at negociation should be made & that the time for it has not entirely passed away.—.

If one or two conservative men who without holding any official position possess influence & weight enough with our people and the Government to inspire confidence in their statements to the leading men of the south, could be found to proceed under the authority or at least with the knowledge of the President to Richmond, in order to open negociations I think success might crown their efforts.—.

It is impossible & would be presumptuous in me to point out the conditions of such a compromise, but I think that propositions would prove acceptable to the south, which contained in their general outline an amnesty for all political offences during the war & the calling of a national convention for the purpose of reconstructing the federal compact with such modifications in the constitution as our late sad experience has demonstrated to have become necessary

The war debts of the North & South might either be borne by each respective section or better still be funded & assumed by the general Government.—

The Monroe doctrine to be strictly and uncompromisingly enforced which would require & Justify a larger standing national army & navy than heretofore, thus give us a chance to make provisions for such of their military leaders, who repenting their past errors are willing again to serve that flag, to which as friends & as foes they owe all the distinction which they have ever acheived.

I know that some of these concessions will be very distasteful to our people — they can be to no one more so than to myself.—.

Every sacrifice must however be made at the alter of our country, when we can restore it to peace & prosperity, and with our blood, & with our treasure we must also be ready to yield our prejudices *& even our convictions*

I firmly beleive that the President would find the hearty support of the vast majority of our people in such a policy and he ought not to lose any time in carrying out these views.—. Such men for instance as yourself and Governor H. Seymour would soon be able to find out, whether the men who are guiding the destinies of the South could be brought to listen to the dictates of reason & moderation.

Before we enter upon a new phase in this terrible war, which must carry with it horrors & misery far greater than what we have witnessed yet, I cannot but think that patriotism & humanity alike call for an earnest effort towards reconciliation & peace.

If our efforts should be spurned & rejected we shall stand Justified before God & men and our good cause will have His blessing & the worlds sympathy.

(signed). August Belmont.

A "SHAMEFUL" DEFEAT:
WASHINGTON, D.C., JULY 1862

Salmon P. Chase to Richard C. Parsons

Secretary of the Treasury Chase reviewed the Seven Days' Battles for an old friend who was serving as U.S. consul in Rio de Janeiro. The new general-in-chief, Henry Halleck, was brought from the western theater along with John Pope. Although Chase dated the letter July 20, the cabinet meeting he describes was held on July 21.

Washington July 20, 1862

My dear Parsons

Day before yesterday your friend, Mr. Bond, called bringing pleasant news of you and yours & those winged jewels converted into wingless uses by being cased in gold. Brazilian gold coffining denizens of Brazilian air now made ornaments of Northern dames. Tell Mrs Parsons I am exceedingly obliged by her gift and hope she will not be displeased by my transfer of it to Nettie, who has now almost grown to be a young lady & while delighted with her sisters presents, evidently thought *she* ought not to be passed by. Now a gift to Nettie is a gift to me & Mrs Parsons has thus been made a double giver and has the thanks of us both.

You will have been mortified & grieved by the news of the disasters which have overtaken us. Since the rebellion broke out I have never been so sad.

The defeat of McClellan before Richmond was shameful, and attributable only to gross neglect & incompetency for which he should at once have been dismissed the service in disgrace.

You may think I speak strongly but you may be assured I do not speak one whit too strongly.

Just think of an army of ninety five thousand men, admirably provided, with unequalled artillery—the Commanding General on the south side of the Chicky. with over sixty probably seventy thousand men and a Corps General Porter with some twenty five thousand on the north bank. The enemy has *at most* not over one hundred thousand men inferior to ours in all respects, except perhaps numbers / Of this force two divisions Hugers & Magruder's are on the James or near it below Richmond—the other four or five divisions are in Richmond & in front of it between our army & the city. The whole of these four or five divisions—except perhaps five or ten thousand men left in Richmond—possibly (including Margruders & Hugers) making thirty thousand men left [ ] south side of the Chicky.—the whole of these four or five divisions, I say, march out & attack Porter. Instead of keeping his line of supply open—instead of giving Porter force enough to ensure a victory on the north bank—McClellan orders his base to be abandoned—his supplies withdrawn from the White House—leaves Porter to be beaten by superior numbers—draws him across the Chickahominy to his own force, kept almost wholly inactive thus far, & commences a disgraceful retreat, only saved from becoming a complete rout by the bravery of the men & skill of the Generals of the Corps & their subordinate officers. After five days retreating & fighting he reaches the James River & there has ever since remained & now remains under the protection of the gunboats.

The smallness of our losses in all these movements compared with the numbers of the army & the hardships & confusions incident to such retreats, show how small relatively to the fears of McClellan the enemys strength must have been. The total loss was about 1500 killed, about ∓5000 wounded & about 8000 missing.

We ought to won a victory and taken Richmond. We lost a battle & narrowly escaped a capitulation of our entire army.

After the battle & after the retreat & after reaching Harrisons Landing McClellan telegraphed the President that he had not more than 50.000 men by their colors. An actual inspection by the President made a few days afterwards proved that he must have had at that very time over eighty thousand.

Can you conceive anything more disgraceful?

Strange as it may seem the President even yet hesitates about superceding McClellan in the command of the Army of the Potomac. He has however resolved to give him at least a Commander by bringing Gen. Halleck here and giving him the

Command in Chief of all the Armies. Meantime also he has brought Pope here and placed him in command of the Army of Virginia, with all the state east of the Fredericksburgh Railroad to operate it. Already a Cavalry detachment inspired by Pope has cut the Virginia Central Railroad west of Richmond & within thirty or forty miles. By day after tomorrow I hope to hear that another detachment has taken Charlottesville & cleared the road towards Lynchburgh at least for a few miles. It is no secret which need be kept from a man beyond the Equinoctial that Pope hopes to be able to concentrate a force in a few days which will enable him to command all the railway approaches to Richmond from the West. We are calling out more men but we don't need them. What we need is activity in Generals & skill & courage.

The Slavery question perplexes the President almost as much as ever and yet I think he is about to emerge from the obscurities where he has been groping into somewhat clearer light.

Today he has had his Secretaries in Consultation & has read us several orders which he is thinking of promulgating:—one, requiring Generals to subsist their troops as far as may be on the enemy; another, authorizing the employment of negroes as laborers by the Generals; a third in form of a proclamation warning the rebels of the confiscations denounced by Congress and declaring his purpose to enfranchise the slaves of all rebels (unless they return to their allegiance in Sixty days) in all the Gulf States. He has also under consideration the question of authorizing the enlistment or employment of negroes as soldiers by Generals in the Gulf States. So you see the world moves. These measures, if all of them are adopted will decide everything. The three first will go near the same result & must necessarily draw the fourth after them. These measures, & the substitution of an able general for McClellan, & the genius & indefatigable labor of Halleck presiding over all, will I hope soon end this rebellion. I say I hope—but I do not hope so confidently as I did. McClellan is not *yet* superceded—Halleck has not *yet* been tried in this sphere. Room for disappointment certainly—but let me trust that disappointment will not come.

What documents do you receive regularly from the U States? What Newspapers? I take the liberty of sending you a paper from the Wall St Review, which rather shocks my modesty.

Katie and Nettie have both retired or they would send all sorts of good wishes & affectionate remembrances.

We are meditating a little excursion Northward. Best regards to Mrs P and believe me as ever

Most faithfully your friend
S P CHASE

Richard Parsons Esq

Don't forget to remember me most cordially to Gen. Webb

PRESIDENTIAL EMANCIPATION:
WASHINGTON, D.C., JULY 1862

Salmon P. Chase: Journal, July 22, 1862

On July 13, the day after his fruitless appeal to border state congressmen to support compensated emancipation, Lincoln revealed privately to Seward and Secretary of the Navy Welles that he had concluded to emancipate the slaves by presidential proclamation. He said, as Welles recorded it, "we must free the slaves or be ourselves subdued." Secretary Chase here reports the President's announcement of his emancipation proclamation to the full cabinet on July 22, drawing on the recent Second Confiscation Act and on his war powers.

TUESDAY, JULY 22D., 1862. This morning, I called on the President with a letter received some time since from Col. Key, in which he stated that he had reason to beleive that if Genl. McClellan found he could not otherwise sustain himself in Virginia, he would declare the liberation of the slaves; and that the President would not dare to interfere with the Order. I urged upon the President the importance of an immediate change in the command of the Army of the Potomac, representing the necessity of having a General in that command who would cordially and efficiently coöperate with the movements of Pope and others; and urging a change before the arrival of Genl. Halleck, in view of the extreme delicacy of his position in this respect, Genl. McClellan being his senior Major-General. I said that I did not regard Genl. McClellan as loyal to the Administration, although I did not question his general loyalty to the country.

I also urged Genl. McClellan's removal upon financial grounds. I told him that, if such a change in the command was made as would insure action to the army and give it power in the ratio of its strength, and if such measures were adopted in respect to slavery as would inspire the country with confidence that no measure would be left untried which promised a speedy and successful result, I would insure that, within ten days, the Bonds of the U.S.—except the 5–20s.—would be so far above par that conversions into the latter stock would take place rapidly and furnish the necessary means for carrying on the Government. If this was not done, it seemed to me impossible to meet necessary expenses. Already there were $10.000.000 of unpaid Requisitions, and this amount must constantly increase.

The President came to no conclusion, but said he would confer with Gen. Halleck on all these matters. I left him, promising to return to Cabinet, when the subject of the Orders discussed yesterday would be resumed.

Went to Cabinet at the appointed hour. It was unanimously agreed that the Order in respect to Colonization should be dropped; and the others were adopted unanimously, except that I wished North Carolina included among the States named in the first order.

The question of arming slaves was then brought up and I advocated it warmly. The President was unwilling to adopt this measure, but proposed to issue a Proclamation, on the basis of the Confiscation Bill, calling upon the States to return to their allegiance—warning the rebels the provisions of the Act would have full force at the expiration of sixty days—adding, on his own part, a declaration of his intention to renew, at the next session of Congress, his recommendation of compensation to States adopting the gradual abolishment of slavery—and proclaiming the emancipation of all slaves within States remaining in insurrection on the first of January, 1863.

I said that I should give to such a measure my cordial support; but I should prefer that no new expression on the subject of compensation should be made, and I thought that the measure of Emancipation could be much better and more quietly accomplished by allowing Generals to organize and arm the slaves (thus avoiding depredation and massacre on the one hand, and support to the insurrection on the other) and by directing the Commanders of Departments to proclaim emancipation within their Districts as soon as practicable; but I regarded this as so much better than inaction on the subject, that I should give it my entire support.

The President determined to publish the first three Orders forthwith, and to leave the other for some further consideration. The impression left upon my mind by the whole discussion was, that while the President thought that the organization, equipment and arming of negroes, like other soldiers, would be productive of more evil than good, he was not unwilling that Commanders should, at their discretion, arm, for purely defensive purposes, slaves coming within their lines.

Mr. Stanton brought forward a proposition to draft 50.000 men. Mr. Seward proposed that the number should be 100.000. The President directed that, whatever number were drafted, should be a part of the 300.000 already called for. No decision was reached, however.

WASHINGTON, D.C., JULY 1862

Abraham Lincoln: First Draft of the Emancipation Proclamation

July 22, 1862

Only the first paragraph of this draft was immediately published, on July 25, in reference to that section of the Second Confiscation Act referring to the potential seizure of property of those in rebellion or abetting rebellion. The following selection explains why the rest of the proclamation—its core—was not immediately made public.

In pursuance of the sixth section of the act of congress entitled "An act to suppress insurrection and to punish treason and rebellion, to seize and confiscate property of rebels, and for other purposes" Approved July 17. 1862, and which act, and the Joint Resolution explanatory thereof, are herewith published, I, Abraham Lincoln, President of the United States, do hereby proclaim to, and warn all persons within the contemplation of said sixth section to cease participating in, aiding, countenancing, or abetting the existing rebellion, or any rebellion against the government of the United States, and to return to their proper allegiance to the United States, on pain of the forfeitures and seizures, as within and by said sixth section provided.

And I hereby make known that it is my purpose, upon the next meeting of congress, to again recommend the adoption of a practical measure for tendering pecuniary aid to the free choice or rejection, of any and all States which may then be recognizing and practically sustaining the authority of the United States, and which may then have voluntarily adopted, or thereafter may voluntarily adopt, gradual abolishment of slavery within such State or States—that the object is to practically restore, thenceforward to be maintained, the constitutional relation between the general government and each, and all the states, wherein that relation is now suspended, or disturbed; and that, for this object, the war, as it has been, will be, prossecuted. And, as a fit and necessary military measure for effecting this object, I, as Commander-in-Chief of the Army and Navy of the United States, do order and declare that on the first day of January in the year of Our Lord one thousand, eight hundred and sixtythree, all persons held as slaves within any state or states, wherein the constitutional authority of the United States shall not then be practically recognized, submitted to, and maintained, shall then, thenceforward, and forever, be free.

Emancipation Proclamation
as first sketched and
shown to the Cabinet in
July 1862.

POSTPONING EMANCIPATION: WASHINGTON, D.C., JULY 1862

Francis B. Carpenter: from Six Months at the White House with Abraham Lincoln

An established portrait painter, Carpenter lived at the White House from February to July 1864 while painting his well-known depiction of Lincoln reading the Emancipation Proclamation to the cabinet. In his 1866 memoir Carpenter related a conversation he had with the President on February 6, 1864, in which Lincoln recalled discussing the initial reaction of his cabinet to the proclamation. While it is unlikely that he recorded the President verbatim, the essence of what Carpenter said Lincoln said is supported by other accounts.

"It had got to be," said he, "midsummer, 1862. Things had gone on from bad to worse, until I felt that we had reached the end of our rope on the plan of operations we had been pursuing; that we had about played our last card, and must change our tactics, or lose the game! I now determined upon the adoption of the emancipation policy; and, without consultation with, or the knowledge of the Cabinet, I prepared the original draft of the proclamation, and, after much anxious thought, called a Cabinet meeting upon the subject. This was the last of July, or the first part of the month of August, 1862." (The exact date he did not remember.) "This Cabinet meeting took place, I think, upon a Saturday. All were present, excepting Mr. Blair, the Postmaster-General, who was absent at the opening of the discussion, but came in subsequently. I said to the Cabinet that I had resolved upon this step, and had not called them together to ask their advice, but to lay the subject-matter of a proclamation before them; suggestions as to which would be in order, after they had heard it read. Mr. Lovejoy," said he, "was in error when he informed you that it excited no comment, excepting on the part of Secretary Seward. Various suggestions were offered. Secretary Chase wished the language stronger in reference to the arming of the blacks. Mr. Blair, after he came in, deprecated the policy, on the ground that it would cost the Administration the fall elections. Nothing, however, was offered that I had not already fully anticipated and settled in my own mind, until Secretary Seward spoke. He said in substance: 'Mr. President, I approve of the proclamation, but I question the expediency of its issue at this juncture. The depression of the public mind, consequent upon our repeated reverses, is so great that I fear the effect of so important a step. It may be viewed as the last measure of an exhausted government, a cry for help; the government stretching forth its hands to Ethiopia, instead of Ethiopia stretching forth her hands to the government.' His idea," said the President, "was that it would be considered our last *shriek*, on the retreat." (This was his *precise* expression.) " 'Now,' continued Mr. Seward, 'while I approve the measure, I suggest, sir, that you postpone its issue, until you can give it to the country supported by military success, instead of issuing it, as would be the case now, upon the greatest disasters of the war!' " Mr. Lincoln continued: "The wisdom of the view of the Secretary of State struck me with very great force. It was an aspect of the case that, in all my thought upon the subject, I had entirely overlooked. The result was that I put the draft of the proclamation aside, as you do your sketch for a picture, waiting for a victory."

SAVING THE GOVERNMENT:
WASHINGTON, D.C., JULY 1862

Abraham Lincoln to Cuthbert Bullitt

Cuthbert Bullitt and Thomas J. Durant, whose letter Bullitt forwarded to the President, were Louisiana unionists. Lincoln's reply to Bullitt forecast his hardening attitude toward prosecuting the conflict.

PRIVATE

Cuthbert Bullitt Esq — Washington D.C.
New Orleans La. — July 28. 1862

Sir: The copy of a letter addressed to yourself by Mr. Thomas J. Durant, has been shown to me. The writer appears to be an able, a dispassionate, and an entirely sincere man. The first part of the letter is devoted to an effort to show that the Secession Ordinance of Louisiana was adopted against the will of a majority of the people. This is probably true; and in that fact may be found some instruction. Why did they allow the Ordinance to go into effect? Why did they not assert themselves? Why stand passive and allow themselves to be trodden down by a minority? Why did they not hold popular meetings, and have a convention of their own, to express and enforce the true sentiment of the state? If preorganization was against them *then*, why not do this *now*, that the United States Army is present to protect them? The paralysis—the dead palsy—of the government in this whole struggle is, that this class of men will do nothing for the government, nothing for themselves, except demanding that the government shall not strike its open enemies, lest they be struck by accident!

Mr. Durant complains that in various ways the relation of master and slave is disturbed by the presence of our Army; and he considers it particularly vexatious that this, in part, is done under cover of an act of Congress, while constitutional guaranties are suspended on the plea of military necessity. The truth is, that what is done, and omitted, about slaves, is done and omitted on the same military necessity. It is a military necessity to have men and money; and we can get neither, in sufficient numbers, or amounts, if we keep from, or drive from, our lines, slaves coming to them. Mr. Durant cannot be ignorant of the pressure in this direction; nor of my efforts to hold it within bounds till he, and such as he shall have time to help themselves.

I am not posted to speak understandingly on all the police regulations of which Mr. Durant complains. If experience shows any one of them to be wrong, let them be set right. I think I can perceive, in the freedom of trade, which Mr. Durant urges, that he would relieve both friends and enemies from the pressure of the blockade. By this he would serve the enemy more effectively than the enemy is able to serve himself. I do not say or believe that to serve the enemy is the purpose of Mr. Durant; or that he is conscious of any purpose, other than national and patriotic ones. Still, if there were a class of men who, having no choice of sides in the contest, were anxious only to have quiet and comfort for themselves while it rages, and to fall in with the victorious side at the end of it, without loss to themselves, their advice as to the mode of conducting the contest would be precisely such as his is. He speaks of no duty—apparently thinks of none—resting upon Union men. He even thinks it injurious to the Union cause that they should be restrained in trade and passage without taking sides. They are to touch neither a sail nor a pump, but to be merely passengers, —dead-heads at that—to be carried snug and dry, throughout the storm, and safely landed right side up. Nay, more; even a mutineer is to go untouched lest these sacred passengers receive an accidental wound.

Of course the rebellion will never be suppressed in Louisiana, if the professed Union men there will neither help to do it, nor permit the government to do it without their help.

Now, I think the true remedy is very different from what is suggested by Mr. Durant. It does not lie in rounding the rough angles of the war, but in removing the necessity for the war. The people of Louisiana who wish protection to person and property, have but to reach forth their hands and take it. Let them, in good faith, reinaugurate the national authority, and set up a State Government conforming thereto under the constitution. They know how to do it, and can have the protection of the Army while doing it. The Army will be withdrawn so soon as such State government can dispense with its presence; and the people of the State can then upon the old Constitutional terms, govern themselves to their own liking. This is very simple and easy.

If they will not do this, if they prefer to hazard all for the sake of destroying the government, it is for them to consider whether it is probable I will surrender the government to save them from losing all. If they decline what I suggest, you scarcely need to ask what I will do. What would you do in my position? Would you drop the war where it is? Or, would you prosecute it in future, with elder-stalk squirts, charged with rose water? Would you deal lighter blows rather than heavier ones? Would you give up the contest, leaving any available means unapplied.

I am in no boastful mood. I shall not do *more* than I can, and I shall do *all* I can to save the government, which is my sworn duty as well as my personal inclination. I shall do nothing in malice. What I deal with is too vast for malicious dealing. Yours truly

A. LINCOLN

COTTON AND EMANCIPATION: MASSACHUSETTS, AUGUST 1862

Charles Sumner to John Bright

Charles Sumner, a Radical Republican senator from Massachusetts who often had the ear of Lincoln on matters of abolition and emancipation, corresponded regularly on the state of the war with the British reformer John Bright, a staunch supporter of the Union cause from his seat in the House of Commons. Bright had written to Sumner on July 14, expressing hopes that the Union capture of New Orleans would allow increased shipments of cotton to English textile mills.

Boston 5th Aug. '62

Dear Mr Bright,

I wish I could sit by the seashore & talk with you again. It is hard to write of events—& of persons, with that fullness & frankness which you require.

The letters which I enclose from Mr Atkinson, a most intelligent & excellent person, will let you see the chance of cotton from the South. *Do not count upon it.* Make yr calculations as if it were beyond reach. His plan of opening Texas reads well on paper, but thus far we have lost by dividing our forces. We must concentrate & crush. The armies of the South must be met & annihilated. If we start an expedition to Texas there will be another diversion. Climate too will be for the present against us.

The correspondence between Genl. Butler & Mr Johnson will shew you that Govt. puts no restraint upon the sale of Cotton. It is the perverseness of the rebels that does it all.

Congress has adjourned. After a few days in Washington, to see the Presdt & cabinet, I have come home—glad of a little rest, but to find new cares here. Our session has been very busy; I doubt if any legislative body ever acted on so many important questions. You who follow our fortunes so kindly, doubtless know what has been done for freedom—for reform generally, &, also in the way of organizing our forces & providing means. There have been differences of opinion on questions of policy—especially on Slavery. This was to be expected. But the Bill of Confiscation & Liberation, which was at last passed, under pressure from our reverses at Richmond, is a practical Act of Emancipation. It was only in this respect that I valued it. The Western men were earnest for reaching the property of the rebels. To this I was indifferent except so far as it was necessary to break up the strongholds of slavery.

I wish that the Cabinet was more harmonious, & that the Presdt. had less *vis inertia*. He is hard to move. He is honest but inexperienced. Thus far he has been influenced by the Border States. I urged him on the 4th July to put forth an edict of Emancipation, telling him he could make the day more sacred & historic than ever. He replied—"I would do it if I were not afraid that half the officers would fling down their arms & three more States would rise." He is plainly mistaken about the officers & I think also with regard to the States. In the cabinet, Chase, who enjoys & deserves public confidence more than any other member, also the Secy of War & Secy of the Navy, are for this policy.—The last call for 300,000 men is recd. by the people with enthusiasm, because it seems to shew a purpose to push the war vigorously.

There is no thought in the cabinet or the Presdt. of abandoning the contest. *Of this be sure.* It will be pushed to the full extent of all the resources of the Republic *including, of course, the slaves.* Strange, it seems to me, that I, who so sincerely accept the principles of Peace, should be mixed up in this terrible war. But I see no way except to go forward; nor do I see any way in which England can get cotton speedily except through our success. England ought to help us with her benedictions; for she is interested next to ourselves. But her adverse sympathies help put off the good day. All here are grateful to you, for yr strong & noble words. God bless you! I say with all my heart.

Ever Yrs, Charles Sumner

The Army of the Potomac once 160,000 men is reduced by death & casualties to 85,000. Yr Walcheren expedition on a larger scale.

EVACUATING THE PENINSULA:
WASHINGTON, D.C., AUGUST 1862

Henry W. Halleck to George B. McClellan

General Halleck, in his new role of general-in-chief, found a strategic puzzle awaiting him when he reached Washington on July 23. John Pope's Army of Virginia lay in northern Virginia between Washington and Richmond. McClellan's Army of the Potomac lay at Harrison's Landing on the James below Richmond. In between was Lee's Army of Northern Virginia, capable of striking in either direction. As Halleck points out here, his decision to withdraw the Potomac army from the Peninsula stemmed largely from McClellan's claim that the Rebel army, with 200,000 men, outnumbered his own by better than two to one. This was McClellan's fixed delusion; after the carnage of the Seven Days, he comfortably outnumbered Lee.

HEADQUARTERS OF THE ARMY,
Washington, August 6, 1862.

GENERAL: Your telegram of yesterday was received this morning, and I immediately telegraphed you a brief reply, promising to write you more fully by mail.

You, general, certainly could not have been more pained at receiving my order than I was at the necessity of issuing it. I was advised by high officers, in whose judgment I had great confidence, to make the order immediately on my arrival here, but I determined not to do so until I could learn your wishes from a personal interview; and even after that interview I tried every means in my power to avoid withdrawing your army, and delayed my decision as long as I dared to delay it. I assure you, general, it was not a hasty and inconsiderate act, but one that caused me more anxious thoughts than any other of my life; but after full and mature consideration of all the pros and cons, I was reluctantly forced to the conclusion that the order must be issued. There was to my mind no alternative.

Allow me to allude to a few of the facts in the case. You and your officers at one interview estimated the enemy's forces in and around Richmond at 200,000 men. Since then you and others report that they have received and are receiving large re-enforcements from the South. General Pope's army covering Washington is only about 40,000. Your effective force is only about 90,000. You are 30 miles from Richmond, and General Pope 80 or 90, with the enemy directly between you, ready to fall with his superior numbers upon one or the other, as he may elect. Neither can re-enforce the other in case of such an attack.

If General Pope's army be diminished to re-enforce you, Washington, Maryland, and Pennsylvania would be left uncovered and exposed. If your force be reduced to strengthen Pope, you would be too weak to even hold the position you now occupy should the enemy turn round and attack you in full force. In other words, the old Army of the Potomac is split into two parts, with the entire force of the enemy directly between them. They cannot be united by land without exposing both to destruction, and yet they must be united. To send Pope's forces by water to the Peninsula is, under present circumstances, a military impossibility. The only alternative is to send the forces on the Peninsula to some point by water, say Fredericksburg, where the two armies can be united.

Let me now allude to some of the objections which you have urged. You say that the withdrawal from the present position will cause the certain demoralization of the army, "which is now in excellent discipline and condition." I cannot understand why a simple change of position to a new and by no means distant base will demoralize an army in excellent discipline, unless the officers themselves assist in that demoralization, which I am satisfied they will not. Your change of front from your extreme right at Hanover Court-House to your present position was over 30 miles, but I have not heard that it demoralized your troops, notwithstanding the severe losses they sustained in effecting it. A new base on the Rappahannock at Fredericksburg brings you within about 60 miles of Richmond, and secures a re-enforcement of 40,000 or 50,000 fresh and disciplined troops. The change, with such advantages, will, I think, if properly represented to your army, encourage rather than demoralize your troops. Moreover, you yourself suggested that a junction might be effected at Yorktown, but that a flank march across the isthmus would be more hazardous than to retire to Fort Monroe. You will remember that Yorktown is 2 or 3 miles farther than Fredericksburg is. Besides, the latter is between Richmond and Washington, and covers Washington from any attack of the enemy. The political effect of the withdrawal may at first be unfavorable; but I think the public are beginning to understand its necessity, and that they will have much more confidence in a united army than in its separated fragments.

But you will reply, why not re-enforce me here, so that I can strike Richmond from my present position? To do this you said at our interview that you required 30,000 additional troops. I told you that it was impossible to give you so many. You finally thought that you would have "some chance" of success with 20,000. But you afterward telegraphed me that you would require 35,000, as the enemy was being largely re-enforced. If your estimate of the enemy's strength was correct, your requisition was perfectly reasonable, but it was utterly impossible to fill it until new troops could be enlisted and organized, which would require several weeks. To keep your army in its present position until it could be so re-enforced would almost destroy it in that climate. The months of August and September are almost fatal to whites who live on that part of James River, and even after you received the re-enforcements asked for, you admitted that you must reduce Fort Darling and the river batteries before you could advance on Richmond. It is by no means certain that the reduction of these fortifications would not require considerable time, perhaps as much as those at Yorktown. This delay might not only be fatal to the health of your army, but in the mean time General Pope's forces would be exposed to the heavy blows of the enemy without the slightest hope of assistance from you.

In regard to the demoralizing effect of a withdrawal from the Peninsula to the Rappahannock I must remark that a large number of your highest officers, indeed a majority of those whose opinions have been reported to me, are decidedly in favor of the movement. Even several of those who originally advocated the line of the Peninsula now advise its abandonment.

I have not inquired, and do not wish to know, by whose advice or for what reasons the Army of the Potomac was separated into two parts, with the enemy between them. I must take things as I find them. I find the forces divided, and I wish to unite them. Only one feasible plan has been presented for doing this. If you or any one else had presented a better plan I certainly should have adopted it. But all of your plans require re-enforcements, which it is impossible to give you. It is very easy to ask for re-enforcements, but it is not so easy to give them when you have no disposable troops at your command.

I have written very plainly as I understand the case, and I hope you will give me credit for having fully considered the matter, although I may have arrived at very different conclusions from your own.

Very respectfully, your obedient servant,

H. W. HALLECK,
General-in-Chief.

Maj. Gen. GEORGE B. MCCLELLAN,
Commanding, &c., Berkeley, Va.

FLEEING SLAVES: GEORGIA, AUGUST 1862

Memorial of a Committee of Citizens of Liberty County, Georgia

Brigadier General Hugh W. Mercer, Confederate commander at Savannah, received no response from Richmond to his forwarding of this citizens' plea. The memorial suggests the dimensions of the problem of runaway slaves in just this one area of coastal Georgia. In April 1862, Union forces had captured Fort Pulaski and occupied the coastal islands off Savannah, which became a haven for the fleeing slaves.

HEADQUARTERS THIRD DIVISION, DISTRICT OF GEORGIA,
Savannah, August 5, 1862.

HON. GEORGE W. RANDOLPH,
Secretary of War:

SIR: I have the honor to inclose a memorial presented by a committee of the citizens of Liberty County, in this State, a community noted for their respectability and worth. The subject presented, I would respectfully submit, is one that demands the early notice of the Congress when it shall reassemble, and the instructions of the War Department (in accordance with such legislation as may be adopted) for the government of military commanders. The evil and danger alluded to may grow into frightful proportions unless checked, but the responsibility of life and death, so liable to be abused, is obviously too great to be intrusted to the hand of every officer whose duties may bring him face to face with this question. It is likely to become one of portentous magnitude if the war continues, and I do not see how it can be properly dealt with except by the supreme legislature of the country. I deem the action of Congress in this regard as needful for the protection of military commanders as for their guidance.

I have the honor to be, sir, very respectfully, your obedient servant,

H. W. MERCER,
Brigadier-General, Commanding.

[Inclosure.]

Brigadier-General MERCER,

Commanding Military District of Georgia, Savannah:

GENERAL: The undersigned, citizens of Liberty County, of the Fifteenth District, would respectfully present for your consideration a subject of grave moment, not to themselves only, but to their fellow-citizens of the Confederate States who occupy not only our territory immediately bordering on that of the old United States, but the whole line of our sea-coast from Virginia to Texas. We allude to the escape of our slaves across the border lines landward, and out to the vessels of the enemy seaward, and to their being also enticed off by those who, having made their escape, return for that purpose, and not infrequently attended by the enemy. The injury inflicted upon the interests of the citizens of the Confederate States by this now constant drain is immense. Independent of the forcible seizure of slaves by the enemy whenever it lies in his power, and to which we now make no allusion, as the indemnity for this loss will in due time occupy the attention of our Government. From ascertained losses on certain parts of our coast, we may set down as a low estimate the number of slaves absconded and enticed off from our sea-board at 20,000, and their value at from $12,000,000 to $15,000,000, to which loss may be added the insecurity of the property along our borders and the demoralization of the negroes that remain, which increases with the continuance of the evil, and may finally result in perfect disorganization and rebellion. The absconding negroes hold the position of traitors, since they go over to the enemy and afford him aid and comfort by revealing the condition of the districts and cities from which they come, and aiding him in creating fortifications and raising provisions for his support, and now that the United States have allowed their introduction into their Army and Navy, aiding the enemy by enlisting under his banners, and increasing his resources in men for our annoyance and destruction. Negroes occupy the position of spies also, since they are employed in secret expeditions for obtaining information by transmission of newspapers and by other modes, and act as guides to expeditions on the land and as pilots to their vessels on the waters of our inlets and rivers.

They have proved of great value thus far to the coast operations of the enemy, and without their assistance he could not have accomplished as much for our injury and annoyance as he has done; and unless some measures shall be adopted to prevent the escape of the negroes to the enemy, the threat of an army of trained Africans for the coming fall and winter campaigns may become a reality.

Meanwhile the counties along the seaboard will become exhausted of the slave population, which should be retained as far as possible for the raising of provisions and supplies for our forces on the coast. In the absence of penalties of such a nature as to insure respect and dread, the temptations which are spread before the negroes are very strong, and when we consider their condition, their ignorance and credulity, and love of change, must prove in too many cases decidedly successful. No effectual check being interposed to their escape, the desire increases among them in proportion to the extent of its successful gratification, and will spread inland until it will draw negroes from counties far in the interior of the State, and negroes will congregate from every quarter in the counties immediately bordering on the sea and become a lawless set of runaways, corrupting the negroes that remain faithful, depredating on property of all kinds, and resorting, it may be, to deeds of violence, which demonstrates that the whole State is interested in the effort to stop this evil; and already have negroes from Middle Georgia made their escape to the sea-board counties, and through Savannah itself to the enemy.

After consulting the laws of the State we can discover none that meet the case and allow of that prompt execution of a befitting penalty which its urgency demands. The infliction of capital punishment is now confined to the superior court, and any indictment before that court would involve incarceration of the negroes for months, with the prospect of postponement of trial, long litigation, large expense, and doubtful conviction; and, moreover, should the negroes be caught escaping in any numbers, there would not be room in all our jails to receive them. The civil law, therefore, as it now stands cannot come to our protection.

Can we find protection under military law? This is the question we submit to the general in command. Under military law the severest penalties are prescribed for furnishing the enemy with aid and comfort and for acting as spies and traitors, all which the negroes can do as effectually as white men, as facts prove, and as we have already suggested. There can be but little doubt that if negroes are detected in the act of exciting their fellow-slaves to escape or of taking them off, or of returning after having gone to the enemy to induce and aid others to escape, they may in each of these cases be summarily punished under military authority. But may not the case of negroes taken in the act of absconding singly or in parties, without being directly incited so to do by one or more others, be also summarily dealt with by military authority? Were our white population to act in the same way, would it not be necessary to make a summary example of them, in order to cure the evil or put it under some salutary control? If it be argued that in case of the negroes it would be hard to mete out a similar punishment under similar circumstances, because of their ignorance, pliability, credulity, desire of change, the absence of the political ties of allegiance, and the peculiar status of the race, it may be replied that the negroes constitute a part of the body politic in fact, and should be made to know their duty; that they are perfectly aware that the act which they commit is one of rebellion against the power and authority of their owners and the Government under which they live. They are perfectly aware that they go over to the protection and aid of the enemy who are on the coast for the purpose of killing their owners and of destroying their property; and they know, further, that if they themselves are found with the enemy that they will be treated as the enemy, namely, shot and destroyed.

To apprehend such transgressors, to confine and punish them privately by owners, or publicly by the citizens of the county by confinement and whipping, and then return them to the plantations, will not abate the evil, for the disaffected will not thereby be reformed, but will remain a leaven of corruption in the mass and stand ready to make any other attempts that may promise success. It is, indeed, a monstrous evil that we suffer. Our negroes are property, the agricultural class of the Confederacy, upon whose order and continuance so much depends—may go off (inflicting a great pecuniary loss, both private and public) to the enemy, convey any amount of valuable information, and aid him by building his fortifications, by raising supplies for his armies, by enlisting as soldiers, by acting as spies and as guides and pilots to his expeditions on land and water, and bringing in the foe upon us to kill and devastate; and yet, if we catch them in the act of going to the enemy we are powerless for the infliction of any punishment adequate to their crime and adequate to fill them with salutary fear of its commission. Surely some remedy should be applied, and that speedily, for the protection of the country aside from all other considerations. A few executions of leading transgressors among them by hanging or shooting would dissipate the ignorance which may be supposed to possess their minds, and which may be pleaded in arrest of judgment.

We do not pray the general in command to issue any order for the government of the citizens in the matter, which, of course, is no part of his duty, but the promulgation of an order to the military for the execution of ringleaders who are detected in stirring up the people to escape, for the execution of all who return, having once escaped, and for the execution of all who are caught in the act of escaping, will speedily be known and understood by the entire slave population, and will do away with all excuses of ignorance, and go very far toward an entire arrest of the evil, while it will enable the citizens to act efficiently in their own sphere whenever circumstances require them to act at all. In an adjoining county, which has lost some 200, since the shooting of two detected in the act of escaping not another attempt has been made, and it has been several weeks since the two were shot.

As law-abiding men we do not desire committees of vigilance clothed with plenary powers, nor meetings of the body of our citizens to take the law into their own hands, however justifiable it may be under the peculiar circumstances, and therefore, in the failure of the civil courts to meet the emergency, we refer the subject to the general in command, believing that he has the power to issue the necessary order to the forces under him covering the whole ground, and knowing that by so doing he will receive the commendation and cordial support of the intelligent and law-abiding citizens inhabiting the military department over which he presides.

All which is respectfully submitted by your friends and fellow-citizens.

R. Q. MALLARD,
T. W. FLEMING,
E. STACY,
Committee of Citizens of the 15th Dist., Liberty County, Ga.

RETALIATION FOR ARMING SLAVES: VIRGINIA, AUGUST 1862

Confederate War Department: General Orders No. 60

The order outlawing Hunter and Phelps was issued at the direction of Jefferson Davis. Brigadier General John W. Phelps had raised five companies of freed slaves in Louisiana in late July, but was ordered by his superior Benjamin F. Butler to use them as laborers instead. After Phelps resigned in protest, Butler began recruiting troops from among free people of color, and by November had formed three regiments of Louisiana Native Guards. On December 23, 1862, Davis issued a proclamation ordering that Butler be immediately hanged if captured.

GENERAL ORDERS, No. 60. } WAR DEPT., ADJT. AND INSP. GENERAL'S OFFICE,

Richmond, August 21, 1862.

I. Whereas, Major-General Hunter, recently in command of the enemy's forces on the coast of South Carolina, and Brigadier-General Phelps, a military commander of the enemy in the State of Louisiana, have organized and armed negro slaves for military service against their masters, citizens of this Confederacy; and whereas, the Government of the United States has refused to answer an inquiry whether said conduct of its officers meets its sanction, and has thus left to this Government no other means of repressing said crimes and outrages than the adoption of such measures of retaliation as shall serve to prevent their repetition:

Ordered, That Major-General Hunter and Brigadier-General Phelps be no longer held and treated as public enemies of the Confederate States, but as outlaws, and that in the event of the capture of either of them, or that of any other commissioned officer employed in drilling, organizing, or instructing slaves with a view to their armed service in this war, he shall not be regarded as a prisoner of war, but held in close confinement for execution as a felon, at such time and place as the President shall order.

By order:

S. COOPER,
Adjutant and Inspector General.

WASHINGTON, D.C., AUGUST 1862

Abraham Lincoln: Address on Colonization

A month after appealing to border state congressmen to adopt compensated emancipation, the President invited a delegation of Washington's black leaders to the White House to promote his plan for colonization. Lincoln's speech to the committee was reported in the *New-York Daily Tribune* on August 15. The Central American site he mentions was the province of Chiriqui, in present-day Panama. Congress had recently appropriated $600,000 to support colonization abroad. The delegation meeting with Lincoln, like the capital's black community in general, was sharply divided on the merits of colonization. Frederick Douglass said it revealed the President's "contempt for Negroes" and "canting hypocrisy." While as many as 500 volunteers did sign up for Chiriqui, the project withered away due to opposition from the surrounding Central American states.

August 14, 1862

This afternoon the President of the United States gave audience to a Committee of colored men at the White House. They were introduced by the Rev. J. Mitchell, Commissioner of Emigration. E. M. Thomas, the Chairman, remarked that they were there by invitation to hear what the Executive had to say to them. Having all been seated, the President, after a few preliminary observations, informed them that a sum of money had been appropriated by Congress, and placed at his disposition for the purpose of aiding the colonization in some country of the people, or a portion of them, of African descent, thereby making it his duty, as it had for a long time been his inclination, to favor that cause; and why, he asked, should the people of your race be colonized, and where? Why should they leave this country? This is, perhaps, the first question for proper consideration. You and we are different races. We have between us a broader difference than exists between almost any other two races. Whether it is right or wrong I need not discuss, but this physical difference is a great disadvantage to us both, as I think your race suffer very greatly, many of them by living among us, while ours suffer from your presence. In a word we suffer on each side. If this is admitted, it affords a reason at least why we should be separated. You here are freemen I suppose.

A VOICE: Yes, sir.

The President—Perhaps you have long been free, or all your lives. Your race are suffering, in my judgment, the greatest wrong inflicted on any people. But even when you cease to be slaves, you are yet far removed from being placed on an equality with the white race. You are cut off from many of the advantages which the other race enjoy. The aspiration of men is to enjoy equality with the best when free, but on this broad continent, not a single man of your race is made the equal of a single man of ours. Go where you are treated the best, and the ban is still upon you.

I do not propose to discuss this, but to present it as a fact with which we have to deal. I cannot alter it if I would. It is a fact, about which we all think and feel alike, I and you. We look to our condition, owing to the existence of the two races on this continent. I need not recount to you the effects upon white men, growing out of the institution of Slavery. I believe in its general evil effects on the white race. See our present condition—the country engaged in war!—our white men cutting one another's throats, none knowing how far it will extend; and then consider what we know to be the truth. But for your race among us there could not be war, although many men engaged on either side do not care for you one way or the other. Nevertheless, I repeat, without the institution of Slavery and the colored race as a basis, the war could not have an existence.

It is better for us both, therefore, to be separated. I know that there are free men among you, who even if they could better their condition are not as much inclined to go out of the country as those, who being slaves could obtain their freedom on this condition. I suppose one of the principal difficulties in the way of colonization is that the free colored man cannot see that his comfort would be advanced by it. You may believe you can live in Washington or elsewhere in the United States the remainder of your life as easily, perhaps more so than you can in any foreign country, and hence you may come to the conclusion that you have nothing to do with the idea of going to a foreign country. This is (I speak in no unkind sense) an extremely selfish view of the case.

But you ought to do something to help those who are not so fortunate as yourselves. There is an unwillingness on the part of our people, harsh as it may be, for you free colored people to remain with us. Now, if you could give a start to white people, you would open a wide door for many to be made free. If we deal with those who are not free at the beginning, and whose intellects are clouded by Slavery, we have very poor materials to start with. If intelligent colored men, such as are before me, would move in this matter, much might be accomplished. It is exceedingly important that we have men at the beginning capable of thinking as white men, and not those who have been systematically oppressed.

There is much to encourage you. For the sake of your race you should sacrifice something of your present comfort for the purpose of being as grand in that respect as the white people. It is a cheering thought throughout life that something can be done to ameliorate the condition of those who have been subject to the hard usage of the world. It is difficult to make a man miserable while he feels he is worthy of himself, and claims kindred to the great God who made him. In the American Revolutionary war sacrifices were made by men engaged in it; but they were cheered by the future. Gen. Washington himself endured greater physical hardships than if he had remained a British subject. Yet he was a happy man, because he was engaged in benefiting his race—something for the children of his neighbors, having none of his own.

The colony of Liberia has been in existence a long time. In a certain sense it is a success. The old President of Liberia, Roberts, has just been with me—the first time I ever saw him. He says they have within the bounds of that colony between 300,000 and 400,000 people, or more than in some of our old States, such as Rhode Island or Delaware, or in some of our newer States, and less than in some of our larger ones. They are not all American colonists, or their descendants. Something less than 12,000 have been sent thither from this country. Many of the original settlers have died, yet, like people elsewhere, their offspring outnumber those deceased.

The question is if the colored people are persuaded to go anywhere, why not there? One reason for an unwillingness to do so is that some of you would rather remain within reach of the country of your nativity. I do not know how much attachment you may have toward our race. It does not strike me that you have the greatest reason to love them. But still you are attached to them at all events.

The place I am thinking about having for a colony is in Central America. It is nearer to us than Liberia—not much more than one-fourth as far as Liberia, and within seven days' run by steamers. Unlike Liberia it is on a great line of travel—it is a highway. The country is a very excellent one for any people, and with great natural resources and advantages, and especially because of the similarity of climate with your native land—thus being suited to your physical condition.

The particular place I have in view is to be a great highway from the Atlantic or Caribbean Sea to the Pacific Ocean, and this particular place has all the advantages for a colony. On both sides there are harbors among the finest in the world. Again, there is evidence of very rich coal mines. A certain amount of coal is valuable in any country, and there may be more than enough for the wants of the country. Why I attach so much importance to coal is, it will afford an opportunity to the inhabitants for immediate employment till they get ready to settle permanently in their homes.

If you take colonists where there is no good landing, there is a bad show; and so where there is nothing to cultivate, and of which to make a farm. But if something is started so that you can get your daily bread as soon as you reach there, it is a great advantage. Coal land is the best thing I know of with which to commence an enterprise.

To return, you have been talked to upon this subject, and told that a speculation is intended by gentlemen, who have an interest in the country, including the coal mines. We have been mistaken all our lives if we do not know whites as well as blacks look to their self-interest. Unless among those deficient of intellect everybody you trade with makes something. You meet with these things here as elsewhere.

If such persons have what will be an advantage to them, the question is whether it cannot be made of advantage to you.

You are intelligent, and know that success does not as much depend on external help as on self-reliance. Much, therefore, depends upon yourselves. As to the coal mines, I think I see the means available for your self-reliance.

I shall, if I get a sufficient number of you engaged, have provisions made that you shall not be wronged. If you will engage in the enterprise I will spend some of the money intrusted to me. I am not sure you will succeed. The Government may lose the money, but we cannot succeed unless we try; but we think, with care, we can succeed.

The political affairs in Central America are not in quite as satisfactory condition as I wish. There are contending factions in that quarter; but it is true all the factions are agreed alike on the subject of colonization, and want it, and are more generous than we are here. To your colored race they have no objection. Besides, I would endeavor to have you made equals, and have the best assurance that you should be the equals of the best.

The practical thing I want to ascertain is whether I can get a number of able-bodied men, with their wives and children, who are willing to go, when I present evidence of encouragement and protection. Could I get a hundred tolerably intelligent men, with their wives and children, to "cut their own fodder," so to speak? Can I have fifty? If I could find twenty-five able-bodied men, with a mixture of women and children, good things in the family relation, I think I could make a successful commencement.

I want you to let me know whether this can be done or not. This is the practical part of my wish to see you. These are subjects of very great importance, worthy of a month's study, instead of a speech delivered in an hour. I ask you then to consider seriously not pertaining to yourselves merely, nor for your race, and ours, for the present time, but as one of the things, if successfully managed, for the good of mankind—not confined to the present generation, but as

"From age to age descends the lay,
To millions yet to be,
Till far its echoes roll away,
Into eternity."

The above is merely given as the substance of the President's remarks.

The Chairman of the delegation briefly replied that "they would hold a consultation and in a short time give an answer." The President said: "Take your full time—no hurry at all."

The delegation then withdrew.

"I WOULD SAVE THE UNION": WASHINGTON, D.C., AUGUST 1862

Abraham Lincoln to Horace Greeley

Horace Greeley, founder and editor of the *New-York Daily Tribune*, addressed Lincoln in "The Prayer of Twenty Millions," a public letter that appeared on August 20. Greeley expressed disappointment with "the policy you seem to be pursuing with regard to the slaves of Rebels . . ." He charged the President with being unduly influenced by "certain fossil politicians" from the border states and with failing to execute the terms of the Second Confiscation Act. With his reply, published in the *Tribune* on August 25, Lincoln sought to prepare the public for his impending proclamation of emancipation.

Hon. Horace Greely: Executive Mansion,
Dear Sir Washington, August 22, 1862.

I have just read yours of the 19th. addressed to myself through the New-York Tribune. If there be in it any statements, or assumptions of fact, which I may know to be erroneous, I do not, now and here, controvert them. If there be in it any inferences which I may believe to be falsely drawn, I do not now and here, argue against them. If there be perceptable in it an impatient and dictatorial tone, I waive it in deference to an old friend, whose heart I have always supposed to be right.

As to the policy I "seem to be pursuing" as you say, I have not meant to leave any one in doubt.

I would save the Union. I would save it the shortest way under the Constitution. The sooner the national authority can be restored; the nearer the Union will be "the Union as it was." If there be those who would not save the Union, unless they could at the same time *save* slavery, I do not agree with them. If there be those who would not save the Union unless they could at the same time *destroy* slavery, I do not agree with them. My paramount object in this struggle *is* to save the Union, and is *not* either to save or to destroy slavery. If I could save the Union without freeing *any* slave I would do it, and if I could save it by freeing *all* the slaves I would do it; and if I could save it by freeing some and leaving others alone I would also do that. What I do about slavery, and the colored race, I do because I believe it helps to save the Union; and what I forbear, I forbear because I do *not* believe it would help to save the Union. I shall do *less* whenever I shall believe what I am doing hurts the cause, and I shall do *more* whenever I shall believe doing more will help the cause. I shall try to correct errors when shown to be errors; and I shall adopt new views so fast as they shall appear to be true views.

I have here stated my purpose according to my view of *official* duty; and I intend no modification of my oft-expressed *personal* wish that all men every where could be free. Yours,

A. LINCOLN

SLAVERY AND THE LAWS OF WAR: TENNESSEE, AUGUST 1862

William T. Sherman to Thomas Hunton

In July 1862 Sherman became the Union commander at Memphis. Hunton, a West Point classmate of Sherman and owner of a Mississippi plantation, wrote to him, citing their old school ties, to ask for the return of his slaves who had fled to the Union camps. He told Sherman that he was willing to come to Memphis himself, but only if he did not have to take the oath of allegiance.

Memphis Tenn. Aug. 24th 1862

Thomas Hunton Esq.
Coahoma, Panolo Co. Miss.
My dear Sir,

I freely admit that when you recall the times when we were schoolfellows, when we were younger than now, you touch me on a tender point, and cause me to deeply regret that even you should style yourself a Rebel. I cannot believe that Tom Hunton the Companion of Gaither, Rankin, and Irvin and many others long since dead, and of Halleck, Ord, Stevens and others still living can of his own free will admit the anarchical principle of secession or be vain enough to suppose the present Politicians can frame a Government better than that of Washington, Hamilton & Jefferson. We cannot realize this but delude ourselves into the belief that by some strange but successful jugglery the managers of our Political Machine have raised up the single issue, North or South, which shall prevail in America? or that you like others have been blown up, and cast into the Mississippi of Secession doubtful if by hard fighting you can reach the shore in safety, or drift out to the Ocean of Death, I know it is no use for us now to discuss this War is on us. We are Enemies, still private friends. In the one Capacity I will do you all the harm I can, yet on the other if here you may have as of old my last Cent, my last shirt and pants. You ask of me your negroes, and I will immediately ascertain if they be under my Military Control and I will moreover see that they are one and all told what is true of all—Boys if you want to go to your master, Go—you are free to choose. You must now think for yourselves, Your master has seceded from his Parent Government and you have seceded from him—both wrong by law—but both exercising an undoubted natural Right to rebel. If your boys want to go, I will enable them to go, but I wont advise, persuade or force them—I confess I have yet seen the "Confiscation Act," but I enclose you my own orders defining my position. I also cut out of a paper Grants Orders, and I assert that the Action of all our Leading Military Leaders, Halleck, McClellan, Buell, Grant & myself have been more conservative of slavery than the Acts of your own men. The Constitution of the United States is your only legal title to slavery. You have another title, that of possession, & force, but in Law & Logic your title to your Boys lay in the Constitution of the United States. You may say you are for the Constitution of the United States, as it was—You know it is unchanged, not a word not a syllable, and I can lay my hand on that Constitution and swear to it without one twang. But your party have made *another* and have another in force. How can you say that you would have the old, when you have a new. By the new if successful you inherit the Right of Slavery, but the new is not law till your Revolution is successful. Therefore we who contend for the old existing Law, contend that you by your own act take away your own title to all property save what is restricted by *our* constitution, your slaves included. You know I don't want your slaves, but to bring you to reason I think as a Military Man I have a Right and it is good policy to make *you all* feel that you are but men—that you have all the wants & despondencies of other men, and must eat, be clad &c to which end you must have property & labor, and that by Rebelling you risk both. Even without the Confiscation Act, by the simple laws of War we ought to take your effective slaves, I don't say to free them, but to use their labor & deprive you of it; as Belligerents we ought to seek the hostile Army and fight it and not the people—We went to Corinth but Beaureguard declined Battle, since which time many are dispersed as Guerillas. We are not bound to follow them, but rightfully make war by any means that will tend to bring about an end and restore

Peace. Your people may say it only exasperates, widens the breach and all that, But the longer the war lasts the more you must be convinced that we are no better & no worse than People who have gone before us, and that we are simply reenacting History, and that one of the modes of bringing People to reason is to touch their Interests pecuniary or property.

We never harbor women or children—we give employment to men, under the enclosed order. I find no negroes Registered as belonging to Hunton, some in the name of McGhee of which the Engineer is now making a list—I see McClellan says that negroes once taken shall never again be restored. I say nothing, my opinion is, we execute not make the Law, be it of Congress or War. But it is manifest that if you wont go into a United States District Court and sue for the recovery of your slave property you can never get it, out of adverse hands. No U.S. Court would allow you to sue for the recovery of a slave under the Fugitive Slave Law, unless you acknowledge allegiance. Believing this honestly, so I must act, though personally I feel strong friendship as ever, for very many in the South. With Great Respect Your friend

W. T. Sherman
Maj. Genl.

EMANCIPATION AND DIPLOMACY: AUSTRIA, AUGUST 1862

John Lothrop Motley to William H. Seward

Motley, a noted historian, served the Lincoln administration as a minister to Austria. He was, as he notes, well versed in European affairs. He offers Secretary of State Seward a shrewd analysis of the ambitions of Louis Napoleon, emperor of the French, and of Great Britain vis-à-vis the American war. Prime Minister Palmerston and Foreign Minister Russell he locates on opposite sides of the slavery question, with their rival John Bright in the wings.

Private & confidential Vienna Aug 26 1862

My dear Mr Seward,

I have to express my thanks for your photograph, which Mr F. Seward was so kind as to enclose to me. I have assured my wife & daughter that it gives a rather better idea of the original than photographs usually do.

I send by this mail a brief despatch, communicating as much in regard to European affairs as you are likely, at this time, to find leisure to read. I have also to acknowledge the receipt of your confidential despatch of July 24. In this you ask me a question, & I esteem it a privilege to answer it very unequivocally. I say, beforehand however, that I dont pretend to offer advice as to home matters. Entertaining a profound conviction that the civil war will never cease, so long as a slave remains in the country, I have refrained from expressing this opinion. To give unsolicited advice on such matters is not within my sphere of duty, & would be almost an impertinence; nor would it be possible for me to say any thing of those belligerent powers of the government in regard to slavery, which slavery, when it drew the sword put into the government's hands, or of the proper time to use those powers with full effect, that is not entirely familiar to you.

I therefore possess my soul in patience, trusting to the wisdom of the President & yourself & his other counsellors, &

hoping that those fatal words, "too late" which have so often rung the knell of nations are not destined to be the response to a policy which, I feel persuaded, must of necessity be one day announced. You can tell much better than I, how much longer it will be necessary to humour the pro-slavery party of the North, & the requirements of the semi-attached border states. But you have asked me a question in regard to matters concerning which I do claim an opinion. There are not many Americans who have had longer or better opportunities of studying European politics & individual opinions than I have had, & it is my duty to advise the government in regard to them to the best of my ability— It sometimes seems to me, as if there were, at home, an unwillingness to contemplate the great danger which is always impending over us from abroad—

You ask me— "are you sure that to day under the seductions & pressure which could be applied to some European populations they would not rise up & resist our attempt to bestow freedom upon the laborers whose capacity to supply cotton & open a market for European fabrics depends or is thought to depend on their continuance in bondage?" I answer, a thousand times, *No.*

A proclamation of emancipation to the blacks, with compensation to owners thenceforth loyal, even altho' it could not be every where immediately enforced, would strike the sword from England's hands. Moreover, the first enforcement would probably be in Virginia where the principal crop is not cotton but negroes—and there is no population in Europe so depraved as to rise up in favour of breeding fellow creatures to be sold in the market. No public man in England dares confront the anti slavery feeling which is universal in the nation. The French emperor, as you are well aware, & as is perfectly well known to the government here, has been perpetually soliciting the English to join him in armed intervention in our affairs. Of course this is officially denied, & will be so until the blow is resolved upon. Qui nescit dissimulare nescit regnere, & neither England nor France is so ingenuous as to tell *us* their little private schemes for our destruction until they are matured. The time when has perhaps not been settled, but I suppose that nobody is so green as to doubt that Louis Napoleon is ready, & desirous of giving the slaveholders' confederacy a lift with a large auxiliary force by sea & land, if he could only get England to join him; & that thus far, England has restrained him— Of course there are many reasons for her withholding her support. She is getting somewhat sick of her magnanimous ally. He stands too thoroughly exposed before the world as the great conspirator against liberty, civilization & humanity; hostis humani generis, to be reputable company. He is siding with *Russia* now in Eastern questions & against Turkey. He is taking measures for crushing Italy, whose freedom, as England has been telling every body for the last two years, was owing to her "moral support" (whatever that may mean). He is cultivating close relations with Prussia, a power never cordial to England, & he is as much at war with Austria, England's only friend on the continent, as he can be without drawing the sword. He had nearly got England involved in his Mexican villainy, the crowning iniquity of his reign, & he is actively pursuing, in company with her, a gigantic scheme for the dismemberment & conquest of China, which is causing much alarm among the peaceful & liberal portion of the British public—

But all these reasons have comparatively little weight. England is restrained from helping France to set up the slaveholders' confederacy partly because it *is* a slaveholders' confederacy. On the other hand, the anti slavery tendency day by day more manifest & more intense of the American people, & the anti slavery legislation of Congress, have hitherto made it difficult for England to accept the propositions of France. A formal proclamation, in unequivocal & bold language, with compensation to loyal masters, would make it *impossible*. In truth, such a proclamation is what our foreign enemies (and they are Legion) most dread. The aristocratic journalists & stump orators of England have done their best to persuade the world that the North (as they call the U S government) is as much in favor of slavery as the South, and they seize upon what pro-slavery demonstrations in New York or Washington they can find, to exhibit as proofs of their charges. The ignorance of Europe in regard to our politics is so universal & profound that malice may practise upon it to almost any extent. But an authoritative & blunt manifesto could not be lied out of existence. There would be any amount of vituperation as to our motives, but the fact would remain, & England *could* not *fight* to establish a separate slave confederacy against the legitimate U S government which had abolished slavery. And it is doubtful whether France—altho' there is no public opinion, & only one man in France—would fight us without her aid. There are very few among the governing classes of England, who do not sympathize with the South. There are fewer still who do not consider the United States as hopelessly gone. But no man in England or in Europe dares publicly to defend African slavery. It is never attempted. The European world has voted it a nuisance which should be buried out of sight.

I *know* from long & intimate conversations with Lord Russell, that he has always, ever since our troubles began, been strongly opposed to the abolition of slavery by our government. You have had proof enough that he wishes the Union dissolved, for he omits no opportunity of publicly proclaiming that wish. Put the two together, & what do you make of it? Simply that abolition would, in his opinion, prevent dissolution, or certainly that it would prevent an English government's lifting its hands to help the dissolution—

Lord Palmerston, who, the last time I talked with him, knew as much of our politics as I do of those of Japan, is a detester of negro slavery. To oppose it is, I firmly believe, the only serious & earnest purpose that he has ever had in his life, except the still more earnest one to remain the rest of his life prime minister. You see that his recent break with the radicals has rather alarmed him, & he will do his best, in the vacation, to conciliate them.

Bright & his men cant govern England but they can upset a government, for they represent the great unrepresented masses, & feel with those masses. You have seen what Bright's views are on our civil war & on slavery. Suppose our government, in the exercise of its war powers, should abolish slavery now—Do you think Lord Palmerston would dare encounter Bright & the radicals, by levying war upon America in order to destroy our government, just as that government had taken this step? To me it is unimaginable.

I can't close this note, without saying a single word in earnest, & not in merely a political view of the most portentous subject of modern times.

So long as I have been old enough to have opinions, I have

hated slavery, as I have hated all forms of oppression; but until now I have felt that we were bound by law to countenance this mighty wrong to humanity, & that worse evils would flow from an illegal attempt to destroy it. But now the slaveholders have committed the great crime from which we shrank. They have aimed a murderous blow at the heart of the country whose destiny they so long controlled, & they have thus, by levying war, put it in our power, without any violation of law to repair the wrongs done for so many generations to a most deeply injured & unhappy race. If we neglect this golden opportunity of doing justice, I feel that we shall perish as a nation, &, what is even worse, that we shall deserve to perish. I feel that we are *now* as much accountable to God for the existence of slavery as were the slaveholders themselves. A thousand millions spent for abolition are better than this or a greater amount spent in war, without a result, perhaps to white or black, & would be noblest debt ever incurred by a people.

You must pardon me saying thus much in my private capacity. Having the ear of a man so wise & so influential I cannot resist the impulse of opening my mind on this subject.

I remain
my dear Mr Seward
with great respect
Very faithfully & sincerely
J Lothrop Motley

Hon. W.H. Seward
etc etc etc

AIDING CONTRABANDS: WASHINGTON, D.C., SUMMER 1862

Harriet Jacobs to William Lloyd Garrison

In the summer of 1862 Harriet Jacobs, the author of *Incidents in the Life of a Slave Girl*, went to the District of Columbia and began relief work among the contrabands who had fled there. She wrote about their situation in a letter to the abolitionist leader William Lloyd Garrison that appeared in his newspaper *The Liberator* on September 5, 1862. (The letter was signed "Linda," after "Linda Brent," the pseudonym under which she had published her autobiography in 1861.) Jacobs would continue her relief efforts in Washington and Alexandria, Virginia, until the end of the war.

Dear Mr. Garrison:

I thank you for the request of a line on the condition of the contrabands, and what I have seen while among them. When we parted at that pleasant gathering of the Progressive Friends at Longwood, you to return to the Old Bay State, to battle for freedom and justice to the slave, I to go to the District of Columbia, where the shackles had just fallen, I hoped that the glorious echo from the blow had aroused the spirit of freedom, if a spark slumbered in its bosom. Having purchased my ticket through to Washington at the Philadelphia station, I reached the capital without molestation. Next morning, I went to Duff Green's Row, Government head-quarters for the contrabands here. I found men, women and children all huddled together, without any distinction or regard to age or sex. Some of them were in the most pitiable condition. Many were sick with measles, diptheria, scarlet and typhoid fever. Some had a few filthy rags to lie on; others had nothing but the bare floor for a couch. There seemed to be no established rules among them; they were coming in at all hours, often through the night, in large numbers, and the Superintendent had enough to occupy his time in taking the names of those who came in, and of those who were sent out. His office was thronged through the day by persons who came to hire these poor creatures, who they say will not work and take care of themselves. Single women hire at four dollars a month; a woman with one child, two and a half or three dollars a month. Men's wages are ten dollars per month. Many of them, accustomed as they have been to field labor, and to living almost entirely out of doors, suffer much from the confinement in this crowded building. The little children pine like prison birds for their native element. It is almost impossible to keep the building in a healthy condition. Each day brings its fresh additions of the hungry, naked and sick. In the early part of June, there were, some days, as many as ten deaths reported at this place in twenty-four hours. At this time, there was no matron in the house, and nothing at hand to administer to the comfort of the sick and dying. I felt that their sufferings must be unknown to the people. I did not meet kindly, sympathizing people, trying to soothe the last agonies of death. Those tearful eyes often looked up to me with the language, "Is this freedom?"

A new Superintendent was engaged, Mr. Nichol, who seemed to understand what these people most needed. He laid down rules, went to work in earnest pulling down partitions to enlarge the rooms, that he might establish two hospitals, one for the men and another for the women. This accomplished, cots and mattresses were needed. There is a small society in Washington—the Freedman's Association—who are doing all they can; but remember, Washington is not New England. I often met Rev. W. H. Channing, whose hands and heart are earnestly in the cause of the enslaved of his country. This gentleman was always ready to act in their behalf. Through these friends, an order was obtained from Gen. Wadsworth for cots for the contraband hospitals.

At this time, I met in Duff Green Row, Miss Hannah Stevenson, of Boston, and Miss Kendall. The names of these ladies need no comment. They were the first white females whom I had seen among these poor creatures, except those who had come in to hire them. These noble ladies had come to work, and their names will be lisped in prayer by many a dying slave. Hoping to help a little in the good work they had begun, I wrote to a lady in New York, a true and tried friend of the slave, who from the first moment had responded to every call of humanity. This letter was to ask for such articles as would make comfortable the sick and dying in the hospital. On the Saturday following, the cots were put up. A few hours after, an immense box was received from New York. Before the sun went down, those ladies who have labored so hard for the comfort of these people had the satisfaction of seeing every man, woman and child with clean garments, lying in a clean bed. What a contrast! They seemed different beings. Every countenance beamed with gratitude and satisfied rest. To me, it was a picture of holy peace within. The next day was the first Christian Sabbath they had ever known. One mother passed away as the setting sun threw its last rays across her dying bed, and as I looked upon her, I could but say—"One day of freedom, and gone to her God." Before the dawn, others were laid beside her. It was a comfort to know that some effort had been made to soothe their dying pillows. Still, there were other places in which I felt, if possible, more interest, where the poor creatures seemed so far removed from the immediate sympathy of those who would help them. These were the contrabands in Alexandria. This place is strongly secesh; the inhabitants are kept quiet only at the point of Northern bayonets. In this place, the contrabands are distributed more over the city. In visiting those places, I had the assistance of two kind friends, women. True at heart, they felt the wrongs and degradation of their race. These ladies were always ready to aid me, as far as lay in their power. To Mrs. Brown, of 3d street, Washington, and Mrs. Dagans, of Alexandria, the contrabands owe much gratitude for the kindly aid they gave me in serving them. In this place, the men live in an old foundry, which does not afford protection from the weather. The sick lay on boards on the ground floor; some, through the kindness of the soldiers, have an old blanket. I did not hear a complaint among them. They said it was much better than it had been. All expressed a willingness to work, and were anxious to know what was to be done with them after the work was done. All of them said they had not received pay for their work, and some wanted to know if I thought it would be paid to their masters. One old man said, "I don't kere if dey don't pay, so dey give me freedom. I bin working for ole maas all de time; he nebber gib me five cent. I like de Unions fuss rate. If de Yankee Unions didn't come long, I'd be working tu de ole place now." All said they had plenty to eat, but no clothing, and no money to buy any.

Another place, the old school-house in Alexandria, is the Government head-quarters for the women. This I thought the most wretched of all the places. Any one who can find an apology for slavery should visit this place, and learn its curse. Here you see them from infancy up to a hundred years old. What but the love of freedom could bring these old people hither? One old man, who told me he was a hundred, said he had come to be free with his children. The journey proved too much for him. Each visit, I found him sitting in the same spot, under a shady tree, suffering from rheumatism. Unpacking a barrel, I found a large coat, which I thought would be so nice for the old man, that I carried it to him. I found him sitting in the same spot, with his head on his bosom. I stooped down to speak to him. Raising his head, I found him dying. I called his wife. The old woman, who seems in her second childhood, looked on as quietly as though we were placing him for a night's rest. In this house are scores of women and children, with nothing to do, and nothing to do with. Their husbands are at work for the Government. Here they have food and shelter, but they cannot get work. The slaves who come into Washington from Maryland are sent here to protect them from the Fugitive Slave Law. These people are indebted to Mr. Rufus Leighton, formerly of Boston, for many comforts. But for their Northern friends, God pity them in their wretched and destitute condition! The Superintendent, Mr. Clarke, a Pennsylvanian, seems to feel much interest in them, and is certainly very kind. They told me they had confidence in him as a friend. That is much for a slave to say.

From this place, I went to Birch's slave-pen in Alexandria. This place forms a singular contrast with what it was two years ago. The habitable part of the building is filled with contrabands, the old jail is filled with secesh prisoners—all within speaking distance of each other. Many a compliment is passed between them on the change in their positions. There is another house on Cameron street, which is filled with very destitute people. To these places I distributed large supplies of clothing, given me by the ladies of New York, New Bedford, and Boston. They have made many a desolate heart glad. They have clothed the naked, fed the hungry. To them, God's promise is sufficient.

Let me tell you of another place, to which I always planned my last visit for the day. There was something about this house to make you forget that you came to it with a heavy heart. The little children you meet at this door bring up pleasant memories when you leave it; from the older ones you carry pleasant recollections. These were what the people call the more favored slaves, and would boast of having lived in the first families in Virginia. They certainly had reaped some advantage from the contact. It seemed by a miracle that they had all fallen together. They were intelligent, and some of the young women and children beautiful. One young girl, whose beauty I cannot describe, although its magnetism often drew me to her side, I loved to talk with, and look upon her sweet face, covered with blushes; besides, I wanted to learn her true position, but her gentle shyness I had to respect. One day, while trying to draw her out, a fine-looking woman, with all the pride of a mother, stepped forward, and said—"Madam, this young woman is my son's wife." It was a relief. I thanked God that this young creature had an arm to lean upon for protection. Here I looked upon slavery, and felt the curse of their heritage was what is considered the best blood of Virginia. On one of my visits here, I met a mother who had just arrived from Virginia, bringing with her four daughters. Of course, they belonged to one of the first families. This man's strong attachment to this woman and her children caused her, with her children, to be locked up one month. She made her escape one day while her master had gone to learn the news from the Union army. She fled to the Northern army for freedom and protection. These people had earned for themselves many little comforts. Their houses had an inviting aspect. The clean floors, the clean white spreads on their cots, and the general tidiness throughout the building, convinced me they had done as well as any other race could have done, under the same circumstances.

Let me tell you of another place—Arlington Heights. Every lady has heard of Gen. Lee's beautiful residence, which has been so faithfully guarded by our Northern army. It looks as though the master had given his orders every morning. Not a tree around that house has fallen. About the forts and camps they have been compelled to use the axe. At the quarters, there are many contrabands. The men are employed, and most of the women. Here they have plenty of exercise in the open air, and seem very happy. Many of the regiments are stationed here. It is a delightful place for both the soldier and the contraband. Looking around this place, and remembering what I had heard of the character of the man who owned it before it passed into the hands of its present owner, I was much inclined to say, Although the wicked prosper for a season, the way of the transgressor is hard.

When in Washington for the day, my morning visit would be up at Duff Green's Row. My first business would be to look into a small room on the ground floor. This room was covered with lime. Here I would learn how many deaths had occurred in the last twenty-four hours. Men, women and children lie here together, without a shadow of those rites which we give to our poorest dead. There they lie, in the filthy rags they wore from the plantation. Nobody seems to give it a thought. It is an every-day occurrence, and the scenes have become familiar. One morning, as I looked in, I saw lying there five children. By the side of them lay a young man. He escaped, was taken back to Virginia, whipped nearly to death, escaped again the next night, dragged his body to Washington, and died, literally cut to pieces. Around his feet I saw a rope; I could not see that put into the grave with him. Other cases similar to this came to my knowledge, but this I saw.

Amid all this sadness, we sometimes would hear a shout of joy. Some mother had come in, and found her long-lost child; some husband his wife. Brothers and sisters meet. Some, without knowing it, had lived years within twenty miles of each other.

A word about the schools. It is pleasant to see that eager group of old and young, striving to learn their A, B, C, and Scripture sentences. Their great desire is to learn to read. While in the school-room, I could not but feel how much these young women and children needed female teachers who could do something more than teach them their A, B, C. They need to be taught the right habits of living and the true principles of life.

My last visit intended for Alexandria was on Saturday. I spent the day with them, and received showers of thanks for myself and the good ladies who had sent me; for I had been careful to impress upon them that these kind friends sent me, and that all that was given by me was from them. Just as I was on the point of leaving, I found a young woman, with an infant, who had just been brought in. She lay in a dying condition, with nothing but a piece of an old soldier coat under her head. Must I leave her in this condition? I could not beg in Alexandria. It was time for the last boat to leave for Washington, and I promised to return in the morning. The Superintendent said he would meet me at the landing. Early the next morning, Mrs. Brown and myself went on a begging expedition, and some old quilts were given us. Mr. Clarke met us, and offered the use of his large Government wagon, with the horses and driver, for the day, and said he would accompany us, if agreeable. I was delighted, and felt I should spend a happy Sabbath in exploring Dixie, while the large bundles that I carried with me would help make others happy. After attending to the sick mother and child, we started for Fairfax Seminary. They send many of the convalescent soldiers to this place. The houses are large, and the location is healthy. Many of the contrabands are here. Their condition is much better than that of those kept in the city. They soon gathered around Mr. Clarke, and begged him to come back and be their boss. He said, "Boys, I want you all to go to Hayti." They said, "You gwine wid us, Mr. Clarke?" "No, I must stay here, and take care of the rest of the boys." "Den, if you aint gwine, de Lord knows I aint a gwine." Some of them will tell Uncle Abe the same thing. Mr. Clarke said they would do anything for him—seldom gave him any trouble. They spoke kindly of Mr. Thomas, who is constantly employed in supplying their wants, as far as he can. To the very old people at this place, I gave some clothing, returned to Alexandria, and bade all good bye. Begging me to come back, they promised to do all they could to help themselves. One old woman said—"Honey tink, when all get still, I kin go an fine de old place? Tink de Union 'stroy it? You can't get nothin on dis place. Down on de ole place, you can raise ebery ting. I ain't seen bacca since I bin here. Neber git a libin here, where de peoples eben buy pasly." This poor old woman thought it was nice to live where tobacco grew, but it was dreadful to be compelled to buy a bunch of parsley. Here they have preaching once every Sabbath. They must have a season to sing and pray, and we need true faith in Christ to go among them and do our duty. How beautiful it is to find it among themselves! Do not say the slaves take no interest in each other. Like other people, some of them are designedly selfish, some are ignorantly selfish. With the light and instruction you give them, you will see this selfishness disappear. Trust them, make them free, and give them the responsibility of caring for themselves, and they will soon learn to help each other. Some of them have been so degraded by slavery that they do not know the usages of civilized life; they know little else than the handle of the hoe, the plough, the cotton pad, and the overseer's lash. Have patience with them. You have helped to make them what they are; teach them civilization. You owe it to them, and you will find them as apt to learn as any other people that come to you stupid from oppression. The negroes' strong attachment no one doubts; the only difficulty is, they have cherished it too strongly. Let me tell you of an instance among the contrabands. One day, while in the hospital, a woman came in to ask that she might take a little orphan child. The mother had just died, leaving two children, the eldest three years old. This woman had five children in the house with her. In a few days, the number would be six. I said to this mother, "What can you do with this child, shut up here with your own? They are as many as you can attend to." She looked up with tears in her eyes, and said—"The child's mother was a stranger; none of her friends cum wid her from de ole place. I took one boy down on de plantation; he is a big boy now, working mong de Unions. De Lord help me to bring up dat boy, and he will help me to take care dis child. My husband work for de Unions when dey pay him. I can make home for all. Dis child shall hab part ob de crust." How few white mothers, living in luxury, with six children, could find room in her heart for a seventh, and that child a stranger!

In this house there are scores of children, too young to help themselves, from eight years old down to the little one-day freeman, born at railroad speed, while the young mother was flying from Virginia to save her babe from breathing its tainted air.

I left the contrabands, feeling that the people were becoming more interested in their behalf, and much had been done to make their condition more comfortable. On my way home, I stopped a few days in Philadelphia. I called on a lady who had sent a large supply to the hospital, and told her of the many little orphans who needed a home. This lady advised me to call and see the Lady Managers of an institution for orphan children supported by those ladies. I did so, and they agreed to take the little orphans. They employed a gentleman to investigate the matter, and it was found impossible to bring them through Baltimore. This gentleman went to the captains of the propellers in Philadelphia, and asked if those orphan children could have a passage on their boats. Oh no, it could not be; it would make an unpleasant feeling among the people! Some of those orphans have died since I left, but the number is constantly increasing. Many mothers, on leaving the plantations, pick up the little orphans, and bring them with their own children; but they cannot provide for them; they come very destitute themselves.

To the ladies who have so nobly interested themselves in behalf of my much oppressed race, I feel the deepest debt of gratitude. Let me beg the reader's attention to these orphans. They are the innocent and helpless of God's poor. If you cannot take one, you can do much by contributing your mite to the institution that will open its doors to receive them.

LINDA.

September 5, 1862

THE SECOND MANASSAS CAMPAIGN:
VIRGINIA, AUGUST 1862

Edward Porter Alexander: *from* Fighting for the Confederacy

As soon as he discovered the Federals' intent to evacuate the Peninsula, General Lee moved north with all speed to strike at Pope's Army of Virginia before McClellan's Army of the Potomac could combine with it. In his reminiscences, Alexander, the ordnance chief for Lee's army, traced the complex movements of what would be known as the Second Bull Run (or Second Manassas) campaign.

OUR CAMPAIGN opened early in August. Pope was concentrating east of the Rappahannock the three armies of Frémont, 13,000, Banks, 11,000, & McDowell, 18,000 inf. & 5,000 cavalry. The best return I can find of their numbers would make his whole available force about 47,000.

To Pope came orders from Halleck to make some demonstrations toward our railroad at Gordonsville so as to attract a part of Gen. Lee's troops from Richmond, in order that McClellan might safely weaken his army by beginning to ship it to the Potomac. Nothing could have suited Gen. Lee better. No sooner did Pope send some of his troops across the Rappahannock, than Lee sent Jackson with his own division, Ewell's & A. P. Hill's to look after him. In fact there is a doubt in my mind whether Lee did not himself start Jackson up to Gordonsville before he ever heard of Pope's demonstrations; intending on his part to *force* Halleck to withdraw McClellan in order to defend Washington, & meanwhile, too, intending to take advantage of his interior position & try & crush Pope before McClellan could reach him. Certainly that whole game was formulated in his mind at the very commencement of the campaign & it was executed with a dash & brilliancy equalled by few campaigns in the world, & with as much success as could possibly have been hoped for, considering the odds & all the circumstances, for Pope had the easiest game to play. Lee lost some time by heavy rains & a freshet in the rivers & Pope did get reinforcements of 3 corps from McClellan (3rd, 4th & 5th I believe) & one, the 9th, from No. Ca., but yet Lee cleaned him up, & ran him off the last battle field while two whole corps, Sumner's & Franklin's, were just 1 & 2 days away. It was a beautifully played game on Lee's part anyway.

And now I'll try & outline briefly the different steps. Jackson crossed the Rapidan with his three divisions & on Aug. 9th had a very sharp battle with Banks's corps on the slope of Cedar Mountain. He drove Banks off the field; but he himself suffered sharply, & he recrossed the Rapidan. Among our casualties was Gen. Winder killed—a very promising officer. One of my special friends, Col. Snowden Andrews, of the arty., received here one of the most desperate wounds from which any one ever recovered. A shell exploded by him & a fragment cut open his side so that his liver protruded. But he still lives to tell how he saw it & pushed it back, & got well in spite of all predictions.

On Aug. 13th Gen. Lee himself left Richmond by rail to join Jackson & took with him Longstreet & his division, and Stuart with the cavalry also followed. That still left R. H. Anderson's, D. H. Hill's, McLaws's & Walker's divns. to observe McClellan's diminishing forces, but they were to follow Longstreet as soon as it was apparent that McClellan was gone. I cannot fix the date, exactly, on which I started, but soon after Gen. Lee got to Gordonsville he wired me to come & bring my train with me. So I put Maj. Duffey in motion that very afternoon, & the next day with my light personal wagon I followed. I can remember very little detail about that march. It was a long, stern chase I had, pursuing our men, who were doing wonderful marching around & beyond the enemy, & I only caught up with them after the battle of 2nd Manassas when I was able to replenish all their ammunition & fix them up as well as when they started, & then by sending back empty wagons to Gordonsville, the nearest rail point, I soon got my own train full again.

Gen. Lee of course was very anxious to attack Pope before he could receive all the reinforcements coming to him, & Gen. Longstreet states that he "gave orders that his army should cross the Rapidan on the 18th & make battle. . . . But for some reason not fully explained our movements were delayed, & we did not cross the Rapidan until the 20th. In the meantime a dispatch to Stuart was captured by Pope which gave information of our presence & contemplated advance. This, with information Pope already had, caused him to withdraw to a very strong position, behind the Rappahannock River, & there instead of at Culpeper C.H., where the attack was first meant to be made, Gen. Lee found him."

So far Pope had handled his army very well indeed. It was his policy indeed to avoid a fight except with great advantages of ground, & these the position on the Rappahannock gave him. Gen. Lee came up to the river on Aug. 21st & felt the position strongly in some severe artillery duels across it. But in spite of his pugnacity he thought better of attacking (which would have been pie for Pope like Malvern Hill was for McClellan) & decided to turn him by a long march, striking his communications far in the rear with one half of his army while the other half, protected by the river against an assault, waited for the results. It was a bold & beautiful play. For back at Manassas Junction 24 miles behind Pope's line of battle were enormous stores & depots of Pope's army. But while the game was in progress the two halves of Lee's army would be necessarily far apart & unable to help each other, & only hard fighting & good marching could save them. From Aug. 21st to 24th Lee was reconnoitering & feeling Pope & was held back too by a freshet in the river, but on the 25th Jackson was able to cross at a point, Hinson's Mill, four miles above Pope's right flank. None of his officers were informed where he was going. His men carried 3 days' cooked rations & a few frying pans. A few ambulances & a few wagon loads of ammunition only were taken along. And Munford's 2nd Va. Cavalry picketed all roads leading to the enemy & screened the march. I should have mentioned, by the way, before that Stuart with part of his cavalry had before this gotten in rear of Pope's line, & had given him a little lesson as to the necessity of looking out for his rear, by capturing his own headquarters wagon, with his baggage & valuable correspondence showing the reinforcements which were coming to him; & this had doubtless stimulated Gen. Lee in his earnestness to get at him.

Jackson had with him his own division under Taliaferro,

Ewell's, & A. P. Hill's, say 21,000 infy. men & 2,500 cavalry (14 brig. of infty., 2 brig. of cav., 18 light batteries). His first day's march was from Jeffersonton via Hinson's Mill & Orlean to Salem—over 26 miles. To give an idea of how much of a march this is I will say that Duane & I coming home from Utah in the fall of 1858 tried to make a good march of it, & having empty wagons let the men put their muskets in the wagons so that they marched light, & had perfect roads, & there being only 64 men, they marched without the annoyance of alternate stoppings & hurryings always attendant on long columns. Under these most favorable possible conditions we averaged 22 miles per day, & the one longest march we ever made was 27 miles. So that 26 miles, including the fording of the Rappahannock, & carrying arms, knapsacks, 60 rounds ammunition, & three days' rations over a very uneven country for a column of 25,000 men with ordnance & artillery & ambulances is a very remarkable march. But in this connection it must be said that such heavy marches will always lose some men from the ranks—not quite able to keep up. And another thing I cannot resist thinking & saying—Ah, if only Gen. Jackson had marched like that from Ashland on June 26.

But perhaps his own conscience had had it out with him about the whole Seven Days business for there was never again in him any trace of his Seven Days behavior.

At dawn on the 26th he started again from Salem, & now he turned sharp to his right flank & marched for Manassas Junction, Pope's great depot of supplies. Parallel to his march most the day before, & between him & Pope, were the Bull Run Mountains, a low outlying development of the Blue Ridge chain. These he crossed at Thoro'fare Gap & soon after he was overtaken by Gen. Stuart with 2 brigades of cavalry (Fitz Lee's & Robertson's) who had crossed the Rappahannock that morning & made a forced march to join him. Together they pushed on & during the night reached Manassas, a distance of 25 miles from Salem, & captured a small force there of 8 guns & 300 men.

During this afternoon of the 26th Pope was waked up to the fact that something was going on in his rear, & he began to abandon the line of the Rappahannock & to come back with his whole army by different roads to see what it meant. And when he found it was only Jackson with 3 divisions he was pleased & made sure that Jackson would be destroyed.

So on the morning of the 27th Pope has gone from the Rappahannock to meet Jackson, & Longstreet with the rest of the army, some thirty-thousand men, he says, started to follow Jackson. Gen. Lee gave him his choice to follow on the straight Warrenton Pike after Pope or to follow Jackson's right angled route & he chose the latter, as less apt to be delayed by an enemy's rear guard in strong positions. His marches were not quite up to Jackson's & he reached Thoro'fare Gap late in afternoon of the 3rd day, the 28th, Jackson having passed it in the morning of his second day. We will leave Longstreet there while we bring Jackson up to the same hour.

He devoted the 27th to plundering & burning the Manassas Depot. Ewell's div. was thrown out towards Bristoe Station to look out for Pope's approach, & in the afternoon it was attacked by Hooker & fell back slowly, fighting until dark when it rejoined Jackson.

Early in the morning of the 27th I forgot to say a New Jersey brigade under a Gen. Taylor had arrived near Manassas by train from Washn. City to drive off what the Washn. authorities supposed to be a cavalry raid. Taylor formed & attacked before he found out any better, & he was killed & many of his men captured & also his train, which was burnt, as also the Bull Run R.R. bridge.

Jackson now knew that by morning of the 28th Pope would be concentrating everything on him. So during the night he marched out toward Bull Run & even sent A. P. Hill's divn. across it & as far as Centreville, but it came around & recrossed Bull Run at Stone Bridge & before the afternoon Jackson had, as we may say, ambushed his army south of Bull Run & west of the Warrenton Turnpike nearly parallel to that pike & not more than a mile off in a large wood. Hill's going around by Centreville was probably only intended to mystify the enemy.

It is worth while to pause here for a moment & take note of Jackson's strategy in thus halting his army & taking position to give battle to the whole of Pope's army, in this open country, when he might have gone on a considerable distance towards Thoro'fare Gap, through which Longstreet was coming to meet him. The main object of his flank movement had been to break up Pope's position, behind the Rapidan, which was too strong to be attacked. He had accomplished this & incidentally destroyed vast quantities of stores & now had Pope's entire army racing back to find him & to reopen their communications. Naturally then he might wish to avoid being brought to battle until Longstreet could be near enough to help him, and Longstreet on this day, the 28th, was still far beyond Thoro'fare Gap. He only approached it at sundown on that day, as stated above, & found a division of the enemy there, under Ricketts, opposing his passage. So Jackson with his three divisions had to contemplate standing off Pope's whole army, of about five corps or fifteen divisions, for all of 24 hours, with all the chances that Pope might detain Longstreet longer, or even crush him separately.

But there was a strong reason why he should fight as soon as it was possible to do so. Two additional whole corps of McClellan's veterans from the James, Franklin's & Sumner's, were on the way, but had not yet arrived, to reinforce Pope. If any choice was left to Pope, he might not make the battle until these had arrived. It was worth taking even desperate chances, & the occasion found the man equal to it. Jackson was no longer the Jackson of the Seven Days, but the Jackson of the Valley. Perhaps the experiences of that campaign had awakened him to at least a sub-conscious appreciation that the Lord helps best those who do not trust in Him for even a row of pins, however devoutly they may talk about it, but who appreciate the whole responsibility & hustle for themselves accordingly. However that may be, the Jackson of the Seven Days was never seen on Earth again. In less than nine months he was to lay down his life, shot by mistake by the fire of his own men, but meanwhile here at 2nd Manassas, & at Harpers Ferry, at Sharpsburg, at Fredericksburg, & at Chancellorsville he was to wipe out from men's memories the fact that he had ever been, even temporarily, anything but the Jackson of the Valley.

So now we see him, at midday of the 28th, in line of battle parallel to the Warrenton Pike & in gun shot of it on the west, ready to try conclusions with whatever might seek to pass on that road. He had not very long to wait. In the latter half of the afternoon King's division of McDowell's corps came along hunting for him. Being attacked, they met it half way, & the ground giving their artillery a good chance, they put up an unusually hot fight which lasted until dark & in which our Gen. Ewell lost his leg—leaving Lawton in command of his division. During the night King abandoned his ground & fell back toward Manassas. Late in the evening Jackson's men had been cheered by hearing Longstreet's guns at Thoro'fare Gap, about 20 miles off, & they knew that help was coming. During that night, Longstreet had sent three brigades through another gap, Hopewell, three miles north, & another brigade or two to occupy the heights on each side of the Thoro'fare road, & when the morning dawned Ricketts's division had retreated without a fight & gone towards Bristoe. So Longstreet pushed on with his troops & Gen. Lee went on with him & by noon they had practically connected with Jackson.

Meanwhile Jackson had been doing some of the most desperate fighting ever done. When Pope learned by his attack on King that Jackson had stayed to fight him he thought that he saw victory in his hands. Jackson was almost sandwiched in between Reno's & Heintzelman's corps on the east & McDowell's & Sigel's corps & Reynolds's division on the west, & Porter's corps was close by in front. Pope attacked at dawn with two corps, Sigel's & Heintzelman's. About noon Reno's corps joined in until about 1:30 P.M. From then until about 4:30 there were intermittent calms & squalls. About 5:30 Reno & Heintzelman renewed their attack on his left & McDowell & Reynolds on his right, Sigel having had all the fight taken out of him during the morning.

It will be noted that Porter's corps was not engaged on the Federal side nor Longstreet's on the Confederate. This happened by our cavalry's reporting the advance of a heavy body of Federal infantry soon after Longstreet's arrival on the ground, & he, expecting to be attacked awaited it. Porter either knew or guessed that a much larger force than his own was before him, & he also preferred the defensive & wanted to be attacked. For this he was court-martialed & cashiered. In 1878 however he got a rehearing, & a board of officers on the testimony of Longstreet & other Confederate officers justified & commended his conduct & he was put on the list of retired officers. No one knowing Fitz John Porter personally would believe that he could deliberately fail in his duty as a soldier.

But no one who knew how Pope was regarded by many of the best officers of the old army can doubt that they found some consolation in the fact that it was Pope who was whipped. Gen. Lee had desired to disregard Porter's proximity & to have Longstreet go to support Jackson's battle soon after his arrival, & doubtless that would have been safer play. Later in the evening, however, near sundown, Longstreet did make an assault with a small force, gained some ground & captured a gun, but later abandoned both & fell back to his original position.

This attack cut no figure as help to Jackson's fight, & it is due both to Jackson & his men to say that these three divisions successfully held off four corps & one division (say ten divisions) from dawn till dark of a long summer day. There was said to have been bayonet fighting at some points, & at one place where there was a rocky hill & an old railroad cut & embankment Starke's Louisiana brigade, its ammunition temporarily running low, defended itself partly by throwing stones at the enemy's lines.

Next morning, Aug. 30th, Gen. Pope thought that Lee's army had begun a retreat to the south. Some of his men who had been captured & paroled from within the Confederate lines brought reports to that effect & his reconnoitering officers confirmed it. It was ten o'clock before he found out any better, his whole army, meanwhile, recuperating from the severe fighting of the 29th. And, on his part, Gen. Lee believed for a time that Pope had either begun to retreat or was preparing to do so. He thought Pope's position & force too strong to be immediately assaulted but he was preparing to pursue vigorously at the earliest moment. About noon Pope, realizing that there was still the bulk of Lee's force before him, formed a powerful assaulting force practically comprising the whole of his army of five corps & one extra division & moved upon Jackson's position. The heavy lines & columns made a magnificent sight as they advanced across the open fields, but their direction was such that from some hills in Longstreet's front they were exposed to an oblique, & almost an enfilading fire.

Longstreet saw this, & immediately brought forward all his available artillery, & opened fire on them. Since the experience of the Seven Days, Gen. Lee had begun to throw his isolated batteries together into battalions of artillery. Usually four batteries (three of 4 guns each & one of 6, making 18 guns in all) constituted a battalion, which was commanded by two field officers. But one of Longstreet's battns. was an unusually large one, comprising 5 batteries—22 guns—under Col. Stephen D. Lee and Maj. Del Kemper. Col. Lee was an excellent officer, as may be guessed from his becoming lieut. general within the next two years. And the battalion itself we will hear much more of also, as I succeeded Lee in the command of it on his promotion early in November. Lee's battalion was conspicuous for its brilliant service upon this occasion. It had a beautiful position in easy range & the weight of its fire was very effective in breaking up the enemy's lines & columns. They endeavored to reform again & again, but were again & again broken & confused by the constantly increasing Confederate fire. While in this condition Longstreet's whole force of infantry was at last launched against them, & even Jackson's tired veterans also took the offensive. The enemy was still in superior force & fought well, but they were gradually driven back everywhere & before darkness ended the fighting they had lost from a half to three quarters of a mile of ground.

During the night Pope retreated across Bull Run. The next day he was joined by Sumner's & Franklin's corps near Centreville, but as Lee moved after him in pursuit he fell back toward Washington City. At Ox Hill on Sep. 1st a part of Jackson's forces encountered a strong rear guard & received a temporary check, but Pope made no halt outside of the strong chain of fortifications guarding Washington on the south. The following are the best returns I can find of the forces engaged & the casualties of this campaign.

"TREACHERY": WASHINGTON, D.C., AUGUST 1862

Charles Francis Adams Jr. to Charles Francis Adams

Lieutenant Adams, 1st Massachusetts Cavalry, wrote to his father, the American minister in London, on the eve of Second Bull Run. As Adams discovered, drawing from his insider army sources, it was a time of great mistrust between the armies of McClellan and Pope and great confusion in the War Department, made all the worse as communications were severed between Washington and Pope's army.

Willard's Hotel, Washington
August 27, 1862

Here I am once more in the city of Washington. Since I last wrote the first detachment of our regiment has arrived at Fortress Monroe, and is now in camp at Acquia Creek, while I have come up here to see about this business of Pope's staff. I find the old city much as usual, but still not the same. It was indeed pleasant for me to get here and at least to see something familiar once more, and I looked at all the public buildings and even at Willard's as at old friends. Once more I have really slept in a bed and I really never enjoyed anything in my life, in its kind, more than the delicious little supper which Gautier got up for me. You don't know how much eight months of coarse fare improve one's faculties for gastronomic enjoyment, and last evening I experienced a new sensation.

Here I am though, and what next? Shall I go onto Pope's staff? I think not. This is a very different place from Hilton Head and here I am learning many strange things which make me open my eyes very wide, which make me sorrow over our past and do not encourage me for the future. Here I have access to certain means of information and I think I can give you a little more light than you now have. Do you know that just before leaving the Peninsula McClellan offered to march into Richmond on his own responsibility? Do you know that in the opinion of our leading military men Washington is in more danger than it ever yet has been? Do you know that but for McDowell's jealousy we should have triumphantly marched into Richmond? Do you know that Pope is a humbug and known to be so by those who put him in his present place? Do you know that today he is so completely outgeneraled as to be cut off from Washington? Yet these are not rumors, but facts, doled out to me by members of McClellan's and Halleck's staffs.

Our rulers seem to me to be crazy. The air of this city seems thick with treachery; our army seems in danger of utter demoralization and I have not since the war begun felt such a tug on my nerves as today in Washington. Everything is ripe for a terrible panic, the end of which I cannot see or even imagine. I always mean to be one of the hopeful, but just now I cast about in vain for something on which to hang my hopes. I still believe in McClellan, but I *know* that the nearest advisers of the President —among them Mr. Holt—distrust his earnestness in this war. Stanton is jealous of him and he and Pope are in bitter enmity. All pin their hope on Halleck and we must do as the rest do; but it is hinted to me that Stanton is likely to be a block in Halleck's way, and the jealousies of our generals are more than a new man can manage. We need a head and we must have it; a man who can keep these jealousies under subordination; and we must have him or go to the wall. Is Halleck going to supply our need? I hope he is, but while the question is in doubt we may lose Washington. You will think that I am in a panic and the most frightened man in Washington. I assure you it is not so. I do consider the outside condition of affairs very critical, but it is my glimpse behind the scenes, the conviction that small men with selfish motives control the war without any central power to keep them in bounds, which terrifies and discourages me.

Take the history of the Peninsular campaign. My authorities are one aid of McClellan's and Halleck's Assistant Adjutant General, but the facts speak for themselves, and the inferences any man may draw. Stanton, contrary to the first principle of strategy and for motives not hard to comprehend, divides Virginia into four independent departments. McClellan takes charge of one and a column is taken from him to form another under charge of McDowell. It is solemnly promised McClellan that McDowell shall join him before Richmond, and meanwhile he is retained where he is to protect Washington. Mark the result. McClellan fights the battle of Hanover Court House, with all its loss of life and time, simply to open the road for McDowell to join him and he does open it. McDowell's advance guard hears his cannon on that day, but McDowell does not stir, and McClellan, still looking for him, forms that fatal Chickahominy front of twenty miles. Doubtless McDowell was kept back by orders, but in how far was he instrumental in procuring these orders to suit himself? McClellan's staff do not hesitate to say that he dictated them on pretence of danger to Washington, in reality because his advance would have absorbed his command in that of McClellan. Take the pretence. Jackson makes his raid in the valley of the Shenandoah, and again McDowell's advance hears the sound of his guns. Washington is in danger now. As before he does not move and Jackson escapes and returns to attack McClellan. Had McDowell done his duty either for McClellan or against Jackson, we should now have Richmond and McClellan would now be the conquering hero. He did neither and is now in disgrace, as subordinated to Pope; but McClellan is not the conquering hero. Not half an hour ago Halleck's nephew and private secretary told me that I could not imagine the trouble these jealousies gave his uncle. Said he, "McDowell and Sigel will not fight under Pope. McClellan and Pope are not in sympathy"; and he added an intimation that McClellan was most restive under Halleck.

Under these circumstances what can we expect? What can we hope for? Sigel stands well, but all our army officers are bitter and jealous against him. In Burnside there is indeed hope. He has been true and generous and, what is much, successful. He did not hesitate to award to McClellan the credit of planning his Carolina campaign, and, unlike McDowell, when told to send to McClellan all the troops he could spare, he at once sent him twenty-eight regiments and six batteries, leaving himself and the Major General under him some 3000 men in all. We have some grim old fighters who do their work and do not scheme. Such they tell me are Sumner and Heintzelman; but even of these the last is outspoken against McClellan because he will not fight with more energy. The simple truth is the man has not come and now we mean to supply his place with vast numbers of undrilled recruits. Shall we succeed? You can judge as well as I.

Thus the war is gloomily enough approaching its last and bloodiest stage. Unless Halleck is the man of iron who can rule, it will be discordant numbers against compact strategy. We must face the music, though we do not like the tune. . . .

"THESE GREAT OPERATIONS": VIRGINIA AND MARYLAND, AUGUST–SEPTEMBER 1862

John Hampden Chamberlayne to Martha Burwell Chamberlayne

Lieutenant "Ham" Chamberlayne's account of Second Bull Run, written to his mother, follows the fortunes of A. P. Hill's division in Stonewall Jackson's wing of the Army of Northern Virginia. In the Ox Hill (or Chantilly) fight Chamberlayne noted the death of two Union generals, Philip Kearny and Isaac Stevens. The campaign cost the Union about 16,000 men killed, wounded, or missing, while Confederate losses totaled about 9,000.

Frederick City, Frederick Co. Maryland
Saturday Sept. 6th 1862

My dear Mother

I am brimful of matter, as an egg of meat. Since my letter, date unknown, from camp in Orange, near Raccoon Ford—there has been no chance to send a letter & therefore I have not written; & now I am at a loss to tell when I can send this.

Let me try to outline our progress, you bearing in mind that I am in Hill's (A. P.) Division in Jackson's Corps, that Corps consisting of Jackson's own Division, in which are Mann, V, Lewis Randolph, & many other friends, Ewells & Hills Divisions; whereby you will not think me egotistical for speaking of Jackson's Corps mostly & of the corps, Hill's Division; for of them I know most & in truth their share was the most memorable even in the almost incredible campaign of the last fortnight. Crossing Rapidan at Somerville, Jackson in front (remember "Jackson," so used, includes Hill Ewell & the Stonewall Division) General Lee without much opposition reached Rappahannock River a few miles above Rappahannock Station, where part of Longstreet's troops had a sharp fight. On friday evening, 22d August, Jackson bivouacked in Culpeper opposite Warrenton Springs, he threw over that evening two Brigades of Ewells; the river rose & destroyed the Bridge;

Saturday the Bridge was rebuilt, that night the two Brigades after some sharp fighting were withdawn.

On Sunday morning the enemy appeared in heavy force & the Batteries of Hills Division were put into position on the hills & shelled their infantry. They retired the infantry & bringing up a large number of Batteries threw a storm of shot & shell at us, we not replying; they must have expended several thousand rounds, & in all, so well sheltered were we, our killed & wounded did not reach 20. That evening Jacksons whole force moved up to Jefferson in Culpeper, Longstreet close to him. The enemy was completely deceived & concluded that we had given the thing up.

Now comes the great wonder. Starting up the bank of the River (on Monday the 25th) we marched through Amosville in Rappahannock Co., still farther up, crossed the Rappahannock within ten miles of the Blue Ridge, marched by strange country paths, across open fields & comfortable homesteads, by a little town called Orleans in Fauquier on & on as if we would never cease—to Salem on the Manassas Gap R. R. reaching it after midnight; up again by day & still on, along the Manassas Gap R. R. meeting crowds along the road, all welcoming, cheering staring with blank amazement, so all day tuesday the 26th through White plains, Haymarket Thoroughfare Gap in Bull Run Mountains, Gainesville to Bristow Station on the Orange & Alexandria R. R., making the distance from Amosville to Bristow (between 45 & 50 miles) within the 48 hours. We burned up at Bristow 2 or three Railway trains & moved on to Manassas Junction on Wednesday taking our prisoners with us. Ewells Division brought up the rear, fighting all the way a force that Pope had sent up from Warrenton supposing us a cavalry party.

Upon reaching the Junction we met a Brigade the 1st New Jersey which had been sent from Alexia on the same supposition, they even were fools enough to send in a flag demanding our surrender; at once & of course we scattered the Brigade, taking several hundred prisoners, killing & wounding many & among them the Brig-Gen. Taylor, who has since died.

At the Junction was a large store depôt, 5 or six pieces of artillery, two trains containing probably 200 large cars loaded down with many millions worth of qr mr. & Commissary stores; beside these there were very large sutlers depôts full of everything; in short there was collected there in a square mile an amount & variety of property such as I had never conceived of (I speak soberly). Twas a curious sight to see our ragged & famished men helping themselves to every imaginable article of luxury or necessity whether of clothing, food or what not; for my part I got a tooth brush, a box of candles, a quantity of lobster salad, a barrel of coffee & other things wh. I forget. But I must hurry on for I have not time to tell the hundredth part & the scene utterly beggars description.

A part of us hunted that Brigade like scattered partridges over the hills just to the right of the Battlefield of the 18th July /61 while the rest were partly plundering partly fighting the forces coming on us from Warrenton. Our men had been living on roasted corn since crossing Rappahannock, & we had brought no wagons so we could carry little away of the riches before us. But the men could eat for one meal at least, so they were marched up and as much of everything eatable served out as they could carry To see a starving man eating lobster salad & drinking rhine wine, barefooted & in tatters was curious; the whole thing is indescribable, I'll tell you sometime may be.

Our situation was now very critical, we were between Alexandria & Warrenton, between the hosts of Mclellan & Pope with our jaded 18000 men, for the Corps had not more then. At nightfall fire was set to the depot, store houses, the loaded trains, several long empty trains, sutler's houses, restaurants & every thing. As the magnificent conflagration began to subside the Stonewall or 1st Division moved off towards the Battlefield of Manassas, the other two to Centreville 6 miles; as day broke we came in sight of Centreville; rested a few hours & towards evening the rear Guard of the Corps crossed Bull Run at Stone Bridge, the scene of the great slaughter of last year, closely pursued by the enemy. A part of their force came up the Warrenton turnpike & in a furious action of two hours, the last two hours of Thursday the 28th August, disputed the possession of a ridge running from Sudley Church Ford to the Warrenton turnpike. We drove them off & on friday morning we held the ridge in front of which runs an incomplete R. R. Cut & embankment. Now we had made a circuit from the Gap in

Bull Run Mt. around to the Junction & Centreville, breaking up the R. R. & destroying their stores, & returned to within six miles of the Gap through which Longstreet *must* come. The enemy disputed his passage & delayed him till late in the day, & meanwhile they threw against our corps all day long vast masses of troops, Sigel, Banks, Pope's own Division; we got out of ammunition, we collected more from cartridge boxes of fallen friend & foe; that gave out, & we charged with the never failing yell & steel.

All day long they threw their masses on us, all day they fell back, shattered & shrieking. When the sun went down their dead were heaped in front of that incomplete Railway, and we sighed with relief for Longstreet could be seen coming into position on our right; the crisis was over, Longstreet never failed yet, but the sun went down *so* slowly. Friday Hill's Division chiefly bore the brunt, on thursday Ewells & Jackson's, tho all were engaged on friday.

On Saturday morning, day even memorable for it broke the back of the great lying nation, our corps still held that ridge & Longstreet formed on our right, obtuse angled to us. So that if they attacked, upon forcing us back, their flank would be exposed to Longstreet, forcing him back, to us. This arrangement was concealed from them, so far that they expected our strength to lie to our left. Skirmishing & distant cannonading lasted till 1 P. M. when the action commenced & soon grew infinitely furious, but they were out generaled & beaten from the start, & at 4 1/2 P. M. or 5 twas plain they were awfully conquered. The fight was by far the most horrible & deadly that I have ever seen. Just at sunset our wings swept round in pursuit; Jackson swinging with his left on the right as a pivot towards the right & Longstreet in the reverse method towards the left. Their dead on the field were in such numbers as to sicken even the veterans of Richmond & the Shenandoah; they left more than 2000 *dead*, rotting clay, & of wounded almost innumerable. Their discipline & the night saved them from a rout. They retreated in tolerable order to Centreville. Twas decisive, their whole army engaged, two corps of ours, & the loss I think was 10 to 1 of ours. Starkes La. Brigade, & the 2nd Brigade of Jackson's 1st Divn., the ammunition partly giving out, fought with the stones from the ground; this *I know* to be fact. Lewis Randolph, it is said, was seen to kill one man with a stone. We lost many valuable men. V. was shot early, in the breast, slightly. I heard of it on Sunday, got leave & found him at the hospital, very dirty in dust & blood but in good hands; I took off my shirt & gave it to him & sent him on his way rejoicing towards Middleburgh where he is now with Tom Dudley. Give him my love & ask him if my outline is not correct. I happened by good luck to have a clean shirt on, having bathed in Bull Run on friday morning & changed my clothing—On Saturday I had the narrowest escape yet, two cannon shot within a minute of each other passed so near to me as almost to take away my breath. The thing was so close that it put me into the wildest spirits.

On Monday our corps moved to Ox Hill between Chantilly and Fairfax C. H. where in the afternoon we had under a driving thunder storm a smart fight, but indecisive, with 3 divisions, in it were killed Generals Kearney & Stephens valuable officers both, worth the battle. Thus this corps fought 6 days out of seven, after enormous marches. On Wednesday the 3rd inst we marched to Drainesville, on thursday, to Leesburg, where we met D. H. Hills Corps, Ripley's Division, & perhaps others. On Yesterday the army crossed the Potomac, D. H. Hill a little earlier in the day than we & at a different ford. We marched till 12 1/2 last night, started today before day & reached this town by 1 P. M. or earlier. It is 24 miles from Leesburg, & within 18 miles of Pennsylvania.

Of the scene at the passage of the Potomac I have not time to speak nor of the battlefield of Leesburg. Saunders, coming on in an independent way captured the telegraph operator, turned him over to Gen. Jackson & heard him send a message to Abe, after which the telegraph was destroyed, the track torn up, B & O. R. R. Stuart yesterday sent a message by another line to Abe. I have seen the Baltimore Sun of today. They are puzzling themselves to guess whether we have really crossed.

I wish, my dear Mother, that I could better tell you of these great matters. But it is easier for you to imagine how tired I am than for me to tell you. In the last 36 hours I have slept two hours & been moving all the rest of the time.

I am proud to have borne even my humble part in these great operations, to have helped, ever so little to consummate the grand plan whose history will be a text book to all young soldiers & whose magnificent, bewildering success places Lee at the side of the Greatest Captains, Hannibal, Caesar, Eugene, Napoleon.

I hope you have preserved my letters in which I have spoken of my faith in Gen. Lee. He & his round table of Generals are worthy of the immortality of Napoleon & his Marshalls. He moves his agencies like a God, secret, complicated, vast, resistless, complete.

John reached me on Sunday the 24th. It was right not to send the horse. I am glad now that he is not here. Give my thanks, with my love to bro. Edward. I hope the colt has recovered. Your letters by John were very grateful. Norborne Starke, I was delighted to see, the day before yesterday. He gave me your most welcome letter. I have never received Sally G's letter nor yours with it. Willy Caskie is in Jackson's 1st Division, but has not been with the army since Cedar Run, August 9th where he was hurt. Please inquire about it. Letters are too scarce & precious to be lost, whether yours or Sally's. I wish I could write better tonight but I am all in a whirl. I write from Maryland, the sickening hope-deferred has at last come to pass.

This part of Md does not welcome us warmly; I have long thought the State was a humbug.

I believe we shall march to Pa tomorrow or next day. John is delighted with the life. Give much love to all my friends. Specially Cousin Harvie & all his house. I think Nannie might write to me a scrap occasionally.

I am truly sorry that the health of Richmond is bad. But the fall weather will improve it. Tell the Grattans that I saw Jimmy this day fortnight. He was well & in fine spirits; anxious to hear from his father about his transfer to a Battery. Norborne Starke wanted me to be Ordnance Officer for his father, but I cant leave this post unless I am offered promotion.

Give no end of love to Hart & bro Edward & Sister. Remember me to the Moores. I hope Dr. Bagby got my letter written from Orange County. Tell Nancy to give my love to Miss Mattie Waller. After what I have seen lately life looks very fleeting & uncertain. If I should never see any of you again, remember that I am in charity with all men, except our enemy whom to hate is lawful, and that many I love very dearly—

Howbeit; care killed a cat. Tell Nancy to sit down when you get this & sing one of her best pieces. So shall I, as I sit here on the banks of Monocacy under the beams of the full, unclouded, moon, fancy that I hear her clear notes welling up in the trills that I remember she used to warble out like a sweet little bird; and straightway from me listening shall flee away all evil thoughts & harsh fancies & the coarse jeer & laughter of camp be hushed leaving only pleasant dreams of home & friends

Your most affectionate son

J. H. C.

Gen. Hill does me the honour always to use me as one of his staff

“UNSOLDIERLY AND DANGEROUS CONDUCT”: VIRGINIA, SEPTEMBER 1862

John Pope to Henry W. Halleck

As the badly beaten Union forces fell back from the Bull Run battlefield toward the defenses of Washington, this dispatch of General Pope's triggered a command crisis. The “commander of a corps” in the Army of the Potomac he mentions was Fitz John Porter, brought to court-martial in December on Pope's charges.

CENTREVILLE, *September* 1—8.50 a.m.

Major-General HALLECK:

All was quiet yesterday and so far this morning. My men are resting; they need it much. Forage for our horses is being brought up. Our cavalry is completely broken down, so that there are not five horses to a company that can raise a trot. The consequence is that I am forced to keep considerable infantry along the roads in my rear to make them secure, and even then it is difficult to keep the enemy's cavalry off the roads. I shall attack again to-morrow if I can; the next day certainly. I think it my duty to call your attention to the unsoldierly and dangerous conduct of many brigade and some division commanders of the forces sent here from the Peninsula. Every word and act and intention is discouraging, and calculated to break down the spirits of the men and produce disaster. One commander of a corps, who was ordered to march from Manassas Junction to join me near Groveton, although he was only 5 miles distant, failed to get up at all, and, worse still, fell back to Manassas without a fight, and in plain hearing, at less than 3 miles' distance, of a furious battle, which raged all day. It was only in consequence of peremptory orders that he joined me next day. One of his brigades, the brigadier-general of which professed to be looking for his division, absolutely remained all day at Centreville, in plain view of the battle, and made no attempt to join. What renders the whole matter worse, these are both officers of the Regular Army, who do not hold back from ignorance or fear. Their constant talk, indulged in publicly and in promiscuous company, is that the Army of the Potomac will not fight; that they are demoralized by withdrawal from the Peninsula, &c. When such example is set by officers of high rank the influence is very bad amongst those in subordinate stations.

You have hardly an idea of the demoralization among officers of high rank in the Potomac Army, arising in all instances from personal feeling in relation to changes of commander-in-chief and others. These men are mere tools or parasites, but their example is producing, and must necessarily produce, very disastrous results. You should know these things, as you alone can stop it. Its source is beyond my reach, though its effects are very perceptible and very dangerous. I am endeavoring to do all I can, and will most assuredly put them where they shall fight or run away. My advice to you—I give it with freedom, as I know you will not misunderstand it—is that, in view of any satisfactory results, you draw back this army to the intrenchments in front of Washington, and set to work in that secure place to reorganize and rearrange it. You may avoid great disaster by doing so. I do not consider the matter except in a purely military light, and it is bad enough and grave enough to make some action very necessary. When there is no heart in their leaders, and every disposition to hang back, much cannot be expected from the men.

Please hurry forward cavalry horses to me under strong escort. I need them badly—worse than I can tell you.

JNO. POPE,
Major-General.

AIDING THE WOUNDED: VIRGINIA AND WASHINGTON, D.C., AUGUST–SEPTEMBER 1862

Clara Barton to John Shaver

Overall the treatment and evacuation of the Union wounded from the battlefield at Manassas were chaotic and inept. In a letter to a friend and supporter, nurse Clara Barton describes the heroic efforts of her small band of volunteers. She recorded the deaths of Generals Kearny and Stevens and Colonel Fletcher Webster, son of Daniel Webster. Barton, a clerk in the Patent Office at the outbreak of the war, operated independently to deliver nursing care right to the scene of the fighting, and she became known in the Union army as the "Angel of the Battlefield." In 1881 she founded the American branch of the Red Cross.

Washington, D.C. Sept. 4 / 62

Mr. Shaver,

Dear friend,

Yours awaited me on my return from Fairfax Tuesday evening (or night rather). I left here on Sunday morning in the rain in company with Mr. Wells, Mrs. Morrell, Mr. Haskell, Mr. Alvord, &c. &c., took the train at Morgan Bulleys office, and soon found ourselves at Fairfax. I can not tell you the scenes which awaited our eyes,—the wounded were constantly arriving—but no hospitals this time, only God's great one under the blue canopy. The men were brot down from the field and laid on the ground beside the train and so back up the hill till they covered acres, the bales of hay for forage were broken open and the ground was "littered" like "bedding" for horses,—they came till dark and then it was dark indeed. *One* lantern on the ground made a requisition for candles drew a few, the wind blew just enough to put them out every few minutes, and the men lay so thick we could not take one step in the dark, by midnight there must have been *three thousand* helpless men lying on that hay.

We had *two* water buckets—5 dippers. The stores which we carried to eat, besides hard crackers,— My one *stew pan* which

I remembered to take, and this made coffee for them, all night we made compresses and slings and bound up and wet wounds, when we could get water, fed what we could, travelled miles in the dark over these poor helpless wretches, in terror lest some ones candle fell *into the hay* and consume them all, at length morning came, and we sent up the train with 1250, next 1000, next 1100, next 950, and so on. Still the ambulances came down, and the cars went out and we worked on, took the meat from our own sandwiches & gave it to them and broke the bread into wine and water to feed the poor sinking wretches as they lay in the ambulances.

On Monday the enemies Cavalry appeared in the wood opposite, & a raid was hourly expected. (I neglected to tell you that *Mrs. Fales* sent to me before I started to know *if she could go with me* and I had the train wait, and sent back an ambulance for her and her stores,—and this made three ladies (Mrs Corner is away)) On Monday PM all the wounded then in were sent off, and the danger became so iminent that Mrs Fales thought it best to leave, although she only "*went for stores.*" I begged to be excused from accompanying her, as the ambulances were up to the field for more, and I knew *I* should *never leave a wounded* man there if I knew it, though I were taken prisoner 40 times. At 6 clock it commenced to thunder an lightning, and all at once the artillery began to play joined by the musketry about *two miles distant*, we sat down in our tent, and waited to see them break in but Reno's forces held them back. The *old 21st Mass.* lay between us and the enemy and they couldnt pass. God only knows who is lost. I do not for the next day *all fell* back. Poor Kearney, Stephens & Webster were brought in, and in the PM, Kearney's and Heintzleman's divisions fell back through our camp on their way to Alexandria. We knew this was the last. We put the thousand wounded we had then into the train. I took one car load of them, Mrs M another. The men took to horse, we steam off, and two hours after there was no Fairfax Station, reached Alexandria at 10 oclock at night. And Oh the repast which met those poor men at the train. The people of the Island are the most noble band I ever saw or heard of. I staid in my car and fed the men till they would eat no more. Then the people *would* take us home and feed us, and after this we came home. I had slept 1 1/4 hours since Saturday night but I am well and strong and wait to go again if I have need.

Our forces are all back again in the old places around the city. McClellans army here again and he in command of it all. I am going to search for my friends now. I have told you nothing of the old friends who met me among the wounded and dying on that bloody field. I have no heart to tell it to day but will some time. Can you read this. Oh how I needed stores on that field. To day 2 huge boxes from Jersey have arrived. I dont know when we shall need them next. I will write you a more readable letter in reply to your last to me.

Yours, C.H. Barton

"McCLELLAN MUST GO DOWN": WASHINGTON, D.C., AUGUST–SEPTEMBER 1862

Gideon Welles: Diary, August 31–September 1, 1862

Navy secretary Welles spells out the case against McClellan, as made by Secretaries Stanton and Chase in their remonstrance, regarding (among other failings) that general's delay in supporting Pope in the Second Bull Run fighting. The forces held back to defend Washington, under McClellan's orders, were William Franklin's Sixth Corps and Edwin Sumner's Second Corps, some 25,000 men in all.

Sunday 31 *August.* For the last two or three days there has been fighting at the front and army movements of interest. McClellan with most of his army arrived at Alexandria a week or more ago, but inertness, inactivity and sluggishness seem to prevail. Some of the troops have moved forward to join Pope, who has been beyond Manassas where he has encountered Jackson and the Rebel forces for the last three days in a severe struggle.

The energy and rapid movements of the Rebels are in such striking contrast with that of some of our own officers, that the War Department is alarmed and I shall not be seriously surprised at any sudden dash. By request, and in anticipation of the worst, though not expecting it, I have ordered Wilkes and a force of fourteen gunboats, including the five light drafts asked for by Burnside, to come round into the Potomac, and have put W. in command of the flotilla here, disbanding that on the James.

Yesterday, Saturday, P.M. when about leaving the Department, Chase called on me with a protest signed by himself and Stanton, against McClellan and demanding his immediate dismissal. Certain grave offenses were enumerated. He said that Smith had seen and would sign it in turn, but as my name preceded his in order, he desired mine in its place. I told him I was not prepared to sign the document—that I preferred a different method of meeting the question—that if asked by the President, and even if not asked, I was prepared to express my opinion—which, as he knew had long been averse to McClellan and was much aggravated from what I had recently learned at the War Department—that I did not choose to denounce McC. for incapacity, or declare him a traitor but I would say, and it was perhaps my duty to say, that I believed his withdrawal from any command was demanded and that even his dismissal would be a blessing.

Chase said that was not sufficient,—that the time had arrived when the Cabinet must act with energy and promptitude, for either the Government or McClellan must go down. He then proceeded to expose certain acts, some of which were partially known to me, and others, more startling, which were new. I said to C. that he and Stanton were familiar with facts of which I was ignorant, and there might therefore be propriety in their stating what they knew which I could not because I had no knowledge of these facts.

I proposed there should be a general consultation with the President. He objected to this until the document was signed, which should be done at once.

This method of getting signatures without an interchange of views from those who were associated in council was repugnant to my ideas of duty and right. When I asked if the Attorney General and Postmaster General, had seen the paper or been consulted, he replied not yet, their turn had not come. I informed C. that I should desire to advise with them in so important a matter,—that I was disinclined to sign the paper—did not like the proceeding—that I could not, though I wished McClellan removed after what I had heard, and should have no hesitation in saying so at the proper time and place, and, in what I considered the right way.

While we were talking Blair came in. Chase was alarmed, for the paper was in my hand and he evidently feared I should address B. on the subject. This, after witnessing his agitation, I could not do without his consent. Blair remained but a few moments; did not even take a seat. After he left, I asked Chase if we should not consult him. C. said No, not now,—it is best he should know nothing of it. I took a different view—that there was no one of the Cabinet whom I would sooner consult on this subject—that I thought his opinion, often very correct. Chase said this was not the time to bring him in. After he left me, he returned to make a special request that I would make no allusion concerning the paper to Blair or any one else.

Met, by invitation, a few friends last evening at Baron Gerolt's. My call was early and feeling anxious concerning affairs in front, I excused myself to go to the War Department for tidings. Found Stanton and Smith alone in the Secretary's room. The conduct of McClellan was soon taken up,—it had, I inferred, been under discussion before I came in.

Stanton began with a statement of his entrance into the Cabinet in January when he found everything in confusion with unpaid bills to the amount of over $20,000,000 against the Department. His inability to procure any satisfactory information from McClellan, who had no plan and no system. Said this vague, indefinite uncertainty was oppressive. That near the close of January, he pressed this subject on the President, who issued the order to him and myself for an advance on the 22d of February. McClellan began at once to interpose objections—yet did nothing,—but talked always vaguely and indefinitely and of various matters except those immediately in hand. The President insisted on, and ordered a forward movement. Then McClellan informed them he intended a demonstration on the upper waters of the Potomac and boats for a bridge were prepared with great labor and expense. He went up there and telegraphed back that two or three officers had done admirably in preparing the bridge and he wished them to be brevetted. The whole thing eventuated in nothing and he was ordered back.

The President then commanded that the army should proceed to Richmond. McClellan delayed, hesitated, said he must go by way of the Peninsula—would take transports at Annapolis. In order that he should have no excuse, but without any faith in his plan, Stanton said he ordered transports and supplies at Annapolis. The President in the mean time urged and pressed forward a movement towards Manassas—its results—the evacuation by the Rebels who fled before the General came, who did not pursue but came back. The transports were then ordered round to the Potomac where the troops were shipped to Fortress Monroe. The plans,—the number of troops to proceed—the number that was to remain Stanton recounted. These arrangements were somewhat deranged by the sudden raid of Jackson towards Winchester, which withdrew Banks from Manassas, leaving no force between Washington and the Rebel army at Gordonsville. He then ordered McDowell and his division, also Franklin's to remain, to the great grief of McDowell, who believed glory and fighting were all to be with the grand army. McClellan had made the withholding of this necessary force his excuse for not being more rapid and effective,—was constantly complaining. The President wrote him how, by his arrangement, only 18,000 troops, the remnants and odd parcels, were left to protect the Capital. Still McClellan was everlastingly complaining and underrating his forces—said he had but 96,000, when his own returns showed he had 123,000. But to stop his complaints and urge him forward, the President finally, on the 10th of June, sent him McCall and his division, with which he promised to proceed at once to Richmond but did not, until finally attacked.

McClellan's excuse for going by way of the Peninsula was that he might have good roads and dry ground, but his complaints were unceasing, after he got there, of bad roads, and water, and swamps.

When finally ordered to withdraw from James River, he delayed obeying the order for thirteen days, and never did comply until General Burnside was sent to supersede him if he did not move.

Since his arrival at Alexandria Stanton says only delay and embarrassment had governed him. General Halleck had, among other things, ordered General Franklin's division to go forward promptly to support Pope at Manassas. When Franklin got as far as Annandale he was stopped by McClellan, against orders and McClellan's excuse was he thought Franklin might be in danger if he proceeded farther. For twenty four hours that large force remained stationary, hearing the whole time the guns of the battle that was raging in front. In consequence of this delay by command of McClellan, against specific orders, he apprehended our army would be compelled to fall back.

Smith left whilst we were conversing after this detailed narrative, and Stanton dropping his voice, though no one was present, said he understood from Chase that I had declined to sign the protest which he had drawn up against McClellan's continuance in command, and asked if I did not think we ought to get rid of him. I told him I might not differ with him on that point, especially after what I had heard in addition to what I had previously known, but that I disliked the method and manner of proceeding—that it was discourteous and disrespectful to the President were there nothing else. Stanton said he knew of no particular obligations he was under to the President who had called him to a difficult position and imposed upon him labors and responsibilities which no man could carry, and which were greatly increased by fastening upon him a commander who was constantly striving to embarrass him. He could not and would not submit to a continuance of this state of things. I admitted they were bad, severe on him, and he could and stated his case strongly, but I could not indorse it, nor did I like the manner in which it was proposed to bring about a dismissal. He said General Pope telegraphed to McClellan for supplies. The latter informed P. they were at Alexandria, and if P. would send an escort he could have them. A general fighting, on the field of battle, sends to a general in the rear, and in repose, an escort!

Watson Assistant Secretary of War gave me this last fact this morning, and reaffirmed others. He informs me that my course on a certain occasion had offended McClellan and was not approved by others; but that both the President and Stanton had since, and now in their private conversations admitted I was right, and that my letter in answer to a curt and impudent demand of McClellan last spring was proper and correct. Watson says that he always told them I was right, and he complimented me on several subjects which others can speak of and judge better than myself.

We hear, this Sunday morning, that our army has fallen back to Centreville. Pope writes in pretty good spirits we have lost no guns, etc. The Rebels were largely reinforced, while our troops, detained at Annandale by McClellan's orders, did not arrive to support our wearied and exhausted men. McClellan telegraphs that he hears Pope is "badly cut up." Schenck who had a wound in his arm left the battle-field, bringing with him for company an Ohio captain. Both arrived *safe at Willard's.*

They met McCall on the other side of Centreville and Sumner on this. Late! late!

Up to this hour, 1 P.M. no specific intelligence beyond the general facts above stated. There is considerable uneasiness in this city, which is mere panic. I see no cause for alarm. It is impossible to feel otherwise than sorrowful and sad over the waste of life and treasure, and energies of the nation—the misplaced confidence in certain men—the errors of some—perhaps the crimes of others who have been trusted. But my faith in present security and of ultimate success is unshaken. We need better generals but can have no better army. There is much latent disloyal feeling in Washington, which should be expelled. And oh, there is great want of capacity among our military leaders.

I hear that all the churches not heretofore seized are now taken for hospital purposes,—private dwellings are taken to be thus used—among others my neighbor Corcoran's fine house and grounds. There is malice in this. I told General Halleck it was vandalism. He said it would be wrong. Halleck walked over with me from the War Department and is, I perceive quite alarmed for the safety of the city,—it is a fatal error, says that we overrate our own strength and underestimate the Rebels'. This has been the talk of McClellan, which none of us have believed.

Monday 1 *September*. The wounded have been coming in to-day in large numbers. From what I can learn, General Pope's estimate of the killed and wounded greatly exceeds the actual number. He should, however, be best informed, but is greatly given to exaggeration.

Chase tells me that McClellan sends word that there are twenty thousand stragglers on the road between Alexandria and Centreville, which C. says is infamously false and done for infamous purposes. He called on me to-day with a more carefully prepared, and less exceptionable address to the President, stating the signers did not deem it safe that McClellan should be intrusted with an army, etc., and that, if required, they would give their reasons for the protest against continuing him in command. This paper was in the handwriting of Attorney-

General Bates. The former was Stanton's. This was signed by Stanton, Chase, Smith and Bates. A space was left between the two last for Blair and myself. Seward is not in town, and if I am not mistaken is purposely absent to be relieved from participation in this movement, which originates with Stanton who is mad—perhaps with reason. Seward and Stanton act in concert, and Seward has opposed the removal of McClellan until since Halleck has been brought here, and Stanton has become fierce, and determined, when Seward gave way and went away. Then Chase, who is sometimes the victim of intrigue, was taken into Stanton's confidence—made to believe that the opportunity of Seward's absence should be improved to shake off McClellan by a combined Cabinet movement to influence the President, who clung to McClellan. It was not difficult under the prevailing feeling of indignation against McClellan to enlist Smith. I am a little surprised that they got Bates, though he has for some time urged this movement. Chase took upon himself to get my name, and then, if possible, Blair was to come in. In all this, Chase flatters himself that he is attaching Stanton to his interest—not but that he is sincere in his opposition to McClellan, who was once his favorite, but whom he now detests.

I told Chase I thought this paper an improvement on the document of Saturday—that in a conference with the President, I would have no hesitation in saying or agreeing mainly in what was there expressed—substituting "advise" in one place—for I am satisfied the country would not be willing McClellan should have the active command of our forces in the field, though I cannot say what is the feeling of the armies. Reflection had more fully satisfied me that this method of combining to influence or control the President was not right—it was unusual, and would justly be deemed offensive. That the President had called us around him as friends and advisers, to counsel and consult with him on all matters affecting the public welfare, not to enter into combinations against him. Nothing of this kind has hitherto taken place in our intercourse. That we had not been sufficiently formal perhaps, and perhaps not sufficiently explicit and decisive in expressing our views.

Chase disclaimed any movement against the President, and thought the manner respectful and correct. Said it was designed to tell President that the Administration must be broken up, or McC. dismissed. The course he said was unusual, but the case was unusual. We had, it was true, been too informal in our meeting. I had been too reserved in the expression of my views which he did me the compliment to say were sound, etc. Conversation, he said amounted to but little with the President on subjects of this importance. It was like throwing water on a duck's back. A more decisive expression must be made and that in writing.

I was satisfied there was a fixed determination to remove, and if possible disgrace McClellan. Chase frankly stated he desired it, that he deliberately believed McClellan ought to be shot, and should, were he President, be brought to a summary punishment. I told him he was aware my faith in McClellan nine months ago. That as early as last December I had, as he would recollect, expressed my disappointment in the man and stated to him, specially, as the friend and indorser of McClellan, my misgivings, in order to have my doubts removed and confirmed. His indifference, and neglect, his failure in many instances to fulfill his promises, when the Rebels were erecting their batteries on the west bank of the Potomac, to close the navigation of the river, had forfeited my confidence in his efficiency and reliability. But at that time he was a general favorite, and neither he (Chase) nor any one heeded my admonitions.

A few weeks after the navigation of the river was first obstructed by the Rebel batteries, I made known to the President and Cabinet how I was put off by General McClellan with frivolous and unsatisfactory answers, until I ceased conversation with him on the subject. To me it seemed he had no plan or policy of his own, or any realizing sense of the condition of affairs. He was occupied with reviews and dress-parades—perhaps with drills and discipline but was regardless of political aspect of the question, the effect which the closing of the only avenue from the National Capital to the ocean, and the embarrassment which would follow to the Government itself. Though deprecating his course and calling his attention to it, I did not think, as Chase says he does, and as I hear others say, that he was imbecile, a coward, a traitor, but it was notorious that he hesitated, doubted, had not self-reliance—innate moral courage, and was wanting in my opinion in several of the essential requisites of a general in chief command. These are my present convictions. Some statements of Stanton and some recent acts indicate delinquencies of a more serious character. The country is greatly incensed against him.

Chase was disappointed I think a little chagrined, because I would not unite in the written demand to the President. He said he had not yet asked Blair and did not propose to till the others had been consulted. This does not look well. It appears as if there was a combination by two to get their associates committed, *seriatim*, in detail, by a skillful *ex parte* movement without general consultation.

McClellan was first invited to Washington under the auspices of Chase—more than of any one else. Seward soon had greater intimacy with him than any one else. Blair acquiesced in McClellan's selection. In the winter, when Chase began to get alienated from McC. in consequence of his hesitancy and reticence, or both, Blair seemed to confide more in the General, yet I do not think he was a favorite.

"WE ARE WHIPPED AGAIN": WASHINGTON, D.C., SEPTEMBER 1862

John Hay: Diary, September 1, 1862

The developing command and military crisis and its effects on the President, as recorded by John Hay, one of Lincoln's secretaries. Herman Haupt, whom Lincoln spoke well of, was chief of construction of U.S. military railroads.

Saturday morning, the 30th of August, I rode out into the country and turned in at the "Soldiers home." The President's horse was standing by the door and in a moment the President appeared and we rode into town together.

We talked about the state of things by Bull Run and Pope's prospect. The President was very outspoken in regard to McClellan's present conduct. He said it really seemed to him that McC wanted Pope defeated. He mentioned to me a despatch of McC.s in which he proposed, as one plan of action, to "leave Pope to get out of his own scrape, and devote ourselves to securing Washington." He spoke also of Mcs dreadful panic in the matter of Chain Bridge, which he had ordered blown up the night before, but which order had been countermanded; and also of his incomprehensible interference with Franklin's corps which he recalled once, and then when they had been sent ahead by Halleck's order, begged permission to recall them again & only desisted after Hallecks sharp injunction to push them ahead till they whipped something or got whipped themselves. The President seemed to think him a little crazy. Envy jealousy and spite are probably a better explanation of his present conduct. He is constantly sending despatches to the President and Halleck asking what is his real position and command. He acts as chief alarmist and grand marplot of the Army.

The President, on my asking if Halleck had any prejudices, rejoined "No! Halleck is wholly for the service. He does not care who succeeds or who fails so the service is benefited."

Later in the day we were in Hallecks room. H. was at dinner

& Stanton came in while we were waiting for him and carried us off to dinner. A pleasant little dinner and a pretty wife as white and cold and motionless as marble, whose rare smiles seemed to pain her. Stanton was loud about the McC. business. He was unqualifiedly severe upon McClellan. He said that after these battles, there should be one Court Martial, if never any more. He said that nothing but foul play could lose us this battle & that it rested with McC. and his friends. Stanton seemed to believe very strongly in Pope. So did the President for that matter.

We went back to the Headquarters and found General Halleck. He seemed quiet and somewhat confident. He said the greatest battle of the Century was now being fought. He said he had sent every man that could go, to the field. At the War Department we found that Mr. Stanton had sent a vast army of Volunteer Nurses out to the field, probably utterly useless, over which he gave Genl. Wadsworth command.

Every thing seemed to be going well and hilarious on Saturday & we went to bed expecting glad tidings at sunrise. But about Eight oclock the President came to my room as I was dressing and calling me out said, "Well John we are whipped again, I am afraid. The enemy reinforced on Pope and drove back his left wing and he has retired to Centerville where he says he will be able to hold his men. I dont like that expression. I dont like to hear him admit that his men need holding."

After a while however things began to look better and peoples spirits rose as the heavens cleared. The President was in a singularly defiant tone of mind. He often repeated, "We must hurt this enemy before it gets away." And this Morning, Monday, he said to me when I made a remark in regard to the bad look of things, "No, Mr Hay, we must whip these people now. Pope must fight them, if they are too strong for him he can gradually retire to these fortifications. If this be not so, if we are really whipped and to be whipped we may as well stop fighting."

It is due in great measure to his indomitable will, that army movements have been characterized by such energy and celerity for the last few days. There is one man who seems thoroughly to reflect and satisfy him in everything he undertakes. This is Haupt the Rail Road man at Alexandria. He has as

Chase says a Major General's head on his shoulders. The President is particularly struck with the businesslike character of his despatch, telling in the fewest words the information most sought for, which contrasted so strongly with the weak whining vague and incorrect despatches of the whilom General-in-chief. If heads or shoulder-straps could be exchanged, it would be a good thing, in either case, here. A good railroader would be spoiled but the General gained would compensate. The corps of Haupt starting from Alexandria have acted as Pioneers advance Guard, voltigeurs and every other light infantry arm of the service.

"THE PREST. WAS IN DEEP DISTRESS": WASHINGTON, D.C., SEPTEMBER 1862

Edward Bates: Remonstrance and Notes on Cabinet Meeting

Attorney General Bates toned down the Stanton-Chase remonstrance against McClellan, and his version gained four signatures from the seven-man cabinet, with Welles promising to support it verbally. The version printed here is Bates's draft of the remonstrance, with the names of the four signers in his handwriting (his fair copy bearing the actual signatures is preserved in Stanton's papers). The attorney general later added his notes on the September 2 cabinet meeting to the draft and wrote an endorsement at the end of the document that suggests the remonstrance was shown or read to the President during the meeting.

The undersigned, who have been honored with your selection, as a part of your confidential advisers, deeply impressed with our great responsibility in the present crisis, do but perform a painful duty in declaring to you our deliberate opinion that, at this time, it is not safe to entrust to Major General McClellan the command of any of the armies of the United States.

And we hold ourselves ready, at any time to explain to you, in detail, the reasons on which this opinion is founded

(Signed by) E.M. Stanton, Secy War
S.P. Chase, Secy Treasury
C.B. Smith Sec Interior
Edwd Bates Atty Genl

To the President—
[Delivered Sept 2d 1862]

Note. Mr. Blair p.m.g. declined to sign (no reason given that I heard, but preserving a cautious reticence)

Gideon Welles, Secy Navy, declined to sign, for some reasons of etiquette, but openly declared in Council, his entire want of confidence in the general

W.H. Seward, Sec of State, *absent*

The Prest. was in deep distress. He had already, with, apparently, Gen Halleck's approbation, assigned Genl McClellan to the command of the forts in & around Washington & entrusted him with the defence of the City. At the opening of the Council, he seemed wrung by the bitterest anguish—said he felt almost ready to hang himself—in ansr to something said by Mr Chase, he sd he was far from doubting our sincerity, but that he was so distressed, precisely because he knew we were earnestly sincere.

He was, manifestly alarmed for the safety of the City— He had been talking with Gen Halleck (who, I think is cowed) & had gotten the idea that Pope's army was utterly demoralized—saying that "if Pope's army came within the lines (of the forts) as *a mob*, the City wd be overrun by the enemy in 48 hours!!"

I said that if Halleck doubted his ability to defend the City, he ought to be instantly, broke— 50.000 men were enough to defend it against all the power of the enemy— If the City fell, it would be by treachery in our leaders, & not by lack of power to defend. The shame was that we were reduced to the defensive, instead of the aggressive policy &c— That all the army was not needed to defend the City, & now was the time, above all others, to strike the enemy behind & at a distance &c

Opinion of Stanton, Chase, Smith & Bates, of want of Confidence in Genl. McClellan.
Given to the President Sept. 2d 1862.

"A SERIES OF FAILURES": WASHINGTON, D.C., SEPTEMBER 1862

Salmon P. Chase: Journal, September 2, 1862

The cabinet meeting of September 2, the most contentious of Lincoln's administration, was recorded in Treasury Secretary Chase's journal. With even Montgomery Blair, a longtime McClellan supporter, admitting that he should no longer be trusted with high command, the cabinet (absent Seward) was unanimous in its condemnation of the general. Lincoln's announcement that he had assigned McClellan to defend Washington, commanding both his army and Pope's, caused Welles to write in his diary, "There was a more disturbed and desponding feeling than I have ever witnessed in council."

TUESDAY, SEPT. 2, 1862. Cabinet met, but neither the President nor Secretary of War were present. Some conversation took place concerning Generals. Mr. F. W. Seward (the Secretary of State being out of town) said nothing. All others agreed that we needed a change in Commander of the Army. Mr. Blair referred to the support he had constantly given McClellan, but confessed that he now thought he could not wisely be trusted with the chief command. Mr. Bates was very decided against his competency, and Mr. Smith equally so. Mr. Welles was of the same judgment, though less positive in expression.

After some time, while the talk was going on, the President came in, saying that not seeing much for a Cabinet Meeting to-day, he had been talking at the Department and Head Quarters about the War. The Secretary of War came in. In answer to some inquiry, the fact was stated, by the President or the Secretary, that McClellan had been placed in command of the forces to defend the Capital—or rather, to use the President's own words, he "had set him to putting these troops into the fortifications about Washington," beleiving that he could do that thing better than any other man. I remarked that this could be done equally well by the Engineer who constructed the Forts; and that putting Genl. McClellan in command for this purpose was equivalent to making him second in command of the entire army. The Secretary of War said that no one was now responsible for the defense of the Capital;—that the Order to McClellan was given by the President direct to McClellan, and that Genl. Halleck considered himself releived from responsibility, although he acquiesced; and approved the Order;—that McClellan could now shield himself, should anything go wrong, under Halleck, while Halleck could and would disclaim all responsibility for the Order given. The President thought Gen. Halleck as much responsible as before; and repeated that the whole scope of the Order was, simply, to direct McClellan to put the troops into the fortifications and command them for the defence of Washington. I remarked that this seemed to me equivalent to making him Commander in Chief for the time being, and that I thought it would prove very difficult to make any substitution hereafter, for active operations;—that I had no feeling whatever against Genl. McClellan;—that he came to the command with my most cordial approbation and support;—that until I became satisfied that his delays would greatly injure our cause, he possessed my full confidence;—that, after I had felt myself compelled to withold that confidence, I had (since the President, notwithstanding my opinion that he should, refrained from putting another in command) given him all possible support in every way, raising means and urging reinforcements;—that his experience as a military commander had been little else than a series of failures;—and that his omission to urge troops forward to the battles of Friday and Saturday, evinced a spirit which rendered him unworthy of trust, and that I could not but feel that giving the command to him was equivalent to giving Washington to the rebels. This and more I said. Other members of the Cabinet expressed a general concurrence, but in no very energetic terms. [Mr. Blair must be excepted, but he did not dissent.]

The President said it distressed him exceedingly to find himself differing on such a point from the Secretary of War and Secretary of the Treasury; that he would gladly resign his place; but he could not see who could do the work wanted as well as McClellan. I named Hooker, or Sumner, or Burnside—either of whom, I thought, would be better.

At length the conversation ended and the meeting broke up, leaving the matter as we found it.

A few Tax Appointments were lying on the table. I asked the President to sign them; which he did, saying he would sign them just as they were and ask no questions. I told him that they had all been prepared in accordance with his directions, and that it was necessary to complete the appointments. They were signed, and I returned to the Department.

RESTORED TO COMMAND:
WASHINGTON, D.C., SEPTEMBER 1862

George B. McClellan to Mary Ellen McClellan

As General McClellan explains in these notes to his wife, his restoration to command was a two-step process—first, command of Washington's defenses, then command of Pope's army as well as his own. The first letter is dated September 2, but it was written in the midnight hours of September 1 and refers to events of that day. While McClellan was never officially removed as head of the Army of the Potomac, he and everyone else understood that he was getting his army back. General Pope was sent to Minnesota to fight the Sioux uprising.

Sept 2 1 am.

. . . Last night I had just finished a very severe application for a leave of absence when I received a dispatch from Halleck begging me to help him out of the scrape & take command here—of course I could not refuse, so I came over this morning, mad as a March hare, & had a pretty plain talk with him & Abe—a still plainer one this evening. The result is that I have reluctantly consented to take command here & try to save the Capital—I don't know whether I can do it or not, for things are far gone—I hope I shall succeed. . . .

I will not work so hard again as I used to—for the next few days I must be at it day & night—once the pressure is over I will make the staff do the work. If when the whole army returns here (if it ever does) I am not placed in command of all I will either insist upon a long leave of absence or resign. . . .

September 2, 1862

Sept 2 12.30 pm.

I was surprised this morning when at bkft by a visit from the Presdt & Halleck—in which the former expressed the opinion that the troubles now impending could be overcome better by me than anyone else. Pope is ordered to fall back upon Washn & as he reenters everything is to come under my command again! A terrible & thankless task—yet I will do my best with God's blessing to perform it. God knows that I need his help. I am too busy to write any more now—Pray that God will help me in the great task now imposed upon me—I assume it reluctantly—with a full knowledge of all its difficulties & of the immensity of the responsibility. I only consent to take it for my country's sake & with the humble hope that God has called me to it—how I pray that he may support me! . . .

Don't be worried—my conscience is clear & I can trust in God.

September 2, 1862

INVADING MARYLAND:
VIRGINIA, SEPTEMBER 1862

Robert E. Lee to Jefferson Davis

In this letter General Lee suggested fairly modest goals in crossing into Maryland, and he started across the Potomac on September 4 without waiting for a response from President Davis. But in suggesting that Braxton Bragg's army, then invading Kentucky, might join him in the eastern campaign, Lee hinted at his greater ambitions.

Head Qurs Alex: & Leesburg Road near
Drainsville 3d. September 1862

Mr. President—

The present seems to be the most propitious time, since the commencement of the war, for the Confederate Army to enter Maryland. The two grand armies of the U. S. that have been operating in Virginia, though now united, are much weakened and demoralized. Their new levees, of which, I understand, sixty thousand men have already been posted in Washington, are not yet organized, and will take some time to prepare for the field. If it is ever desired to give material aid to Maryland, and afford her an opportunity of throwing off the oppression to which she is now subject, this would seem the most favorable. After the enemy had disappeared from the vicinity of Fairfax C. H. and taken the road to Alexandria & Washington, I did not think it would be advantageous to follow him further. I had no intention of attacking him in his fortifications, and am not prepared to invest them. If I possessed the necessary munitions, I should be unable to supply provisions for the troops. I therefore determined while threatening the approaches to Washington to draw the troops into Loudon, where forage and some provisions can be obtained, menace their possession of the Shenandoah Valley, and if found practicable, to cross into Maryland.

The purpose, if discovered, will have the effect of carrying the enemy north of the Potomac, and if prevented, will not result in much evil. The army is not properly equipped for an invasion of an enemy's territory. It lacks much of the material of war, is feeble in transportation, the animals being much reduced, and the men are poorly provided with clothes, and in thousands of instances, are destitute of shoes. Still we cannot afford to be idle, and though weaker than our opponents in men and military equipments, must endeavor to harass, if we cannot destroy them. I am aware that the movement is attended with much risk, yet I do not consider success impossible, and shall endeavor to guard it from loss. As long as the army of the enemy are employed on this frontier, I have no fears for the safety of Richmond, yet I earnestly recommend that advantage be taken of this period of comparative safety, to place its defence, both by land and water, in the most, perfect condition. A respectable force can be collected to defend its approaches by land, and the steamer Richmond I hope is now ready to clear the river of hostile vessels. Should Genl Bragg find it impracticable to operate to advantage on his present frontier, his army, after leaving sufficient garrisons, could be advantageously employed in opposing the overwhelming numbers which it seems to be the intention of the enemy now to concentrate in Virginia. I have already been told by prisoners that some of Buell's Cavalry have been joined to Gen'l. Pope's Army, and have reason to beleive that the whole of McClellan's, the larger portions of Burnside's & Coxe's, and a portion of Hunter's, are united to it, what occasions me most concern is the fear of getting out of ammunition. I beg you will instruct the Ordnance Dept: to spare no pains in manufacturing a sufficient amount of the best kind, & to be particular in preparing that for the Artillery, to provide three times as much of the long range ammunition, as of that for smooth bore or short range guns.

The points to which I desire the ammunition to be forwarded, will be made known to the Department in time. If the Qur. Master's Department can furnish any shoes, it would be the greatest releif.

We have entered upon September, and the nights are becoming cool.

I have the honor to be with high respect Your Ob't Servant,

R. E. Lee. Gen'l:

"A STATE OF NAUSEA": NEW YORK, SEPTEMBER 1862

George Templeton Strong: Diary, September 3–4, 1862

Strong was a New York lawyer and treasurer of the U.S. Sanitary Commission, a civilian organization dedicated to improving conditions in army camps and the care of the sick and wounded; Henry W. Bellows was its president. In his diary Strong appraised the gloomy war news in both eastern and western theaters.

September 3. It has been a day of depressing malignant dyspepsia, not only private and physical, but public and moral. *Egomet Ipse*, George T. Strong, to wit, and we the people have been in a state of nausea and irritation all day long. The morning papers and an extra at mid-day turned us livid and blue. Fighting Monday afternoon at Chantilly, the enemy beat back (more or less), and Pope retreating on Alexandria and Washington to our venerable field-worn fortresses of a year ago. Stonewall Jackson (our national bugaboo) about to invade Maryland, 40,000 strong. General advance of the rebel line threatening our hold on Missouri and Kentucky. Cincinnati in danger. A rebel army within forty miles of the Queen City of the West. Martial law proclaimed in her pork shops. On the other hand, we hear that General Stahel and General Kearny have come to life again, or were only "kilt," not killed, after all. Everybody talks down McClellan and McDowell. McDowell *is said* to have lost us the battle of Saturday afternoon by a premature movement to the rear, though his supports were being hurried up. He is an unlucky general.

September 4. It is certain now that the army has fallen back to its old burrows around Washington. It will probably hibernate there. So, after all this waste of life and money and material, we are at best where we were a year ago. McClellan is chief under Halleck. Many grumble at this, but whom can we find that is proved his superior? He is certainly as respectable as any of the mediocrities that make up our long muster roll of generals. The army believes in him, undoubtingly; that is a material fact. And I suppose him very eminently fitted for a campaign of redoubts and redans, though incapable of vigorous offensive operations. There is reason to hope that Stanton is trembling to his fall. May he fall soon, for he is a public calamity. McDowell and Pope are "universally despised"; so writes Bellows. Poor General Kearny is dead and no mistake and will be buried in Trinity Churchyard next Saturday; so says Meurer the sexton. He's a great loss. I don't know whether he understood strategy, but he was a dashing, fearless sabreur who had fought in Mexico, Algeria, and Lombardy, and loved war from his youth up. I remember my father talking thirty years ago about young Kearny, who was studying law in his office, and about this strange, foolish passion for a military life. He was under a very dark cloud six years ago and was cut by many of his friends. But, bad as it was, the lady's family were horribly to blame—most imprudent; and Kearny made all the reparation he could. He married her and treated her with all possible affection and loyalty. Whatever his faults, we shall miss him.

Our Sanitary Commission stores were first on the field after the battle of Saturday and did great service, for all the forty-two wagon loads of the Medical Department were bagged by the rebels at Manassas. Dr. Chamberlain, our inspector in charge, was taken prisoner, but the rebels let him go. Stanton is reported rancorously hostile to the Commission; probably because Bellows has talked to him once or twice like a Dutch uncle, with plainness of speech that was certainly imprudent, though quite justifiable.

A DEMORALIZED ARMY: WASHINGTON, D.C., SEPTEMBER 1862

William Thompson Lusk to Elizabeth Freeman Lusk

A medical student at Heidelberg and Berlin who had returned home in 1861 to enlist in the 79th New York Infantry, Captain Lusk served on the staff of Major General Isaac Stevens, a division commander in the Ninth Corps who was killed at Chantilly on September 1. The views Lusk expresses to his mother were common among Union soldiers in the aftermath of the Second Bull Run debacle.

HEADQUARTERS 1ST DIVISION,
9th ARMY CORPS,
MERIDIAN HILL, WASHINGTON, D. C.
Sept. 6th, 1862.

My dear Mother:

Now that our General is dead, a Colonel commands the old Division temporarily, and I continue to superintend the office, running the old machine along until different arrangements can be made, when I suppose I shall be set adrift with no pleasant prospects before me. I would resign, were I permitted to do so, and would gladly return to my medical studies this winter, tired as I am of the utter mismanagement which characterizes the conduct of our public affairs. Disheartened by the termination of a disastrous campaign—disasters which every one could and did easily foresee from the course pursued—we find as a consolation, that our good honest old President has told a new story apropos of the occasion, and the land is ringing with the wisdom of the rail-splitting Solomon. Those who were anxious and burning to serve their country, can only view with sullen disgust the vast resources of the land directed not to make our arms victorious, but to give political security to those in power. Men show themselves in a thousand ways incompetent, yet still they receive the support of the Government. Politicians, like Carl Schurz, receive high places in the army without a qualification to recommend them. Stern trusty old soldiers like Stevens are treated with cold neglect. The battle comes—there is no head on the field—the men are handed over to be butchered—to die on inglorious fields. Lying reports are written. Political Generals receive praises where they deserve execration. Old Abe makes a joke. The army finds that nothing has been learned. New preparations are made, with all the old errors retained. New battles are prepared for, to end in new disasters. Alas, my poor country! The army is sadly demoralized. Men feel that there is no honor to be gained by the sword. No military service is recognized unless coupled with political interest. The army is exhausted with suffering—its enthusiasm is dead. Should the enemy attack us here however, we should be victorious. The men would never yield up their Capitol. There is something more though than the draft needed to enable us to march a victorious host to the Gulf of Mexico. Well, I have been writing freely enough to entitle me to accommodations in Fort Lafayette, but I can hardly express the grief and indignation I feel at the past. God grant us better things in future.

I had said my own prospects are somewhat gloomy. When the changes are made in this command, and new hands shall take charge of it, I will have to return to the 79th Regiment—a fate at which I shudder. The Regiment has been in five large battles, and in ten or twelve smaller engagements. While adding on each occasion new luster to its own reputation, it has never taken part in a successful action. The proud body that started from the city over a thousand strong, are now a body of cripples. The handful (230) that remains are foreigners whose patriotism misfortunes have quenched. The *morale* is destroyed—discipline relaxed beyond hope of restoration. The General and all the true friends of the Regiment were of the opinion that it should be mustered out of the service. After performing hard duties in the field for fifteen months I find there is nothing left me, but to sink into disgrace with a Regiment that is demoralized past hope of restoration. This for a reward. I am writing this from the old scene of the mutiny of last year. A strange year it has been. God has marvellously preserved my life through every danger. May he be merciful to my mother in the year to come. My old friend Matteson is dead. He was a Major in Yates' Regiment of Sharpshooters which distinguished itself at Corinth. He died at Rosecrans' Headquarters, of typhoid fever.

We are going to move from here to-morrow, but your safest direction will be Capt. W. T. Lusk, A. A. A. G., 1st Div. 9th Army Corps, Washington (or elsewhere). All the letters sent me since I left Fredericksburg have miscarried, and I am very anxious for news.

Affec'y.,
WILL.

"GOD WILLS THIS CONTEST": WASHINGTON, D.C., SEPTEMBER 1862

Abraham Lincoln: Meditation on the Divine Will

c. early September 1862

This manuscript is undated. It is thought to have been written in the immediate aftermath of Second Bull Run and the army's command crisis, when the President's fortunes seemed to reach a new low.

The will of God prevails. In great contests each party claims to act in accordance with the will of God. Both *may* be, and one *must* be wrong. God can not be *for*, and *against* the same thing at the same time. In the present civil war it is quite possible that God's purpose is something different from the purpose of either party—and yet the human instrumentalities, working just as they do, are of the best adaptation to effect His purpose. I am almost ready to say this is probably true—that God wills this contest, and wills that it shall not end yet. By his mere quiet power, on the minds of the now contestants, He could have either *saved* or *destroyed* the Union without a human contest. Yet the contest began. And having begun He could give the final victory to either side any day. Yet the contest proceeds.

BRITAIN CONSIDERS MEDIATION: SEPTEMBER 1862

Lord Palmerston and Lord Russell: An Exchange

When news crossed the Atlantic of the Union defeat at Second Bull Run, following the earlier reports of the collapse of McClellan's Peninsula campaign against Richmond, it raised prospects among Britain's rulers for mediation in the American war—which in turn raised prospects for recognition of the Confederacy. In exploring the possibility, Prime Minister Palmerston and Foreign Secretary Russell thought to bring in the Continental powers to strengthen their hand in the mediation process.

---

94 Piccadilly: September 14, 1862.

My dear Russell,—The detailed accounts given in the 'Observer' to day of the battles of August 29 and 30 between the Confederates and the Federals show that the latter got a very complete smashing; and it seems not altogether unlikely that still greater disasters await them, and that even Washington or Baltimore may fall into the hands of the Confederates.

If this should happen, would it not be time for us to consider whether in such a state of things England and France might not address the contending parties and recommend an arrangement upon the basis of separation? . . . —Yours sincerely,

PALMERSTON.

Lord Russell replied—

Gotha: September 17, 1862.

My dear Palmerston,—Whether the Federal army is destroyed or not, it is clear that it is driven back to Washington, and has made no progress in subduing the insurgent States. Such being the case, I agree with you that the time is come for offering mediation to the United States Government, with a view to the recognition of the independence of the Confederates. I agree further, that, in case of failure, we ought ourselves to recognise the Southern States as an independent State. For the purpose of taking so important a step, I think we must have a meeting of the Cabinet. The 23rd or 30th would suit me for the meeting.

We ought then, if we agree on such a step, to propose it first to France, and then, on the part of England and France, to Russia and other powers, as a measure decided upon by us.

We ought to make ourselves safe in Canada, not by sending more troops there, but by concentrating those we have in a few defensible posts before the winter sets in.

I hope to get home on Sunday, but a letter sent to the Foreign Office is sure to reach me.

If Newcastle has not set off, you might as well speak to him before he goes.

The Queen is, I think, much the better for the new interest which has opened for her.—Yours truly,

J. RUSSELL

Broadlands: September 23, 1862.

My dear Russell,—Your plan of proceedings about the mediation between the Federals and Confederates seems to be excellent. Of course, the offer would be made to both the contending parties at the same time; for, though the offer would be as sure to be accepted by the Southerns as was the proposal of the Prince of Wales by the Danish Princess, yet, in the one case as in the other, there are certain forms which it is decent and proper to go through.

A question would occur whether, if the two parties were to accept the mediation, the fact of our mediating would not of itself be tantamount to an acknowledgment of the Confederates as an independent State.

Might it not be well to ask Russia to join England and France in the offer of mediation? . . .

We should be better without her in the mediation, because she would be too favourable to the North; but on the other hand her participation in the offer might render the North the more willing to accept it.

The after communication to the other European powers

would be quite right, although they would be too many for mediation.

As to the time of making the offer, if France and Russia agree,—and France, we know, is quite ready, and only waiting for our concurrence—events may be taking place which might render it desirable that the offer should be made before the middle of October.

It is evident that a great conflict is taking place to the north-west of Washington, and its issue must have a great effect on the state of affairs. If the Federals sustain a great defeat, they may be at once ready for mediation, and the iron should be struck while it is hot. If, on the other hand, they should have the best of it, we may wait awhile and see what may follow . . .—Yours sincerely,

PALMERSTON.

"RECOGNITION OF OUR INDEPENDENCE": MARYLAND, SEPTEMBER 1862

Robert E. Lee to Jefferson Davis

Writing after his army had crossed the Potomac, Lee revealed to Davis the strategic ambitions behind his invasion of Maryland. The mid-term elections in the Northern states Lee sought to influence were due to begin in mid-October.

Headquarters, Near Fredericktown, Maryland
September 8, 1862

Mr. President:

The present posture of affairs, in my opinion, places it in the power of the Government of the Confederate States to propose with propriety to that of the United States the recognition of our independence.

For more than a year both sections of the country have been devastated by hostilities which have brought sorrow and suffering upon thousands of homes, without advancing the objects which our enemies proposed to themselves in beginning the contest.

Such a proposition coming from us at this time, could in no way be regarded as suing for peace, but being made when it is in our power to inflict injury upon our adversary, would show conclusively to the world that our sole object is the establishment of our independence, and the attainment of an honorable peace. The rejection of this offer would prove to the country that the responsibility of the continuance of the war does not rest upon us, but that the party in power in the United States elect to prosecute it for purposes of their own. The proposal of peace would enable the people of the United States to determine at their coming elections whether they will support those who favor a prolongation of the war, or those who wish to bring it to a termination, which can but be productive of good to both parties without affecting the honor of either.

I have the honor to be with high respect, your obt servt

R. E. LEE
Genl Comdg

A "DIRTY AND REPULSIVE" ARMY:
MARYLAND, SEPTEMBER 1862

Lewis H. Steiner: Diary, September 5–6, 1862

Steiner was a physician who served as an inspector for the U.S. Sanitary Commission. His diary of the Confederate occupation of Frederick, Maryland, his native town, was submitted as a report to the commission and then published as a pamphlet. As a Confederate column marched out of town on September 10, Steiner wrote: "The ill-suppressed expressions of delight on the countenances of the citizens could not be interpreted into indications of sympathy with Secession. They manifested only profound delight at the prospect of its speedy departure."

Friday, September 5.—Left Washington at 6 o'clock, under the impression that the Confederate army had crossed the Potomac the preceding evening and were then in Frederick. Anxiety as to the fate of my friends, as well as to the general treatment my native place would receive at rebel hands, made the trip by no means a pleasant one.

Along the road, at different stopping-places, reports reached us as to the numbers of the Confederates that had crossed into Maryland. The passengers began to entertain fears that the train would not be able to reach Frederick. These were, however, quieted by a telegram received at a station near Monrovia, which announced the road open. Arriving at 12 o'clock, M., I found the town full of surmises and rumors. Such information had been received by the Post Quarter Master and the Surgeon in charge of Hospital, that they were busy all the afternoon making arrangements to move off their valuable stores. The citizens were in the greatest trepidation. Invasion by the Southern army was considered equivalent to destruction. Impressment into the ranks as common soldiers, or immurement in a *Southern* prison—these were not attractive prospects for quiet, Union-loving citizens!

Towards nightfall it became pretty certain that a force had crossed somewhere about the mouth of the Monocacy. Telegrams were crowding rapidly on the army officers located here, directing that what stores could not be removed should be burned, and that the sick should as far as possible be sent on to Pennsylvania. Here began a scene of terror seldom witnessed in this region. Lieut. Castle, A. Q. M., burned a large quantity of his stores at the depot. Assist. Surg. Weir fired his storehouse on the Hospital grounds and burned the most valuable of his surplus bedding contained in Kemp Hall, in Church street near Market. Many of our prominent citizens, fearing impressment, left their families and started for Pennsylvania in carriages, on horseback, and on foot. All the convalescents at the Hospital that could bear the fatigue, were started also for Pennsylvania, in charge of Hospital Steward Cox. The citizens removed their trunks containing private papers and other valuables from the bank-vaults, under the firm belief that an attack would be made on these buildings for the sake of the specie contained in them.

About 1 1/2 o'clock, A. M., it was ascertained that Jackson's force—the advance guard of the Southern army—was encamped on Moffat's farm, near Buckeystown, and that this force would enter Frederick after daylight; for what purpose no one knew. Having possession of this amount of information, I retired about two o'clock, being willing to wait the sequel, whatever it might be.

Saturday, September 6.—Found, on visiting the market in the morning, that a very large number of our citizens had "*skedaddled*" (i. e. retired rapidly in good order) last night. Every mouth was full of rumors as to the numbers, whereabouts, and whatabouts of the Confederate force. One old gentleman, whose attachment to McClellan has become proverbial, declared that it was an impossibility for the rebels to cross the Potomac; and another, who looks upon Banks as the greatest of generals, declared that Banks' force had been taken for Confederates, and that the supposed enemies were friends.

At length uncertainty was changed into certainty. About nine o'clock two seedy-looking individuals rode up Market street as fast as their jaded animals could carry them. Their dress was a dirty, faded gray, their arms rusty and seemingly uncared for, their general appearance raffish or vagabondish. They shouted for Jeff. Davis at the intersection of Patrick and

Market street, and then riding to the intersection of Church and Market, repeated the same *strange* jubilant shout. No one expressing an opinion as to the propriety or impropriety of this proceeding, they countermarched and trotted down the street. Then followed some fifty or a hundred horsemen, having among them Bradley T. Johnson, *soi-disant* Colonel C. S. A. These were received with feeble shouts from some secession-sympathizers. They said, "the time of your deliverance has come." It was plain that the deliverance they meant was from the rule of law and order. The sidewalks were filled with Union-loving citizens, who felt keenly that their humiliation was at hand, and that they had no course but submission, at least for a time.

As this force of cavalry entered the town from the south, Capt. Yellot's company retreated west from the town, and disappeared no one knew whither. One ruffian cavalry soldier rode up to Sergt. Crocker (in charge of hospital stores in Kemp Hall) and accosted him with "Sa-ay, are you a Yankee?" "No, I am a Marylander." "What are you doing in the Yankee army?" "I belong to the United States army," said the old man, proudly. "If you don't come along with me, I'll cut your head off." Having waved his sabre over the *unarmed* old man's head, he demanded his keys, and rode off with the sergeant as a prisoner. This display of chivalry did not infuse great admiration of the Southern army into the hearts of the bystanders.

A force of cavalry entered the hospital grounds and took possession of hospital and contents. All the sick were carefully paroled, not excepting one poor fellow then in a moribund condition. After some hours, the medical officers and hospital stewards were allowed to go about town on passes.

At ten o'clock Jackson's advance force, consisting of some five thousand men, marched up Market street and encamped north of the town. They had but little music; what there was gave us "My Maryland" and Dixie in execrable style. Each regiment had a square red flag, with a cross, made of diagonal blue stripes extending from opposite corners: on these blue stripes were placed thirteen white stars. A dirtier, filthier, more unsavory set of human beings never *strolled* through a town—marching it could not be called without doing violence to the word. The distinctions of rank were recognized on the coat collars of officers; but all were alike dirty and repulsive. Their arms were rusty and in an unsoldierly condition. Their uniforms, or rather multiforms, corresponded only in a slight predominance of grey over butternut, and in the prevalence of filth. Faces looked as if they had not been acquainted with water for weeks: hair, shaggy and unkempt, seemed entirely a stranger to the operations of brush or comb. A motlier group was never herded together. But *these* were the chivalry—the deliverers of Maryland from Lincoln's oppressive yoke.

During the afternoon a Provost Marshal was appointed for the town, and he occupied the same office which had been the headquarters of the U. S. Provost Marshal. Guards were posted along our streets, and pickets on the roads leading from Frederick. Our stores were soon thronged with crowds. The shoe stores were most patronized, as many of their men were shoeless and stockingless. The only money most of them had was Confederate scrip, or shinplasters issued by banks, corporations, individuals, etc.—all of equal value. To use the expression of an old citizen "the notes depreciated the paper on which they were printed." The crowded condition of the stores enabled some of the chivalry to *take* what they wanted, (confiscate is the technical expression,) without going through the formality of even handing over Confederate rags in exchange. But guards were placed at the stores wherever requested, and only a few men allowed to enter at a time. Even this arrangement proved inadequate, and the stores were soon necessarily closed. The most intense hatred seems to have been encouraged and fostered in the men's hearts towards Union people, or *Yankees* as they style them; and this word *Yankee* is employed with any and every manner of emphasis possible to indicate contempt and bitterness. The men have been made to believe that "to kill a Yankee" is to do a duty imperatively imposed on them. The following incident will illustrate this: A gentleman was called aside, while talking with some ladies, by an officer who wished information as to shoes. He said he was in want of shoes for his men, that he had United States money if the dealers were so foolish as to prefer it, or he would procure them gold; but if they wouldn't sell he was satisfied to wait until they reached Baltimore, where he had no doubt but that shoes in quantity could be procured. No reply was made. Changing the subject, he inquired how the men were behaving. The answer was *very well*; there was no complaint, although some few had been seen intoxicated on the street. "Who gave them the liquor," said the officer. "Townsmen who sympathize with you and desire to show their love for you." "The only way to do that," said the officer, "is to kill a Yankee: kill a Yankee, sir, if you want to please a Southerner." This was uttered with all imaginable expression of vindictiveness and venom.

Our houses were besieged by hungry soldiers and officers. They ate everything offered them with a greediness that fully sustained the truth of their statement, that their entire subsistence lately had been *green corn, uncooked, and eaten directly from the stalk.* Union families freely gave such food as they had. "If thine enemy hunger, feed him," seemed the principle acted on by our good people. But few of our secession citizens aided them. They seemed ashamed of their Southern brethren. The Union people stood out for their principles, and took care to remind them that they were getting their food from those they had come to destroy. A gentleman relates the following: "In the evening, after having had one of their officers to tea—one whom I had known in former days—two officers came to the door and begged that something might be given them for which they wished to pay. On giving them the last biscuits in the house, one of them offered *pay.* The reply was, 'No sir, whenever you meet a Federal soldier wanting food, recollect that a Union man in Frederick gave you the last morsel of food in his house when *you* were famishing.' The officer's face flushed up, and he replied, 'You are right, sir, I am very, very much obliged to you.' The coals of fire had been heaped on his head."

Outrages were committed on the National flag whenever one fell into the hands of the soldiers. These simply strengthened the Union feeling, and made the men and women of Frederick more attached than ever to the National cause for which their fathers had fought and died. Stauncher, stouter, stronger did Unionism in Frederick grow with each passing hour. We were conquered, not enslaved,—humiliated greatly with the thought that rebel feet were pressing on our soil, but not disposed to bow the knee to Baal.

An attack on the *Examiner* Printing Office being anticipated, a small guard was placed at the door. About nine o'clock, P. M., a rush was made on the guard by some of the Southern soldiers, the door was driven in and the contents of the office thrown into the street. W. G. Ross, Esq., a prominent lawyer of Frederick, called on the Provost Marshal, who soon arrived with a strong force, suppressed the riot, and, having obliged the rioters to return every thing belonging to the office, put them in the guard-house. During the continuance of this disturbance, the oaths and imprecations were terrific. Every one in the neighborhood expected that a general attack would be made on the Union houses. Fortunately, a quiet night ensued.

A CONFEDERATE IN MARYLAND: SEPTEMBER 1862

James Richmond Boulware: Diary, September 4–14, 1862

Boulware was a surgeon in the 6th South Carolina, Jenkins's Brigade, Longstreet's Corps. In his diary he traces his brigade's march from the crossing of the Potomac through Frederick (where he found a welcome rather warmer than Dr. Steiner suggests) and across South Mountain to Boonsboro and Hagerstown. On September 14 Longstreet backtracked to Boonsboro and the fight at Turner's Gap (or Boonsboro Gap) in South Mountain.

Thursday, 4th:

After eating roast corn for supper last night laid down and slept well. Cooked rations and marched in the direction of Leesburg. Halted a few miles from town and camped for the night.

Friday, 5th:

After cooking rations six days and leaving a number of sick for the hospital at Leesburg, passed through the town. It was a pretty, business looking place. There were quite a number of pretty ladies, they seemed to have on *their finest dresses.* I had not seen so many in such a long time, it was quite a treat. Marched on until 11 o'clock at night and camped about 2 or 3 miles from Potomac River.

Saturday, 6th:

Leaving some sick who were unable to stand long marches (among them was Lt. Brice) we proceeded on towards the river. Came to it, pulled off, for it was nearly waist deep in places, and waded across. I fortunately had my horse and rode over. It was 3/4 of a mile wide—was very clear, could see every rock in the bottom and they were not a few—the bottom was covered with round rocks. We got over and was several hours in getting fixed to move off. Getting ready we moved off in the hot sun. Travelled until dark, rested and set out again and about 11 o'clock camped at Buckey's Town for the night—at a late hour. I could not get any feed for my horse until late the next day.

Sunday, 7th:

Late in the day we began to march and early in the evening arrived in the vicinity of Frederick City, Maryland. On the road we passed through a rich little valley—crossing the Monocacy River twice—there were some neat little towns—beautifully laid out showing taste as well as superior management. We were pretty well tired when we arrived at Frederick, but when the ranks were broken orders were read that soap would be issued to us and it was required of us to wash both ourselves and clothes. I never was so anxious to get a piece of soap in my remembrance before, for our Hosp. wagon and Ambulance were still behind. I went and washed but would not undertake to wash my clothes for I can not wash clothes. So I put on my dirty clothes thinking my Hosp. wagon would come up in a few days.

Monday, 8th:

I arose this morning having had quite a refreshing sleep, went to the wagon train and found that our hospital wagon and ambulance had arrived during the night very late and Brother Frank and I. D. Gaillord with them. I went to get corn from our Q. M. and received somewhat of a short answer from his Emissary (Blake) or rather his wagonmaster. I proceeded to Col. Steedman and reported no corn for me. Col. went to Q. M. and I soon had corn for my mare for she had been doing without for several days—so I had a fuss on hand. I went to Frederick late in the day—got my mare shod. I happened to meet with some clever Artillerists belonging to Jackson's command and they drove on four shoes for me. They would not take pay but were anxious to get something to drink—so, I being a Surg. managed (by going to Provost Martial) to get at some Jamaica Rum and treated them to two canteens full. We drank out one together and I made a present of the other. I carried one full with me to camp and treated the boys all. It was very good rum too. I took a second wash and putting on a new shirt Bro. Frank brought me, felt a little like myself once more. Capt. Cureton was taken very sick also several others in the Regiment so I could not buy anything in Frederick for the stores were all closed etc.

Tuesday, 9th:

The day was passing away without anything transpiring worth noting. In the afternoon W. E. Boggs and myself walked into the city (for it was a place of considerable importance for an inland town) to get a private house for Capt. Cureton to go to for he was too ill to go any farther with us. So, after making efforts at various houses, we fortunately met with a kind lady—who was an avowed Secessionist—who gave her consent to take him in. In walking about we found other Secessionists—got acquainted with several nice, pretty young ladies, and really had a good time chatting with them. We were doing so well we did not realize the fact that it was dark and yet we had to walk two miles to get to our camp. When we arrived at camp I was told that the Q.M. had refused to give any feed for my horse—without a requisition—So I went to work and made out one according to Army Regulations and presented it. Corn was given me and I refused to take it until I saw it weighed to me. The reply was they had no scales and could not do it. I replied that he had made me come to the Regulations and that I required him to do the same or I would report him again in the morning. I had him. The result was he gave me feed without the requisition. So, after talking for some time as to the cause of our ill feeling, we found out that things were told him and to me that were false, so we quit on good terms.

Wednesday, 10th:

We took up our line of march this morning, passing through Frederick City. Saw a number of pretty ladies and amid waving of Secession flags by the ladies and cheering of the soldiers had a lively time. The ladies bowed gracefully to us and once more I was caught lifting my cap, and not a few times either. After passing the town the march was dull and wearisome. We passed Middletown during the afternoon. It was eight miles distant from Frederick. Marched until near South Mountain Gap and camped for the night.

Thursday, 11th:

I arose, eat my breakfast on sweet milk, apple butter and raised bread—thought it was the best I had eaten in a long time (and without doubt it was). Crossed the mountain and got a splendid view of the valley which had some fine farms on the road. All the people seem to live well and not only *stay there* but *live.* One thing I notice is they every one have a *large fine barn*—finer than the dwelling houses in Virginia—most of them built of hewn stone. Maryland is the finest state I have been in. At one house I noticed a spring—very bold indeed—under a fine dwelling house. The spring house was nicely fixed and in every way betokened a tasty and wealthy citizen. Boonsboro is Union town of the deepest dye—we passed through it without stopping and crossed several streams, having fine bridges over them. Passed Funk's Town—a Union hole. I rode up to a house and asked to purchase some Tomatoes. The lady told me she was Union and could not take our money. I told her I was not surprised to find people Union in sentiment and liked to hear them come out plain and say so. I told them we were not come to pilfer or destroy but to give them a chance to come with if they choosed to do so. Orders not to pillage apple orchards and corn fields were strictly enjoined on us. The lady kindly gave me as many as I wished to carry. The ladies would have buckets of water at their doors and give to the thirsty soldiers as they marched by. One said "*remember a Union lady is giving you water*". In one instance a *woman*, as we passed through Middletown, came out in her yard and bemeaned our soldiers at a terrible rate. I am glad to say it is the only instance so far. We camped—no name for the place—drew rations and went to sleep, after eating my supper on beef kidney.

Friday, 12th:

We began to march as usual this morning and in the direction of Hagers Town, which was not more than four miles distant. Passed through the town, found it to be a considerable place, yet, like all the others, the stores were closed, and only at a few places would they take Confederate money. We camped two miles from the town. Upon arriving at camp I set out to try my hand at foraging. I bought some apple butter, bread, etc., got as many apples as I could carry, had a long chat with a pretty nice cross-eyed girl—who claimed to be a Secesh. and returned to camp feeling well satisfied as to my excursion besides having something for the boys to eat. I never saw apple butter until I came to Maryland. I am fond of it.

Saturday, 13th:

I went to town this morning but could not buy anything for want of gold or Yankee money (either), yet they tell me Hagers Town is a Secession Town. I believe they (our officers) did get quite a number to enlist in our cause; also at Frederick about 800 joined us. In all so far 1400 joined us since we came into Maryland. I went to the 15th Regt. S.C.V. and to James' Battalion and saw the boys of my acquaintance. Late in the afternoon went back and saw my little cross-eyed girl again, got more apples, etc.

Sunday, 14th:

We began our march this morning and found ourselves retracing our steps towards Boonsboro. Having gone six or eight miles we heard the booming of cannon in the distance and go on met couriers who told us that D. H. Hill was fighting the Yankees at South Mountain near Boonsboro. When we started this morning every one thought we were going into Pennsylvania (for, when at Hagers Town, we were only five miles from the line) but soon saw that were going to engage in battle. About the middle of afternoon we got to Boonsboro, having come sixteen miles, and went on to battle but was near night when we went into battle. We were on the top of high hills and the enemy also on adjacent hills. We merely wished to hold the position and done so. We lost only a few in our (Jenkins) Brigade, yet some of our forces cut up badly. James' Bat. was all killed and taken prisoners with some exceptions. Our Brigade was among the last to leave that night. Our forces were ordered to fall back.

I give a list of killed and wounded at Boonsboro Gap, South Mountain, Md. on 14th September, 1862.

List of Casualties in 6th Regt. S.C.V. on 14th Sept. at Boonsboro Gap, South Mountain, Maryland

Co. C Priv.	Robert Borwick	Killed
" " "	C. C. Stuckey	"
Co. K "	T. S. Chandler	Wounded thigh (broken) severe
Co. I Lt.	Grandison Williams	" elbow slight
		Total 4

THE LOST ORDER:
MARYLAND, SEPTEMBER 1862

Alpheus S. Williams to George B. McClellan
Robert E. Lee: Special Orders No. 191

On September 13, in a roadside field, an Indiana soldier found a lost copy of General Lee's instructions for dividing his army to accomplish the capture of the Union garrison at Harpers Ferry. The Lost Order made its way to Alpheus Williams, commanding the Twelfth Corps, who forwarded it, along with a covering note, to General McClellan. "Here is a paper," McClellan told one of his generals, "with which if I cannot whip Bobbie Lee, I will be willing to go home."

Head Qts Banks Corps
Near Fredrick Sept 13/62

General

I enclose a Special order of Genl. Lee Commanding Rebel forces—which was found on the field where my corps is encamped.

It is a document of interest & is no doubt genuine.

I am General
with much respect
Your obt svt
A S Williams
Brig Genl Cdg

The Document was found by a corporal of 27 Ind. Rgt, Col. Colgrove, Gordon's Brigade. AW

(Confidential)

Hd Qrs Army of Northern Va
Sept 9th 1862

Special Orders)
Nr 191)

III The Army will resume its march to-morrow taking the Hagerstown road. Gen Jacksons Command will form the advance and after passing Middleton with such portion as he may select take the route towards Sharpsburg, cross the Potomac at the most convenient point & by Friday morning take possession of the Baltimore & Ohio RR, capture such of the enemy as may be at Martinsburg and intercept such as may attempt to escape from Harpers Ferry.

IV Gen Longstreets Command will pursue the main road as far as Boonsboro where it will halt, with reserve supply and baggage trains of the Army.

V Gen McLaws with his own division and that of Gen R.H. Anderson will follow Gen Longstreet. On reaching Middleton will take the route to Harpers Ferry and by Friday morning possess himself of the Maryland heights and endeavor to capture the enemy at Harpers Ferry and vacinity.

VI Gen Walker with his division after ac. the object in which he is now engaged will cross the Potomac at Cheeks ford ascend its right bank to Lovettsville take possession of Loudoun Heights if practicable by Friday morning Keys ford on his left and the road between the end of mountain and the Potomac on his right. He will as far as practicable cooperate with Gen McLaws & Genl Jacks in intercepting the retreat of the enemy.

VII Gen D.H. Hill's division will form the rear guard of the Army pursuing the road taken by the main body. The reserve artillery ordnance and supply trains will precede Gen Hill

VIII Gen Stuart will detach a squadron of Cavalry to accompany the Commands of Gen Longstreet Jackson and McLaws and with the main body of the Cavalry will cover the route of the Army & bring up all stragglers that may have been left behind.

IX the commands of Gen Jackson McLaws & Walker after accomplishing the objects for which they have been detached will join the main body of the Army at Boonsboro or Hagerstown.

X Each Regiment on the march will habitually carry its axes in the Regimental ordnance wagons for use of the men at their encampments to procure wood &c

By command of Gen R.E. Lee
R.H. Chilton
AA General

For
Maj Gen D.H. Hill
Cmdg Division

BATTLE OF ANTIETAM:
MARYLAND, SEPTEMBER 1862

George W. Smalley: Narrative of Antietam

September 19, 1862

With the Lost Order in hand, but setting out some eighteen hours too late to divide and conquer his enemy, McClellan forced his way across South Mountain on September 14. Lee fell back, intending to recross the Potomac. Then Stonewall Jackson reported the capture of the 12,000-man garrison at Harpers Ferry, and Lee took up a defensive position behind Antietam Creek at Sharpsburg and began to reassemble his army. This was neither where nor when he had intended to give battle. He would write after the war, "the loss of the dispatch changed the character of the campaign." After further delays, McClellan elected September 17 as the day of battle. Correspondent George W. Smalley of the *New-York Daily Tribune* witnessed the battle, then rode to Frederick, where he took a train to Baltimore and then New York. His overview of the fighting appeared in the *Tribune* on September 19, and drew a salute from William Cullen Bryant, editor of the rival New York *Evening Post*, as one of "the best battle pieces in literature."

BATTLE-FIELD OF ANTIETAM,
WEDNESDAY EVENING, Sept. 17, 1862.

Fierce and desperate battle between two hundred thousand men has raged since daylight, yet night closes on an uncertain field. It is the greatest fight since Waterloo—all over the field contested with an obstinacy equal even to Waterloo. If not wholly a victory to-night, I believe it is the prelude to a victory to-morrow. But what can be foretold of the future of a fight in which from five in the morning till seven at night the best troops of the continent have fought without decisive result?

I have no time for speculation—no time even to gather details of the battle—only time to state its broadest features, then mount and spur for New-York.

After the brilliant victory near Middletown, Gen. McClellan

pushed forward his army rapidly, and reached Keedysville with three corps on Monday night. That march has already been described. On the day following the two armies faced each other idly until night. Artillery was busy at intervals; once in the morning opening with spirit, and continuing for half an hour with vigor, till the rebel battery, as usual, was silenced.

McClellan was on the hill where Benjamin's battery was stationed, and found himself suddenly under a rather heavy fire. It was still uncertain whether the rebels were retreating or reënforcing. Their batteries would remain in position in either case, and as they had withdrawn nearly all their troops from view, there was only the doubtful indication of columns of dust to the rear.

On the evening of Tuesday, Hooker was ordered to cross the Antietam Creek with his corps, and feeling the left of the enemy, to be ready to attack next morning. During the day of apparent inactivity, McClellan, it may be supposed, had been maturing his plan of battle, of which Hooker's movement was one development.

The position on either side was peculiar. When Richardson advanced on Monday he found the enemy deployed and displayed in force on a crescent-shaped ridge, the outline of which followed more or less exactly the course of Antietam Creek. Their lines were then forming, and the revelation of force in front of the ground which they really intended to hold, was probably meant to delay our attack until their arrangements to receive it were complete.

During that day they kept their troops exposed and did not move them even to avoid the artillery-fire, which must have been occasionally annoying. Next morning the lines and columns which had darkened corn-fields and hill-crests had been withdrawn. Broken and wooded ground behind the sheltering hills concealed the rebel masses. What from our front looked like only a narrow summit fringed with woods was a broad tableland of forest and ravine; cover for troops every where, nowhere easy access for an enemy. The smoothly sloping surface in front and the sweeping crescent of slowly mingling lines was all a delusion. It was all a rebel stronghold beyond.

Under the base of these hills runs the deep stream called Antietam Creek, fordable only at distant points. Three bridges cross it, one on the Hagerstown road, one on the Sharpsburgh pike, one to the left in a deep recess of steeply falling hills. Hooker passed the first to reach the ford by which he crossed, and it was held by Pleasanton with a reserve of cavalry during the battle. The second was close under the rebel centre, and no way important to yesterday's fight. At the third, Burnside attacked and finally crossed. Between the first and third lay most of the battle-lines. They stretched four miles from right to left.

Unaided attack in front was impossible. McClellan's forces lay behind low, disconnected ridges in front of the rebel summits, all or nearly all unwooded. They gave some cover for artillery, and guns were therefore massed on the centre. The enemy had the Shepherdstown road and the Hagerstown and Williamsport road both open to him in rear for retreat. Along one or the other, if beaten, he must fly. This among other reasons determined, perhaps, the plan of battle which McClellan finally resolved on.

The plan was generally as follows: Hooker was to cross on the right, establish himself on the enemy's left if possible, flanking his position, and to open the fight. Sumner, Franklin, and Mansfield were to send their forces also to the right, coöperating with and sustaining Hooker's attack while advancing also nearer the centre. The heavy work in the centre was left mostly to the batteries, Porter massing his infantry supports in the hollows. On the left, Burnside was to carry the bridge already referred to, advancing then by a road which enters the pike at Sharpsburgh, turning at once the rebel flank and destroying his line of retreat. Porter and Sykes were held in reserve. It is obvious that the complete success of a plan contemplating widely divergent movements of separate corps, must largely depend on accurate timing—that the attacks should be simultaneous and not successive.

Hooker moved Tuesday afternoon at four, crossing the creek at a ford above the bridge and well to the right, without opposition. Fronting southwest, his line advanced not quite on the rebel flank but overlapping and threatening it. Turning off from the road after passing the stream, he sent forward cavalry skirmishers straight into the woods and over the fields beyond. Rebel pickets withdrew slowly before them, firing scattering and harmless shots. Turning again to the left, the cavalry went down on the rebel flank, coming suddenly close to a battery which met them with unexpected grape and canister. It being the nature of cavalry to retire before batteries, this company loyally followed the law of its being, and came swiftly back without pursuit.

Artillery was sent to the front, infantry was rapidly deployed, and skirmishers went out in front and on either flank. The corps moved forward compactly, Hooker as usual reconnoitring in person. They came at last to an open grass-sown field inclosed on two sides with woods, protected on the right by a hill, and entered through a corn-field in the rear. Skirmishers penetrating these woods were instantly met by rebel shots, but held their ground, and as soon as supported, advanced and cleared the timber. Beyond, on the left and in front, volleys of musketry opened heavily, and a battle seemed to have begun a little sooner than it was expected.

General Hooker formed his lines with precision and without hesitation. Ricketts's division went into the woods on the left in force. Meade with the Pennsylvania reserves formed in the centre. Doubleday was sent out on the right, planting his guns on the hill, and opening at once on a rebel battery that began to enfilade the central line. It was already dark, and the rebel position could only be discovered by the flashes of their guns. They pushed forward boldly on the right after losing ground on the other flank, but made no attempt to regain their hold on the woods. The fight flashed, and glimmered, and faded, and finally went out in the dark.

Hooker had found out what he wanted to know. When the firing ceased, the hostile lines lay close to each other—their pickets so near that six rebels were captured during the night. It was inevitable that the fight should recommence at daylight. Neither side had suffered considerable loss; it was a skirmish, not a battle. "We are through for to-night, gentlemen," remarked the General, "but to-morrow we fight the battle that will decide the fate of the republic."

Not long after the firing ceased, it sprang up again on the left. General Hooker, who had taken his headquarters in a barn which had been nearly the focus of the rebel artillery, was out at once. First came rapid and unusually frequent picket-shots, then several heavy volleys. The General listened a moment and smiled grimly. "We have no troops there. The rebels are shooting each other. It is Fair Oaks over again." So every body lay down again, but all the night through there were frequent alarms.

McClellan had been informed of the night's work, and of the certainties awaiting the dawn. Sumner was ordered to move his corps at once, and was expected to be on the ground at daylight. From the extent of the rebel lines developed in the evening, it was plain that they had gathered their whole army behind the heights and were waiting for the shock.

The battle began with the dawn. Morning found both armies just as they had slept, almost close enough to look into each other's eyes. The left of Meade's reserves and the right of Ricketts's line became engaged at nearly the same moment, one with artillery, the other with infantry. A battery was almost immediately pushed forward beyond the central woods, over a ploughed field near the top of the slope where the corn-field began. On this open field, in the corn beyond, and in the woods which stretched forward into the broad fields like a promontory into the ocean, were the hardest and deadliest struggles of the day.

For half an hour after the battle had grown to its full strength, the line of fire swayed neither way. Hooker's men were fully up to their work. They saw their General every where in front, never away from the fire, and all the troops believed in their commander, and fought with a will. Two thirds of them were the same men who under McDowell had broken at Manassas.

The half-hour passed, the rebels began to give way a little—only a little, but at the first indication of a receding fire, Forward, was the word, and on went the line with a cheer and a rush. Back across the corn-field, leaving dead and wounded behind them, over the fence, and across the road, and then back again into the dark woods which closed around them went the retreating rebels.

Meade and his Pennsylvanians followed hard and fast—followed till they came within easy range of the woods, among which they saw their beaten enemy disappearing—followed still, with another cheer, and flung themselves against the cover.

But out of those gloomy woods came suddenly and heavily terrible volleys—volleys which smote, and bent, and broke in a moment that eager front, and hurled them swiftly back for half the distance they had won. Not swiftly, nor in panic, any further. Closing up their shattered lines, they came slowly away; a regiment where a brigade had been; hardly a brigade where a whole division had been victorious. They had met at the woods the first volleys of musketry from fresh troops—had met them and returned them till their line had yielded and gone down before the weight of fire, and till their ammunition was exhausted.

In ten minutes the fortune of the day seemed to have changed; it was the rebels now who were advancing, pouring out of the woods in endless lines, sweeping through the corn-field from which their comrades had just fled. Hooker sent in his nearest brigade to meet them, but it could not do the work. He called for another. There was nothing close enough, unless he took it from his right. His right might be in danger if it was weakened, but his centre was already threatened with annihilation. Not hesitating one moment, he sent to Doubleday: "Give me your best brigade instantly."

The best brigade came down the hill to the right on the run, went through the timber in front through a storm of shot and bursting shell and crashing limbs, over the open field beyond and straight into the corn-field, passing as they went the fragments of three brigades shattered by the rebel fire and streaming to the rear. They passed by Hooker, whose eyes lighted as he saw those veteran troops, led by a soldier whom he knew he could trust. "I think they will hold it," he said.

General Hartsuff took his troops very steadily, but, now that they were under fire, not hurriedly, up the hill from which the corn-field begins to descend, and formed them on the crest. Not a man who was not in full view—not one who bent before the storm. Firing at first in volleys, they fired then at will with wonderful rapidity and effect. The whole line crowned the hill and stood out darkly against the sky, but lighted and shrouded ever in flame and smoke. They were the Twelfth and Thirteenth

Massachusetts and another regiment which I cannot remember—old troops all of them.

There for half an hour they held the ridge, unyielding in purpose, exhaustless in courage. There were gaps in the line, but it nowhere bent. Their General was severely wounded early in the fight, but they fought on. Their supports did not come—they determined to win without them. They began to go down the hill and into the corn; they did not stop to think that their ammunition was nearly gone; they were there to win that field, and they won it. The rebel line for the second time fled through the corn and into the woods. I cannot tell how few of Hartsuff's brigade were left when the work was done, but it was done. There was no more gallant, determined, heroic fighting in all this desperate day. General Hartsuff is very severely wounded, but I do not believe he counts his success too dearly purchased.

The crisis of the fight at this point had arrived. Ricketts's division, vainly endeavoring to advance and exhausted by the effort, had fallen back. Part of Mansfield's corps was ordered in to their relief, but Mansfield's troops came back again, and their General was mortally wounded. The left nevertheless was too extended to be turned, and too strong to be broken. Ricketts sent word he could not advance, but could hold his ground. Doubleday had kept his guns at work on the right, and had finally silenced a rebel battery that for half an hour had poured in a galling enfilading fire along Hooker's central line. There were woods in front of Doubleday's hill which the rebels held, but so long as those guns pointed toward them they did not care to attack.

With his left, then, able to take care of itself, with his right impregnable, with two brigades of Mansfield still fresh and coming rapidly up, and with his centre a second time victorious, Gen. Hooker determined to advance. Orders were sent to Crawford and Gordon—the two Mansfield brigades—to move forward at once, the batteries in the centre were ordered to advance, the whole line was called on, and the General himself went forward.

To the right of the corn-field and beyond it was a point of woods. Once carried and firmly held, it was the key of the position. Hooker determined to take it. He rode out in front of his furthest troops on a hill to examine the ground for a battery. At the top he dismounted and went forward on foot, completed his reconnoissance, returned, and remounted. The musketry-fire from the point of woods was all the while extremely hot. As he put his foot in the stirrup a fresh volley of rifle-bullets came whizzing by. The tall, soldierly figure of the General, the white horse which he rode, the elevated place where he was, all made him a most dangerously conspicuous mark. So he had been all day, riding often without a staff-officer or an orderly near him—all sent off on urgent duty—visible every where on the field. The rebel bullets had followed him all day, but they had not hit him, and he would not regard them.

Remounting on this hill, he had not ridden five steps when he was struck in the foot by a ball. Three men were shot down at the same moment by his side. The air was alive with bullets. He kept on his horse a few minutes, though the wound was severe and excessively painful, and would not dismount till he had given his last order to advance. He was himself in the very front. Swaying unsteadily on his horse, he turned in his seat to look about him. "There is a regiment to the right. Order it forward! Crawford and Gordon are coming up. Tell them to carry those woods and hold them—and it is our fight!"

It was found that the bullet had passed completely through his foot. The surgeon who examined it on the spot could give no opinion whether bones were broken, but it was afterward ascertained that though grazed they were not fractured. Of course the severity of the wound made it impossible for him to keep the field, which he believed already won, so far as it belonged to him to win it. It was nine o'clock. The fight had been furious since five. A large part of his command was broken, but with his right still untouched, and with Crawford's and Gordon's brigades just up; above all, with the advance of the whole central line, which the men had heard ordered with cheers, and with a regiment already on the edge of the woods he wanted, he might well leave the field, thinking the battle was won—that *his* battle was won, for I am writing only about the attack on the rebel left.

I see no reason why I should disguise my admiration of Gen. Hooker's bravery and soldierly ability. Remaining nearly all the morning on the right, I could not help seeing the sagacity and promptness of his movements, how completely his troops were kept in hand, how devotedly they trusted him, how keen was his insight into the battle, how every opportunity was seized and every reverse was checked and turned into another success. I say this the more unreservedly, because I have no personal relation whatever with him, never saw him till the day before the fight, and don't like his politics or opinions in general. But what are politics in such a battle?

Sumner arrived just as Hooker was leaving, and assumed command. Crawford and Gordon had gone into the woods, and were holding them stoutly against heavy odds. As I rode over toward the left I met Sumner at the head of his column, advancing rapidly through the timber, opposite where Crawford was fighting. The veteran General was riding alone in the forest, far ahead of his leading brigade, his hat off, his gray hair and beard and moustache strangely contrasting with the fire in his eyes and his martial air, as he hurried on to where the bullets were thickest.

Sedgwick's division was in advance, moving forward to support Crawford and Gordon. Rebel reënforcements were approaching also, and the struggle for the roads was again to be renewed. Sumner sent forward two divisions—Richardson and French—on the left. Sedgwick, moving in column of divisions through the woods in rear, deployed and advanced in line over the corn-field. There was a broad interval between him and the nearest division, and he saw that if the rebel line were complete, his own division was in immediate danger of being flanked. But his orders were to advance, and those are the orders which a soldier—and Sedgwick is every inch a soldier—loves best to hear.

To extend his own front as far as possible, he ordered the Thirty-fourth New-York to move by the left flank. The manœuvre was attempted under a fire of the greatest intensity, and the regiment broke. At the same moment the enemy, perceiving their advantage, came round on that flank. Crawford was obliged to give way on the right, and his troops pouring in confusion through the ranks of Sedgwick's advance brigade, threw it into disorder and back on the second and third lines. The enemy advanced, their fire increasing.

Gen. Sedgwick was three times wounded, in the shoulder, leg, and wrist, but he persisted in remaining on the field so long as there was a chance of saving it. His Adjutant-General, Major Sedgwick, bravely rallying and trying to re-form the troops, was shot through the body, the bullet lodging in the spine, and fell from his horse. Severe as the wound is, it is probably not mortal. Lieut. Howe, of Gen. Sedgwick's staff, endeavored vainly to rally the Thirty-fourth New-York. They were badly cut up and would not stand. Half their officers were killed or wounded, their colors shot to pieces, the color-sergeant killed, every one of the color-guard wounded. Only thirty-two were afterward got together.

The Fifteenth Massachusetts went into action with seventeen officers and nearly six hundred men. Nine officers were killed or wounded, and some of the latter are prisoners. Capt. Simons, Capt. Saunders of the sharp-shooters, Lieut. Derby, and Lieut. Berry are killed. Capt. Bartlett and Capt. Jocelyn, Lieut. Spurr, Lieut. Gale, and Lieut. Bradley are wounded. One hundred and thirty-four men were the only remains that could be collected of this splendid regiment.

Gen. Dana was wounded. Gen. Howard, who took command of the division after Gen. Sedgwick was disabled, exerted himself to restore order; but it could not be done there. Gen. Sumner ordered the line to be re-formed. The test was too severe for volunteer troops under such a fire. Sumner himself attempted to arrest the disorder, but to little purpose. Lieut.-Col. Revere and Capt. Audenried of his staff were wounded severely, but not dangerously. It was impossible to hold the position. Gen. Sumner withdrew the division to the rear, and once more the corn-field was abandoned to the enemy.

French sent word he could hold his ground. Richardson, while gallantly leading a regiment under a heavy fire, was severely wounded in the shoulder. Gen. Meagher was wounded at the head of his brigade. The loss in general officers was becoming frightful.

At one o'clock affairs on the right had a gloomy look. Hooker's troops were greatly exhausted, and their General away from the field. Mansfield's were no better. Sumner's command had lost heavily, but two of his divisions were still comparatively fresh. Artillery was yet playing vigorously in front, though the ammunition of many of the batteries was entirely exhausted, and they had been compelled to retire.

Doubleday held the right inflexibly. Sumner's headquarters were now in the narrow field where the night before Hooker had begun the fight. All that had been gained in front had been lost! The enemy's batteries, which if advanced and served vigorously might have made sad work with the closely-massed troops, were fortunately either partially disabled or short of ammunition. Sumner was confident that he could hold his own, but another advance was out of the question. The enemy, on the other hand, seemed to be too much exhausted to attack.

At this crisis Franklin came up with fresh troops and formed on the left. Slocum, commanding one division of the corps, was sent forward along the slopes lying under the first ranges of the rebel hills, while Smith with the other division was ordered to retake the corn-fields and woods which all day had been so hotly contested. It was done in the handsomest style. His Maine and Vermont regiments and the rest went forward on the run, and cheering as they went, swept like an avalanche through the corn-fields, fell upon the woods, cleared them in ten minutes, and held them. They were not again retaken.

The field and its ghastly harvest which the Reaper had gathered in those fatal hours remained finally with us. Four times it had been lost and won. The dead are strewn so thickly that as you ride over it you cannot guide your horse's steps too carefully. Pale and bloody faces are every where upturned. They are sad and terrible, but there is nothing which makes one's heart beat so quickly as the imploring look of sorely wounded men who beckon wearily for help which you cannot stay to give.

Gen. Smith's attack was so sudden that his success was accomplished with no great loss. He had gained a point, however, which compelled him to expect every moment an attack, and to hold which, if the enemy again brought up reserves, would task his best energies and best troops. But the long strife, the heavy losses, incessant fighting over the same ground repeatedly lost and won inch by inch, and more than all, perhaps, the fear of Burnside on the left and Porter in front, held the enemy in check. For two or three hours there was a lull even in the cannonade on the right, which hitherto had been incessant. McClellan had been over on the field after Sumner's repulse, but had speedily returned to his headquarters. Sumner again sent word that he was able to hold his position, but could not advance with his own corps.

Meantime where was Burnside, and what was he doing? On the right where I had spent the day until two o'clock, little was known of the general fortunes of the field. We had heard Porter's guns in the centre, but nothing from Burnside on the left. The distance was, perhaps, too great to distinguish the sound of his artillery from Porter's. There was no immediate prospect of more fighting on the right, and I left the field which all day long had seen the most obstinate contest of the war, and rode over to McClellan's headquarters. The different battle-fields were shut out from each other's view, but all partially visible from the central hill which Gen. McClellan had occupied during the day. But I was more than ever impressed, on returning, with the completely deceitful appearance of the ground the rebels had chosen, when viewed from the front.

Hooker's and Sumner's struggle had been carried on over an uneven and wooded surface, their own line of battle extending in a semi-circle not less than a mile and a half. Perhaps a better notion of their position can be got by considering their right, centre, and left as forming three sides of a square. So long, therefore, as either wing was driven back, the centre became exposed to a very dangerous enfilading fire, and the further the centre was advanced the worse off it was, unless the lines on its side and rear were firmly held. This formation resulted originally from the efforts of the enemy to turn both flanks. Hooker at the very outset threw his column so far into the heart of the rebel lines that they were compelled to threaten him on the flank to secure their own centre.

Nothing of all this was perceptible from the hills in front. Some directions of the rebel lines had been disclosed by the smoke of their guns, but the whole interior formation of the country beyond the hills was completely concealed. When McClellan arranged his order of battle, it must have been upon information, or have been left to his corps and division commanders to discover for themselves.

Up to three o'clock Burnside had made little progress. His attack on the bridge had been successful, but the delay had been so great that to the observer it appeared as if McClellan's plans must have been seriously disarranged. It is impossible not to suppose that the attacks on right and left were meant in a measure to correspond, for otherwise the enemy had only to repel Hooker on the one hand, then transfer his troops, and push them against Burnside.

Here was the difference between Smith and Burnside. The former did his work at once, and lost all his men at once—that is, all whom he lost at all; Burnside seems to have attacked cautiously in order to save his men, and sending successively insufficient forces against a position of strength, distributed his loss over a greater period of time, but yet lost none the less in the end.

Finally, at four o'clock, McClellan sent simultaneous orders to Burnside and Franklin—to the former to advance and carry the batteries in his front at all hazards and at any cost; to the latter to carry the woods next in front of him to the left, which the rebels still held. The order to Franklin, however, was practically countermanded, in consequence of a message from Gen. Sumner that if Franklin went on and was repulsed, his own corps was not yet sufficiently reörganized to be depended on as a reserve. Franklin, thereupon, was directed to run no risk of losing his present position, and instead of sending his infantry into the woods, contented himself with advancing his batteries over the breadth of the fields in front, supporting them with heavy columns of infantry, and attacking with energy the rebel batteries immediately opposed to him. His movement was a success, so far as it went, the batteries maintaining their new ground, and sensibly affecting the steadiness of the rebel fire. That being once accomplished, and all hazard of the right being again forced back having been dispelled, the movement of Burnside became at once the turning-point of success, and the fate of the day depended on him.

How extraordinary the situation was may be judged from a moment's consideration of the facts. It is understood that from the outset Burnside's attack was expected to be decisive, as it certainly must have been if things went well elsewhere, and if he succeeded in establishing himself on the Sharpsburgh road in the rebel rear. Yet Hooker and Sumner and Franklin and Mansfield were all sent to the right three miles away, while Porter seems to have done double duty with his single corps in front, both supporting the batteries and holding himself in reserve. With all this immense force on the right, but sixteen thousand men were given to Burnside for the decisive movement of the day.

Still more unfortunate in its results was the total failure of these separate attacks on the right and left to sustain, or in any manner coöperate with each other. Burnside hesitated for hours in front of the bridge which should have been carried at once by a *coup de main*. Meantime Hooker had been fighting for four hours with various fortune, but final success. Sumner had come up too late to join in the decisive attack which his earlier arrival would probably have converted into a complete success; and Franklin reached the scene only when Sumner had been repulsed. Probably before his arrival the rebels had transferred a considerable number of troops to their right to meet the attack of Burnside, the direction of which was then suspected or developed.

Attacking first with one regiment, then with two, and delaying both for artillery, Burnside was not over the bridge before two o'clock—perhaps not till three. He advanced slowly up the slopes in his front, his batteries in rear covering, to some extent, the movements of the infantry. A desperate fight was going on in a deep ravine on his right; the rebel batteries were in full play and apparently very annoying and destructive, while heavy columns of rebel troops were plainly visible, advancing, as if careless of concealment, along the road and over the hills in the direction of Burnside's forces. It was at this point of time that McClellan sent him the order above given.

Burnside obeyed it most gallantly. Getting his troops well in hand, and sending a portion of his artillery to the front, he advanced with rapidity and the most determined vigor straight up the hill in front, on top of which the rebels had maintained their most dangerous battery. The movement was in plain view of McClellan's position, and as Franklin on the other side sent his batteries into the field about the same time, the battle seemed to open in all directions with greater activity than ever.

The fight in the ravine was in full progress, the batteries in the centre were firing with new vigor, Franklin was blazing away on the right, and every hill-top, ridge and woods along the whole line was crested and veiled with white clouds of smoke. All day had been clear and bright since the early cloudy morning, and now this whole magnificent, unequalled scene shone with the splendor of an afternoon September sun. Four miles of battle, its glory all visible, its horrors all hidden, the fate of the Republic hanging on the hour—could any one be insensible of its grandeur?

There are two hills on the left of the road, the farthest the lowest. The rebels have batteries on both. Burnside is ordered to carry the nearest to him, which is the farthest from the road. His guns opening first from this new position in front, soon entirely controlled and silenced the enemy's artillery. The infantry came on at once, advancing rapidly and steadily; their long, dark lines and broad masses plainly visible without a glass as they moved over the green hill-side.

The next moment the road in which the rebel battery was planted was canopied with clouds of dust swiftly descending into the valley. Underneath was a tumult of wagons, guns, horses, and men, flying at speed down the road. Blue flashes of smoke burst now and then among them, a horse or a man or half a dozen went down, and then the whirlwind swept on.

The hill was carried, but could it be held? The rebel columns, before seen moving to the left, increase their pace. The guns on the hill above send an angry tempest of shell down among Burnside's guns and men. He has formed his columns apparently in the near angles of two fields bordering the road—high ground about them every where except in rear.

In another moment a rebel battle-line appears on the brow of the ridge above them, moves swiftly down in the most perfect order, and though met by incessant discharges of musketry, of which we plainly see the flashes, does not fire a gun. White spaces show where men are falling, but they close up instantly, and still the line advances. The brigades of Burnside are in heavy column; they will not give way before a bayonet-charge in line, and the rebels think twice before they dash into those hostile masses.

There is a halt, the rebel left gives way and scatters over the field, the rest stand fast and fire. More infantry comes up; Burnside is outnumbered, flanked, compelled to yield the hill he took so bravely. His position is no longer one of attack; he defends himself with unfaltering firmness, but he sends to McClellan for help.

McClellan's glass for the last half-hour has seldom been turned away from the left. He sees clearly enough that Burnside is pressed—needs no messenger to tell him that. His face grows darker with anxious thought. Looking down into the valley where fifteen thousand troops are lying, he turns a half-questioning look on Fitz-John Porter, who stands by his side, gravely scanning the field. They are Porter's troops below, are fresh and only impatient to share in this fight. But Porter slowly shakes his head, and one may believe that the same thought is passing through the minds of both generals. "They are the only reserves of the army; they cannot be spared."

McClellan remounts his horse, and with Porter and a dozen officers of his staff rides away to the left in Burnside's direction. Sykes meets them on the road—a good soldier, whose opinion is worth taking. The three Generals talk briefly together. It is easy to see that the moment has come when every thing may turn on one order given or withheld, when the history of the battle is only to be written in thoughts and purposes and words of the General.

Burnside's messenger rides up. His message is: "I want troops and guns. If you do not send them, I cannot hold my position half an hour." McClellan's only answer for the moment is a glance at the western sky. Then he turns and speaks very slowly: "Tell Gen. Burnside this is the battle of the war. He must hold his ground till dark at any cost. I will send him Miller's battery. I can do nothing more. I have no infantry." Then as the messenger was riding away he called him back. "Tell him if he *cannot* hold his ground, then the bridge, to the last man!—always the bridge! If the bridge is lost, all is lost."

The sun is already down; not half an hour of daylight is left. Till Burnside's message came it had seemed plain to every one that the battle could not be finished to-day. None suspected how near was the peril of defeat, of sudden attack on exhausted forces—how vital to the safety of the army and the nation were those fifteen thousand waiting troops of Fitz-John Porter in the hollow. But the rebels halted instead of pushing on; their vindictive cannonade died away as the light faded. Before it was quite dark the battle was over. Only a solitary gun of Burnside's thundered against the enemy, and presently this also ceased, and the field was still.

The peril came very near, but it has passed, and in spite of the peril, at the close the day was partly a success; not a victory, but an advantage had been gained. Hooker, Sumner, and Franklin held all the ground they had gained, and Burnside still held the bridge and his position beyond. Every thing was favorable for a renewal of the fight in the morning. If the plan of the battle is sound, there is every reason why McClellan should win it.

He may choose to postpone the battle to await his reënforcements. The rebels may choose to retire while it is possible. Fatigue on both sides may delay the deciding battle, yet if the enemy means to fight at all, he cannot afford to delay. His reënforcements may be coming, but where are his supplies? His losses are enormous. His troops have been massed in woods and hollows, where artillery has had its most terrific effect. Ours have been deployed and scattered. From infantry fire there is less difference.

It is hard to estimate losses on a field of such extent, but I think ours cannot be less than six thousand killed and wounded—it may be much greater. Prisoners have been taken from the enemy; I hear of a regiment captured entire, but I doubt it. All the prisoners whom I saw agree in saying that the whole army is there.

FIGHT FOR THE CORNFIELD: MARYLAND, SEPTEMBER 1862

Rufus R. Dawes: from Service with the Sixth Wisconsin Volunteers

The Battle of Antietam opened at daybreak on September 17 with the advance of Joseph Hooker's First Corps against the Confederate left, on the northern part of the battlefield. Major Dawes was second in command of the 6th Wisconsin Infantry, part of a brigade commanded by John Gibbon. In an 1890 memoir he remembered the struggle for farmer David R. Miller's cornfield.

About daylight, General Doubleday came galloping along the line, and he ordered that our brigade be moved at once out of its position. He said we were in open range of the rebel batteries. The men were in a heavy slumber. After much shaking and kicking and hurrying, they were aroused, and stood up in their places in the lines. Too much noise was probably made, which appears to have aroused the enemy. The column hurriedly changed direction, according to orders, and commenced moving away from the perilous slope which faced the hostile batteries.

We had marched ten rods, when whiz-z-z! bang! burst a shell over our heads; then another; then a percussion shell struck and exploded in the very center of the moving mass of men. It killed two men and wounded eleven. It tore off Captain David K. Noyes's foot, and cut off both arms of a man in his company. This dreadful scene occurred within a few feet of where I was riding, and before my eyes. The column pushed on without a halt, and in another moment had the shelter of a barn. Thus opened the first firing of the great battle of Antietam, in the early morning of September 17th, 1862. The regiment continued moving forward into a strip of woods, where the column was deployed into line of battle. The artillery fire had now increased to the roar of an hundred cannon. Solid shot and shell whistled through the trees above us, cutting off limbs which fell about us. In front of the woods was an open field; beyond this was a house, surrounded by peach and apple trees, a garden, and outhouses.* The rebel skirmishers were in this cover, and they directed upon us a vigorous fire. But company "I" deployed as skirmishers, under command of Captain John A. Kellogg, dashed across the field at a full run and drove them out, and the line of the regiment pushed on over the green open field, the air above our heads filled with the screaming missiles of the contending batteries. The right of the regiment was now on the Sharpsburg and Hagerstown Turnpike. The left wing was obstructed in its advance by the picket fence around the garden before mentioned. As the right wing passed on, I ordered the men of the left wing to take hold all together and pull down the fence. They were unable to do so. I had, therefore, to pass the left wing by the flank through a gate with the utmost haste, and form again in the garden. Here Captain Edwin A. Brown, of company "E," was instantly killed. There is in my mind as I write, the spectacle of a young officer, with uplifted sword, shouting in a loud imperative voice the order I had given him, "Company 'E,' on the right by file into line!" A bullet passes into his open mouth, and the voice is forever silent. I urged the left wing forward with all possible speed. The men scrambled over briars and flower-beds in the garden. Beyond the garden, we entered a peach orchard. I hurried forward to a rail fence skirting the front edge of the orchard, where we overtook the right wing. Before us was a strip of open-field, beyond which on the left-hand side of the turnpike, was rising ground, covered by a large cornfield, the stalks standing thick and high. The rebel skirmishers ran into the corn as we appeared at the fence. Owing to our headlong advance, we were far ahead of the general lines of battle. They were in open fields, and we had the cover of the houses and orchard. Colonel Bragg, however, with his usual battle ardor, ordered the regiment forward. We climbed the fence, moved across the open space, and pushed on into the corn-field. The three right companies of the regiment were crowded into an open field on the right-hand side of the turnpike. Thus we pushed up the hill to the middle of the corn-field.

At this juncture, the companies of the right wing received a

*David R. Miller's house.

deadly fire from the woods on their right. To save them, Colonel Bragg, with a quickness and coolness equal to the emergency, caused them to change front and form behind the turnpike fence, from whence they returned the fire of the enemy. Meanwhile, I halted the left wing, and ordered them to lie down on the ground. The bullets began to clip through the corn, and spin through the soft furrows—thick, almost, as hail. Shells burst around us, the fragments tearing up the ground, and canister whistled through the corn above us. Lieutenant Bode of company "F," was instantly killed, and Lieutenant John Ticknor was badly wounded. Sergeant Major Howard J. Huntington now came running to me through the corn. He said: "Major, Colonel Bragg wants to see you, quick, at the turnpike." I ran to the fence in time to hear Bragg say: "Major, I am shot," before he fell upon the ground. I saw a tear in the side of his overcoat which he had on. I feared that he was shot through the body. I called two men from the ranks, who bundled him quickly into a shelter tent, and hurried away with him. Colonel Bragg was shot in the first fire from the woods and his nerve, in standing up under the shock until he had effected the maneuver so necessary for the safety of his men, was wonderful. I felt a great sense of responsibility, when thrown thus suddenly in command of the regiment in the face of a terrible battle. I stood near the fence in the corn-field, overlooking the companies on the turnpike which were firing on the enemy in the woods, and where I could see the left wing also. I noticed a group of mounted rebel officers, whom I took to be a general and staff. I took a rest over the turnpike fence, and fired six shots at the group, the men handing me loaded muskets. They suddenly scattered.

Our lines on the left now came sweeping forward through the corn and the open fields beyond. I ordered my men up to join in the advance, and commanded: "Forward—guide left—march!" We swung away from the turnpike, and I sent the sergeant-major (Howard J. Huntington) to Captain Kellogg, commanding the companies on the turnpike, with this order: "If it is practicable, move forward the right companies, aligning with the left wing." Captain Kellogg said: "Please give Major Dawes my compliments, and say it is impracticable; the fire is murderous."

As we were getting separated, I directed Sergeant Huntington to tell Captain Kellogg that he could get cover in the corn, and to join us, if possible. Huntington was struck by a bullet, but delivered the order. Kellogg ordered his men up, but so many were shot that he ordered them down again at once. While this took place on the turnpike, our companies were marching forward through the thick corn, on the right of a long line of battle. Closely following was a second line. At the front edge of the corn-field was a low Virginia rail fence. Before the corn were open fields, beyond which was a strip of woods surrounding a little church, the Dunkard church. As we appeared at the edge of the corn, a long line of men in butternut and gray rose up from the ground. Simultaneously, the hostile battle lines opened a tremendous fire upon each other. Men, I can not say fell; they were knocked out of the ranks by dozens. But we jumped over the fence, and pushed on, loading, firing, and shouting as we advanced. There was, on the part of the men, great hysterical excitement, eagerness to go forward, and a reckless disregard of life, of every thing but victory. Captain Kellogg brought his companies up abreast of us on the turnpike.

The Fourteenth Brooklyn Regiment, red legged Zouaves, came into our line, closing the awful gaps. Now is the pinch. Men and officers of New York and Wisconsin are fused into a common mass, in the frantic struggle to shoot fast. Every body tears cartridges, loads, passes guns, or shoots. Men are falling in their places or running back into the corn. The soldier who is shooting is furious in his energy. The soldier who is shot looks around for help with an imploring agony of death on his face. After a few rods of advance, the line stopped and, by common impulse, fell back to the edge of the corn and lay down on the ground behind the low rail fence. Another line of our men came up through the corn. We all joined together, jumped over the fence, and again pushed out into the open field. There is a rattling fusilade and loud cheers. "Forward" is the word. The men are loading and firing with demoniacal fury and shouting and laughing hysterically, and the whole field before us is covered with rebels fleeing for life, into the woods. Great numbers of them are shot while climbing over the high post and rail fences along the turnpike. We push on over the open fields half way to the little church. The powder is bad, and the guns have become very dirty. It takes hard pounding to get the bullets down, and our firing is becoming slow. A long and steady line of rebel gray, unbroken by the fugitives who fly before us, comes sweeping down through the woods around the church. *They raise the yell and fire. It is like a scythe running through our line. "Now, save, who can." It is a race for life that each man runs for the cornfield. A sharp cut, as of a switch, stings the calf of my leg as I run. Back to the corn, and back through the corn, the headlong flight continues. At the bottom of the hill, I took the blue color of the state of Wisconsin, and waving it, called a rally of Wisconsin men. Two hundred men gathered around the flag of the Badger state. Across the turnpike just in front of the haystacks, two guns of Battery "B," 4th U. S. artillery were in action. The pursuing rebels were upon them. General John Gibbon, our brigade commander, who in regular service was captain of this battery, grimed and black with powder smoke in himself sighting these guns of his old battery, comes running to me, "Here, major, move your men over, we must save these guns." I commanded "Right face, forward march," and started ahead with the colors in my hand into the open field, the men following. As I entered the field, a report as of a thunderclap in my ear fairly stunned me. This was Gibbon's last shot at the advancing rebels. The cannon was double charged with canister. The rails of the fence flew high in the air. A line of union blue charged swiftly forward from our right across the field in front of the battery, and into the corn-field. They drove back the rebels who were firing upon us. It was our own gallant 19th Indiana, and here fell dead their leader, Lieutenant Colonel A. F. Bachman; but the youngest captain in their line, William W. Dudley, stepped forward and led on the charge. I gathered my men on the turnpike, reorganized them, and reported to General Doubleday, who was himself there. He ordered me to move back to the next woods in the rear, to remain and await instruction. Bullets, shot, and shell, fired by the enemy in the corn-field, were still flying thickly around us, striking the trees in this woods, and cutting off the limbs. I placed my men under

*Hood's old Texas brigade, and Law's brigade.

the best shelter I could find, and here we figured up, as nearly as we could, our dreadful losses in the battle. Three hundred and fourteen officers and men had marched with us into battle. There had been killed and wounded, one hundred and fifty-two. Company "C" under Captain Hooe, thirty-five men, was not in the fight in front of the corn-field. That company was on skirmish duty farther to our right. In this service they lost two men. Of two hundred and eighty men who were at the corn-field and turnpike, one hundred and fifty were killed or wounded. This was the most dreadful slaughter to which our regiment was subjected in the war. We were joined in the woods by Captain Ely, who reported to me, as the senior officer present, with the colors and eighteen men of the second Wisconsin. They represented what remained for duty of that gallant regiment.

"THE INFERNAL MUSIC": MARYLAND, SEPTEMBER 1862

Alpheus S. Williams to Irene and Mary Williams

Brigadier General Williams, a former officer in the Michigan militia, was temporarily commanding the Twelfth Corps as the Maryland campaign opened. On September 15 he turned the corps over to Major General Joseph K. F. Mansfield, a regular officer and West Point graduate; when Mansfield was killed on the 17th, Williams resumed the corps command. In a letter to his daughters, he described the early morning fighting in the East Woods, Miller's Cornfield, and the West Woods.

Camp near Sandy Hook,
Near Harpers Ferry, Sept. 22, 1862.

My Dear Daughters:

I wrote you last from Damascus, I think, on the 11th inst. On the 12th we moved to the neighborhood of Urbana, after a circuitous and tedious march. On the 13th we marched to Frederick expecting an attack all the way. We forded the Monocacy and encamped about a mile east of the city. It was a year ago nearly that we marched through Frederick with flying banners. Alas! of those gallant troops (the old 3rd Brigade) how few remain. On Sunday the 14th we were ordered forward from Frederick crossing the Catoctin Mountain by a very rough road, east of the pike upon which we were encamped a year ago. The road took us very near our old campground at a small hamlet called Shookstown. I found all the people knew me, and I was fairly deluged with peaches, apples, etc. Ascending the mountain, we heard the reports of distant artillery and once on the summit could see that a fierce engagement was going on across the valley and in the gorges of the opposite range of mountains.

We were hurried down and marched over rough roads and finally about sundown I got an order to bivouac the corps.

Before, however, the regiments had filed into the fields a new order came to follow Gen. Sumner's corps over the ploughed fields toward the musketry firing heard in front. I had ordered a supper (after a meal-less day) at a farmhouse and went back to get it and to look after my artillery which had got astray in our field and erratic marches. We had a good meal and I mounted to follow the command when I heard that Capt. Abert, U.S. Topographical Engineers, of my staff had been seriously injured by the fall of his horse. Having directed his removal to the house where Dr. Antisell was, I rode back but met a staff officer on the way with a report that the corps was ordered to Middletown to report to Gen. McClellan. Thither I started in the darkest of nights, but at Middletown could hear nothing of my corps. So I rode from there toward the mountain gap where the fighting had been and got as far as our advanced pickets but could not find my corps.

Back I went to Middletown again, but could get no knowledge of my command. But here I heard with sad heart that Gen. Reno, one of the best officers and bravest fellows, had been killed in the engagement. But one day before he had spent at Damascus half a day with me, full of spirits, full of confidence, and full of good feeling. Of all the major generals he was my *beau ideal* of a soldier. You will remember that he commanded a corps which followed ours along the Rappahannock. I had been thrown much with him. His frankness, absence of pomp and parade, his cheerfulness under all circumstances—that indescribable something in manner, had made me love him at first sight. I could have cried when I heard of his death, but for the thousand cares that oppressed me and for the heavy duties which close up the tender impulses of the heart.

Hearing nothing of my command I again rode to the front and on the pike found a portion of our regiment sleeping calmly with no knowledge of the rest. Soon afterward I found a mounted orderly, who directed me to a by-road leading up through the mountain defiles, and following this I at length at 2 o'clock in the morning found the rear division of my command bivouacking near the column of Hooker, which had been engaged with the enemy. I lodged under the best tree I could find, and at daylight got my whole command under arms and went forward to see what was to be done. On the top of the pass I met almost the first man I knew, Gen. Willcox, who commands a division. The dead lay thick in front, but I could see nothing beyond as the mist hung heavily on the mountain. Our troops, however, were already in motion and skirmishers were firing right and left as they pushed the Rebels forward.

Going back to my command, I met Gen. Mansfield, who had just arrived from Washington to take command of the corps. He is a most veteran-looking officer, with head as white as snow. You may have seen him in Washington. His home is at Middletown, Conn. and he has been inspector general of the army for a long time. With this new commander came an order to march. I went back to my division, rather pleased that I had got rid of an onerous responsibility. We crossed the fields to the Hagerstown pike. Our new commander was very fussy. He had been an engineer officer and never before had commanded large bodies of troops.

Onward we went after being delayed for other columns to pass. Crossing the South Mountain we descended rapidly to Boonsboro where the people, as at Frederick, received us with great rejoicing. I did not tell you that in marching my corps through Frederick we were greatly cheered and ladies brought bouquets to me as commander. The same enthusiasm followed us everywhere. Citizens met us on horseback and the whole population seemed rejoiced that we were chasing the Rebels from the state. At Boonsboro we passed south towards Sharpsburg, taking across lots and in all sorts of out of the ways. We encamped at a crossroads and for the first time for weeks I slept in a house, the home of a Mr. Nicodemus. As I was getting my division into camp I saw other troops arriving and an officer darting up to me put out his hand eagerly to greet me. It was the topographical engineer captain with whom Alph. and Ez. went to New Mexico, now Col. Scammon of an Ohio regiment. I did not feel very kindly, I fear, and yet he looked so changed and so glad to see me that I greeted him in return. He went away and I have not seen him since.

The next morning we were ordered hurriedly to the front, Gen. Mansfield, in an excited and fussy way, announcing that we should be in a general engagement in half an hour. Over we went across lots till we struck a road and after a three-mile march we were *massed* in close column in a small space where the shells of the enemy's guns fell close to us. A high ridge in front did not seem much protection. We lay here all day, and at night fancied we were going to rest. I sought a tent with one of my colonels, who gave me the best bed I had seen for weeks.

During the afternoon, amongst the troops marching up I had seen Col. Stockton and other old friends. It was evident that the Rebels were standing for a fight. Their lines were plainly visible from the elevation in front and one battery had been playing all day with ours. I had got fairly asleep when along came a message to get under arms at once. Oh, how sleepy I was, but there is no help at such times. Up I got and in a few moments the head of my division was moving along an unknown road. We passed a stone bridge over the Antietam and then branched off into the fields. Gen. Mansfield and his escort led the way, but it was so dark and the forests and woods so deep that I could not follow and was obliged to send ahead to stop our leaders repeatedly.

After a weary march we halted in some ploughed ground and I was told to put my division in column in mass. It took a long time as I had five new regiments who knew absolutely nothing of maneuvering. At length about two o'clock in the morning I got under the corner of a rail fence, but the pickets in front of us kept firing and as often as I got asleep Gen. Mansfield would come along and wake me with some new directions. At length I got fairly asleep and for two hours was dead to all sounds or sensations. I shall not, however, soon forget that night; so dark, so obscure, so mysterious, so uncertain; with the occasional rapid volleys of pickets and outposts, the low, solemn sound of the command as troops came into position, and withal so sleepy that there was a half-dreamy sensation about it all; but with a certain impression that the morrow was to be great with the future fate of our country. So much responsibility, so much intense, future anxiety! and yet I slept as soundly as though nothing was before me.

At the first dawn of day the cannon began work. Gen. Hooker's command was about a mile in front of us and it was his corps upon which the attack began. By a common impulse our men stood to arms. They had slept in ranks and the matter of toilet was not tedious, nor did we have time to linger over the breakfast table. My division being in advance, I was ordered to move up in close column of companies—that is a company front to each regiment and the other companies closed up to within six paces. When so formed a regiment looks like a solid mass. We had not moved a dozen rods before the shells and round shot came thick over us and around us. If these had struck our massed regiments dozens of men would have been killed by a single shot.

I had five new regiments without drill or discipline. Gen. Mansfield was greatly excited. Though an officer of acknowledged gallantry, he had a very nervous temperament and a very impatient manner. Feeling that our heavy masses of raw troops were sadly exposed, I begged him to let me deploy them in line of battle, in which the men present but *two* ranks or rows instead of *twenty*, as we were marching, but I could not move him. He was positive that all the new regiments would run away. So on we went over ploughed ground, through cornfields and woods, till the line of infantry fight began to appear.

It was evident that Hooker's troops were giving way. His general officers were hurrying toward us begging for support in every direction. First one would come from the right; then over from the center, and then one urging support for a battery on the left. I had ridden somewhat in advance to get some idea of the field and was standing in the center of a ploughed field, taking directions from Gen. Hooker and amidst a very unpleasant shower of bullets, when up rode a general officer begging for immediate assistance to protect a battery. He was very earnest and absorbed in the subject, as you may well suppose, and began to plead energetically, when he suddenly stopped, extended his hand, and very calmly said, "How are you?" It was Gen. Meade. He darted away, and I saw him no more that day. Hooker's troops were soon withdrawn and I think were not again brought into the field. Was it not a strange encounter?

I had parted with Gen. Mansfield but a moment before this and in five minutes afterward his staff officer reported to me that he was mortally wounded and the command of the corps devolved on me. I began at once to deploy the new regiments. The old ones had already gotten themselves into line. Taking hold of one, I directed Gens. Crawford and Gordon to direct the others. I got mine in line pretty well by having a fence to align it on and having got it in this way I ordered the colonel to go forward and open fire the moment he saw the Rebels. Poor fellow! He was killed within ten minutes. His regiment, advancing in line, was split in two by coming in contact with a barn. One part did very well in the woods but the trouble with this regiment and the others was that in attempting to move them forward or back or to make any maneuver they fell into inextricable confusion and fell to the rear, where they were easily rallied. The men were of an excellent stamp, ready and willing, but neither officers nor men knew anything, and there was an absence of the mutual confidence which drill begets. Standing still, they fought bravely.

When we engaged the enemy he was in a strip of woods, long but narrow. We drove him from this, across a ploughed field and through a cornfield into another woods, which was full of ravines. There the enemy held us in check till 9 1/2 o'clock, when there was a general cessation of musketry. All over the ground we had advanced on, the Rebel dead and wounded lay thick, much more numerous than ours, but ours were painfully mingled in. Our wounded were rapidly carried off and some of the Rebels'. Those we were obliged to leave begged so piteously to be carried away. Hundreds appealed to me and I confess that the rage of battle had not hardened my heart so that I did not feel a pity for them. Our men gave them water and as far as I saw always treated them kindly.

The necessities of the case were so great that I was obliged to put my whole corps into action at once. The roar of the infantry was beyond anything conceivable to the uninitiated. Imagine from 8,000 to 10,000 men on one side, with probably a larger number on the other, all at once discharging their muskets. If all the stone and brick houses of Broadway should tumble at once the roar and rattle could hardly be greater, and amidst this, hundreds of pieces of artillery, right and left, were thundering as a sort of bass to the infernal music.

At 9 1/2 o'clock Gen. Sumner was announced as near at hand with his corps. As soon as his columns began to arrive I withdrew mine by degrees to the shelter of the woods for the purpose of rest, to collect stragglers, and to renew the ammunition. Several of the old regiments had fired nearly forty rounds each man. They had stood up splendidly and had forced back the enemy nearly a mile. The new regiments were badly broken up, but I collected about one-half of them and placed them in support of batteries. The regiments had up to this time suffered comparatively little. The 3rd Wisconsin and the 27th Indiana had lost a good many men, but few officers. I began to hope that we should get off, when Sumner attacked, with but little loss. I rode along where our advanced lines had been. Not an enemy appeared. The woods in front were as quiet as any sylvan shade could be. Presently a single report came and a ball whizzed close to my horse. Two or three others followed all in disagreeable closeness to my person. I did not like to hurry, but I lost as little time as possible in getting out of the range of sharpshooters.

I should have mentioned that soon after I met Gen. Hooker he rode toward the left. In a few minutes I heard he was wounded. While we were talking the dust of the ploughed ground was knocked up in little spurts all around us, marking the spot where musket balls struck. I had to ride repeatedly over this field and every time it seemed that my horse could not possibly escape. It was in the center of the line of fire, slightly elevated, but along which *my* troops were extended. The peculiar singing sound of the bullet becomes a regular whistle and it seems strange that everybody is not hit.

While the battle was raging fiercest with that division the 2nd Division came up and I was requested to support our right with one brigade. I started one over to report to Gen. Doubleday and soon followed to see what became of them. As I entered the narrow lane running to the right and front a battery opened a cross-fire and Pittman and myself had the excitement of riding a mile or so out and back under its severest salutations. We found Gen. Doubleday sheltered in a ravine and apparently in bland ignorance of what was doing on his front or what need he had of my troops, except to relieve his own, but I left the brigade and came back. Finding a battery, I put it in position to meet the flank fire of the Rebel battery and some one else had the good sense to establish another farther in the rear. The two soon silenced this disagreeable customer.

It was soon after my return to the center that Sumner's columns began to arrive. They were received with cheers and went fiercely toward the wood with too much haste, I thought, and too little reconnoitering of the ground and positions held by us. They had not reached the road before a furious fire was opened on them and we had the infernal din over again. The Rebels had been strongly reinforced, and Sumner's troops, being formed in three lines in close proximity, after his favorite idea, we lost a good deal of our fire without any corresponding benefit or advantage. For instance, the second line, within forty paces of the front, suffered almost as much as the front line and yet could not fire without hitting our own men. The colonel of a regiment in the second line told me he lost sixty men and came off without firing a gun.

Sumner's force in the center was soon used up, and I was called upon to bring up my wearied and hungry men. They advanced to the front and opened fire, but the force opposed was enormously superior. Still they held on, under heavy losses, till one o'clock. Some of the old regiments were fairly broken up in this fight and what was left were consolidated and mixed up afterward with the new regiments. The 46th Pennsylvania, Col. Knipe, and the 28th New York, Capt. Mapes, commanding, were especially broken. Col. Knipe has just returned to duty from his wounds. He had but one captain (Brooks) in his regiment present and he was killed early. The 2nd Massachusetts, which had done excellent service in the first engagement, was badly cut up and its lieut. col. (Dwight), mortally wounded. At 1 1/2 o'clock I ordered them back, as reinforcements were at hand.

While this last attack was going on, Gen. Greene, 2nd Division, took possession and held for an hour or more the easterly end of the wood—struggled for so fiercely—where it abuts on the road to Sharpsburg. A small brick school house stands by the road, which I noticed the next day was riddled by our shot and shell. Greene held on till Sumner's men gave way towards the left, when he was drawn out by a rush and his men came scampering to the rear in great confusion. The Rebels followed with a yell but three or four of our batteries being in position they were received with a tornado of canister which made them vanish before the smoke cloud cleared away. I was near one of our brass twelve-pound Napoleon gun batteries and seeing the Rebel colors appearing over the rolling ground I directed the two left pieces charged with canister to be turned on the point. In the moment the Rebel line appeared and both guns were discharged at short range. Each canister contains several hundred balls. They fell in the very front of the line and all along it apparently, stirring up a dust like a thick cloud. When the dust blew away no regiment and not a living man was to be seen.

Just then Gen. Smith (Baldy Smith) who was at Detroit on the light-house duty, came up with a division. They fairly rushed toward the left and front. I hastily called his attention to the woods full of Rebels on his right as he was advancing. He dispatched that way one regiment and the rest advanced to an elevation which overlooked the valley on our left, where the left wing had been fighting for several hours. The regiment sent toward the woods got a tremendous volley and saved itself by rushing over the hillside for shelter. The rest of the brigade got an enfilading fire on a Rebel line and it broke and ran to the rear. One regiment only charged the front, as if on parade, but a second battery sent it scampering.

On this ground the contest was kept up for a long time. The multitude of dead Rebels (I saw them) was proof enough how hotly they contested the ground. It was getting toward night. The artillery took up the fight. We had driven them at all points, save the one woods. It was thought advisable not to attack further. We held the main battlefield and all our wounded, except a few in the woods. My troops slept on their arms well to the front. All the other corps of the center seemed to have vanished, but I found Sumner's the next morning and moved up to it and set to work gathering up our stragglers. The day was passed in comparative quietness on both sides. Our burial parties would exchange the dead and wounded with the Rebels in the woods.

It was understood that we were to attack again at daylight on the 19th, but as our troops moved up it was found the Rebels had departed. Some of the troops followed, but we lay under arms all day, waiting orders. I took the delay to ride over the field of battle. The Rebel dead, even in the woods last occupied by them, was very great. In one place, in front of the position of my corps, apparently a whole regiment had been cut down in line. They lay in two ranks, as straightly aligned as on a dress parade. There must have been a brigade, as part of the line on the left had been buried. I counted what appeared to be a single regiment and found 149 dead in the line and about 70 in front and rear, making over 200 dead in one Rebel regiment. In riding over the field I think I must have seen at least 3,000. In one place for nearly a mile they lay as thick as autumn leaves along a narrow lane cut below the natural surface, into which they seemed to have tumbled. Eighty had been buried in one pit, and yet no impression had apparently been made on the unburied host. The cornfield beyond was dotted all over with those killed in retreat.

The wounded Rebels had been carried away in great numbers and yet every farmyard and haystack seemed a large hospital. The number of dead horses was high. They lay, like the men, in all attitudes. One beautiful milk-white animal had died in so graceful a position that I wished for its photograph. Its legs were doubled under and its arched neck gracefully turned to one side, as if looking back to the ball-hole in its side. Until you got to it, it was hard to believe the horse was dead. Another feature of the field was the mass of army accouterments, clothing, etc. scattered everywhere or lying in heaps where the contest had been severest. I lost but two field officers killed, Col. Croasdale, 128th Pennsylvania and Col. Dwight, 2nd Massachusetts, several men wounded. Gen. Crawford of the 1st Brigade was wounded, not severely. I marvel, not only at my own escape, as I was particularly exposed, on account of raw troops to be handled, but at the escape of any mounted officer.

The newspapers will give you further particulars, but as far as I have seen them, nothing reliable. . . . The "big staff generals" get the first ear and nobody is heard of and no corps mentioned till their voracious maws are filled with puffing. I see it stated that Sumner's corps relieved Hooker's. So far is this from true that my corps was engaged from sunrise till 9 1/2 o'clock before Sumner came up, though he was to be on the ground at daylight. Other statements picked up by reporters from the principal headquarters are equally false and absurd. To me they are laughably *canard*.

On the afternoon of the 18th I received orders to occupy Maryland Heights with my corps. They are opposite Harpers Ferry, and had just been surrendered by Col. Miles. I marched till 2 o'clock in the morning, reaching Brownsvllle. Halted till daylight, men sleeping in the road. I slept on hay in a barn. Started by sunrise up the Heights and marched along a rocky path on the ridge to the Heights overlooking Harpers Ferry. I left my artillery and train at Brownsville. Occupied the Heights without opposition. Found there was no water there; left a strong guard and took the command down the mountain on the east side. Sent a brigade over the river and a regiment to Sandy Hook. This morning (Gen. Sumner's corps having come up) I have sent one division over the river to Loudon Heights and one part way up Maryland Heights in front. The Rebels are in sight in and about and this side Charleston and to the west toward Shepardstown. What is to be done next I know not. It will be my fate, I fear, to go a third time up the valley. Heaven forbid! The valley has been an unfortunate land for me. My friends think I shall get a major generalship. I should if I was of the regular army; but not being such nor a graduated fool I suppose I shall remain a brigadier. Gen. Banks never moves for any of his command, unless solicited personally. Nobody in his corps has received promotion, though he seems to have gathered some newspaper laurels. . . .

It is now nearly six weeks that I have hardly halted a whole day, and when I have it was under orders to be ready to move at a moment. I am so tired and uneasy of this kind of sleepless life. On the march up my command was one day eighteen hours under arms and marching most of the time. But I am well and bear it better than anyone.

Affectionately, my Daughters,
Your Father,
A.S.W.

A LANDSCAPE TURNED RED: MARYLAND, SEPTEMBER 1862

David L. Thompson: With Burnside at Antietam

As the day wore on, the fighting shifted from the northern sector to the center and finally to the southern end of the battleground. Ambrose Burnside's Ninth Corps forced its way across a stone bridge (known thereafter as Burnside's Bridge) and pushed on to the outskirts of Sharpsburg. A. P. Hill's Confederate division, rushing from Harpers Ferry, caught Burnside's corps in the flank, drove it back to the bridge, and ended the day's fighting. Private Thompson, 9th New York Infantry, narrated his modest role amidst the confusing battle scene for *Battles and Leaders of the Civil War.*

AT ANTIETAM our corps—the Ninth, under Burnside—was on the extreme left, opposite the stone bridge. Our brigade stole into position about half-past 10 o'clock on the night of the 16th. No lights were permitted, and all conversation was carried on in whispers. As the regiment was moving past the 103d New York to get to its place, there occurred, on a small scale and without serious results, one of those unaccountable panics often noticed in crowds, by which each man, however brave individually, merges his individuality for the moment, and surrenders to an utterly causeless fear. When everything was at its darkest and stealthiest one of the 103d stumbled over the regimental dog, and, in trying to avoid treading on it, staggered against a stack of muskets and knocked them over. The giving way of the two or three men upon whom they fell was communicated to others in a sort of wave movement of constantly increasing magnitude, reënforced by the ever-present apprehension of attack, till two regiments were in confusion. In a few seconds order was restored, and we went on to our place in the line—a field of thin corn sloping toward the creek, where we sat down on the plowed ground and watched for a while the dull glare on the sky of the Confederate campfires behind the hills. We were hungry, of course, but, as no fires were allowed, we could only mix our ground coffee and sugar in our hands and eat them dry. I think we were the more easily inclined to this crude disposal of our rations from a feeling that for many of us the need of drawing them would cease forever with the following day.

All through the evening the shifting and placing had gone on, the moving masses being dimly descried in the strange half lights of earth and sky. There was something weirdly impressive yet unreal in the gradual drawing together of those whispering armies under cover of the night—something of awe and dread, as always in the secret preparation for momentous deeds. By 11 o'clock the whole line, four miles or more in length, was sleeping, each corps apprised of its appointed task, each battery in place.

It is astonishing how soon, and by what slight causes, regularity of formation and movement are lost in actual battle. Disintegration begins with the first shot. To the book-soldier all order seems destroyed, months of drill apparently going for nothing in a few minutes. Next after the most powerful factor in this derangement—the enemy—come natural obstacles and the inequalities of the ground. One of the commonest is a patch of trees. An advancing line lags there inevitably, the rest of the line swinging around insensibly, with the view of keeping the alignment, and so losing direction. The struggle for the possession of such a point is sure to be persistent. Wounded men crawl to a wood for shelter, broken troops re-form behind it, a battery planted in its edge will stick there after other parts of the line have given way. Often a slight rise of ground in an open field, not noticeable a thousand yards away, becomes, in the keep of a stubborn regiment, a powerful head-land against which the waves of battle roll and break, requiring new dispositions and much time to clear it. A stronger fortress than a casual railroad embankment often proves, it would be difficult to find; and as for a sunken road, what possibilities of victory or disaster lie in that obstruction, let Waterloo and Fredericksburg bear witness.

At Antietam it was a low, rocky ledge, prefaced by a corn-field. There were woods, too, and knolls, and there were other corn-fields; but the student of that battle knows one corn-field only—*the* corn-field, now historic, lying a quarter of a mile north of Dunker Church, and east of and bordering the Hagerstown road. About it and across it, to and fro, the waves of battle swung almost from the first, till by 10 o'clock in the morning, when the struggle was over, hundreds of men lay dead among its peaceful blades.

While these things were happening on the right, the left was not without its excitement. A Confederate battery discovered our position in our corn-field, as soon as it was light enough to see, and began to shell us. As the range became better we were moved back and ordered to boil coffee in the protection of a hollow. The general plan of battle appears to have been to break through the Confederate left, following up the advantage with a constantly increasing force, sweep him away from the fords, and so crowd his whole army down into the narrow peninsula formed by the Potomac and Antietam Creek. Even the non-military eye, however, can see that the tendency of such a plan would be to bring the two armies upon concentric arcs, the inner and shorter of which must be held by the enemy, affording him the opportunity for reënforcement by interior lines—an immense advantage only to be counteracted by the utmost activity on our part, who must attack vigorously where attacking at all, and where not, imminently threaten. Certainly there was no imminence in the threat of our center or left—none whatever of the left, only a vague consciousness of whose existence even seems to have been in the enemy's mind, for he flouted us all the morning with hardly more than a meager skirmish line, while his coming troops, as fast as they arrived upon the ground, were sent off to the Dunker Church.

So the morning wore away, and the fighting on the right ceased entirely. That was fresh anxiety—the scales were turning perhaps, but which way? About noon the battle began afresh. This must have been Franklin's men of the Sixth Corps, for the firing was nearer, and they came up behind the center. Suddenly a stir beginning far up on the right, and running like a wave along the line, brought the regiment to its feet. A silence fell on every one at once, for each felt that the momentous "now" had come. Just as we started I saw, with a little shock, a line-officer take out his watch to note the hour, as though the affair beyond the creek were a business appointment which he was going to keep.

When we reached the brow of the hill the fringe of trees along the creek screened the fighting entirely, and we were deployed as skirmishers under their cover. We sat there two hours. All that time the rest of the corps had been moving over the stone bridge and going into position on the other side of the creek. Then we were ordered over at a ford which had been found below the bridge, where the water was waist-deep. One man was shot in mid-stream. At the foot of the slope on the opposite side the line was formed and we moved up through the thin woods. Reaching the level we lay down behind a battery which seemed to have been disabled. There, if anywhere, I should have remembered that I was soaking wet from my waist down. So great was the excitement, however, that I have never been able to recall it. Here some of the men, going to the rear for water, discovered in the ashes of some hay-ricks which had been fired by our shells the charred remains of several Confederates. After long waiting it became noised along the line that we were to take a battery that was at work several hundred yards ahead on the top of a hill. This narrowed the field and brought us to consider the work before us more attentively.

Right across our front, two hundred feet or so away, ran a country road bordered on each side by a snake fence. Beyond this road stretched a plowed field several hundred feet in length, sloping up to the battery, which was hidden in a cornfield. A stone fence, breast-high, inclosed the field on the left, and behind it lay a regiment of Confederates, who would be directly on our flank if we should attempt the slope. The prospect was far from encouraging, but the order came to get ready for the attempt.

Our knapsacks were left on the ground behind us. At the word a rush was made for the fences. The line was so disordered by the time the second fence was passed that we hurried forward to a shallow undulation a few feet ahead, and lay down among the furrows to re-form, doing so by crawling up into line. A hundred feet or so ahead was a similar undulation to which we ran for a second shelter. The battery, which at first had not seemed to notice us, now, apprised of its danger, opened fire upon us. We were getting ready now for the charge proper, but were still lying on our faces. Lieutenant-Colonel Kimball was ramping up and down the line. The discreet regiment behind the fence was silent. Now and then a bullet from them cut the air over our heads, but generally they were reserving their fire for that better shot which they knew they would get in a few minutes. The battery, however, whose shots at first went over our heads, had depressed its guns so as to shave the surface of the ground. Its fire was beginning to tell. I remember looking behind and seeing an officer riding diagonally across the field—a most inviting target—instinctively bending his head down over his horse's neck, as though he were riding through driving rain. While my eye was on him I saw, between me and him, a rolled overcoat with its straps on bound into the air and fall among the furrows. One of the enemy's grape-shot had plowed a groove in the skull of a young fellow and had cut his overcoat from his shoulders. He never stirred from his position, but lay there face downward—a dreadful spectacle. A moment after, I heard a man cursing a comrade for lying on him heavily. He was cursing a dying man. As the range grew better, the firing became more rapid, the situation desperate and exasperating to the last degree. Human nature was on the rack, and there burst forth from it the most vehement, terrible swearing I have ever heard. Certainly the joy of conflict was not ours that day. The suspense was only for a moment, however, for the order to charge came just after. Whether the regiment was thrown into disorder or not, I never knew. I only remember that as we rose and started all the fire that had been held back so long was loosed. In a second the air was full of the hiss of bullets and the hurtle of grape-shot. The mental strain was so great that I saw at that moment the singular effect mentioned, I think, in the life of Goethe on a similar occasion—the whole landscape for an instant turned slightly red. I see again, as I saw it then in a flash, a man just in front of me drop his musket and throw up his hands, stung into vigorous swearing by a bullet behind the ear. Many men fell going up the hill, but it seemed to be all over in a moment, and I found myself passing a hollow where a dozen wounded men lay—among them our sergeant-major, who was calling me to come down. He had caught sight of the blanket rolled across my back, and called me to unroll it and help to carry from the field one of our wounded lieutenants.

When I returned from obeying this summons the regiment (?) was not to be seen. It had gone in on the run, what there was left of it, and had disappeared in the corn-field about the battery. There was nothing to do but lie there and await developments. Nearly all the men in the hollow were wounded, one man—a recruit named Devlin, I think—frightfully so, his arm being cut short off. He lived a few minutes only. All were calling for water, of course, but none was to be had. We lay there till dusk,—perhaps an hour, when the fighting ceased. During that hour, while the bullets snipped the leaves from a young locust-tree growing at the edge of the hollow and powdered us with the fragments, we had time to speculate on many things—among others, on the impatience with which men clamor, in dull times, to be led into a fight. We heard all through the war that the army "was eager to be led against the enemy." It must have been so, for truthful correspondents said so, and editors confirmed it. But when you came to hunt for this particular itch, it was always the next regiment that had it. The truth is, when bullets are whacking against tree-trunks and solid shot are cracking skulls like egg-shells, the consuming passion in the breast of the average man is to get out of the way. Between the physical fear of going forward and the moral fear of turning back, there is a predicament of exceptional awkwardness from which a hidden hole in the ground would be a wonderfully welcome outlet.

Night fell, preventing further struggle. Of 600 men of the regiment who crossed the creek at 3 o'clock that afternoon, 45 were killed and 176 wounded. The Confederates held possession of that part of the field over which we had moved, and just after dusk they sent out detachments to collect arms and bring in prisoners. When they came to our hollow all the unwounded and slightly wounded there were marched to the rear—prisoners of the 15th Georgia. We slept on the ground that night without protection of any kind; for, with a recklessness quite common throughout the war, we had thrown away every incumbrance on going into the fight. The weather, however, was warm and pleasant, and there was little discomfort.

The next morning we were marched—about six hundred of us, fragments of a dozen different commands—to the Potomac, passing through Sharpsburg. We crossed the Potomac by the Shepherdstown ford, and bivouacked in the yard of a house near the river, remaining there all day. The next morning (the 19th) shells began to come from over the river, and we were started on the road to Richmond with a mixed guard of cavalry and infantry. When we reached Winchester we were quartered for a night in the court-house yard, where we were beset by a motley crew who were eager to exchange the produce of the region for greenbacks.

On the road between Shepherdstown and Winchester we fell in with the Maryland Battalion—a meeting I have always remembered with pleasure. They were marching to the front by companies, spaced apart about 300 or 400 feet. We were an ungainly, draggled lot, about as far removed as well could be from any claim to ceremonious courtesy; yet each company, as it passed, gave us the military salute of shouldered arms. They were noticeable, at that early stage of the war, as the only organization we saw that wore the regulation Confederate gray, all other troops having assumed a sort of revised regulation uniform of homespun butternut—a significant witness, we thought, to the efficacy of the blockade.

From Winchester we were marched to Staunton, where we were put on board cattle-cars and forwarded at night, by way of Gordonsville, to Richmond, where we entered Libby Prison. We were not treated with special severity, for Libby was not at that time the hissing it afterward became. Our time there, also, was not long. Only nine days after we entered it we were sent away, going by steamer to Camp Parole, at Annapolis. From that place I went home without ceremony, reporting my address to my company officers. Three weeks afterward they advised me that I was exchanged—which meant that I was again, legally and technically, food for powder.

AFTER THE BATTLE:
MARYLAND, SEPTEMBER 1862

Samuel W. Fiske to the Springfield Republican

After defiantly standing his ground on September 18, General Lee fell back across the Potomac into Virginia. McClellan made no serious effort at pursuit. Lieutenant Fiske of the 14th Connecticut Infantry described the aftermath of the struggle in one of his regular letters to the *Springfield* (Massachusetts) *Republican*, writing under his nom de plume Dunn Browne. The combined casualties of the Battle of Antietam reached 22,717 killed, wounded, or missing (Union 12,401, Confederate 10,316), making it the bloodiest single day in American history.

AFTER THE BATTLE

Field of Battle, near Sharpsburg, Md.
Saturday, Sept. 20

The excitement of battle comes in the day of it, but the horrors of it two or three days after. I have just passed over a part of the field, I suppose only a small part of it, and yet I have counted nearly a thousand dead bodies of rebels lying still unburied in groves and corn-fields, on hill sides and in trenches. Three hundred and fifty I was told by one who helped to bury them, were taken this morning from one long rifle pit which lay just in front of where the 14th (among other regiments) made their fight, and were buried in one trench. The air grows terribly offensive from the unburied bodies, and a pestilence will speedily be bred if they are not put under ground. The most of the Union soldiers are now buried, but some of them only slightly. Think now of the horrors of such a scene as lies all around us, for there are hundreds of horses too, all mangled and putrefying, scattered everywhere. Then there are the broken gun carriages, and wagons, the thousands of muskets and all sorts of equipments, the clothing all torn and bloody, and cartridges and cannon shot and pieces of shell, the trees torn with shot and scarred with bullets, the farm houses and barns knocked to pieces and burned down, the crops trampled and wasted, the whole country forlorn and desolate. And yet I saw over all this scene of devastation and horror, yesternight, one of the loveliest double rainbows that ever mortal eyes looked upon. It was as if heaven sat serene over human woes and horrors, and crowned all the earthly evils with the promise of ultimate most glorious good. I took it as an emblem of success to our blessed Union cause, that out of the horrors of battle shall arise the blessings of a more secure freedom and stable system of liberal government.

The enemy has retired in disgrace from his bold invasion of the North with at least 40,000 or 50,000 less men than he entered upon it—and after all our disasters and blunders and waste, let us hope that the successful end is beginning to draw nigh. The waste of this war is tremendous beyond all conception. It would take a long time to reckon that of this one battle. Thousands and thousands and tens of thousands of muskets, stacks of guns, piles of guns like big piles of rails, muskets laid up against rocks and trees and muskets scattered yet over the ground and choking up water courses, muskets rusty and broken and dirty, spoiled and half-spoiled, that a few days ago were bright in the hands of living men, are only one item of the waste. Whole regiments threw away their overcoats and blankets and everything that encumbered them, and they were trampled in the rush of conflicting hosts, and so with equipments and stores and ammunition and everything else. Waste, waste, ruin and destruction. Why, I saw a whole immense stack of unthreshed wheat, big as a barn, scattered in a few minutes over a hundred acre field (the same I think from which it had been reaped) just as bedding for the soldiers for a single night. Much of this waste is unavoidable. Much of it might be helped. Just as it is said that out of the waste of an American kitchen a French family would live comfortably, so it might almost be said that out of the waste of an American war a European war might be carried on. But I must make no more waste of ink now. Yours truly,

DUNN BROWNE

September 20, 1862

"OUR MEN HAD WON": MARYLAND, SEPTEMBER 1862

Clifton Johnson: from Battleground Adventures

In 1913 Clifton Johnson, a travel writer from Massachusetts, interviewed almost three score civilians about their recollections of the wartime events they had witnessed, publishing his interviews in 1915. This "elderly gentlewoman," as Johnson described her, still lived in her ancestral home in Sharpsburg, and shared her memories of that September day a half-century before.

A MARYLAND MAIDEN[1]

WE WERE all up in the Lutheran Church at Sunday-school on the Sunday before the battle when the Rebel cavalry came dashing through the town. The whole assembly flocked out, and there was nothing but excitement from that on. We just imagined something was going to happen, and the children ran home from church in terror. There was no dinner eaten that day. The people were too frightened. We'd go out the front door and stand waiting to see what would be next to come.

I was twenty years old then. My father was a blacksmith, and we lived in this same big stone house on the main street of the town. I suppose the house was built a hundred and fifty or more years ago.

Most of us in this region favored the Union, and the ladies had made a big flag out of material that the townspeople bought. For a while we had it on a pole in the square, but some of the Democratic boys cut the flag rope every night. So we took the flag down and hung it on a rope stretched across from our garret window to that of the house opposite. In

[1]We chatted in one of the old-fashioned, wood-panelled rooms of her ancestral village home. She was a slender, elderly gentlewoman, but though the years had left their mark they had in nowise subdued her natural alertness and enthusiasm.

pleasant weather it was out all the time. But when we heard that Lee had crossed the Potomac Pa began to be uneasy, and he says, "Girls, what you goin' to do with that flag? If the Rebels come into town they'll take it sure as the world."

He thought we'd better hide it in the ground somewhere. So a lady friend of mine and I put it in a strong wooden box, and buried it in the ash pile behind the smokehouse in the garden.

When the Rebel cavalry went through that Sunday we had no idea what they were up to, and we could n't help being fearful that we were in danger. We expected trouble that night, but all was quiet until the next day. Then more Rebels came, and they nearly worried us to death asking for something to eat. They were half famished and they looked like tramps—filthy and ragged.

By Tuesday there was enough going on to let us know we were likely to have a battle near by. Early in the day two or three Rebels, who'd been informed by some one that a Union flag was concealed at my father's place, came right to the house, and I met 'em at the door. Their leader said: "We've come to demand that flag you've got here. Give it up at once or we'll search the house."

"I'll not give it up, and I guess you'll not come any farther than you are, sir," I said.

They were impudent fellows, and he responded, "If you don't tell me where that flag is I'll draw my revolver on you."

"It's of no use for you to threaten," I said. "Rather than have you touch a fold of that starry flag I laid it in ashes."

They seemed to be satisfied then and went away without suspecting just how I'd laid it in ashes.

Tuesday afternoon the neighbors began to come in here. Our basement was very large with thick stone walls, and they wanted to take refuge in it if there was danger. There were women and children of all ages and some very old men. Mostly they stood roundabout in the yard listening and looking. The cannonading started late in the day, and when there was a very loud report they scampered to the cellar.

A lot of townspeople run out of the village to a cave about three miles from here near the Potomac. The cave was just an overhanging ledge of rocks, but shells and cannon balls would fly over it and could n't hurt the people under the cliff. I reckon seventy-five went to that cave.

Before day, on Wednesday, a cannon ball tore up the pavement out in front of our house. Oh my soul! we thought we were gone. There was no more sleep, but most of us were awake anyhow. After that, you know, we all flew to the cellar. Very little was stored in there at that time of year. We carried down some seats, and we made board benches around, and quite a number of us got up on the potato bunks and the apple scaffolds. We were as comfortable as we could possibly be in a cellar, but it's a wonder we did n't all take our deaths of colds in that damp place.

We did n't have any breakfast—you bet we did n't—and no dinner was got that day, or supper—no, indeed! We had to live on fear. But a few of the women thought enough to bring some food in their baskets for the children. The battle did n't prevent the children from eating. They did n't understand the danger.

A number of babies were there, and several dogs, and every time the firing began extra hard the babies would cry and the dogs would bark. Often the reports were so loud they shook the walls. Occasionally a woman was quite unnerved and hysterical, and some of those old aged men would break out in prayer.

In the height of the fighting six Rebel soldiers opened the basement door and said, "We're comin' in, but we're not a-goin' to hurt you."

We had a spring in the cellar. The water filled a shallow tank, and that was where our family got what water was used in the house. Those refugee soldiers went back in a little nook right next to the spring. There they stood like sardines in a box, and every once in a while one would slip down into the water.

We had two cows and a horse in our stable, and at dinner time Mother and I went to feed 'em. We climbed up to pull down some hay and found the haymow just full of Rebels a-layin' there hiding.

"Madam, don't be frightened," one of 'em said to Mother. "We're hidin' till the battle is over. We're tired of fightin'. We were pressed into service, and we're goin' to give ourselves up as soon as the Yankees get here."

And that was what they did. When the Yankees rushed into

town these Rebels came through the garden and gave themselves up as prisoners.

There were deserters hid in every conceivable place in the town. We had a lot of sacks of seed wheat on our back porch, and some of the skulkers piled the sacks up on the outside of the porch three or four feet high, as a sort of bulwark, which they lay down behind to shelter themselves. How they did curse their leaders for bringing them into this slaughter pen. They said they hoped the hottest place in hell would be their leaders' portion.

Some of the townsmen in the cellar would come up and venture out under the porch, but they were afraid to stay out; and the danger was n't just fancied either. A shell exploded right out here at our front gate and killed or wounded seven men.

And yet, mind you, on Wednesday afternoon, another girl and myself went up to the attic, and though the bullets were raining on the roof, we threw open the shutter and looked out toward the battleground. We were curious to know what was going on. The bullets could have struck us just as easy, but we did n't seem to fear them. On all the distant hills around were the blue uniforms and shining bayonets of our men, and I thought it was the prettiest sight I ever saw in my life. Yes, there were our men, advancing cautiously, driven back again and again, but persistently returning and pushing nearer. My! it was lovely, and I felt so glad to think that we were going to get them into town shortly. We stayed up there I suppose a couple of hours at that little window, and then old Dr. Kelsey came hunting for us and made us come down. I shall always remember what we saw from that window, and many times I go up to the attic and look out, and the view brings it all back.

In the evening mother and I slipped down to the stable and did the milking. But afterward we went back to the cellar, for the firing kept up till ten o'clock. Then we came up and snatched what little bit we could to eat. We did n't cook anything but took what was prepared, like bread and butter and milk. Our neighbors who had been in the cellar did n't attempt to go home. Some of the older ones we accommodated in beds, others lay on the floors, but the best part of the people sat up all night and watched, for we did n't know what was going to come on us.

About midnight we heard the Rebels retreating. Oh! the cannon just came down the hill bouncing. And the cavalry—my! if they did n't dash through here! The infantry, too, were going on a dead run, and some of the poor, hungry fellows were so weak they were saying to their stronger comrades, "Take hold of my hand, and help me along." A lot of 'em were drownded in going across the Potomac.

We were overjoyed to know that our men had won—yes, we certainly were happy. Well, the next morning everything was quiet. It was an unearthly quiet after all the uproar of the battle. The people who had taken refuge with us saw that the danger was over, and they scattered away to their homes. Father and I went out on the front pavement. We could see only a few citizens moving about, but pretty soon a Federal officer came cautiously around the corner by the church. He asked Father if any one was hurt in the town and said they had tried to avoid shelling it, and he was awful sorry they could n't help dropping an occasional shell among the houses.

I lost no time now in getting our flag from the ash heap so I could have it where it would be seen when our men marched into the town. I draped it on the front of the house, but I declare to goodness! I had to take that flag down. It made the officers think our house was a hotel, and they'd ride up, throw their reins to their orderlies, and come clanking up the steps with their swords and want something to eat. So I hurried to get it swung across the street, and after that, as the officers and men passed under it they all took off their hats. Their reverence for the flag was beautiful, and so was the flag.

I had a little flag in my hand, and while I was waving and waving it and cheering our victorious troops some prisoners marched by, and, bless your soul! among them I saw the very men who had demanded the big flag that was now suspended across the street. They looked at the flag and at me and shouted, "You said it was burned!" and they cursed me till some of our men drew their swords and quieted 'em down. "We'll settle with you when we come through here again," they called back, but they never came.

Our men were much cleaner and better fed than the Rebels, and their clothing was whole. The trains soon arrived with the hardtack, and there were baggage wagons and ambulances and everything. We had our men here with us quite a while camped in the town woods, and so constant was the coming and going of troops and army conveyances on the highways that we did n't get to speak to our neighbors across the street for weeks. Those were exciting times, but we felt safe. Of course there were some common, rough fellows among the soldiers, but as a general thing we found them very nice and we became much attached to them. When they went away it left us decidedly lonely here.

As for the day of the battle, it was tragic, but after the fighting was all over and I just sat and studied everything that had transpired a good deal was really laughable.

Well, the region was dreadfully torn to pieces by the conflict, but now you see no trace of it only the cemeteries.

“NOISE, CONFUSION, DUST”: VIRGINIA, SEPTEMBER 1862

Mary Bedinger Mitchell: A Woman’s Recollections of Antietam

Mary Bedinger was twelve years old at the time of Antietam and lived with her widowed mother and younger brother and sister in Shepherdstown, Virginia. Her reminiscences were published in 1887 in *Battles and Leaders of the Civil War*, having first appeared as “In the Wake of Battle” in the July 1886 *Century Magazine* under the pseudonym Maria Blunt.

SEPTEMBER, 1862, was in the skies of the almanac, but August still reigned in ours; it was hot and dusty. The railroads in the Shenandoah Valley had been torn up, the bridges had been destroyed, communication had been made difficult, and Shepherdstown, cornered by the bend of the Potomac, lay as if forgotten in the bottom of somebody’s pocket. We were without news or knowledge, except when some chance traveler would repeat the last wild and uncertain rumor that he had heard. We had passed an exciting summer. Winchester had changed hands more than once; we had been “in the Confederacy” and out of it again, and were now waiting, in an exasperating state of ignorance and suspense, for the next move in the great game.

It was a saying with us that Shepherdstown was just nine miles from everywhere. It was, in fact, about that distance from Martinsburg and Harper’s Ferry—oft-mentioned names—and from Williamsport, where the armies so often crossed, both to and from Maryland. It was off the direct road between those places and lay, as I said, at the foot of a great sweep in the river, and five miles from the nearest station on the Baltimore and Ohio railroad. As no trains were running now, this was of little consequence; what was more important was that a turnpike road—unusually fine for that region of stiff, red clay—led in almost a straight line for thirty miles to Winchester on the south, and stretched northward, beyond the Potomac, twenty miles to Hagerstown. Two years later it was the scene of "Sheridan's ride." Before the days of steam this had been part of the old posting-road between the Valley towns and Pennsylvania, and we had boasted a very substantial bridge. This had been burned early in the war, and only the massive stone piers remained; but a mile and a half down the Potomac was the ford, and the road that led to it lay partly above and partly along the face of rocky and precipitous cliffs. It was narrow and stony, and especially in one place, around the foot of "Mount Misery," was very steep and difficult for vehicles. It was, moreover, entirely commanded by the hills on the Maryland side, but it was the ford over which some part of the Confederate army passed every year, and in 1863 was used by the main body of infantry on the way to Gettysburg. Beyond the river were the Cumberland Canal and its willow-fringed tow-path, from which rose the soft and rounded outlines of the hills that from their farther slopes looked down upon the battle-field of Antietam. On clear days we could see the fort at Harper's Ferry without a glass, and the flag flying over it, a mere speck against the sky, and we could hear the gun that was fired every evening at sunset.

Shepherdstown's only access to the river was through a narrow gorge, the bed of a small tributary of the Potomac, that was made to do much duty as it slipped cheerily over its rocks and furnished power for several mills and factories, most of them at that time silent. Here were also three or four stone warehouses, huge empty structures, testifying mutely that the town had once had a business. The road to the bridge led through this cleft, down an indescribably steep street skirting the stream's ravine to whose sides the mills and factories clung in most extraordinary fashion; but it was always a marvel how anything heavier than a wheelbarrow could be pulled up its tedious length, or how any vehicle could be driven down without plunging into the water at the bottom.

In this odd little borough, then, we were waiting "developments," hearing first that "our men" were coming, and then that they were not coming, when suddenly, on Saturday, the 13th of September, early in the morning, we found ourselves surrounded by a hungry horde of lean and dusty tatterdemalions, who seemed to rise from the ground at our feet. I did not know where they came from, or to whose command they belonged; I have since been informed that General Jackson recrossed into Virginia at Williamsport, and hastened to Harper's Ferry by the shortest roads. These would take him some four miles south of us, and our haggard apparitions were perhaps a part of his force. They were stragglers, at all events,—professional, some of them, but some worn out by the incessant strain of that summer. When I say that they were hungry, I convey no impression of the gaunt starvation that looked from their cavernous eyes. All day they crowded to the doors of our houses, with always the same drawling complaint: "I've been a-marchin' an' a-fightin' for six weeks stiddy, and I ain't had n-a-r-thin' to eat 'cept green apples an' green cawn, an' I wish you'd please to gimme a bite to eat."

Their looks bore out their statements, and when they told us they had "clean gin out," we believed them, and went to get what we had. They could be seen afterward asleep in every fence corner, and under every tree, but after a night's rest they "pulled themselves together" somehow and disappeared as suddenly as they had come. Possibly they went back to their commands, possibly they only moved on to repeat the same tale elsewhere. I know nothing of numbers, nor what force was or was not engaged in any battle, but I saw the troops march past us every summer for four years, and I know something of the appearance of a marching army, both Union and Southern. There are always stragglers, of course, but never before or after did I see anything comparable to the demoralized state of the Confederates at this time. Never were want and exhaustion more visibly put before my eyes, and that they could march or fight at all seemed incredible.

As I remember, the next morning—it was Sunday, September 14th—we were awakened by heavy firing at two points on the mountains. We were expecting the bombardment of Harper's Ferry, and knew that Jackson was before it. Many of our friends were with him, and our interest there was so intense that we sat watching the bellowing and smoking Heights, for a long time, before we became aware that the same phenomena were to be noticed in the north. From our windows both points could be observed, and we could not tell which to watch more keenly. We knew almost nothing except that there was fighting, that it must be very heavy, and that our friends were surely in it somewhere, but whether at South Mountain or Harper's Ferry we had no means of discovering. I remember how the day wore on, how we staid at the windows until we could not endure the suspense; how we walked about and came back to them; and how finally, when night fell, it seemed cruel and preposterous to go to bed still ignorant of the result.

Monday afternoon, about 2 or 3 o'clock, when we were sitting about in disconsolate fashion, distracted by the contradictory rumors, our negro cook rushed into the room with eyes shining and face working with excitement. She had been down in "de ten-acre lot to pick a few years ob cawn," and she had seen a long train of wagons coming up from the ford, and "dey is full ob wounded men, and de blood runnin' outen dem dat deep," measuring on her outstretched arm to the shoulder. This horrible picture sent us flying to town, where we found the streets already crowded, the people all astir, and the foremost wagons, of what seemed an endless line, discharging their piteous burdens. The scene speedily became ghastly, but fortunately we could not stay to look at it. There were no preparations, no accommodations—the men could not be left in the street—what was to be done?

A Federal soldier once said to me, "I was always sorry for your wounded; they never seemed to get any care." The remark was extreme, but there was much justice in it. There was little mitigation of hardship to our unfortunate armies. We were fond of calling them Spartans, and they were but too truly called upon to endure a Spartan system of neglect and privation. They were generally ill-fed and ill-cared for. It would have been possible at this time, one would think, to send a courier back to inform the town and bespeak what comforts it could provide for the approaching wounded; but here they were, unannounced, on the brick pavements, and the first thing was to find roofs to cover them. Men ran for keys and opened the shops, long empty, and the unused rooms; other people got brooms and stirred up the dust of ages; then swarms of children began to appear with bundles of hay and straw, taken from anybody's stable. These were hastily disposed in heaps, and covered with blankets—the soldiers' own, or blankets begged or borrowed. On these improvised beds the sufferers were placed, and the next question was how properly to dress their wounds. No surgeons were to be seen. A few men, detailed as nurses, had come, but they were incompetent, of course. Our women set bravely to work and washed away the blood or stanched it as well as they could, where the jolting of the long rough ride had disarranged the hasty binding done upon the battle-field. But what did they know of wounds beyond a cut finger, or a boil? Yet they bandaged and bathed, with a devotion that went far to make up for their inexperience. Then there was the hunt for bandages. Every housekeeper ransacked her stores and brought forth things new and old. I saw one girl, in despair for a strip of cloth, look about helplessly, and then rip off the hem of her white petticoat. The doctors came up, by and by, or I suppose they did, for some amputating was done—rough surgery, you may be sure. The women helped, holding the instruments and the basins, and trying to soothe or strengthen. They stood to their work nobly; the emergency brought out all their strength to meet it.

One girl who had been working very hard helping the men on the sidewalks, and dressing wounds afterward in a close, hot room, told me that at one time the sights and smells (these last were fearful) so overcame her that she could only stagger to the staircase, where she hung, half conscious, over the banisters, saying to herself, "Oh, I hope if I faint some one will kick me into a corner and let me lie there!" She did not faint, but went back to her work in a few moments, and through the whole of what followed was one of the most indefatigable and useful. She was one of many; even children did their part.

It became a grave question how to feed so many unexpected guests. The news spread rapidly, and the people from the country neighborhoods came pouring in to help, expecting to stay with friends who had already given up every spare bed and every inch of room where beds could be put up. Virginia houses are very elastic, but ours were strained to their utmost. Fortunately some of the farmers' wives had been thoughtful enough to bring supplies of linen, and some bread and fruit, and when our wants became better known other contributions flowed in; but when all was done it was not enough.

We worked far into the night that Monday, went to bed late,

and rose early next morning. Tuesday brought fresh wagon-loads of wounded, and would have brought despair, except that they were accompanied by an apology for a commissariat. Soon more reliable sources of supply were organized among our country friends. Some doctors also arrived, who—with a few honorable exceptions—might as well have staid away. The remembrance of that worthless body of officials stirs me to wrath. Two or three worked conscientiously and hard, and they did all the medical work, except what was done by our own town physicians. In strong contrast was the conduct of the common men detailed as nurses. They were as gentle as they knew how to be, and very obliging and untiring. Of course they were uncouth and often rough, but with the wounded dying about us every day, and with the necessity that we were under for the first few days, of removing those who died at once that others not yet quite dead might take their places, there was no time to be fastidious; it required all our efforts to be simply decent, and we sometimes failed in that.

We fed our men as well as we could from every available source, and often had some difficulty in feeding ourselves. The townspeople were very hospitable, and we were invited here and there, but could not always go, or hesitated, knowing every house was full. I remember once, that having breakfasted upon a single roll and having worked hard among sickening details, about 4 o'clock I turned wolfishly ravenous and ran to a friend's house down the street. When I got there I was almost too faint to speak, but my friend looked at me and disappeared in silence, coming back in a moment with a plate of hot soup. What luxury! I sat down then and there on the front doorstep and devoured the soup as if I had been without food for a week.

It was known on Tuesday that Harper's Ferry had been taken, but it was growing evident that South Mountain had not been a victory. We had heard from some of our friends, but not from all, and what we did hear was often most unsatisfactory and tantalizing. For instance, we would be told that some one whom we loved had been seen standing with his battery, had left his gun an instant to shake hands and send a message, and had then stepped back to position, while our civilian informant had come away for safety, and the smoke of conflict had hidden battery and all from view. As night drew nearer, whispers of a great battle to be fought the next day grew louder, and we shuddered at the prospect, for battles had come to mean to us, as they never had before, blood, wounds, and death.

On the 17th of September cloudy skies looked down upon the two armies facing each other on the fields of Maryland. It seems to me now that the roar of that day began with the light, and all through its long and dragging hours its thunder formed a background to our pain and terror. If we had been in doubt as to our friends' whereabouts on Sunday, there was no room for doubt now. There was no sitting at the windows now and counting discharges of guns, or watching the curling smoke. We went about our work with pale faces and trembling hands, yet trying to appear composed for the sake of our patients, who were much excited. We could hear the incessant explosions of artillery, the shrieking whistles of the shells, and the sharper, deadlier, more thrilling roll of musketry; while every now and then the echo of some charging cheer would come, borne by the wind, and as the human voice pierced that demoniacal clangor we would catch our breath and listen, and try not to sob, and turn back to the forlorn hospitals, to the suffering at our feet and before our eyes, while imagination fainted at thought of those other scenes hidden from us beyond the Potomac.

On our side of the river there were noise, confusion, dust; throngs of stragglers; horsemen galloping about; wagons blocking each other, and teamsters wrangling; and a continued din of shouting, swearing, and rumbling, in the midst of which men were dying, fresh wounded arriving, surgeons amputating limbs and dressing wounds, women going in and out with bandages, lint, medicines, food. An ever-present sense of anguish, dread, pity, and, I fear, hatred—these are my recollections of Antietam.

When night came we could still hear the sullen guns and hoarse, indefinite murmurs that succeeded the day's turmoil. That night was dark and lowering and the air heavy and dull. Across the river innumerable camp-fires were blazing, and we could but too well imagine the scenes that they were lighting. We sat in silence, looking into each other's tired faces. There were no impatient words, few tears; only silence, and a drawing close together, as if for comfort. We were almost hopeless, yet clung with desperation to the thought that we were hoping. But in our hearts we could not believe that anything human could have escaped from that appalling fire. On Thursday the two armies lay idly facing each other, but we could not be idle. The wounded continued to arrive until the town was quite unable to hold all the disabled and suffering. They filled every building and overflowed into the country round, into farm-houses, barns, corn-cribs, cabins,—wherever four walls and a roof were found together. Those able to travel were sent on to Winchester and other towns back from the river, but their departure seemed to make no appreciable difference. There were six churches, and they were all full; the Odd Fellows' Hall, the Freemasons', the little Town Council room, the barn-like place known as the Drill Room, all the private houses after their capacity, the shops and empty buildings, the school-houses,—every inch of space, and yet the cry was for room.

The unfinished Town Hall had stood in naked ugliness for many a long day. Somebody threw a few rough boards across the beams, placed piles of straw over them, laid down single planks to walk upon, and lo, it was a hospital at once. The stone warehouses down in the ravine and by the river had been passed by, because low and damp and undesirable as sanitariums, but now their doors and windows were thrown wide, and, with barely time allowed to sweep them, they were all occupied,—even the "old blue factory," an antiquated, crazy, dismal building of blue stucco that peeled off in great blotches, which had been shut up for years, and was in the last stages of dilapidation.

On Thursday night we heard more than usual sounds of disturbance and movement, and in the morning we found the Confederate army in full retreat. General Lee crossed the Potomac under cover of the darkness, and when the day broke the greater part of his force—or the more orderly portion of it—had gone on toward Kearneysville and Leetown. General McClellan followed to the river, and without crossing got a battery in position on Douglas's Hill, and began to shell the retreating army and, in consequence, the town. What before was confusion grew worse; the retreat became a stampede. The battery may not have done a very great deal of execution, but it made a fearful noise. It is curious how much louder guns sound when they are pointed at you than when turned the other way! And the shell, with its long-drawn screeching, though no doubt less terrifying than the singing minie-ball, has a way of making one's hair stand on end. Then, too, every one who has had any experience in such things, knows how infectious fear is, how it grows when yielded to, and how, when you once begin to run, it soon seems impossible to run fast enough; whereas, if you can manage to stand your ground, the alarm lessens and sometimes disappears.

Some one suggested that yellow was the hospital color, and immediately everybody who could lay hands upon a yellow rag hoisted it over the house. The whole town was a hospital; there was scarcely a building that could not with truth seek protection under that plea, and the fantastic little strips were soon flaunting their ineffectual remonstrance from every roof-tree and chimney. When this specific failed the excitement became wild and ungovernable. It would have been ludicrous had it not produced so much suffering. The danger was less than it seemed, for McClellan, after all, was not bombarding the town, but the army, and most of the shells flew over us and exploded in the fields; but aim cannot be always sure, and enough shells fell short to convince the terrified citizens that their homes were about to be battered down over their ears. The better people kept some outward coolness, with perhaps a feeling of "*noblesse oblige*"; but the poorer classes acted as if the town were already in a blaze, and rushed from their houses with their families and household goods to make their way into the country. The road was thronged, the streets blocked; men were vociferating, women crying, children screaming; wagons, ambulances, guns, caissons, horsemen, footmen, all mingled—nay, even wedged and jammed together—in one struggling, shouting mass. The negroes were the worst, and with faces of a ghastly ash-color, and staring eyes, they swarmed into the fields, carrying their babies, their clothes, their pots and kettles, fleeing from the wrath behind them. The comparison to a hornet's nest attacked by boys is not a good one, for there was no "fight" shown; but a disturbed ant-hill is altogether inadequate. They fled widely and camped out of range, nor would they venture back for days.

Had this been all, we could afford to laugh now, but there was another side to the picture that lent it an intensely painful aspect. It was the hurrying crowds of wounded. Ah me! those maimed and bleeding fugitives! When the firing commenced the hospitals began to empty. All who were able to pull one foot after another, or could bribe or beg comrades to carry them, left in haste. In vain we implored them to stay; in vain we showed them the folly, the suicide, of the attempt; in vain we argued, cajoled, threatened, ridiculed; pointed out that we were remaining and that there was less danger here than on the road. There is no sense or reason in a panic. The cannon were bellowing upon Douglas's Hill, the shells whistling and shrieking, the air full of shouts and cries; we had to scream to make ourselves heard. The men replied that the "Yankees" were crossing; that the town was to be burned; that *we* could not be made prisoners, but they could; that, anyhow, they were going as far as they could walk, or be carried. And go they did. Men with cloths about their heads went hatless in the sun, men with cloths about their feet limped shoeless on the stony road; men with arms in slings, without arms, with one leg, with bandaged sides and backs; men in ambulances, wagons, carts, wheelbarrows, men carried on stretchers or supported on the shoulder of some self-denying comrade—all who could crawl went, and went to almost certain death. They could not go far, they dropped off into the country houses, where they were received with as much kindness as it was possible to ask for; but their wounds had become inflamed, their frames were weakened by fright and over-exertion: erysipelas, mortification, gangrene set in; and long rows of nameless graves still bear witness to the results.

Our hospitals did not remain empty. It was but a portion who could get off in any manner, and their places were soon taken by others, who had remained nearer the battle-field, had attempted to follow the retreat, but, having reached Shepherdstown, could go no farther. We had plenty to do, but all that day we went about with hearts bursting with rage and shame, and breaking with pity and grief for the needless, needless waste of life. The amateur nurses all stood firm, and managed to be cheerful for the sake of keeping their men quiet, but they could not be without fear. One who had no thought of leaving her post desired to send her sister—a mere child—out of harm's way. She, therefore, told her to go to their home, about half a mile distant, and ask their mother for some yellow cloth that was in the house, thinking, of course, that the mother would never permit the girl to come back into the town. But she miscalculated. The child accepted the commission as a sacred trust, forced her way out over the crowded road, where the danger was more real than in the town itself, reached home, and made her request. The house had its own flag flying, for it was directly in range and full of wounded. Perhaps for this reason the mother was less anxious to keep her daughter with her; perhaps in the hurry and excitement she allowed herself to be persuaded that it was really necessary to get that strip of yellow flannel into Shepherdstown as soon as possible. At all events, she made no difficulty, but with streaming tears kissed the girl, and saw her set out to go alone, half a mile through a panic-stricken rabble, under the fire of a battery and into a town whose escape from conflagration was at best not assured. To come out had been comparatively easy, for she was going with the stream. The return was a different matter. The turbulent tide had now to be stemmed. Yet she managed to work her way along, now in the road, now in the field, slipping between the wagon wheels, and once, at least, crawling under a stretcher. No one had noticed her coming out, she was but one of the crowd; and now most were too busy with their own safety to pay much heed to anything else. Still, as her face seemed alone set toward the town, she attracted some attention. One or two spoke to her. Now it was, "Look-a here, little gal! don't you know you're a-goin' the wrong way?" One man looked at the yellow thing she had slung across her shoulder and said, with an approving nod: "That's right, that's right; save the wounded if ye kin." She meant to do it, and finally reached her sister, breathless but triumphant, with as proud a sense of duty done as if her futile errand had been the deliverance of a city.

I have said that there was less danger than appeared, but it must not be supposed that there was none. A friend who worked chiefly in the old blue factory had asked me to bring her a bowl of gruel that some one had promised to make for one of her patients. I had just taken it to her, and she was walking across the floor with the bowl in her hands, when a shell crashed through a corner of the wall and passed out at the opposite end of the building, shaking the rookery to its foundations, filling the room with dust and plaster, and throwing her upon her knees to the floor. The wounded screamed, and had they not been entirely unable to move, not a man would have been left in the building. But it was found that no one was hurt, and things proceeded as before. I asked her afterward if she was frightened. She said yes, when it was over, but her chief thought at the time was to save the gruel, for the man needed it, and it had been very hard to find any one composed enough to make it. I am glad to be able to say that he got his gruel in spite of bombs. That factory was struck twice. A school-house, full of wounded, and one or two other buildings were hit, but I believe no serious damage was done.

On Saturday morning there was a fight at the ford. The negroes were still encamped in the fields, though some, finding that the town was yet standing, ventured back on various errands during the day. What we feared were the stragglers and hangers-on and nondescripts that circle round an army like the great buzzards we shuddered to see wheeling silently over us. The people were still excited, anticipating the Federal crossing and dreading a repetition of the bombardment or an encounter in the streets. Some parties of Confederate cavalry rode through, and it is possible that a body of infantry remained drawn up in readiness on one of the hills during the morning, but I remember no large force of troops at any time on that day.

About noon, or a little after, we were told that General McClellan's advance had been checked, and that it was not believed he would attempt to cross the river at once—a surmise that proved to be correct. The country grew more composed. General Lee lay near Leetown, some seven miles south of us, and General McClellan rested quietly in Maryland. On Sunday we were able to have some short church services for our wounded, cut still shorter, I regret to say, by reports that the "Yankees" were crossing. Such reports continued to harass us, especially as we feared the capture of our friends, who would often ride down to see us during the day, but who seldom ventured to spend a night so near the river. We presently passed into debatable land, when we were in the Confederacy in the morning, in the Union after dinner, and on neutral ground at night. We lived through a disturbed and eventful autumn, subject to continual "alarms and excursions," but when this Saturday came to an end, the most trying and tempestuous week of the war for Shepherdstown was over.

"OUR VICTORY WAS COMPLETE": MARYLAND, SEPTEMBER 1862

George B. McClellan to Mary Ellen McClellan

General McClellan expresses to his wife his pride in repelling an enemy he believed greatly outnumbered him. In fact, he overcounted Lee's troops by a factor of three. The meeting of twelve Northern governors at Altoona, Pennsylvania, in late September that McClellan hoped would help rid him of Secretary Stanton and General Halleck had a quite different outcome: it came close to passing a resolution recommending his dismissal.

Sept 20 8 am. Camp near Sharpsburg

. . . Yesterday the enemy completed his evacuation of Maryland —completely beaten—we got many prisoners, muskets, colors, cannon etc—his loss in killed & wounded was very great—so was ours, unfortunately.

Genl Mansfield was killed (or rather died of his wounds)—Genls Sedgwick, Richardson, Dana, Brooks, Hooker, Weber, Rodman—& two others whose names I cannot recall were wounded on Wednesday. Poor Henry Kingsbury died of his wounds the day after the battle.

The battle lasted 14 hours & was without doubt the most severe ever fought on this continent, & few more desperate were ever fought anywhere.

9 am. . . . Am glad to say that I am much better today—for to tell you the truth I have been under the weather since the battle—the want of rest & anxiety brought on my old disease. The battle of Wednesday *was* a terrible one. I presume the loss will prove not less than 10,000 on each side. Our victory was complete & the disorganized rebel army has rapidly returned to Virginia—its dreams of "invading Penna" dissipated for ever. I feel some little pride in having with a beaten and demoralized army defeated Lee so utterly, & saved the North so completely. Well—one of these days history will I

trust do me justice in deciding that it was not my fault that the campaign of the Peninsula was not successful. An opportunity has presented itself through the Governors of some of the states to enable me to take my stand—I have insisted that Stanton shall be removed & that Halleck shall give way to me as Comdr in Chief. I will *not* serve under him—for he is an incompetent fool—in no way fit for the important place he holds. Since I left Washn Stanton has again asserted that *I* not *Pope* lost the battle of Manassas No 2! The only safety for the country & for me is to get rid of both of them—no success is possible with them. I am tired of fighting against such disadvantages & feel that it is now time for the country to come to my help, & remove these difficulties from my path. If my countrymen will not open their eyes & assert themselves they must pardon me if I decline longer to pursue the thankless avocation of serving them. . . .

Thank Heaven for one thing—my military reputation is cleared—I have shown that I can fight battles & *win* them! I think my enemies are pretty effectively killed by this time! May they remain so!!

September 20, 1862

Ephraim Anderson: from Memoirs: Historical and Personal

After a cautious monthlong advance from the Shiloh battlefield, Union forces occupied Corinth, Mississippi, on May 30, gaining control of a major rail junction. In the hot, dry summer that followed, the Union armies commanded by Ulysses S. Grant and William S. Rosecrans (who succeeded John Pope when Pope went east) occupied northern Mississippi and western Tennessee, repairing and guarding railroads against guerrillas and cavalry raids. Don Carlos Buell, meanwhile, began slowly advancing eastward toward Chattanooga. In September Braxton Bragg began his invasion of Kentucky and ordered Sterling Price, the Confederate commander in northern Mississippi, to prevent Rosecrans from reinforcing Buell. On September 19 Price and 14,000 Confederates fought 9,000 men under Rosecrans south of Iuka, Mississippi, while another Union force under Edward O. C. Ord approached the town from the west. The battle ended on September 20 when Price retreated after losing 1,516 men killed, wounded, or missing; Union losses totaled 782. Corporal Ephraim Anderson of the Confederate 2nd Missouri Infantry recalled the battle in his 1868 memoir.

OUR BRIGADE was soon drawn up about two hundred yards in the rear of the line engaged; our regiment had several men wounded while forming, when we laid down, expecting every moment that our line in front, which had been engaged for some time, and was now fighting almost muzzle to muzzle, would in all probability be overwhelmed by superior numbers, and we would then confront the enemy's lines.

The sun, like a molten ball of fire, hung just above the horizon, and was falling slowly behind a faint streak of crimson clouds low in the west. The fighting on our part was up a gentle slope of thickly timbered land, and extended on into an old field in front, upon the most of which a dense growth of blackjack had sprung up, from seven to fifteen feet high. In the cleared ground upon this field a battery had been charged and taken by our troops at the very muzzles of the pieces; but the infantry gave back step by step, stubbornly clinging to the cover of the bushes, and only leaving their pieces behind after the most desperate struggle to save them.

There was no intermission in the fierceness of the combat until after dark: the Third Louisiana and Third Texas, dismounted cavalry, armed with double-barreled shot-guns, and using buck-shot at close range, assisted by the Seventeenth Arkansas and another regiment, also, I believe, from Arkansas, pressed steadily on and drove the enemy slowly before them. When the fighting ceased for the night, our lines were over two hundred yards in advance of the position occupied by the captured battery, and all the ground that had been fought over was in our possession.

A little after dark our brigade was ordered to the front, to relieve the command that had been fighting: as we advanced up the road we met several detachments rolling down the Federal artillery; among those engaged in this service were some of our acquaintances of the Texas company that had assisted us on provost duty; their regiment had charged in front of the battery and was badly cut to pieces.

The artillery captured was of the best, as fine as is ever found upon the field; the pieces were entirely new and had never been in action before: it was the Tenth Ohio battery from Cincinnati, containing ten guns, and was supported by a division of Ohio troops.

Proceeding to the front, upon the ground where the hardest fighting had been done, the brigade formed, and our company was thrown out at a short distance as pickets and skirmishers, covering the line of the regiment. One of our detachment stepped accidentally upon a wounded soldier, who was lying upon the ground and spoke out—"Don't tread on me." He was asked, "What regiment do you belong to?"

"The Thirty-ninth Ohio."

"How many men has Rosecrans here?"

"Near forty-five thousand."

A little Irishman of our party curtly observed, "Our sixty-five thousand are enough for them."

The moon was nearly full, and threw a strong light upon the pale and ghastly faces of the thickly strewn corpses, while it glanced and sparkled upon the polished gun-barrels and bright sword bayonets of the enemy's guns, which lay scattered around. Everything bore evidence of the bloody character of the action. The dead were so thick, that one could very readily have stepped about upon them, and the bushes were so lapped and twisted together—so tangled up and broken down in every conceivable manner, that the desperate nature of the struggle was unmistakable.

The carnage around the battery was terrible. I do not think a single horse escaped, and most of the men must have shared the same fate. One of the caissons was turned upside down, having fallen back upon a couple of the horses, one of which lay wounded and struggling under it; and immediately behind was a pile of not less than fifteen men, who had been killed and wounded while sheltering themselves there. They were all Federals, and most of them artillery-men. Some of the limbers were standing with one wheel in the air, and strewn thickly around all were the bloody corpses of the dead, while the badly wounded lay weltering in gore. I have been on many battle-fields, but never witnessed so small a space comprise as many dead as were lying immediately around this battery.

That night is well remembered as one marked by many conflicting emotions. Though already much hardened to the rough usages of war and the fearful events which inevitably accompany it—though somewhat accustomed to look upon the faces of the dead and fields of carnage as certain and natural results, yet the groans and cries of the wounded for help and water, the floundering of crippled horses in harness, and the calls of the infirmary corps, as it passed to and fro with litters in search of and bearing off the wounded, rendered the scene very gloomy, sad and impressive. As the night wind rose and fell, swelling with louder, wilder note, or sinking into a gentle, wailing breath, it seemed an invocation from the ghosts of the dead, and a requiem to the departing spirits of the dying.

There were few grey-coats among the dead around, and I gazed upon the blue ones with the feeling that they had come from afar and taken much pains to meet such a fate. It was but little akin to compassion, for war hardens men—especially when their country, their homes and firesides are invaded and laid waste.

Only a few feet from me a groan escaped the lips of a dying man, and I stepped to his side to offer the slight relief that my situation could afford. He was lying almost upon his face, with a thick covering of the bruised bushes twisted over him. Putting them aside, I spoke to him, and turned him in a more comfortable position. He was unable to speak, but looked as though he wanted something, and I placed my canteen to his lips, from which he eagerly drank. After this an effort to speak was made: he could only murmur something inarticulate and unintelligible, and at the same time a look of intense gratitude spread over his countenance. He was a Federal officer, as was easily perceived from his sword, dress and shoulder-straps. Some of the infirmary corps soon passed, and I asked them if they had any brandy or could do anything for him. Their answer was that he was too far gone to lose time with, and their brandy had given out. A few minutes after, he died.

A wounded soldier some distance off, hallooed at intervals until after midnight, repeatedly calling, "Caldwell guards!"—the name of his company, which belonged to the Third Louisiana. The regiment had gone to the rear. I could not leave my post to go to his assistance, and his cries ceased after midnight. Whether he received attention in time or died unnoticed where he had fallen, I never knew.

From our picket lines to those of the Federals it was not more than seventy yards, and at some points even nearer. One of our company unguardedly struck a match to light his pipe, when several shots were immediately fired at him without effect. This was the only firing through the night, and the blaze from the enemy's guns was but a little distance in the brush beyond us.

It seemed certain that a general engagement would take place on the morrow, and our brigade would occupy the post of honor—the front of the line. Though the enemy had a decided advantage in point of numbers, yet our troops were in admirable condition and their spirit was buoyant, fearless, and in every way promising. We were not, however, destined to fight the next morning, and, as the shades of night began to break into faint streaks of approaching day, we were withdrawn slowly from the field.

"THE CAUSE OF EMANCIPATION": WASHINGTON, D.C., SEPTEMBER 1862

Gideon Welles: Diary, September 22, 1862

Appraising the outcome at Antietam as victory enough for his purposes, Lincoln called together his cabinet to announce he was making the proclamation of emancipation public. Secretary Chase noted in his journal that the President opened the momentous occasion by reading a chapter from humorist Artemus Ward's new book, "and seemed to enjoy it very much—the Heads also (except Stanton) of course. . . . The President then took a graver tone. . . ."

September 22. *Monday* A special Cabinet meeting. The subject was the Proclamation for emancipating the slaves after a certain date, in States that should be in rebellion. For several weeks the subject has been suspended, but never lost sight of. When it was submitted, and in taking up the Proclamation, the President stated that the question was finally decided, the act and the consequences were his, but that he felt it due to us to make us acquainted with the fact and to invite criticism on the paper which he had prepared. There were, he had found, some differences in the Cabinet, but he had, after consulting each and all, individually and collectively, formed his own conclusions and made his own decision. In the course of the discussion which was long, earnest, and on the general principle involved, harmonious, he remarked that he had made a vow, a covenant, that if God gave us the victory in the approaching battle, he would consider it an indication of Divine will, and that it was his duty to move forward in the cause of emancipation. It might be thought strange, he said, that he had in this way submitted the disposal of matters—when the way was not clear to his mind what he should do. God had decided this question in favor of the slaves. He was satisfied it was right, was confirmed and strengthened in his action by the vow and the results. His mind was fixed, his decision made, but he wished his paper announcing his course as correct in terms as it could be made without any change in his determination.

He read the document. One or two unimportant emendations suggested by Seward were approved. It was handed to the Secretary of State to publish to-morrow. After this, Blair remarked that he did not concur in the expediency of the measure at this time, though he approved of the principle, and should therefore wish to file his objections. He stated at some length his views, which were that we ought not to put in greater jeopardy the patriotic element in the Border States, that the results of this Proclamation would be to carry over those States *en masse* to the Secessionists as soon as it was read, and that there was a class of partisans in the Free States endeavoring to revive old parties, who would have a club put into their hands of which they would avail themselves to beat the Administration.

The President said he had considered the danger to be apprehended from the first objection, which was undoubtedly serious, but the objection was certainly as great not to act; as regarded the last, it had not much weight with him. The question of power, authority in the Government was not much discussed at this meeting, but had been canvassed individually by the President in private conversation with the members. Some thought legislation advisable but Congress was clothed with no authority on this subject, nor is the Executive, except under the war power,—military necessity, martial law, when there can be no legislation. This was the view which I took when the President first presented the subject to Seward and myself as we were returning from the funeral of Stanton's child, which we attended—two or three miles beyond Georgetown. Seward was at that time not at all communicative, and I think not willing to advise the movement. It is momentous both in its immediate and remote results, and an exercise of extraordinary power, which cannot be justified on mere humanitarian principles, and would never have been attempted but to preserve the national existence. These were my convictions and this the drift of the discussion.

The effect which the Proclamation will have on the public mind is a matter of some uncertainty. In some respects, it would, I think have been better to have issued it when formerly considered. There is an impression that Seward has opposed and is opposed to the measure. I have not been without that impression chiefly from his hesitation to commit himself, and perhaps because action was suspended but in the final discussion he has as cordially supported the measure as Chase.

For myself the subject has, from its magnitude and its consequences oppressed me, aside from the ethical features of the question. It is a step in the progress of this war which will extend into the distant future. The termination of this terrible conflict seems more remote with every movement, and unless the Rebels hasten to avail themselves of the alternative presented, of which I see little probability, the war can scarcely be other than one of subjugation. There is in the Free States a very general impression that this measure will insure a speedy peace. I cannot say that I so view it. No one in those States dare advocate peace as a means of prolonging slavery if it is his honest opinion, and the pecuniary, industrial and social sacrifice impending will intensify the struggle before us. While however these dark clouds are above and around us, I cannot see how the subject could be avoided. Perhaps it is not desirable it should be.

WASHINGTON, D.C., SEPTEMBER 1862

Abraham Lincoln: Preliminary Emancipation Proclamation; Proclamation Suspending the Writ of Habeas Corpus

While incorporating provisions of the Second Confiscation Act, the Emancipation Proclamation was drawn primarily on the president's war powers, which Lincoln interpreted as not authorizing him to free slaves in loyal states. Thus the proclamation applied only to those states in rebellion, where the Union armies had to be depended upon to free the slaves. The proclamation suspending the writ of habeas corpus nationwide was occasioned in part by resistance to the militia draft instituted in the summer of 1862 to help fill state militia regiments called up for nine months' service. Both proclamations were denounced as unconstitutional exercises of executive power by anti-administration Democrats in the fall elections.

September 22, 1862

By the President of the
United States of America
A Proclamation.

I, Abraham Lincoln, President of the United States of America, and Commander-in-chief of the Army and Navy thereof, do hereby proclaim and declare that hereafter, as heretofore, the war will be prossecuted for the object of practically restoring the constitutional relation between the United States, and each of the states, and the people thereof, in which states that relation is, or may be suspended, or disturbed.

That it is my purpose, upon the next meeting of Congress to again recommend the adoption of a practical measure tendering pecuniary aid to the free acceptance or rejection of all slave-states, so called, the people whereof may not then be in rebellion against the United States, and which states, may then have voluntarily adopted, or thereafter may voluntarily adopt, immediate, or gradual abolishment of slavery within their respective limits; and that the effort to colonize persons of African descent, with their consent, upon this continent, or elsewhere, with the previously obtained consent of the Governments existing there, will be continued.

That on the first day of January in the year of our Lord, one thousand eight hundred and sixty-three, all persons held as slaves within any state, or designated part of a state, the people whereof shall then be in rebellion against the United States shall be then, thenceforward, and forever free; and the executive government of the United States, including the military and naval authority thereof, will recognize and maintain the freedom of such persons, and will do no act or acts to repress such persons, or any of them, in any efforts they may make for their actual freedom.

That the executive will, on the first day of January aforesaid, by proclamation, designate the States, and parts of states, if any, in which the people thereof respectively, shall then be in rebellion against the United States; and the fact that any state, or the people thereof shall, on that day be, in good faith represented in the Congress of the United States, by members chosen thereto, at elections wherein a majority of the qualified voters of such state shall have participated, shall, in the absence of strong countervailing testimony, be deemed conclusive evidence that such state and the people thereof, are not then in rebellion against the United States.

That attention is hereby called to an act of Congress entitled "An act to make an additional Article of War" approved March 13, 1862, and which act is in the words and figure following:

Be it enacted by the Senate and House of Representatives of the United States of America in Congress assembled, That hereafter the following shall be promulgated as an additional article of war for the government of the army of the United States, and shall be obeyed and observed as such:

Article—. All officers or persons in the military or naval service of the United States are prohibited from employing any of the forces under their respective commands for the purpose of returning fugitives from service or labor, who may have escaped from any persons to whom such service or labor is claimed to be due, and any officer who shall be found guilty by a court-martial of violating this article shall be dismissed from the service.

SEC. 2. *And be it further enacted,* That this act shall take effect from and after its passage.

Also to the ninth and tenth sections of an act entitled "An Act to suppress Insurrection, to punish Treason and Rebellion, to seize and confiscate property of rebels, and for other purposes," approved July 17, 1862, and which sections are in the words and figures following:

SEC. 9. *And be it further enacted,* That all slaves of persons who shall hereafter be engaged in rebellion against the government of the United States, or who shall in any way give aid or comfort thereto, escaping from such persons and taking refuge within the lines of the army; and all slaves captured from such persons or deserted by them and coming under the control of the government of the United States; and all slaves of such persons found *on* (or) being within any place occupied by rebel forces and afterwards occupied by the forces of the United States, shall be deemed captives of war, and shall be forever free of their servitude and not again held as slaves.

SEC. 10. *And be it further enacted,* That no slave escaping into any State, Territory, or the District of Columbia, from any other State, shall be delivered up, or in any way impeded or hindered of his liberty, except for crime, or some offence against the laws, unless the person claiming said fugitive shall first make oath that the person to whom the labor or service of such fugitive is alleged to be due is his lawful owner, and has not borne arms against the United States in the present rebellion, nor in any way given aid and comfort thereto; and no person engaged in the military or naval service of the United States shall, under any pretence whatever, assume to decide on the validity of the claim of any person to the service or labor of any other person, or surrender up any such person to the claimant, on pain of being dismissed from the service.

And I do hereby enjoin upon and order all persons engaged in the military and naval service of the United States to observe, obey, and enforce, within their respective spheres of service, the act, and sections above recited.

And the executive will in due time recommend that all citizens of the United States who shall have remained loyal thereto throughout the rebellion, shall (upon the restoration of the constitutional relation between the United States, and their respective states, and people, if that relation shall have been suspended or disturbed) be compensated for all losses by acts of the United States, including the loss of slaves.

In witness whereof, I have hereunto set my hand, and caused the seal of the United States to be affixed.

Done at the City of Washington, this twenty second day of September, in the year of our Lord, one thousand eight hundred and sixty two, and of the Independence of the United States, the eighty seventh.

By the President: ABRAHAM LINCOLN

WILLIAM H. SEWARD, Secretary of State.

September 24 1862

By the President of the United States of America:
A Proclamation.

Whereas, it has become necessary to call into service not only volunteers but also portions of the militia of the States by draft in order to suppress the insurrection existing in the United States, and disloyal persons are not adequately restrained by the ordinary processes of law from hindering this measure and from giving aid and comfort in various ways to the insurrection;

Now, therefore, be it ordered, first, that during the existing insurrection and as a necessary measure for suppressing the same, all Rebels and Insurgents, their aiders and abettors within the United States, and all persons discouraging volunteer enlistments, resisting militia drafts, or guilty of any disloyal practice, affording aid and comfort to Rebels against the authority of the United States, shall be subject to martial law and liable to trial and punishment by Courts Martial or Military Commission:

Second. That the Writ of Habeas Corpus is suspended in respect to all persons arrested, or who are now, or hereafter during the rebellion shall be, imprisoned in any fort, camp, arsenal, military prison, or other place of confinement by any military authority or by the sentence of any Court Martial or Military Commission.

In witness whereof, I have hereunto set my hand, and caused the seal of the United States to be affixed.

Done at the City of Washington this twenty fourth day of September, in the year of our Lord one thousand eight hundred and sixty-two, and of the Independence of the United States the 87th.

By the President: ABRAHAM LINCOLN.

WILLIAM H. SEWARD, Secretary of State.

"THE AIR IS THICK WITH REVOLUTION": WASHINGTON, D.C., SEPTEMBER 1862

L. A. Whitely to James Gordon Bennett

Whitely was chief Washington correspondent for editor Bennett's *New York Herald*, the nation's largest newspaper, and he, like other reporters (and not a few generals), hastened to evaluate reactions to the President's emancipation decree in the highly politicized Army of the Potomac. The army was in the field, in Maryland, and Whitely wondered if its officers felt the same as the ones he spoke to in the capital.

Confidential

Washington Sep 24" 1862

My dear Sir

A deep and earnest feeling pervades the army, if we are to judge from the Generals, Colonels, Captains and Lieutenants who are here, in reference to the recent proclamation of the President. The army is dissatisfied and the air is thick with revolution. It has been not only thought of but talked of and the question now is where can the man be found. McClellan is idolised but he seems to have no political ambition. The sentiment throughout the whole army seems to be in favor of a change of dynasty. They are unwilling to submit to the control of the faction which has attempted to direct the Government and whose policy is enunciated in the recent proclamation. They demur to this policy and claim that as they are fighting the battles, risking their lives and limbs and really stand as the conservators of all there is in the Government they have a right to dictate its policy. God knows what will be the consequence but at present matters look dark indeed, and there is large promise of a fearful revolution which will sweep before it not only the administration but popular government. As I telegraphed you in one of my despatches, Kentuckians here approve the President's Proclamation. They say that sooner or later it will have to come and I have been strongly importuned by such men as Cassius M. Clay to give, at once, an earnest and hearty support to the policy thus enunciated. I have no doubt that the result will be as Abolitionists desire: Slavery is already practically abolished but the Proclamation is a different affair and if it should not be received more kindly by other Officers of the Army than those whom I have seen it will go far towards producing an expression on the part of the Army that will startle the Country and give us a Military Dictator.

I send this information only as the result of my observations during the last twenty four hours in order that you may know what is to be the condition of affairs here if the expression from the Army of McClellan corresponds to that of the position of the army around Washington. There may be a change in the Government and in the form of Government within a very few days. Your article of a few days ago suggesting that McClellan should dictate to the administration was regarded then as revolutionary, but I have heard a hundred of the same men, who then found fault with it, express today the same opinion.

Very Respectfully
L.A. Whitely

"SERVILE WAR" AND "DESPOTISM": MARYLAND, SEPTEMBER 1862

George B. McClellan to William H. Aspinwall

Correspondent Whitely thought General McClellan not political enough to consider taking a public stance against the two proclamations, but this letter of McClellan's to one of his home front supporters, New York businessman and prominent Democrat William H. Aspinwall, suggests otherwise.

Head-Quarters Army of the Potomac,
Sharpsburg Sept 26, 1862

My dear Sir

I am very anxious to know how you and men like you regard the recent Proclamations of the Presdt inaugurating servile war, emancipating the slaves, & at one stroke of the pen changing our free institutions into a despotism—for such I regard as the natural effect of the last Proclamation suspending the Habeas Corpus throughout the land.

I shall probably be in this vicinity for some days &, if you regard the matter as gravely as I do, would be glad to communicate with you.

In haste I am sincerely yours
Geo B McClellan

Wm H Aspinwall esq
New York City

“THAT IS NOT THE GAME”:
WASHINGTON, D.C., SEPTEMBER 1862

Abraham Lincoln: Record of Dismissal of John J. Key

In this time of alarming unrest in the Army of the Potomac, Lincoln was told of an allegedly treasonable remark by Major John J. Key, of the War Department staff, and he determined to act on it. The President carefully wrote out this record of the case. Afterward, when Key appealed his dismissal, Lincoln refused to restore him to duty, explaining: “I had been brought to fear that there was a class of officers in the army, not very inconsiderable in numbers, who were playing a game to not beat the enemy when they could. . . . I dismissed you as an example and a warning to that supposed class.”

September 26–27, 1862

We have reason to believe that the following is an exact copy of the record upon which Major John J. Key was dismissed from the military service of the United States.

Executive Mansion

Major John J. Key Washington, Sept. 26. 1862.

Sir: I am informed that in answer to the question “Why was not the rebel army bagged immediately after the battle near Sharpsburg?” propounded to you by Major Levi C. Turner, Judge Advocate &c. you answered “That is not the game” “The object is that neither army shall get much advantage of the other; that both shall be kept in the field till they are exhausted, when we will make a compromise and save slavery.”

I shall be very happy if you will, within twentyfour hours from the receipt of this, prove to me by Major Turner, that you did not, either litterally, or in substance, make the answer stated. Yours,

A. LINCOLN

(Indorsed as follows)

"Copy delivered to Major Key at 10.25 A.M. September 27th. 1862.

JOHN HAY."

At about 11 o'clock, A.M. Sept. 27. 1862, Major Key and Major Turner appear before me. Major Turner says: "As I remember it, the conversation was, I asked the question why we did not bag them after the battle at Sharpsburg? Major Key's reply was that was not the game, that we should tire the rebels out, and ourselves, that that was the only way the Union could be preserved, we come together fraternally, and slavery be saved"

On cross-examination, Major Turner says he has frequently heard Major Key converse in regard to the present troubles, and never heard him utter a sentiment unfavorable to the maintainance of the Union. He has never uttered anything which he Major T. would call disloyalty. The particular conversation detailed was a private one A. LINCOLN.

(Indorsed on the above)

In my view it is wholly inadmissable for any gentleman holding a military commission from the United States to utter such sentiments as Major Key is within proved to have done. Therefore let Major John J. Key be forthwith dismissed from the Military service of the United States. A. LINCOLN.

The foregoing is the whole record, except the simple order of dismissal at the War Department. At the interview of Major Key and Major Turner with the President, Major Key did not attempt to controvert the statement of Major Turner; but simply insisted, and sought to prove, that he was true to the Union. The substance of the President's reply was that if there was a "game" ever among Union men, to have our army not take an advantage of the enemy when it could, it was his object to break up that game.

"PROCLAMATIONS OF A POLITICAL COWARD": MARYLAND, SEPTEMBER 1862

Fitz John Porter to Manton Marble

General Porter, acting as McClellan's confidant and spokesman, corresponded regularly with *New York World* editor Manton Marble, whose paper was a major Democratic anti-administration voice. Here Porter explains why there was no follow-up to the Antietam battle (falling back on the myth of being outnumbered), and projects his view of the Emancipation Proclamation as the army's view.

(*Excuse brevity* and conciseness)

September 30" '62

My dear friend,

My frequent change of location, together with the irregularity of the mails which I believe are made up in Washington, have deprived me of the pleasures always received for the perusal of your sheets—and kept me in darkness for the past month. I see however from quotations in the Clipper and Phil. Enquirer (the only ones which have reached this benighted region) that you still hammer away at the good cause, relying I presume upon the old simile that the continued dripping of water will wear away stone. But don't you suppose that some of the late orders fulminated at the War Department are aimed at such as you, and fear that some dark morning you will find yourself in Lafayette for being guilty of disloyal practices, of which some ignorant constable is the judge?

I have been expecting daily to hear that the "World" has been upset and eclipsed and no longer permitted to reflect the light of the sun and enlighten the darkened masses of abolitionists, secessionists and other enemies of their country. But you have been spared, no doubt for a good purpose.

You have no doubt been much gratified at our successes, and the rise once more of Genl McClellan. He appreciates the services of the World and the kind sympathy it has extended to him in times of darkness. You have no doubt also been anxious for a continued advance and pursuit of the enemy—and as the radicals say, smite him. T'is easier said than done, but as there *seems* to be a misunderstanding of matters here I will give you (though perhaps unnecessary) our status and the reasons therefor.

First—What was one of the first causes of the rebels having been whipped in Maryland. Because they passed the Potomac and got so far from his base of supplies that starvation had accomplished half the victory.

When he recrossed the Potomac, so difficult was it for us to go and form sufficient head on the opposite bank (having difficult and narrow fords) that he stopped just beyond reach of our guns and yet so close that he could rush upon and annihilate any force before it was half over just as was done at Ball's Bluff, while the other half could render no assistance.

Again we could get insufficient supplies over the river from Frederick and Hagerstown to sustain this army, and of course we would be committing the same blunder as they did, and in two days be half whipped while they, getting nearer their base, would be growing stronger.

They selected a beautiful position behind the Opequon, every foot of which was well swept by them, and every bridge over which was destroyed.

The bridge at Harpers Ferry is not completed and will not be for five or six days. Until then the rail road will be of no use to our one half the army this side of Frederick. When that is completed you may expect a resumption of operations. It will enable supplies to be thrown to Charlestown & towards Martinsburg. But the enemy will not then be at Winchester, or will not be there long. He will try to draw us on. Knowing we would not operate till the R.R. bridge is complete, he leisurely halted at Martinsburg, permitted all his trains to get behind him towards Winchester and has moved off himself in time not to permit us to strike him so soon. Had we crossed in full force at Harpers Ferry or Shepherdstown ford, we would have had to leave Wmport unguarded and Hagerstown and he would have walked into that depot with considerable gusto, and into the B & O. rail road, which is now safe—also the canal.

Now for another material reason. This army is (or was not) in a condition to renew the contest. On Wednesday the 17th Inst. General Sumner who has ever been one of the most anxious to fight declared "his command demoralized and scattered—that he could not risk another attack—but if Genl McClellan was willing to risk a total defeat if he failed, he would advance." So much alarmed was he for his portion of the line, that over one third of my little force (6500) was sent to support him. On Thursday he was opposed to a renewal of the attack and so I believe were other officers. Our artillery ammunition was nearly expended and was not renewed till Friday. A large portion of this army was composed of recruits—new regiments, and Wednesdays fighting had proved they could not be relied upon—and that the loss of General officers and others on whom the troops looked to lead them, had caused want of confidence.

He had then lost about 10000 men in killed and wounded and some 10000 in stragglers. We were much less than the acknowledged strength of the enemy. The battles though apparently easily gained in the first instance were not so, and made many of the troops very cautious, and *slow*, in some cases culpably slow. We are now doing all we can to recover our losses and establish discipline and good drill. One week will do much, but we must re-organize. We must have some good officers—new general officers for those disabled—and confidence must be restored. We want troops to fill up the ranks of our small old regiments. The Governors give us none, and the government has sent no new regiments to us. A promise of 20 new regts is given. How long will it be before fulfilled. Long enough to cause delay and the delay attributed to Genl McClellan.

The fact that no one but political aspirants, and those strongly favoring the party of the administration, can attain favor is producing its effect. The proclamation was ridiculed in the army—caused disgust, discontent, and expressions of disloyalty to the views of the administration, and amounting I have heard, to insubordination. And for this reason. All such bulletins tend only to prolong the war by rousing the bitter feelings of the South—and causing unity of action among them—while the reverse with us. Those who have to fight the battles of the country are tired of the war and wish to see it ended and honorably, by a restoration of the Union. Not merely a suppression of the rebellion—for there is a wide difference, though the President would fain make us think by his working for a "suppression of the rebellion" that they are one & the same. How is this rebellion to be put down except by hard fighting, and who is to do it. We—and who are the sufferers. Look at the number of high officers wounded & killed in the late battles. Without their individual efforts no success would have been attained. As soon as they fell fighting ceased. The army rested on its arms. So it has been in every battle. Every officer of standing and worth must expose himself to an unprecedented degree—without he does so, nothing is accomplished. If he is wounded, all fall with him. He strives to end the contest & finds politicians working to prolong it. All his efforts, all his dangers, are useless. His labor is upset by the absurd proclamation of a political coward, who has not the manliness to sustain opinions expressed but a few days before, and can unblushingly see published side by side, his proclamation and his reasons for not issuing it. What a ruler for us to admire! Yet he holds in his hands the lives of thousands and trifles with them. Surely every father, mother, brother, sister, and friend at home should remember this and when an Election comes exert themselves to hurl such s______ls from power and restore their relatives to their places. I believe God in his own particular way will punish these wicked rulers and abettors and bring peace to our country in due time. I believe you have full faith in Genl Halleck. I have never known a hypocrite to succeed—nor one who worked for his own ends alone—nor one who professed strong friendship and acted the Enemy—who played the part of Iago. Nor will Halleck. I told you long since he would fall. I expected it earlier, because I expected Stanton to fall, both for the same reason—they deserved it—both have brought all our disasters upon us, in Virginia & Kentucky, and soon I expect to hear of another—that is the crushing of a force which I fear they will throw towards Manassas to interrupt the retreat of the enemy from Winchester. A force they will throw there in the hope the leader will be successful and become prominent over McClellan. I fear they will do this and take from Washington good defensive forces and put in the field to oppose veterans, a raw army—undisciplined, not drilled—and ignorant of their officers and of themselves. If that is done, Lee will suddenly turn his back upon us, as Joe Johnston did on Patterson, and rush to Manassas to wipe out the pride of the north. There will we be—like Patterson—unable to follow, too far to move around by Washington, and accused of treachery to cover the want of skill of those in authority. We suffered once for the mismanagement of Pope and the following such councils as his and Hallecks, and the country was near ruin. Are we to be so again? Watch the movements.

I hope for peace, but I do not see it in the course of the administration or of its supporters the radical elements at the north. I see but one course to "suppress this rebellion and restore the Union." Military matters must be left to the control of him who knows his business and been tried, and politics must not enter therein. We must overcome the armies opposed to us. In doing that we crush or destroy the military, and many of the political, leaders who keep alive the rebellion. We must scatter and break the army, and let the constituent elements (now tired of the war) return to their homes, where by a consistent just and firm policy we can soon make them through the ballot box, express their opinions and assume their rights. We must occupy their seaport towns & cities and by the blockade make them suffer. Hold their cities and counties by military power compel the inhabitants to defray all expenses of the civil functionaries placed over them to execute their own laws as far as applicable and show by a conservative reign, that there is no intention to oppress. In this way I believe the opinion of the people will be softened, the poor enlightened and a new reign established, and before summer returns, peace reign over all the country. But on our part—the part of those at the North—must be done. The monied men, the capitalists (the power now behind the throne) must declare their policy, their demands & they must be a conservative political policy—a military General-in-Chief who is honest and in whom they have confidence—exclusion of politics from the military sphere—support by continued reinforcements when the General-in-Chief shall want them—Energetic prosecution of the task assigned to each commander, and the removal of such men as Mitchell & Butler. In this way the army will penetrate farther into the interior, and one object of the Radicals (professed?) the extinction of slavery more effectually accomplished, for where the army goes slavery disappears. Such men as Stanton Chase and Halleck must be got rid of, and such conservative men—honest and energetic in the prosecution of the war—as Dix & Banks substituted. They can be found.

To day, October 3d I have seen many troops under arms—mine I have been watching and working at for a time, yet I see gross deficiencies. Troops anxious to be instructed are commanded by ignorant men, who have seen no service, and in some cases whole regiments have not one officer who has seen service, because Secretary Stanton published an order that no volunteer would be permitted to leave the Army of the Potomac to assume positions more elevated in the new regiments. At that time the officers would have made many friends for Genl McClellan and proclaimed opinions prejudicial to the Sec of War. Jealousy prevented the promotion of meritorious men, and now the country should thank him for inefficient regiments and inefficient officers. Regiments which have been in service months are as green in all their duties and more innocent of their drill than regiments under experienced officers of three weeks standing. Did Sec Stanton wish an effective army? Did he, and does he, wish to put down this rebellion at an early day, or is he combined with the radical members of the north to prolong it. I should be very loth to go into action with such troops, but if advance now is the order, go I will and we will do our best. I feel we shall be victorious but it will be at great loss. But two weeks will make a wonderful difference. Why dont our governors encourage the filling up the old regiments. The men are discouraged. They get no increase. Every battle reduces their numbers and the men think the next one will be their last. They would not feel so if the regiments were full. They would feel too more could be accomplished. They say the Governors are raising their power to the injury of these men, and when the chance offers they will make the powers that be suffer. There are many causes working in the army to break down the power and influence of the ruling authorities in states. No wonder the radicals wish not for peace. They read the handwriting on the wall and know they are doomed.

The R R bridge over the Potomac is completed. I know not what will be done immediately—if anything. I hope however ere long we can move & will move and that the rebels will be compelled to go south of Richmond, and we be there. A combined movement all over the country by land & sea will crush the rebellion—but it must be done under McClellan's mind—not the present chief—and I think t'will be well done if directed by him. I would like to see Banks in the War Dept, to work with Genl. McC. He is firm, thoughtful, energetic, pure and honest—a patriot. I intended to have given you some interesting items of Popes campaign (or as he declares, the campaign of President & Halleck) but I've been too prolix now. T'will take a week to read this. So good by till you hear of a defeat off yonder or a victory here.

The course of the administration is shaking some of the officers. Sumner has asked for a leave of absence, and is inclined to resign. He is getting old, has been promised command of a department, but does not get it—while such as Mitchell, Curtis & Butler do. Hooker is working for promotion to the General-in-Chief and will turn a somerset to get it. He will soon gone north, or will go. Watch him. He has been a professed friend of Genl McC. He will say what the radicals will state is against McC. or draw inferences which discredit. He is ambitious & unscrupulous. The President is here. His visits have been always followed by injury, so look out. Another proclamation or War Order. Good by till next year—The enemy have only a few men in front of us, and stretch with 8000 men (cvly) from Bunker Hill through Stevensons Station to Berry's.

A CONFEDERATE INVASION:
KENTUCKY, SEPTEMBER 1862

Braxton Bragg: To the People of the Northwest

In the western theater two Confederate armies, under Edmund Kirby Smith and Braxton Bragg, invaded Kentucky in August. Bragg issued this proclamation four days after occupying Bardstown, thirty miles south of Louisville. He had twin hopes for his proclamation—to split off the northwestern states from the Union through economic arguments; and to rouse Democratic voters in the midterm elections. "A plain, unvarnished argument based on their interests I presumed would have the most effect," Bragg explained to President Davis. But Bragg would find little support and few recruits in the Bluegrass State. "Enthusiasm runs high," he told Davis, "but exhausts itself in words."

HEADQUARTERS C. S. ARMY IN KENTUCKY,
Bardstown, Ky., September 26, 1862.

To the PEOPLE OF THE NORTHWEST:

On approaching your borders at the head of a Confederate army, it is proper to announce to you the motives and the purposes of my presence. I therefore make known to you—

First. That the Confederate Government is waging this war solely for self-defense; that it has no designs of conquest, nor any other purpose than to secure peace and the abandonment by the United States of its pretensions to govern a people who never have been their subjects, and who prefer self-government to a union with them.

Second. That the Confederate Government and people, deprecating civil strife from the beginning and anxious for a peaceful adjustment of all difference growing out of a political separation which they deemed essential to their happiness and well-being, at the moment of its inauguration sent commissioners to Washington to treat for these objects, but that their commissioners were not received or even allowed to communicate the object of their mission; and that on a subsequent occasion a communication from the President of the Confederate States to President Lincoln remained without answer, although a reply was promised by General Scott, into whose hands the communication was delivered.

Third. That among the pretexts urged for the continuance of the war is the assertion that the Confederate Government desires to deprive the United States of the free navigation of the Western rivers, although the truth is that the Confederate Congress, by public act, prior to the commencement of the war, enacted that "the peaceful navigation of the Mississippi River is hereby declared free to the citizens of any of the States upon its borders, or upon the borders of its tributaries," a declaration to which our Government has always been and is still ready to adhere.

From these declarations, people of the Northwest, it is made manifest that, by the invasion of our territories by land and from sea, we have been unwillingly forced into a war for self-defense, and to vindicate a great principle, once dear to all Americans, to wit, that no people can be rightly governed except by their own consent. We desire peace now. We desire to see a stop put to a useless and cruel effusion of blood and that waste of national wealth rapidly leading to, and sure to end in, national bankruptcy. We are, therefore, now, as ever, ready to treat with the United States, or any one or more of them, on terms of mutual justice and liberality. And at this juncture, when our arms have been successful on many hard-fought fields; when our people have exhibited a constancy, a fortitude, and a courage worthy of the boon of self-government, we restrict ourselves to the same moderate demands that we made at the darkest period of our reverses—the demand that the people of the United States cease to war upon us and permit us in peace to pursue our path to happiness, while they in peace pursue theirs. We are, however, debarred from the renewal of former proposals for peace, because the relentless spirit that actuates the Government at Washington leaves us no reason to expect that they would be received with the respect naturally due by nations in their intercourse, whether in peace or war.

It is under these circumstances that we are driven to protect our own country by transferring the seat of war to that of an enemy who pursues us with an implacable and apparently aimless hostility. If the war must continue, its theater must be changed, and with it the policy that has heretofore kept us on the defensive on our own soil. So far, it is only our fields that have been laid waste, our people killed, our homes made desolate, and our frontiers ravaged by rapine and murder. The sacred right of self-defense demands that henceforth some of the consequences of the war shall fall upon those who persist in their refusal to make peace. With the people of the Northwest rests the power to put an end to the invasion of their homes, for, if unable to prevail upon the Government of the United States to conclude a general peace, their own State governments, in the exercise of their sovereignty, can secure immunity from the desolating effects of warfare on their soil by a separate treaty of peace, which our Government will be ready to conclude on the most just and liberal basis.

The responsibility, then, rests with you, the people of the Northwest, of continuing an unjust and aggressive warfare upon the people of the Confederate States. And in the name of reason and humanity I call upon you to pause and reflect what cause of quarrel so bloody have you against these States, and what are you to gain by it. Nature has set her seal upon these States and marked them out to be your friends and allies. She has bound them to you by all the ties of geographical contiguity and conformation and the great mutual interests of commerce and productions. When the passions of this unnatural war shall have subsided and reason resumes her sway, a community of interest will force commercial and social coalition between the great grain and stock growing States of the Northwest and the cotton, tobacco, and sugar regions of the South. The Mississippi River is a grand artery of their mutual national lives which men cannot sever, and which never ought to have been suffered to be disturbed by the antagonisms, the cupidity, and the bigotry of New England and the East. It is from the East that have come the germs of this bloody and most unnatural strife. It is from the meddlesome, grasping, and fanatical disposition of the same people who have imposed upon you and us alike those tariffs, internal-improvement, and fishing-bounty laws whereby we have been taxed for their aggrandizement. It is from the East that will come the tax-gatherer to collect from you the mighty debt which is being amassed mountain high for the purpose of ruining your best customers and natural friends.

When this war ends, the same antagonisms of interest, policy, and feeling which have been pressed upon us by the East, and forced us from a political union where we had ceased to find safety for our interests or respect for our rights, will bear down upon you and separate you from a people whose traditional policy it is to live by their wits upon the labor of their neighbors. Meantime you are being used by them to fight the battle of emancipation, a battle which, if successful, destroys our prosperity, and with it your best markets to buy and sell. Our mutual dependence is the work of the Creator. With our peculiar productions, convertible into gold, we should, in a state of peace, draw from you largely the products of your labor. In us of the South you would find rich and willing customers. In the East you must confront rivals in productions and trade, and the tax-gatherer in all the forms of partial legislation. You are blindly following abolitionism to this end, whilst they are nicely calculating the gain of obtaining your trade on terms that would impoverish your country. You say you are fighting for the free navigation of the Mississippi. It is yours, freely, and has always been, without striking a blow. You say you are fighting to maintain the Union. That Union is a thing of the past. A union of consent was the only union ever worth a drop of blood. When force came to be substituted for consent, the casket was broken and the constitutional jewel of your patriotic adoration was forever gone.

I come, then, to you with the olive branch of peace, and offer it to your acceptance in the name of the memories of the past and the ties of the present and future. With you remains the responsibility and the option of continuing a cruel and wasting war, which can only end, after still greater sacrifices, in such treaty of peace as we now offer, or of preserving the blessings of peace by the simple abandonment of the design of subjugating a people over whom no right of dominion has been conferred on you by God or man.

BRAXTON BRAGG,
General, C. S. Army.

"AN EVENT WORTH THE DREADFUL WAR": MASSACHUSETTS, SEPTEMBER 1862

Ralph Waldo Emerson: The President's Proclamation

September 1862

In January 1862 the poet-philosopher Ralph Waldo Emerson, a dedicated abolitionist, had given a lecture on the theme "Emancipation is the demand of civilization." He delivered an address on Lincoln's proclamation in Boston in late September and published it in the November 1862 *Atlantic Monthly*.

IN so many arid forms which States incrust themselves with, once in a century, if so often, a poetic act and record occur. These are the jets of thought into affairs, when, roused by danger or inspired by genius, the political leaders of the day break the else insurmountable routine of class and local legislation, and take a step forward in the direction of catholic and universal interests. Every step in the history of political liberty is a sally of the human mind into the untried future, and has the interest of genius, and is fruitful in heroic anecdotes. Liberty is a slow fruit. It comes, like religion, for short periods, and in rare conditions, as if awaiting a culture of the race which shall make it organic and permanent. Such moments of expansion in modern history were the Confession of Augsburg, the plantation of America, the English Commonwealth of 1648, the Declaration of American Independence in 1776, the British emancipation of slaves in the West Indies, the passage of the Reform Bill, the repeal of the Corn-Laws, the Magnetic Ocean-Telegraph, though yet imperfect, the passage of the Homestead Bill in the last Congress, and now, eminently, President Lincoln's Proclamation on the twenty-second of September. These are acts of great scope, working on a long future, and on permanent interests, and honoring alike those who initiate and those who receive them. These measures provoke no noisy joy, but are received into a sympathy so deep as to apprise us that mankind are greater and better than we know. At such times it appears as if a new public were created to greet the new event. It is as when an orator, having ended the compliments and pleasantries with which he conciliated attention, and having run over the superficial fitness and commodities of the measure he urges, suddenly, lending himself to some happy inspiration, announces with vibrating voice the grand human principles involved,—the bravoes and wits who greeted him loudly thus far are surprised and overawed: a new audience is found in the heart of the assembly,—an audience hitherto passive and unconcerned, now at last so searched and kindled that they come forward, every one a representative of mankind, standing for all nationalities.

The extreme moderation with which the President advanced to his design,—his long-avowed expectant policy, as if he chose to be strictly the executive of the best public sentiment of the country, waiting only till it should be unmistakably pronounced, —so fair a mind that none ever listened so patiently to such extreme varieties of opinion,—so reticent that his decision has taken all parties by surprise, whilst yet it is the just sequel of his prior acts,—the firm tone in which he announces it, without inflation or surplusage,—all these have bespoken such favor to the act, that, great as the popularity of the President has been, we are beginning to think that we have underestimated the capacity and virtue which the Divine Providence has made an instrument of benefit so vast. He has been permitted to do more for America than any other American man. He is well entitled to the most indulgent construction. Forget all that we thought shortcomings, every mistake, every delay. In the extreme embarrassments of his part, call these endurance, wisdom, magnanimity, illuminated, as they now are, by this dazzling success.

When we consider the immense opposition that has been neutralized or converted by the progress of the war, (for it is not long since the President anticipated the resignation of a large number of officers in the army, and the secession of three States, on the promulgation of this policy,)—when we see how the great stake which foreign nations hold in our affairs has recently brought every European power as a client into this court, and it became every day more apparent what gigantic and what remote interests were to be affected by the decision of the President,—one can hardly say the deliberation was too long. Against all timorous counsels he had the courage to seize the moment; and such was his position, and such the felicity attending the action, that he has replaced Government in the good graces of mankind. "Better is virtue in the sovereign than plenty in the season," say the Chinese. 'T is wonderful what power is, and how ill it is used, and how its ill use makes life mean, and the sunshine dark. Life in America had lost much of its attraction in the later years. The virtues of a good magistrate undo a world of mischief, and, because Nature works with rectitude, seem vastly more potent than the acts of bad governors, which are ever tempered by the good-nature in the people, and the incessant resistance which fraud and violence encounter. The acts of good governors work at a geometrical ratio, as one midsummer day seems to repair the damage of a year of war.

A day which most of us dared not hope to see, an event worth the dreadful war, worth its costs and uncertainties, seems now to be close before us. October, November, December will have passed over beating hearts and plotting brains: then the hour will strike, and all men of African descent who have faculty enough to find their way to our lines are assured of the protection of American law.

It is by no means necessary that this measure should be suddenly marked by any signal results on the negroes or on the Rebel masters. The force of the act is that it commits the country to this justice,—that it compels the innumerable officers, civil, military, naval, of the Republic to range themselves on the line of this equity. It draws the fashion to this side. It is not a measure that admits of being taken back. Done, it cannot be undone by a new Administration. For slavery overpowers the disgust of the moral sentiment only through immemorial usage. It cannot be introduced as an improvement of the nineteenth century. This act makes that the lives of our heroes have not been sacrificed in vain. It makes a victory of our defeats. Our hurts are healed; the health of the nation is repaired. With a victory like this, we can stand many disasters. It does not promise the redemption of the black race: that lies not with us:

but it relieves it of our opposition. The President by this act has paroled all the slaves in America; they will no more fight against us; and it relieves our race once for all of its crime and false position. The first condition of success is secured in putting ourselves right. We have recovered ourselves from our false position, and planted ourselves on a law of Nature.

> "If that fail,
> The pillared firmament is rottenness,
> And earth's base built on stubble."

The Government has assured itself of the best constituency in the world: every spark of intellect, every virtuous feeling, every religious heart, every man of honor, every pest, every philosopher, the generosity of the cities, the health of the country, the strong arms of the mechanics, the endurance of farmers, the passionate conscience of women, the sympathy of distant nations,—all rally to its support.

Of course, we are assuming the firmness of the policy thus declared. It must not be a paper proclamation. We confide that Mr. Lincoln is in earnest, and, as he has been slow in making up his mind, has resisted the importunacy of parties and of events to the latest moment, he will be as absolute in his adhesion. Not only will he repeat and follow up his stroke, but the nation will add its irresistible strength. If the ruler has duties, so has the citizen. In times like these, when the nation is imperilled, what man can, without shame, receive good news from day to day, without giving good news of himself? What right has any one to read in the journals tidings of victories, if he has not bought them by his own valor, treasure, personal sacrifice, or by service as good in his own department? With this blot removed from our national honor, this heavy load lifted off the national heart, we shall not fear henceforward to show our faces among mankind. We shall cease to be hypocrites and pretenders, but what we have styled our free institutions will be such.

In the light of this event the public distress begins to be removed. What if the brokers' quotations show our stocks discredited, and the gold dollar costs one hundred and twenty-seven cents? These tables are fallacious. Every acre in the Free States gained substantial value on the twenty-second of

September. The cause of disunion and war has been reached, and begun to be removed. Every man's house-lot and garden are relieved of the malaria which the purest winds and the strongest sunshine could not penetrate and purge. The territory of the Union shines to-day with a lustre which every European emigrant can discern from far: a sign of inmost security and permanence. Is it feared that taxes will check immigration? That depends on what the taxes are spent for. If they go to fill up this yawning Dismal Swamp, which engulfed armies and populations, and created plague, and neutralized hitherto all the vast capabilities of this continent,—then this taxation, which makes the land wholesome and habitable, and will draw all men unto it, is the best investment in which property-holder ever lodged his earnings.

Whilst we have pointed out the opportuneness of the Proclamation, it remains to be said that the President had no choice. He might look wistfully for what variety of courses lay open to him: every line but one was closed up with fire. This one, too, bristled with danger, but through it was the sole safety. The measure he has adopted was imperative. It is wonderful to see the unseasonable senility of what is called the Peace party, through all its masks, blinding their eyes to the main feature of the war, namely, its inevitableness. The war existed long before the cannonade of Sumter, and could not be postponed. It might have begun otherwise or elsewhere, but war was in the minds and bones of the combatants, it was written on the iron leaf, and you might as easily dodge gravitation. If we had consented to a peaceable secession of the Rebels, the divided sentiment of the Border States made peaceable secession impossible, the insatiable temper of the South made it impossible, and the slaves on the border, wherever the border might be, were an incessant fuel to rekindle the fire. Give the Confederacy New Orleans, Charleston, and Richmond, and they would have demanded St. Louis and Baltimore. Give them these, and they would have insisted on Washington. Give them Washington, and they would have assumed the army and navy, and, through these, Philadelphia, New York, and Boston. It looks as if the battle-field would have been at least as large in that event as it is now. The war was formidable, but could not be avoided. The war was and is an immense mischief, but brought with it the immense benefit of drawing a line, and rallying the Free States to fix it impassably,—preventing the whole force of Southern connection and influence throughout the North from distracting every city with endless confusion, detaching that force and reducing it to handfuls, and, in the progress of hostilities, disinfecting us of our habitual proclivity, through the affection of trade, and the traditions of the Democratic party, to follow Southern leading.

These necessities which have dictated the conduct of the Federal Government are overlooked, especially by our foreign critics. The popular statement of the opponents of the war abroad is the impossibility of our success. "If you could add," say they, "to your strength the whole army of England, of France, and of Austria, you could not coerce eight millions of people to come under this Government against their will." This is an odd thing for an Englishman, a Frenchman, or an Austrian to say, who remembers the Europe of the last seventy years,—the condition of Italy, until 1859,—of Poland, since 1793,—of France, of French Algiers,—of British Ireland, and British India. But, granting the truth, rightly read, of the historical aphorism, that "the people always conquer," it is to be noted, that, in the Southern States, the tenure of land, and the local laws, with slavery, give the social system not a democratic, but an aristocratic complexion; and those States have shown every year a more hostile and aggressive temper, until the instinct of self-preservation forced us into the war. And the aim of the war on our part is indicated by the aim of the President's Proclamation, namely, to break up the false combination of Southern society, to destroy the piratic feature in it which makes it our enemy only as it is the enemy of the human race, and so allow its reconstruction on a just and healthful basis. Then new affinities will act, the old repulsions will cease, and, the cause of war being removed, Nature and trade may be trusted to establish a lasting peace.

We think we cannot overstate the wisdom and benefit of this act of the Government. The malignant cry of the Secession press within the Free States, and the recent action of the Confederate Congress, are decisive as to its efficiency and correctness of aim. Not less so is the silent joy which has greeted it in all generous hearts, and the new hope it has breathed into the world.

It was well to delay the steamers at the wharves, until this edict could be put on board. It will be an insurance to the ship as it goes plunging through the sea with glad tidings to all people. Happy are the young who find the pestilence cleansed out of the earth, leaving open to them an honest career. Happy the old, who see Nature purified before they depart. Do not let the dying die: hold them back to this world, until you have charged their ear and heart with this message to other spiritual societies, announcing the melioration of our planet.

"Incertainties now crown themselves assured,
And Peace proclaims olives of endless age."

Meantime that ill-fated, much-injured race which the Proclamation respects will lose somewhat of the dejection sculptured for ages in their bronzed countenance, uttered in the wailing of their plaintive music,—a race naturally benevolent, joyous, docile, industrious, and whose very miseries sprang from their great talent for usefulness, which, in a more moral age, will not only defend their independence, but will give them a rank among nations.

"YOUR DELIVERANCE DRAWS NIGH!": OCTOBER 1862

Frederick Douglass: Emancipation Proclaimed

October 1862

Douglass believed emancipation long overdue, yet his welcome for Lincoln's action was wholehearted. He published this analysis in his journal *Douglass' Monthly.*

EMANCIPATION PROCLAIMED

Common sense, the necessities of the war, to say nothing of the dictation of justice and humanity have at last prevailed. We shout for joy that we live to record this righteous decree. *Abraham Lincoln*, President of the United States, Commander-in-Chief of the army and navy, in his own peculiar, cautious, forbearing and hesitating way, slow, but we hope sure, has, while the loyal heart was near breaking with despair, proclaimed and declared: "*That on the First of January, in the Year of Our Lord One Thousand, Eight Hundred and Sixty-three, All Persons Held as Slaves Within Any State or Any Designated Part of a State, The People Whereof Shall Then be in Rebellion Against the United States, Shall be Thenceforward and Forever Free.*" "Free forever" oh! long enslaved millions, whose cries have so vexed the air and sky, suffer on a few more days in sorrow, the hour of your deliverance draws nigh! Oh! Ye millions of free and loyal men who have earnestly sought to free your bleeding country from the dreadful ravages of revolution and anarchy, lift up now your voices with joy and thanksgiving for with freedom to the slave will come peace and safety to your country. President Lincoln has embraced in this proclamation the law of Congress passed more than six months ago, prohibiting the employment of any part of the army and naval forces of the United States, to return fugitive slaves to their masters, commanded all officers of the army and navy to respect and obey its provisions. He has still further declared his intention to urge upon the Legislature of all the slave States not in rebellion the immediate or gradual abolishment of slavery. But read the proclamation for it is the most important of any to which the President of the United States has ever signed his name.

Opinions will widely differ as to the practical effect of this measure upon the war. All that class at the North who have not lost their affection for slavery will regard the measure as the very worst that could be devised, and as likely to lead to endless mischief. All their plans for the future have been projected with a view to a reconstruction of the American Government upon the basis of compromise between slaveholding and non-slaveholding States. The thought of a country unified in sentiments, objects and ideas, has not entered into their political calculations, and hence this newly declared policy of the Government, which contemplates one glorious homogeneous people, doing away at a blow with the whole class of compromisers and corrupters, will meet their stern opposition. Will that opposition prevail? Will it lead the President to reconsider and retract? Not a word of it. Abraham Lincoln may be slow, Abraham Lincoln may desire peace even at the price of leaving our terrible national sore untouched, to fester on for generations, but Abraham Lincoln is not the man to reconsider, retract and contradict words and purposes solemnly proclaimed over his official signature.

The careful, and we think, the slothful deliberation which he has observed in reaching this obvious policy, is a guarantee against retraction. But even if the temper and spirit of the President himself were other than what they are, events greater than the President, events which have slowly wrung this proclamation from him may be relied on to carry him forward in the same direction. To look back now would only load him with heavier evils, while diminishing his ability, for overcoming those with which he now has to contend. To recall his proclamation would only increase rebel pride, rebel sense of power and would be hailed as a direct admission of weakness on the part of the Federal Government, while it would cause heaviness of heart and depression of national enthusiasm all over the loyal North and West. No, Abraham Lincoln will take no step backward. His word has gone out over the country and the world, giving joy and gladness to the friends of freedom and progress wherever those words are read, and he will stand by them, and carry them out to the letter. If he has taught us to confide in nothing else, he has taught us to confide in his word. The want of Constitutional power, the want of military power, the tendency of the measure to intensify Southern hate, and to exasperate the rebels, the tendency to drive from him all that class of Democrats at the North, whose loyalty has been conditioned on his restoring the union as it was, slavery and all, have all been considered, and he has taken his ground notwithstanding. The President doubtless saw, as we see, that it is not more absurd to talk about restoring the union, without hurting slavery, than restoring the union without hurting the rebels. As to exasperating the South, there can be no more in the cup than the cup will hold, and that was full already. The whole situation having been carefully scanned, before Mr. Lincoln could be made to budge an inch, he will now stand his ground. Border State influence, and the influence of half-loyal men, have been exerted and have done their worst. The end of these two influences is implied in this proclamation. Hereafter, the inspiration as well as the men and the money for carrying on the war will come from the North, and not from half-loyal border States.

The effect of this paper upon the disposition of Europe will be great and increasing. It changes the character of the war in European eyes and gives it an important principle as an object, instead of national pride and interest. It recognizes and declares the real nature of the contest, and places the North on the side of justice and civilization, and the rebels on the side of robbery and barbarism. It will disarm all purpose on the part of European Government to intervene in favor of the rebels and thus cast off at a blow one source of rebel power. All through the war thus far, the rebel ambassadors in foreign countries have been able to silence all expression of sympathy with the North as to slavery. With much more than a show of truth, they said that the Federal Government, no more than the Confederate Government, contemplated the abolition of slavery.

But will not this measure be frowned upon by our officers and men in the field? We have heard of many thousands who have resolved that they will throw up their commissions and lay down their arms, just so soon as they are required to carry on a war against slavery. Making all allowances for exaggeration there are doubtless far too many of this sort in the loyal army. Putting this kind of loyalty and patriotism to the test, will be one of the best collateral effects of the measure. Any man who leaves the field on such a ground will be an argument in favor of the proclamation, and will prove that his heart has been more with slavery than with his country. Let the army be cleansed from all such proslavery vermin, and its health and strength will be greatly improved. But there can be no reason to fear the loss of many officers or men by resignation or desertion. We have no doubt that the measure was brought to the attention of most of our leading Generals, and blind as some of them have seemed to be in the earlier part of the war, most of them have seen enough to convince them that there can be no end to this war that does not end slavery. At any rate, we may hope that for every pro-slavery man that shall start from the ranks of our loyal army, there will be two anti-slavery men to fill up the vacancy, and in this war one truly devoted to the cause of Emancipation is worth two of the opposite sort.

Whether slavery will be abolished in the manner now proposed by President Lincoln, depends of course upon two conditions, the first specified and the second implied. The first is that the slave States shall be in rebellion on and after the first day of January 1863 and the second is we must have the ability to put down that rebellion. About the first there can be very little doubt. The South is thoroughly in earnest and confident. It has staked everything upon the rebellion. Its experience thus far in the field has rather increased its hopes of final success than diminished them. Its armies now hold us at bay at all points, and the war is confined to the border States slave and free. If Richmond were in our hands and Virginia at our mercy, the vast regions beyond would still remain to be subdued. But the rebels confront us on the Potomac, the Ohio, and the Mississippi. Kentucky, Maryland, Missouri, and Virginia are in debate on the battlefields and their people are divided by the line which separates treason from loyalty. In short we are yet, after eighteen months of war, confined to the outer margin of the rebellion. We have scarcely more than touched the surface of the terrible evil. It has been raising large quantities of food during the past summer. While the masters have been fighting abroad, the slaves have been busy working at home to supply them with the means of continuing the struggle. They will not down at the bidding of this Proclamation, but may be safely relied upon till January and long after January. A month or two will put an end to general fighting for the winter. When the leaves fall we shall hear again of bad roads, winter quarters and spring campaigns. The South which has thus far withstood our arms will not fall at once before our pens. All fears for the abolition of slavery arising from this apprehension may be dismissed. Whoever, therefore, lives to see the first day of next January, should Abraham Lincoln be then alive and President of the United States, may confidently look in the morning papers for the final proclamation, granting freedom, and freedom forever, to all slaves within the rebel States. On the next point nothing need be said. We have full power to put down the rebellion. Unless one man is more than a match for four, unless the South breeds braver and better men than the North, unless slavery is more precious than liberty, unless a just cause kindles a feebler enthusiasm than a wicked and villainous one, the men of the loyal States will put down this rebellion and slavery, and all the sooner will they put down that rebellion by coupling slavery with that object. Tenderness towards slavery has been the loyal weakness during the war. Fighting the slaveholders with one hand and holding the slaves with the other, has been fairly tried and has failed. We have now inaugurated a wiser and better policy, a policy which is better for the loyal cause than an hundred thousand armed men. The Star Spangled Banner is now the harbinger of Liberty and the millions in bondage, inured to hardships, accustomed to toil, ready to suffer, ready to fight, to dare and to die, will rally under that banner wherever they see it gloriously unfolded to the breeze. Now let the Government go forward in its mission of Liberty as the only condition of peace and union, by weeding out the army and navy of all such officers as the late Col. Miles, whose sympathies are now known to have been with the rebels. Let only the men who assent heartily to the wisdom and the justice of the anti-slavery policy of the Government be lifted into command; let the black man have an arm as well as a heart in this war, and the tide of battle which has thus far only waved backward and forward, will steadily set in our favor. The rebellion suppressed, slavery abolished, and America will, higher than ever, sit as a queen among the nations of the earth.

Now for the work. During the interval between now and next January, let every friend of the long enslaved bondman do his utmost in swelling the tide of anti-slavery sentiment, by writing, speaking, money and example. Let our aim be to make the North a unit in favor of the President's policy, and see to it that our voices and votes, shall forever extinguish that latent and malignant sentiment at the North, which has from the first cheered on the rebels in their atrocious crimes against the union, and has systematically sought to paralyze the national arm in striking down the slaveholding rebellion. We are ready for this service or any other, in this, we trust the last struggle with the monster slavery.

Debate in the Confederate Senate on Retaliation for the Emancipation Proclamation

When the Confederate Senate adjourned on October 13 it adopted a resolution declaring support for whatever retaliatory measures Jefferson Davis chose to adopt. In a proclamation of December 23, 1862, outlawing Union general Benjamin F. Butler, Davis denounced the Emancipation Proclamation as an "effort to excite servile war" and ordered Union officers captured while leading freed slaves to be turned over to state authorities for trial.

SEVERAL propositions under the form of bills, were introduced into the Senate respecting retaliatory measures. These propositions were brought forward in consequence of the proclamation of President Lincoln, issued on the 22d of September, declaring that on the 1st of January ensuing an emancipation proclamation would be issued. The subject came up for the first time on the 29th of Sept., when Mr. Semmes, of Louisiana, offered the following resolution:

Resolved by the Congress of the Confederate States, That the proclamation of Abraham Lincoln, President of the United States of America, issued in the city of Washington, in the year 1862, wherein he declares "that on the first day of January, in the year of our Lord 1863, all persons held as slaves within any State, or designated parts of a State, whereof the people shall be in rebellion against the United States shall be henceforth and forever free," is levelled against the citizens of the Confederate States, and as such is a gross violation of the usuages of civilized warfare, an outrage on the rights of private property, and an invitation to an atrocious servile war, and therefore should be held up to the execration of mankind, and counteracted by such retaliatory measures as in the judgment of the President may be best calculated to secure its withdrawal or arrest its execution.

Mr. Clark, of Missouri, moved that the resolution be referred to the Committee on Foreign Affairs. He was in favor of declaring every citizen of the Southern Confederacy a soldier, authorized to put to death every man caught on our soil in arms against the Government.

Mr. Semmes, of Louisiana, said that the resolution had not been drawn without reflection. The question of retaliation was exclusively an Executive one, to be regulated by circumstances. But it was proper that the legislative department of the Government should express its approval of the retaliation contemplated by the resolution.

Mr. Henry, of Tennessee, said that the resolution did not go far enough. He favored the passage of a law providing that, upon any attempt being made to execute the proclamation of Abraham Lincoln, we immediately hoist the "black flag," and proclaim a war of extermination against all invaders of our soil.

Mr. Phelan, of Mississippi, said that he had always been in favor of conducting the war under the "black flag." If that flag had been raised a year ago the war would be ended now.

Mr. Burnett, of Kentucky, moved that all of said resolutions be referred to the Committee on the Judiciary. This was agreed to.

Subsequently, on the 1st of October, a majority of the Judiciary Committee made a report recommending the passage of the following bill:

Whereas, these States, exercising a right consecrated by the blood of our Revolutionary forefathers, and recognized as fundamental in the American system of government, which is based on the consent of the governed, dissolved the compact which united them to the Northern States, and withdrew from the Union created by the Federal Constitution; and whereas, the Government of the United States, repudiating the principles on which its founders, in their solemn appeal to the civilized world, justified the American Revolution, commenced the present war to subjugate and enslave these States under the pretext of repressing rebellion and restoring the Union; and whereas, in the prosecution of the war for the past seventeen months, the rights accorded to belligerents by the usages of civilized nations have been studiously denied to the citizens of these States, except in cases where the same have been extorted by the apprehension of retaliation, or by the adverse fortune of the war; and whereas, from the commencement of this unholy invasion to the present moment, the invaders have inflicted inhuman miseries on the people of these States, exacting of them treasonable oaths, subjecting unarmed citizens, women, and children to confiscation, banishment and imprisonment; burning their dwelling houses, ravaging the land, plundering private property; murdering men for pretended offences; organizing the abduction of slaves by government officials and at government expense; promoting servile insurrection, by tampering with slaves, and protecting them in resisting their masters; stealing works of art and destroying public libraries; encouraging and inviting a brutal soldiery to commit outrages on women by the unrebuked orders of military commanders, and attempting to ruin cities by filling up the entrances to their harbors with stone: And, whereas, in the same spirit of barbarous ferocity the Government of the United States enacted a law, entitled "An act to suppress insurrection, to prevent treason and rebellion, to seize and confiscate the property of rebels, and for other purposes," and has announced by a proclamation, issued by Abraham Lincoln, the President thereof, that in pursuance of said law, "on the 1st of January, 1863, all persons held as slaves within any State, or designated part of a State, the people whereof shall be in rebellion against the United States, shall be thenceforward and forever free," and has, thereby, made manifest that this conflict has ceased to be a war as recognized among civilized nations, but on the part of the enemy has become an invasion of an organized horde of murderers and plunderers, breathing hatred and revenge for the numerous defeats sustained on legitimate battle fields, and determined, if possible, to exterminate the loyal population of these States, to transfer their property to their enemies, and to emancipate their slaves, with the atrocious design of adding servile insurrection and the massacre of families to the calamities of war; and, whereas, justice and humanity require this Government to endeavor to repress the lawless practices and designs of the enemy by inflicting severe retribution: Therefore, the Confederate States of America do enact,

1. That on and after the 1st of January, 1863, all commissioned and non-commissioned officers of the enemy, except as hereinafter mentioned, when captured, shall be imprisoned at hard labor, or otherwise put at hard labor, until the termination of the war, or until the repeal of the act of the Congress of the United States, herein before recited, or until otherwise determined by the President.

2. Every white person who shall act as a commissioned or non-commissioned officer, commanding negroes or mulattoes against the Confederate States, or who shall arm, organize, train, or prepare negroes or mulattoes for military service, or aid them in any military enterprise against the Confederate States, shall, if captured, suffer death.

3. Every commissioned or non-commissioned officer of the enemy who shall incite slaves to rebellion, or pretend to give them freedom,

under the aforementioned act of Congress and proclamation, by abducting, or causing them to be abducted, or inducing them to abscond, shall, if captured, suffer death.

4. That every person charged with an offence under this act shall be tried by such military courts as the President shall direct; and after conviction, the President may commute the punishment, or pardon unconditionally, or on such terms as he may see fit.

5. That the President is hereby authorized to resort to such other retaliatory measures as in his judgment may be best calculated to repress the atrocities of the enemy.

Mr. Phelan, of Mississippi, submitted a minority report from the same committee, in the form of a lengthy preamble, and the following resolution:

Be it resolved, &c., That from this day forth all rules of civilized warfare should be discarded in the future defence of our country, our liberties and our lives, against the fell design now openly avowed by the Government of the United States to annihilate or enslave us: and that a war of extermination should henceforth be waged against every invader whose hostile foot shall cross the boundaries of these Confederate States.

Mr. Hill, of Georgia: I must be allowed to say for myself that I regard the proclamation of Mr. Lincoln as a mere *brutum fulmen*, and so intended by its author. It is to serve a temporary purpose at the North. I fear we are dignifying it beyond its importance. As the Senate has concluded to notice it, I am in favor of the simplest and most legal action. We must confine our action within the line of right, under the laws of nations. In my opinion we have the right to declare certain acts as crimes, being in conflict with civilized war, and the actors as criminals; and a criminal, though a soldier, is not entitled to be considered a prisoner of war. While, therefore, I approve the general idea to treat persons guilty of certain acts as criminals, contained in the bill reported by the Senator from Louisiana (Mr. Semmes), and agreed to that report as being the one most favored by the majority of the committee, I also, in accordance with the understanding of the committee, propose the following bill, and ask that it be printed for the consideration of the Senate:

1. That if any person singly, or in organized bodies, shall, under pretence of waging war, kill or maim, or in any wise injure the person of any unarmed citizen of the Confederate States, or shall destroy, or seize, or damage the property, or invade the house or domicil, or insult the family of each unarmed citizen; or shall persuade or force any slave to abandon his owner, or shall, by word or act, counsel or incite to servile insurrection within the limits of the Confederate States, all such persons, if captured by the forces of the Confederate States, shall be treated as criminals and not as prisoners of war, and shall be tried by a military court, and, on conviction, suffer death.

2. That every person pretending to be a soldier or officer of the United States, who shall be captured on the soil of the Confederate States, after the 1st day of January, 1863, shall be presumed to have entered the territory of the Confederate States with intent to incite insurrection and abet murder, and unless satisfactory proof be adduced to the contrary, before the military court before which the trial shall be had, shall suffer death. This section shall continue in force until the proclamation issued by Abraham Lincoln, dated at Washington, on the 22d day of September, 1862, shall be rescinded, and the policy therein announced shall be abandoned, and no longer.

Mr. Clark, of Missouri, read a preamble and resolution embracing his views on the subject under consideration. The resolution proposed to recognize the enemy as "savage, relentless, and barbarous," and declares that it "is the duty of the Government of the Confederate States neither to ask quarter for its soldiers nor extend it to the enemy until an awakened or created sense of decency and humanity, or the sting of retaliation, shall have impelled our enemy to adopt or practise the usages of war which prevail among Christian and civilized nations."

On the motion of Mr. Semmes, of Louisiana, the several bills and resolutions were ordered to be printed.

The whole matter was finally disposed of on the last day of the session by the passage of a resolution, declaring that Congress would sustain the President in such retaliatory measures as he might adopt.

"THIS GIGANTIC WICKEDNESS": LONDON, OCTOBER 1862

The Times of London: Editorial on the Emancipation Proclamation

October 7, 1862

The lordly *Times*, known as "the Thunderer," achieved maximum volume in its condemnation of the Emancipation Proclamation. The *Times* had strongly favored the Confederacy from the beginning of the war, but this editorial marked a new level of ferocity. It appeared as the Palmerston government debated whether Britain should offer to mediate an end to the conflict.

LONDON, TUESDAY, OCTOBER 7, 1862.

It is rarely that a man can be found to balance accurately mischief to another against advantage to himself. President LINCOLN is, as the world says, a good-tempered man, neither better nor worse than the mass of his kind—neither a fool nor a sage, neither a villain nor a saint, but a piece of that common useful clay out of which it delights the American democracy to make great Republican personages. Yet President LINCOLN has declared that from the 1st of January next to come every State that is in rebellion shall be in the eye of Mr. LINCOLN a Free State. After that date Mr. LINCOLN proposes to enact that every slave in a rebel State shall be for ever after free, and he promises that neither he, nor his army, nor his navy will do anything to repress *any* efforts which the negroes in such rebel States may make for the recovery of their freedom. This means, of course, that Mr. LINCOLN will, on the 1st of next January, do his best to excite a servile war in the States which he cannot occupy with his arms. He will run up the rivers in his gunboats; he will seek out the places which are left but slightly guarded, and where the women and children have been trusted to the fidelity of coloured domestics. He will appeal to the black blood of the African; he will whisper of the pleasures of spoil and of the gratification of yet fiercer instincts; and when blood begins to flow and shrieks come piercing through the darkness, Mr. LINCOLN will wait till the rising flames tell that all is consummated, and then he will rub his hands and think that revenge is sweet. This is what Mr. LINCOLN avows before the world that he is about to do. Now, we are in Europe thoroughly convinced that the death of slavery must follow as necessarily upon the success of the Confederates in this war as the dispersion of darkness occurs upon the rising of the sun; but sudden and forcible emancipation resulting from "the efforts the negroes may make for their actual freedom" can only be effected by massacre and utter destruction. Mr. LINCOLN avows, therefore, that he proposes to excite the negroes of the Southern plantations to murder the families of their masters while these are engaged in the war. The conception of such a crime is horrible. The employment of Indians sinks to a level with civilized warfare in comparison with it; the most detestable doctrines of MAZZINI are almost less atrocious; even Mr. LINCOLN'S own recent achievements of burning by gunboats the defenceless villages on the Mississippi are dwarfed by this gigantic wickedness. The single thing to be said for it is that it is a wickedness that holds its head high and scorns hypocrisy. It does not pretend to attack slavery as slavery. It launches this threat of a servile rebellion as a means of war against certain States, and accompanies it with a declaration of general protection to all other slavery.

Where he has no power Mr. LINCOLN will set the negroes free; where he retains power he will consider them as slaves. "Come to me," he cries to the insurgent planters, "and I will preserve your rights as slaveholders; but set me still at defiance, and I will wrap myself in virtue and take the sword of freedom in my hand, and, instead of aiding you to oppress, I will champion the rights of humanity. Here are whips for you who are loyal; go forth and flog or sell your black chattels as you please. Here are torches and knives for employment against you who are disloyal; I will press them into every black hand, and teach their use." Little Delaware, with her 2,000 slaves, shall still be protected in her loyal tyranny. Maryland, with her 90,000 slaves, shall "freely accept or freely reject" any project for either gradual or immediate abolition; but if Mississippi and South Carolina, where the slaves rather outnumber the masters, do not repent, and receive from Mr. LINCOLN a licence to trade in human flesh, that human flesh shall be adopted by Mr. LINCOLN as the agent of his vengeance. The position is peculiar for a mere layman. Mr. LINCOLN, by this proclamation, constitutes himself a sort of moral American Pope. He claims to sell indulgences to own votaries, and he offers them with full hands to all who will fall down and worship him. It is his to bind, and it is his to loose. His decree of emancipation is to go into remote States, where his temporal power cannot be made manifest, and where no stars and stripes are to be seen; and in those distant swamps he is, by a sort of Yankee excommunication, to lay the land under a slavery interdict.

What will the South think of this? The South will answer with a hiss of scorn. But what will the North think of it? What will Pennsylvania say—Pennsylvania, which is already unquiet under the loss of her best customers, and not easy under the absolute despotism of the present Government at Washington? What Boston may say or think is not, perhaps, of much consequence. But what will New York say? It would not answer the purpose of any of these cities to have the South made a howling wilderness. They want the handling of the millions which are produced by the labour of the black man. Pennsylvania desires to sell her manufactures in the South; New York wishes to be again broker, banker, and merchant to the South. This is what the Union means to these cities. They would rather have a live independent State to deal with than a dead dependency where nothing could be earnt. To these practical persons President LINCOLN would be, after his black revolution had succeeded, like a dogstealer who should present the anxious owner with the head of his favourite pointer. They want the useful creature alive. The South without its cotton and its sugar and its tobacco would be of small use to New York, or even to Philadelphia; and the South without the produce of its rice and cotton, and its sugar and tobacco, would be but a sorry gain, even if it could be obtained. If President LINCOLN wants such a conquest as this, the North is, perhaps, yet strong enough to conquer Hayti. A few fanatics, of course, will shout, but we cannot think that, except in utter desperation and vindictiveness, any real party in the North will applaud this nefarious resolution to light up a servile war in the distant homesteads of the South.

As a proof of what the leaders of the North, in their passion and their despair, would do if they could, this is a very sad document. As a proof of the hopelessness and recklessness which prompt their actions, it is a very instructive document. But it is not a formidable document. We gather from it that Mr. LINCOLN has lost all hope of preserving the Union, and is now willing to let any quack try his nostrum. As an act of policy it is, if possible, more contemptible than it is wicked. It may possibly produce some partial risings, for let any armed power publish an exhortation to the labouring class of any community to plunder and murder, and there will be some response. It might happen in London, or Paris, or New York. That Mr. LINCOLN's emancipation decrees will have any general effect bearing upon the issue of the war we do not, however, believe. The negroes have already abundantly discovered that the tender mercies of the Northerners are cruelties. The freedom which is associated with labour in the trenches, military discipline, and frank avowals of personal abhorrence momentarily repeated does not commend itself to the negro nature. General BUTLER could, if he pleased, tell strange stories of the ill success of his tamperings with the negroes about New Orleans. We do not think that even now, when Mr. LINCOLN plays his last card, it will prove to be a trump. Powerful malignity is a dreadful reality, but impotent malignity is apt to be a very contemptible spectacle. Here is a would-be conqueror and a would-be extirpator who is not quite safe in his seat of government, who is reduced to such straits that he accepts a defeat as a glorious escape, a capitulation of 8,000 men as an unimportant event, a drawn battle as a glorious victory, and the retreat of an invading army which retires laden with plunder and rich in stores as a deliverance. Here is a President who has just, against his will, supplied his antagonists with a hundred and twenty guns and millions of stores, and who is trembling for the very ground on which he stands. Yet, if we judged only by his pompous proclamations, we should believe that he had a garrison in every city of the South. This is more like a Chinaman beating his two swords together to frighten his enemy than like an earnest man pressing on his cause in steadfastness and truth.

OBEYING CIVIL AUTHORITY:
MARYLAND, OCTOBER 1862

George B. McClellan to Abraham Lincoln

General McClellan had second thoughts about taking a public stance against the Emancipation Proclamation after his political advisor William Aspinwall visited him on October 4 and warned him off the idea, suggesting he "quietly continue doing" his "duty as a soldier." Several army officers McClellan consulted gave him the same advice. Still he felt it necessary to address his army on the matter, pointing to the ballot box as "the remedy for political error."

Hd Quarters Army Potomac

The President, U.S. 7th

I have issued the following order on your proclamation.

"Hd Quarters Army Potomac Camp near Sharpsburg Md Oct 7th 1862 Genl Order No. 163. The attention of the officers & soldiers of the Army of the Potomac is called to Genl Order No. 139 War Dept Sept 24th 1862, publishing to the Army the Presidents proclamation of Sept 22d.

A proclamation of such grave moment to the Nation officially communicated to the Army affords to the Genl Commanding an opportunity of defining specifically to the officers & soldiers under his Command the relation borne by all persons in the Military service of the U.S. towards the Civil Authorities of the Government. The Constitution confides to the Civil Authorities legislative judicial and executive, the power and duty of making expounding & executing the federal laws. Armed forces are raised & supported simply to sustain the Civil Authorities and are to be held in strict subordination thereto in all respects. This fundamental rule of our political system is essential to the security of our Republican Institutions & should be thoroughly understood & observed by every soldier. The principle upon which & the objects for which Armies shall be employed in suppressing Rebellion must be determined & declared by the Civil Authorities and the Chief Executive, who is charged with the administration of the

National affairs, is the proper & only source through which the views & orders of the Government can be made known to the Armies of the Nation. Discussions by officers & soldiers concerning public measures determined upon and declared by the Government when carried at all beyond temperate and respectful expressions of opinion tend greatly to impair & destroy the discipline & efficiency of troops by substituting the spirit of political faction for that firm steady & earnest support of the Authority of the Government which is the highest duty of the American soldier. The remedy for political error if any are committed is to be found only in the action of the people at the polls. In thus calling the attention of this Army to the true relation between the soldiers and the Government the Genl Commanding merely adverts to an evil against which it has been thought advisable during our whole history to guard the Armies of the Republic & in so doing he will not be considered by any right minded person as casting any reflection upon that loyalty & good conduct which has been so fully illustrated upon so many battle fields. In carrying out all measures of public policy this Army will of course be guided by the same rules of mercy and Christianity that have ever controlled its conduct toward the defenceless.

By Command of Maj Genl McClellan. James Hardie Lt Col Aide de Camp Acting Ajt. A Genl."

Geo B McClellan
M.G. Comdg

BATTLE OF CORINTH: MISSISSIPPI, OCTOBER 1862

Oscar L. Jackson: from The Colonel's Diary

After the battle of Iuka, Sterling Price was reinforced by troops from central Mississippi under the command of Earl Van Dorn. On October 3 Van Dorn and Price led 22,000 men in an attack on the 23,000 Union troops at Corinth under William S. Rosecrans and pushed the defenders back to their inner defensive line. When the battle resumed the following morning, some of the fiercest fighting took place around Battery Robinett. Oscar L. Jackson, a company commander in the 63rd Ohio Infantry, recalled the battle in a narrative posthumously published in 1922.

About ten o'clock the rebels began pouring out of the timber and forming storming columns. All the firing ceased and everything was silent as the grave. They formed one column of perhaps two thousand men in plain view, then another, and crowding out of the woods another, and so on. I thought they would never stop coming out of the timber. While they were forming, the men were considerable distance from us but in plain sight and as soon as they were ready they started at us with a firm, slow, steady step.

> "Firm paced and slow a fearful front they form,
> Still as the breeze but dreadful as the storm."

So it seemed to us. In my campaigning I had never seen anything so hard to stand as that slow, steady tramp. Not a sound was heard but they looked as if they intended to walk over us. I afterwards stood a bayonet charge when the enemy came at us on the double-quick with a yell and it was not so trying on the nerves as that steady, solemn advance.

I could see that my men were affected by it. They were in line and I knew that they would stand fire but this was a strong test. I noticed one man examining his gun to see if it was clean; another to see if his was primed right; a third would stand a while on one foot then on the other; whilst others were pulling at their blouses, feeling if their cartridge boxes or cap-pouches were all right, and so on, but all the time steadily watching the advancing foe. It is customary in engagements to have some motto or battle cry given by some commander, such as "Fire low," "Stick to your company," "Remember some battle," (naming it). To draw the attention of my company while the charge was advancing I said: "Boys, I guess we are going to have a fight." This is always a doubtful question to an old soldier until he sees it, but they all believed it this time. "I have two things I want you to remember today. One is, we own all the ground behind us. The enemy may go over us but all the rebels yonder can't drive Company H back. The other is, if the butternuts come close enough, remember you have good bayonets on your rifles and use them." And well did they remember what I said.

When the enemy had advanced about one-third of the distance toward us, we got orders to lie down, and then, when the enemy got close enough, we were to fire by companies. The unevenness of the ground now screened us from their view and the second line of infantry, some distance to the rear, appeared to the rebels to be the first they would have to fight, and when they came upon us it was a surprise to them. My company being on the left of the regiment, and our regiment on the left of the brigade, I was among the nearest to the enemy.

The enemy had to come over a bluffish bank a few yards in front of me and as soon as I saw their heads, still coming slowly, I jumped up and said: "Company H, get up." The column was then in full view and only about thirty yards distant. Captain Smith of our regiment thought only about twenty-five yards. Just in front of me was a bush three or four feet high with sear leaves on it. Hitting this with my sword, I said: "Boys, give them a volley just over this. Ready! aim! (and jumping around my company to get from in front of their guns) fire!" In a few seconds the fire was continued along the whole line.

It seems to me that the fire of my company had cut down the head of the column that struck us as deep back as my company was long. As the smoke cleared away, there was apparently ten yards square of a mass of struggling bodies and butternut clothes. Their column appeared to reel like a rope shaken at the end. I had heard this idea advanced and here I saw it plainly. The enemy were stopped, but deploying their column, returned the fire, and, a fine thing for us, fired too low, striking the ground, knocking the dirt and chips all over us, wounding a very few, not one in my company. We got ahead of them with the next volley which we delivered right in their faces. (The guns were all muzzle-loading). At this close distance we fought for perhaps five minutes, when the enemy gave back in confusion. The leafy bush I struck with my sword, on giving the first command to fire, was stripped almost clean. The boys made a fine volley. The enemy came at us in fine order, moving handsomely, but in retreating, every fellow went as suited him, and it appeared to suit all to go fast.

The column that fought us was led by General Rodgers of Texas who fell dead but a few feet from me. When I saw the enemy retreating in such confusion, I remarked to a comrade that we would not have to fight those men any more today, as I thought it would be impossible to rally them again, but strange to say, in some forty minutes I saw them reformed and coming at us again with that slow, steady step, but they made a change in their tactics, for as they came over the bank, or rather out of ravine in front of us, they came at us with a yell on the double-quick. Our men stood firm with loaded guns and fixed bayonets and gave them a volley that threw them somewhat into confusion, slaughtering them fearfully, but pressing on, and firing at us rapidly, they dashed themselves against us like water against a rock and were a second time repulsed and gave back.

Colonel Sprague had all the while been in the thickest of the fight. I think I see him now rush to where the line wavered and with sabre sweeping the air, exclaim, "What does this mean, men? Company —, close up!" He then spoke and said, "Men, it is your time to cheer now," and with a hearty good will did they respond.

Some distance to the left and front of me were a pair of parrot guns, that we called Battery Robinett in distinction from the small fort of the same name a short distance in the rear of them. Captain Brown and his Company A supported these guns immediately, that is, were between me and them. He was almost annihilated by the first two charges and between me and the guns was clear ground. Colonel Sprague gave me this order: "Captain Jackson, move your company up to those guns and hold them." Saluting, I replied, "I will do it," and turning to my command I added, "Left face, forward march." It was like moving into dead men's shoes, for I had seen one company carried away from there on litters, but without a moment's hesitation we moved up.

I had scarce posted my men in rear of the guns when I saw that the enemy were again coming at us, and that a detachment was moving from the main column toward my guns. I knew what they wanted and, as the guns were not for close action, I moved my men in front of them and waited their approach. On they came, formed in their favorite manner, namely, in a solid square or column. I now had but twenty-four men in line formed in two ranks, but even the detachment of the enemy which veered off towards me were formed in a square. As I afterwards learned, they were dismounted Texan rangers and very few of their guns had bayonets. I am told Colonel Sprague asked permission to move up to my support, but permission was denied.

The rebel officer in command of the Texans was marching at the left of his men and when he came nigh us he turned and walked backwards and said to his men, "Boys, when you charge, give a good yell." I heard his command distinctly and it almost made the hair stand up on my head. The next instant the Texans began yelling like savages and rushed at us without firing. The ground in front of us was about like that where we stood previously and at the proper moment I gave them a volley that halted them, cutting down their entire front. I saw they meant to overwhelm us and drive us from the guns, as they out-numbered us. I estimated their force at one hundred men. My men began loading at will and the Texan, by a dexterous movement, was putting his bayonets to the front, doing the thing among and literally over his dead and wounded comrades. I saw that he would strike us before we could get another volley at them and I gave the command, "Don't load, boys; they are too close on you; let them have the bayonet." In a second every bayonet was brought down to a charge. I have never lived through moments of such intense excitement. Events happened quicker than I can record them. The rebels rushed toward us and just before they struck us, I yelled, "Charge!" in order to give my men momentum to meet the shock. My men sprang at the enemy as one man. It reminded me of a man cutting heavy grain, striking at a thick place. The hostile guns clashed. For an instant we parried like boxers, when the enemy gave back, firing at us now for the first as they retired.

Never have I felt so proud of anything as I was of my men. I thought that no such company was in that army. Hand to hand we fought them. A few of the enemy rushed around my left to my rear to get at the guns and two rebels were killed in rear of my line in single-handed combat. Corporal Selby, then a private, killed a rebel with his bayonet there, which is a remarkable thing in a battle and was spoken of in the official report. Selby called on the Texan to surrender, but he replied, "We'll see who surrenders," and made a lunge at Selby with his bayonet. Selby's skill in the bayonet exercise, in which they had been well drilled, gave him the advantage and he parried the stroke and plunged his own bayonet through the body of the Texan, who fell dead with Selby's bayonet sticking in his body. Thomas Lady also killed a man with his bayonet. Lady was mortally wounded. During this time, terrible fighting was being done along the whole line.

My company was fearfully cut up in this last charge. I had but eleven men standing when I thought the enemy was repulsed, but just as they went into the ravine, one of the rebels turned toward us and fired. I was at the head of my command and a little in front. I saw the fire was aimed at me and tried to avoid it but fate willed otherwise and I fell right backwards, indeed "with my back to the field and my feet to the foe." I was struck in the face. I felt as if I had been hit with a piece of timber, so terrible was the concussion and a stunning pain went through my head. I thought I was killed. It was my impression that I would never rise, but I was not alarmed or distressed by the thought that I was dying; it seemed a matter of indifference to me. In a little while I tried to rise and found I could do so. I got up and tried to walk to the rear. There was no one wounded in my company after I fell. Just at that time our supports charged and pursued the retreating foe, and the battle closed. The victory was ours.

When I got on my feet I walked to the rear a few yards till I came to the trunk of a fallen tree. I was too weak to cross it, but I observed Private Frank Ingmire standing on the tree trunk and I said "Ingmire, help me over." "Yes," he replied, "let me help you across," and gave me his left hand. I then noticed that his right arm was dangling at his side, his hand dripping blood. His wrist had been shattered by a ball. He helped me over the log and I took hold of his left arm with both my hands to support myself, saying, "Ingmire, don't leave me," but I only walked a short distance till I felt my hands slipping off his arm, my knees doubling under me, and I sank to the ground unconscious, and knew nothing more until I came to, in the field hospital two days later.

I took into action thirty-three men with myself, an aggregate of thirty-four. The Lieutenants of my company had both resigned and two of my non-commissioned officers were Acting Lieutenants, Sergeant Terry and Corporal Ferris. Acting 1st Sergeant Casey was killed. Acting Lieutenant Sergeant Terry was killed and Acting Lieutenant Corporal Ferris was severely wounded. The Left Guide of the company, Acting Sergeant, Corporal Wilson, was killed. I had six men killed and sixteen wounded, just two-thirds of the company, and myself wounded in addition, making twenty-three killed and wounded out of a company of thirty-four officers and men. Some of the wounded died from their wounds. Nearly all of the remaining eleven had something to show of the fight, such as bullet holes in the clothing, and abrasions of the skin by the balls. I had five bullet holes through my coat, each one of which cut the coat in two places. One that passed through the left breast of the coat, I felt when it went through, but the others I knew nothing about till afterwards. My pistol was knocked out of my hand and I never saw it again. My sword was lost off me in some way after I was wounded. Both Lieutenant Howard of Company G and Corporal Savely of my own company saw me fall when I was hit. They say I fell backwards to the ground and my limbs quivered convulsively, the blood spurted from my face in a stream several inches high. They both thought I was dead, and someone exclaimed, "The Captain is killed!" Both comrades were so intensely occupied in the fight that they could not go to my assistance, but Lieutenant Howard says he saw me when I rose to my feet and started to walk to the rear.

I was struck just below the right eye. It was not a musket ball but something smaller, either a buckshot or a ball from a squirrel rifle, with which some Texan rangers may have been armed. The ball broke through the cheek bone, passing under the inside corner of the eye. The surgeons probed the wound and tried to take the ball out but did not succeed. I was insensible when the wound was dressed. Doctor A. B. Monahan, Assistant Surgeon of our regiment, dressed the wound and he says he quit probing it lest he would entirely destroy my eye. F. M. Green of the 43rd Ohio, who nursed me, says I was unconscious for three days.

I have recollection of almost nothing that happened till I recovered consciousness the second or third day after the battle, when I aroused from my stupor but could scarcely recollect what had happened. Both eyes were swelled completely shut from the wound and although it was day time I supposed it was night, and my first conscious words were, "It is dark." Soon I was able to remember where I had, as it were, quit the world two days before, but I was not really certain whether any of the men of my company were dead. I knew they had nearly all fallen but had no time during the action to examine their wounds. My time was fully occupied with those who could fight.

Corporal Harrison, afterwards Captain, was standing beside me. I hurriedly asked him, "How are my men?" He replied, "The company is badly cut up, Captain." "For God's sake tell me who were killed," I shrieked, and the words are ringing in my ears to this day, every time I think of that fearful question. He replied, "Corporal Wilson is dead, and Sergeant Terry, and Sergeant Casey," and went on with the details. I thought he named the whole company. As soon as I got the news of how terribly my men had suffered, actually a feeling of gladness came over me that I had been wounded and had something to suffer.

Charles B. Labruzan: Journal, October 4, 1862

Lieutenant Labruzan, a company commander in the 42nd Alabama Infantry, fought in the Confederate attack on Battery Robinett. The Confederates failed to break through the inner defenses at Corinth and retreated when the Union counterattacked on the afternoon of October 4. Confederate casualties in the battle were 4,233 men killed, wounded, or missing, while the Union losses totaled 2,520. Labruzan was captured along with his journal, the Corinth section of which found its way into print in 1864 in a regimental history of the 9th Illinois Infantry. Labruzan was paroled and returned to his Alabama regiment, only to become a prisoner again at the surrender of Vicksburg in 1863.

Saturday, Oct. 4th.—An awful day. At 4 o'clock, before day, our Brigade was ordered to the left about one-fourth of a mile, and halted, throwing out lines of skirmishers, which kept up a constant fire. A Battery in front of the right of our Regiment opened briskly, and the enemy replied the same. The cannonading was heavy for an hour and a half. Our Regiment lay down close, and stood it nobly. The shell flew thick and fast, cutting off large limbs and filling the air with fragments. Many burst within 20 feet, and the pieces popped within 2 or 3 feet. It was extremely unpleasant, and I prayed for forgiveness of my sins, and made up my mind to go through. Col. Sawier called for volunteers to assist the 2d Texas skirmishers. I volunteered, and took my company. Captain Perkins and Lieutenant Wumson being taken sick directly after the severe bombardment, I had the Co. all the time. I went skirmishing at 7 1/2, and returned at 9 1/2 o'clock. We got behind trees and logs, and the way the bullets did fly, was unpleasant to see. I think 20 must have passed within a few feet of me, humming prettily. Shells tore off large limbs and splinters. Struck my tree several times. We could only move from tree to tree, and bending low to the ground, while moving. Oh, how anxiously I watched for the bursting of the shells when the heavy roar of the cannon proclaimed their coming. At 9 1/2 o'clock I had my skirmishers relieved, by Captain Rouse's Company. Sent my men to their places, and went behind a log with Major Furges. At 10 o'clock, suddenly the fight fairly opened, with heavy volleys of musketry and the double thundering cannon. This was on the right. In a few minutes the left went into action in splendid style. At 10 1/4 o'clock, Col. Rogers came up by us, only saying "Alabama forces." Our Regiment, with the Brigade rose, unmindful of the shell or shot, and moved forward, marching about 250 yards and rising the crest of a hill. The whole of Corinth, with its enormous fortifications, burst upon our view. The U. S. flag was floating over the forts and in town. We were now met by a perfect storm of grape, cannister, cannon balls and Minnie balls. Oh, God! I have never seen the like! The men fell like grass, even here. Giving one tremendous cheer, we dashed to the bottom of the hill on which the fortifications are situated. Here we found every foot of ground covered with large trees and brush, cut down to impede our progress. Looking to the right and left, I saw several Brigades charging at the same time. What a sight was there. I saw men running at full speed, stop suddenly and fall upon their faces, with their brains scattered all around. Others, with legs and arms cut off, shrieking with agony. They fell behind, beside, and within a few feet of me. I gave myself to God, and got ahead of my company. The ground was literally strewed with mangled corpses. One ball passed through my pants, and they cut twigs right by me. It seemed, by holding out my hand I could have caught a dozen. They buzzed and hissed by me in all directions, but I still pushed forward. I seemed to be moving right in the mouth of cannon, for the air was filled with hurling grape and cannister. Ahead was one continuous blaze. I rushed to the ditch of the fort, right between some large cannon. I grappled into it, and half way up the sloping wall. The enemy were only three or four feet from me on the other side, but could not shoot us for fear of having their heads blown off. Our men were in the same predicament. Only 5 or 6 were on the wall, and 30 or 40 in and around the ditch. Catesby on the wall by my side. A man within two feet of me, put his head cautiously up, to shoot into the fort. But he suddenly dropped his musket, and his brains were dashed in a stream over my fine coat, which I had in my arms, and on my shirt sleeves. Several were killed here, on top one another, and rolled down the embankment in ghastly heaps. This was done by a Regiment of Yankees coming about 40 yards on our left, after finding us entirely cut off, and firing into us. Several of our men cried "put down the flag," and it was lowered, or shot into the ditch. Oh, we were butchered like dogs, as we were not supported. Some one placed a white handkerchief on Sergeant Buck's musket, and he took it to a port hole. But the Yankees snatched it off and took him prisoner. The men fell 10 at a time. The ditch being full, and finding we had no chance, the survivors tried to save themselves as best they could. I was so far up, I could not get off quickly. I do not recollect of seeing Catesby after this, but think he got off before. I trust in God he has. I and Capt. Foster started together, and the air was literally filled with hissing balls. I got about 20 steps, as quick as I could, about a dozen being killed in that distance. I fell down and scrambled behind a large stump. Just then, I saw poor Foster throw up his hands, and saying "Oh, my God!" jumped about two feet from the ground, falling on his face. The top of his head seemed to cave in, and the blood spouted straight up several feet. I could see men fall as they attempted to run, some with their heads to pieces, and others with the blood streaming from their backs. It was horrible. One poor fellow being almost on me, told me his name, and asked me to take his pocket-book if I escaped and give it to his mother, and tell her that he died a brave man. I asked him if he was a Christian, and told him to pray, which he did, with the cannon thundering a deadly accompaniment. Poor fellow. I forgot his request in the excitement. His legs were literally cut to pieces. As our men returned, the enemy poured in their fire, and I was hardly 30 feet from the mouth of the cannon. Minnie balls filled the stump I was behind, and the shells bursted within three feet of me. One was so near it stunned me, and burned my face with powder. The grape-shot hewed large pieces off my stump, gradually wearing it away. I endured the horrors of death here for half an hour, and endeavored to resign myself and prayed. Our troops formed in line in the woods, and advanced a second time to the charge with cheers. They began firing when about half way, and I had to endure it all. I was feigning death. I was right between our own and the enemies fire. In the first charge our men did not fire a gun, but charged across the ditch, and to the very mouth of the cannon, with the bayonet. So also the second charge, but they fired. Thank God, I am unhurt, and I think it was a merciful Providence. Our troops charged by, when I seized a rifle and endeavored to fire it several times, but could not, for the cap was bad. Our boys were shot down like hogs, and could not stand it, and fell back each man for himself. Then the same scene was enacted as before. This time the Yankees charged after them, and as I had no chance at all, and all around we were surrendering, I was compelled to do so, as a rascal threatened to shoot me. I had to give up my sword to him. He demanded my watch also. Took it; but I appealed to an officer, and got it back. I had no means of defending myself for the first time in many years. I cried to see our brave men slaughtered so, and thought where Catesby might be. I have never felt so in all my life. It is now said that our Brigade was never ordered to charge such a place, and that it was a mistake. If so, it was a sad one. Being brought behind the works we found three Regiments drawn up in line, and all of them were fighting our 42d Alabama alone. I helped to carry a wounded man to the Depot, with Lieutenants Marshall, Contra and Preston, they being the only unhurt officers who were prisoners from our Regiment. We and the privates were soon marched to a large house, having a partition for the officers. The men, about 400, in next room. I heard firing again, but I fear we can do nothing. We are treated very politely—more so than I had expected.

BATTLE OF PERRYVILLE:
KENTUCKY, OCTOBER 1862

J. Montgomery Wright: Notes of a Staff-Officer at Perryville

Don Carlos Buell's army reached Louisville on September 25 while Braxton Bragg's Confederate forces were still thirty miles to the south at Bardstown. When Buell began advancing south from Louisville in early October, Bragg tried to unite his army with Edmund Kirby Smith's, which had occupied Frankfort in early September. Before Bragg and Smith could combine forces, Buell brought Bragg to battle at Perryville, some fifty miles southeast of Louisville, on October 8. Major Wright, of Buell's staff, was one of many Union officers surprised by the fighting at Perryville, due to a phenomenon known as acoustic shadow—layers of air of differing densities that muffled sound. Buell was prevented from hearing the battle being fought less than three miles from his headquarters; as a result, most of his army remained unengaged. Union losses in the battle totaled about 4,200 men killed, wounded, or missing, while Confederate casualties were close to 3,400. Wright's account appeared in *Battles and Leaders of the Civil War*.

THE SITUATION at Louisville in the latter part of September, 1862, was not unlike that at Washington after the first battle of Bull Run. The belief was entertained by many that Bragg would capture the city, and not a few had removed their money and valuables across the Ohio River, not over-assured that Bragg might not follow them to the lakes. Nelson had sworn that he would hold the city so long as a house remained standing or a soldier was alive, and he had issued an order that all the women, children, and non-combatants should leave the place and seek safety in Indiana. He had only raw troops and convalescent veterans, and few citizens believed that he could hold out against an attack. His tragic death occurred a few days later.

Buell's arrival changed the situation of affairs. The uncertain defensive suddenly gave way to an aggressive attitude, and speculation turned from whether Bragg would capture Louisville to whether Buell would capture Bragg.

The country through which Buell's army marched is almost destitute of water, but at Perryville a stream flowed between the contending armies, and access to that water was equally important to both armies. Buell accompanied the center corps (Gilbert's), and the advance reached this stream on the evening of October 7th. From that time until the stream was crossed there was constant fighting for access to it, and the only restriction on this fighting was that it should not bring on an engagement until the time for the general attack should arrive. An incident will illustrate the scarcity of water. I obtained a canteenful, and about dark on October 7th, after giving myself a good brushing and a couple of dry rubs without feeling much cleaner, my careless announcement that I was about to take a tin-dipper bath brought General Buell out of his tent with a rather mandatory suggestion that I pour the water back into my canteen and save it for an emergency. The emergency did not come to me, but on the morning of October 9th that water helped to relieve the suffering of some wounded men who lay between the two armies.

At Buell's headquarters, on the 8th, preparations were going on for the intended attack, and the information was eagerly waited for that Crittenden had reached his position on the right. Fighting for water went on in our front, and it was understood that it extended all along the line, but no battle was expected that day. McCook was at Buell's headquarters in the morning, and received, I believe, some oral instructions regarding the contemplated attack. It was understood that care would be taken not to bring on a general engagement, and no importance was attached to the sounds that reached us of artillery-firing at the front of the center. Of course the young officers of the staff, of whom I was one, were not taken into conference by General Buell, but we all knew that the subject of attention that morning was the whereabouts of Crittenden's corps, and the placing it in position on the right for the general engagement that was to be brought on as soon as the army was in line. We all saw McCook going serenely away like a general carrying his orders with him.

In the afternoon we moved out for a position nearer Crittenden, as I inferred from the direction taken. A message came from the line on the left center to General Buell, and in a few moments Colonel James B. Fry, our chief of staff, called me up, and sent me with an order to General Gilbert, commanding the center corps, to send at once two brigades to reënforce General McCook, commanding the left corps. Thus I came to be a witness to some of the curious features of Perryville.

I did not know what was going on at the left, and Colonel Fry did not inform me. He told me what to say to General Gilbert, and to go fast, and taking one of the general's orderlies with me, I started on my errand. I found General Gilbert at the front, and as he had no staff-officer at hand at the moment, he asked me to go to General Schoepf, one of his division commanders, with the order. Schoepf promptly detached two brigades, and he told me I had better go on ahead and find out where they were to go. There was no sound to direct me, and as I tried to take an air line I passed outside the Union lines and was overtaken by a cavalry officer, who gave me the pleasing information that I was riding toward the enemy's pickets. Now up to this time I had heard no sound of battle; I had heard no artillery in front of me, and no heavy infantry-firing. I rode back, and passed behind the cavalry regiment which was deployed in the woods, and started in the direction indicated to me by the officer who called me back. At some distance I overtook an ambulance train, urged to its best speed, and then I knew that something serious was on hand. This was the first intimation I had that one of the fiercest struggles of the war was at that moment raging almost within my sight.

Directed by the officers in charge of the ambulances I made another detour, and pushing on at greater speed I suddenly turned into a road, and there before me, within a few hundred yards, the battle of Perryville burst into view, and the roar of the artillery and the continuous rattle of the musketry first broke upon my ear. It was the finest spectacle I ever saw. It was wholly unexpected, and it fixed me with astonishment. It was like tearing away a curtain from the front of a great picture, or the sudden bursting of a thunder-cloud when the sky in front seems serene and clear. I had seen an unlooked-for storm at sea, with hardly a moment's notice, hurl itself out of the clouds and lash the ocean into a foam of wild rage. But here there was not the warning of an instant. At one bound my horse carried me from stillness into the uproar of battle. One turn from a lonely bridle-path through the woods brought me face to face with the bloody struggle of thousands of men.

Waiting for news to carry back, I saw and heard some of the unhappy occurrences of Perryville. I saw young Forman, with the remnant of his company of the 15th Kentucky regiment, withdrawn to make way for the reënforcements, and as they silently passed me they seemed to stagger and reel like men who had been beating against a great storm. Forman had the colors in his hand, and he and several of his little group of men had their hands upon their chests and their lips apart as though they had difficulty in breathing. They filed into a field, and without thought of shot or shell they lay down on the ground apparently in a state of exhaustion. I joined a mounted group about a young officer, and heard Rumsey Wing, one of Jackson's volunteer aides, telling of that general's death and the scattering of the raw division he commanded. I remembered how I had gone up to Shiloh with Terrill's battery in a small steamer, and how, as the first streak of daylight came, Terrill, sitting on the deck near me, had recited a line about the beauty of the dawn, and had wondered how the day would close upon us all. I asked about Terrill, who now commanded a brigade, and was told that he had been carried to the rear to die. I thought of the accomplished, good, and brave Parsons,—whom I had seen knocked down seven times in a fight with a bigger man at West Point, without ever a thought of quitting so long as he could get up, and who lived to take orders in the church, and die at Memphis of the yellow fever, ministering to the last to the spiritual wants of his parishioners,—and I asked about Parsons's battery. His raw infantry support had broken, and stunned by the disaster that he thought had overtaken the whole army, he stood by his guns until every horse and every man had gone, and the enemy was almost touching him, and had been dragged away at last by one of his men who had come back to the rescue. His battery was a wreck and no one knew then where he was. And so the news came in of men I knew and men with friends about me.

"THIS GRAND HAVOC OF BATTLE": KENTUCKY, OCTOBER 1862

Sam R. Watkins: from "Co. Aytch," Maury Grays, First Tennessee Regiment

In his 1882 memoir Private Watkins recalls the unrivaled pleasures of the Confederates' march into Kentucky (although overstating the number of new recruits) and the badly led but bloody fighting at Perryville. The battle's results were inconclusive, but Bragg lost his enthusiasm for the offensive and he and Smith withdrew into Tennessee. When Buell failed to pursue the retreating Confederates, Lincoln replaced him with William S. Rosecrans.

WE GO INTO KENTUCKY.

After being thoroughly reorganized at Tupelo, and the troops had recovered their health and spirits, we made an advance into Kentucky. We took the cars at Tupelo and went to Mobile, from thence across Mobile Bay to Montgomery, Alabama, then to Atlanta, from there to Chattanooga, and then over the mountains afoot to the blue-grass regions of Kentucky—the dark and bloody ground. Please remember, patient reader, that I write entirely from memory. I have no data or diary or anything to go by, and memory is a peculiar faculty. I find that I cannot remember towns and battles, and remember only the little things. I remember how gladly the citizens of Kentucky received us. I thought they had the prettiest girls that God ever made. They could not do too much for us. They had heaps and stacks of cooked rations along our route, with wine and cider everywhere, and the glad shouts of "Hurrah for our Southern boys," greeted and welcomed us at every house. Ah, the boys felt like soldiers again. The bands played merrier and livelier tunes. It was the patient convalescing; the fever had left him, he was getting fat and strong; the old fire was seen to illuminate his eyes; his step was buoyant and proud; he felt ashamed that he had ever been "hacked;" he could fight now. It was the same old proud soldier of yore. The bands played "Dixie" and the "Bonnie Blue Flag," the citizens cheered, and the ladies waved their handkerchiefs and threw us bouquets. Ah, those were halcyon days, and your old soldier, kind reader, loves to recall that happy period. Mumfordsville had been captured with five thousand prisoners. New recruits were continually joining our ranks.

Camp Dick Robinson, that immense pile of army stores, had fallen into our hands. We rode upon the summit of the wave of success. The boys had got clean clothes, and had their faces washed. I saw then what I had long since forgotten—a "cockade." The Kentucky girls made cockades for us, and almost every soldier had one pinned on his hat. But stirring events were hastening on, the black cloud of battle and war had begun then to appear much larger than a man's hand, in fact we could see the lightning flash and hear the thunder roar.

We were at Harrodsburg; the Yankees were approaching Perryville under General Buell. The Yankees had been dogging our rear, picking up our stragglers and capturing some of our wagon trains.

This good time that we were having was too good to last. We were in an ecstasy akin to heaven. We were happy; the troops were jubilant; our manhood blood pulsated more warmly; our patriotism was awakened; our pride was renewed and stood ready for any emergency; we felt that one Southern man could whip twenty Yankees. All was lovely and the goose hung high. We went to dances and parties every night.

When General Chalmers marched to Perryville, in flanking and surrounding Mumfordsville, we marched the whole night long. We, the private soldiers, did not know what was going on among the Generals. All that we had to do was march, march, march. It mattered not how tired, hungry, or thirsty we were. All that we had to do was to march that whole night long, and every staff officer who would pass, some fellow would say, "Hey, mister, how far is it to Mumfordsville?" He would answer, "Five miles." It seemed to me we traveled a hundred miles and were always within five miles of Mumfordsville. That night we heard a volley of musketry in our immediate front, and did not know what it meant, but soon we came to where a few soldiers had lighted some candles and were holding them over the body of a dead soldier. It was Captain Allison, if I remember rightly, of General Cheatham's staff. He was very bloody, and had his clothes riddled with balls. I heard that he rode on in front of the advance guard of our army, and had no doubt discovered the Yankee picket, and came galloping back at full speed in the dark, when our advance guard fired on and killed him.

We laid down in a graveyard that night and slept, and when we awoke the sun was high in the heavens, shining in our faces. Mumfordsville had surrendered. The next day Dr. C. T. Quintard let me ride his horse nearly all day, while he walked with the webfeet.

THE BATTLE OF PERRYVILLE.

In giving a description of this most memorable battle, I do not pretend to give you figures, and describe how this General looked and how that one spoke, and the other one charged with drawn sabre, etc. I know nothing of these things—see the history for that. I was simply a soldier of the line, and I only write of the things I saw. I was in every battle, skirmish and march that was made by the First Tennessee Regiment during the war, and I do not remember of a harder contest and more evenly fought battle than that of Perryville. If it had been two men wrestling, it would have been called a "dog fall." Both sides claim the victory—both whipped.

I stood picket in Perryville the night before the battle—a Yankee on one side of the street, and I on the other. We got very friendly during the night, and made a raid upon a citizen's pantry, where we captured a bucket of honey, a pitcher of sweet milk, and three or four biscuit. The old citizen was not at home—he and his whole household had gone visiting, I believe. In fact, I think all of the citizens of Perryville were taken with a sudden notion of promiscuous visiting about this time; at least they were not at home to all callers.

At length the morning dawned. Our line was drawn up on one side of Perryville, the Yankee army on the other. The two enemies that were soon to meet in deadly embrace seemed to be eyeing each other. The blue coats lined the hillside in plain view. You could count the number of their regiments by the number of their flags. We could see the huge war dogs frowning at us, ready at any moment to belch forth their fire and smoke, and hurl their thunderbolts of iron and death in our very midst.

I wondered why the fighting did not begin. Never on earth were our troops more eager for the engagement to open. The Yankees commenced to march toward their left, and we marched almost parallel to our right—both sides watching each other's maneuvers and movements. It was but the lull that precedes the storm. Colonel Field was commanding our brigade, and Lieutenant-Colonel Patterson our regiment. About 12 o'clock, while we were marching through a corn field, in which the corn had been shocked, they opened their war dogs upon us. The beginning of the end had come. Here is where Captain John F. Wheless was wounded, and three others, whose names I have forgotten. The battle now opened in earnest, and from one end of the line to the other seemed to be a solid sheet of blazing smoke and fire. Our regiment crossed a stream, being preceded by Wharton's Texas Rangers, and we were ordered to attack at once with vigor. Here General Maney's horse was shot. From this moment the battle was a mortal struggle. Two lines of battle confronted us. We killed almost every one in the first line, and were soon charging over the second, when right in our immediate front was their third and main line of battle, from which four Napoleon guns poured their deadly fire.

We did not recoil, but our line was fairly hurled back by the leaden hail that was poured into our very faces. Eight color-bearers were killed at one discharge of their cannon. We were right up among the very wheels of their Napoleon guns. It was death to retreat now to either side. Our Lieutenant-Colonel, Patterson, halloed to charge and take their guns, and we were soon in a hand-to-hand fight—every man for himself—using the buts of our guns and bayonets. One side would waver and fall back a few yards, and would rally, when the other side would fall back, leaving the four Napoleon guns; and yet the battle raged. Such obstinate fighting I never had seen before or since. The guns were discharged so rapidly that it seemed the earth itself was in a volcanic uproar. The iron storm passed through our ranks, mangling and tearing men to pieces. The very air seemed full of stifling smoke and fire, which seemed the very pit of hell, peopled by contending demons.

Our men were dead and dying right in the very midst of this grand havoc of battle. It was a life to life and death to death grapple. The sun was poised above us, a great red ball, sinking slowly in the west, yet the scene of battle and carnage continued. I cannot describe it. The mantle of night fell upon the scene. I do not know which side whipped, but I know that I helped bring off those four Napoleon guns that night, though we were mighty easy about it.

They were given to Turner's Battery of our brigade, and had the name of our Lieutenant-Colonel, Patterson, and our color-bearer, Mitchell, both of whom were killed, inscribed on two of the pieces. I have forgotten the names inscribed on the other two pieces. I saw these very four guns surrendered at Missionary Ridge. But of this another time.

The battle of Perryville presented a strange scene. The dead, dying, and wounded of both armies, Confederate and Federal, were blended in inextricable confusion. Now and then a cluster of dead Yankees and close by a cluster of dead Rebels. It was like the Englishman's grog—'alf and 'alf. Now, if you wish, kind reader, to find out how many were killed and wounded, I refer you to the histories.

I remember one little incident that I laughed at while in the very midst of battle. We were charging through an old citizen's yard, when a big yellow cur dog ran out and commenced snapping at the soldiers' legs—they kicking at him to keep him off. The next morning he was lying near the same place, but he was a dead dog.

I helped bring off our wounded that night. We worked the whole night. The next morning about daylight a wounded comrade, Sam Campbell, complained of being cold, and asked me to lie down beside him. I did so, and was soon asleep; when I awoke the poor fellow was stiff and cold in death. His spirit had flown to its home beyond the skies.

After the battle was over, John T. Tucker, Scott Stephens, A. S. Horsley and I were detailed to bring off our wounded that night, and we helped to bring off many a poor dying comrade—Joe Thompson, Billy Bond, Byron Richardson, the two Allen boys—brothers, killed side by side—and Colonel Patterson, who was killed standing right by my side. He was first shot through the hand, and was wrapping his handkerchief around it, when another ball struck and killed him. I saw W. J. Whittorne, then a strippling boy of fifteen years of age, fall, shot through the neck and collar-bone. He fell apparently dead, when I saw him all at once jump up, grab his gun and commence loading and firing, and I heard him say, "D—n 'em, I'll fight 'em as long as I live." Whit thought he was killed, but he is living yet. We helped bring off a man by the name of Hodge, with his under jaw shot off, and his tongue lolling out. We brought off Captain Lute B. Irvine. Lute was shot through the lungs and was vomiting blood all the while, and begging us to lay him down and let him die. But Lute is living yet. Also, Lieutenant Woldridge, with both eyes shot out. I found him rambling in a briar-patch. About fifty members of the Rock City Guards were killed and nearly one hundred wounded. They were led by Captains W. D. Kelley, Wheless, and Steele. Lieutenant Thomas H. Maney was badly wounded. I saw dead on the battle-field a Federal General by the name of Jackson. It was his brigade that fought us so obstinately at this place, and I did hear that they were made up in Kentucky. Colonel Field, then commanding our brigade, and on his fine gray mare, rode up almost face to face with General Jackson, before he was killed, and Colonel Field was shooting all the time with his seven-shooting rifle. I cannot tell the one-half, or even remember at this late date, the scenes of blood and suffering that I witnessed on the battle-field of Perryville. But its history, like all the balance, has gone into the history of the war, and it has been twenty years ago, and I write entirely from memory. I remember Lieutenant Joe P. Lee and Captain W. C. Flournoy standing right at the muzzle of the Napoleon guns, and the next moment seemed to be enveloped in smoke and fire from the discharge of the cannon. When the regiment recoiled under the heavy firing and at the first charge, Billy Webster and I stopped behind a large oak tree and continued to fire at the Yankees until the regiment was again charging upon the four Napoleon guns, heavily supported by infantry. We were not more than twenty paces from them; and here I was shot through the hat and cartridge-box. I remember this, because at that time Billy and I were in advance of our line, and whenever we saw a Yankee rise to shoot, we shot him; and I desire to mention here that a braver or more noble boy was never created on earth than was Billy Webster. Everybody liked him. He was the flower and chivalry of our regiment. His record as a brave and noble boy will ever live in the hearts of his old comrades that served with him in Company H. He is up yonder now, and we shall meet again. In these memoirs I only tell what I saw myself, as every one ought to tell what he saw himself, and in this way the world will know the truth. Now, citizen, let me tell you what you never heard before, and that is this—there were many men with the rank and pay of General, who were not Generals; there were many men with the rank and pay of privates who would have honored and adorned the name of General. Now, I will state further that a private soldier was a private.

It mattered not how ignorant a Corporal might be, he was always right; it mattered not how intelligent the private might be (and so on up); the Sergeant was right over the Corporal, the Sergeant-major over the Sergeant, the Lieutenant over him, and the Captain over him, and the Major over him, and the Colonel over him, and the General over him, and so on up to Jeff Davis. You see, a private had no right to know anything, and that is why Generals did all the fighting, and that is to-day why Generals and Colonels and Captains are great men. They fought the battles of our country. The privates did not. The Generals risked their reputation, the private soldier his life. No one ever saw a private in battle. His history would never be written. It was the Generals that everybody saw charge such and such, with drawn sabre, his eyes flashing fire, his nostrils dilated, and his clarion voice ringing above the din of battle—"in a horn," over the left.

Bill Johns and Marsh Pinkard would have made Generals that would have distinguished themselves and been an honor to the country.

I know to-day many a private who would have made a good General. I know of many a General who was better fitted to be excused from detail and fights, to hang around a camp and draw rations for the company. A private had no way to distinguish himself. He had to keep in ranks, either in a charge or a retreat. But now, as the Generals and Colonels fill all the positions of honor and emoluments, the least I say, the better.

“YOUR OVER-CAUTIOUSNESS”:
WASHINGTON, D.C., OCTOBER 1862

Abraham Lincoln to George B. McClellan

When two weeks passed after Antietam and McClellan made no move to resume campaigning, Lincoln traveled to Sharpsburg to confer with him. McClellan wrote to his wife that the president “does feel very kindly towards me personally,” while Lincoln told his friend David Davis he sought to make the general understand he would “be a ruined man if he did not move forward, move rapidly & effectively.” On his return to Washington, the President issued orders through Halleck on October 6 for the Army of the Potomac to advance. After yet another week passed, this carefully thought-out letter marked Lincoln’s final effort to reason with the Young Napoleon.

Major General McClellan Executive Mansion,
My dear Sir Washington, Oct. 13, 1862.

You remember my speaking to you of what I called your over-cautiousness. Are you not over-cautious when you assume that you can not do what the enemy is constantly doing? Should you not claim to be at least his equal in prowess, and act upon the claim?

As I understand, you telegraph Gen. Halleck that you can not subsist your army at Winchester unless the Railroad from Harper’s Ferry to that point be put in working order. But the enemy does now subsist his army at Winchester at a distance nearly twice as great from railroad transportation as you would have to do without the railroad last named. He now wagons from Culpepper C.H. which is just about twice as far as you would have to do from Harper’s Ferry. He is certainly not more than half as well provided with wagons as you are. I certainly should be pleased for you to have the advantage of the Railroad from Harper’s Ferry to Winchester, but it wastes all the remainder of autumn to give it to you; and, in fact ignores the question of *time*, which can not, and must not be ignored.

Again, one of the standard maxims of war, as you know, is “to operate upon the enemy’s communications as much as possible without exposing your own." You seem to act as if this applies *against* you, but can not apply in your *favor*. Change positions with the enemy, and think you not he would break your communication with Richmond within the next twenty-four hours? You dread his going into Pennsylvania. But if he does so in full force, he gives up his communications to you absolutely, and you have nothing to do but to follow, and ruin him; if he does so with less than full force, fall upon, and beat what is left behind all the easier.

Exclusive of the water line, you are now nearer Richmond than the enemy is by the route that you *can*, and he *must* take. Why can you not reach there before him, unless you admit that he is more than your equal on a march. His route is the arc of a circle, while yours is the chord. The roads are as good on yours as on his.

You know I desired, but did not order, you to cross the Potomac below, instead of above the Shenandoah and Blue Ridge. My idea was that this would at once menace the enemies' communications, which I would seize if he would permit. If he should move Northward I would follow him closely, holding his communications. If he should prevent our seizing his communications, and move towards Richmond, I would press closely to him, fight him if a favorable opportunity should present, and, at least, try to beat him to Richmond on the inside track. I say "try"; if we never try, we shall never succeed. If he make a stand at Winchester, moving neither North or South, I would fight him there, on the idea that if we can not beat him when he bears the wastage of coming to us, we never can when we bear the wastage of going to him. This proposition is a simple truth, and is too important to be lost sight of for a moment. In coming to us, he tenders us an advantage which we should not waive. We should not so operate as to merely drive him away. As we must beat him somewhere, or fail finally, we can do it, if at all, easier near to us, than far away. If we can not beat the enemy where he now is, we never can, he again being within the entrenchments of Richmond.

Recurring to the idea of going to Richmond on the inside track, the facility of supplying from the side away from the enemy is remarkable—as it were, by the different spokes of a wheel extending from the hub towards the rim—and this whether you move directly by the chord, or on the inside arc, hugging the Blue Ridge more closely. The chord-line, as you see, carries you by Aldie, Hay-Market, and Fredericksburg; and you see how turn-pikes, railroads, and finally, the Potomac by Acquia Creek, meet you at all points from Washington. The same, only the lines lengthened a little, if you press closer to the Blue Ridge part of the way. The gaps through the Blue Ridge I understand to be about the following distances from Harper's Ferry, towit: Vestal's five miles; Gregorie's, thirteen, Snicker's eighteen, Ashby's, twenty-eight, Mannassas, thirty-eight, Chester fortyfive, and Thornton's fifty-three. I should think it preferable to take the route nearest the enemy, disabling him to make an important move without your knowledge, and compelling him to keep his forces together, for dread of you. The gaps would enable you to attack if you should wish. For a great part of the way, you would be practically between the enemy and both Washington and Richmond, enabling us to spare you the greatest number of troops from here. When at length, running for Richmond ahead of him enables him to move this way; if he does so, turn and attack him in rear. But I think he should be engaged long before such point is reached. It is all easy if our troops march as well as the enemy; and it is unmanly to say they can not do it.

This letter is in no sense an order.

Yours truly A. LINCOLN.

RECONSIDERING MEDIATION:
ENGLAND, OCTOBER 1862

Lord Palmerston to Lord Russell

By the date of this first letter, Lord Palmerston was uncertain of the significance of Lee's check in Maryland and still considering the consequences of some form of intervention in the American war. Support from the Continental powers seemed to him essential, but he admitted it was a difficult case. By October 22, however, Palmerston's turnabout was complete. He had scheduled a cabinet meeting for October 23 to set policy for intervening by proposing mediation to the warring sides. But the Emancipation Proclamation, coming on the heels of Antietam, caused a general backing away in Britain from any appearance of supporting a slavery regime. The cabinet was postponed and finally never held, and schemes of intervention faded away.

October 2, 1862.

I return you Granville's letter, which contains much deserving of serious consideration. There is no doubt that the offer of mediation upon the basis of separation would be accepted by the South. Why should it not be accepted? It would give the South in principle the points for which they are fighting. The refusal, if refusal there was, would come from the North, who would be unwilling to give up the principle for which they have been fighting, so long as they had a reasonable expectation that by going on fighting they would carry their point. The condition of things therefore which would be favourable to an offer of mediation would be great success of the South against the North. That state of things seemed ten days ago to be approaching. Its advance has now been lately checked, but we do not yet know the real course of recent events, and still less can we foresee what is about to follow; ten days or a fortnight more may throw a clearer light upon future prospects. As regards possible resentment on the part of the Northerns following upon our acknowledgement of the independence of the South, it is quite true that we should have less to care about that resentment in the spring when communication with

Canada opens, and when our naval force could more easily operate upon the American coast than in winter, when we are cut off from Canada and the American coast is not so safe. But if the acknowledgement were made at one and the same time by England, France and some other Powers, the Yankee would probably not seek a quarrel with us alone, and would not like one against a European Confederation. Such a quarrel would render certain and permanent that southern independence, the acknowledgement of which would have caused it.

The first communication to be made by England and France to the contending parties might be not an absolute offer of mediation but a friendly suggestion whether the time was not come when it might be well for the two parties to consider whether the war, however long continued, would lead to any other result than separation, and whether it might not, therefore, be best to avoid the great evils, which must necessarily flow from a prolongation of hostilities, by at once coming to an agreement to meet upon that principle of separation which must apparently be the inevitable result of the contest, however long it may last. The best thing would be that the two parties should settle details by direct negotiation with each other, though perhaps with the rancorous hatred now existing between them this might be difficult. But their quarrels in negotiation would do us no harm if they did not lead to a renewal of war. An armistice if not accompanied by a cessation of blockades would be all in favour of the North, especially if New Orleans remained in the hands of the North. The whole matter is full of difficulty, and can only be cleared up by some more decided events between the contending armies.

October 22, 1862.

Have just read through your Memorandum on American affairs and Lewis's observations. Your description of the state of things between the two parties is most comprehensive and just. I am, however, much inclined to agree with Lewis that at present we could take no step nor make any communication of a distinct proposition with any advantage. What he says of the effect of an armistice is quite true; unless it is founded upon the acceptance by both parties of some basis of negotiation it is a mere temporary suspension of movements and action, and such suspension would probably be more disadvantageous to one party than to the other. If both parties stood equally in need of a respite they would equally remain quiet; if one party thought its antagonist would gain most by an armistice, that party would refuse it. All that we could possibly do without injury to our position would be to ask the two parties, not whether they would agree to an armistice, but whether they might not lean their thoughts towards an arrangement between themselves. But the answer of each might be written by us beforehand. The Northerners would say that the only condition of arrangement would be the restoration of the Union; the South would say their only condition would be an acknowledgement by the North of Southern independence. We should not be more advanced, and should only have pledged each party more strongly to the object for which they are fighting. I am therefore inclined to change the opinion on which I wrote to you when the Confederates seemed to be carrying all before them, and I am very much come back to our original view of the matter, that we must continue merely to be lookers-on till the war shall have taken a more decided turn.

"THE PRESDT. IS IN EARNEST": MASSACHUSETTS, OCTOBER 1862

Charles Sumner to John Bright

Senator Sumner wrote to reassure Bright, a member of Parliament and prominent supporter of the Union cause, who had observed that the Emancipation Proclamation "means that you will preserve the Union even tho' it involve a social revolution in the South," and he asked if the government "be thoroughly supported by all the free States in such a policy?" While the Democrats made gains in Congress and governorships and state legislatures in the midterm elections, Republican control of Congress was not at risk.

---

private

Boston 28th Oct. '62

Dear Mr Bright,

I wish that I were at Landudno where for a day I could talk on our affairs, & enjoy a little repose.

The Presdt. is in earnest. He has no thought of any backward step. Of this be assured. Since I last wrote you I have been in Washington, where I saw him daily, & became acquainted precisely with his position at that time. There is nobody in the cabinet who is for "backing-down." It is not talked of or thought of.

The Presdt. was brought slowly to the Proclamation. It was written six weeks before it was put forth, & delayed, waiting for a victory; & the battle of Antietam was so regarded. I protested against the delay, & wished it to be put forth—the sooner the better—without any reference to our military condition. In the cabinet it was at first opposed strenuously by Seward, who, from the beginning has failed to see this war in its true character, & whose contrivances & anticipation have been those merely of a politician, who did not see the elemental forces engaged. But he countersigned the Proclamation, which was written by the Presdt himself, as you may infer from the style.

The old Democracy (more than half of which is now in armed Rebellion) are rallying against the Proclamation. At this moment our chief if not only danger is from the division which they may create at the North. The recent elections have shewn losses for the Administration; but these may be explained by the larger proportion of Republicans who have gone to the war. I regret these losses; but I do not think it possible that we can be without a determined working majority in the House, who will not hearken to any proposition, except the absolute submission of the rebels.

The hesitation of the Administration to adopt the policy of Emancipation led democrats to feel that the President was against it & they have gradually rallied. I think a more determined policy months ago would have prevented them from shewing their heads. The President himself has played the part of the farmer in the fable who warmed the frozen snake at his fire.

But from this time forward our whole policy will be more vigorous, & I should not be astonished to see the whole Rebellion crumble like yr Sepoy Rebellion, which for a while seemed as menacing to yr Indian Empire as ours has been to our Republic. I believe that I have avoided in my letters any very confident predictions. I have never seen our affairs with Mr Seward's eyes. But I have from the beginning seen that our only chance against the Rebellion was by striking Slavery, &, it seemed to me that these mighty armaments on both sides & their terrible shock were intended to insure its destruction. It is time for it to come to an end.

I am grateful to you that you have kept yr faith in us, & I pray you to persevere. I write to you sincerely, as I feel, & I beg you to believe that I would not excite any confidence which I do not believe well-founded.—Of course, we have before us the whole reconstruction of Southern Society. I have seen it so from the beginning. But I have hope that our people will rise to the grandeur of the occasion. The Colonization delusion is from Montgomery Blair, Post-Master Genl. who has made a convert of the President. But thus far I have thought it best to allow it to have a free course & thus to avoid a difference with the Presdt. Our generals are inefficient; but our troops are excellent. I have loved England, & now deplore her miserable & utterly false position towards my country. God bless you.

Ever Yrs   Charles Sumner

"AN AUGER TOO DULL TO TAKE HOLD": WASHINGTON, D.C., NOVEMBER 1862

Francis Preston Blair to Montgomery Blair

The wily Washington political veteran explains to his son, the postmaster general, the advice he gave the President regarding the politics of either retaining or dismissing McClellan—politics that bore on the Democrats' presidential nominee for 1864. Should there be a new Army of the Potomac commander, Blair recommends his son Frank, now a general serving in the western theater, to be the new man's chief of staff. The President did not reveal to Blair that he had already reached a decision regarding General McClellan.

I had a long talk with the President last night in his solitude. The torpidity of McClellan, will I fear prove fatal to him & our cause—I urged on the Prest. Mc's late success and the armys devotion to him. The difficulty of finding any other capable of wielding so great a force & to be trusted with working so complicated a machine under increased difficulties impending. His answer was that "he had tried long enough to bore with an auger too dull to take hold"—

I represented to him, the probable effect of superseding Mc & yielding to the pressure which it is known looked to succeed through the fast process of Pope, McDowell &c. Their catastrophe ought to be a warning. Yielding again to the ultras who seek to accomplish our purposes by unusual & extravagant means would give countenance to the charges of late triumph & consequently hold on the public mind—If on the contrary, Mc could be pushed on in the line he has taken & compelled to make a winter campaign, if successful the Democrats in Congress who are in heart on the side of Oligarchy & the South,—would be compelled to make war on him, & he would be compelled to take sides with the President bringing to his support in Congress the real war Democrats, while those who would resuscitate that party to carry the next Presidency, would necessarily take an antiMcClellan man for their candidate—whereas if Mc should fail as a general, he would fail on their conclusive policy and as the chief of that party they would fail with him—

In every aspect in which I can view it, the cause I think would be best served by retaining Mc at least until he makes a failure if that cannot be averted & not change him for an untried man while the Laurels of South Mountain & Antietam are fresh.

I entreated the President to send some common friend to Mc to have an explicit understanding with him—telling him what the President expected him to do & when & telling him that absolute & prompt obedience was the tenure by which alone he held his command. If it be given to Hooker or some others, mere fighting men, who want Brains tell the President I would be glad Frank were appointed Chief of Staff— He could supply strength at least.

Yours afta. F. P. Blair

November 7, 1862

McCLELLAN'S DISMISSAL:
VIRGINIA, NOVEMBER 1862

George G. Meade to Margaret Meade

On November 5 Lincoln ordered the dismissal of McClellan and his replacement by Ambrose Burnside. Meade, a division commander in the Army of the Potomac—and future commanding general of that army—told his wife of the reaction in the army to McClellan's removal. He found McClellan's situation similar to that of General Zachary Taylor in the Mexican War—and Taylor ended up in the White House.

Camp near Warrenton Va
Nov. 8. 1862

Dear Margaret,

I wrote you yesterday a long and dismal letter founded on a report that Seymour gave me which I have reason to believe to day was founded in mis-apprehension. This morning I found myself accidentally at Reynolds with Gibbons. Some conversation took place about Gibbons position, when Gibbons said that Col. S. Meredith of Indiana, (an old politician utterly incompetent who had been made a Brigadier) had told him he was going to have him made a Major General. Well said Reynolds he has succeeded for I understand *you & I & Meade* are to be promoted. Ah said I I understood yesterday just the reverse. Reynolds observed well but you were told before you would be. The conversation here stopped as I did not wish to let Reynolds know what Seymour had said but I was satisfied Reynolds never told him, it was decided *not* to promote me but may have remained silent, when Seymour referred to my case, thinking he (S) would not like my promotion.

Afterwards in a conversation with Gibbon he told me that McClellan had said to him that he had recommended both of us. I am glad to do McClellan this justice, because altho' I do not think he has treated me altogether as well as I had a right to expect yet I am thankful for what he has done, & wish to give him all the credit that is due particularly as to day the order has been received relieving him from duty with this Army & placing *Burnside* in command.—I must confess I was surprised at this, as I thought the storm had blown over. If he had been relieved immediately after the battle of Antietam, or at any period before he moved, I could have seen some show of reason on *military* grounds. This removal *now* proves conclusively that the cause is political, and the date of the order *Nov. 5* (the day after the N. Yk election) confirms it. I presume they have said—Well if the Democrats choose to come out openly against us & organise a formidable opposition, we will not permit them to have the comd. Genl. of the Army, and as they look on McClellan as the military representative of the Democracy, they have struck a blow at the party thro' him. But they never made a greater mistake in their lives, and like the attempt to put down Taylor in Mexico it will most certainly result in making a martyr of McClellan, and putting him in the White house. Indeed I should not be surprised if it results in bringing about a revolution at the North & in the *people* demanding his restoration.—I understand he takes it very quietly, except that he says all consideration for the administration on his part is now gone, and that it shall be war to the knife between him & them. It is a pity he did not take this stand some time ago, and not have submitted as he has done so long in silence to the outrages perpetrated on him. The army is filled with gloom and their spirit greatly depressed. —Burnside it is said wept like a child, and is the most distressed man in the army—openly says he is not fit for the position, and that McClellan is the only man we have who can handle the large army now collected together, 120,000 men.

It will be a great triumph to the South, will raise & inspirit their army, for McClellan is the only man they respect & fear, and in its moral effect can not but be most injurious to our cause.—I am sick & tired of the whole business, and most heartily wish I could be honorably released. I am sure if I were in McClellans place I would feel most grateful to them for letting me retire without any fault on my part.

I trust this letter will reach you before you have done any action, on my last. Still I would advise the stirring up of our friends, and the interesting personally Gov. Curtin on my behalf, if it can be done quietly without attracting notice—also

Senator Cowan if you can find any mode of approaching him. It is always to one's interest to be identified with a state, and I have at last succeeded in becoming known as a Pennsylvanian.

Every thing has been quiet today, and no indication of the enemy in any force between the Rapidan & Rappahannock. They do not seem disposed to dispute our crossing of the latter river, whatever they may do when we get to the former.—

I understand Porters corps has come up and I will try to see Willie Townsend.—We (the Generals) are going tomorrow in a body to pay our respects & bid farewell to McClellan who leaves in the afternoon. He is ordered to Trenton, N. Jersey to await further orders. I wish I could be with you & remain with you & the dear children. Kiss them all and try & be cheerful.

Ever yours, Geo. G. Meade

LINCOLN AND McCLELLAN: WASHINGTON, D.C., NOVEMBER 1862

Orville H. Browning: Diary, November 29, 1862

Lincoln unburdened himself on the topic of General McClellan and other matters to his old Illinois friend Senator Browning. His reference to proclamations are those of emancipation and habeas corpus. The allegations the president mentions against General Fitz John Porter at Second Bull Run led to Porter's court-martial in December. By this date Burnside had initiated a winter campaign against the Confederates at Fredericksburg on the Rappahannock.

Saturday Nov 29, 1862 Sheffield arrived this morning before breakfast. At 12 I called on the President. He was apparently very glad to see me, and received me with much cordiality. We had a long familiar talk. When speaking of the result of the recent elections I told him that his proclamations had been disasterous to us. That prior to issuing them all loyal people were united in support of the war and the administration. That the masses of the democratic party were satisfied with him, and warmly supporting him, and that their disloyal leaders could not rally them in opposition—They had no issue without taking ground against the war, and upon that we would annihilate them. But the proclamations had revived old party issues—given them a rallying cry—capitol to operate upon and that we had the results in our defeat. To this he made no reply.

I added that the Republican party could not put down the rebellion—that no party could do it—that it required a union of all loyal men in the free states to give us success, and that without that union we must disasterously fail. To all this he fully assented.

I asked him whether Genl Pope was a failure, or whether he had been sacrificed by the bad faith of his officers. He replied that he knew no reason to suspect any one of bad faith except Fitz John Porter, and that he very much hoped an investigation would relieve him from suspicion, but that at present he believed his disobedience of orders, and his failure to go to Popes aid in the battle of Friday had occasioned our defeat, and deprived us of a victory which would have terminated the war. That all Popes orders, and all his movements had met with the full approval of Genl Halleck and himself with one exception. That during the conflict between Popes and the rebel army, he Pope, had placed a portion of his army in a position, which he pointed out to me on the map, which alarmed him, but that no bad results followed—in fact it had turned out fortunately

That after the last battle fought by Pope the army was much demoralized, and it was feared the enemy would be down on Washington. In this emergency he had called McClellan here to take upon him the defence of the City—That he soon brought order out of chaos, and got the army in good condition. That for such work McClellan had great talents—Indeed for organizing, disciplining and preparing an army for the field and handling it in the field he was superior to any of our Genls That when the rebels crossed into Maryland he sent for Burnsides and told him he must take command of our army, march against the enemy and give him battle. Burnsides declined—said the responsibility was too great—the consequences of defeat too momentous—he was willing to command a Corps under McClellan, but was not willing to take the chief command of the army—hence McClellan was reinstated. The battles of South Mountain and Antietam were fought with ability—as well as any Genl could have fought them, but McClellan was too slow in his movements. He could and ought to have prevented the loss of Harper's Ferry, but was six days marching 40 miles, and it was surrendered. He did not follow up his advantages after Antietam. The army of the enemy should have been annihilated, but it was permitted to recross the Potomac without the loss of a man, and McClellan would not follow. He coaxed, urged & ordered him, but all would not do. At the expiration of two weeks after a peremptory order to that effect he had only 3/4 of his army across the River, and was six days doing that, whereas the rebel army had effected a crossing in one day

He concluded as he has in all the conversations I have had

with him about McClellan by saying that his great defect was his excess of caution I asked him about what Butler told me in Springfield that Fitz John Porter & Genl Griffing had sent a despatch to McClellan to hold on, that they had Pope where they could ruin, and that this despatch was in the Presidents hands—He said there was no shadow of foundation for such a story and no truth in it. I asked him about Burnsides army before Fredericksburg, and whether it was likely soon to accomplish any thing. He answered that Burnsides was now here consulting upon that subject—That he and Halleck had just left the room as I entered. That to get at the enemy he had to cross the Rappanhannock, and that to cross in the face of an opposing army was very hazardous, especially as he did not know its strength, and could not ascertain it. They had just been debating whether to move immediately, or whether to wait a few days till some collateral movement could be made to create a diversion which would render the passage less difficult, and that the question would be decided to day Burnside had then gone with Halleck and would receive his final orders before he left him.

Sheffield arrived this morning, and Cowan at night. Also Giffin and his wife

WASHINGTON, D.C., DECEMBER 1862

Abraham Lincoln: Annual Message to Congress

Lincoln began his message of December 1 routinely enough, reporting on foreign affairs and financial matters and various domestic concerns, using material supplied by various cabinet officers. But then he elevated both his purpose and his rhetoric, seeking to eliminate the war's root cause, slavery, by means of compensated emancipation and colonization, to be achieved through constitutional amendments. "Mr Lincoln's whole soul is absorbed in his plan of remunerative emancipation," his friend David Davis wrote, "and he thinks if Congress dont fail him that the problem is solved." Congress did fail him, showing little favor for the proposed amendments. Still, Lincoln's closing appeal moved Horace Greeley's *Tribune* to claim, "Sentiments so noble, so forcible, so profoundly true, have very rarely found their way into the manifestoes of rulers and Governments."

December 1, 1862

Fellow-citizens of the Senate and House of Representatives:

Since your last annual assembling another year of health and bountiful harvests has passed. And while it has not pleased the Almighty to bless us with a return of peace, we can but press on, guided by the best light He gives us, trusting that in His own good time, and wise way, all will yet be well.

The correspondence touching foreign affairs which has taken place during the last year is herewith submitted, in virtual compliance with a request to that effect, made by the House of Representatives near the close of the last session of Congress.

If the condition of our relations with other nations is less gratifying than it has usually been at former periods, it is certainly more satisfactory than a nation so unhappily distracted as we are, might reasonably have apprehended. In the month of June last there were some grounds to expect that the maritime powers which, at the beginning of our domestic difficulties, so unwisely and unnecessarily, as we think, recognized the insurgents as a belligerent, would soon recede from that position, which has proved only less injurious to themselves, than to our own country. But the temporary reverses which afterwards befell the national arms, and which were exaggerated by our own disloyal citizens abroad have hitherto delayed that act of simple justice.

The civil war, which has so radically changed for the moment, the occupations and habits of the American people, has necessarily disturbed the social condition, and affected very deeply the prosperity of the nations with which we have carried on a commerce that has been steadily increasing throughout a period of half a century. It has, at the same time, excited political ambitions and apprehensions which have produced a profound agitation throughout the civilized world. In this unusual agitation we have forborne from taking part in any controversy between foreign states, and between parties or factions in such states. We have attempted no propagandism, and acknowledged no revolution. But we have left to every nation the exclusive conduct and management of its own affairs. Our struggle has been, of course, contemplated by foreign nations with reference less to its own merits, than to its supposed, and often exaggerated effects and consequences resulting to those nations themselves. Nevertheless, complaint on the part of this government, even if it were just, would certainly be unwise.

The treaty with Great Britain for the suppression of the slave trade has been put into operation with a good prospect of complete success. It is an occasion of special pleasure to acknowledge that the execution of it, on the part of Her Majesty's government, has been marked with a jealous respect for the authority of the United States, and the rights of their moral and loyal citizens.

The convention with Hanover for the abolition of the stade dues has been carried into full effect, under the act of Congress for that purpose.

A blockade of three thousand miles of sea-coast could not be established, and vigorously enforced, in a season of great commercial activity like the present, without committing occasional mistakes, and inflicting unintentional injuries upon foreign nations and their subjects.

A civil war occurring in a country where foreigners reside

and carry on trade under treaty stipulations, is necessarily fruitful of complaints of the violation of neutral rights. All such collisions tend to excite misapprehensions, and possibly to produce mutual reclamations between nations which have a common interest in preserving peace and friendship. In clear cases of these kinds I have, so far as possible, heard and redressed complaints which have been presented by friendly powers. There is still, however, a large and an augmenting number of doubtful cases upon which the government is unable to agree with the governments whose protection is demanded by the claimants. There are, moreover, many cases in which the United States, or their citizens, suffer wrongs from the naval or military authorities of foreign nations, which the governments of those states are not at once prepared to redress. I have proposed to some of the foreign states, thus interested, mutual conventions to examine and adjust such complaints. This proposition has been made especially to Great Britain, to France, to Spain, and to Prussia. In each case it has been kindly received, but has not yet been formally adopted.

I deem it my duty to recommend an appropriation in behalf of the owners of the Norwegian bark Admiral P. Tordenskiold, which vessel was, in May, 1861, prevented by the commander of the blockading force off Charleston from leaving that port with cargo, notwithstanding a similar privilege had, shortly before, been granted to an English vessel. I have directed the Secretary of State to cause the papers in the case to be communicated to the proper committees.

Applications have been made to me by many free Americans of African descent to favor their emigration, with a view to such colonization as was contemplated in recent acts of Congress. Other parties, at home and abroad—some from interested motives, others upon patriotic considerations, and still others influenced by philanthropic sentiments—have suggested similar measures; while, on the other hand, several of the Spanish-American republics have protested against the sending of such colonies to their respective territories. Under these circumstances, I have declined to move any such colony to any state, without first obtaining the consent of its government, with an agreement on its part to receive and protect such emigrants in all the rights of freemen; and I have, at the same time, offered to the several states situated within the tropics, or having colonies there, to negotiate with them, subject to the advice and consent of the Senate, to favor the voluntary emigration of persons of that class to their respective territories, upon conditions which shall be equal, just, and humane. Liberia and Hayti are, as yet, the only countries to which colonists of African descent from here, could go with certainty of being received and adopted as citizens; and I regret to say such persons, contemplating colonization, do not seem so willing to migrate to those countries, as to some others, nor so willing as I think their interest demands. I believe, however, opinion among them, in this respect, is improving; and that, ere long, there will be an augmented, and considerable migration to both these countries, from the United States.

The new commercial treaty between the United States and the Sultan of Turkey has been carried into execution.

A commercial and consular treaty has been negotiated, subject to the Senate's consent, with Liberia; and a similar negotiation is now pending with the republic of Hayti. A considerable improvement of the national commerce is expected to result from these measures.

Our relations with Great Britain, France, Spain, Portugal, Russia, Prussia, Denmark, Sweden, Austria, the Netherlands, Italy, Rome, and the other European states, remain undisturbed. Very favorable relations also continue to be maintained with Turkey, Morocco, China and Japan.

During the last year there has not only been no change of our previous relations with the independent states of our own continent, but, more friendly sentiments than have heretofore existed, are believed to be entertained by these neighbors, whose safety and progress, are so intimately connected with our own. This statement especially applies to Mexico, Nicaragua, Costa Rica, Honduras, Peru, and Chile.

The commission under the convention with the republic of New Granada closed its session, without having audited and passed upon, all the claims which were submitted to it. A proposition is pending to revive the convention, that it may be able to do more complete justice. The joint commission between the United States and the republic of Costa Rica has completed its labors and submitted its report.

I have favored the project for connecting the United States with Europe by an Atlantic telegraph, and a similar project to extend the telegraph from San Francisco, to connect by a Pacific telegraph with the line which is being extended across the Russian empire.

The Territories of the United States, with unimportant exceptions, have remained undisturbed by the civil war, and they are exhibiting such evidence of prosperity as justifies an expectation that some of them will soon be in a condition to be organized as States, and be constitutionally admitted into the federal Union.

The immense mineral resources of some of those Territories ought to be developed as rapidly as possible. Every step in that direction would have a tendency to improve the revenues of the government, and diminish the burdens of the people. It is worthy of your serious consideration whether some extraordinary measures to promote that end cannot be adopted. The means which suggests itself as most likely to be effective, is a scientific exploration of the mineral regions in those Territories, with a view to the publication of its results at home and in foreign countries—results which cannot fail to be auspicious.

The condition of the finances will claim your most diligent consideration. The vast expenditures incident to the military and naval operations required for the suppression of the rebellion, have hitherto been met with a promptitude, and certainty, unusual in similar circumstances, and the public credit has been fully maintained. The continuance of the war, however, and the increased disbursements made necessary by the augmented forces now in the field, demand your best reflections as to the best modes of providing the necessary revenue, without injury to business and with the least possible burdens upon labor.

The suspension of specie payments by the banks, soon after the commencement of your last session, made large issues of United States notes unavoidable. In no other way could the payment of the troops, and the satisfaction of other just demands, be so economically, or so well provided for. The judicious legislation of Congress, securing the receivability of these notes for loans and internal duties, and making them a legal tender for other debts, has made them an universal currency;

and has satisfied, partially, at least, and for the time, the long felt want of an uniform circulating medium, saving thereby to the people, immense sums in discounts and exchanges.

A return to specie payments, however, at the earliest period compatible with due regard to all interests concerned, should ever be kept in view. Fluctuations in the value of currency are always injurious, and to reduce these fluctuations to the lowest possible point will always be a leading purpose in wise legislation. Convertibility, prompt and certain convertibility into coin, is generally acknowledged to be the best and surest safeguard against them; and it is extremely doubtful whether a circulation of United States notes, payable in coin, and sufficiently large for the wants of the people, can be permanently, usefully and safely maintained.

Is there, then, any other mode in which the necessary provision for the public wants can be made, and the great advantages of a safe and uniform currency secured?

I know of none which promises so certain results, and is, at the same time, so unobjectionable, as the organization of banking associations, under a general act of Congress, well guarded in its provisions. To such associations the government might furnish circulating notes, on the security of United States bonds deposited in the treasury. These notes, prepared under the supervision of proper officers, being uniform in appearance and security, and convertible always into coin, would at once protect labor against the evils of a vicious currency, and facilitate commerce by cheap and safe exchanges.

A moderate reservation from the interest on the bonds would compensate the United States for the preparation and distribution of the notes and a general supervision of the system, and would lighten the burden of that part of the public debt employed as securities. The public credit, moreover, would be greatly improved, and the negotiation of new loans greatly facilitated by the steady market demand for government bonds which the adoption of the proposed system would create.

It is an additional recommendation of the measure, of considerable weight, in my judgment, that it would reconcile, as far as possible, all existing interests, by the opportunity offered to existing institutions to reorganize under the act, substituting only the secured uniform national circulation for the local and various circulation, secured and unsecured, now issued by them.

The receipts into the treasury from all sources, including loans and balance from the preceding year, for the fiscal year ending on the 30th June, 1862, were $583,885,247 06, of which sum $49,056,397 62 were derived from customs; $1,795,331,73 from the direct tax; from public lands $152,203,77; from miscellaneous sources, $931,787 64; from loans in all forms, $529,692,460 50. The remainder, $2,257,065 80, was the balance from last year.

The disbursements during the same period were for congressional, executive, and judicial purposes, $5,939,009 29; for foreign intercourse, $1,339,710,35; for miscellaneous expenses, including the mints, loans, post office deficiencies, collection of revenue, and other like charges, $14,129,771 50; for expenses under the Interior Department, $3,102,985 52; under the War Department, $394,368,407,36; under the Navy Department, $42,674,569 69; for interest on public debt, $13,190,324 45; and for payment of public debt, including reimbursement of temporary loan, and redemptions, $96,096,922 09; making an aggregate of $570,841,700 25; and leaving a balance in the treasury on the first day of July, 1862, of $13,043,546,81.

It should be observed that the sum of $96,096,922 09, expended for reimbursements and redemption of public debt, being included also in the loans made, may be properly deducted, both from receipts and expenditures, leaving the actual receipts for the year $487,788,324 97; and the expenditures, $474,744,778 16.

Other information on the subject of the finances will be found in the report of the Secretary of the Treasury, to whose statements and views I invite your most candid and considerate attention.

The reports of the Secretaries of War, and of the Navy, are herewith transmitted. These reports, though lengthy, are scarcely more than brief abstracts of the very numerous and extensive transactions and operations conducted through those departments. Nor could I give a summary of them here, upon any principle, which would admit of its being much shorter than the reports themselves. I therefore content myself with laying the reports before you, and asking your attention to them.

It gives me pleasure to report a decided improvement in the financial condition of the Post Office Department, as compared with several preceding years. The receipts for the fiscal year 1861 amounted to $8,349,296 40, which embraced the revenue from all the States of the Union for three quarters of that year. Notwithstanding the cessation of revenue from the so-called seceded States during the last fiscal year, the increase of the correspondence of the loyal States has been sufficient to produce a revenue during the same year of $8,299,820 90, being only $50,000 less than was derived from all the States of the Union during the previous year. The expenditures show a still more favorable result. The amount expended in 1861 was $13,606,759 11. For the last year the amount has been reduced to $11,125,364 13, showing a decrease of about $2,481,000 in the expenditures as compared with the preceding year and about $3,750,000 as compared with the fiscal year 1860. The deficiency in the department for the previous year was $4,551,966.98. For the last fiscal year it was reduced to $2,112,814.57. These favorable results are in part owing to the cessation of mail service in the insurrectionary States, and in part to a careful review of all expenditures in that department in the interest of economy. The efficiency of the postal service, it is believed, has also been much improved. The Postmaster General has also opened a correspondence, through the Department of State, with foreign governments, proposing a convention of postal representatives for the purpose of simplifying the rates of foreign postage, and to expedite the foreign mails. This proposition, equally important to our adopted citizens, and to the commercial interests of this country, has been favorably entertained, and agreed to, by all the governments from whom replies have been received.

I ask the attention of Congress to the suggestions of the Postmaster General in his report respecting the further legislation required, in his opinion, for the benefit of the postal service.

The Secretary of the Interior reports as follows in regard to the public lands:

"The public lands have ceased to be a source of revenue.

From the 1st July, 1861, to the 30th September, 1862, the entire cash receipts from the sale of lands were $137,476 26—a sum much less than the expenses of our land system during the same period. The homestead law, which will take effect on the 1st of January next, offers such inducements to settlers, that sales for cash cannot be expected, to an extent sufficient to meet the expenses of the General Land Office, and the cost of surveying and bringing the land into market"

The discrepancy between the sum here stated as arising from the sales of the public lands, and the sum derived from the same source as reported from the Treasury Department arises, as I understand, from the fact that the periods of time, though apparently, were not really, coincident at the beginning point—the Treasury report including a considerable sum now, which had previously been reported from the Interior—sufficiently large to greatly overreach the sum derived from the three months now reported upon by the Interior, and not by the Treasury.

The Indian tribes upon our frontiers have, during the past year, manifested a spirit of insubordination, and, at several points, have engaged in open hostilities against the white settlements in their vicinity. The tribes occupying the Indian country south of Kansas, renounced their allegiance to the United States, and entered into treaties with the insurgents. Those who remained loyal to the United States were driven from the country. The chief of the Cherokees has visited this city for the purpose of restoring the former relations of the tribe with the United States. He alleges that they were constrained, by superior force, to enter into treaties with the insurgents, and that the United States neglected to furnish the protection which their treaty stipulations required.

In the month of August last the Sioux Indians, in Minnesota, attacked the settlements in their vicinity with extreme ferocity, killing, indiscriminately, men, women, and children. This attack was wholly unexpected, and, therefore, no means of defence had been provided. It is estimated that not less than eight hundred persons were killed by the Indians, and a large amount of property was destroyed. How this outbreak was induced is not definitely known, and suspicions, which may be unjust, need not to be stated. Information was received by the

Indian bureau, from different sources, about the time hostilities were commenced, that a simultaneous attack was to be made upon the white settlements by all the tribes between the Mississippi river and the Rocky mountains. The State of Minnesota has suffered great injury from this Indian war. A large portion of her territory has been depopulated, and a severe loss has been sustained by the destruction of property. The people of that State manifest much anxiety for the removal of the tribes beyond the limits of the State as a guarantee against future hostilities. The Commissioner of Indian Affairs will furnish full details. I submit for your especial consideration whether our Indian system shall not be remodelled. Many wise and good men have impressed me with the belief that this can be profitably done.

I submit a statement of the proceedings of commissioners, which shows the progress that has been made in the enterprise of constructing the Pacific railroad. And this suggests the earliest completion of this road, and also the favorable action of Congress upon the projects now pending before them for enlarging the capacities of the great canals in New York and Illinois, as being of vital, and rapidly increasing importance to the whole nation, and especially to the vast interior region hereinafter to be noticed at some greater length. I purpose having prepared and laid before you at an early day some interesting and valuable statistical information upon this subject. The military and commercial importance of enlarging the Illinois and Michigan canal, and improving the Illinois river, is presented in the report of Colonel Webster to the Secretary of War, and now transmitted to Congress. I respectfully ask attention to it.

To carry out the provisions of the act of Congress of the 15th of May last, I have caused the Department of Agriculture of the United States to be organized.

The Commissioner informs me that within the period of a few months this department has established an extensive system of correspondence and exchanges, both at home and abroad, which promises to effect highly beneficial results in the development of a correct knowledge of recent improvements in agriculture, in the introduction of new products, and in the collection of the agricultural statistics of the different States.

Also that it will soon be prepared to distribute largely seeds, cereals, plants and cuttings, and has already published, and liberally diffused, much valuable information in anticipation of a more elaborate report, which will in due time be furnished, embracing some valuable tests in chemical science now in progress in the laboratory.

The creation of this department was for the more immediate benefit of a large class of our most valuable citizens; and I trust that the liberal basis upon which it has been organized will not only meet your approbation, but that it will realize, at no distant day, all the fondest anticipations of its most sanguine friends, and become the fruitful source of advantage to all our people.

On the twenty-second day of September last a proclamation was issued by the Executive, a copy of which is herewith submitted.

In accordance with the purpose expressed in the second paragraph of that paper, I now respectfully recall your attention to what may be called "compensated emancipation."

A nation may be said to consist of its territory, its people, and its laws. The territory is the only part which is of certain durability. "One generation passeth away, and another generation cometh, but the earth abideth forever." It is of the first importance to duly consider, and estimate, this ever-enduring part. That portion of the earth's surface which is owned and inhabited by the people of the United States, is well adapted to be the home of one national family; and it is not well adapted for two, or more. Its vast extent, and its variety of climate and productions, are of advantage, in this age, for one people, whatever they might have been in former ages. Steam, telegraphs, and intelligence, have brought these, to be an advantageous combination, for one united people.

In the inaugural address I briefly pointed out the total inadequacy of disunion, as a remedy for the differences between the people of the two sections. I did so in language which I cannot improve, and which, therefore, I beg to repeat:

"One section of our country believes slavery is *right*, and ought to be extended, while the other believes it is *wrong*, and ought not to be extended. This is the only substantial dispute. The fugitive slave clause of the Constitution, and the law for the suppression of the foreign slave trade, are each as well enforced, perhaps, as any law can ever be in a community where the moral sense of the people imperfectly supports the law itself. The great body of the people abide by the dry legal obligation in both cases, and a few break over in each. This, I think, cannot be perfectly cured; and it would be worse in both cases *after* the separation of the sections, than before. The foreign slave trade, now imperfectly suppressed, would be ultimately revived without restriction in one section; while fugitive slaves, now only partially surrendered, would not be surrendered at all by the other.

"Physically speaking, we cannot separate. We cannot remove our respective sections from each other, nor build an impassable wall between them. A husband and wife may be divorced, and go out of the presence, and beyond the reach of each other; but the different parts of our country cannot do this. They cannot but remain face to face; and intercourse, either amicable or hostile, must continue between them. Is it possible, then, to make that intercourse more advantageous, or more satisfactory, *after* separation than *before*? Can aliens make treaties, easier than friends can make laws? Can treaties be more faithfully enforced between aliens, than laws can among friends? Suppose you go to war, you cannot fight always; and when, after much loss on both sides, and no gain on either, you cease fighting, the identical old questions, as to terms of intercourse, are again upon you."

There is no line, straight or crooked, suitable for a national boundary, upon which to divide. Trace through, from east to west, upon the line between the free and slave country, and we shall find a little more than one-third of its length are rivers, easy to be crossed, and populated, or soon to be populated, thickly upon both sides; while nearly all its remaining length, are merely surveyor's lines, over which people may walk back and forth without any consciousness of their presence. No part of this line can be made any more difficult to pass, by writing it down on paper, or parchment, as a national boundary. The fact of separation, if it comes, gives up, on the part of the seceding section, the fugitive slave clause, along with all other constitutional obligations upon the section seceded from, while

I should expect no treaty stipulation would ever be made to take its place.

But there is another difficulty. The great interior region, bounded east by the Alleghanies, north by the British dominions, west by the Rocky mountains, and south by the line along which the culture of corn and cotton meets, and which includes part of Virginia, part of Tennessee, all of Kentucky, Ohio, Indiana, Michigan, Wisconsin, Illinois, Missouri, Kansas, Iowa, Minnesota and the Territories of Dakota, Nebraska, and part of Colorado, already has above ten millions of people, and will have fifty millions within fifty years, if not prevented by any political folly or mistake. It contains more than one-third of the country owned by the United States—certainly more than one million of square miles. Once half as populous as Massachusetts already is, it would have more than seventy-five millions of people. A glance at the map shows that, territorially speaking, it is the great body of the republic. The other parts are but marginal borders to it, the magnificent region sloping west from the rocky mountains to the Pacific, being the deepest, and also the richest, in undeveloped resources. In the production of provisions, grains, grasses, and all which proceed from them, this great interior region is naturally one of the most important in the world. Ascertain from the statistics the small proportion of the region which has, as yet, been brought into cultivation, and also the large and rapidly increasing amount of its products, and we shall be overwhelmed with the magnitude of the prospect presented. And yet this region has no sea-coast, touches no ocean anywhere. As part of one nation, its people now find, and may forever find, their way to Europe by New York, to South America and Africa by New Orleans, and to Asia by San Francisco. But separate our common country into two nations, as designed by the present rebellion, and every man of this great interior region is thereby cut off from some one or more of these outlets, not, perhaps, by a physical barrier, but by embarrassing and onerous trade regulations.

And this is true, *wherever* a dividing, or boundary line, may be fixed. Place it between the now free and slave country, or place it south of Kentucky, or north of Ohio, and still the truth remains, that none south of it, can trade to any port or place north of it, and none north of it, can trade to any port or place south of it, except upon terms dictated by a government foreign to them. These outlets, east, west, and south, are indispensable to the well-being of the people inhabiting, and to inhabit, this vast interior region. *Which* of the three may be the best, is no proper question. All, are better than either, and all, of right, belong to that people, and to their successors forever. True to themselves, they will not ask *where* a line of separation shall be, but will vow, rather, that there shall be no such line. Nor are the marginal regions less interested in these communications to, and through them, to the great outside world. They too, and each of them, must have access to this Egypt of the West, without paying toll at the crossing of any national boundary.

Our national strife springs not from our permanent part; not from the land we inhabit; not from our national homestead. There is no possible severing of this, but would multiply, and not mitigate, evils among us. In all its adaptations and aptitudes, it demands union, and abhors separation. In fact, it would, ere long, force reunion, however much of blood and treasure the separation might have cost.

Our strife pertains to ourselves—to the passing generations of men; and it can, without convulsion, be hushed forever with the passing of one generation.

In this view, I recommend the adoption of the following resolution and articles amendatory to the Constitution of the United States:

"*Resolved by the Senate and House of Representatives of the United States of America in Congress assembled*, (two thirds of both houses concurring,) That the following articles be proposed to the legislatures (or conventions) of the several States as amendments to the Constitution of the United States, all or any of which articles when ratified by three-fourths of the said legislatures (or conventions) to be valid as part or parts of the said Constitution, viz:

"Article ——.

"Every State, wherein slavery now exists, which shall abolish the same therein, at any time, or times, before the first day of

January, in the year of our Lord one thousand and nine hundred, shall receive compensation from the United States as follows, to wit:

"The President of the United States shall deliver to every such State, bonds of the United States, bearing interest at the rate of —— per cent, per annum, to an amount equal to the aggregate sum of for each slave shown to have been therein, by the eighth census of the United States, said bonds to be delivered to such State by instalments, or in one parcel, at the completion of the abolishment, accordingly as the same shall have been gradual, or at one time, within such State; and interest shall begin to run upon any such bond, only from the proper time of its delivery as aforesaid. Any State having received bonds as aforesaid, and afterwards reintroducing or tolerating slavery therein, shall refund to the United States the bonds so received, or the value thereof, and all interest paid thereon.

"Article ——.

"All slaves who shall have enjoyed actual freedom by the chances of the war, at any time before the end of the rebellion, shall be forever free; but all owners of such, who shall not have been disloyal, shall be compensated for them, at the same rates as is provided for States adopting abolishment of slavery, but in such way, that no slave shall be twice accounted for.

"Article ——.

"Congress may appropriate money, and otherwise provide, for colonizing free colored persons, with their own consent, at any place or places without the United States."

I beg indulgence to discuss these proposed articles at some length. Without slavery the rebellion could never have existed; without slavery it could not continue.

Among the friends of the Union there is great diversity, of sentiment, and of policy, in regard to slavery, and the African race amongst us. Some would perpetuate slavery; some would abolish it suddenly, and without compensation; some would abolish it gradually, and with compensation; some would remove the freed people from us, and some would retain them with us; and there are yet other minor diversities. Because of these diversities, we waste much strength in struggles among ourselves.

By mutual concession we should harmonize, and act together. This would be compromise; but it would be compromise among the friends, and not with the enemies of the Union. These articles are intended to embody a plan of such mutual concessions. If the plan shall be adopted, it is assumed that emancipation will follow, at least, in several of the States.

As to the first article, the main points are: first, the emancipation; secondly, the length of time for consummating it—thirty-seven years; and thirdly, the compensation.

The emancipation will be unsatisfactory to the advocates of perpetual slavery; but the length of time should greatly mitigate their dissatisfaction. The time spares both races from the evils of sudden derangement—in fact, from the necessity of any derangement—while most of those whose habitual course of thought will be disturbed by the measure will have passed away before its consummation. They will never see it. Another class will hail the prospect of emancipation, but will deprecate the length of time. They will feel that it gives too little to the now living slaves. But it really gives them much. It saves them from the vagrant destitution which must largely attend immediate emancipation in localities where their numbers are very great; and it gives the inspiring assurance that their posterity shall be free forever. The plan leaves to each State, choosing to act under it, to abolish slavery now, or at the end of the century, or at any intermediate time, or by degrees, extending over the whole or any part of the period; and it obliges no two states to proceed alike. It also provides for compensation, and generally the mode of making it. This, it would seem, must further mitigate the dissatisfaction of those who favor perpetual slavery, and especially of those who are to receive the compensation. Doubtless some of those who are to pay, and not to receive will object. Yet the measure is both just and economical. In a certain sense the liberation of slaves is the destruction of property—property acquired by descent, or by purchase, the same as any other property. It is no less true for having been often said, that the people of the south are not more responsible for the original introduction of this property, than are the people of the north; and when it is remembered how unhesitatingly we all use cotton and sugar, and share the profits of dealing in them, it may not be quite safe to say, that the south has been more responsible than the north for its continuance. If then, for a common object, this property is to be sacrificed is it not just that it be done at a common charge?

And if, with less money, or money more easily paid, we can preserve the benefits of the Union by this means, than we can by the war alone, is it not also economical to do it? Let us consider it then. Let us ascertain the sum we have expended in the war since compensated emancipation was proposed last March, and consider whether, if that measure had been promptly accepted, by even some of the slave States, the same sum would not have done more to close the war, than has been otherwise done. If so the measure would save money, and, in that view, would be a prudent and economical measure. Certainly it is not so easy to pay *something* as it is to pay *nothing*; but it is easier to pay a *large* sum than it is to pay a larger one. And it is easier to pay any sum *when* we are able, than it is to pay it *before* we are able. The war requires large sums, and requires them at once. The aggregate sum necessary for compensated emancipation, of course, would be large. But it would require no ready cash; nor the bonds even, any faster than the emancipation progresses. This might not, and probably would not, close before the end of the thirty-seven years. At that time we shall probably have a hundred millions of people to share the burden, instead of thirty one millions, as now. And not only so, but the increase of our population may be expected to continue for a long time after that period, as rapidly as before; because our territory will not have become full. I do not state this inconsiderately. At the same ratio of increase which we have maintained, on an average, from our first national census, in 1790, until that of 1860, we should, in 1900, have a population of 103,208,415. And why may we not continue that ratio far beyond that period? Our abundant room—our broad national homestead—is our ample resource. Were our territory as limited as are the British Isles, very certainly our population could not expand as stated. Instead of receiving the foreign born, as now, we should be compelled to send part of the native born away. But such is not our condition. We have two millions nine hundred and sixty-three thousand square miles.

Europe has three millions and eight hundred thousand, with a population averaging seventy-three and one-third persons to the square mile. Why may not our country, at some time, average as many? Is it less fertile? Has it more waste surface, by mountains, rivers, lakes, deserts, or other causes? Is it inferior to Europe in any natural advantage? If, then, we are, at some time, to be as populous as Europe, how soon? As to when this *may* be, we can judge by the past and the present; as to when it *will* be, if ever, depends much on whether we maintain the Union. Several of our States are already above the average of Europe—seventy three and a third to the square mile. Massachusetts has 157; Rhode Island, 133; Connecticut, 99; New York and New Jersey, each, 80; also two other great States, Pennsylvania and Ohio, are not far below, the former having 63, and the latter 59. The States already above the European average, except New York, have increased in as rapid a ratio, since passing that point, as ever before; while no one of them is equal to some other parts of our country, in natural capacity for sustaining a dense population.

Taking the nation in the aggregate, and we find its population and ratio of increase, for the several decennial periods, to be as follows:—

1790	3,929,827		
1800	5,305,937	35.02 per cent.	ratio of increase
1810	7,239,814	36.45	"
1820	9,638,131	33.13	"
1830	12,866,020	33.49	"
1840	17,069,453	32.67	"
1850	23,191,876	35.87	"
1860	31,443,790	35.58	"

This shows an average decennial increase of 34.60 per cent. in population through the seventy years from our first, to our last census yet taken. It is seen that the ratio of increase, at no one of these seven periods, is either two per cent. below, or two per cent. above, the average; thus showing how inflexible, and, consequently, how reliable, the law of increase, in our case, is. Assuming that it will continue, gives the following results:—

1870	42,323,341	1910	138,918,526
1880	56,967,216	1920	186,984,335
1890	76,677,872	1930	251,680,914
1900	103,208,415		

These figures show that our country *may* be as populous as Europe now is, at some point between 1920 and 1930—say about 1925—our territory, at seventy-three and a third persons to the square mile, being of capacity to contain 217,186,000.

And we *will* reach this, too, if we do not ourselves relinquish the chance, by the folly and evils of disunion, or by long and exhausting war springing from the only great element of national discord among us. While it cannot be foreseen exactly how much one huge example of secession, breeding lesser ones indefinitely, would retard population, civilization, and prosperity, no one can doubt that the extent of it would be very great and injurious.

The proposed emancipation would shorten the war, perpetuate peace, insure this increase of population, and proportionately the wealth of the country. With these, we should pay all the emancipation would cost, together with our other debt, easier than we should pay our other debt, without it. If we had allowed our old national debt to run at six per cent. per annum, simple interest, from the end of our revolutionary struggle until to day, without paying anything on either principal or interest, each man of us would owe less upon that debt now, than each man owed upon it then; and this because our increase of men, through the whole period, has been greater than six per cent.; has run faster than the interest upon the debt. Thus, time alone relieves a debtor nation, so long as its population increases faster than unpaid interest accumulates on its debt.

This fact would be no excuse for delaying payment of what is justly due; but it shows the great importance of time in this connexion—the great advantage of a policy by which we shall not have to pay until we number a hundred millions, what, by a different policy, we would have to pay now, when we number but thirty one millions. In a word, it shows that a dollar will be much harder to pay for the war, than will be a dollar for emancipation on the proposed plan. And then the latter will cost no blood, no precious life. It will be a saving of both.

As to the second article, I think it would be impracticable to return to bondage the class of persons therein contemplated. Some of them, doubtless, in the property sense, belong to loyal owners; and hence, provision is made in this article for compensating such.

The third article relates to the future of the freed people. It does not oblige, but merely authorizes, Congress to aid in colonizing such as may consent. This ought not to be regarded as objectionable, on the one hand, or on the other, in so much as it comes to nothing, unless by the mutual consent of the people to be deported, and the American voters, through their representatives in Congress.

I cannot make it better known than it already is, that I strongly favor colonization. And yet I wish to say there is an objection urged against free colored persons remaining in the country, which is largely imaginary, if not sometimes malicious.

It is insisted that their presence would injure, and displace white labor and white laborers. If there ever could be a proper time for mere catch arguments, that time surely is not now. In times like the present, men should utter nothing for which they would not willingly be responsible through time and in eternity. Is it true, then, that colored people can displace any more white labor, by being free, than by remaining slaves? If they stay in their old places, they jostle no white laborers; if they leave their old places, they leave them open to white laborers. Logically, there is neither more nor less of it. Emancipation, even without deportation, would probably enhance the wages of white labor, and, very surely, would not reduce them. Thus, the customary amount of labor would still have to be performed; the freed people would surely not do more than their old proportion of it, and very probably, for a time, would do less, leaving an increased part to white laborers, bringing their labor into greater demand, and, consequently, enhancing the wages of it. With deportation, even to a limited extent, enhanced wages to white labor is mathematically certain. Labor is like any other commodity in the market—increase the demand for it, and you increase the price of it. Reduce the supply of black labor, by colonizing the black laborer out of the country, and, by precisely so much, you increase the demand for, and wages of, white labor.

But it is dreaded that the freed people will swarm forth, and cover the whole land? Are they not already in the land? Will liberation make them any more numerous? Equally distributed among the whites of the whole country, and there would be but one colored to seven whites. Could the one, in any way, greatly disturb the seven? There are many communities now, having more than one free colored person, to seven whites; and this, without any apparent consciousness of evil from it. The District of Columbia, and the States of Maryland and Delaware, are all in this condition. The District has more than one free colored to six whites; and yet, in its frequent petitions to Congress, I believe it has never presented the presence of free colored persons as one of its grievances. But why should emancipation south, send the free people north? People, of any color, seldom run, unless there be something to run from. *Heretofore* colored people, to some extent, have fled north from bondage; and *now*, perhaps, from both bondage and destitution. But if gradual emancipation and deportation be adopted, they will have neither to flee from. Their old masters will give them wages at least until new laborers can be procured; and the freed men, in turn, will gladly give their labor for the wages, till new homes can be found for them, in congenial climes, and with people of their own blood and race. This proposition can be trusted on the mutual interests involved. And, in any event, cannot the north decide for itself, whether to receive them?

Again, as practice proves more than theory, in any case, has there been any irruption of colored people northward, because of the abolishment of slavery in this District last spring?

What I have said of the proportion of free colored persons to the whites, in the District, is from the census of 1860, having no reference to persons called contrabands, nor to those made free by the act of Congress abolishing slavery here.

The plan consisting of these articles is recommended, not but that a restoration of the national authority would be accepted without its adoption.

Nor will the war, nor proceedings under the proclamation

of September 22, 1862, be stayed because of the *recommendation* of this plan. Its timely *adoption*, I doubt not, would bring restoration and thereby stay both.

And, notwithstanding this plan, the recommendation that Congress provide by law for compensating any State which may adopt emancipation, before this plan shall have been acted upon, is hereby earnestly renewed. Such would be only an advance part of the plan, and the same arguments apply to both.

This plan is recommended as a means, not in exclusion of, but additional to, all others for restoring and preserving the national authority throughout the Union. The subject is presented exclusively in its economical aspect. The plan would, I am confident, secure peace more speedily, and maintain it more permanently, than can be done by force alone; while all it would cost, considering amounts, and manner of payment, and times of payment, would be easier paid than will be the additional cost of the war, if we rely solely upon force. It is much—very much—that it would cost no blood at all.

The plan is proposed as permanent constitutional law. It cannot become such without the concurrence of, first, two-thirds of Congress, and, afterwards, three-fourths of the States. The requisite three-fourths of the States will necessarily include seven of the Slave states. Their concurrence, if obtained, will give assurance of their severally adopting emancipation, at no very distant day, upon the new constitutional terms. This assurance would end the struggle now, and save the Union forever.

I do not forget the gravity which should characterize a paper addressed to the Congress of the nation by the Chief Magistrate of the nation. Nor do I forget that some of you are my seniors, nor that many of you have more experience than I, in the conduct of public affairs. Yet I trust that in view of the great responsibility resting upon me, you will perceive no want of respect to yourselves, in any undue earnestness I may seem to display.

Is it doubted, then, that the plan I propose, if adopted, would shorten the war, and thus lessen its expenditure of money and of blood? Is it doubted that it would restore the national authority and national prosperity, and perpetuate both indefinitely? Is it doubted that we here—Congress and Executive—can secure its adoption? Will not the good people respond to a united, and earnest appeal from us? Can we, can they, by any other means, so certainly, or so speedily, assure these vital objects? We can succeed only by concert. It is not "can *any* of us *imagine* better?" but "can we *all* do better?" Object whatsoever is possible, still the question recurs "can we do better?" The dogmas of the quiet past, are inadequate to the stormy present. The occasion is piled high with difficulty, and we must rise with the occasion. As our case is new, so we must think anew, and act anew. We must disenthrall our selves, and then we shall save our country.

Fellow-citizens, *we* cannot escape history. We of this Congress and this administration, will be remembered in spite of ourselves. No personal significance, or insignificance, can spare one or another of us. The fiery trial through which we pass, will light us down, in honor or dishonor, to the latest generation. We *say* we are for the Union. The world will not forget that we say this. We know how to save the Union. The world knows we do know how to save it. We—even *we here*—hold the power, and bear the responsibility. In *giving* freedom to the *slave*, we *assure* freedom to the *free*—honorable alike in what we give, and what we preserve. We shall nobly save, or meanly lose, the last best, hope of earth. Other means may succeed; this could not fail. The way is plain, peaceful, generous, just—a way which, if followed, the world will forever applaud, and God must forever bless.

December 1, 1862. ABRAHAM LINCOLN

BATTLE OF FREDERICKSBURG: VIRGINIA, DECEMBER 1862

Edward Porter Alexander: from Fighting for the Confederacy

General Burnside took command of the Army of the Potomac on November 7, and in ten days reached the Rappahannock opposite Fredericksburg. He had stolen a march on Lee and Fredericksburg was undefended. A pontoon train for bridging the river was to have been waiting for Burnside, but due to negligence in Washington it did not arrive until well after Lee had assembled his army and readied it to meet an attack. In his memoir, Edward Porter Alexander, now commanding an artillery battalion under James Longstreet's First Corps of the Army of Northern Virginia, spells out the deadly, nearly impregnable defenses awaiting the Union assault.

WITHIN A few days after I had given up my position on Gen. Lee's staff & taken command of my battn. of artillery, news reached us that Gen. McClellan had been deposed from command of the Army of the Potomac & succeeded by Gen. Burnside. No one was surprised then, & still less should anyone be surprised now when McClellan's inability to fight an army stands out so clearly in the light of his whole career, & particularly in his Sharpsburg campaign. Burnside did not want the position, but took it with the advice of his friends, to keep it from being offered to Hooker; of whom the old army influence by no means approved. Burnside was a man almost universally popular, though few thought him, & he did not apparently think himself, any great general. In my mind his name is associated with "Benny Havens's" near West Point, for he was old Benny's greatest admiration of all cadets ever at the Academy. He had graduated long before me, & had left the army but old Benny was always talking, even in my day, of "Ambrose Burnside."

The Federal army gave McClellan immense demonstrations of affection in telling him good-bye, & he devoted a day to receiving them. The men liked him because he had them well cared for, & they believed he would never expose them in action unnecessarily, which was most certainly true. But there was no kick against Burnside. Burnside was understood to have changed McClellan's plan of campaign for one of his own device—McC. had started to operate on a line towards Gordonsville. Burnside changed direction to Fredericksburg. It was certainly a great improvement, giving him a water base & a nearer one, & chances for new water bases, if successful, as he advanced on to Richmond. But he lost his campaign, & his excellent chances, from the miserable slowness & hesitation with which he executed his first step. He had six army corps of infantry, over 100,000 men. Lee was with Longstreet at Culpeper with about 30,000 men, & Jackson was up in the Valley with about the same number. Our pickets held the line of the Rappahannock, & there was a regiment of cavalry, perhaps, and a field battery at Fredericksburg.

On Nov. 17th the leading corps of Burnside's army arrived at Falmouth on the north side of the Rappahannock opposite Fred. but made no serious effort to cross. The news came to Gen. Lee about the _____ & on the 20th Longstreet's columns began to arrive on our side of the river. Burnside could easily with his immense force have crossed & at least occupied the town & a fortified camp on our side of the river. His excuse was the absence of his pontoon trains but he could have torn down houses & made boats or forded plenty of men to have taken the town. And at that time our army was, indeed, dangerously divided; Jackson being still in the Valley. And he did not come down to join us until about Dec. 3rd. Of course my battalion came down with Longstreet's infantry from Culpeper, & I encamped it west of the Plank Road, a mile or so out of town, nearly opposite Mr. Guest's house. I had been dined at that house, & also at Marye's, Stansbury's & Lacy's, when last at Fredbg., with my wife a few weeks after our wedding.

Very soon after my arrival I was directed to assist Gen. Lee's engineer officers in locating & constructing some pits for artillery at various points along the range of hills overlooking the town & valley of the river. The idea was that the enemy was likely to shell the town at any time, & our pits were ordered to be located so as to fire upon their batteries, if they did. But, in selecting the positions, I persuaded the engineers always to advance the guns to the brows of the hills so as to be able to sweep the approaches to the hills if it became necessary. And this brought about a little incident with Gen. Lee which, in the end, I enjoyed immensely. One day when the pits were nearly finished I was with a party working upon one on Marye's Hill, when Captain Sam Johnston, Gen. Lee's engineer in charge of the whole business, came up to tell me that Gen. Lee was inspecting the line man near by, & was blaming him for not having located the pits further back on the hill. He said, "You made me put them here. Now you come along & help me take the cussin." So I rode with him & when I came up Gen. Lee said, "Ah, Col. Alexander, just see what a mistake Captain Johnston has made here in the location of his gun pits, putting them forward at the brow of the hill!" I said, "Gen., I told him to put the pits there, where they could see all this canister & short range ground this side of the town. Back on the hill they can see nothing this side of the river." "But," he says, "you have lost some feet of command you might have had back there." I answered that that was a refinement which would cut no figure in comparison with the increased view, but he rather sat on me & had the last word, though I knew I was right & did not give it up.

Well, when the battle came on, Burnside's most powerful effort was made at that exact point, & the guns there never fired a shot at their distant view, but thousands of rounds into infantry swarming over the canister & short range ground, & contributed greatly to the enemy's bloody repulse. And a few evenings afterward, visiting Gen. Lee's camp, I took the opportunity, when the general was near enough to hear, to say loudly to Johnston, "Sam, it was a mighty good thing those guns about Marye's were located on the brows of the hills when the Yankees charged them!" I was half afraid the general might think me impertinent, though I could not resist the temptation to have one little dig at him. But he took it in silence & never let on that he was listening to us. I was however frequently put at location jobs afterward, &, thence to the close of the war, I never got but one more scolding (Oct. 7th, 1864) which I will tell of when I get to it.

Longstreet's corps at this time consisted of four regular divisions of infantry—Hood's, Pickett's, McLaws's, & Anderson's, & beside these Walker's temporary division of his own & Ransom's brigades was attached to us. Each division had some artillery attached to it, & these division batteries had in the fall gradually been made into battalions, & these battalions marched with the divisions & fought under control of the generals commanding them. Gen. Lee had on his staff a so called chief of artillery, Gen. Pendleton, but at this period his duties consisted principally in commanding a collection of some nine or ten batteries in 3 battalions called the Reserve Artillery, belonging to no corps, but kept ready to reinforce either which should need extra help. Later this command was broken up, & Gen. Pendleton after that was more directly looked on as the official head of all the artillery of the whole army. We made returns to him & drew supplies through him. And, later, each infantry corps had its own chief of artillery who, more & more, took direct command of all the battalions of the corps in battle, as well as on the march & in camp. But, at this time, I am not sure that even the title of "chief of artillery" of a corps was used. At first it was little more than a title given to the ranking battalion commander. But in battle he occupied himself principally with his own battalion. In Longstreet's corps the senior artillery officer was Col. Walton, who commanded the Washington Artillery from New Orleans—three small companies manning only 9 guns. His battalion & my 26 were called Longstreet's reserve artillery, & I made my returns & received orders through Col. Walton.

As I had had so much to do with selecting the line & positions I was practically allowed to choose for myself whether I would take any of the gun-pits on the line, in the approaching battle. But I decided not to take any. I never conceived for a moment that Burnside would make his main attack right where we were the strongest—at Marye's Hill, & I determined to keep most of my guns out in reserve, behind our left flank, expecting the brunt of the attack to fall there; but foot loose & ready to go anywhere. I thought he would try to turn our left flank on the river above Falmouth where his superior artillery, & a cloud of sharpshooters, on the north side could certainly destroy a part of our line near the river bank & enable his storming columns to make a lodgment. The ground is there yet to be looked at, and I submit that Burnside made a great mistake in not directing his attack there. I placed one light battery, Parker's, up that way, in the Stansbury yard & I placed Rhett, who had some heavy 20 pr. Parrott rifles, in pits on a high central hill near the Plank Road which overlooked our whole line & the plateau in rear of it, as a nucleus for a second line in case we were compelled to fall back or change front. The other four batteries I determined to hold in reserve in a little hollow west of the Plank Road whence I had roads in every direction.

Our pickets & the enemy's occupied opposite sides of the river in full view & short range but without firing on each other. It was the first time in the war, I believe, that this had ever happened. Before that they would keep up constant sharpshooting whenever they were within a half mile. But now both sides were willing to postpone killing each other until the grand struggle should be prepared. And, afterward, it became the general custom, to the close of the war, for pickets not to fire when there were no active operations on foot. So we built our batteries on our side & the enemy built a lot on his side, all without disturbance; and, beside our batteries, we very quietly constructed a good many rifle pits, on the edge of the town along the river, preparing to make it warm for them whenever they came to cross. As to the front of Marye's Hill, Gen. Longstreet says that I reported to him that a chicken could not find room to scratch where I could not rake the ground. I don't recall it, but very possibly I said something of the sort. It was exaggeration, but the ground was so thoroughly covered that I never thought Burnside would choose that point for attack.

At this time the enemy got to using his balloons on us again. We had not seen them since the Peninsula campaign. Now he used two of them constantly, endeavoring to locate our roads & encampments.

Jackson had joined us from the Valley about the 3rd. On the afternoon of Dec. 10th I received notice that the enemy intended to move on us the next morning at day break. Stuart had had some scouts within his lines & they had brought the news. Orders had been issued to the whole army that two guns, fired near headquarters, would be a signal upon which all troops must move to their assigned stations. About 4 A.M.

on the 11th, clear, cold, & still, the shots rang out, putting our 60,000 men in motion for their positions, & letting the enemy's 120,000 know that we were ready for them. Fredericksburg was the most dramatic of all our battles; the opposing hills & intermediate plain affording some wonderful & magnificent scenes. And I expect few who heard those two cannon shot, that cold morning, and rose & ate & hastened to their posts by starlight ever forgot the occasion.

The town itself was held by Barksdale's brigade (four Mississippi, & one Florida, regts.) of McLaws's division. McLaws was about the best general in the army for that sort of a job, being very painstaking in details, & having a good eye for ground. He had fixed up his sharpshooters all along the river to the Queen's taste. It was not expected that we could prevent the enemy from crossing but only designed to delay & annoy him as much as possible. Barksdale's men had reported, early in the night, the noise of boats & material being unloaded on the enemy's side, & long before daylight they could hear boats being put in the water & work commenced. But they were ordered to let the enemy get well committed to his work & to wait for good daylight before opening fire. Meanwhile, the guns which served as a signal to us, were also taken as a signal by most of the population of Fredericksburg to abandon the town. By every road there came numbers generally on foot, with carts loaded with bedding, &c. preparing to encamp in the woods back of our lines until the battle was over. The woods were full of them, mostly women & children. A few persons remained in the town, & though it was severely shelled, as will be told presently, no one I think was killed. But Gen. Couch, in the *Century*, speaks of the Federal soldiers looting the houses, & implies that no objection was offered by the officers.

Soon after day there rose from the river the merry popping of Barksdale's rifles. He had waited patiently until the light was good & the enemy getting careless, & he then opened suddenly a deadly fire upon them which ran them all to cover immediately. They deployed a large force of sharpshooters to try & keep down his fire & opened with their artillery & made many fresh attempts to continue their bridge-building, but were invariably driven back with loss. Meanwhile the morning wore on, calm, clear, & cold, but a very heavy smoky mist, something like that of an Indian summer, hung in the river valley in the early hours, gradually disappearing as the sun got power. The troops were all at ease along the line of battle, & looked across at the Federal army grandly displayed on the open slopes & bare hills on the north side; & listened to the fight of the sharpshooters on the river bank, which rose & fell from time to time, & in which from daylight a few Federal guns were taking a hand.

At last, near noon, Burnside out of all patience with the delay, thought to crush out the sharpshooters with one tremendous blow. He already had about 170 guns in position extending from Falmouth, above, to nearly two miles below Fredericksburg. He ordered that every gun within range should be turned upon the town & should throw fifty shells into it as fast as they could do it. Then I think was presented the most impressive exhibition of military force, by all odds, which I ever witnessed. The whole Federal army had broken up their camps, packed their wagons & moved out on the hills, ready to cross the river as soon as the bridges were completed. Over 100,000 infantry were visible, standing apparently in great solid squares upon the hilltops, for a space of three miles, scattered all over the slopes were endless parks of ambulances, ordnance, commissary, quartermaster & regimental white-topped wagons, also parked in close squares & rectangles, & very impressive in the sense of order & system which they conveyed. And still more impressive to military eyes though less conspicuous & showy were the dark colored parks of batteries of artillery scattered here & there among them. Then, in front, was the three mile line of angry blazing guns firing through white clouds of smoke & almost shaking the earth with their roar. Over & in the town the white winkings of the bursting shells reminded one of a countless swarm of fire-flies. Several buildings were set on fire, & their black smoke rose in remarkably slender, straight, & tall columns for two hundred feet, perhaps, before they began to spread horizontally & unite in a great black canopy. And over the whole scene there hung, high in the air, above the rear of the Federal lines, two immense black, captive balloons, like two great spirits of the air attendant on the coming struggle.

To all this cannonade not one of our guns replied with a single shot! We were saving every single round of ammunition we had for the infantry struggle which we knew would come. I had come forward to Marye's Hill to watch events & I sat there quietly & took it all in. And I could not but laugh out heartily, at times, to catch in the roar of the Federal guns the faint drownded pop of a musket which told that Barksdale's men were still in their rifle pits & still defiant. The contrast in the noises the two parties were making was very ludicrous. In fact the sharpshooters scattered in their pits were very little hurt. The one casualty which was severe was caused by the falling of the chimney of Mr. Roy Mason, Jr.'s, house, which fell upon a Mississippi company held in reserve behind the house, and killed, I was told, seven, who were buried in the yard. But when Burnside advanced his bridge-builders again, on the cessation of the cannonade they were driven back just as promptly as before.

Then the Federals, at last, resorted to what they should have done at first, before daylight in the morning. They ran two or three regiments down into the pontoon boats, & rowed across. They suffered some loss of course but, as the boats drew near our shore, they got under cover of the bank & out of fire. The rest was easy: to form under cover & then take the pits singly and in flank. But Barksdale was now ready to withdraw anyhow. Two or three miles below the town, where there was no cover on our shore, the Federals had already completed a bridge, & were crossing in force. So Barksdale was now ordered to withdraw back out of the town, which he did very succesfully, having however a few isolated men cut off & captured. And so the whole day passed with no more fighting, & at night everything slept on the line of battle. I recall that the night was very cold & indeed the cold spell lasted throughout the battle. I was told that there were one or two cases of pickets without fire being frozen to death (one in the 15th So. Ca.).

The next day was rather uneventful. It was entirely occupied by Burnside in crossing over his army & ours lay quietly on its arms. We could not attack him, for our advance would have been swept by his artillery on the north side, besides which the ground he occupied near the river was also very strong & favorable for defense. Our rifle guns however would fire occasionally at bodies of infantry exposing themselves within range & the enemy's batteries would retaliate at them; & the opposing picket lines in the valley had bullets to spare for any body who would show himself within a thousand yards. Joe Haskell joined me & offered his services as an aid which I gladly availed myself of, & found him exceedingly useful as well as a delightful companion. Our friendship, commenced then, has only grown closer every day since.

Again we slept in position & then dawned Saturday the 13th, which we all knew would bring the struggle. In the early morning all the valley was shrouded in the strange sort of Indian summer mist before referred to. About 9 o'clock the heights on each side became visible & perhaps about ten the plain could be seen from the hills. Infantry pickets & sharpshooters all along the line began firing as soon as they could see, and the Federal heavy batteries from the hills north of the river began to feel for us also. We let them do most of the shooting, but occasionally Rhett's 20 pr. Parrots, or a Whitworth rifle of Lane's battery (the company from Washington, Geo.), from a high hill on our left—or some other rifle gun which got a chance, would try a shot at something offering an attractive target. But we devoted very little fire to their batteries.

Some half mile to the rear and a little to the right of Marye's Hill was a very high & commanding hill called Telegraph Hill (afterwards Lee's Hill) overlooking the entire field down to Hamilton's Crossing—five miles away—where Jackson's right flank rested. Gen. Lee made his headquarters on this hill, & on it were some half a dozen, or more, guns in scattered pits. And among these guns were two 30 pr. Parrot rifles. It was the only time in war that we ever had such heavy guns in the field. They were, however, the right things in the right place here, & filled a great want, until they, unfortunately, both exploded towards the middle of the day, one at the 37th round & one at the 42nd. At one of the explosions Genls. Lee & Longstreet & many staff officers were standing very near, & fragments flew all about them, but none was hurt. And, to finish with these guns, one of these fragments furnished a good story on a green youngster serving on Pickett's staff. He had brought a message to Gen. Lee & he saw the base of one of these large guns, with all in front of the trunnions blown away. He told Gen. P. that "the Yankees had thrown the biggest shell at Gen. Lee that he ever saw. It was about 6 feet long & three feet in diameter with two knobs on one end as thick as his leg & it must weigh over two thousand pounds."

About ten o'clock, the firing in Jackson's front began to indicate serious battle. From Gen. Lee's hill the enemies' lines of battle, preceded by a heavy skirmish line & accompanied with many batteries, could be seen advancing across the plain upon Jackson's position on the wooded hills about Hamilton's Crossing. And there was one very petty little incident. "Sallie" Pelham, as we called him at West Point, major commanding Stuart's horse artillery, was with our cavalry upon the enemy's left flank. When their long lines of infantry advanced & when Pelham found himself almost in their prolongation the temptation to enfilade them was irresistible. With only two guns he galloped forward to where an old gate stood on a small knoll & opened fire on them & soon began to produce a good deal of confusion & delay. They brought up battery after battery to crush him, until he sustained the fire of six 6 gun batteries, when he retired without much damage. Gen. Lee told of the action in a dispatch to Richmond that night in which he spoke of "the gallant Pelham," by which name his memory is still dear to all survivors of the Army of Northern Virginia. Poor fellow, he was killed in the April following, charging with a cavalry squadron, up on the Rapidan, just before Chancellorsville. He was a very young looking, handsome, & attractive fellow, slender, blue eyes, light hair, smooth, red & white complexion, & with such a modest & refined expression that his classmates & friends never spoke of him but as "Sallie" and there never was a Sallie whom a man could love more!

Having started on Jackson's fight I will finish it before I take up Longstreet's, for the two were entirely distinct. As the Federals advanced, in three lines of battle after the little Pelham episode, Jackson's artillery along his whole line opened on them very effectively. They developed a very heavy artillery fire in reply, & their infantry pushed on in very handsome style & making a fine show. But, when they came near enough to receive Jackson's infantry fire, their advance was checked. Several efforts were made to push them on but all failed except at one point upon the line of A. P. Hill's division. I have never known exactly how it came about, but his second brigade from the right, Gregg's, was not in the line between Archer's, the first, & Thomas's, the 3rd, but was back some 200 or 300 yards in the woods, which were quite swampy where the straight line would have been. The error was probably due to the fact that a considerable part of Jackson's force had only arrived that morning from Port Royal, 18 miles below Fredericksburg, where Burnside had been making some demonstrations. So the character of the field was not throughly known to all of his officers.

It happened that Meade's division had the luck to strike that soft spot where it met no infantry fire, & of course it went in. Naturally Archer & Thomas soon began to crumble away on the left flank of Archer & the right of Thomas. Gregg, in the rear, did not seem to know the gap existed, for when the advancing Federals surprised his brigade he thought they were friends & was actually trying to stop his men from firing upon them when he received his mortal wound. Some of the men, & officers too, of Archer's right—finding their left falling back, at first actually fired upon the fugitives, believing that they were deserting their posts without cause. A severe fight now took place in the woods. Gibbon's division, & part of Birney's, reinforced Meade. But Jackson had Early's division in reserve & sent it to repair the breach. They struck like a cyclone & not only whirled the enemy—all of them—out of the woods, but pursued him far out into the plain across the railroad & toward his bridges. That was the end of the battle on the right. After that there was nothing but sharpshooting & some shelling. Gen. Jackson did propose a night attack upon the enemy, & Gen. Lee gave him permission to try it, but after more careful study he decided not to venture it. So now we can take up Longstreet's fight.

About 11 that morning, I had gotten a little uneasy lest all the fighting would go Jackson's way & none of it come ours, for we were practically doing nothing, while the noise Jackson was making now filled the heavens. So I rode over to Gen. Lee's hill to find out what was going on. It took but a few minutes to see that we had no occasion to be jealous of Jackson's luck. The town was evidently already crammed as full of troops as it could hold, &, beside these, dense black columns still pouring into it, or headed for it, were visible coming up the river from below & also moving down to the bridges from the north bank. Evidently more than half of Burnside's whole army was preparing to assault us, & the assault too was not going to be where I had imagined it would be—up along the river bank—but it was going to come right out from the town, & strike where we were strongest. If we couldn't whip it we couldn't whip anything, & had better give up the war at once & go back to our homes. From that moment I felt the elation of a certain & easy victory, & my only care then was to get into it somehow & help do the enemy all the harm I could.

And, very soon, I thought I saw a good chance. I got glimpses of a heavy column of infantry on the north side evidently in motion across a bridge and into the town. My knowledge of the town made me quite sure that they would march up a certain street. Intervening hills, trees, &c. would prevent my seeing even the tops of the houses on the sides of the street, but they would not prevent my cannon shot from a distance flying high over those obstacles & then coming down in the street & bouncing along it where they would meet that advancing column. In fact all three streets must have been full of men anyhow. The only question was whether we could afford to use ammunition in that way, where it could, indeed, worry the enemy & kill some of them, but yet where we could not certainly know what we were doing, & where there was no special issue to be determined.

While I was debating this in my mind I saw a long line of battle advance from the eastern side of the town toward Marye's Hill. A long cut of an unfinished railroad ran obliquely across the open ground they had to cross. They were evidently receiving some long range infantry fire, & also a few shells, & as they came up to this railroad cut, say ten feet deep, the whole brigade of them swarmed into it. They had hardly done so when one of the 30 pr. Parrott guns, right by me, roared out, & I saw the bloodiest shot I ever saw in all my life. The gun exactly enfiladed the cut & it sent its shell right into the heart of the blue mass of men where it exploded. I think it could not have failed to kill or wound as many as 20 men. The sight of that shot excited me so that I felt bound to have some share, so I determined to send forty shot, anyhow, down that street.

So I did not wait to see any more, but started for my battalion to get Moody's Napoleons for the job. After a little reconnoitering I was able to locate them upon the prolongation of the street leading to the bridge & then we fired the forty shots at an elevation to take them nearly to the river. What harm they did, of course, we could not tell, but there were lots of people about where they fell & bounced. The enemy's batteries across the river opened on us & dropped some of their shell very close, but we had no one hurt.

Meanwhile Burnside had ordered his troops in Fredericksburg to carry Marye's Hill. Of his six corps of infantry, two were already in the town, & two more, just below, were brought up during the action which followed. Our line here was held by McLaws's division, with three brigades in line of battle at the foot of the hill: Cobb's Georgians; Kershaw's South Carolinians; & Barksdale's Mississippians, in order from left to right with Semmes's Georgians in reserve. Walker with his own & Ransom's brigade were also in reserve close by in the rear. The Washington Artillery, 9 guns, were in the pits above & also near the Plank Road was Maurin's battery—4 guns of Cabell's battalion. A sunken road, for a part of the way, gave the infantry a beautiful line, &, where that was lacking, McLaws, with his usual painstaking care & study of detail, had utilized ditches & dug trenches & provided for supplies of water & of ammunition & care of the wounded. But there was one feature of the ground which was very favorable to the enemy. There was a little sort of flat ravine running parallel to our position, & about four hundred yards in front of it, in which there was perfect cover from our sight & direct fire, for twenty thousand men or more, & this covered ground could be reached without any serious difficulty.

So the military dimensions of the task were as follows—to charge out of cover, over 400 yards of open ground, broken by a few scattered houses & garden fences, under the direct fire of fourteen guns & three brigades of infantry (say 5,000 muskets)—mostly under cover of pits & walls or trenches. To be sure there were in reserve, behind, three more brigades of infantry & say 22 guns—four of them in pits, but the rest, & the infantry, would have had to fight out in the open. But these reserves were not found necessary to repel the attacks, although toward the last, one brigade of them, Cooke's North Carolina, was brought into action. Had the case been reversed I cannot believe but that the morale of the Army of Northern Virginia would at least have taken them over the guns at the first dash. The difficulties do not begin to compare with what our men went through at either Malvern Hill or Gettysburg, where we went over the guns at the first go, charging those times as far & against five times as many men & guns. I don't wish to seem to brag about our men unduly, but I think that any professional military critic will say that that ravine ought to have enabled the Federals to, at least, have crossed bayonets with us. As it was, none of their lines of battle came within 75 yards, though a few officers & individuals got up nearer—the nearest to about 30 yards.

The first assault was made by a column of 6 brigades who advanced from the ravine above mentioned, each one after the first letting the one in advance get 200 yards' start. Practically every brigade broke up & retreated at or about the 100 yards line: which was where our infantry fire began to get in its full strength. For our men would not fire at long range but would purposely let them get nearer. The fugitives crowded behind the scattered houses, fences and in little depressions here & there, whence they fired back at our guns & line of battle. There were enough of them to keep the air, as it were, swarming with bullets, but the pits & banks enabled us to hold on in spite of them. Meanwhile, too, their siege guns, from the north bank, concentrated & pounded at us, their very best & heaviest, but we just paid no attention to them & let them shoot. One of them however killed Gen. T. R. R. Cobb, with a fragment of shell, smashing his thigh. He was a great loss to us. A man more brave, noble, & lovely in character & disposition, never lived, & he was making his mark as a soldier as rapidly as he had made it in civil & political life before the war.

It is not necessary to go into detail as to the different Federal charges, & how they brought up reinforcements, & made a number of efforts, but none of them any stronger or more serious looking, to us, than the first. A popular impression has seemed to prevail that the Irish Brigade of Thomas Francis Meagher exceeded all others in its dash & gallantry. But while it may be true that his men went as far as the farthest,

Gen. Meagher's official report of the battle shows that personally he was not in the charge, but that as it began he "being lame" started back to town to get his horse & he was soon joined in town by the remnants of his brigade whom he led back to the river bank.

So the battle in front of Marye's Hill would occasionally rise to the intensity of a charge, & decrease to severe sharpshooting & more or less shelling, from about noon till late in the afternoon. About half past three a note came to me from Col. Walton saying that the Washington Artillery was nearly out of ammunition, & calling upon me to relieve it with an equal number of guns from my battalion. Had I not been new to my command, I would have proposed to send in ammunition, & men too, if necessary, but to object to the exposure necessary of both his teams & mine in his gun's being withdrawn & my guns going in. For all the pits were in open ground & some were a little troublesome to get to. But it was my first fight in command of troops, & I was only too glad of the chance to get into those pits, & I determined at once, not only to go, but, once there, to stay to the end of the fight, if it were a week. So I at once selected 9 guns—Woolfolk's 4, Donnell Smith 2, & 3 of Moody's—& started with them for Marye's.

As we came up to the Plank Road, I asked Joe Haskell to ride up to Rhett's battery, which was firing at the time right over the route we had to take, & order it to stop until we passed; as its shells sometimes exploded prematurely. As he spurred ahead we both saw a Parrott shell from the enemy coming which had struck about 100 yards off & ricocheted & was now whirling end over end like a stick. I was just in the line of it as we could both see. Haskell reined up his horse expecting to see me cut down. I merely realized that I had no time to dodge, & wondered where it would hit. It passed under the horse's belly somehow—without touching & struck about fifteen feet beyond her. When we got nearly to Marye's Hill, keeping in low places & under cover as much as possible, the leading driver in trying to avoid the bodies of two dead men in the road got into a narrow deep ditch with both his team & the guns, & made some delay in righting things. Meanwhile the Washington Artillery ran up their teams, limbered up & came out. It was only a few minutes however before we were on hand & went in at a gallop. The sharpshooters & the enemy's guns all went for us, but we were emulating greased lightning just then & we got off very lightly, some 6 men & 12 horses, I think it was, only who were struck. Then we dismounted ammunition chests, & sent running gear & horses back under cover.

Up on Gen. Lee's hill they did not know that Walton had asked me to relieve him, & Gen. Lee, happening to look & see his guns coming out, thought they were retreating. He caught Longstreet's arm & said, "Look there, what does that mean?" Longstreet turned to Maj. Fairfax of his staff & said, "Go & order Walton to go back there and to stay there," but in a few minutes they saw my guns going in, & then they understood.

Meanwhile it happened that the enemy had just brought up a fresh division under command of Gen. Humphreys, of my old corps—the engineers, a splendid old soldier; and they were preparing to make an extra effort. Just as they were getting good & ready for the charge, back in the flat ravine, before mentioned, word was sent back to them that our artillery on the hill had been withdrawn. This raised their hopes, & Humphreys, to diminish the temptation to stop & fire, which is the bane & danger in all charges, ordered that his whole division should go with empty muskets, & rely on the bayonet alone. And so it resulted that we were hardly in our pits & good & ready, when there arose a great hurrah back at the Federal ravine & there swarmed out some three or four long lines of battle and started for us in fine style. That was just what we wanted. Our chests were crammed full of ammunition, & the sun was low; so we set in to improve each shining hour, & get rid of as much as possible of that ammunition before dark. It was for just this sort of chance that we had been saving it up since the beginning. So now we gave them our choicest varieties, canister and shrapnel, just as fast as we could put it in. It was plainly a disagreeable surprise to them, but they faced it very well & came along fairly until our infantry at the foot of the hill opened. There were now six ranks of infantry for a part of the way, & their fire was very heavy.

Then Humphreys broke all up. General Couch, in describing this charge of Humphreys's division, in the Century War Book, writes as follows: "The musketry fire was very heavy &

the artillery fire was simply terrible. I sent word, several times, to our artillery on the right of Falmouth that they were firing into us & tearing our own men to pieces. I thought they had made a mistake in the range. But I learned later that the fire came from the guns of the enemy on their extreme left." This last fire mentioned came from Parker's battery near the Stansbury house. His line got no further than the others had come & his men scattered about, & laid down & fired from behind houses, but the charge was over.

And then, between sundown & dark still one more division, Getty's, was sent in on Humphreys's left. If they had not started with a cheer I don't think that I, at least, would have known they were coming; for I could not see them, but only—when they began to fire—the flashes of their muskets. I was in a pit near the right with one of Jordan's guns, & we had almost ceased to fire for lack of a good target, when this disturbance began, & I ordered them to fire canister at the gun flashes. The gunner, who was a Corporal Logwood, from Bedford Co., Va., aimed & stepped back & ordered fire. But I was watching his aiming, & I thought he had not given quite enough elevation to his gun, so I stopped the man about to pull the lanyard & told Logwood to give the screw another turn or two down. He stepped to the breech to obey, but as he reached out his hand there was a thud, & the poor fellow fell with a bullet through & through the stomach. We had to remove him from under the wheels, & then I aimed the gun myself, & fired until after it got dark when, gradually, the whole field became quiet. Poor Logwood lived for two days, but his case was hopeless from the first.

That was an awful night upon the wounded; especially on the Federal wounded left between the lines, where their friends could give them no relief or assistance. Gen. Couch writes of it, "It was a night of dreadful suffering. Many died of wounds & exposure, and as fast as men died they stiffened in the wintry air, & on the front line were rolled forward for protection to the living. Frozen men were placed for dumb sentries."

"MURDEROUS BUTCHERY": VIRGINIA, DECEMBER 1862

Samuel W. Fiske to the Springfield Republican

Lieutenant Fiske, ill with typhoid and dysentery, could only watch as his regiment, the 14th Connecticut, lost 120 men in the assault on Marye's Heights behind Fredericksburg. The Army of the Potomac lost more than 12,600 men killed, wounded, or missing in the battle, while Confederate casualties totaled about 5,300.

DUNN BROWNE ON THE BATTLE FIELD

Fredericksburg
December 15

Oh, Republican! My heart is sick and sad. Blood and wounds and death are before my eyes; of those who are my friends, comrades, brothers; of those who have marched into the very mouth of destruction as coolly and cheerfully as to any ordinary duty. Another tremendous, terrible, murderous butchery of brave men has made Saturday, the 13th of December, a memorable day in the annals of this war.

On Friday, Fredericksburg was taken with comparatively little trouble and loss. On Saturday, the grand army corps of Sumner marched up against the heights back of the city, where the enemy lay behind strong fortifications, all bristling with cannon and protected by rifle pits; while our men must cross a wide space of clear, open ground, and then a canal whose every crossing was swept by artillery so perfectly trained beforehand that every discharge mowed down whole ranks of men. Into this grand semi-circle of death our divisions marched with rapid and unflinching step. French's division (to which we belong) behaved splendidly, and the others no less so if we may judge by the losses. Of whole companies and regiments not a man flinched. The grape and canister tore through their ranks, the fearful volleys of musketry from invisible foes decimated their numbers every few moments; the conflict was hopeless; they could inflict scarcely any damage upon the foe; our artillery couldn't cover them, for they would do more damage to friend than to enemy; yet our gallant fellows pressed on, determined to scale those breastworks and take the position of the rebels. But there were none left to do that work. A little handful of a great division approached, and even in a few instances began to climb the works, but only to leave their mangled bodies on the bloody field; a few torn and blackened remnants of the fine regiments sternly retired to the city. The wounded were mainly brought off, though hundreds were killed in the benevolent task. The city is filled with the pieces of brave men who went whole into the conflict. Every basement and floor is covered with pools of blood. Limbs in many houses lie in heaps, and surgeons are exhausted with their trying labors.

But I will not sicken you with a recital of the horrors before us. Why our noble fellows were pushed on into such a hopeless and desperate undertaking I am not military man enough to say. Or why the grand division of Hooker were marching and countermarching all through the day on the other side of the river, and didn't cross over till just at night to help in the bloody business, if it must be undertaken, I do not know either. Indeed I don't know anything hardly save that I am sick at such a destruction of noble human lives, necessary or unnecessary, useful or useless.

Personally, dear Republican, I was not much in the fight except to be under the shell fire a considerable part of the day in my anxiety to reach my regiment, and failing that to get as near as possible, as a spectator of the terrible scene. Sick for two weeks of a fever and diarrhoea, I heard the heavy firing of Thursday from a hospital ten miles distant, got permission from the surgeon in charge to mount a U.S. wagon laden with medical stores and start for the regiment. But the fearful roads of corduroy under a foot or two of mud, and the feeble state of the teams living for weeks on half forage, hindered us, and prevented your correspondent from reaching his post till the day after the battle. And doubtless the sight of the poor remnants of his regiment—one hundred men only reported for duty—and of his brigade, not enough to make half a regiment —and then not having been in the scene where the change was effected, have come over his feelings more powerfully than would otherwise have been the case, and given a sad tinge to what he ever wishes to write cheerfully. For God is over all, and even this thing is right, and shall come out in a result of good, sometime. God grant we may see it!

December 17: Night before last, quietly and without disturbance from the enemy, we evacuated Fredericksburg, and marched back to our respective old camps on this side the Rappahannock. In the darkness and through the deep mud the tired soldiers plodded wearily on their way, and then on their arrival were obliged to lie down on the ground and make the best of a rainy winter's night, before they could proceed to arrange themselves any comfortable quarters. Let us hope that the shattered divisions that bore the brunt of the fatal fight behind Fredericksburg may be left to a little rest before meeting any more of the horrors of a winter's campaign in this terrible country. Oh for a month of that beautiful weather that we wasted in the autumn. We hear rumors of the capture of Fort Darling and of Richmond, but do not credit it. If it only could be so, and that our desperate attack at Fredericksburg could have the excuse of being a part of the preconcerted plan to occupy the attention of the enemy and keep his forces here, it would much relieve many sore and discouraged hearts.

We brought off all our wounded from the city, and have left little that is valuable on the other side, save our unburied heroes on the field of battle. The pontoon bridges too are saved and ready to throw across again, and our heavy artillery command the passage of the river at any time, I suppose.

DUNN BROWNE

December 15 and 17, 1862

“THOROUGHLY LICKED”: VIRGINIA, DECEMBER 1862

Henry Livermore Abbott to Josiah Gardner Abbott and to George B. Perry

Captain Abbott, an 1860 Harvard graduate, commanded Company I in the 20th Massachusetts, Norman J. Hall's brigade, O. O. Howard's division, Darius N. Couch's corps. In these letters to his father and to Perry, a former comrade in the 20th who had been invalided out of service that fall, Abbott is unsparing of the Union generalship at Fredericksburg. Leander F. Alley was a close friend in his company. Abbott's brother Edward had been killed at Cedar Mountain in August, and another soldier brother, Fletcher, was then home on sick leave.

Fredericksburg Va
Dec 14 / 62

My dear Papa,

We are still in Fredericksburg (Sunday). The very moment I finished my last letter to mama we were ordered again to the front. Howard, a most conscientious man, but a very poor general, had heard of batteries stormed & rifle pits taken &c, & without stopping to think whether the rifle pits in question were an analogous case, he took the weakest brigade in the army, one which besides was considerably demoralized by the fight of the previous day & the shelling they had suffered, to say nothing of the recollection of their awful loss & defeat at Antietam, he took this brigade & ordered it to advance not altogether, but regt. after regt. The result was that the 19th which first got into position, no sooner reached the brow of the hill than they tumbled right back head over heels into us. Then came our turn. We had about 200 men. We advanced 2 or 3 rods over the brow of the hill under a murderous fire, without the slightest notion of what was intended to be accomplished. Our men however, though they couldn't be got to advance in double-quick against the rifle pits which we soon perceived, didn't on the other hand like the 19th, break & run. They held their position firmly until Col. Hall seeing that the pits could only be carried at the run, & that if carried they were completely enfiladed by a rebel battery on the hill, ordered us to retire, which we did in good order, below the brow of the hill where the whole brigade lay till 2 next morning. Crowds of troops were ordered up, but none found courage even to undertake what the poor little brigade of 1000 men had been unable to accomplish. At 2 oclock, we were relieved by the regulars who were ordered up as a last resort since Hall's brigade had failed to take the pits, which they were to storm this morning. However the generals have changed their minds since & consider the assault impracticable, so nothing has been done to day, except a little shelling—(3 oclock). Hall stoutly condemned the whole attempt by such a weak exhausted brigade, as simply ridiculous. But Howard is so pious that he thought differently. & hinc illae &c. Hooker suffered terribly yesterday & accomplished nothing. The enthusiasm of the soldiers has been all gone for a long time. They only fight from discipline & old associations. McClellan is the only man who can revive it. Macy commanded our regiment as well as it could possibly be commanded. This morning, Gen Howard called him to the front of the regt. & at the same time that he praised the regiment, complimented Macy publicly in the handsomest manner. The regiment during the few minutes they were engaged lost about 60 men & 3 officers. We have now a hundred odd men & 5 company officers with the regiment. I lost only 4 men as all but 10 I had sent out under cover to watch our flanks, which were otherwise entirely unprotected. Alley was killed instantaneously by a bullet through the eye. You will know how I feel about this loss, when I tell you that for a moment I felt the same pang as when I first heard of our great loss. I don't want to say any thing more about him now, for thinking on such a subject makes a man bluer than he ought to be in the presence of the enemy. I have sent his body home by Sergt. Summerhayes with orders to call on you for funds, as I have no money. I will settle it from

Alley's account. For God's sake, don't let Fletcher get on till after Richmond is taken. I couldn't stand the loss of a third brother, for I regard Alley almost as a brother.

I am in excellent health. My scabbard was smashed by a bullet, but I myself was uninjured. Don't you or mama worry yourself about our fighting any more. Howard told us we were so used up that we shouldn't fight again except in direst necessity.

Love to all
Your aff. son
H. L. Abbott

Near Falmouth Va
AM Wednesday

Dear George,

I suppose the letters I have written home, describing the battles have got there. So I will only say as a summing up of them, that we took over 320 men & lost 165 men & 8 officers. However we are getting back the men in the hospitals, the detailed men & that sort of thing, so that we shall soon have a respectable number again. Holmes & Willard will soon return to duty, too. As it is, we have only 5 officers. Macy & our regiment covered itself with glory & have received no end of compliments. The army generally didn't fight well. The new regiments behaved shamefully, as well as many of the old ones. The whole army is demoralized. The 15 Mass was seized with a panic at nothing at all & broke & ran like sheep. They have always been considered one of the most trustworthy regiments in the army. Hooker's troops broke & ran. He is played out. Our loss was 10000. The rebels may have lost 3000. Burnside, who is a noble man, but not a general is going to leave the army entirely. He rode through the town, the last day without a single cheer. That conscientious donkey, Howard, after keeping our brigade shivering & freezing for an hour yesterday afternoon listening to a sermon & benediction from him, proposed (N. B. he may be summed up in the words, devilish *green*) three cheers for Burnside. Several men in a new regiment, the 127th Penn. gave a mockery of 3 cheers. Not a man in the other regiments opened their mouths, except to mutter three cheers for McClellan. We can never win another victory till he comes back, & even then, not till, after 3 months of winter quarters, he has had time to reorganize the army. Financial troubles & foreign intervention may stop the thing before that time expires, but any other course is *certain* destruction. The only two generals left that this brigade believes in are Couch & Hall. We dont know much about the former, except that he protested in the strongest manner against the whole thing. The army went over with the conviction, almost the determination, of getting licked & they have got thoroughly licked. If you people at home, are going to allow us to be butchered any longer by Halleck & Stanton, you will find the enemy at your own doors.

Your aff. friend,
H. L. Abbott

Tell the governor that I have sent an order for $75 on him to pay for embalming the body of Alley. I will pay it from Alley's money, as soon as the funds come.

I was devlish sorry to hear that Fletch met with an accident. Don't let him come back before something new turns up. Old heads like Johnny Sedgwick know too much to come before McClellan.

I forgot to say, that we are in our old quarters, with every prospect of remaining.

December 17, 1862

Clifton Johnson: *from* Battleground Adventures

At the time of the battle, this free black man was a barrel maker in Fredericksburg, and when Clifton Johnson interviewed him in 1913 he was still working at his cooperage there. Johnson referred to him as "The Colored Cooper," but he has since been identified as Joseph Lawson, born in 1831.

The Colored Cooper[1]

Me and my wife was both free born. We could have gone away befo' the battle, but we had a house hyar in Fredericksburg and four small chil'en, and I had work in town makin' barrels. So we stayed all the whole time. There was n't many who did that.

As soon as the Yankees got hyar the slaves began to run away from their mistresses and masters. They went by hundreds. You'd see 'em gittin' out of hyar same as a rabbit chased by a dog. Some carried little bundles tied up, but they could n't tote much. Often one of the women would walk along carrying a child wrapped up in a blanket. Fifteen miles from hyar they got to the Potomac, and the Yankee gunboats would take 'em right to Washington. Then they'd pile in wherever they could git. They never come back this way.

A good many of the Rebel soldiers stole off, too, so they could git into the Yankee lines, and not have to fight.

We had such cold weather that December when the battle was fought that the ice formed quite thick on a pond up hyar in the early days of the month. I promised Mr. Roe, who carried on butchery, that I'd help draw to fill his icehouse. He was to start work on the 13th. The night before was cold—

[1]That his years were many was evident in his stooping form and thin white hair, but he was still working. I visited him in the shop where he was making barrels as of yore, and he continued at his task while he told his story.

bitter cold. I wanted to be at the pond early, and when a noise waked me, after I'd been asleep a good long time, I thought it must be near about daybreak. So I got up and went to the barn and fed my horse. But what I'd heard was the Yankees fixin' to come over hyar from the other side of the Rappahannock on pontoon bridges.

Colonel Lang was camped up the lane, and pretty soon he marched right past my door with one thousand Confederate troops. They went down in intrenchments along the river. Then the old signal gun went off, and there was somethin' doin'. I did n't know what it meant—a gun goin' off at that time in the morning. Lang killed about seventy-five men who were makin' the pontoon bridges—swept 'em off clean as a whistle—but later in the day the Yankees come across in their boats and swept him off.

Early in the morning word was sent around that they was goin' to shell the town, and they done it, too. But I did n't git no warning and did n't know a thing of it till I saw people running. Some ran with their nightclothes on. They did n't have any time to play, I tell you. All that could, got out into the country and the woods was full of 'em—white and colored. But I stayed in the town. I think there was two hundred Yankee cannon over the river on the hills. The shelling begun about five o'clock, as near as I can come at it, and the gunners could shoot the bombs and balls just where they wanted to. I know two people was killed dead in bed that morning—an old man and an old woman. We had rough times hyar. I don't want any mo' of that bumbarding in this world. I don't want it in the next world either, if I'm ever able to git there.

Tom Knox who owned the hotel had a narrow escape. He got up when the signal gun fired and put on his clothes as quick as he could and got out of town on foot. He left everything he had behind him, and he was hardly out of the house when a shell come in and split his pillow open. It did n't hurt the bed, but they tell me a knife could n't have cut that pillow into two parts any better than the shell did. The shell was lookin' for Mr. Knox, but it did n't git him. It would have split *him* open if he'd stayed there. Yes, fifteen or twenty minutes longer in his bed would have fixed him.

The neighbors come into my house when the shells begun

to fly. Oh! we had the greatest quantity of women and children there. The house was full. They all wanted to have plenty of company so if any of 'em got hurt the others could help 'em. By and by a solid shot—a twelve-pounder—come right through my house. The Yankees had been firin' a right smart while, and I s'pose the sun was 'bout half an hour high. I was settin' up by the fire with some of the others in my bedroom. The ball cut one of the big house timbers plumb in two, and I never saw so much dirt flyin' around in my life. It took the end off the bureau just as clean as you could with a circular saw, and it left dust and everything else all over the room as if some one had been sowin' seed. Ah, man! I never want to see that pass over no mo'. It was terrible.

I had a splendid cellar under my house, and we all went down into that. We did n't have no breakfast. But I did n't bother my mind at all about that. I was n't hungry a bit. I was already filled up with skeer. The chil'en would have liked breakfast, but 'deed and they did n't git it. They was not so skeered as the grown folks because they did n't know the danger. The older people was just skeered to death, all hands of 'em, and some was mo' uneasy 'bout the chil'en than they was 'bout themselves. We had a tejious time of it with nothin' to do but talk of how the shells was running.

That was an awful day—awful day, but the firin' stopped up some by noon, and we all come up and took a peep. I went out in the back yard where I could look and see the Yankees like bees on them heights across the river. A ball had struck a haystack I had piled up in my lot, and I expected my horse would be killed tied right there in the stable, but he wa'n't hurt a bit. The town seemed to be deserted. I walked up as far as the corner, and looked up and down and could n't see a soul—man or woman, cat or dog. The neighbors stayed at our house until night, and then they went home and give the chil'en something to eat, I reckon.

Next day the place was full of Yankee troops. One of the citizens had a good deal of whiskey in his cellar, and I had helped hide it. The cellar had a brick floor, and we took up a part of it and dug a hole. All the liquor was in jimmy-johns, and we put the whole parcel of 'em down in the ground, covered 'em up with dirt, and laid back the bricks. Nobody would have known anything was buried there if they'd walked over that hyar cellar floor all day. Some one must have told, for the Irish brigade found the whiskey, and the men got so drunk they did n't know what they was doing.

The Rebels was on Marye's Heights. That was a hot place—a hot place! The Yankees never had no chance to win there. They kept chargin' a stone wall at the foot of the Heights. But Lord 'a' mercy! they was all cut to pieces every time. Some got up to the wall so they could put their hands on it, but they couldn't git no further. That wall still stands, and when there comes a rain they say the blood stains show on it even yet.

One of the leading Southern generals in this fight was Stonewall Jackson—you've heard talk of him. He was a plague, he was a honey, old Stonewall was—he was a honey! He wanted his men to take off their pants and just have on drawers so he'd know 'em. They would n't do it, and I don't blame 'em. They did n't have much to take off nohow, I reckon, and it was winter weather. Jackson's men did n't wear no shoes. Instead, they had on each foot a piece of leather tied up behind and before with leather strings. I found one of those foot protectors where they camped. Old Stonewall was a terrible man. He did n't think anything of marching his troops thirty mile in a night. They had the hardest time of any soldiers I heard of in the war. Ha, ha! do you know what kind of food he gave 'em? Three times a day each man got one year of corn—a raw year of corn. They did n't have to stop marching to eat it, but gnawed and chewed it as they tramped along.

I went to the battlefield and took a look around when things got cool, and I can tell you I don't never want to see no mo' war in my day. The battlefield 'peared like somebody had been doin' something—it 'peared awful bad! The dead was scattered around, and some looked like they was fast asleep. When a man had been hit by a shell that exploded it bust him up in such little pieces you would n't 'a' known he was ever the shape of a man. A good many bodies was all laid in a row side of the stone wall with blankets over their faces. I saw some old gray fellers among the dead. They had no business to be in the war at their age. Out in front of the stone wall was the Yankees where they'd fallen one 'pon top of t' other.

The Southern troops took possession of the town after the

battle. Some of 'em was so smoked up I did n't know whether they was white men or black men. They was nasty and dirty, and their clothes was dreadful. If a Rebel wanted a good pair of pants or shoes he had to shoot a Yankee to git 'em. Every Union man that was killed was stripped, and you often could n't tell the Rebels in their borrowed clothing from the Northern soldiers.

A heap of 'em on both sides suffered mightily for food. Some had the rashions but no chance to cook what they had. 'Bout noon one day two Rebel soldiers come up to our house off of the river, and they said to my wife, "Aunty, we've got some fish we want you to fry."

They'd been on picket duty. The Rebel pickets was on this side of the river and the Yankee pickets on the other side layin' there watchin' one another, and these fellers had put in some of their time fishing. They'd caught a mess of herrings, but they did n't have no salt nor nothing to cook 'em with. So my wife took a piece of meat and fried the herrings nicely and gave the men some bread to eat with their fish. Their rashions could n't have been much. Some of the soldiers pulled up wild onions and e't 'em.

"HUNDREDS DIE EVERY DAY": VIRGINIA, DECEMBER 1862

Walt Whitman: from Specimen Days

Walt Whitman was living in Brooklyn and working as a freelance journalist when he learned that his brother George, a captain with the 51st New York Infantry, had been wounded at Fredericksburg. Whitman traveled to Falmouth, across the Rappahannock from the battlefield, and discovered that his brother's wound was slight. After visiting army hospitals and camps around Falmouth, he accompanied a group of wounded soldiers as they were evacuated to Washington by train and steamboat. Whitman would remain in the capital for the next eighteen months, visiting military hospitals while working as a government clerk. He described his time with the Army of the Potomac in *Specimen Days* (1882), drawing on accounts he had previously published in *The New York Times* in 1864; in "'Tis But Ten Years Since," a series of six articles that appeared in the *New York Weekly Graphic* in 1874; and in *Memoranda During the War* (1875).

DOWN AT THE FRONT

FALMOUTH, VA., *opposite Fredericksburgh, December 21, 1862.*—Begin my visits among the camp hospitals in the army of the Potomac. Spend a good part of the day in a large brick mansion on the banks of the Rappahannock, used as a hospital since the battle—seems to have receiv'd only the worst cases. Out doors, at the foot of a tree, within ten yards of the front of the house, I notice a heap of amputated feet, legs, arms, hands, &c., a full load for a one-horse cart. Several dead bodies lie near, each cover'd with its brown woolen blanket. In the dooryard, towards the river, are fresh graves, mostly of officers, their names on pieces of barrel-staves or broken boards, stuck in the dirt. (Most of these bodies were subsequently taken up and transported north to their friends.) The large mansion is quite crowded upstairs and down, everything impromptu, no system, all bad enough, but I have no doubt the best that can be done; all the wounds pretty bad, some frightful, the men in their old clothes, unclean and bloody. Some of the wounded are rebel soldiers and officers, prisoners. One, a Mississippian, a captain, hit badly in leg, I talk'd with some time; he ask'd me for papers, which I gave him. (I saw him three months afterward in Washington, with his leg amputated, doing well.) I went through the rooms, downstairs and up. Some of the men were dying. I had nothing to give at that visit, but wrote a few letters to folks home, mothers, &c. Also talk'd to three or four, who seem'd most susceptible to it, and needing it.

After First Fredericksburg

December 23 to 31.—The results of the late battle are exhibited everywhere about here in thousands of cases, (hundreds die every day,) in the camp, brigade, and division hospitals. These are merely tents, and sometimes very poor ones, the wounded lying on the ground, lucky if their blankets are spread on layers of pine or hemlock twigs, or small leaves. No cots; seldom even a mattress. It is pretty cold. The ground is frozen hard, and there is occasional snow. I go around from one case to another. I do not see that I do much good to these wounded and dying; but I cannot leave them. Once in a while some youngster holds on to me convulsively, and I do what I can for him; at any rate, stop with him and sit near him for hours, if he wishes it.

Besides the hospitals, I also go occasionally on long tours through the camps, talking with the men, &c. Sometimes at night among the groups around the fires, in their shebang enclosures of bushes. These are curious shows, full of characters and groups. I soon get acquainted anywhere in camp, with officers or men, and am always well used. Sometimes I go down on picket with the regiments I know best. As to rations, the army here at present seems to be tolerably well supplied, and the men have enough, such as it is, mainly salt pork and hard tack. Most of the regiments lodge in the flimsy little shelter-tents. A few have built themselves huts of logs and mud, with fire-places.

"TORN AND SHATTERED":
DISTRICT OF COLUMBIA, DECEMBER 1862

Louisa May Alcott: from Hospital Sketches

A schoolteacher, writer, and dedicated abolitionist, Louisa May Alcott left her home in Concord, Massachusetts, in December 1862 to volunteer as a nurse at a military hospital in the District of Columbia. Her first experience was with the gravely wounded from Fredericksburg. After a month she contracted typhoid fever, ending her nursing experience. Her book *Hospital Sketches*, in which Alcott appears under the name "Tribulation Periwinkle," was published in August 1863.

CHAPTER III.

A DAY.

"THEY'VE COME! they've come! hurry up, ladies—you're wanted."

"Who have come? the rebels?"

This sudden summons in the gray dawn was somewhat startling to a three days' nurse like myself, and, as the thundering knock came at our door, I sprang up in my bed, prepared

> "To gird my woman's form,
> And on the ramparts die,"

if necessary, but my room-mate took it more coolly, and, as she began a rapid toilet, answered my bewildered question,—

"Bless you, no child; it's the wounded from Fredericksburg; forty ambulances are at the door, and we shall have our hands full in fifteen minutes."

"What shall we have to do?"

"Wash, dress, feed, warm and nurse them for the next three months, I dare say. Eighty beds are ready, and we were getting impatient for the men to come. Now you will begin to see hospital life in earnest, for you won't probably find time to sit down all day, and may think yourself fortunate if you get to bed by midnight. Come to me in the ball-room when you are ready; the worst cases are always carried there, and I shall need your help."

So saying, the energetic little woman twirled her hair into a button at the back of her head, in a "cleared for action" sort of style, and vanished, wrestling her way into a feminine kind of pea-jacket as she went.

I am free to confess that I had a realizing sense of the fact that my hospital bed was not a bed of roses just then, or the prospect before me one of unmingled rapture. My three days' experiences had begun with a death, and, owing to the defalcation of another nurse, a somewhat abrupt plunge into the superintendence of a ward containing forty beds, where I spent my shining hours washing faces, serving rations, giving medicine, and sitting in a very hard chair, with pneumonia on one side, diptheria on the other, five typhoids on the opposite, and a dozen dilapidated patriots, hopping, lying, and lounging about, all staring more or less at the new "nuss," who suffered untold agonies, but concealed them under as matronly an aspect as a spinster could assume, and blundered through her trying labors with a Spartan firmness, which I hope they appreciated, but am afraid they didn't. Having a taste for "ghastliness," I had rather longed for the wounded to arrive, for rheumatism was n't heroic, neither was liver complaint, or measles; even fever had lost its charms since "bathing burning brows" had been used up in romances, real and ideal; but when I peeped into the dusky street lined with what I at first had innocently called market carts, now unloading their sad freight at our door, I recalled sundry reminiscences I had heard from nurses of longer standing, my ardor experienced a sudden chill, and I indulged in a most unpatriotic wish that I was safe at home again, with a quiet day before me, and no necessity for being hustled up, as if I were a hen and had only to hop off my roost, give my plumage a peck, and be ready for action. A second bang at the door sent this recreant desire to the right about, as a little woolly head popped in, and Joey, (a six years' old contraband,) announced—

"Miss Blank is jes' wild fer ye, and says fly round right away. They's comin' in, I tell yer, heaps on 'em—one was took out dead, and I see him,—ky! warn't he a goner!"

With which cheerful intelligence the imp scuttled away,

singing like a blackbird, and I followed, feeling that Richard was *not* himself again, and wouldn't be for a long time to come.

The first thing I met was a regiment of the vilest odors that ever assaulted the human nose, and took it by storm. Cologne, with its seven and seventy evil savors, was a posy-bed to it; and the worst of this affliction was, every one had assured me that it was a chronic weakness of all hospitals, and I must bear it. I did, armed with lavender water, with which I so besprinkled myself and premises, that, like my friend, Sairy, I was soon known among my patients as "the nurse with the bottle." Having been run over by three excited surgeons, bumped against by migratory coal-hods, water-pails, and small boys; nearly scalded by an avalanche of newly-filled tea-pots, and hopelessly entangled in a knot of colored sisters coming to wash, I progressed by slow stages up stairs and down, till the main hall was reached, and I paused to take breath and a survey. There they were! "our brave boys," as the papers justly call them, for cowards could hardly have been so riddled with shot and shell, so torn and shattered, nor have borne suffering for which we have no name, with an uncomplaining fortitude, which made one glad to cherish each as a brother. In they came, some on stretchers, some in men's arms, some feebly staggering along propped on rude crutches, and one lay stark and still with covered face, as a comrade gave his name to be recorded before they carried him away to the dead house. All was hurry and confusion; the hall was full of these wrecks of humanity, for the most exhausted could not reach a bed till duly ticketed and registered; the walls were lined with rows of such as could sit, the floor covered with the more disabled, the steps and doorways filled with helpers and lookers on; the sound of many feet and voices made that usually quiet hour as noisy as noon; and, in the midst of it all, the matron's motherly face brought more comfort to many a poor soul, than the cordial draughts she administered, or the cheery words that welcomed all, making of the hospital a home.

The sight of several stretchers, each with its legless, armless, or desperately wounded occupant, entering my ward, admonished me that I was there to work, not to wonder or weep; so I corked up my feelings, and returned to the path of duty, which was rather "a hard road to travel" just then. The house had been a hotel before hospitals were needed, and many of the doors still bore their old names; some not so inappropriate as might be imagined, for my ward was in truth a *ball-room*, if gun-shot wounds could christen it. Forty beds were prepared, many already tenanted by tired men who fell down anywhere, and drowsed till the smell of food roused them. Round the great stove was gathered the dreariest group I ever saw—ragged, gaunt and pale, mud to the knees, with bloody bandages untouched since put on days before; many bundled up in blankets, coats being lost or useless; and all wearing that disheartened look which proclaimed defeat, more plainly than any telegram of the Burnside blunder. I pitied them so much, I dared not speak to them, though, remembering all they had been through since the route at Fredericksburg, I yearned to serve the dreariest of them all. Presently, Miss Blank tore me from my refuge behind piles of one-sleeved shirts, odd socks, bandages and lint; put basin, sponge, towels, and a block of brown soap into my hands, with these appalling directions:

"Come, my dear, begin to wash as fast as you can. Tell them to take off socks, coats and shirts, scrub them well, put on clean shirts, and the attendants will finish them off, and lay them in bed."

If she had requested me to shave them all, or dance a hornpipe on the stove funnel, I should have been less staggered; but to scrub some dozen lords of creation at a moment's notice, was really—really——. However, there was no time for nonsense, and, having resolved when I came to do everything I was bid, I drowned my scruples in my washbowl, clutched my soap manfully, and, assuming a business-like air; made a dab at the first dirty specimen I saw, bent on performing my task *vi et armis* if necessary. I chanced to light on a withered old Irishman, wounded in the head, which caused that portion of his frame to be tastefully laid out like a garden, the bandages being the walks, his hair the shrubbery. He was so overpowered by the honor of having a lady wash him as he expressed it, that he did nothing but roll up his eyes, and bless me, in an irresistible style which was too much for my sense of the ludicrous; so we laughed together, and when I knelt down to take off his shoes, he "flopped" also and wouldn't hear of my touching "them dirty craters. May your bed above be aisy darlin', for the day's work ye are doon!—Whoosh! there ye are, and bedad, it's hard tellin' which is the dirtiest, the fut or the shoe." It was; and if he hadn't been to the fore, I should have gone on pulling, under the impression that the "fut" was a boot; for trousers, socks, shoes and legs were a mass of mud. This comical tableau produced a general grin, at which propitious beginning I took heart and scrubbed away like any tidy parent on a Saturday night. Some of them took the performance like sleepy children, leaning their tired heads against me as I worked, others looked grimly scandalized, and several of the roughest colored like bashful girls. One wore a soiled little bag about his neck, and, as I moved it, to bathe his wounded breast, I said,

"Your talisman didn't save you, did it?"

"Well, I reckon it did, marm, for that shot would a gone a couple a inches deeper but for my old mammy's camphor bag," answered the cheerful philosopher.

Another, with a gun-shot wound through the cheek, asked for a looking-glass, and when I brought one, regarded his swollen face with a dolorous expression, as he muttered—

"I vow to gosh, that's too bad! I warn't a bad looking chap before, and now I'm done for; won't there be a thunderin' scar? and what on earth will Josephine Skinner say?"

He looked up at me with his one eye so appealingly, that I controlled my risibles, and assured him that if Josephine was a girl of sense, she would admire the honorable scar, as a lasting proof that he had faced the enemy, for all women thought a wound the best decoration a brave soldier could wear. I hope Miss Skinner verified the good opinion I so rashly expressed of her, but I shall never know.

The next scrubbee was a nice looking lad, with a curly brown mane, and a budding trace of gingerbread over the lip, which he called his beard, and defended stoutly, when the barber jocosely suggested its immolation. He lay on a bed, with one leg gone, and the right arm so shattered that it must evidently follow; yet the little Sergeant was as merry as if his afflictions were not worth lamenting over, and when a drop or two of salt water mingled with my suds at the sight of this strong young body, so marred and maimed, the boy looked up, with a brave smile, though there was a little quiver of the lips, as he said,

"Now don't you fret yourself about me, miss; I'm first rate here, for it's nuts to lie still on this bed, after knocking about in those confounded ambulances, that shake what there is left of a fellow to jelly. I never was in one of these places before, and think this cleaning up a jolly thing for us, though I'm afraid it isn't for you ladies."

"Is this your first battle, Sergeant?"

"No, miss; I've been in six scrimmages, and never got a scratch till this last one; but it's done the business pretty thoroughly for me, I should say. Lord! what a scramble there'll be for arms and legs, when we old boys come out of our graves, on the Judgment Day: wonder if we shall get our own again? If we do, my leg will have to tramp from Fredericksburg, my arm from here, I suppose, and meet my body, wherever it may be."

The fancy seemed to tickle him mightily, for he laughed blithely, and so did I; which, no doubt, caused the new nurse to be regarded as a light-minded sinner by the Chaplain, who roamed vaguely about, informing the men that they were all worms, corrupt of heart, with perishable bodies, and souls only to be saved by a diligent perusal of certain tracts, and other equally cheering bits of spiritual consolation, when spirituous ditto would have been preferred.

"I say, Mrs.!" called a voice behind me; and, turning, I saw a rough Michigander, with an arm blown off at the shoulder, and two or three bullets still in him—as he afterwards mentioned, as carelessly as if gentlemen were in the habit of carrying such trifles about with them. I went to him, and, while administering a dose of soap and water, he whispered, irefully:

"That red-headed devil, over yonder; is a reb, damn him! You'll agree to that, I'll bet? He's got shet of a foot, or he'd a cut like the rest of the lot. Don't you wash him, nor feed him, but jest let him holler till he's tired. It's a blasted shame to fetch them fellers in here, along side of us; and so I'll tell the chap that bosses this concern; cuss me if I don't."

I regret to say that I did not deliver a moral sermon upon the duty of forgiving our enemies, and the sin of profanity, then and there; but, being a red-hot Abolitionist, stared fixedly at the tall rebel, who was a copperhead, in every sense of the word, and privately resolved to put soap in his eyes, rub his nose the wrong way, and excoriate his cuticle generally, if I had the washing of him.

My amiable intentions, however, were frustrated; for, when I approached, with as Christian an expression as my principles would allow, and asked the question—"Shall I try to make you more comfortable, sir?" all I got for my pains was a gruff—

"No; I'll do it myself."

"Here's your Southern chivalry, with a witness," thought I, dumping the basin down before him, thereby quenching a strong desire to give him a summary baptism, in return for his ungraciousness; for my angry passions rose, at this rebuff, in a way that would have scandalized good Dr. Watts. He was a disappointment in all respects, (the rebel, not the blessed Doctor,) for he was neither fiendish, romantic, pathetic, or anything interesting; but a long, fat man, with a head like a burning bush, and a perfectly expressionless face: so I could hate him without the slightest drawback, and ignored his existence from that day forth. One redeeming trait he certainly did possess, as the floor speedily testified; for his ablutions were so vigorously performed, that his bed soon stood like an isolated island, in a sea of soapsuds, and he resembled a dripping merman, suffering from the loss of a fin. If cleanliness is a near neighbor to godliness, then was the big rebel the godliest man in my ward that day.

Having done up our human wash, and laid it out to dry, the second syllable of our version of the word war-fare was enacted with much success. Great trays of bread, meat, soup and coffee appeared; and both nurses and attendants turned waiters, serving bountiful rations to all who could eat. I can call my pinafore to testify to my good will in the work, for in ten minutes it was reduced to a perambulating bill of fare, presenting samples of all the refreshments going or gone. It was a lively scene; the long room lined with rows of beds, each filled by an occupant, whom water, shears, and clean raiment, had transformed from a dismal ragamuffin into a recumbent hero, with a cropped head. To and fro rushed matrons, maids, and convalescent "boys," skirmishing with knives and forks; retreating with empty plates; marching and counter-marching, with unvaried success, while the clash of busy spoons made most inspiring music for the charge of our Light Brigade:

"Beds to the front of them,
Beds to the right of them,
Beds to the left of them,
Nobody blundered.
Beamed at by hungry souls,
Screamed at with brimming bowls,
Steamed at by army rolls,
Buttered and sundered.
With coffee not cannon plied,
Each must be satisfied,
Whether they lived or died;
All the men wondered."

Very welcome seemed the generous meal, after a week of suffering, exposure, and short commons; soon the brown faces began to smile, as food, warmth, and rest, did their pleasant work; and the grateful "Thankee's" were followed by more graphic accounts of the battle and retreat, than any paid reporter could have given us. Curious contrasts of the tragic and comic met one everywhere; and some touching as well as ludicrous episodes, might have been recorded that day. A six foot New Hampshire man, with a leg broken and perforated by a piece of shell, so large that, had I not seen the wound, I should have regarded the story as a Munchausenism, beckoned me to come and help him, as he could not sit up, and both his bed and beard were getting plentifully anointed with soup. As I fed my big nestling with corresponding mouthfuls, I asked him how he felt during the battle.

"Well, 'twas my fust, you see, so I aint ashamed to say I was a trifle flustered in the beginnin', there was such an allfired racket; for ef there's anything I do spleen agin, it's noise. But when my mate, Eph Sylvester, caved, with a bullet through his head, I got mad, and pitched in, licketty cut. Our part of the fight didn't last long; so a lot of us larked round Fredericksburg, and give some of them houses a pretty consid'able of a rummage, till we was ordered out of the mess. Some of our fellows cut like time; but I warn't a-goin to run for nobody; and, fust thing I knew, a shell bust, right in front of us, and I keeled over, feelin' as if I was blowed higher'n a kite. I sung out, and the boys come back for me, double quick; but the way they chucked me over them fences was a caution, I tell you. Next day I was most as black as that darkey yonder, lickin' plates on the sly. This is bully coffee, ain't it? Give us another pull at it, and I'll be obleeged to you."

I did; and, as the last gulp subsided, he said, with a rub of his old handkerchief over eyes as well as mouth:

"Look a here; I've got a pair a earbobs and a handkercher pin I'm a goin' to give you, if you'll have them; for you're the very moral o' Lizy Sylvester, poor Eph's wife: that's why I signalled you to come over here. They aint much, I guess, but they'll do to memorize the rebs by."

Burrowing under his pillow, he produced a little bundle of what he called "truck," and gallantly presented me with a pair of earrings, each representing a cluster of corpulent grapes, and the pin a basket of astonishing fruit, the whole large and coppery enough for a small warming-pan. Feeling delicate about depriving him of such valuable relics, I accepted the earrings alone, and was obliged to depart, somewhat abruptly, when my friend stuck the warming-pan in the bosom of his night-gown, viewing it with much complacency, and, perhaps, some tender memory, in that rough heart of his, for the comrade he had lost.

Observing that the man next him had left his meal untouched, I offered the same service I had performed for his neighbor, but he shook his head.

"Thank you, ma'am; I don't think I'll ever eat again, for I'm shot in the stomach. But I'd like a drink of water, if you aint too busy."

I rushed away, but the water-pails were gone to be refilled, and it was some time before they reappeared. I did not forget my patient patient, meanwhile, and, with the first mugful, hurried back to him. He seemed asleep; but something in the tired white face caused me to listen at his lips for a breath. None came. I touched his forehead; it was cold: and then I knew that, while he waited, a better nurse than I had given him a cooler draught, and healed him with a touch. I laid the sheet over the quiet sleeper, whom no noise could now disturb; and, half an hour later, the bed was empty. It seemed a poor requital for all he had sacrificed and suffered,—that hospital bed, lonely even in a crowd; for there was no familiar face for him to look his last upon; no friendly voice to say, Good bye; no hand to lead him gently down into the Valley of the Shadow; and he vanished, like a drop in that red sea upon whose shores so many women stand lamenting. For a moment I felt bitterly indignant at this seeming carelessness of the value of life, the sanctity of death; then consoled myself with the thought that, when the great muster roll was called, these nameless men might be promoted above many whose tall monuments record the barren honors they have won.

All having eaten, drank, and rested, the surgeons began their rounds; and I took my first lesson in the art of dressing wounds. It wasn't a festive scene, by any means; for Dr. P., whose Aid I constituted myself, fell to work with a vigor which soon convinced me that I was a weaker vessel, though nothing would have induced me to confess it then. He had served in the Crimea, and seemed to regard a dilapidated body very much as I should have regarded a damaged garment; and, turning up his cuffs, whipped out a very unpleasant looking housewife, cutting, sawing, patching and piecing, with the enthusiasm of an accomplished surgical seamstress; explaining the process, in scientific terms, to the patient, meantime; which, of course, was immensely cheering and comfortable. There was an uncanny sort of fascination in watching him, as he peered and probed into the mechanism of those wonderful bodies, whose mysteries he understood so well. The more intricate the wound, the better he liked it. A poor private, with both legs off, and shot through the lungs, possessed more attractions for him than a dozen generals, slightly scratched in some "masterly retreat;" and had any one appeared in small pieces, requesting to be put together again, he would have considered it a special dispensation.

The amputations were reserved till the morrow, and the merciful magic of ether was not thought necessary that day, so the poor souls had to bear their pains as best they might. It is all very well to talk of the patience of woman; and far be it from me to pluck that feather from her cap, for, heaven knows, she isn't allowed to wear many; but the patient endurance of these men, under trials of the flesh, was truly wonderful; their fortitude seemed contagious, and scarcely a cry escaped them, though I often longed to groan for them, when pride kept their white lips shut, while great drops stood upon their foreheads, and the bed shook with the irrepressible tremor of their tortured bodies. One or two Irishmen anathematized the doctors with the frankness of their nation, and ordered the Virgin to stand by them, as if she had been the wedded Biddy to whom they could administer the poker, if she didn't; but, as a general thing, the work went on in silence, broken only by some quiet request for roller, instruments, or plaster, a sigh from the patient, or a sympathizing murmur from the nurse.

It was long past noon before these repairs were even partially made; and, having got the bodies of my boys into something like order, the next task was to minister to their minds, by writing letters to the anxious souls at home; answering questions, reading papers, taking possession of money and valuables; for the eighth commandment was reduced to a very fragmentary condition, both by the blacks and whites, who ornamented our hospital with their presence. Pocket books, purses, miniatures, and watches, were sealed up, labelled, and handed over to the matron, till such times as the owners thereof were ready to depart homeward or campward again. The letters dictated to me, and revised by me, that afternoon, would have made an excellent chapter for some future history of the war; for, like that which Thackeray's "Ensign Spooney" wrote his mother just before Waterloo, they were "full of affection, pluck, and bad spelling;" nearly all giving lively accounts of the battle, and ending with a somewhat sudden plunge from patriotism to provender, desiring "Marm," "Mary Ann," or "Aunt Peters," to send along some pies, pickles, sweet stuff, and apples, "to yourn in haste," Joe, Sam, or Ned, as the case might be.

My little Sergeant insisted on trying to scribble something with his left hand, and patiently accomplished some half dozen lines of hieroglyphics, which he gave me to fold and direct, with a boyish blush, that rendered a glimpse of "My Dearest Jane," unnecessary, to assure me that the heroic lad had been more successful in the service of Commander-in-Chief Cupid than that of Gen. Mars; and a charming little romance blossomed instanter in Nurse Periwinkle's romantic fancy, though no further confidences were made that day, for Sergeant fell asleep, and, judging from his tranquil face, visited his absent sweetheart in the pleasant land of dreams.

At five o'clock a great bell rang, and the attendants flew, not to arms, but to their trays, to bring up supper, when a second uproar announced that it was ready. The new comers woke at the sound; and I presently discovered that it took a very bad wound to incapacitate the defenders of the faith for the consumption of their rations; the amount that some of them sequestered was amazing; but when I suggested the probability of a famine hereafter, to the matron, that motherly lady cried out: "Bless their hearts, why shouldn't they eat? It's their only amusement; so fill every one, and, if there's not enough ready to-night, I'll lend my share to the Lord by giving it to the boys." And, whipping up her coffee-pot and plate of toast, she gladdened the eyes and stomachs of two or three dissatisfied heroes, by serving them with a liberal hand; and I haven't the slightest doubt that, having cast her bread upon the waters, it came back buttered, as another large-hearted old lady was wont to say.

Then came the doctor's evening visit; the administration of medicines; washing feverish faces; smoothing tumbled beds; wetting wounds; singing lullabies; and preparations for the night. By eleven, the last labor of love was done; the last "good night" spoken; and, if any needed a reward for that day's work, they surely received it, in the silent eloquence of those long lines of faces, showing pale and peaceful in the shaded rooms, as we quitted them, followed by grateful glances that lighted us to bed, where rest, the sweetest, made our pillows soft, while Night and Nature took our places, filling that great house of pain with the healing miracles of Sleep, and his diviner brother, Death.

A CABINET CRISIS:
WASHINGTON, D.C., DECEMBER 1862

Orville H. Browning: Diary, December 18, 1862

The Fredericksburg debacle fed mounting frustration among Republicans, particularly the radical Republicans, in the Senate over the administration's management of the war. On December 17, meeting in caucus, they passed a resolution calling for "a change in and partial reconstruction of the Cabinet." The caucus's target was Secretary of State Seward, thought to be the frequent architect of bad policies and a malign power behind the throne. These complaints had been fed in backstairs fashion to the radicals by their favorite, Secretary of the Treasury Chase, who hoped to replace Seward's influence with his own. Senator Browning records Lincoln's response to this burgeoning cabinet crisis.

Thursday Decr 18, 1862 With Boone & Head at the Treasury Department in the morning. In the evening went with Mr D W Wise of Boston to the Presidents The Servant at the door reported that he was not in his office—was in the house but had directed them to say that he could not be seen to night.

I told the boy to tell him I wished to see him a moment and went up in to his room. He soon came in. I saw in a moment that he was in distress—that more than usual trouble was pressing upon him. I introduced Mr Wise who wished to get some items for the preparation of a biography, but soon discovered that the President was in no mood to talk upon the subject. We took our leave. When we got to the door the President called to me saying he wished to speak to me a moment. Mr Wise passed into the hall and I returned. He asked me if I was at the caucus yesterday. I told him I was and the day before also. Said he "What do these men want?" I answered "I hardly know Mr President, but they are exceedingly violent towards the administration, and what we did yesterday was the gentlest thing that could be done. We had to do that or worse." Said he "They wish to get rid of me, and I am sometimes half disposed to gratify them." I replied "Some of them do wish to get rid of you, but the fortunes of the Country are bound up with your fortunes, and you stand firmly at your post and hold the helm with a steady hand—To relinquish it now would bring upon us certain and inevitable ruin." Said he "We are now on the brink of destruction. It appears to me the Almighty is against us, and I can hardly see a ray of hope." I answered "Be firm and we will yet save the Country. Do not be driven from your post. You ought to have crushed the ultra, impracticable men last summer. You could then have done it, and escaped these troubles. But we will not talk of the past. Let us be hopeful and take care of the future Mr Seward appears now to be the especial object of their hostility. Still I believe he has managed our foreign affairs as well as any one could have done. Yet they are very bitter upon him, and some of them very bitter upon you." He then said "Why will men believe a lie, an absurd lie, that could not impose upon a child, and cling to it and repeat it in defiance of all evidence to the contrary." I understood this to refer to the charges against Mr Seward.

He then added "the Committee is to be up to see me at 7 O'clock. Since I heard last night of the proceedings of the caucus I have been more distressed than by any event of my life." I bade him good night, and left him

LINCOLN RESOLVES THE CRISIS:
WASHINGTON, D.C., DECEMBER 1862

Gideon Welles: Diary, December 19–20, 1862

Secretary of the Navy Welles picks up the story with the cabinet session the morning of December 19, at which the president reported on his meeting the previous evening with a committee from the Republican caucus, its demands, and reveals that Seward has submitted his resignation. That evening Lincoln arranged a showdown at the White House, with the cabinet (absent Seward) meeting face-to-face with eight Republicans from the caucus. Chase, put on the spot, was forced to side with Lincoln's view of the cabinet's cooperative workings as against the challengers' view. Welles reveals the dénouement on December 20, with the president extracting from Chase his resignation. "Now I can ride," Lincoln told Senator Ira Harris. "I have got a pumpkin in each end of my bag." With both resignations in hand, he announced he would accept neither. To the senators the lessons were clear: to be rid of Seward would cost the cabal its favorite, Chase; and Congress could not dictate to the Executive in such matters as retaining or dismissing cabinet members.

Friday 19 December. Soon after reaching the Department this A.M. I received a note from Nicolay the President's secretary requesting me to attend a special Cabinet meeting at half past ten. All the members were punctually there except Seward.

The President desired that what he had to communicate should not be the subject of conversation elsewhere, and proceeded to inform us that on Wednesday evening, about six o'clock, Senator Preston King and F. W. Seward came into his room each bearing a communication. That which Mr. King presented was the resignation of the Secretary of State, and Mr. F. W. Seward handed in his own.

Mr. King then informed him that at a Republican caucus held that day a pointed and positive opposition had shown itself against the Secretary of State which terminated in a unanimous expression, with one exception, against him and a wish for his removal. The feeling finally shaped itself into resolutions of a general character, and the appointment of a committee of nine to bear them to the President, and to communicate to him the sentiments of the Republican Senators. Mr. King, the former colleague and the friend of Mr. Seward, being also from the same State, felt it to be a duty to inform the Secretary at once of what had occurred. On receiving this information Mr. Seward immediately tendered his resignation. Mr. King suggested it would be well for the committee to wait upon the President at an early moment, and the President agreeing with him, Mr. King on Wednesday morning notified Judge Collamer the chairman, who sent word to the President that they would call at the Executive Mansion at any hour after six that evening, and the President sent word he would receive them at seven.

The committee came at the time specified and the President says the evening was spent in a pretty free discussion and animated conversation. No opposition was manifested towards any other member of the Cabinet than Mr. Seward. Some not very friendly feelings were shown towards one or two others, but no wish that any one should leave but the Secretary of State. Him they charged if not with infidelity with indifference, with want of earnestness in the War, with want of sympathy with the country in this great struggle and with many things objectionable, and especially with a too great ascendency and control of the President. This he said was the point and pith of their complaint.

The President in reply to the committee stated how this movement shocked and grieved him. That the Cabinet he had selected in view of impending difficulties and of all the responsibilities upon him that the members and himself had gone on harmoniously—that there had never been serious disagreements though there had been differences—that in the overwhelming troubles of the country which had borne heavily upon him he had been sustained and consoled by the good feeling and the mutual and unselfish confidence and zeal that pervaded the Cabinet.

He expressed a hope that there would be no combined movement on the part of other members of the Cabinet to resist this assault whatever might be the termination. Said the movement was uncalled for, that there was no such charge, admitting all that was said, as should break up or overthrow a Cabinet, nor was it possible for him to go on with a total abandonment of old friends.

Mr. Bates stated the difference between our system and that of England where a change of ministry involved a new election, dissolution of Parliament, etc.

Three or four members of the Cabinet said they had heard of the resignation: Blair the day preceding, Stanton through the President, on whom he had made a business call. Mr. Bates when coming to the meeting.

The President requested that we should, with him, meet the committee. This did not receive the approval of Mr. Chase, who said he had no knowledge whatever of the movement, or the resignation, until since he had entered the room.

Mr. Bates knew of no good that would come of an interview. I stated that I could see no harm in it, and if the President wished it I thought it a duty. Mr. Blair thought it would be well for us to be present, and finally, all acquiesced. The President named half past seven this evening.

Saturday 20 December. At the meeting last evening there were present of the committee Senators Collamer, Fessenden, Harris, Trumbull, Grimes, Howard, Sumner, and Pomeroy. Wade was absent. The President, and all the Cabinet but Seward were present. The subject was opened by the President, who read the resolutions and stated the substance of his interviews with the committee—their object and purpose. He spoke of the unity of his Cabinet, and how, though they could not be expected to think and speak alike on all subjects, all had acquiesced in measures when once decided. The necessities of the times, he said, had prevented frequent and long sessions of the Cabinet, and the submission of every question at the meetings.

Secretary Chase indorsed the President's statement fully and entirely, but regretted that there was not a more full and thorough consideration and canvass of all important measure in open Cabinet.

Senator Collamer, however, the chairman of the committee succeeded the President, and calmly and fairly presented the views of the committee and of those whom they represented. They wanted united counsels, combined wisdom, and energetic action. If there is truth in the maxim, that in a multitude of counselors there is safety, it might be well that those advisers who were near the President and selected by him, and all of whom were more or less responsible, should be consulted on the great questions which affected the national welfare, and that the ear of the Executive should be open to all and that he should have the minds of all.

Senator Fessenden was skillful but a little tart,—felt, it could be seen, more than he cared to say,—wanted the whole Cabinet to consider and decide great questions, and that no one should absorb the whole Executive. Spoke of a remark which he had heard from J.Q. Adams on the floor of Congress in regard to a measure of his administration. Mr. Adams said the measure was adopted against his wishes and opinion, but he was outvoted by Mr. Clay and others. He wished an administration so conducted.

Grimes, Sumner and Trumbull were pointed, emphatic and unequivocal in their hostility to Mr. Seward, each was unrelenting and unforgiving.

Blair spoke earnestly and well. Sustained the President and dissented most decidedly from the idea of a plural Executive,—claimed that the President was accountable for his administration, might ask opinions or not of either and as many as he pleased, of all or none, of his Cabinet. Mr. Bates took much the same view.

The President managed his own case, speaking freely, and showed great tact and ability provided such a subject were a proper one for such a meeting and discussion. I have no doubt he considered it most judicious to conciliate the Senators with respectful deference, whatever may have been his opinion of their interference. When he closed his remarks, he said it would be a gratification to him if each member of the committee would state whether he now thought it advisable to dismiss Mr. Seward, and whether his exclusion would strengthen or weaken the Administration, and the Union cause in their respective States. Grimes, Trumbull and Sumner, who had expressed themselves decidedly against the continuance of Mr. Seward in the Cabinet indicated no change of opinion. Collamer and Fessenden declined committing themselves on the subject—were not prepared to answer the questions. Senator

Harris felt it a duty to say that while many of the friends of the Administration would be gratified, others would feel deeply wounded, and the effect of Mr. Seward's retirement would, on the whole be calamitous in the State of New York. Pomeroy of Kansas said, personally, he believed the withdrawal of Mr. Seward would be a good movement and he sincerely wished it might take place. Howard of Michigan declined answering the question.

During the discussion the volume of diplomatic correspondence, recently published, was alluded to—some letters denounced as unwise and impolitic were specified, one of which, a confidential dispatch to Mr. Adams, was read. If it was unwise to write, it was certainly injudicious and indiscreet to publish the document. Mr. Seward has genius and talent, no one better knows it than himself, but he is often wanting in true wisdom, sound judgment, and discreet statesmanship. The committee believe that he thinks more of the glorification of Seward than the welfare of the country. He has unwittingly and unwarily begotten a vast amount of distrust and hostility on the part of Senators by his endeavors to impress them and others with the belief that he is the Administration. It is a mistake, they have measured and know him.

It was nearly midnight when we left the President; and it could not be otherwise than that all my wakeful moments should be absorbed with a subject which, time and circumstances considered, was of grave importance to the Administration and the country. A Senatorial combination to dictate to the President in regard to his political family in the height of a civil war which threatens the existence of the Republic cannot be permitted even if the person to whom they object is as obnoxious as they represent. After fully canvassing the subject in all its phases my mind was clear as to the course which it was my duty to pursue, and what I believed was the President's duty also.

My first movement this morning was to call on the President as soon as I supposed he could have breakfasted. Governor Robertson of Kentucky was with him when I went in but soon left. I informed the President I had pondered the events of yesterday and last evening, and felt it incumbent on me to advise him not to accept the resignation of Mr. Seward. That if there were objections, real or imaginary, against Mr. Seward, the time, manner and circumstances—the occasion, and the method of presenting what the Senators considered objections were all inappropriate and wrong. That no party or faction should be permitted to dictate to the President in regard to his Cabinet,—that it would be of evil example and fraught with incalculable injury to the Government and country,—that the legislative department, or the Senate should not be allowed to encroach on the Executive prerogatives,—that it devolved on him, and was his duty to assert and maintain the rights and independence of the Executive,—that he ought not, against his own convictions, to yield one iota of the authority intrusted to him on the demand of either branch of Congress or both combined, or to any party, whatever might be its views and intentions,—that Mr. Seward had his infirmities and errors,—that he and I differed on many things, as did other members of the Cabinet—that he was disposed to step beyond his own legitimate bounds and not duly respect the rights of his associates, but these were matters that did not call for Senatorial interference. In short I considered it for the true interest of the country, now as in the future, that this scheme should be defeated,—that so believing I had, at the earliest moment given him my conclusions.

The President was much gratified—said the whole thing had struck him as it had me, and if carried out as the Senators prescribed the whole Government must cave in. It could not stand. Could not hold water,—the bottom would be out.

I added that, having expressed my wish that he would not accept Mr. Seward's resignation, I thought it equally important that Seward should not press its acceptance. In this he also concurred, and asked if I had seen Seward. I replied I had not, my first duty was with him, and having ascertained that we agreed I would now go over and see him. He earnestly desired me to do so.

I went immediately to Seward's house. Stanton was with him. Seward was excited, talking vehemently to Stanton of the course pursued and the results that must follow if the scheme succeeded,—told Stanton he would be the next victim, that there was a call for a meeting at the Cooper Institute this evening. Stanton said he had seen it. I had not. Seward got the

Herald for me to read but Stanton seized the paper, as Seward and myself then entered into conversation, when he related what the President had already communicated,—how Preston King had come to him, he wrote his resignation at once, and so did Fred, etc., etc. In the mean time Stanton rose and remarking he had much to do and that Governor S. had been over this matter with him, he would leave.

I then stated my interview with the President, my advice that the President must not accept, nor he press, his resignation. Seward was greatly pleased with my views,—said he had but one course before him when the doings of the Senators were communicated, but that if the President and country required from him any duty in this emergency he did not feel at liberty to refuse it. He spoke of his long political experience, dwelt on his own sagacity and his great services, feels deeply this movement which was wholly unexpected,—tries to suppress any exhibition of personal grievance or disappointment, but is painfully wounded, mortified, and chagrined.

I told him I should return and report to the President our interview and that he acquiesced. He said he had no objections, but he thought the subject should be disposed of one way or the other at once. He is disappointed I see that the President did not promptly refuse to consider his resignation, and dismiss, or refuse to parley with the committee.

When I returned to the White House, Chase and Stanton were in the President's office, but he was absent. A few words were interchanged on the great topic in hand. I was very emphatic in my opposition to the acceptance of Seward's resignation. Neither gave me a direct answer or expressed an opinion on the subject, though I think both wished to be understood as acquiescing.

When the President came in, which was in a few moments, his first address was to me, asking if I "had seen the man." I replied that I had, and that he assented to my views. He then turned to Chase and said I sent for you, for this matter is giving me great trouble. At our first interview he rang and directed that a message be sent to Mr. Chase.

Chase said he had been painfully affected by the meeting last evening, which was a total surprise to him, and, after some, not very explicit remarks as to how he was affected, informed the

President he had prepared his resignation. Where is it, said the President quickly, his eye lighting up in a moment. I brought it with me, said Chase, taking it from his pocket—I wrote it this morning. Let me have it, said the President, reaching his long arm and fingers towards C., who held on, seemingly reluctant to part with the letter which was sealed, and which he apparently hesitated to surrender. Something further he wished to say, but the President was eager and did not perceive it, but took the letter.

This said he, looking towards me with a triumphal laugh cuts the Gordian knot. An air of satisfaction spread over his countenance such as I have not seen for some time. I can dispose of this subject now he added, as he turned on his chair and broke the seal. I see my way clear.

Chase sat by Stanton fronting the fire—the President beside the fire his face towards them, Stanton nearest him. I was on the sofa near the east window. While the President was reading the note which was brief, Chase turned round towards me a little perplexed and would, I think have been better satisfied could this interview with the President been without the presence of others, or at least if I was away. The President was delighted and saw not how others were affected.

Mr. President, said Stanton with solemnity, I informed you day before yesterday that I was ready to tender you my resignation. I wish you sir to consider my resignation at this time in your possession.

You may go to your Department said the President, I don't want yours. This, holding out Chase's letter is all I want—this relieves me—my way is clear—the trouble is ended. I will detain neither of you longer. We all rose to leave, but Stanton held back as we reached the door. Chase and myself came downstairs together. He was moody and taciturn. Some one stopped him on the lower stairs and I passed on, but C. was not a minute behind me. Before I reached the Department, Stanton came staving along.

"SICKNESS, DISGUST, AND DESPAIR": DECEMBER 1862

Harper's Weekly: The Reverse at Fredericksburg

December 27, 1862

The blunder-ridden campaign and battle of Fredericksburg, with its deadly toll of casualties—for the Union, greater even than at Antietam—plunged Northern morale to its lowest point of the war. This *Harper's Weekly* editorial, while thin factually, reflected the national discouragement.

THE REVERSE AT FREDERICKSBURG.

WE HAVE again to report a disastrous reverse to our arms. Defeated with great slaughter in the battle of 13th, General Burnside has now withdrawn the army of the Potomac to the north side of Rappahannock, where the people congratulate themselves that it is at least in safety. And now, who is responsible for this terrible repulse?

General Burnside was appointed to the command of the army of the Potomac on 9th November, and began at once to prepare to shift the base and line of march of his army toward Fredericksburg. In view of such a movement General McClellan had, before his removal, suggested the propriety of rebuilding and occupying the railroad from Aquia Creek to Falmouth; but, for some reason not apparent, the War Department had not acted upon the suggestion. About 12th November General Burnside notified the Department that he would arrive at Fredericksburg in about a week, and that pontoons must be there by that time, in order to enable him to cross and occupy the hills on the south side of the river. On the 21st General Sumner arrived at Fredericksburg, and found that there was not a pontoon there, and the railroad between Aquia Creek and Falmouth being out of order, there was no means of getting any, and no means of procuring supplies. It was absolutely impossible to cross the river, and the enemy were already arriving on the south side and throwing up earth-works.

General Burnside, on discovering this state of things, repaired instantly to Washington to ascertain why he was being sacrificed. What satisfaction he obtained no one knows. But a general officer, one of the most distinguished in the service, not in the army of the Potomac, as early as 23d November, made no secret of his opinion that the movement *via* Fredericksburg "*was a failure*," because Burnside had been unable to occupy the south bank of the Rappahannock in time.

In the course of two weeks pontoons were furnished to the army, the railroad was repaired, and supplies were forthcoming. But, on the other hand, Lee, with 150,000 men, was strongly intrenched on the opposite side of the river, on two ranges of hills which command the slope at the foot of which the Rappahannock runs and Fredericksburg lies. The question was, what was to be done? A council of war was held on the night of 11th. At that council it is understood, that Generals Sumner, Franklin, Hooker, and all the corps commanders who had been invited were decidedly opposed to a movement across the river and up the slope. IT IS RUMORED THAT BURNSIDE THEN SAID THAT HE WAS ORDERED TO CROSS THE RIVER AND ATTACK THE BATTERIES IN FRONT, AND THAT WE WOULD DO IT, NO MATTER WHAT THE COST. This of course closed the discussion, and the Generals made their preparations accordingly. On 12th the river was crossed without serious resistance. On 13th the rebel batteries were attacked in front by the bulk of Burnside's army, and our troops were repulsed with a loss which is now variously estimated at from twelve to seventeen thousand men. The rebel loss is not known, but they can not have lost many score of men. On the night of 15–16th, General Burnside withdrew his army to the north side of the river.

We are indulging in no hyperbole when we say that these events are rapidly filling the heart of the loyal North with sickness, disgust, and despair. Party lines are becoming effaced by such unequivocal evidences of administrative imbecility; it is the men who have given and trusted the most, who now feel most keenly that the Government is unfit for its office, and that the most gallant efforts ever made by a cruelly tried people are being neutralized by the obstinacy and incapacity of their leaders. Where this will all end no one can see. But it must end soon. The people have shown a patience, during the past year, quite unexampled in history. They have borne, silently and grimly, imbecility, treachery, failure, privation, loss of friends and means, almost every suffering which can afflict a brave people. But they can not be expected to suffer that such massacres as this at Fredericksburg shall be repeated. Matters are rapidly ripening for a military dictatorship.

LINCOLN AND EMANCIPATION: NEW YORK, DECEMBER 1862

George Templeton Strong: Diary, December 27, 1862

As Strong suggests, there were doubters of Lincoln's promise to issue the Emancipation Proclamation. The pamphlet by the lawyer and writer Charles Stillé, titled *How a Free People Conduct a Long War*, would be widely distributed by the U.S. Sanitary Commission, in which both Stillé and Strong were active. The Jefferson Davis proclamation Strong mentions listed a long bill of particulars against General Butler's administration in New Orleans, and declared Butler "a felon, deserving of capital punishment." As for the *brutum fulmen*, back on September 13, replying to a delegation of ministers demanding immediate emancipation, Lincoln said he would not make an empty gesture "inoperative, like the pope's bull against the comet!" (The comet was Halley's, the date 1486, and the tale popular but apocryphal.) On December 30 Strong returned to the subject of the proclamation: "If he come out fair and square, he will do the 'biggest thing' an Illinois jury-lawyer has ever had a chance of doing, and take high place among the men who have controlled the destinies of nations. If he postpone or dilute his action, his name will be a byword and a hissing till the annals of the nineteenth century are forgotten."

December 27. Public affairs unchanged. Will Uncle Abe Lincoln stand firm and issue his promised proclamation on the first of January, 1863? Nobody knows, but I think he will. Charles J. Stillé of Philadelphia has published a clever pamphlet, comparing our general condition as to blunders, imbecility, failures, popular discontent, financial embarrassment, and so on with that of shabby old England during the first years of her Peninsular War. He makes out a strong case in our favor. It is a valuable paper, and we must have it reprinted here, for there are many feeble knees in this community that want to be confirmed and corroborated. It had an excellent effect on Bidwell; a bad case of typhoid despondency in a state of chronic collapse and utter prostration. He rallied a little after reading it, and was heard to remark that "we might possibly come out all right after all."

Jefferson Davis's precious proclamation!! Butler and all Butler's commissioned officers to be hanged, whenever caught. Ditto all armed Negroes, and all white officers commanding them. This is the first great blunder Jeff has committed since the war began. It's evidence not only of barbarism but of weakness, and will disgust his foreign admirers (if anything can) and strengthen the backbone of the North at the same time. If he attempts to carry it out, retaliation becomes a duty, and we can play at extermination quite as well as Jeff Davis.

George Wright, who was here Christmas evening, recounted a talk with some South Carolina woman about the policy of forming nigger regiments. The lady was furious. "Just think how infamous it is that our *gentlemen* should have to go out and fight niggers, and that every nigger they shoot is a thousand dollars out of their own pockets! Was there ever anything so outrageous?" "And then," said Wright, "she was so mad that she just jumped straight up and down a minute or two." No wonder. The liberating proclamation we hope for next Thursday, January 1, 1863, may possibly prove a *brutum fulmen*, "a pope's bull against the comet" (a clever mot of Abe Lincoln's), but the enlisting, arming, and drilling of a few thousand muscular athletic buck niggers, every one of whom knows he will be certainly hanged and probably tortured besides if made prisoner, is a material addition to the national force. How strange that patriotic, loyal people should deny its expediency. This generation is certainly overshadowed by a superstition, not yet quite exploded, that slaveholding rights possess peculiar sanctity and inviolability, that everybody who doubts their justice is an Abolitionist, and that an Abolitionist is a social pariah, a reprobate and caitiff, a leper whom all decent people are bound to avoid and denounce. We shall feel otherwise ten years hence, unless subjugated meanwhile by the pluck and ferocity of the slaveholders' rebellion, and look back on Northern reverence for slavery and slaveholders A.D. 1862, even after the long experience of war with treason arrayed in support of slavery, as we now regard the gross superstitions of ten centuries ago, or the existing superstitions of the Mandingoes and the Zulu Kaffirs. I trust we may not have to remember it as a signal instance of judicial blindness, a paralyzing visitation of divine vengeance on a whole people at the very moment when their national existence depended on their seeing the truth and asserting it.

PORTER'S COURT-MARTIAL: WASHINGTON, D.C., DECEMBER 1862

Fitz John Porter to Samuel L.M. Barlow

On December 3 a general court-martial was convened in the case of Fitz John Porter, charged with failing to obey orders and misbehavior before the enemy at Second Bull Run. Dispatches and letters were introduced to show Porter's animus toward General Pope, and witnesses testified that at critical points in the first day's fighting he failed to obey Pope's orders. But as Porter points out here, writing to New York lawyer Barlow, the court was neither unbiased nor unaffected by the unrest in the army's high command. Porter's prediction of its verdict was borne out. He was found guilty and cashiered in January 1863. In 1879 an army review board exonerated Porter, yet his conduct at Second Bull Run remains controversial.

Washington.
Dec. 29" 62

My dear Friend.

I missed you the day you left. I caused to be sent you by express, a package of papers, more with a view you might see how biased is the court against me, than for any action. Since then I have seen sufficient of the court—or of the minds of a few of them, the most of them—to know their conclusion is a foregone one, if not determined by order or the wish of those high in power. Within the past two days I have seen sufficient to convince me of their intent and no matter what the record may be, to find a verdict against me. T'is hard that I should be accused of acts so much at variance with my character, and after exposure of life since the dates of these charges, to be accused of these acts, and to be charged with bad faith towards any one. Yet such is the case. Confident of my own innocence I can, not withstanding any decision rendered by the court—(some members of which expect reward either by restoration to command or appointment of relations, or promotion) I can lay my hand on my heart as say there is no guile there or intention to injure our cause or be a defaulter in effort to any one or to my country. God knows I have risked life in too many battles and skirmishes to be criminal now. I intend to make the record plain and honest, and if declared by the court guilty, will show to the world that the court (not I am) is guilty before my maker— I have too many personal enemies & enemies of Genl McClellan on the court.

The army will soon I expect make another effort to turn the enemy's right, lower down the river. If so you may expect to hear that the enemy have flown—and are behind the North Anna—where they cannot be reached—and where the same obstacles will be raised against them as at Fredericksburg—and if the army advances beyond that place—the rail road will not supply their men & animals.—A longer line will have to be guarded and their security diminished. I believe *the policy of the rebels is now* (I judge from their activity.) *to abandon Fredericksburg and induce our army to advance and remain on the line it is now attempting to follow*, the worst line it can take, and to keep it going to James River, and we are fools enough to go where they pull us by the nose. Whatever they wish we have done, and will do as much as if their consils governed.

Banks I have reason to believe is to ascend the Mississippi, and wherever his army may go either Texas or Miss, it is understood freedom to slaves is to be declared, and *insurrection encouraged.* It seems hard to believe Banks has lent himself to such base and inhuman policy, but I believe it is so. You will soon see. I also hear Seward and Chase are as thick as two peas, and their policy the same. So closely connected are they, that the communications between the department buildings are such each can visit the other without being seen. You may rest assured the most intimate relations exist, and that Chase resigned because Seward was to leave, & he was determined to keep him. You may also expect the proclamation to be issued, and commanders of troops directed not to interfere in case of servile insurrections—or the Law of last Congress pointed to—God help us. —Our men & officers are discouraged. The rebels appear to be prospering, and the fear exists that the west may slide from New England and unite with the South. An Effort is being made to solder NYork & the west by the Erie canal being made into a ship canal as an outlet to produce in opposition to the Miss. and thus buy off the west— A game is being played and if the good men of the north dont work. I fear another split will ensue. I do believe if we had one good strong man of influence and character to work the matter through, preliminaries to a settlement might be commenced, and by operating on the fears *of* the chief power, peace might be restored. The wire pullers, by working on the interests of the monied men can effect it. But there must be change—and Butler must not go into the cabinet or be promoted, which he is brought home for—because he is thrown overboard by the Democrats. He will take the bribe unless New York men can bribe higher as soon as he arrives & he should be at once worked upon cautiously. He is to be brought home to work for the radicals. I believe to go into the War Dept, but certainly for no good for *our* party.

I send you these thoughts—to put you in possession of some opinions desired from parties here, & let you see if your own are confirmed. Conservative men are to be pushed to the wall, and radicalism is to rule. Seymour [ ] & Parker & Curtis can check all this.

LOOTING IN HOLLY SPRINGS: MISSISSIPPI, DECEMBER 1862

Cyrus F. Boyd: Diary, December 22–25, 1862

In November 1862 Ulysses S. Grant began advancing southward along the Mississippi Central Railroad toward the Confederate bastion at Vicksburg. After reaching Oxford, Mississippi, in early December, Grant planned to move against the Confederate army defending Grenada, forty miles to the south, while William T. Sherman led an expedition from Memphis down the Mississippi to Vicksburg. His plans were thwarted on December 20 by Earl Van Dorn, who led 3,500 cavalrymen in a raid on Grant's supply depot at Holly Springs. Sergeant Cyrus F. Boyd of the 15th Iowa Infantry recorded the aftermath of Van Dorn's attack.

Camp at Holly Springs Mississippi

Dec 22d Weather warm and *roads good* Started at day break toward Holly Springs Had Knapsacks guns and 40 rounds and traveled very fast At noon we ate dinner at the Tallahatchie on our old camp ground. Made a hard march until 7 P M After dark we entered Holly Springs and went through the town and halted on the North side Soon as the men could get their things off they commenced going for things generaly. Every one was gone except those who could not travel from fatigue As for myself I was so far gone that I could not get up to move I could hear hogs squeal and chickens squall in all directions By 11 oclock we had devoured some fresh pig Sergt Gray had secured for our mess a fine Pig. He can hear a hog grunt or a chicken breathe as far as any other man in this Army . . .

Dec 23d Reveille at 4 A. M. The men were very tired and sore but with about the average amount of groaning and *swearing* they got out. At 8 A M we were told that we should not march to-day The wagons were unloaded and foraging parties sent out Almost all the men left Camp and were soon scattered all over the town in a few hours Soldiers could be seen everywhere Out of the cellar of a large brick residence close to our camp there came a constant stream of men and others kept going in and it resembled a *hive of bees* I went over and found the molasses running about 2 inches deep on the floor of the cellar and the men were wading through and carrying off various articles The occupants of the house were inside and locked up and no one outside except a little Negro boy Around were all the indications of Wealth Beautiful shrubbery and trees and vines and flowers and arbors While I was looking around I heard a *row* inside and soon seen a soldier come through the kitchen window heels first and a boot close to his *rear* and attached to a pair of *shoulder straps* About this time I had *business* toward camp

Going down to the "Clayton House" a large frame building I noticed a great crowd around the front door with their arms full of books and papers. I came around the house and just then a lady raised the window and called to me and asked me if I was an officer I replied that I was not a commissioned officer Said she for Gods sake keep the "soldiers from breaking into my room they have possession of the house and I fear they will *Kill me*" I told her not to fear as no man would disturb her. She was a rather good looking woman and had four little children with her This evening this *same* woman was arrested for *shooting* one of our men who was on guard at the "Clayton House" (2 days ago) She cowardly shot him although he was guarding her property This whole town was literly gutted to-day

Van Dorn was here two days ago with a large force of Cavalry and surprised what few men we had here Then the Rebs blew up several buildings right in the Centre of the town and burned the Depots and all the rolling stock and Warehouses and destroyed more than one million Dollars worth of our supplies and also captured several of our Pay Masters with large amounts of Money. Long trains of cars were burned with all their contents and nothing but the irons and trucks stand on the track for almost a *mile* There has been a fearful destruction of property and many of the citizens were killed by the explosions The 101st Ills Infty and the 2d Ills Cavalry had been left to guard the Post The Cav fought as long as they could and then had to *retreat* The Infantry *surrendered* at the first summons and scarcely fired a gun Col Murphy of the 8th Wisconsin commanded

I found the Court House square filled with horses, cannon

ammunition Women with band-boxes and other traps were leaving in all directions The soldiers were in every house and garret and cellar, store and church, and nook and corner. The streets were white with all kinds of paper and men were running with their arms full of books and ledgers and one lot of soldiers had their arms full of Confederate *bank notes* which were perfect in all except the Presidents signature (I think the President did not have time to sign) The boys said they could do that *themselves* On the east side of the square the large brick buildings which we saw there two weeks ago were now one vast shapeless mass of ruins Some of these buildings had been stored with shell and other ammunition and explosive Material Fully one half the fine buildings on North side of the square were likewise blown to pieces

There had been a Bank in one of them and some gold and silver had been melted among the rubbish and the soldiers wete in digging to their knees in the brick bats Sudden and complete destruction has overtaken this city When we went down through here the women and even the children could insult us in every way and we did not disturb a hair of their heads But it remained for their *own friends* to complete their woe If the Confederates treat their own people thus what would they do with their enemies I came to Genl Grants headquarters and saw him talking to an Officer He stood with his hands in his pockets like a common farmer and looked as unconcerned as if he was selling eggs at 2 cts per dozen Everyone thinks Grant has made another big blunder in allowing the Army thus to be cut off from our base of supplies The Col Murphy who surrendered here is the same man who surrendered about 100,000 000$ worth of supplies at Iuka to Price He is called a *traitor*

I came by a fine large Roman Catholic Church A lot of soldiers were in the building some were taking the organ to pieces and had the pipes out blowing on them and throwing them away Up in the pulpit was a squad playing *cards* and another lot were scattering the library over the floor One daring and reckless soldier climbed to the pinnacle of the temple and took off the little silver image of "Jesus" that stood there. It was at a giddy height but he got it—said to be worth several hundred dollars Every portion of the *fated city* seemed given over to *pillage* and destruction and no hand was raised to save anything from the general *sack and ruin*

Finely dressed ladies were leaving on all the streets and going God knows where Women and children were standing in their houses wailing with the most piteous cries Young girls whose eyes were red with weeping peered from behind the curtains of the windows and gazed listlessly upon the passing throngs that crowded the streets No insults were offered any women or citizen that I saw or heard of

When I had witnessed all this destruction and terror my heart almost ceased to beat when I thought of the sadness and woe that is caused by this inhuman war of brother against brother and how the innocent shall suffer in the cause of treason and Rebellion

Railroad communication is completely broken up and we are about out of provisions and Memphis now our base of supplies which is a long way off Marion Mart one of our Co left here was taken prisoner and parolled by the enemy

Dec 24th From poverty and want we have suddenly become rich and *stuck* up. We have been sleeping on slanting rails and on the cold frosty earth or under a mule wagon or indeed we have slept in all kinds of places with a stone for a pillow But we are above that now We have mahogany bedsteads and the finest lounges that this Market affords The tents are not large enough to hold all the fine furniture now on hands. Dan Embree, Gray, Harv Reid and I are all in one tent We have fine Carpet down, a stove and more stuff than we actually *need*. We are short of provisions but shall *trust* to Gray

Dec 25th Christmas We are not so *merry* as we might be. No demonstration in Camp would indicate this Holiday Have nothing to eat but a little Corn bread and some tough beef Genl Logans Division went North to-day

JACKSON, DECEMBER 1862

Jefferson Davis: Address to the Mississippi Legislature

The Confederate defeats at Iuka and Corinth, the failure of Bragg's campaign in Kentucky, and the continued Union threat to Vicksburg caused grave concern in Richmond about the war in the western theater. In November Jefferson Davis placed Joseph E. Johnston in overall command of both Bragg's army in Tennessee and the army defending Vicksburg, now led by John C. Pemberton. Davis then decided to appraise the situation in person. After conferring with Bragg in Tennessee, he traveled with Johnston to Mississippi, where they inspected the Vicksburg defenses and met with Pemberton at Grenada. Before returning to Richmond, Davis addressed the Mississippi legislature in Jackson.

December 26, 1862

Friends and Fellow-Citizens, Gentlemen of the House of Representatives and Senate of the State of Mississippi:

After an absence of nearly two years I again find myself among those who, from the days of my childhood, have ever been the trusted objects of my affections, those for whose good I have ever striven, and whose interest I have sometimes hoped I may have contributed to subserve. Whatever fortunes I may have achieved in life have been gained as a representative of Mississippi, and before all, I have labored for the advancement of her glory and honor. I now, for the first time in my career, find myself the representative of a wider circle of interest; but a circle in which the interests of Mississippi are still embraced. Two years ago, nearly, I left you to assume the duties which had devolved on me as the representative of the new Confederacy. The responsibilities of this position have occupied all my time, and have left me no opportunity for mingling with my friends in Mississippi, or for sharing in the dangers which have menaced them. But, wherever duty may have called me, my heart has been with you and the success of the cause in which we are all engaged has been first in my thoughts and in my prayers. I thought when I left Mississippi that the service to which I was called would prove to be but temporary. The last time I had the honor of addressing you from this stand, I was influenced by that idea. I then imagined that it might be my fortune again to lead Mississippians in the field, and to be with them where danger was to be braved and glory won. I thought to find that place which I believed to be suited to my capacity: that of an officer in the service of the State of Mississippi. For, although in the discharge of my duties as President of the Confederate States, I had determined to make no distinction between the various parts of the country—to know no separate State—yet my heart has always beat more warmly for Mississippi, and I have looked on Mississippi soldiers with a pride and emotion such as no others inspired. But it was decided differently. I was called to another sphere of action. How, in that sphere, I have discharged the duties and obligations imposed on me, it does not become me to constitute myself the judge. It is for others to decide that question. But, speaking to you with that frankness and that confidence with which I have always spoken to you, and which partakes of the nature of thinking aloud, I can say with my hand upon my heart, that whatever I have done, has been done with the sincere purpose of promoting the noble cause in which we are engaged. The period which has elapsed since I left you is short; for the time, which may appear long in the life of man, is short in the history of a nation. And in that short period remarkable changes have been wrought in all the circumstances by which we are surrounded. At the time of which I speak, the question presented to our people was "will there be war!" This was the subject of universal speculation. We had chosen to exercise an indisputable right—the right to separate from those with whom we conceived association to be no longer possible, and to establish a government of our own. I was among those who, from the beginning, predicted war as the consequence of secession, although I must admit that the contest has assumed proportions more gigantic than I had anticipated. I predicted war not because our right to secede and to form a government of our own was not indisputable and clearly defined in the spirit of that declaration which rests the right to govern on the consent of the governed, but because I foresaw that the wickedness of the North would precipitate a war upon us. Those who supposed that the exercise of this right of separation could not produce war, have had cause to be convinced that they had credited their recent associates of the North with a moderation, a sagacity, a morality they did not possess. You have been involved in a war waged for the gratification of the lust of power and of aggrandizement, for your conquest and your subjugation, with a malignant ferocity and with a disregard and a contempt of the usages of civilization, entirely unequalled in history. Such, I have ever warned you, were the characteristics of the Northern people—of those with whom our ancestors entered into a Union of consent, and with whom they formed a constitutional compact. And yet, such was the attachment of our people for that Union, such their devotion to it, that those who desired preparation to be made for the inevitable conflict, were denounced as men who only wished to destroy the Union. After what has happened during the last two years, my only wonder is that we consented to live for so long a time in association with such miscreants, and have loved so much a government rotten to the core. Were it ever to be proposed again to enter into a Union with such a people, I could no more consent to do it than to trust myself in a den of thieves.

You in Mississippi, have but little experienced as yet the horrors of the war. You have seen but little of the savage manner in which it is waged by your barbarous enemies. It has been my fortune to witness it in all its terrors; in a part of the country where old men have been torn from their homes, carried into captivity and immured in distant dungeons, and where delicate women have been insulted by a brutal soldiery and forced even to cook for the dirty Yankee invaders; where property has been wantonly destroyed, the country ravaged, and every outrage committed. And it is with these people that our fathers formed a union and a solemn compact. There is indeed a difference between the two peoples. Let no man hug the delusion that there can be renewed association between them. Our enemies are a traditionless and a homeless race; from the time of Cromwell to the present moment they have been disturbers of the peace of the world. Gathered together by Cromwell from the bogs and fens of the North of Ireland and of England, they commenced by disturbing the peace of their own country; they disturbed Holland, to which they fled, and they disturbed England on their return. They persecuted Catholics in England, and they hung Quakers and witches in America. Having been hurried into a war with a people so devoid of every mark of civilization you have no doubt wondered that I have not carried out the policy, which I had intended should be our policy, of fighting our battles on the fields of the enemy instead of suffering him to fight them on ours. This was not the result of my will, but of the power of the enemy. They had at their command all the accumulated wealth of seventy years—the military stores which had been laid up during that time. They had grown rich from the taxes wrung from you for the establishing and supporting their manufacturing institutions. We have entered upon a conflict with a nation contiguous to us in territory, and vastly superior to us in numbers. In the face of these facts the wonder is not that we have done little, but that we have done so much. In the first year of the war our forces were sent into the field poorly armed, and were far inferior in number to the enemy. We were compelled even to arm ourselves by the capture of weapons taken from the foe on the battle-field. Thus in every battle we exchanged our arms for those of the invaders. At the end of twelve months of the war, it was still necessary for us to adopt some expedient to enable us to maintain our ground. The only expedient remaining to us was to call on those brave men who had entered the service of their country at the beginning of the war, supposing that the conflict was to last but a short time, and that they would not be long absent from their homes. The only expedient, I say, was to call on these gallant men; to ask them to maintain their position in front of the enemy, and to surrender for a time their hopes of soon returning to their families and their friends. And nobly did they respond to the call. They answered that they were willing to stay, that they were willing to maintain their position and to breast the tide of invasion. But it was not just that they should stand alone. They asked that the men who had stayed at home—who had thus far been sluggards in the cause—should be forced, likewise, to meet the enemy. From this, resulted the law of Congress, which is known as the conscription act, which declared all men, from the age of eighteen to the age of thirty-five, to be liable to enrolment in the Confederate service. I regret that there has been some prejudice excited against that act, and that it has been subjected to harsher criticism than it deserves. And here I may say that an erroneous impression appears to prevail in regard to this act. It is no disgrace to be brought into the army by conscription. There is no more reason to expect from the citizen voluntary service in the army than to expect voluntary labor on the public roads or the voluntary payment of taxes. But these things we do not expect. We assess the property of the citizen, we appoint tax-gatherers; why should we not likewise distribute equally the labor, and enforce equally the obligation of defending the country from its enemies? I repeat that it is no disgrace to any one to be conscribed, but it is a glory for those who do not wait for the conscription. Thus resulted the conscription act; and thence arose the necessity for the exemption act. That necessity was met; but when it was found that under these acts enough men were not drawn into the ranks of the army to fulfill the purposes intended, it became necessary to pass another exemption act, and another conscription act. It is only of this latter that I desire now to speak. Its policy was to leave at home those men needed to conduct the administration, and those who might be required to support and maintain the industry of the country—in other words, to exempt from military service those whose labor, employed in other avocations, might be more profitable to the country and to the government, than in the ranks of the army.

I am told that this act has excited some discontent and that it has provoked censure, far more severe, I believe, than it deserves. It has been said that it exempts the rich from military service, and forces the poor to fight the battles of the country. The poor do, indeed, fight the battles of the country. It is the poor who save nations and make revolutions. But is it true that in this war the men of property have shrunk from the ordeal of the battle-field? Look through the army; cast your eyes upon the maimed heroes of the war whom you meet in your streets and in the hospitals; remember the martyrs of the conflict; and I am sure you will find among them more than a fair proportion drawn from the ranks of men of property. The object of that portion of the act which exempts those having charge of twenty or more negroes, was not to draw any distinction of classes, but simply to provide a force, in the nature of a police force, sufficient to keep our negroes in control. This was the sole object of the clause. Had it been otherwise, it would never have received my signature. As I have already said, we have no cause to complain of the rich. All of our people have done well; and, while the poor have nobly discharged their duties, most of the wealthiest and most distinguished families of the South have representatives in the ranks. I take, as an example, the case of one of your own representatives in Congress, who was nominated for Congress and elected; but still did a sentinel's duty until Congress met. Nor is this a solitary instance, for men of the largest fortune in Mississippi are now serving in the ranks.

Permit me now to say that I have seen with peculiar pleasure the recommendation of your Governor in his message, to make some provision for the families of the absent soldiers of Mississippi. Let this provision be made for the objects of his affection and his solicitude, and the soldier engaged in fighting the battles of his country will no longer be disturbed in his slumber by dreams of an unprotected and neglected family at home. Let him know that his mother Mississippi has spread her protecting mantle over those he loves, and he will be ready to fight your battles, to protect your honor, and, in your cause, to die. There is another one of the governor's propositions to which I wish to allude. I mean the proposition to call upon those citizens who are not subject to the Confederate conscription law, and to form them into a reserve corps for the purpose of aiding in the defense of the State. Men who are exempted by law from the performance of any duty, do not generally feel the obligation to perform that duty unless called upon by the law. But I am confident that the men of Mississippi have only to know that their soil is invaded, their cities menaced, to rush to meet the enemy, even if they serve only for thirty days. I see no reason why the State may not, in an exigency like that which now presses on her, call on her reserved forces and organize them for service. Such troops could be of material benefit, by serving in intrenchments, and thus relieving the veteran and disciplined soldiers for the duties of the field, where discipline is so much needed. At the end of a short term of service they could return to their homes and to their ordinary avocations, resuming those duties necessary to the public prosperity.

The exemption act, passed by the last Congress, will probably be made the subject of revision and amendment. It seems to me that some provision might be made by which those who are exempt from enrollment now, might, on becoming subject to conscription, be turned over by the State to the Confederate authorities. But let it never be said that there is a conflict between the States and the Confederate government, by which a blow may be inflicted on the common cause. If such a page is to be written on the history of any State, I hope that you, my friends, will say that that State shall not be Mississippi. Let me repeat that there is much that the reserved corps can do. They can build bridges, construct fortifications, act as a sort of police to preserve order and promote the industrial interests of the State and to keep the negroes under control. Being of the people among whom they would act, those misunderstandings would thus be avoided which are apt to arise when strangers are employed in such a service. In this manner the capacity of the army for active operations against the enemy would be materially increased. I hope I shall not be considered intrusive for having entered into these details. The measures I have recommended are placed before you only in the form of suggestions, and, by you, I know I shall not be misinterpreted.

In considering the manner in which the war has been conducted by the enemy, nothing arrests the attention more than the magnitude of the preparations made for our subjugation. Immense navies have been constructed, vast armies have been accumulated, for the purpose of crushing out the rebellion. It has been impossible for us to meet them in equal numbers; nor have we required it. We have often whipped them three to one, and in the eventful battle of Antietam, Lee whipped them four to one. But do not understand me as saying that this will always be the case. When the troops of the enemy become disciplined, and accustomed to the obedience of the camp, they will necessarily approach more nearly to an equality with our own men. We have always whipped them in spite of disparity of numbers, and on any fair field, fighting as man to man, and relying only on those natural qualities with which men are endowed, we should not fear to meet them in the proportion of one to two. But troops must be disciplined in order to develop their efficiency; and in order to keep them at their posts. Above all, to assure this result, we need the support of public opinion. We want public opinion to frown down those who come from the army with sad tales of disaster, and prophecies of evil, and who skulk from the duties they owe their country. We rely on the women of the land to turn back these deserters from the ranks. I thank the Governor for asking the legislature to make the people of the State tributary to this service. In addition to this, it is necessary to fill up those regiments which have for so long a time been serving in the field. They have stood before the foe on many hard fought fields and have proven their courage and devotion on all. They have won the admiration of the army and of the country. And here I may repeat a compliment I have heard which, although it seems to partake of levity, appears an illustration of the esteem in which Mississippians are held. It happened that several persons were conversing of a certain battle, and one of them remarked that the Mississippians did not run. "Oh no!" said another "Mississippians never run." But those who have passed through thirteen pitched battles are not unscathed. Their ranks are thinned, and they look back to Mississippi for aid to augment their diminished numbers. They look back expecting their brothers to fly to their rescue; but it sometimes seems as if the long anticipated relief would never come. A brigade which may consist of only twelve hundred men is expected to do the work of four thousand. Humanity demands that these depleted regiments be filled up. A mere skeleton cannot reasonably be expected to perform the labor of a body with all its flesh and muscle on it. You have many who might assist in revivifying your reduced regiments—enough to fill up the ranks if they would only consent to throw off the shackles of private interest, and devote themselves to the noblest cause in which a man can be engaged. You have now in the field old men and gentle boys who have braved all the terrors and the dangers of war. I remember an instance of one of these, a brave and gallant youth who, I was told, was but sixteen years of age. In one of those bloody battles by which the soil of Virginia has been consecrated to liberty, he was twice wounded, and each time bound up the wound with his own hands, while refusing to leave the field. A third time he was struck, and the life-blood flowed in a crimson stream from his breast. His brother came to him to minister to his wants; but the noble boy said "brother, you cannot do me any good now; go where you can do the Yankees most harm." Even then, while lying on the ground, his young life fast ebbing away, he cocked his rifle and aimed it to take one last shot at the enemy. And so he died, a hero and a martyr. This was one of the boys whose names shed glory on Mississippi, and who, looking back from their distant camps, where they stand prepared to fight your battles, and to turn back the tide of Yankee invasion, ask you now to send them aid in the struggle —to send them men to stand by them in the day of trial, on the right hand and on the left.

When I came to Mississippi I was uncertain in which direction the enemy intended to come, or what point they intended to attack. It had been stated indeed in their public prints, that they would move down upon Mississippi from the North, with the object of taking Vicksburg in the rear, while their navy would attack that place in front. Such was the programme which had been proclaimed for the invasion and subjugation of your State. But when I went to Grenada, I found that the enemy had retired from our front, and that nothing was to be seen of them but their backs. It is probable that they have abandoned that line, with the intention of reinforcing the heavy column now descending the river. Vicksburg and Port Hudson are the real points of attack. Every effort will be made to capture those places with the object of forcing the navigation of the Mississippi, of cutting off our communications with the trans Mississippi department, and of severing the Western from the Eastern portion of the Confederacy. Let, then, all who have at heart the safety of the country, go without delay to Vicksburg and Port Hudson; let them go for such length of time as they can spare—for thirty, for sixty, or for ninety days. Let them assist in preserving the Mississippi river, that great artery of the country, and thus conduce more than in any other way to the perpetuation of the Confederacy and the success of the cause.

I may say here that I did not expect the Confederate enrolling officers to carry on the work of conscription. I relied for this upon the aid of the State authorities. I supposed that State officers would enroll the conscripts within the limits of their respective States, and that Confederate officers would then receive them in camps of instruction. This I believe to be the policy of your Governor's arguments. We cannot too strongly enforce the necessity of harmony between the Confederate Government and the State Governments. They must act together if our cause is to be brought to a successful issue. Of this you may rest assured, whatever the Confederate government can do for the defense of Mississippi will be done. I feel equal confidence that whatever Mississippi can do will likewise be done. It undoubtedly requires legislation to cause men to perform those duties which are purely legal. Men are not apt to feel an obligation to discharge duties from which they may have been exempted. Ours is a representative government, and it is only through the operation of the law that the obligations toward it can be equally distributed. When the last Congress proclaimed that a certain number of men were required to fill up the ranks of the army, that class of men who were already in the field and who were retained in service, would not have been satisfied had there been no conscription of those who had remained at home. I may state also, that I believe this to be the true theory for the military defense of the Confederacy. Cast your eyes forward to that time at the end of the war, when peace shall nominally be proclaimed—for peace between us and our hated enemy will be liable to be broken at short intervals for many years to come—cast your eyes forward to that time, and you will see the necessity for continued preparation and unceasing watchfulness. We have but few men in our country who will be willing to enlist in the army for a soldier's pay. But if every young man shall have served for two or three years in the army, he will be prepared when war comes to go into camp and take his place in the ranks an educated and disciplined soldier. Serving among his equals, his friends and his neighbors, he will find in the army no distinction of class. To such a system I am sure there can be no objection.

The issue before us is one of no ordinary character. We are not engaged in a conflict for conquest, or for agrandizement, or for the settlement of a point of international law. The question for you to decide is, "will you be slaves or will you be independent?" Will you transmit to your children the freedom and equality which your fathers transmitted to you or will you bow down in adoration before an idol baser than ever was worshipped by Eastern idolators? Nothing more is necessary than the mere statement of this issue. Whatever may be the personal sacrifices involved, I am sure that you will not shrink from them whenever the question comes before you. Those men who now assail us, who have been associated with us in a common Union, who have inherited a government which they claim to be the best the world ever saw—these men, when left to themselves, have shown that they are incapable of preserving their own personal liberty. They have destroyed the freedom of the press; they have seized upon and imprisoned members of State Legislatures and of municipal councils, who were suspected of sympathy with the South. Men have been carried off into captivity in distant States without indictment, without a knowledge of the accusations brought against them, in utter defiance of all rights guaranteed by the institutions under which they live. These people, when separated from the South and left entirely to themselves, have, in six months, demonstrated their utter incapacity for self-government. And yet these are the people who claim to be your masters. These are the people who have determined to divide out the South among their Yankee troops. Mississippi they have devoted to the direst vengeance of all. "But vengeance is the Lord's," and beneath his banner you will meet and hurl back these worse than vandal hordes.

The great end and aim of the government is to make our struggle successful. The men who stand highest in this contest would fall the first sacrifice to the vengeance of the enemy in case we should be unsuccessful. You may rest assured then for that reason if for no other that whatever capacity they possess will be devoted to securing the independence of the country. Our government is not like the monarchies of the Old World, resting for support upon armies and navies. It sprang from the people and the confidence of the people is necessary for its success. When misrepresentations of the government have been circulated, when accusations have been brought against it of weakness and inefficiency, often have I felt in my heart the struggle between the desire for justice and the duty not to give information to the enemy—because at such times the correction of error would have been injurious to the safety of the cause. Thus, that great and good man, Gen. A. Sidney Johnston, was contented to rest beneath public contumely and to be pointed at by the finger of scorn, because he did not advance from Bowling Green with the little army under his command. But month after month he maintained his post, keeping the enemy ignorant of the paucity of his numbers, and thus holding the invaders in check. I take this case as one instance; it is not the only one by far.

The issue then being: will you be slaves; will you consent to be robbed of your property; to be reduced to provincial dependence; will you renounce the exercise of those rights with which you were born and which were transmitted to you by your fathers? I feel that in addressing Mississippians the answer will be that their interests, even life itself, should be willingly laid down on the altar of their country.

By the memories of the past; by the glories of the field of Chalmette, where the Mississippians, in a general order of the day, were addressed as the bravest of the brave; by the glorious dead of Mexico; by the still more glorious dead of the battle fields of the Confederacy; by the desolate widows and orphans, whom the martyrs of the war have left behind them; by your maimed and wounded heroes—I invoke you not to delay a moment, but to rush forward and place your services at the disposal of the State. I have been one of those who, from the beginning, looked forward to a long and bloody war; but I must frankly confess that its magnitude has exceeded my expectations. The enemy have displayed more power and energy and resources than I had attributed to them. Their finances have held out far better than I imagined would be the case. But I am also one of those who felt that our final success was certain, and that our people had only to be true to themselves to behold the Confederate flag among those of the recognized nations of the earth. The question is only one of time. It may be remote but it may be nearer than many people suppose. It is not possible that a war of the dimensions that this one has assumed, of proportions so gigantic, can be very long protracted. The combatants must be soon exhausted. But it is impossible, with a cause like ours, we can be the first to cry, "Hold, enough."

The sacrifices which have already been made, have perhaps fallen heavily upon a portion of the people, especially upon the noble little city of Vicksburg. After Memphis and New Orleans had fallen, two points which were considered to be admirably defended, two points which we had no reason to believe would fall, Vicksburg became the object of attack. A few earthworks were thrown up, a few guns were mounted, and Vicksburg received the shock of both fleets; the one which, under Commodore Foote had descended the river, and the one which, under Farragut, had achieved the capture of New Orleans. Nobly did the little city receive the assault, and even the women said, "Rather than surrender let us give them the soil, but with the ashes of our dwellings upon it."

This was the heroic devotion of a people who deserve to be free. Your Governor left his chair, and went himself to the scene of danger. Nothing more profoundly touched me amid my duties in a distant land, than to hear that the chief magistrate of my own State was defending the town which the enemy had made the object of his attack, and that the defense was successful. Now we are far better prepared in that quarter. The works, then weak, have been greatly strengthened; the troops assigned for their defense are better disciplined and better instructed, and that gallant soldier who came with me, has been pouring in his forces to assist in its protection. Himself the son of a Revolutionary hero, he has emulated his father's glorious example upon other fields, and comes to Mississippi to defend, and, as I believe, to protect you.

In the course of this war our eyes have been often turned abroad. We have expected sometimes recognition and sometimes intervention at the hands of foreign nations, and we have had a right to expect it. Never before in the history of the world had a people for so long a time maintained their ground, and showed themselves capable of maintaining their national existence, without securing the recognition of commercial nations. I know not why this has been so, but this I say, "put not your trust in princes," and rest not your hopes in foreign nations. This war is ours; we must fight it out ourselves, and I feel some pride in knowing that so far we have done it without the good will of anybody. It is true that there are now symptoms of a change in public opinion abroad. They give us their admiration—they sometimes even say to us God speed—and in the remarkable book written by Mr. Spence, the question of secession has been discussed with more of ability than it ever has been even in this country. Yet England still holds back, but France, the ally of other days, seems disposed to hold out to us the hand of fellowship. And when France holds out to us her hand, right willingly will we grasp it.

During the last year, the war has been characterized by varied fortunes. New Orleans fell; a sad blow it was to the valley of the Mississippi, and as unexpected to me as to any one. Memphis also fell, and besides these we have lost various points on the Atlantic coast. The invading armies have pressed upon us at some points; at others they have been driven back; but take a view of our condition now and compare it with what it was a year ago—look at the enemy's position as it then was and as it now is; consider their immense power, vast numbers, and great resources; look at all these things and you will be convinced that our condition now will compare favorably with what it was then. Armies are not composed of numbers alone. Officers and men are both to be disciplined and instructed. When the war first began the teacher and the taught were in the condition of the blind leading the blind; now all this is changed for the better. Our troops have become disciplined and instructed. They have stripped the gunboat of its terrors; they have beaten superior numbers in the field; they have discovered that with their short range weapons they can close upon the long range of the enemy and capture them. Thus, in all respects, moral as well as physical, we are better prepared than we were a year ago.

There are now two prominent objects in the programme of the enemy. One is to get possession of the Mississippi river and to open it to navigation in order to appease the clamors of the West and to utilize the capture of New Orleans, which has thus far rendered them no service. The other is to seize upon the capital of the Confederacy, and hold this out as a proof that the Confederacy has no existence. We have recently repulsed them at Fredericksburg, and I believe that under God and by the valor of our troops the capital of the Confederacy will stand safe behind its wall of living breasts. Vicksburg and Port Hudson have been strengthened, and now we can concentrate at either of them a force sufficient for their protection. I have confidence that Vicksburg will stand as before, and I hope that Johnston will find generals to support him if the enemy dare to land. Port Hudson is now strong. Vicksburg will stand, and Port Hudson will stand; but let every man that can be spared from other vocations, hasten to defend them, and thus hold the Mississippi river, that great artery of the Confederacy, preserve our communications with the trans-Mississippi department, and thwart the enemy's scheme of forcing navigation through to New Orleans. By holding that section of the river between Port Hudson and Vicksburg, we shall secure these results, and the people of the West, cut off from New Orleans, will be driven to the East to seek a market for their products, and will be compelled to pay so much in the way of freights that those products will be rendered almost valueless. Thus, I should not be surprised if the first daybreak of peace were to dawn upon us from that quarter.

Some time since, for reasons not necessary to recapitulate, I sent to this State a general unknown to most of you, and, perhaps, even by name, known but to few among you. This was the land of my affections. Here were situated the little of worldly goods I possessed. I selected a general who, in my view, was capable of defending my State and discharging the duties of this important service. I am happy to state, after an attentive, examination, that I have not been mistaken in the general of my choice. I find that, during his administration here everything has been done that could be accomplished with the means at his command. I recommend him to your confidence as you may have confidence in me, who selected him. For the defense of Vicksburg, I selected one from the army of the Potomac, of whom it is but faint praise to say he has no superior. He was sent to Virginia at the beginning of the war, with a little battery of three guns. With these he fought the Yankee gunboats, drove them off, and stripped them of their terrors. He was promoted for distinguished services on various fields. He was finally made a colonel of cavalry, and I have reason to believe that, at the last great conflict on the field of Manassas, he served to turn the tide of battle and consummate the victory.

On succeeding fields he has won equal distinction. Though yet young he has fought more battles than many officers who have lived to an advanced age and died in their beds. I have therefore sent Lee to take charge of the defenses of Vicksburg. I can say then that I have every confidence in the skill and energy of the officers in command. But when I received dispatches and heard rumors of alarm and trepidation and despondency among the people of Mississippi; when I heard even that people were fleeing to Texas in order to save themselves from the enemy; when I saw it stated by the enemy that they had handled other States with gloves, but Mississippi was to be handled without gloves, every impulse of my heart dragged me hither in spite of duties which might have claimed my attention elsewhere. When I heard of the sufferings of my own people, of the danger of their subjugation by a ruthless foe, I felt that if Mississippi were destined for such a fate, I would wish to sleep in her soil. On my way here I stopped at the headquarters of Gen. Johnston. I knew his capacity and his resolution. I imparted to him my own thoughts and asked him to come with me. I found that his ideas were directed in the same channel. He came in the shortest time for preparation; but whatever man can do will be done by him. I have perfect confidence that with your assistance and support he will drive the enemy from the soil of Mississippi. After having visited the army—after having mingled among the people of the State—I shall go away from among you with a lighter heart. I do not think the people of Mississippi are despondent or depressed; those who are so are those on whom the iron tread of the invader has fallen, or those who, skulking from their duty, go home with fearful tales to justify their desertion.

Nor is the army despondent; on the contrary, it is confident of victory. At Grenada I found the only regret to be that the enemy had not come on. At Vicksburg, even without reinforcements, the troops did not dream of defeat. I go, therefore, anxious but hopeful. My attachment to Mississippi, and my esteem for her people, have risen since the war began. I have been proud of her soldiers. I have endeavored to conceal my pride, for I wished to make no distinction between the States of the Confederacy; but I cannot deny that my heart has warmed with a livelier emotion when I have seen those letters upon the boy's cap that have marked him for a Mississippian. Man's affections are not subject to his will; mine are fixed upon Mississippi. And when I return to where I shall find Mississippians fighting for you in a distant State, ween I shall tell them that you are safe here, that you can be defended without calling upon them, and that they are necessary to guard the capital and to prevent the inroads of the enemy in Georgia and Alabama, I shall be proud to say to them for you that they are welcome to stay.

As to the States on the other side of the Mississippi, I can say that their future is bright. The army is organized and disciplined, and it is to be hoped that at no distant day it may be able to advance into that land which has been trodden under the foot of despotism, where old men have been torn from their homes and immured in dugeons, where even the women have been subjected to the insults of the brutal Yankee soldiery—that under the flag of the Confederacy Missouri will again be free.

Kentucky, too, that gallant State whose cause is our cause, the gallantry of whose sons has never been questioned, is still the object of the ardent wishes of Gen. Bragg. I heard him say in an address to his troops, that he hoped again to lead them into Kentucky, and to the banks of the Ohio river.

I can then say with confidence that our condition is in every respect greatly improved over what it was last year. Our armies have been augmented, our troops have been instructed and disciplined. The articles necessary for the support of our troops, and our people, and from which the enemy's blockade has cut us off, are being produced in the Confederacy. Our manufactories have made rapid progress, so much is this the case that I learn with equal surprise and pleasure from the general commanding this department, that Mississippi alone can supply the army which is upon her soil.

Our people have learned to economize and are satisfied to wear home spun. I never see a woman dressed in home spun that I do not feel like taking off my hat to her; and although our women never lose their good looks, I cannot help thinking that they are improved by this garb. I never meet a man dressed in home spun but I feel like saluting him. I cannot avoid remarking with how much pleasure I have noticed the superior morality of our troops, and the contrast which in this respect they present to those of the invader. I can truly say that an army more pious and more moral than that defending our liberties, I do not believe to exist. On their valor and the assistance of God I confidently rely.

BATTLE OF CHICKASAW BAYOU:
MISSISSIPPI, DECEMBER 1862

William T. Sherman to John Sherman

Grant was forced to abandon his advance on Vicksburg by Van Dorn's attack on Holly Springs, but was unable to tell Sherman that he was retreating because Confederate raiders had torn down the telegraph lines. Sherman landed his troops on the Yazoo River north of Vicksburg and on December 29 assaulted the bluffs overlooking Chickasaw Bayou in an attempt to reach high ground. The unsuccessful attack cost the Union forces nearly 1,800 men killed, wounded, or missing, while Confederate casualties totaled about 200. Sherman wrote to his brother John, now a Republican senator from Ohio.

Steamer *Forest Queen*,
January 6, 1863.

Dear Brother,

You will have heard of our attack on Vicksburg and failure to succeed. The place is too Strong, and without the cooperation of a large army coming from the Interior it is impracticable. Innumerable batteries prevent the approach of Gun boats to the city or to the first bluff up the Yazoo, and the only landing between is on an insular space of low boggy ground with innumerable bayous or deep sloughs. I did all that was possible to reach the main Land but was met at every point by Batteries & Rifle pits that we could not pass, and in the absence of Genl. Grants cooperating force I was compelled to reembark my command. My Reports to General Grant a copy of which I send to General Halleck who will let you see it is very full, and more than I could write to you with propriety. Whatever you or the absent may think, not a soldier or officer who was present but will admit I pushed the attack as far as prudence would justify, and that I reembarked my command in the nick of time, for a heavy rain set in which would have swamped us and made it impossible to withdraw artillery & Stores. Up to that time I was acting on the Right Wing of Genl. Grants army, but Gen. McClernand has arrived and we now have a new organization—

McClernand commanding the whole, and our present force divided into two commands or Corps d'Armee one of which is commanded by me and one by Morgan of Cumberland Gap. We are now en route for the Arkansas. Up that River about 50 miles the enemy is entrenched, and has sent down to the Mississipi and captured two steamboats carrying to the fleet supplies. Now it is unwise to leave such a force on our rear and flank and inasmuch as Genl. Grant is not prepared to march down to Vicksburg by Land, we can attack this Post of Arkansas and maybe reach Little Rock. Success in this quarter will have a good Effect on the Main River. But in the end Vicksburg must be reduced, and it is going to be a hard nut to crack—It is the strongest place I ever saw, both by nature and art, and so far as we could observe it is defended by a Competent form of artillery Infantry and Cavalry, besides its Rail Road connections with the interior give them great advantage. I wish you would ask Halleck to allow you to See my Report, and as soon as all the Reports of the Division & Brigade commanders reach Washington from Genl. Grant to where they must first go, you will have a complete picture. Of course newspaper men will first flood the country with their stories and what they will be no one can tell, they having their purposes to Serve and not Knowing my orders or plans. My orders from Grant were to leave Memphis by the 18th and I got off the 20th and I was exactly on time to cooperate with Grant. I did not know that he was delayed by the breaking of his Railroad Communications to his Rear. Indeed I supposed him to be advancing south towards the Yazoo River. My entire force was 30,000, and was every man I could raise at Memphis & Helena, and Grant & Halleck were fully advised of my strength & plans. I suppose you are now fully convinced of the stupendous energy of the South, and their ability to prolong this war indefinitely, but I am further satisfied that if it last thirty years we must fight it out, for the moment the North relaxes its energies, the South will assume the offensive, and it is wonderful how well disciplined and provided they have their men—we found everywhere abundant supplies, even on the Yazoo, and all along the River we found cattle & fat ones feeding quietly. The Country everywhere abounds with corn, and the Soldiers though coarsely are well clad. We hear of the manufacture of all sorts of cloth and munitions of war. The River Plantations are mostly abandoned, and all families negros, stock & cotton removed 25 miles back. All corn has been carried in advance to Vicksburg. We find a few old people along the River but all the Young & middle aged have gone to the war. I see no symptoms of a relaxation of their fierce energy, so that I still regard the war as but fairly begun. Young Henry Sherman was under fire, but is well. He is in Lindseys Brigade of Morgans Division. In time I will move for his promotion.

I think I see at the North & in the discussions in the Senate & Cabinet symptoms of that anarchy which I fear more than war. Stand by the Constituted authorities even if it lead to despotism rather than anarchy which will result if popular clamor is to be the Ruling Power. yrs.

Sherman

MISTREATMENT OF CONTRABANDS: ARKANSAS, DECEMBER 1862

Samuel Sawyer, Pearl P. Ingalls, and Jacob G. Forman to Samuel R. Curtis

Slaves who came within the Union lines often suffered from neglect and abuse at the hands of Northern soldiers. Three Union army chaplains sent this appeal to Major General Samuel R. Curtis, the commander of the Department of the Missouri. Sawyer was subsequently appointed superintendent of contrabands at Helena, with Forman serving as his assistant.

Helena Arkansas Dec 29th 1862

General The undersigned Chaplains and Surgeons of the army of the Eastern Destrict of Arkansas would respectfully call your attention to the Statements & Suggestions following

The Contrabands within our lines are experiencing hardships oppression & neglect the removal of which calls loudly for the intervention of authority. We daily see & deplore the evil and leave it to your wisdom to devise a remedy. In a great degree the contrabands are left entirely to the mercy and rapacity of the unprincipled part of our army (excepting only the limited jurisdiction of capt Richmond) with no person clothed with Specific authority to look after & protect them. Among their list of grievances we mention these:

Some who have been paid by individuals for cotton or for labor have been waylaid by soldiers, robbed, and in several instances fired upon, as well as robbed, and in no case that we can now recal have the plunderers been brought to justice—

The wives of some have been molested by soldiers to gratify thier licentious lust, and thier husbands murdered in endeavering to defend them, and yet the guilty parties, though known, were not arrested. Some who have wives and families are required to work on the Fortifications, or to unload Government Stores, and receive only their meals at the Public table, while their families, whatever provision is intended for them, are, as a matter of fact, left in a helpless & starving condition

Many of the contrabands have been employed, & received in numerous instances, from officers & privates, only counterfeit money or nothing at all for their services. One man was employed as a teamster by the Government & he died in the service (the government indebted to him nearly fifty dollars) leaving an orphan child eight years old, & there is no apparent provision made to draw the money, or to care for the orphan child. The negro hospital here has become notorious for filth, neglect, mortality & brutal whipping, so that the contrabands have lost all hope of kind treatment there, & would almost as soon go to their graves as to their hospital. These grievances reported to us by persons in whom we have confidence, & some of which we know to be true, are but a few of the many wrongs of which they complain— For the sake of humanity, for the sake of christianity, for the good name of our army, for the honor of our country, cannot something be done to prevent this oppression & to stop its demoralizing influences upon the Soldiers themselves? Some have suggested that the matter be laid before the War Department at Washington, in the hope that they will clothe an agent with authority, to register all the names of the contrabands, who will have a benevolent regard for their welfare, though whom all details of fatigue & working parties shall be made though whom rations may be drawn & money paid, & who shall be empowered to organize schools, & to make all needfull Regulations for the comfort & improvement of the condition of the contrabands; whose accounts shall be open at all times for inspection, and who shall make stated reports to the Department— All which is respectfully submitted

Samuel Sawyer
committee Pearl P Ingalls
J. G. Forman

BATTLE OF STONES RIVER:
TENNESSEE, DECEMBER 1862–JANUARY 1863

Ira S. Owens: from Greene County in the War

After replacing Don Carlos Buell in late October, William S. Rosecrans built up supplies and reorganized his command, now named the Army of the Cumberland. On December 26 Rosecrans began advancing from Nashville toward Braxton Bragg's Army of Tennessee at Murfreesboro, thirty miles to the southeast. By December 30 Rosecrans and his army of 42,000 men faced Bragg and 35,000 Confederates along Stones River outside of Murfreesboro. Bragg struck first on December 31 and succeeded in nearly doubling the Union battle line back on itself. Private Ira S. Owens of the 74th Ohio Infantry fought as part of James S. Negley's division in the corps commanded by George H. Thomas. He recalled his first (and only) battle in an 1874 regimental history.

ON THE 26th of December 1862 we received orders to march to Murfreesboro, Tennessee, where the rebels were in strong force. Accordingly we packed up and started, the Army of the Cumberland moving at the same time. We were then going to our first battle. We had not marched far before it began to rain and rained very hard. We marched on through the mud and rain until nearly night, when we halted within two miles of Nashville. We had prepared our suppers and eaten them, and were preparing to spend the night by spreading our blankets on the ground for beds, when the bugle sounded and we were ordered to fall in. Then we marched some two or three miles farther, passing through the town of Nolensville, and halted in the woods. It will be remembered that we had neither shelter tents nor gum blankets, consequently we were exposed to all the rain, which continued nearly all night, so that we had to sit up nearly the whole time. The next day we advanced on toward Murfreesboro, skirmishing in front, as they had been all the day before. Colonel Moody urging us on, telling us if we did not hurry up the battle would be over before we should get there. We marched on until we came to the Nashville pike, some eight or nine miles from Murfreesboro. We halted just at night wet, cold and hungry. It was not long, however, before we had a fire built of rails, and after getting warm and dry we became tolerably comfortable. After getting and eating our suppers we prepared to spend the night. After spreading our blankets down on the ground around the fire we addressed ourselves to sleep. During the night the fire popped out on blankets and burned several large holes in them. Rained some during the night. The next day the being Sunday, we rested and spread out our blankets to dry.

Monday, the 29th, the regiment advanced toward Murfreesboro, except Company C, which was ordered back to Nolensville, to guard some teams which were sent back for part of the baggage, which was left behind, owing to the bad condition of the roads. We arrived at Nolensville, and loaded the teams, and started back. We had left the town but a short time when it was entered by some rebel scouts and plundered of everything. Had we remained an hour longer, in all probability, we should all have been captured. We arrived at the place where we left the regiment, but they had gone on; so we halted and remained all night, and the next morning we advanced toward Murfreesboro, where we found the regiment in line of battle, and skirmishing going on in front. We remained in line through the day and until about 11 o'clock at night, our position being on the center, amid a thick growth of cedars. About 11 o'clock at night we were ordered out to support a battery in front. We remained in line until morning. It was quite cool, and the ground considerably frozen. I had lost my knapsack, putting it in a wagon the day we arrived on the battle ground, and never saw it any more. Consequently I had neither coat nor blanket. I suffered very much during the night with cold. Could not lie down but a few minutes at a time, and dare not go back to the fire, rebels being but a few yards in. I was chilled through and exposed to the enemy, there being no breastworks. It was considered a mark of cowardice to get behind anything to fight. Had the same policy been adopted then as was toward the close of the war, that is, of building works, a great many lives might have been saved. About 6 o'clock on the morning of the 31st of

December, we were relieved by the 37th Indiana Volunteer Infantry. We returned where the regiment lay the day previous, and commenced breakfast, but did not have time to eat it before we were ordered into line. Not having time to drink my coffee, I poured it into my canteen, and swung it around my neck. We marched out to fight, forming double column at half distance. We advanced a short distance, when we formed line and were ordered to lie down. Then it was that the balls and the shrieking shells came whistling over us, and there were to be seen batteries wheeling into position, orderlies riding back and forth, horses without riders, while the yelling of the rebels like so many fiends, and the roar of artillery and musketry, filled the air with horrid din. The battle was raging fiercely. In a short time we were ordered to arise and move forward. We accordingly moved forward in line a few yards, and were then ordered to halt, make ready, aim—fire. Then the Seventy-Fourth opened its first fire on the enemy. For a description of the battle of Stone River, and an account of the same, I refer the reader to "Rosecrans' Campaign with the 14th Army Corps." I was kneeling in a fence corner, loading and firing when we received orders to move to the left to make room for a battery. When I was just in the act of rising, I felt something hit me on the leg, which did not produce much pain at the time, only a smarting sensation. I thought I would say nothing about it. However it began to grow stiff, and I had not proceeded but a short distance before I had to call for help. I was then helped off the field.

We went back the same way we came. But it was getting to be a hot place in the rear. Balls and shells were flying thick and fast around us, striking trees, and cutting off leaves and branches. The rebels were getting around, and we scarcely knew which way to go, for fear of running right into their midst. At last we got out to the pike. On our way we stopped in an old building where several of our wounded boys were. The rebels soon commenced shelling us; so we had to get away as fast as we could. We proceeded about half a mile, when we were overtaken by some ambulances, where I was taken in and taken to the field hospital, five miles distant. Some of the boys who read this will remember the field hospital at the brick house, near Stewart's creek. It was impossible to supply all the wounded with tents. Rails were hauled and thrown in piles similar to farmers when they wish to build fence, and large fires built apart. The wounded were brought and lain by these fires. Men were wounded in every conceivable way, some with their arms shot off, some wounded in the body, some in the head. It was heart-rending to hear their cries and groans. One poor fellow who was near me was wounded in the head. He grew delirious during the night, and would very frequently call his mother. He would say: "Mother, O, Mother, come and help me!" The poor fellow died before morning with no mother near, to soothe him in his dying moments, or wipe the cold sweat from off his brow. I saw the surgeons amputate limbs, then throw the quivering flesh into a pile. Every once in a while a man would stretch himself out and die. Next morning rows of men were laid out side by side ready for the soldier's burial. No weeping friends stood around, no coffin and hearse to bear them away to the grave, no funeral orations delivered; but there, away from home and kindred, they were wrapped in the soldiers' blanket, a trench dug, and their bodies placed side by side, like they fought, a few shovelfulls of earth thrown upon them, when they were left alone.

Lot D. Young: from Reminiscences of a Soldier of the Orphan Brigade

The new Union battle line held on the afternoon of December 31. After a lull on New Year's Day, the battle resumed on the afternoon of January 2 when Bragg attacked the Union positions on the eastern bank of Stones River. Bragg ordered a retreat on January 3, allowing the North to claim victory at Stones River (or Murfreesboro), a battle that cost the Union 12,906 men killed, wounded, or missing and the Confederacy 11,739—about a third of each army. Lieutenant Lot D. Young served in the Confederate 1st Kentucky Brigade, which became known as the "Orphan Brigade" because its members were unable to return to their native state. He remembered the fighting on January 2 in a 1918 memoir.

THE BATTLE progressed steadily and satisfactorily to the Confederates until about four o'clock, when they, in the language of the "bum," "run against a snag." Woods' and Sheridan's divisions, with other of Rosecrans' forces had concentrated upon his extreme left, which was his strongest position for a final and last stand. The conflict here was desperate and bloody, neither party seeming to have much the advantage.

The National cemetery now occupies this identical ground and in which there are more than 6,000 Federal soldiers buried. A beautiful and fit place for the remains of these brave Western soldiers to rest, for here upon this field was displayed a courage that all men must admire.

Both armies slept that night upon the field with the greater part of the field in possession of the Confederates and the advantages and results of the day almost wholly in their favor.

The Orphans spent the night in the rear of and among the artillery they had been supporting. When morning came we found that the enemy was still in our front instead of on the road to Nashville as Bragg believed. Both parties seemed willing that a truce should prevail for the day and scarcely a shot was heard. Bragg believed that Rosecrans' army was "demolished" and would surely retreat to his base (Nashville), and so informed President Davis.

But old "Rosy" had something else in his mind. He was planning and scheming and matured a plan for a trap and Bragg walked right into it with the innocence of a lamb and the ignorance of a man that had never known anything of the art of war, and the butchery of the next day followed as a result of his obstinacy and the lack of military skill. Had he listened to the protestations of General Breckinridge and his officers he might have saved for the time being his military reputation and the lives of several hundred brave and noble men.

The recounting of the steps that led up to this ill-conceived and fatal denouement and the efforts by General Breckinridge to prevent its consummation, by one while not high in rank, but who claims to know something of the facts in the case, may not go amiss even at this late day.

Early on the morning of January 2, Captain Bramblett, commanding Company H, Fourth Kentucky, and who had served with General Breckinridge in Mexico, received orders from him (Breckinridge), to make a thorough reconnaissance of the enemy's position, Company H being at that time on the skirmish line. Captain Bramblett with two of his lieutenants, myself one of them, crawled through the weeds a distance of several hundred yards to a prominent point of observation from which through his field glass and even the naked eye we could see the enemy's concentrated forces near and above the lower ford on the opposite side of the river, his artillery being thrown forward and nearest to the river. His artillery appeared to be close together and covering quite a space of ground; we could not tell how many guns, but there was quite a number. The infantry was seemingly in large force and extended farther down toward the ford. Captain Bramblett was a man of no mean order of military genius and information, and after looking at, and studying the situation in silence for some minutes, he said to us boys, "that he believed Rosecrans was setting a trap for Bragg." Continuing, he said, "If he means to attack us on this side, why does he not reinforce on this side? Why concentrate so much artillery on the bluff yonder? He must be expecting us to attack that force yonder," pointing to Beatty's position on the hill North of us, "and if we do, he will use that artillery on us as we move to the attack." At another time during the afternoon I heard him while discussing the situation with other officers of the regiment use substantially the same argument. I accompanied Captain Bramblett to General Breckinridge's headquarters and heard him make substantially in detail a report containing the facts above recited. Captain Tom Steele was ordered (his company having relieved ours) on the skirmish line to make a reconnaissance also, and made a similar report, and lastly General Breckinridge, to thoroughly and unmistakably understand the situation and satisfy himself, in company with one or two of his staff examined the situation as best he could and I presume reached the same conclusion, and when he (Breckinridge) repaired to Bragg's headquarters and vouchsafed this information and suggested the presumptive plan of the enemy, Bragg said: "Sir, my information is different. I have given the order to attack the enemy in your front and expect it to be obeyed."

What was General Breckinridge to do but attempt to carry out his orders, though in carrying out this unwise and ill-conceived order it should cost in one hour and ten minutes 1,700 of as brave and chivalrous soldiers as the world ever saw. What a terrible blunder, what a bloody and useless sacrifice! And all because General Breckinridge had resented the imputation that the cause of the failure of Bragg's Kentucky campaign was the "disloyalty of her people to the Confederate cause." Could anyone of the thousands of Kentuckians that espoused the cause of the South, complacently acquiesce in this erroneous charge and endorse the spirit that prompted this order and led to the slaughter of so many of her noble boys? This was the view that many of us took of Bragg's course.

How was this wicked and useless sacrifice brought about? "That subordinate must always obey his superior"—is the military law. In furtherance of Bragg's order we were assembled about three o'clock on the afternoon of January 2, 1863 (Friday, a day of ill luck) in a line North of and to the right of Swain's hill, confronting Beatty's and Growes' brigades, with a battery or two of artillery as support. They being intended for the bait that had been thrown across the river at the lower ford, and now occupied an eminence some three-quarters of a mile to the right-front of the Orphan's position on Swain's hill.

This was the force, small as it was that Bragg was so anxious to dislodge. Between the attacking line and federal position was a considerable scope of open ground, fields and pastures, with here and there a clump of bushes or briars, but the entire space was in full view of and covered by the enemy's batteries to the left of the line on the opposite side of the river previously referred to. If the reader will only carry these positions in his eye, he can readily discover the jaws of the trap in this murderous scheme.

A more imposing and thoroughly disciplined line of soldiers never moved to the attack of an enemy than responded to the signal gun stationed immediately in our rear, which was fired exactly at four o'clock. Every man vieing with his fellowman, in steadiness of step and correct alignment, with the officers giving low and cautionary commands, many knowing that it was their last hour on earth, but without hesitating moved forward to their inevitable doom and defeat. We had gotten only fairly started, when the great jaws of the trap on the bluff from the opposite side of the river were sprung, and bursting shells that completely drowned the voice of man were plunging and tearing through our columns, ploughing up the earth at our feet in front and behind, everywhere. But with steadiness of step we moved on. Two companies of the Fourth regiment, my own and adjoining company, encountered a pond, and with a dexterous movement known to the skilled officer and soldier was cleared in a manner that was perfectly charming, obliquing to the right and left into line as soon as passed.

By reason of the shorter line held by the enemy, our line, which was much longer and the colors of each of our battalions being directed against this shorter line, caused our lines to interlap, making it necessary, in order to prevent confusion and crowding, that some of the regiments halt, until the others had passed forward out of the way. When thus halted they would lie down in order to shield themselves from the enemy infantry fire in front, who had by this time opened a lively fusillade from behind their temporary works.

While lying on the ground momentarily a very shocking and disastrous occurrence took place in Company E, immediately on my left and within a few feet of where I lay. A shell exploded right in the middle of the company, almost literally tearing it to pieces. When I recovered from the shock the sight I witnessed was appalling. Some eighteen or twenty men hurled in every direction, including my dear friend, Lieut. George Burnley of Frankfort. But these circumstances were occurring every minute now while the battle was raging all around and about us. Men moved intuitively—the voice being silenced by the whizzing and bursting shells. On we moved, Beatty's and Growes' lines giving way seemingly to allow the jaws of the trap to press with more and ever increasing vigor upon its unfortunate and discomfited victims. But, on we moved, until the survivors of the decoy had passed the river and over the lines stationed on the other side of the river, when their new line of infantry opened on our confused and disordered columns another destructive and ruinous fire.

Coupled with this condition and correlative to it, a battery of Growes and a part of their infantry had been cut off from the ford and seeing our confused condition, rallied, reformed and opened fire on our advanced right now along the river bank. Confronted in front by their infantry, with the river intervening; swept by their artillery from the left and now attacked by both infantry and artillery by an oblique fire from the right, we found ourselves in a helpless condition, from which it looked like an impossibility to escape; and but for the fact that two or three batteries had been ordered into position to check the threatened advance of the enemy and thereby distract their attention, we doubtless would have fared still worse.

We rallied some distance to the right of where we started and found that many, very many, of our noblest, truest and best had fallen. Some of them were left on the field, among whom was my military preceptor, advisor and dear friend, Captain Bramblett, who fell into the hands of the enemy and who died a few days after in Nashville. I shall never forget our parting, a moment or two before, he received his wound—never forget the last quick glance and the circumstances that called it forth. He was a splendid soldier and his loss grieved me very much. Many another gallant Kentuckian, some of our finest line and field officers, were left on the field, a sacrifice to stupidity and revenge. Thirty-seven per cent in one hour and ten minutes—some say one hour—was the frightful summary. Among the first of these was the gallant and illustrious Hanson, whose coolness and bearing was unsurpassed and whose loss was irreparable. He with Breckinridge, understood and was fully sensible of—as indicated by the very seriousness of his countenance—the unwisdom of this move and as shown in their protest to Bragg. What a pity that a strict observance of military rule compelled it to be obeyed against his mature military mind and judgment, causing the loss of such a magnificent soldier and gentleman—uselessly and foolishly.

Comtemplating this awful sacrifice, as he rode by the dead and dying in the rear of our lines, General Breckinridge, with tears falling from his eyes, was heard to say in tones of anguish, "My poor Orphans! My poor Orphans!" little thinking that he was dedicating to them a name that will live throughout the annals of time and crown the history of that dear little band with everlasting immortality.

AN OFFER TO RESIGN: WASHINGTON, D.C., JANUARY 1863

Ambrose E. Burnside to Abraham Lincoln

Following the Fredericksburg debacle, a cabal of Army of the Potomac general officers conspired against Burnside, going over his head and behind his back to the President to challenge his plans. They succeeded: Burnside's orders for a renewed campaign in the Fredericksburg sector were cancelled on Lincoln's order. On December 31 Burnside met with Lincoln, Stanton, and Halleck to debate the matter but they reached no decision. Believing he had lost the confidence of his lieutenants, Burnside determined to resign his command, and on the morning of January 1 he handed the President this letter ("this morning" in the first line actually refers to the previous day's meeting). Lincoln did not accept the resignation, and when Burnside repeated the offer on January 5, replied that he did "not yet see how I could profit by changing the command." Still, the poisonous matter of the Potomac army command would require resolution in the new year.

WASHINGTON, D.C., *January* 1, 1863.

HIS EXCELLENCY THE PRESIDENT OF THE UNITED STATES:

Since leaving you this morning, I have determined that it is my duty to place on paper the remarks which I made to you, in order that you may use them or not, as you see proper.

I am in command, as you know, of nearly 200,000 men, 120,000 of whom are in the immediate presence of the enemy, and I cannot conscientiously retain the command without making an unreserved statement of my views.

The Secretary of War has not the confidence of the officers and soldiers, and I feel sure that he has not the confidence of the country. In regard to the latter statement, you are probably better informed than I am. The same opinion applies with equal force in regard to General Halleck. It seems to be the universal opinion that the movements of the army have not been planned with a view to co-operation and mutual assistance.

I have attempted a movement upon the enemy, in which I have been repulsed, and I am convinced, after mature deliberation, that the army ought to make another movement in the same direction, not necessarily at the same points on the river; but I am not sustained in this by a single grand division commander in my command. My reasons for having issued the order for making this second movement I have already given you in full, and I can see no reasons for changing my views. Doubtless this difference of opinion between my general officers and myself results from a lack of confidence in me. In this case it is highly necessary that this army should be commanded by some other officer, to whom I will most cheerfully give way.

Will you allow me, Mr. President, to say that it is of the utmost importance that you be surrounded and supported by men who have the confidence of the people and of the army, and who will at all times give you definite and honest opinions in relation to their separate departments, and at the same time give you positive and unswerving support in your public policy, taking at all times their full share of the responsibility for that policy? In no positions held by gentlemen near you are these conditions more requisite than those of the Secretary of War and General-in-Chief and the commanders of your armies. In the struggle now going on, in which the very existence of our Government is at stake, the interests of no one man are worth the value of a grain of sand, and no one should be allowed to stand in the way of accomplishing the greatest amount of public good.

It is my belief that I ought to retire to private life. I hope you will not understand this to savor of anything like dictation. My only desire is to promote the public good. No man is an accurate judge of the confidence in which he is held by the public and the people around him, and the confidence in my management may be entirely destroyed, in which case it would be a great wrong for me to retain this command for a single day; and, as I before said, I will most cheerfully give place to any other officer.

I have the honor to be, very respectfully, your obedient servant,

A. E. BURNSIDE,
Major-General, Commanding Army of the Potomac.

"YOU FAIL ME PRECISELY":
WASHINGTON, D.C., JANUARY 1863

Abraham Lincoln to Henry W. Halleck

Burnside's was not the only high-level command resignation the President received on New Year's Day 1863. After the confrontation with Burnside, Lincoln turned to his general-in-chief to settle the military stalemate on the Rappahannock. Henry Halleck, quailing at the responsibility, replied, "there is a very important difference of opinion in regard to my relations toward generals commanding armies in the field," and submitted his resignation. With no better candidate for general-in-chief, Lincoln withdrew his letter and Halleck remained in his position.

Major Gen. Halleck — Executive Mansion,
My dear Sir: — Washington, January 1. 1863.

Gen. Burnside wishes to cross the Rappahannock with his army, but his Grand Division commanders all oppose the movement. If in such a difficulty as this you do not help, you fail me precisely in the point for which I sought your assistance. You know what Gen. Burnside's plan is; and it is my wish that you go with him to the ground, examine it as far as practicable, confer with the officers, getting their judgment, and ascertaining their temper, in a word, gather all the elements for forming a judgment of your own; and then tell Gen. Burnside that you *do* approve, or that you do *not* approve his plan. Your military skill is useless to me, if you will not do this. Yours very truly

A LINCOLN

Withdrawn, because considered harsh by Gen. Halleck. A.L.
Jan. 1. 1863

WASHINGTON, D.C., JANUARY 1863

Abraham Lincoln: Final Emancipation Proclamation

Despite his trials with his generals, Lincoln marked January 1, 1863, as memorable—the signing and issuing of the Emancipation Proclamation. He later termed it "the central act of my administration and the great event of the nineteenth century." Mention of compensated emancipation and colonization and the Second Confiscation Act in the September 22 preliminary document was absent in this final version. Added to it were the specific "States and parts of States" in rebellion to which the proclamation applied. And there was a further major addition, made at Secretary Chase's suggestion: beyond an exercise of presidential war powers, the Proclamation was "an act of justice." At the signing Lincoln remarked that at the White House New Year's reception he had been shaking hands for three hours "till my arm is stiff and numb." His signature, he said, would be closely examined, "and if they find my hand trembled, they will say 'he had some compunctions.'" But he did not hesitate, and slowly and firmly he signed in a bold hand. With a smile he said, "That will do."

January 1, 1863

By the President of the United States of America:
A Proclamation.

Whereas, on the twentysecond day of September, in the year of our Lord one thousand eight hundred and sixty two, a proclamation was issued by the President of the United States, containing, among other things, the following, towit:

"That on the first day of January, in the year of our Lord one thousand eight hundred and sixty-three, all persons held as slaves within any State or designated part of a State, the people whereof shall then be in rebellion against the United States, shall be then, thenceforward, and forever free; and the Executive Government of the United States, including the military and naval authority thereof, will recognize and maintain the freedom of such persons, and will do no act or acts to repress such persons, or any of them, in any efforts they may make for their actual freedom.

"That the Executive will, on the first day of January aforesaid, by proclamation, designate the States and parts of States, if any, in which the people thereof, respectively, shall then be in rebellion against the United States; and the fact that any State, or the people thereof, shall on that day be, in good faith, represented in the Congress of the United States by members chosen thereto at elections wherein a majority of the qualified voters of such State shall have participated, shall, in the absence of strong countervailing testimony, be deemed conclusive evidence that such State, and the people thereof, are not then in rebellion against the United States."

Now, therefore I, Abraham Lincoln, President of the United States, by virtue of the power in me vested as Commander-in-Chief, of the Army and Navy of the United States in time of actual armed rebellion against authority and government of the United States, and as a fit and necessary war measure for suppressing said rebellion, do, on this first day of January, in the year of our Lord one thousand eight hundred and sixty three, and in accordance with my purpose so to do publicly proclaimed for the full period of one hundred days, from the day first above mentioned, order and designate as the States and parts of States wherein the people thereof respectively, are this day in rebellion against the United States, the following, towit:

Arkansas, Texas, Louisiana, (except the Parishes of St. Bernard, Plaquemines, Jefferson, St. Johns, St. Charles, St. James, Ascension, Assumption, Terrebonne, Lafourche, St. Mary, St. Martin, and Orleans, including the City of New-Orleans) Mississippi, Alabama, Florida, Georgia, South-Carolina, North-Carolina, and Virginia, (except the fortyeight counties designated as West Virginia, and also the counties of Berkley, Accomac, Northampton, Elizabeth-City, York, Princess Ann, and Norfolk, including the cities of Norfolk & Portsmouth); and which excepted parts are, for the present, left precisely as if this proclamation were not issued.

And by virtue of the power, and for the purpose aforesaid, I do order and declare that all persons held as slaves within said designated States, and parts of States, are, and henceforward shall be free; and that the Executive government of the United States, including the military and naval authorities thereof, will recognize and maintain the freedom of said persons.

And I hereby enjoin upon the people so declared to be free to abstain from all violence, unless in necessary self-defence; and I recommend to them that, in all cases when allowed, they labor faithfully for reasonable wages.

And I further declare and make known, that such persons of suitable condition, will be received into the armed service of the United States to garrison forts, positions, stations, and other places, and to man vessels of all sorts in said service.

And upon this act, sincerely believed to be an act of justice, warranted by the Constitution, upon military necessity, I invoke the considerate judgment of mankind, and the gracious favor of Almighty God.

In witness whereof, I have hereunto set my hand and caused the seal of the United States to be affixed.

Done at the City of Washington, this first day of January, in the year of our Lord one thousand eight hundred and sixty three, and of the Independence of the United States of America the eighty-seventh.

By the President: ABRAHAM LINCOLN

WILLIAM H. SEWARD, Secretary of State.

CELEBRATING EMANCIPATION:
PHILADELPHIA, JANUARY 1863

Benjamin Rush Plumly to Abraham Lincoln

Plumly, a Quaker abolitionist, wrote to the President about the celebrations greeting the proclamation in Philadelphia. And there were other celebrations that day. In Beaufort, South Carolina, more than five thousand former slaves gathered; in Chicago, Osborne Perry Anderson, the sole black survivor of John Brown's raid on Harpers Ferry, spoke in a church; in Boston, William Wells Brown and Frederick Douglass addressed a crowd of three thousand at Tremont Temple.

Philadelphia,
New Year, 1863,
Midnight.

Mr President
Dear Sir,

I have been, all day, from early morning intil a short time ago, in the Crowded Churches of the Colored People of this City.

During thirty years of active Anti-Slavery life, I have never witnessed, such intense, intelligent and devout "Thanksgiving." It was like unto the solemn joy of an old Jewish Passover.

Occasionally, they sang and shouted and wept and prayed. God knows, I cried, with them.

Your Proclamation not having reached us, I took with me Genl Saxton's, and read it, in some of the Churches. The mention of your name, in *that*, evoked a spontaneous benediction from the whole Congregation. No doubt of the coming of Your Proclamation beset any one of them.

As one of their speakers was explaining the effect of your Act, he was interrupted by a sudden outburst, from four or five hundred voices, singing "The Year of Jubilee."

An old Anti-Slavery song, that commemorates some of our great names, which we sang, stirringly, in the dark days of mobs & outrage, was so changed as to include Your name. It was sung with wonderful effect.

The whole rejoicing took the devotional direction. At the close of the morning Meeting, in one Church, the whole Congregation passed up one aisle to the Communion table, each one receiving a piece of Cake, and depositing a small sum for the Contrabands; all the while singing their moving hymns.

In the Episcopal (Col) Church, the service for the 4th of July, was read.

The places of business, controlled by the Colored people were, generally, closed. In the private houses of the better class, festivals and Love feasts, were held.

There are, in this City, about *30-000*, Colored People.

They have *20* Churches. They all go to Church; for the Black man, like all Oriental or Tropical races, is devout.

To day, all the Churches were open & filled.

They have among them, many men of talent, education and property. There are several excellent orators. All of these,—Ministers and laymen, exhorted the people, to accept the Great Gift, with reverent joy; to make no public demonstration, no procession or parade; To indulge in no resentment for the past, and no impatience for the future, but to "work and wait," trusting in God, for the final triumph of Justice.

Never was demonstration so touching. Many wet eyes of white people, testified to the profound pathos of the occasion.

The Black people all trust *you*. They *beleive* that you desire to do them Justice. They do not beleive that *You*, *wish* to expatriate them, or to enforce upon them, any disability, but—that you *cannot* do *all*, that you would.

The spontaneous outburst of this faith in you, was touching, beyond expression. Some one intimated, that You might be forced into some, form of Colinization. "God wont let him," shouted an old woman. "God's in his *heart*", said another, and the response of the Congregation was emphatic.

Another, thought, there must be some design of God, in having your name "Abraham" that if you were not the "Father" You were to be the "Liberator" of a People. One Minister advised them to thank God, that *He* had raised up an honest man, for the White House, whereupon, they broke forth, five hundred strong, in that ringing hymn, "The Year of Jubilee".

It is a great thing Sir, to be the President of the U. States, even though, thorns are in the Seat of Power. But, it is a greater thing, to be enshrined in the Religious sense of a People, yet in its plastic infancy, but destined to, a distant but grand maturity. I would rather be there, as you are, than be President for Life

Very truly
Your ob St
B. Rush Plumly.

PS. An Editor of the Tribune has just asked me to furnish some account of the matter. I shall take the liberty to use the substance of this letter.

"BROKEN EGGS CAN NOT BE MENDED": WASHINGTON, D.C., JANUARY 1863

Abraham Lincoln to John A. McClernand

Major General McClernand, a former Democratic congressman from Illinois, wrote to Lincoln from Memphis on December 29 that a "gentleman of the first respectability" had arrived from northern Mississippi, claiming to speak for "officers of high rank in the rebel service, who were formerly my warm personal and political friends." These officers desired "the restoration of peace and are represented to be willing to wheel their columns into the line of that policy," but sought reassurances that the President would not "subvert the institutions of any state," implying that the Emancipation Proclamation stood in the way of peace. On that point Lincoln was unyielding: "it must stand."

Executive Mansion,
Major General McClernand Washington, January 8. 1863.

My dear Sir Your interesting communication by the hand of Major Scates is received. I never did ask more, nor ever was willing to accept less, than for all the States, and the people thereof, to take and hold their places, and their rights, in the Union, under the Constitution of the United States. For this alone have I felt authorized to struggle; and I seek neither more nor less now. Still, to use a coarse, but an expressive figure, broken eggs can not be mended. I have issued the emancipation proclamation, and I can not retract it.

After the commencement of hostilities I struggled nearly a year and a half to get along without touching the "institution"; and when finally I conditionally determined to touch it, I gave a hundred days fair notice of my purpose, to all the States and people, within which time they could have turned it wholly aside, by simply again becoming good citizens of the United States. They chose to disregard it, and I made the peremptory proclamation on what appeared to me to be a military necessity. And being made, it must stand. As to the States not included in it, of course they can have their rights in the Union as of old. Even the people of the states included, if they choose, need not to be hurt by it. Let them adopt systems of apprenticeship for the colored people, conforming substantially to the most approved plans of gradual emancipation; and, with the aid they can have from the general government, they may be nearly as well off, in this respect, as if the present trouble had not occurred, and much better off than they can possibly be if the contest continues persistently.

As to any dread of my having a "purpose to enslave, or exterminate, the whites of the South," I can scarcely believe that such dread exists. It is too absurd. I believe you can be my personal witness that no man is less to be dreaded for undue severity, in any case.

If the friends you mention really wish to have peace upon the old terms, they should act at once. Every day makes the case more difficult. They can so act, with entire safety, so far as I am concerned.

I think you would better not make this letter public; but you may rely confidently on my standing by whatever I have said in it. Please write me if any thing more comes to light. Yours very truly

A. LINCOLN

CHRONOLOGY

BIOGRAPHICAL NOTES

NOTE ON THE TEXTS

NOTES

INDEX

Chronology
January 1862–January 1863

1862 President Abraham Lincoln and his cabinet meet with the congressional Joint Committee on the Conduct of the War, January 6. Lincoln rejects demand of its chairman, Ohio Republican senator Benjamin F. Wade, that General George B. McClellan be replaced as commander of the Army of the Potomac. (McClellan has served as both commander of the Army of the Potomac and as general-in-chief of the Union army since November 1861.) Appoints Edwin M. Stanton, a Democrat who had served as attorney general in the final months of the Buchanan administration, as secretary of war on January 13, replacing Simon Cameron. The same day, Lincoln meets with McClellan and several cabinet members and military advisers to discuss future operations, but McClellan will not reveal his campaign plans. Union force commanded by General George H. Thomas defeats Confederates at Mill Springs on January 19, breaking the Confederate defensive line in southern Kentucky. Lincoln issues President's General War Order No. 1 on January 27, calling for an advance by Union forces in several war theaters by February 22. President's Special War Order No. 1, issued January 31, directs McClellan and the Army of the Potomac to advance against the Confederate army at Manassas outside Washington.

McClellan responds by submitting a campaign plan on February 3 that would outflank the Confederate army at Manassas and strike at Richmond from lower Chesapeake Bay. General Ulysses S. Grant begins offensive against Forts Henry and Donelson on the Tennessee and Cumberland rivers, just south of the Kentucky-Tennessee border. Fort Henry on the Tennessee surrenders on February 6 after bombardment by Union gunboats. On the Atlantic coast, General Ambrose Burnside captures the Confederate outpost on Roanoke Island in North Carolina's Pamlico Sound, February 7–8. General Charles P. Stone, who had commanded the Union forces defeated at Ball's Bluff, Virginia, in October 1861, is arrested on Stanton's orders in Washington, D.C., on February 9 for alleged treachery.

(Stone is imprisoned without charges for six months before being released.) Grant's army begins siege of Fort Donelson on the Cumberland, February 12. In response to Grant's offensive, Confederates evacuate Bowling Green, Kentucky, on February 14. Confederate counterattack at Fort Donelson is defeated, February 15, and the 12,000-man garrison surrenders on February 16. First Confederate Congress, elected in November 1861, convenes in Richmond on February 18. Confederate force advancing up the Rio Grande Valley from Texas defeats Union troops at Valverde in southern New Mexico Territory, February 21. Jefferson Davis is inaugurated in Richmond on February 22 for a six-year term as president of the Confederacy (Davis had served as provisional president since February 1861). Union troops occupy Nashville, Tennessee's capital, on February 25. The same day, Lincoln signs Legal Tender Act authorizing the U.S. Treasury to issue paper money ("greenbacks") not secured by specie. Confederate Congress gives Davis authority to declare martial law and suspend habeas corpus in areas threatened by Union attack, February 27.

Confederates evacuate Columbus, their last outpost in Kentucky, on March 2. Lincoln sends message to Congress on March 6 calling for federal financial aid to states adopting gradual compensated emancipation. General Samuel R. Curtis defeats Confederates in battle of Elkhorn Tavern (or Pea Ridge) in northwestern Arkansas, March 7–8, securing Missouri for the Union. In Virginia, Confederate General Joseph E. Johnston begins withdrawing his army from Manassas to a new position behind the Rappahannock River on March 8. The same day, the ironclad ram C.S.S. *Virginia* attacks the Union blockading squadron in Hampton Roads, Virginia, destroying two wooden warships and damaging a third. Union ironclad U.S.S. *Monitor* reaches Hampton Roads from New York on evening of March 8. The *Virginia* and *Monitor* fight to a draw on March 9 in the first battle in naval history between ironclad ships. Lincoln removes McClellan as general-in-chief (leaving that post vacant) on March 11, retaining him in command of the Army of the Potomac. In response to the Confederate withdrawal from Manassas, McClellan and his corps commanders meet on March 13 and change the starting point for the campaign against Richmond to Fort Monroe on the Virginia Peninsula. Lincoln signs into law new article of war passed by Congress forbidding Union officers from returning fugitive slaves, March 13. General John Pope captures Confederate outpost at New Madrid,

Missouri, on March 14, initiating a campaign to open the Mississippi River. The same day, Ambrose Burnside expands the Union foothold on the North Carolina coast by defeating the Confederates at New Bern. Peninsula campaign begins on March 17 as the first Union troops embark for Fort Monroe. Grant's army moves up the Tennessee (southward) to Pittsburg Landing, just north of the Mississippi-Tennessee border, where it waits to be joined by General Don Carlos Buell's army before planned advance on Corinth, Mississippi. Davis appoints Judah P. Benjamin to replace Robert M. T. Hunter as Confederate secretary of state, George W. Randolph to succeed Benjamin as secretary of war, and Thomas H. Watts to succeed Thomas Bragg as attorney general. Despite U.S. diplomatic protests, British authorities allow newly built warship *Oreto* to sail from Liverpool on March 22. (Commissioned as C.S.S. *Florida* in the Bahamas, the ship begins raiding Union commerce in January 1863.) General Thomas J. (Stonewall) Jackson, the Confederate commander in the Shenandoah Valley of Virginia, is defeated at Kernstown on March 23. Confederates occupy Santa Fe, New Mexico Territory, March 23, but are then defeated at Glorieta, March 26–28, and forced by lack of supplies to retreat down the Rio Grande to Texas.

In Virginia, McClellan advances from Fort Monroe, April 4, then halts before the Confederate defensive lines extending across the Peninsula from Yorktown on April 5. McClellan decides upon a siege and protests he will be outnumbered after Lincoln withholds General Irvin McDowell's corps to defend Washington. Confederate General Albert Sidney Johnston attacks Union forces at Pittsburg Landing on morning of April 6 and drives them back toward the Tennessee River. General Pierre G. T. Beauregard takes command of Confederate army after Johnston is killed in the afternoon. After being reinforced by Buell's army, Grant counterattacks on April 7 and Confederates retreat toward Corinth. Battle of Shiloh (named after country church on the battlefield) costs the Union about 13,000 men killed, wounded, or missing, the Confederates about 10,700. General John Pope captures Island No. 10 in the Mississippi near New Madrid, April 7. Congress passes resolution approving gradual compensated emancipation on April 10, but plan fails to win support in the border states. Fort Pulaski, guarding the entrance to the Savannah River, surrenders to Union forces on April 11 after a two-day bombardment. Confederate Congress passes conscription act, April 16. The same day, Lincoln signs act abolishing slavery in the District of Columbia. On night of April 24 Union fleet commanded by Flag Officer David Farragut forces passage between Forts Jackson and St. Philip on the lower Mississippi, then sails upriver to New Orleans, which surrenders on April 25. The same day, Union forces continue their gains on the North Carolina coast by capturing Fort Macon at Beaufort. General Jackson begins diversionary campaign in the Shenandoah Valley designed to prevent reinforcements from being sent to McClellan.

On the Virginia Peninsula, General Joseph E. Johnston evacuates Yorktown defenses on May 3, ending month-long siege. The same day, 100,000-man Union army led by General Henry W. Halleck begins slow advance from Pittsburg Landing toward Corinth, Mississippi. Confederates fight rear-guard action at Williamsburg, Virginia, on May 5 against McClellan's pursuing forces. Jackson defeats Union forces at McDowell, Virginia, May 8. President Lincoln visits Fort Monroe and organizes the capture of Norfolk, May 9. The same day, Union General David Hunter orders the military emancipation of slaves in Florida, Georgia, and South Carolina (order is revoked by Lincoln on May 19). In naval battle at Plum Run Bend on the Tennessee shore of the Mississippi, a Confederate flotilla sinks two Union gunboats but suffers heavy damage and is forced to retreat downriver, May 10. Ironclad C.S.S. *Virginia* is blown up on May 11 after Union capture of Norfolk leaves the ship without a port. Union flotilla is repulsed by batteries at Drewry's Bluff on the James River, eight miles below Richmond, on May 15. General Benjamin F. Butler, Union commander in New Orleans, issues controversial "Woman's Order" intended to prevent the city's women from insulting Union soldiers, May 15. Advance division of Farragut's fleet reaches Vicksburg, Mississippi, on May 18, but is unable to compel the garrison to surrender. Lincoln signs Homestead Act, May 20, granting settlers 160 acres of public land. (Absence of Southern representatives and senators from Thirty-seventh Congress will enable Republican majority to pass series of domestic measures, including Pacific Railroad Act and Morrill Act, providing land grants for agricultural colleges, both signed by Lincoln on July 2.) Jackson marches down the Shenandoah Valley (northward) and captures the garrison of Front Royal on May 23. The next day, Lincoln countermands an order sending Irvin McDowell's corps to the Peninsula and orders McDowell and other Union commanders in the

Valley to cut off and capture Jackson. On May 25 Jackson routs Union troops led by General Nathaniel P. Banks at Winchester, then pursues Banks toward Harper's Ferry at the northern end of the Valley. Beauregard evacuates Corinth, Mississippi, May 29–30. After driving Banks from the Valley, Jackson marches south on May 30 and evades Union attempts to trap his command. Joseph E. Johnston attacks the left wing of McClellan's army south of the Chickahominy River near Richmond on May 31, beginning battle of Fair Oaks (or Seven Pines).

Fighting at Fair Oaks ends in draw on June 1 after Confederates lose about 6,100 men killed, wounded, or missing and the Union about 5,000. General Robert E. Lee replaces Johnston, who was badly wounded on May 31, as commander of the Army of Northern Virginia. Confederates begin evacuating Fort Pillow, near Memphis, Tennessee, on June 3. Confederate river flotilla is destroyed by Union gunboats at Memphis on June 6, and the city surrenders. Jackson defeats Union forces in the southern Shenandoah Valley at Cross Keys, June 8, and Port Republic, June 9. Confederate General J.E.B. Stuart leads cavalry reconnaissance that rides completely around McClellan's army on the Peninsula, June 12–15. Union forces attempting to close Charleston Harbor are defeated at Secessionville, South Carolina, on June 16. Jackson leaves the Shenandoah Valley and moves his command to join Lee on the Peninsula. Cumberland Gap, mountain pass in the Appalachians at the juncture of Kentucky, Tennessee, and Virginia, is occupied by Union troops on June 18. Lincoln signs act prohibiting slavery in the territories, June 19. Lee meets with his principal generals on June 23 to plan an offensive against McClellan's army. Lincoln travels to West Point to seek military advice from former general-in-chief Winfield Scott, June 24–25, then returns to Washington and on June 26 names General John Pope to command new Army of Virginia formed from scattered Union commands in the Shenandoah Valley and Northern Virginia. Seven Days' Battles outside of Richmond begin on June 25 with small Union advance at Oak Grove. On June 26 Lee seizes the initiative, attacking McClellan's right wing at Mechanicsville, north of the Chickahominy, and is repulsed. Lee renews his offensive at Gaines's Mill on June 27 and drives the Union forces south across the Chickahominy. McClellan abandons plans for siege of Richmond and orders a retreat across the Peninsula to the James River and the protection of the navy's gunboats. Farragut runs his fleet past the Confederate batteries at Vicksburg on June 28. Union rear guard fights off Confederate pursuers at Savage's Station, June 29, as McClellan's army retreats toward the James. In battle of Glendale (or White Oak Swamp), June 30, Lee narrowly misses his best chance to cut the Army of the Potomac in two.

Seven Days' Battles end on July 1 with Union artillery repelling Lee's attacks at Malvern Hill on the James. Confederates lose 20,204 men killed, wounded, or missing in the Seven Days, while Union casualties total 15,855. Lincoln calls for 300,000 volunteers and signs revenue act establishing federal income tax, July 1. McClellan ends retreat at Harrison's Landing on the James, July 2. Confederate cavalryman John Hunt Morgan conducts extended raid into Kentucky, July 4–28. Lincoln visits Harrison's Landing, July 8–9, to confer with McClellan and his corps commanders. Henry W. Halleck is named general-in-chief on July 11. Union forces occupy Helena, Arkansas, on July 12. Lincoln makes appeal for compensated emancipation to border state representatives, July 12, but the majority of the delegation rejects his plan on July 14. Confederate ironclad C.S.S. *Arkansas* fights its way through Farragut's fleet on the Yazoo River and the Mississippi before reaching protection of the Vicksburg batteries, July 15. Lincoln signs Second Confiscation Act, authorizing the seizure of slaves of persons inciting or supporting rebellion, and Militia Act, authorizing the president to enroll blacks as soldiers or military laborers, on July 17. Pope issues series of orders, July 18–23, permitting the Army of Virginia to live off the land and authorizing the harsh treatment of disloyal civilians. Union General John A. Dix and Confederate General D. H. Hill sign cartel governing prisoner paroles and exchanges (treatment of prisoners had previously been decided mainly by commanders in the field). Lincoln reads draft of preliminary emancipation proclamation to the cabinet on July 22, but after discussion agrees to delay issuing it until there is a Union battlefield victory. British authorities allow another commerce raider built in English shipyards to sail from Liverpool on July 29 despite protests from U.S. diplomats. (Ship is commissioned as C.S.S. *Alabama* in the Azores on August 24, and will capture and burn twenty-two Northern merchant and whaling ships by the end of 1862.) Farragut takes fleet downriver from Vicksburg on July 24, ending Union attempt to capture the city with naval forces alone.

Over McClellan's protests, on August 3 General-in-Chief

Halleck orders the Army of the Potomac to evacuate the Peninsula and combine with Pope's Army of Virginia in northern Virginia. Union garrison at Baton Rouge, Louisiana, repulses Confederate attack on August 5. Confederate ironclad C.S.S. *Arkansas* runs aground near Baton Rouge on August 6 and is burned by her crew. Jackson defeats part of Pope's army at Cedar Mountain on August 9 as new campaign begins in northern Virginia. First detachment of the Army of the Potomac leaves Harrison's Landing, August 14. In White House meeting on August 14 Lincoln urges a delegation of free blacks to embrace colonization project in present-day Panama. Confederates begin fortifying Port Hudson, Louisiana, on August 15, giving them a second bastion on the Mississippi. Confederate General Edmund Kirby Smith begins invasion of eastern Kentucky on August 16. Sioux Indians begin uprising in southwestern Minnesota on August 17 (fighting continues until U.S. victory at Wood Lake on September 23). In response to Horace Greeley's editorial "The Prayer of Twenty Millions," Lincoln writes public letter on slavery and the Union on August 22 (published August 25). Union War Department authorizes recruitment of freed slaves in the coastal islands of Georgia and South Carolina, August 25. Lee sends Jackson's wing of the Army of Northern Virginia on flanking march to the west of Pope's army, August 25. Jackson destroys Pope's supply base at Manassas Junction, August 27. Pope withdraws his army from the northern bank of the Rappahannock River and marches toward Jackson. General Braxton Bragg advances north from Chattanooga, Tennessee, August 28, beginning second Confederate invasion of Kentucky. Second Battle of Bull Run (or Second Manassas) begins August 28 when Jackson attacks a Union column in order to draw Pope into battle. On August 29 Pope unsuccessfully attacks Jackson's position as Lee brings the other wing of his army, commanded by General James Longstreet, onto the field. Longstreet attacks the left wing of Pope's army on August 30 and drives it into retreat. In Kentucky, Kirby Smith defeats a Union force at Richmond, August 29–30. Buell retreats from central Tennessee into Kentucky.

Union forces block flanking move by Jackson at Chantilly, Virginia, on September 1. The Second Bull Run campaign costs the Union about 16,000 men killed, wounded, or missing, the Confederates about 9,200. Despite opposition by his cabinet, on September 2 Lincoln puts McClellan in charge of the Washington defenses, then in command of Pope's army as well as the Army of the Potomac. In Kentucky, Kirby Smith's Confederate forces occupy Lexington, September 2, and Frankfort, September 3. Lee's army begins crossing the Potomac September 4, and occupies Frederick, Maryland, on September 6. Pope is relieved of command and ordered to Minnesota to fight the Sioux uprising, September 5. McClellan starts his army into Maryland in pursuit of the Confederates on September 7. Lee issues order on September 9 dividing his army for an attack on Harper's Ferry, Virginia. A lost copy of Lee's order is found by a Union soldier and given to McClellan on September 13, giving him an opportunity to defeat Lee's divided forces. In London, Prime Minister Lord Palmerston writes to Lord Russell, the foreign secretary, on September 14 that if "greater disasters" befall the Union after Second Bull Run, Britain and France might "address the contending parties and recommend an arrangement upon the basis of separation." In Maryland, McClellan's army fights its way through passes in South Mountain on September 14. Jackson captures 12,000-man Union garrison at Harper's Ferry, September 15. Lee reunites his army behind Antietam Creek near Sharpsburg, Maryland, September 15–16. McClellan attacks Lee's army on September 17. Battle of Antietam ends in a tactical draw; the combined casualties of nearly 23,000 men killed, wounded, or missing make it the bloodiest single day of the war. In Kentucky, Bragg captures the 4,000-man Union garrison at Munfordville, September 17. Lee withdraws his army across the Potomac into Virginia on the night of September 18. Union forces led by General William S. Rosecrans defeat Confederates led by General Sterling Price at Iuka in northern Mississippi on September 19. Lincoln issues preliminary Emancipation Proclamation on September 22, to take effect January 1, 1863, in all territory still in rebellion. Bragg's army occupies Bardstown, Kentucky, September 22. On September 24 Lincoln suspends the writ of habeas corpus nationwide and orders military trials for persons aiding the rebellion. Buell's army reaches Louisville, Kentucky, on September 25.

Buell begins advancing south from Louisville on October 1. Lincoln confers with McClellan at Sharpsburg, October 2–4. Rosecrans successfully defends Corinth, Mississippi, against Confederate attack, October 3–4, ending attempt by General Earl Van Dorn to recapture western Tennessee. Union navy captures Galveston, Texas, October 4 (city is retaken by the Confederates on January 1,

1863). Lincoln orders McClellan to take the offensive, October 6. Buell and Bragg fight inconclusive battle at Perryville, Kentucky, on October 8. J.E.B. Stuart and his cavalry ride around McClellan's army for a second time, reaching as far north as Chambersburg, Pennsylvania, on October 9–12. After uniting his army with Kirby Smith's, Bragg decides on October 12 to abandon his campaign in Kentucky and retreat to Tennessee. British foreign secretary Lord Russell proposes to the cabinet on October 13 that the European powers intervene to arrange an armistice in the American war. Midterm elections are held in Ohio, Indiana, and Pennsylvania, October 14. Prime Minister Lord Palmerston writes to Lord Russell on October 22, expressing doubts about intervention. Buell's failure to pursue the Confederates after Perryville results in his replacement by Rosecrans, October 24. McClellan begins crossing the Potomac into Virginia on October 26. Napoleon III proposes on October 31 that France, Britain, and Russia mediate the American war.

Northern midterm elections conclude on November 4. Democrats win the governorships of New Jersey and New York, legislative majorities in Illinois, Indiana, and New Jersey, and gain thirty-four seats in the House of Representatives, although the Republicans retain control of Congress. Lincoln dismisses McClellan as commander of the Army of the Potomac on November 5 and replaces him with Ambrose Burnside. Nathaniel P. Banks replaces Benjamin F. Butler as commander of the Department of the Gulf on November 8. British cabinet debates and rejects French mediation proposal, November 11–12. Burnside opens winter campaign in Virginia on November 15, advancing from Warrenton toward Fredericksburg. Union troops reach Falmouth, across the Rappahannock from Fredericksburg, on November 17, but then wait for more than a week for pontoon bridges needed to cross the river. Longstreet's corps of Lee's army arrives at Fredericksburg, November 20–23. After George W. Randolph resigns as secretary of war, Jefferson Davis names James A. Seddon as his successor, November 21, and appoints Joseph E. Johnston as overall Confederate commander in the western theater, November 24, with responsibility for Bragg's army in Tennessee and John C. Pemberton's forces in Mississippi. Attorney General Edward Bates issues opinion on November 29 declaring that free black persons born in the United States are American citizens.

In his annual message to Congress on December 1,

Lincoln recommends the adoption of constitutional amendments authorizing gradual, compensated emancipation. Jackson's corps arrives at Fredericksburg, December 1–3, completing the buildup of Lee's army. Grant's army occupies Oxford, Mississippi, December 2, as it prepares to advance down the Mississippi Central Railroad toward Vicksburg. General court-martial of Union General Fitz John Porter begins on December 3 for his alleged misconduct at Second Bull Run (Porter is found guilty on January 10, 1863, and cashiered). Union forces maintain control of northwest Arkansas by defeating Confederate offensive at Prairie Grove, December 7. Jefferson Davis visits Tennessee, December 11–14, and Mississippi, December 19–29, during inspection tour of the western theater. Burnside's engineers bridge the Rappahannock under fire on December 11 as Union troops capture Fredericksburg. On December 13 a series of Union frontal attacks against the Confederate positions on the heights behind Fredericksburg are repulsed, with the Union losing 12,653 men killed, wounded, or missing and the Confederates 5,309. Burnside withdraws his army across the Rappahannock on the night of December 15. Senate Republican caucus votes on December 17 to seek the dismissal of Secretary of State William H. Seward, who submits his resignation after learning of the vote. Lincoln and the cabinet (excluding Seward) meet with a committee from the caucus, December 19. As a result of the meeting, Secretary of the Treasury Salmon P. Chase, Seward's chief cabinet critic, submits his resignation on December 20; Lincoln rejects both resignations, resolving the crisis. Confederate General Nathan Bedford Forrest leads cavalry raid that damages Grant's railroad supply lines in western Tennessee, December 18–20. Van Dorn leads raid that destroys Grant's main supply depot at Holly Springs, Mississippi, on December 20, forcing Grant to retreat. Rosecrans advances from Nashville toward Bragg's army at Murfreesboro, Tennessee, on December 26. Unaware of Grant's retreat, General William T. Sherman leads expedition up the Yazoo River north of Vicksburg on December 26. Sherman attacks Confederate positions on the bluffs above Chickasaw Bayou on December 29 and is repulsed. Bragg attacks Rosecrans's army along Stones River outside of Murfreesboro, December 31. The same day, Lincoln signs statehood bill for West Virginia that provides for gradual emancipation.

1863 Lincoln issues final Emancipation Proclamation on January 1. Sherman withdraws his troops from the Yazoo River to Milliken's Bend, Louisiana, about fifteen miles above Vicksburg, January 2. After lull on New Year's Day, Bragg resumes attacks at Stones River, January 2, then orders retreat on January 3 to Tullahoma, Tennessee, thirty-five miles to the south. Battle costs the Union about 13,000 men killed, wounded, or missing, the Confederates about 12,000. Lincoln nominates John P. Usher on January 5 to succeed Caleb B. Smith as secretary of the interior. On January 8 Lincoln writes to Union General John A. McClernand that "being made," the Emancipation Proclamation "must stand."

Biographical Notes

Henry Livermore Abbott (January 21, 1842–May 6, 1864) Born in Lowell, Massachusetts, the son of a lawyer active in Democratic politics. Graduated from Harvard College in 1860 and began studying law in his father's office. Commissioned second lieutenant, 20th Massachusetts Volunteer Infantry Regiment, July 10, 1861. Formed close friendship with his fellow officer Oliver Wendell Holmes Jr. Fought at Ball's Bluff. Promoted to first lieutenant, November 1861. Fought at Fair Oaks and in the Seven Days' Battles, where he was wounded in the arm at Glendale. Older brother Edward killed at Cedar Mountain. Fought at Fredericksburg (December 1862 and May 1863) and Gettysburg; promoted to captain, December 1862, and major, October 1863. Became acting commander of the 20th Massachusetts after all of the regimental officers senior to him were killed or wounded at Gettysburg. Led the regiment at Briscoe Station and at the battle of the Wilderness, where he was fatally wounded on May 6, 1864.

Charles Francis Adams (August 18, 1807–November 21, 1886) Born in Boston, Massachusetts, the son of John Quincy Adams and Louisa Johnson Adams and grandson of John and Abigail Adams. Graduated from Harvard in 1825. Admitted to the bar in 1829. Married Abigail Brown Brooks the same year. Served as a Whig in the Massachusetts house of representatives, 1841–43, and in the state senate, 1844–45. Vice-presidential candidate of the Free Soil Party in 1848. Edited *The Works of John Adams* (1850–56). Served in Congress as a Republican, 1859–61. As U.S. minister to Great Britain, 1861–68, helped maintain British neutrality in the Civil War. Served as the U.S. representative on the international arbitration tribunal that settled American claims against Great Britain for losses caused by Confederate commerce raiders built in British shipyards, 1871–72. Edited the *Memoirs of John Quincy Adams* (1874–77). Died in Boston.

Charles Francis Adams Jr. (May 27, 1835–March 20, 1915) Born in Boston, Massachusetts, brother of Henry Adams, son of lawyer Charles Francis Adams and Abigail Brooks Adams, grandson of John Quincy Adams, great-grandson of John Adams. Graduated Harvard College, 1856. Read law in Boston and passed bar, 1858. Commissioned first lieutenant, 1st Massachusetts Cavalry, December 1861.

Served at Hilton Head, South Carolina, 1862, and with the Army of the Potomac, 1862–63, including Antietam and Gettysburg campaigns; promoted to captain, October 1862. Commanded detached company on guard service at Army of the Potomac headquarters, spring 1864. Commissioned as lieutenant colonel of the 5th Massachusetts Cavalry, a black regiment, in July 1864, and as its colonel, February 1865; the regiment guarded Confederate prisoners at Point Lookout, Maryland, until March 1865, when it was sent to Virginia. Left army and married Mary Ogden in November 1865. Served on Massachusetts Railroad Commission, 1869–79. President of Union Pacific Railroad, 1884–90. Published series of historical works, including *Three Episodes of Massachusetts History* (1892) and biographies of Richard Henry Dana (1890) and Charles Francis Adams (1900). Died in Washington, D.C.

Louisa May Alcott (November 29, 1832–March 6, 1888) Born in Germantown, Pennsylvania, the daughter of schoolteacher and educational reformer Amos Bronson Alcott. Became a teacher and began publishing poetry and stories in the 1850s. Supported abolitionism, temperance, woman's suffrage, woman's rights, and other reform movements. Traveled to Washington, D.C., in December 1862 to serve as nurse in an army hospital, but soon fell ill with typhoid fever and returned to Massachusetts; described her nursing experiences in *Hospital Sketches* (1863). Her novels include *Little Women* (1868–69), *An Old-Fashioned Girl* (1870), *Little Men* (1871), and *Jo's Boys* (1886). Died in Boston.

Edward Porter Alexander (May 26, 1835–April 28, 1910) Born in Washington, Georgia, the son of a plantation owner. Graduated from West Point in 1857. Married Bettie Mason in 1860. Resigned from U.S. Army in April 1861 and accepted Confederate commission as captain in May 1861. Served as chief of ordnance and chief signal officer of the Army of Northern Virginia, July 1861–November 1862. Promoted to major, April 1862, and lieutenant colonel, July 1862. Assigned command of an artillery battalion in James Longstreet's corps in November 1862, and led it at Fredericksburg. Promoted to colonel in April 1863. Commanded artillery battalion at Chancellorsville, Gettysburg, Chattanooga, and Knoxville. Promoted to brigadier general in February 1864 and became chief of artillery for the corps in March 1864. Served in Overland campaign and was wounded at Petersburg on June 30, 1864. Returned to duty in August 1864 and served until Lee's surrender at Appomattox Court House, April 9, 1865. Professor of mathematics and engineering at the University of South Carolina, 1866–69. Served as president of several Southern railroad companies,

1871–93. Drafted personal reminiscences of the war in 1897–99 (published in 1989 as *Fighting for the Confederacy*) while serving on boundary arbitration commission in Greytown, Nicaragua. Following the death of his wife in 1899, married her niece, Mary Mason, in 1901. Published *Military Memoirs of a Confederate: A Critical Narrative* in 1907. Died in Savannah, Georgia.

Ephraim McDowell Anderson (June 29, 1843–January 10, 1916) Born in Knoxville, Tennessee, the son of a farmer. Family moved in his youth to Monroe County, Missouri. In 1861, became a member of the secessionist Missouri State Guard under General Sterling Price, and participated in the battles of Carthage, Springfield, and Lexington. Joined Company G, 2nd Regiment, 1st Missouri Confederate Brigade, in 1862. Fought at Elkhorn Tavern, Iuka, and Corinth. Surrendered at Vicksburg in July 1863 and was exchanged in September 1863. Served as commissary clerk at Demopolis, Alabama, after illness ended his field service. Invalided out of the Confederate army in late 1864. Returned to farming in Missouri after the war. Published *Memoirs: Historical and Personal; including the campaigns of the First Missouri Confederate Brigade* (1868). Moved in late 1915 to the Confederate Soldiers Home at Higginsville, Missouri, where he died.

John Russell Bartlett (September 26, 1843–November 22, 1904) Born in New York City, the son of a merchant and bookseller. Entered U.S. Naval Academy in 1859. Served as midshipman on the *Mississippi* in the Gulf of Mexico, 1861–62, and on the *Brooklyn* during the passage of Forts Jackson and St. Philip and the capture of New Orleans, April 1862, and the naval attack on Vicksburg, June 1862. Promoted to ensign, September 1863, and lieutenant, February 1864. Served on the *Susquehanna* during the Union attacks on Fort Fisher, North Carolina, December 1864 and January 1865. Promoted to lieutenant commander, 1866, and commander, 1877. Married Jeanie Jenckes in 1872. Retired as a captain in July 1897, then returned to active duty during the Spanish-American War. Died in St. Louis, Missouri.

Clara Barton (December 25, 1821–April 12, 1912) Born Clarissa Howe Barton in North Oxford, Massachusetts, the daughter of a farmer and miller. Taught school in Massachusetts, 1839–50. Attended Clinton Liberal Institute, Oneida County, New York, 1850–51. Taught school at Hightstown, New Jersey, 1851–52, and founded a free public school in nearby Bordentown, New Jersey. Worked as recording clerk and copyist in the U.S. Patent Office in Washington, D.C., 1854–57. Lived in Massachusetts, 1857–60, then returned to Patent Office as copyist in December 1860. Helped care for wounded soldiers in Washington after First Bull Run in July 1861. Operating independently of the army and the U.S. Sanitary Commission, she began furnishing nursing care and supplies directly to the battlefields in August 1862, serving at Cedar Mountain, Second Bull Run, South Mountain, Antietam, and Fredericksburg. Provided assistance to soldiers in coastal South Carolina during the siege of Charleston, April–December 1863. Served as head nurse for field hospital in the Army of the James during the Petersburg campaign, June 1864–January 1865. Established office that traced missing Union soldiers, 1865–69, and spent summer of 1865 identifying graves at the former Confederate prisoner-of-war camp at Andersonville, Georgia. Traveled in Europe, 1869–73, and engaged in relief work during the Franco-Prussian War. Founded the American Red Cross in 1881 and served as its president until 1904. Published *The Red Cross in Peace and War* (1898) and *The Story of My Childhood* (1907). Died in Glen Echo, Maryland.

Edward Bates (September 4, 1793–March 25, 1869) Born in Belmont, Virginia, the son of a planter and merchant. Attended Charlotte Hall Academy in Maryland for three years. Served in militia company in 1813 but did not see action. Moved to St. Louis, Missouri, in 1814. Admitted to the bar, 1816. Delegate to the state constitutional convention in 1820. Attorney general of Missouri, 1820–21. Married Julia Coalter in 1823. Served in state house of representatives, 1822–24 and 1834–36, and state senate, 1830–34. U.S. attorney for Missouri, 1824–26. Served in Congress, 1827–29, but was defeated for reelection. Became leader of Whig Party in Missouri. Candidate for 1860 Republican presidential nomination. Served as attorney general in the Lincoln administration, March 1861–November 1864, before resigning. Opposed Radical Reconstruction in Missouri. Died in St. Louis.

August Belmont (December 8, 1813–November 24, 1890) Born in Alzey in the Rhenish Palatinate, the son of a farmer and trader. Apprenticed to Rothschild banking office in Frankfurt-am-Main, 1828. Arrived in New York City during the Panic of 1837 and founded August Belmont and Company, becoming the Rothschilds' new agent in the United States and soon emerging as one of the leading bankers in the country. Wounded in duel, 1841. Became naturalized citizen in 1844. Married Caroline Slidell Perry, daughter of Commodore Matthew Perry, in 1849. Actively supported Democrat Franklin Pierce in 1852 election. Served as U.S. minister to the Netherlands, 1853–57. Supported Stephen A. Douglas in the 1860 election, and was appointed chairman of the Democratic National Committee, a position he held until 1872. Traveled in Europe, 1861–62, and urged political and financial leaders not to support the Confederacy. Supported

George B. McClellan for the 1864 Democratic presidential nomination. Resigned as party chairman in 1872 when the Democratic convention endorsed Liberal Republican candidate Horace Greeley. Died in New York City.

Francis Preston Blair (April 12, 1791–October 18, 1876) Born in Abingdon, Virginia, the son of a lawyer. Family moved to Kentucky in the early 1790s. Graduated from Transylvania University in 1811. Married Eliza Violet Gist, 1812. Served as Franklin County circuit court clerk, 1812–30. Became editor of the Frankfort *Argus of Western America*. Supported Andrew Jackson in the 1828 presidential election. Moved to Washington, D.C., in 1830 to edit new pro-administration newspaper, *The Globe*. Became a member of Jackson's "Kitchen Cabinet" of unofficial advisers. Cofounded the *Congressional Globe* in 1833 to report debates and proceedings in Congress. Gave up editorship of *The Globe* in 1845 due to differences with the new Polk administration. Moved to estate at Silver Spring, Maryland. Supported Free Soil candidacy of Martin Van Buren in 1848. Helped organize first Republican national convention in 1856. Served as advisor to Abraham Lincoln. Opposed Republican Reconstruction after Lincoln's death and returned to the Democratic Party. Died in Silver Spring, Maryland.

John Boston An escaped slave from Maryland who took refuge with soldiers in the New York State militia who were stationed in Upton Hill, Virginia. It is not known whether his wife, Elizabeth Boston, and his son, Daniel, were free as well.

James Richmond Boulware (May 29, 1835–November 13, 1869) Born and died in Fairfield County, South Carolina. Trained as a doctor, he enlisted at Columbia as an assistant surgeon in the 6th South Carolina Infantry and served in the Army of Northern Virginia until at least the end of 1863. Married Eliza Milling after the war.

Cyrus F. Boyd (May 1837–July 25, 1914) Born in Ohio. Enlisted in Company G, 15th Iowa Infantry, in October 1861 as orderly sergeant. Saw action at Shiloh, April 1862, and Corinth, October 1862, and in the early phases of the Vicksburg campaign. Resigned to become lieutenant in the 34th Iowa Infantry in March 1863, with which he served in the Vicksburg and Red River campaigns. Mustered out in November 1864. Later married and lived in Ainsworth, Nebraska.

Braxton Bragg (March 22, 1817–September 27, 1876) Born in Warrenton, North Carolina, the son of a contractor and builder. Graduated West Point 1837. Served as an artillery officer in the Second Seminole

War and the U.S.-Mexican War. Married Eliza Brooks Ellis, 1849. Resigned from the army in 1856 to become a sugar planter in Louisiana. Joined the Confederate army as a brigadier general, March 1861. Promoted to major general, September 1861, and full general, April 12, 1862. Commanded a corps at Shiloh. Succeeded Pierre G. T. Beauregard as commander of the Army of Mississippi in June 1862. Invaded Kentucky in late August, but withdrew into Tennessee following the battle of Perryville, October 8, 1862. Became commander of the Army of Tennessee in November 1862, and commanded it at battle of Stones River (Murfreesboro), December 31, 1862–January 2, 1863. Won battle of Chickamauga, September 19–20, 1863, but was defeated at Chattanooga, November 23–25, 1863. Resigned from his command, November 29, 1863. Served as military advisor to Jefferson Davis in Richmond until November 1864, then commanded troops in North Carolina. Worked after the war as civil engineer in Mobile, Alabama, and railroad engineer in Galveston, Texas, where he died.

Sallie Brock (March 18, 1831–March 22, 1911) Born Sarah Ann Brock in Madison County, Virginia, the daughter of a hotel owner. Moved with her family to Richmond in 1858. Began working as a tutor in King and Queen County, Virginia, in 1860, but returned to Richmond in 1861 and remained there for the duration of the war. Moved to New York City in 1865. Published *Richmond During the War: Four Years of Personal Observations* (1867). Edited *The Southern Amaranth* (1869), a collection of poetry about the Confederacy and the war, and published a novel, *Kenneth, My King* (1873). Married Richard F. Putnam in 1882. Died in Brooklyn.

Orville H. Browning (February 10, 1806–August 10, 1881) Born in Cynthiana, Kentucky, the son of a farmer and merchant. Studied at Augusta College. Admitted to the bar in 1831 and moved to Quincy, Illinois. Married Eliza Caldwell in 1836. Served as a Whig in the state senate, 1836–40, and in the state house of representatives, 1842–43. Became friends with Abraham Lincoln. Delegate to the convention that founded the Illinois Republican Party in 1856 and to the Republican national convention in 1860. Appointed in June 1861 to U.S. Senate seat left vacant by the death of Stephen A. Douglas and served until January 1863. Practiced law in Washington and served as secretary of the interior in the Andrew Johnson administration, 1866–69. Returned to his law practice in Quincy, Illinois, where he later died.

Ambrose Burnside (May 23, 1824–September 3, 1881) Born in Liberty, Indiana, the son of a court clerk. Graduated from West Point in 1847. Married Mary Richmond Bishop, 1852. Resigned from the army in 1853 to manufacture a breech-loading carbine of his own design at Bristol, Rhode Island. Company failed to win government contract, and Burnside gave up his interest in the venture in 1858. With the aid of his friend George B. McClellan, obtained position with the Illinois Central Railroad and worked in Chicago and New York, 1858–60. Appointed colonel of the 1st Rhode Island Infantry in May 1861. Led a brigade at First Bull Run. Promoted to brigadier general of volunteers, August 1861. Commanded expeditionary force that gained a foothold on the North Carolina coast, winning engagements at Roanoke Island, New Bern, and Beaufort, February–April 1862. Promoted to major general, March 1862. Led a corps at South Mountain and Antietam, September 1862. Refused command of the Army of the Potomac following the Peninsula and Second Bull Run campaigns, but accepted order to replace McClellan on November 7, 1862. Defeated at Fredericksburg on December 13, 1862. Replaced as army commander on January 26, 1863. Commanded the Department of the Ohio, March–December 1863. Occupied Knoxville in September 1863 and withstood Confederate siege, November–December. Commanded the Ninth Corps during the Overland campaign in Virginia, May–June 1864, and during the siege of Petersburg, June–July. After his failure at the battle of the Crater at Petersburg on July 30, 1864, was sent on leave for the remainder of the war. Became president of several railroad companies after the war. Republican governor of Rhode Island, 1866–69, and served as a Republican in the U.S. Senate from 1875 until his death in Bristol, Rhode Island.

Francis Bicknell Carpenter (August 6, 1830–May 23, 1900) Born in Homer, New York, the son of a farmer. Studied with painter Sandford Thayer in Syracuse, New York, for five months before opening studio in Homer in 1846. Moved to New York City at age twenty-one and opened portrait studio. Painted portraits of Millard Fillmore and Franklin Pierce. Married Augusta Prentiss in 1853. Worked in the White House from February to July 1864 on his best-known painting, *First Reading of the Emancipation Proclamation of President Lincoln*, depicting the cabinet meeting held on July 22, 1862. Published *Six Months at the White House with Abraham Lincoln: The Story of a Picture* in 1866. Attended ceremonial donation of the *First Reading* to Congress in 1878. Died in New York City.

John Hampden Chamberlayne (June 2, 1838–February 18, 1882) Born in Richmond, Virginia, the son of a physician. Attended the University of Virginia, 1855–58, read law in Richmond, and was admitted to Virginia bar in 1860. Enlisted in the 21st Virginia Regiment and served in western Virginia, 1861–62. Became artillery sergeant in the

Army of Northern Virginia, February 1862, and was promoted to lieutenant, June 1862. Served at Mechanicsville, Gaines's Mill, Glendale, Cedar Mountain, Second Manassas, Antietam, Fredericksburg, and Chancellorsville. Captured at Millerstown, Pennsylvania, on June 28, 1863. Exchanged in March 1864. Served in Overland campaign and the siege of Petersburg. Promoted to captain, August 1864. Evaded surrender at Appomattox Court House and joined Confederate forces in North Carolina before giving his parole at Atlanta, Georgia, on May 12, 1865. Became journalist at the Petersburg *Index* in 1869. Married Mary Walker Gibson in 1873. Edited the Norfolk *Virginian*, 1873–76. Founded *The State* newspaper in Richmond in 1876 and edited it until his death. Died in Richmond.

Salmon P. Chase (January 13, 1808–May 7, 1873) Born in Cornish, New Hampshire, the son of a farmer. After the death of his father in 1817, he was raised in Worthington, Ohio, by his uncle, Philander Chase, an Episcopal bishop. Graduated from Dartmouth College in 1826. Read law in Washington with Attorney General William Wirt and was admitted to the bar in 1829. Established law practice in Cincinnati, Ohio, in 1830. Married Catherine Jane Garniss, 1834; after her death, Eliza Ann Smith, 1839; and after Smith's death, Sarah Bella Dunlop Ludlow, 1846. Began defending fugitive slaves and those who aided them in 1837. Became a leader in the antislavery Liberty Party and campaigned for the Free Soil ticket in 1848. Served in the U.S. Senate as a Free Soil Democrat, 1849–55. Republican governor of Ohio, 1856–60. Candidate for the Republican presidential nomination in 1860. Won election to the U.S. Senate in 1860, but resigned in March 1861 to become secretary of the treasury. Helped found national banking system and successfully financed Union war effort. Resigned June 29, 1864, after making unsuccessful attempt to challenge Lincoln for the Republican nomination. Appointed chief justice of the U.S. Supreme Court on December 6, 1864, and served until his death. Upheld Radical Reconstruction measures and presided over the 1868 Senate impeachment trial of President Andrew Johnson. Died in New York City.

Jefferson Davis (June 3, 1808–December 6, 1889) Born in Christian (now Todd) County, Kentucky, the son of a farmer. Moved with his family to Mississippi. Graduated from West Point in 1828 and served in the Black Hawk War. Resigned his commission in 1835 and married Sarah Knox Taylor, who died later in the year. Became a cotton planter in Warren County, Mississippi. Married Varina Howell in 1845. Elected to Congress as a Democrat and served 1845–46, then resigned to command a Mississippi volunteer regiment in Mexico,

1846–47, where he fought at Monterrey and was wounded at Buena Vista. Elected to the Senate and served from 1847 to 1851, when he resigned to run unsuccessfully for governor. Secretary of war in the cabinet of Franklin Pierce, 1853–57. Elected to the Senate and served from 1857 to January 21, 1861, when he withdrew following the secession of Mississippi. Inaugurated as provisional president of the Confederate States of America on February 18, 1861. Elected without opposition to six-year term in November 1861 and inaugurated on February 22, 1862. Captured by Union cavalry near Irwinville, Georgia, on May 10, 1865. Imprisoned at Fort Monroe, Virginia, and indicted for treason. Released on bail on May 13, 1867; the indictment was dropped in 1869 without trial. Published *The Rise and Fall of the Confederate Government* in 1881. Died in New Orleans.

Rufus R. Dawes (July 4, 1838–August 1, 1899) Born in Malta, Ohio. Attended the University of Wisconsin; graduated from Marietta College in 1860. Commissioned as captain in 6th Wisconsin Infantry in July 1861. Promoted to major in June 1862 and lieutenant colonel in March 1863. Fought as part of the "Iron Brigade" at Second Bull Run, Antietam, Fredericksburg, Chancellorsville, Gettysburg, the Overland campaign, and Petersburg. Married Mary Beman Gates in January 1864 while on furlough. Mustered out in August 1864 with the rank of colonel. Became a wholesale lumber merchant in Marietta. Served as a Republican congressman, 1881–83. Published *Service with the Sixth Wisconsin Volunteers* in 1890. Died in Marietta, Ohio.

George W. Dawson (July 19, 1831–June 13, 1862) Born in New Madrid, Missouri, the son of a doctor. Became a farmer and married Laura Amanda Lavalle in 1852. Enlisted in June 1861, and was elected second lieutenant in Company I, 1st Missouri Infantry, the state's first Confederate regiment. Elected captain in April 1862 shortly before the battle of Shiloh. Contracted typhoid fever at Corinth, Mississippi, in May 1862 and died in New Madrid.

Emily Dickinson (December 10, 1830–May 15, 1886) Born in Amherst, Massachusetts, the daughter of a lawyer. Attended Mount Holyoke Female Seminary in South Hadley, Massachusetts, 1847–48. Returned to family home and lived there for the remainder of her life, rarely leaving except for trips to Washington, D.C., where her father served in Congress as a Whig, 1853–55, to Philadelphia in 1855, and to Boston and Cambridge in 1864–65. Composed over 1,700 brief lyric poems, most intensively in the years 1859–65; only a few were published during her lifetime, primarily in the *Springfield Daily Republican*, most without her consent and in heavily edited form. Initiated correspondence in April 1862 with writer, reformer, and abolitionist

Thomas Wentworth Higginson, who later commanded the 1st South Carolina Volunteers, the first black regiment in the Union army. They exchanged letters for more than twenty years. In later years she rarely left her house. Fell ill in June 1884, and never fully recovered. Died in Amherst.

Frederick Douglass (February 1818–February 20, 1895) Born Frederick Bailey in Talbot County, Maryland, the son of a slave mother and an unknown white man. Worked on farms and in Baltimore shipyards. Escaped to Philadelphia in 1838. Married Anna Murray, a free woman from Maryland, and settled in New Bedford, Massachusetts, where he took the name Douglass. Became a lecturer for the American Anti-Slavery Society, led by William Lloyd Garrison, in 1841. Published *Narrative of the Life of Frederick Douglass, An American Slave* (1845). Began publishing *North Star*, first in a series of antislavery newspapers, in Rochester, New York, in 1847. Broke with Garrison and became an ally of Gerrit Smith, who advocated an antislavery interpretation of the Constitution and participation in electoral politics. Published *My Bondage and My Freedom* (1855). Advocated emancipation and the enlistment of black soldiers at the outbreak of the Civil War. Met with Abraham Lincoln in Washington in August 1863 and August 1864, and wrote public letter supporting his reelection in September 1864. Continued his advocacy of racial equality and woman's rights after the Civil War. Served as U.S. marshal for the District of Columbia, 1877–81, and as its recorder of deeds, 1881–86. Published *Life and Times of Frederick Douglass* (1881). After the death of his wife Anna, married Helen Pitts in 1884. Served as minister to Haiti, 1889–91. Died in Washington, D.C.

Thomas Haines Dudley (October 9, 1819–April 15, 1893) Born in Burlington County, New Jersey, the son of a farmer. Read law and was admitted to the bar in 1845. Married Emmaline Matlack in 1846. Active in Whig and Republican politics. Attended 1860 Republican national convention and helped swing the New Jersey delegation to Abraham Lincoln on the third ballot. Served as U.S. consul in Liverpool, England, 1861–72. Collected intelligence during the Civil War on Confederate shipbuilding and blockade-running activities, and helped prevent two ironclad rams built for the Confederate navy in the Laird shipyards from sailing in 1863. Provided evidence for the international tribunal arbitrating American claims against Great Britain for losses caused by Confederate commerce raiders built in British shipyards, 1871–72. Resumed law practice and involvement in Republican politics after returning to the United States in 1872. Helped found the American Protective Tariff League. Died in Philadelphia.

Ralph Waldo Emerson (May 25, 1803–April 27, 1882) Born in Boston, Massachusetts, the son of a minister. Graduated from Harvard College in 1821. Studied briefly at Harvard Divinity School in 1825. Ordained pastor of Second Church of Boston in March 1829. Married Ellen Tucker, 1829; she died in 1831. Gave up pastorate in 1832 and sailed for Europe. Settled in Concord, Massachusetts, in 1834. Married Lydia Jackson, 1835. Formed informal discussion group (later called the Transcendental Club), whose members included Margaret Fuller, Bronson Alcott, Orestes Brownson, and Theodore Parker. Published essay *Nature* (1836), *Essays* (1841), and *Essays: Second Series* (1844) while lecturing extensively. Opposed the U.S.-Mexican War and became involved in the abolitionist movement. Published *Representative Men* (1850), *English Traits* (1856), and *The Conduct of Life* (1860). Spoke at meetings held to benefit John Brown's family after his execution. Published verse collection *May-Day and Other Pieces* (1867). Continued to lecture until his health began to fail in 1872. Died in Concord.

John Kennerly Farris (April 18, 1836–August 7, 1910) Born in Franklin County, Tennessee. Studied medicine under a physician in Pleasant Hill, Tennessee. Married Mary Elisabeth Austell in 1857. Practiced in Arkansas before returning to Tennessee in 1860. Enlisted in the 41st Tennessee Infantry on November 26, 1861, and became a hospital steward in January 1862. Captured at Fort Donelson in February 1862, he was exchanged in September 1862. Served with the 41st Tennessee at Port Hudson, Louisiana, and in the Vicksburg campaign. Injured in railroad accident in Georgia in early September 1863. Rejoined regiment in early November and fought in the battle of Chattanooga. Served in Atlanta campaign and in Hood's invasion of Tennessee. Captured at Franklin on December 17, 1864. Escaped and returned to his medical practice in Coffee County, Tennessee. Died in Prairie Plains, Tennessee.

Samuel W. Fiske (July 23, 1828–May 22, 1864) Born in Shelburne, Massachusetts. Graduated from Amherst College in 1848. Taught school, studied for three years at Andover Theological Seminary, then returned to Amherst in 1853 as a tutor. Traveled in Europe and the Middle East. Published *Dunn Browne's Experiences in Foreign Parts* (1857), travel letters written to the *Springfield Republican* under a nom de plume. Became pastor of the Congregational church in Madison, Connecticut, in 1857. Married Elizabeth Foster in 1858. Became second lieutenant in the 14th Connecticut Infantry in August 1862. Signing himself Dunn Browne, wrote weekly letters to the *Springfield Republican* describing campaigns and camp life (collected in 1866 under the title *Mr. Dunn Browne's Experiences in the Army*). Served at Antietam and Fredericksburg. Promoted to captain in early 1863. Captured at Chancellorsville on May 3, 1863, was paroled in late May and exchanged in June. Served at Gettysburg. Wounded in the battle of the Wilderness on May 6, 1864, and died in Fredericksburg, Virginia.

Thomas W. Fleming (September 16, 1815–February 7, 1894) Born in Liberty County, Georgia. Attended Franklin College in Athens (later University of Georgia). Married Susan Eliza Wilson in 1837. Became a plantation owner in Liberty County, and later in Baker County, Georgia.

Jacob Gilbert Forman (January 21, 1820–February 7, 1885) Born in Queensbury, New Brunswick, Canada. Became merchant's clerk in Peekskill, New York, in 1836. Graduated from Transylvania University in Lexington, Kentucky, with law degree in 1843. Married Sarah Elizabeth Carpenter in 1844. Practiced law in Cincinnati before becoming Unitarian minister in Akron, Ohio; later served as pastor in Massachusetts and Illinois. During the Civil War, served as chaplain of the 3rd Missouri Infantry, as acting chaplain of the 1st Missouri Cavalry and the 3rd U.S. Infantry, as superintendent of refugees in St. Louis, and as secretary of the Western Sanitary Commission. Published *The Christian Martyrs: or, The Conditions of Obedience to the Civil Government* (1851) and *The Western Sanitary Commission: A Sketch of Its Origin* (1864). Moved to Lynn, Massachusetts, in 1869 and opened a drugstore. Died in Lynn.

Ulysses S. Grant (April 22, 1822–July 23, 1885) Born in Point Pleasant, Ohio, the son of a tanner. Graduated from West Point in 1843. Served in the U.S.-Mexican War, 1846–48, and promoted to first lieutenant in 1847. Married Julia Dent in 1848. Promoted to captain, 1854, and resigned commission. Worked as a farmer, real estate agent, and general store clerk, 1854–61. Commissioned colonel, 21st Illinois Volunteers, June 1861, and brigadier general of volunteers, August 1861. Promoted to major general of volunteers, February 1862, after victories at Forts Henry and Donelson. Defeated Confederates at Shiloh, April 1862, and captured Vicksburg, Mississippi, July 1863. Promoted to major general in the regular army, July 1863, and assigned to command of Military Division of the Mississippi, covering territory between the Alleghenies and the Mississippi, October 1863. Won battle of Chattanooga, November 1863. Promoted to lieutenant general, March 1864, and named general-in-chief of the Union armies. Accepted surrender of Robert E. Lee at Appomattox Court House, April 9, 1865. Promoted to general, July 1866. Served as secretary of war ad interim,

August 1867–January 1868. Nominated for president by the Republican Party in 1868. Defeated Democrat Horatio Seymour, and won reelection in 1872 by defeating Liberal Republican Horace Greeley. President of the United States, 1869–77. Made world tour, 1877–79. Failed to win Republican presidential nomination, 1880. Worked on Wall Street, 1881–84, and was financially ruined when private banking firm of Grant & Ward collapsed. Wrote *Personal Memoirs of U.S. Grant*, 1884–85, while suffering from throat cancer, and completed them days before his death at Mount McGregor, New York.

Henry W. Halleck (January 16, 1814–January 9, 1872) Born in Westernville, New York, the son of a farmer. Educated at Union College. Graduated from West Point in 1839. Published *Elements of Military Art and Science* (1846). Served in California during the U.S.-Mexican War. Resigned from the army in 1854 as captain. Married Elizabeth Hamilton, granddaughter of Alexander Hamilton, in 1855. Practiced law in California. Published *International Law, or, Rules Regulating the Intercourse of States in Peace and War* (1861). Commissioned as a major general in the regular army in August 1861. Commanded the Department of the Missouri, November 1861–March 1862, and the Department of the Mississippi, March–July 1862. General-in-chief of the Union army from July 11, 1862, to March 12, 1864, when he was succeeded by Ulysses S. Grant. Served as chief of staff for the remainder of the war. Commanded military division of the Pacific, 1866–69, and the division of the South, 1869–72. Died in Louisville, Kentucky.

Nathaniel Hawthorne (July 4, 1804–May 19, 1864) Born in Salem, Massachusetts, the son of a ship's captain. Graduated in 1825 from Bowdoin College, where he formed a lifelong friendship with Franklin Pierce. Began writing short fiction, collected in *Twice-told Tales* (1837), *Mosses from an Old Manse* (1846), and *The Snow-Image, and Other Twice-told Tales* (1851). Worked in customhouses in Boston, 1839–41, and Salem, 1846–49. Married Sophia Peabody in 1842. Published novels *The Scarlet Letter* (1850), *The House of the Seven Gables* (1851), and *The Blithedale Romance* (1852). Wrote campaign biography of Pierce for 1852 election. Served as U.S. consul in Liverpool, England, 1853–57. Published novel *The Marble Faun* (1860). Died in Plymouth, New Hampshire.

John Hay (October 8, 1838–July 1, 1905) Born in Salem, Indiana, the son of a doctor. Family moved to Warsaw, Illinois. Graduated from Brown University in 1858. Studied law in office of his uncle in Springfield, Illinois. Traveled to Washington in 1861 as assistant private secretary to Abraham Lincoln, serving until early in 1865. First secretary to American legation in Paris, 1865–67, chargé d'affaires in Vienna, 1867–68, and legation secretary in Madrid, 1868–70. Published *Castilian Days* (1871) and *Pike County Ballads and Other Pieces* (1871). Married Clara Louise Stone in 1874. Served as assistant secretary of state, 1879–81. Political novel *The Bread-Winners*, an attack on labor unions, published anonymously in 1884. In collaboration with John G. Nicolay, wrote *Abraham Lincoln: A History* (10 volumes, 1890) and edited *Complete Works of Abraham Lincoln* (2 volumes, 1894). Ambassador to Great Britain, 1897–98. Served as secretary of state in the administrations of William McKinley and Theodore Roosevelt, 1898–1905. Among first seven members elected to American Academy of Arts and Letters in 1904. Died in Newbury, New Hampshire.

Charles B. Haydon (1834–March 14, 1864) Born in Vermont. Raised in Decatur, Michigan. Graduated from the University of Michigan in 1857, then read law in Kalamazoo. Joined the Kalamazoo Home Guard on April 22, 1861, then enlisted on May 25 for three years' service in the 2nd Michigan Infantry. Fought at Blackburn's Ford during the First Bull Run campaign. Commissioned second lieutenant in September 1861 and promoted to first lieutenant in February 1862. Fought at Williamsburg, Fair Oaks, the Seven Days' Battles, Second Bull Run, and Fredericksburg; promoted to captain in September 1862. Regiment was sent to Kentucky in April 1863 and to Vicksburg in June as part of the Ninth Corps. Wounded in the shoulder while leading his company at Jackson, Mississippi, on July 11, 1863. Returned to active duty in December 1863 and was made lieutenant colonel of the 2nd Michigan. Died of pneumonia in Cincinnati while returning to Michigan on a thirty-day furlough after reenlisting.

Julia Ward Howe (May 27, 1819–October 17, 1910) Born in New York City, the daughter of a banker. Married the Boston educator and reformer Samuel Gridley Howe in 1843. Edited the antislavery newspaper *Commonwealth* with her husband in the early 1850s, and published poetry collections *Passion Flowers* (1854) and *Words for the Hour* (1857), and travel book *A Trip to Cuba* (1860). Published "The Battle Hymn of the Republic" in the February 1862 *Atlantic Monthly*. Campaigned after the war for woman's suffrage, prison reform, and international peace. Published *Later Lyrics* (1866), *Sex and Education* (1874), *Modern Society* (1881), *Margaret Fuller* (1883), *Reminiscences, 1819–1899* (1899), and a poetry collection, *At Sunset* (1910). In 1907 she became the first woman to be elected to the American Academy of Arts and Sciences. Died in Newport, Rhode Island.

David Hunter (July 21, 1802–February 2, 1886) Born in Princeton, New Jersey, the son of a Presbyterian minister. Graduated from West Point in 1822. Married Maria Indiana Kinzie, 1829. Resigned commission in July 1836, but reentered the army in November 1841 as paymaster. Commissioned as brigadier general of volunteers, May 1861, and promoted to major general, August 1861. Led brigade at First Bull Run, where he was wounded. Commanded Department of Kansas, November 1861–March 1862, and Department of the South, March–September 1862 and January–June 1863. Declared military emancipation of slaves in Department of the South, May 9, 1862; his order was revoked by President Lincoln on May 19. Attempted to recruit black regiments in the spring of 1862 but failed to receive War Department authorization. Served as president of the court-martial that convicted General Fitz John Porter in January 1863. Commanded the Army of West Virginia in the Shenandoah Valley, May–June 1864. Retreated from the valley following his defeat at Lynchburg, and resigned command in August 1864. President of the military commission that tried the conspirators in the Lincoln assassination, May–June 1865. Resigned commission on July 31, 1866. Died in Washington, D.C.

Pearl Parker Ingalls (February 1, 1823–May 18, 1887) Born in Franklin, Ohio, the son of a chair maker. Graduated from Ohio Wesleyan University and became a Methodist minister, holding pastorates for the next forty years in Ohio and Iowa. Became chaplain of the 3rd Iowa Cavalry in 1861. Mustered out in 1863 and returned to Keokuk, Iowa. Helped found the Iowa Soldiers' Orphans' Home in Davenport, serving as secretary, raising donations, and securing financial support from the Iowa legislature. Became editor of the *Iowa State Tribune* in 1879. Died in White City, Kansas.

Oscar Lawrence Jackson (September 2, 1840–February 16, 1920) Born in Shenango Township, Pennsylvania, the son of a storekeeper. Taught school in Shenango Township, 1858–59, and Hocking County, Ohio, 1859–61. Became captain of Company H, 63rd Ohio Infantry, in January 1862. Served at New Madrid, Island No. 10, the siege of Corinth, and the battle of Iuka. Seriously wounded at Corinth, October 4, 1862, and spent seven weeks in the hospital. Rejoined regiment at Corinth in February 1863 and spent remainder of the year on occupation duty in Tennessee and Mississippi. Served in the 1864 Atlanta campaign and the march through Georgia and the Carolinas. Promoted to major in March 1865 and assumed command of the 63rd Ohio. Mustered out on June 30, 1865, as lieutenant colonel. Returned to Pennsylvania and was admitted to the bar in 1866. Served as district attorney of Lawrence County, 1868–71; as county solicitor,

1874–80; and as a Republican member of the U.S. House of Representatives, 1885–89. Died in New Castle, Pennsylvania.

Harriet Ann Jacobs (1813–March 7, 1897) Born in Edenton, North Carolina, the daughter of slaves. After the death of her mother in 1819, she was raised by her grandmother and her white mistress, Margaret Horniblow, who taught her to read, write, and sew. In 1825 Horniblow died, and Jacobs was sent to the household of Dr. James Norcom. At sixteen, to escape Norcom's repeated sexual advances, Jacobs began a relationship with a white lawyer, Samuel Tredwell Sawyer (later a member of the U.S. House of Representatives), with whom she had two children, Joseph (b. 1829) and Louisa Matilda (b. 1833). In 1835, Jacobs ran away and spent the next seven years hiding in a crawl space above her freed grandmother's storeroom. In 1842, she escaped to New York City, where she was reunited with her children. Worked as a nurse for the family of Nathaniel Parker Willis; moved to Boston in 1843 to avoid recapture by Norcom. Moved to Rochester in 1849, where she became part of a circle of abolitionists surrounding Frederick Douglass. In 1852, Cornelia Grinnell Willis, second wife of Nathaniel Parker Willis, purchased Jacobs's manumission. Published *Incidents in the Life of a Slave Girl, Written by Herself*, pseudonymously in 1861. From 1862 to 1868 engaged in Quaker-sponsored relief work among former slaves in Washington, D.C.; Alexandria, Virginia; and Savannah, Georgia. She then lived with her daughter in Cambridge, Massachusetts, and in Washington, D.C., where she died.

Clifton Johnson (January 25, 1865–January 22, 1940) Born in Hadley, Massachusetts. Attended Hopkins Academy, but left in 1880 to work in a book and stationery store to help pay the family mortgage. In the mid-1880s began to write and illustrate for local newspapers and magazines. Attended the Art Students League in New York City in 1887. Johnson wrote, illustrated, or edited 125 books between 1892 and 1938, including biographies of naturalist John Burroughs and inventor Hudson Maxim, a series of travel books, and volumes of children's literature. Interviewed fifty-four civilian witnesses to Civil War battles in 1913 and published their accounts in *Battleground Adventures* (1915). Died in Brattleboro, Vermont.

Catesby ap Roger Jones (April 15, 1821–June 21, 1877) Born at Fairfield, estate in Frederick (now Clarke) County, Virginia, the son of an army officer. Entered U.S. Navy in 1836 as a midshipman. Promoted to lieutenant in 1849. Became specialist in naval ordnance and helped develop the Dahlgren gun. Resigned his commission on April 17, 1861, and entered the Confederate navy in June as a lieutenant. Served as executive officer of the ironclad *Virginia* in battle of Hampton Roads, March 8, 1862, and commanded the ship during its fight with the Union ironclad *Monitor* on March 9. Along with the crew of the now-scuttled *Virginia*, helped defend Drewry's Bluff on the James River against Union naval attack on May 15, 1862. Commanded gunboat *Chattachoochee*, 1862–63. Served as head of the naval foundry and ordnance works at Selma, Alabama, from May 1863 until the end of the war. Married Gertrude Tartt in 1865. Supplied ordnance to South American governments after the war, then returned to Selma, where he was fatally shot in a dispute with a neighbor.

John B. Jones (March 6, 1810–February 4, 1866) Born in Baltimore, Maryland. Lived in Kentucky and Missouri as a boy. Married Frances Custis in 1840. Became editor of the *Saturday Visiter* in Baltimore, 1841. Published several novels, including *Wild Western Scenes* (1841), *The War Path* (1858), and *Wild Southern Scenes* (1859). Established weekly newspaper *Southern Monitor* in Philadelphia, 1857. Fearing arrest as a Confederate sympathizer, Jones moved in 1861 to Richmond, Virginia, where he worked as a clerk in the Confederate war department. Died in Burlington, New Jersey, shortly before the publication of *A Rebel War Clerk's Diary.*

Charles B. Labruzan (February 29, 1840–June 17, 1930) A merchant from Mobile, Alabama, Labruzan became a lieutenant in the 42nd Alabama Infantry. Served as the acting commander of Company F during the battle of Corinth, where he was captured on October 4, 1862. Paroled and exchanged, he became a prisoner again at the surrender of Vicksburg in July 1863. Died in Little River, Alabama.

Elizabeth Blair Lee (June 20, 1818–September 13, 1906) Born in Frankfort, Kentucky, daughter of journalist Francis Preston Blair and Elizabeth Gist Blair, sister of Montgomery Blair (postmaster general, 1861–64) and Frank Blair (a Union major general, 1862–65). Moved with family in 1830 to Washington, D.C., where her father edited the *Globe* and advised Andrew Jackson. Educated at boarding school in Philadelphia. Married naval officer Samuel Phillips Lee, a cousin of Robert E. Lee, in 1843. Became board member and active patron of the Washington City Orphan Asylum in 1849. Lived in Washington and at the Blair estate in Silver Spring, Maryland. Died in Washington.

Robert E. Lee (January 19, 1807–October 12, 1870) Born in Westmoreland County, Virginia, the son of Revolutionary War hero Henry "Light-Horse Harry" Lee and Ann Carter Lee. Graduated from West Point in 1829. Married Mary Custis, great-granddaughter of Martha Washington, in 1831. Served in the U.S.-Mexican War, and as superintendent of West Point, 1852–55. Promoted to colonel in March 1861. Resigned commission on April 20, 1861, after declining offer of field command of the Federal army. Served as commander of Virginia military forces, April–July 1861; commander in western Virginia, August–October 1861; commander of the southern Atlantic coast, November 1861–March 1862; and military advisor to Jefferson Davis, March–May 1862. Assumed command of the Army of Northern Virginia on June 1, 1862, and led it until April 9, 1865, when he surrendered to Ulysses S. Grant at Appomattox. Named general-in-chief of all Confederate forces, February 1865. Became president of Washington College (now Washington and Lee), September 1865. Died in Lexington, Virginia.

Abraham Lincoln (February 12, 1809–April 15, 1865) Born near Hodgenville, Kentucky, the son of a farmer and carpenter. Family moved to Indiana in 1816 and to Illinois in 1830. Settled in New Salem, Illinois, and worked as a storekeeper, surveyor, and postmaster. Served as a Whig in the state legislature, 1834–41. Began law practice in 1836 and moved to Springfield in 1837. Married Mary Todd in 1842. Elected to Congress as a Whig and served from 1847 to 1849. Became a public opponent of the extension of slavery after the passage of the Kansas-Nebraska Act in 1854. Helped found the Republican Party of Illinois in 1856. Campaigned in 1858 for Senate seat held by Stephen A. Douglas and debated him seven times on the slavery issue; although the Illinois legislature reelected Douglas, the campaign brought Lincoln national prominence. Received Republican presidential nomination in 1860 and won election in a four-way contest; his victory led to the secession of seven Southern states. Responded to the Confederate bombardment of Fort Sumter by calling up militia, proclaiming the blockade of Southern ports, and suspending habeas corpus. Issued preliminary and final emancipation proclamations on September 22, 1862, and January 1, 1863. Appointed Ulysses S. Grant commander of all Union forces in March 1864. Won reelection in 1864 by defeating Democrat George B. McClellan. Died in Washington, D.C., after being shot by John Wilkes Booth.

William Thompson Lusk (May 23, 1838–June 12, 1897) Born in Norwich, Connecticut, the son of a merchant. Attended Yale College, 1855–56, then studied medicine in Heidelberg and Berlin, 1858–61. Enlisted as private in the 79th New York Infantry in June 1861. Served at First Bull Run. Commissioned second lieutenant in September 1861. Served in Port Royal expedition, November 1861. Promoted to captain in February 1862. Served at Secessionville, Second Bull Run,

Chantilly, South Mountain, Antietam, and Fredericksburg. Became assistant adjutant general to General Daniel Tyler, commander of Eighth Corps, in 1863. Commanded troops in New York City during the July 1863 draft riots. Resigned commission, September 17, 1863. Married Mary Hartwell Chittenden in 1864. Studied medicine at Edinburgh, Prague, and Vienna, 1864–65. Returned to New York City and began medical career at Bellevue Hospital. Held chair in obstetrics at Bellevue Medical College, 1871–97. Following the death of his wife in 1871, married Matilda Myer Thorn in 1876. Published *The Science and Art of Midwifery* (1882). President of the faculty of Bellevue Medical College, 1889–97. Died in New York City.

Robert Q. Mallard (September 7, 1830–March 3, 1904) Born in Walthourville, Liberty County, Georgia, the son of a plantation owner. Graduated from Franklin College in 1850 and the Columbia Theological College in 1855. Served as pastor of the Walthourville Presbyterian Church, 1856–63. Married Mary Sharpe Jones, the daughter of the Reverend Charles Colcock Jones and Mary Jones of Liberty County, in 1857. Pastor of the Central Presbyterian Church in Atlanta, 1863–66. Moved to New Orleans in 1866, where he continued to serve as a pastor. Published *Plantation Life Before Emancipation* (1892) and *Montevideo-Maybank: Some Memories of a Southern Christian Household in the Olden Times* (1898). After the death of his wife in 1889, married Amarintha Mary Witherspoon. Died in New Orleans.

Dabney H. Maury (May 21, 1822–January 11, 1900) Born in Fredericksburg, Virginia, the son of a naval officer. Graduated from the University of Virginia in 1842 and from West Point in 1846. Wounded at Cerro Gordo in the U.S.-Mexican War. Taught at West Point, 1847–52, and served on the Texas frontier, 1852–56. Published *Skirmish Drill for Mounted Troops* (1859) while serving as superintendent of the cavalry school at Carlisle, Pennsylvania, 1856–60. Resigned from the U.S. Army in May 1861 and joined the Confederacy as a lieutenant colonel of cavalry in July. Served as chief of staff to General Earl Van Dorn at battle of Elkhorn Tavern (Pea Ridge), Arkansas, March 1862. Promoted to brigadier general, March 1862. Fought at Iuka and Corinth, September–October 1862. Promoted to major general, November 4, 1862. Commanded District of the Gulf at Mobile, Alabama, July 1863–April 1865. Taught school in Fredericksburg after the war before becoming an express agent and merchant in New Orleans. Founded Southern Historical Society in Richmond, Virginia, and served as its chairman until 1886. U.S. minister to Colombia, 1886–89.

Published *Recollections of a Virginian in the Mexican, Indian, and Civil Wars* (1894). Died in Peoria, Illinois.

George B. McClellan (December 3, 1826–October 29, 1885) Born in Philadelphia, the son of a surgeon. Graduated from West Point in 1846. Served in the U.S.-Mexican War. Resigned from the army in 1857 to become chief engineer of the Illinois Central Railroad. Became president of the Ohio & Mississippi Railroad in 1860. Married Ellen Marcy, 1860. Appointed major general in the regular army, May 1861. Commanded offensive that drove Confederate troops from western Virginia, July 1861. Assumed command of the Military Division of the Potomac on July 25, 1861, following the Union defeat at First Bull Run. Served as general-in-chief of the Union armies, November 1861–March 1862. Commanded the Army of the Potomac on the Peninsula, in the Second Bull Run campaign, and at Antietam. Relieved of command by President Lincoln on November 7, 1862. Nominated for president by the Democratic Party in 1864, but was defeated by Lincoln. Governor of New Jersey, 1878–81. Died in Orange, New Jersey.

Judith W. McGuire (March 19, 1813–March 21, 1897) Born Judith White Brockenbrough near Richmond, Virginia, the daughter of a judge. Married John P. McGuire, an Episcopalian rector, in 1846. Moved to Alexandria in 1852 when husband became principal of the Episcopal High School of Virginia. Fled Alexandria in May 1861 and settled in Richmond in February 1862. Worked as a clerk in the Confederate commissary department, November 1863–April 1864. Published *Diary of a Southern Refugee, During the War* (1867). Kept a school with her husband in Essex County in the 1870s. Published *General Robert E. Lee: The Christian Soldier* (1873). Died in Richmond.

George G. Meade (December 31, 1815–November 6, 1872) Born in Cádiz, Spain, the son of an American merchant. Family returned to Philadelphia in 1816. Graduated from West Point in 1835. Resigned in 1836 to work as engineer and surveyor. Married Margaretta Sergeant in 1840. Reentered army in 1842 as topographical engineer. Served under Zachary Taylor in the U.S.-Mexican War at Palo Alto, Resaca de la Palma, and Monterrey, and under Winfield Scott in the siege of Veracruz. Engaged in engineering and surveying duties in Delaware Bay, Florida, and the northern lakes, 1847–61. Commissioned as brigadier general of volunteers, August 1861. Became brigade commander in the Army of the Potomac, October 1861. Fought at Mechanicsville, Gaines's Mill, and Glendale, where he was wounded. Returned to duty in August 1862. Commanded brigade at Second Bull Run and a division at South Mountain and Antietam, where he temporarily led the First Corps after Joseph Hooker was wounded. Promoted to major general of volunteers, November 1862. Commanded division at Fredericksburg. Appointed commander of the Fifth Corps in December 1862 and led it at Chancellorsville. Replaced Hooker as commander of the Army of the Potomac on June 28, 1863, and led it until the end of the war. Received the thanks of Congress for his victory at Gettysburg. Promoted to major general in the regular army, September 23, 1864. Held postwar commands in the South and in the mid-Atlantic states. Died in Philadelphia.

Herman Melville (August 1, 1819–September 28, 1891) Born in New York City, the son of a merchant. Educated at schools in New York City and in upstate New York. Worked as bank clerk, bookkeeper, and schoolteacher. Sailed for Pacific on whaling ship in 1841 and returned in 1844 on frigate *United States.* Published *Typee* (1846) and *Omoo* (1847), fictionalized accounts of his experiences in the South Seas. Married Elizabeth Shaw in 1847. Published *Mardi* (1849), *Redburn* (1849), *White-Jacket* (1850), *Moby-Dick* (1851), *Pierre; or, The Ambiguities* (1852), *Israel Potter* (1855), *The Piazza Tales* (1856), and *The Confidence-Man* (1857). Visited Union troops in Virginia in spring 1864. Published poetry collection *Battle-Pieces and Aspects of the War* (1866). Worked as customs inspector in New York City, 1866–85. Published long poem *Clarel* (1876) and two small books of poetry, *John Marr and Other Sailors* (1888) and *Timoleon* (1891). Died in New York City, leaving *Billy Budd, Sailor*, in manuscript.

Hugh W. Mercer (November 27, 1808–June 9, 1877) Born in Fredericksburg, Virginia. Graduated from West Point in 1828. Served as artillery officer until 1835, when he resigned his commission. Married Mary Stites Anderson in 1834. Commissioned as brigadier general, October 1861. Commanded Confederate forces at Savannah, 1862–64. Led a brigade and then a division in the Atlanta campaign, May–July 1864, until poor health caused him to return to Savannah. After the war he was a banker in Savannah, 1866–69, and a commission merchant in Baltimore, 1869–72. Died in Baden Baden, Germany.

Mary Bedinger Mitchell (August 3, 1850–August 17, 1896) Born in Shepherdstown, Virginia (now West Virginia), the daughter of a lawyer and former congressman. Lived in Copenhagen, 1853–56, where father served as U.S. minister to Denmark, and with mother's family in Flushing, New York, 1856–58, before returning to Shepherdstown, where she spent the war. Married John F. B. Mitchell, a former Union officer, in 1871, and moved to Flushing. Published short stories under the name Maria Blunt in *Scribner's*, *Century*, and other magazines. Died in Flushing.

Thomas O. Moore (April 10, 1804–June 25, 1876) Born near Clinton, North Carolina, the son of a plantation owner. Moved to Rapides Parish, Louisiana, in 1829 to manage uncle's plantation. Married Bethiah Johnston Leonard, 1830. Acquired his own plantation, raising cotton and later sugar. Served as a Democrat in the state house of representatives, 1848–49, and in the state senate, 1856–60. Elected governor of Louisiana in 1859 and served January 1860–January 1864. Strongly supported secession after Lincoln's election. Following the Union occupation of New Orleans in April 1862, moved state capital from Baton Rouge to Opelousas and later Shreveport. Fled to Texas in spring of 1864 to escape Union troops, and to Mexico and Cuba following the Confederate surrender. Returned to Louisiana after being paroled by President Andrew Johnson, and received full pardon on January 15, 1867. Died at his plantation near Alexandria, Louisiana.

Benjamin Moran (August 1, 1820–June 20, 1886) Born in West Marlboro, Pennsylvania, the son of a cotton mill owner. Worked for bookseller and printer John Grigg in Philadelphia. Traveled to England in 1851. Published *The Footpath and Highway: or, Wanderings of an American in Great Britain, in 1851 and '52* (1853). Married Catherine Goulder, an English mill worker. Became private secretary to James Buchanan, then U.S. minister to Great Britain, in 1854. Assistant secretary of the American legation in London, 1857–64, and secretary, 1864–74. Served as minister resident in Portugal, 1874–76, and as chargé d'affaires at Lisbon, 1876–82. Returned to England in 1882 and died at Braintree, Essex.

John Lothrop Motley (April 15, 1814–May 29, 1877) Born in Dorchester, Massachusetts, the son of a merchant. Graduated from Harvard College in 1831. Continued university studies at Göttingen and Berlin, then traveled through Austria, Italy, France, and Britain, 1831–35. Admitted to the bar in 1836. Married Mary Benjamin in 1837. Published novels *Morton's Hope* (1839) and *Merrymount* (1849). Served term in the Massachusetts house of representatives, 1849. Traveled to Europe in 1851 for research on Dutch history. Published *The Rise of the Dutch Republic* (3 vols., 1856) and *History of the United Netherlands* (2 vols., 1860; 2 vols., 1867). Served as U.S. minister to the Austrian Empire, 1861–67, and to Great Britain, 1869–70. Published *The Life and Death of John of Barneveld* (2 vols., 1874). Died near Dorchester, England.

Robert Henry Newell (December 13, 1836–early July 1901) Born in New York City, the son of a lock manufacturer. Assistant editor of the *New York Sunday Mercury*, 1858–62. Began writing satiric letters signed "Orpheus C. Kerr" in March 1861 and continued through April 1865; they were collected in three volumes, published in 1862, 1863, and 1865. Married actress and writer Adah Isaacs Menken in 1862; she divorced him in 1865. Worked at the *New York World*, 1869–74, *New York Daily Graphic*, and *Hearth and Home* before retiring from journalism in 1876. Published poetry collections *The Palace Beautiful* (1865), *Versatilities* (1871), *Studies in Stanzas* (1882); novels *Avery Gliburn* (1867), *The Cloven Foot* (1870), *The Walking Doll* (1872), *There Once Was a Man* (1884); and *Smoked Glass* (1868), a collection of Orpheus C. Kerr letters satirizing Reconstruction politics. Died in Brooklyn, New York.

Ira S. Owens (March 1, 1830–February 19, 1913) Born in Greene County, Ohio. Enlisted in October 1861 from Xenia, Ohio, in the 74th Ohio Infantry as a private. Wounded in the left leg on December 31, 1862, at battle of Stones River (Murfreesboro), his only engagement. Reenlisted in January 1864, promoted to corporal, January 1865, and discharged in July 1865. Resumed farming in Montgomery County, Ohio. Later became a merchant and public notary. Published *Greene County in the War* (1872) and *Greene County Soldiers in the Late War* (1884). Died in Dayton, Ohio.

Charles A. Page (May 22, 1838–May 1873) Born near Dixon, Illinois, the son of a farmer. Graduated from Cornell College in Mount Vernon, Iowa, in 1859. Edited *The Mount Vernon News*, 1859–61. Worked as treasury department clerk in Washington, D.C., 1861, before becoming a correspondent for the *New-York Daily Tribune*, 1862–65, covering campaigns of the Army of the Potomac. Served as U.S. consul in Zurich, Switzerland, 1865–69. Founded successful condensed-milk company. Died in London.

Henry John Temple, third Viscount Palmerston (October 20, 1784–October 18, 1865) Born in Westminster, the son of an Irish peer whose title did not grant him a seat in the House of Lords. Educated at Harrow School, the University of Edinburgh, 1800–3, and St. John's College, Cambridge, 1803–6. Succeeded to his father's peerage in 1802. Entered the House of Commons as a Tory in 1807. Served as secretary at war, 1809–28 (the position made Palmerston responsible for managing the finances of the British army, but did not make him a member of the cabinet). Married Emily, Lady Cowper, a sister of Lord Melbourne, in 1839. Joined the Whigs in 1830 and served as foreign secretary, 1830–34, 1835–41, 1846–51; home secretary, 1852–55;

and prime minister, 1855–58. Became prime minister of the first Liberal government, 1859–65. Died in office at Brocket Hall, Hertfordshire.

George Hamilton Perkins (October 20, 1836–October 24, 1899) Born in Hopkinton, New Hampshire, the son of a lawyer. Graduated from the U.S. Naval Academy in 1856. Returned to the United States from West Africa in summer 1861 and was assigned to the gunboat *Cayuga* as first lieutenant in December 1861. Served in passage of Forts Jackson and St. Philip and the capture of New Orleans, April 1862. Patrolled the lower Mississippi River and served on blockade duty off Mobile and the Texas coast, 1862–64. Promoted to lieutenant commander, December 1862. Assumed command of the ironclad monitor *Chickasaw* in July 1864. Fought in battle of Mobile Bay, August 5, 1864. Commanded *Chickasaw* on Gulf blockade duty for remainder of the war. Married Anna Minot Weld in 1870. Retired as captain in 1891. Died in Boston.

Benjamin Rush Plumly (May 15, 1816–December 29, 1887) Born in Newton, Pennsylvania, the son of a Quaker physician. Worked as a merchant while active in the abolitionist and social reform movements. Married Rebecca Wilson. Served on staff of General John C. Frémont in Missouri, 1861, with rank of major. In 1863 went to New Orleans as an appraiser of abandoned property for the treasury department. Joined the staff of General Nathaniel P. Banks and recruited black soldiers for Banks's Corps d'Afrique. Chairman of the New Orleans Board of Education for Freedmen, 1864–65. Moved to Galveston, Texas, in 1866, where he founded a street railway company. After his wife's death, married Agnes Maria Garland in 1869. Served in the Texas house of representatives, 1870–73, 1881–83, and in 1887. Died in Galveston.

John Pope (March 16, 1822–September 23, 1892) Born in Louisville, Kentucky, the son of a federal district judge. Graduated from West Point in 1842. Joined topographical engineers and conducted surveys in Florida and along the northeastern border. Served in U.S.-Mexican War. Continued survey work in Minnesota, Texas, and New Mexico. Promoted to captain in 1856. Married Clara Pomeroy Horton in 1859. Appointed brigadier general of volunteers in May 1861. Led troops in Missouri, July 1861–February 1862. Became commander of the Army of the Mississippi in February 1862, and captured New Madrid, Missouri, and Island No. 10, March–April 1862. Promoted to major general of volunteers in March 1862. Joined Union advance on Corinth, Mississippi, in May 1862. Named commander of the new Army of Virginia, June 26. Defeated at Second Bull Run, August 28–30, and assigned to the Department of the Northwest on September 6, 1862. After the war he held a series of commands in the West before retiring in 1886. Died in Sandusky, Ohio.

Fitz John Porter (August 31, 1822–May 21, 1901) Born in Portsmouth, New Hampshire, the son of a naval officer. Graduated from West Point in 1845. Served in the U.S.-Mexican War, and as an instructor at West Point, 1849–55. Married Harriet Pierson Cook in 1857. Served as chief of staff of the Union command in the Shenandoah Valley, April–August 1861. Commissioned brigadier general of volunteers, May 1861. Commanded division in the Army of the Potomac, October 1861–May 1862. Appointed commander of the Fifth Corps, Army of the Potomac, May 1862. Served in the Peninsula campaign and in the Seven Days' Battles, where he commanded the Union forces at Mechanicsville, Gaines's Mill, and Malvern Hill. Promoted to major general of volunteers in July 4, 1862. Led Fifth Corps in the Second Bull Run campaign and at Antietam. Relieved of command in November 1862. Convicted by general court-martial of misconduct and disobedience at Second Bull Run and cashiered from the army, January 21, 1863. Worked as mining engineer in Colorado, as merchant in New York City, and as construction engineer and railroad executive in New Jersey. An army board of inquiry exonerated him of all charges in 1879, and in 1886 he was reinstated in the army and placed on the retired list. Served as a New York City police commissioner, 1884–88, and fire commissioner, 1888–89. Died in Morristown, New Jersey.

Sara Agnes Pryor (February 19, 1830–February 15, 1912) Born Sara Agnes Rice in Halifax County, Virginia, the daughter of a Baptist minister. Married Roger Atkinson Pryor in 1848. Lived in Charlottesville, Petersburg, Richmond, and Washington, D.C., while her husband studied law, edited several newspapers, and served in the U.S. Congress, 1859–61. Moved around Virginia, 1861–63, while her husband commanded a regiment and then a brigade the Confederate army. Served as a nurse in Richmond during the Seven Days' Battles. Returned to Petersburg in the autumn of 1863 and remained there during the 1864–65 siege. Moved in 1867 to New York, where her husband was now practicing law, and lived in Brooklyn and later Manhattan. Published *The Mother of Washington and Her Times* (1903), *Reminiscences of Peace and War* (1904), *The Birth of the Nation: Jamestown, 1607* (1907), *My Day: Reminiscences of a Long Life* (1909), and a novel, *The Colonel's Story* (1911). Died in New York City.

Whitelaw Reid (October 27, 1837–December 15, 1912). Born near Cedarville, Ohio, the son of a farmer. Graduated from Miami University in 1856. Edited and published the *Xenia News*, 1857–60. Supported Abraham Lincoln in the 1860 presidential election. In 1861 began contributing to the *Cincinnati Times*, *Cleveland Herald*, and *Cincinnati Gazette*. Reported on the 1861 Union offensive in western Virginia and the battle of Shiloh for the *Gazette*. Became the Washington correspondent for the *Gazette* in June 1862, signing his dispatches "Agate," while also contributing reports to the *Chicago Tribune* and newspapers in St. Louis, Cleveland, Detroit, and Pittsburgh. Reported from the field at Gettysburg. Published *After the War* (1866), describing his travels through the South following the Confederate surrender. Unsuccessfully tried to raise cotton in Louisiana and Alabama, 1866–67. Published *Ohio in the War: Her Statesmen, Her Generals, and Soldiers* (1868). Reported on the impeachment trial of President Andrew Johnson and the 1868 political conventions for the *Gazette*. Joined the *New York Tribune* in 1868 and served as its managing editor, 1869–72. Following the death of Horace Greeley, he became the *Tribune*'s editor, 1872–1905, and publisher, 1872–1912. Served as U.S. minister to France, 1889–92. Nominated by the 1892 Republican convention as vice-presidential running mate for President Benjamin Harrison (election was won by former president Grover Cleveland). Served as member of the commission that negotiated peace treaty with Spain in 1898 and as U.S. ambassador to Great Britain, 1905–12. Died in London.

Henry Ropes (May 16, 1839–July 3, 1863) Born in London, England, the son of an American merchant. Family returned to Boston in 1842. Entered Harvard College in 1858. Commissioned as second lieutenant in Company K, 20th Massachusetts Infantry, on November 25, 1861. Fought in the Peninsula campaign, in the Seven Days' Battles, and at Antietam. Promoted to first lieutenant on October 2, 1862. Fought at Fredericksburg (December 1862 and May 1863) and at Gettysburg, where he was killed by the premature explosion of a Union shell.

Lord John Russell, first Earl Russell (August 18, 1792–May 28, 1878) Born in Westminster, the third son of the future Duke of Bedford. Educated at Westminster School and the University of Edinburgh. Entered the House of Commons as a Whig M. P. in 1813. Published series of historical works, essays, novels, and plays beginning in 1819. Helped draft the Reform Bill of 1832. Married Adelaide, Lady Riblesdale, in 1835; after her death, married Lady Fannie Elliot in 1841. Served as home secretary, 1835–41; prime minister, 1846–52; foreign secretary, 1852–53; colonial secretary, 1855; foreign secretary in the Palmerston government, 1859–65; and prime minister after Palmerston's death, 1865–66. Created Earl Russell in 1861. Died in Richmond Park, Surrey.

Samuel Sawyer (June 20, 1823–May 23, 1902) Born in Goshen, New York, the son of a farmer. Graduated from the College of New Jersey (Princeton) in 1842. Attended Union Theological Seminary, 1845–48. Ordained as Presbyterian minister in 1849. Held pastorate in Rodgersville, Tennessee, 1848–57. President of the College of Indiana in Marion, 1857–61. Appointed chaplain of the 47th Indiana Infantry in 1861. After the capture of Memphis in 1862, edited a Unionist newspaper in the city until it was closed by General William T. Sherman. Served as superintendent of contrabands at Helena, Arkansas, and St. Louis, 1863. Mustered out in 1864. Held church positions in Knoxville and Maryville, Tennessee, 1864–68; in Chillicothe, Missouri, where he edited a newspaper, 1868–72; and in East St. Louis, Illinois, and Pleasant Grove, New Jersey. Returned to Marion, Indiana, in 1880. Died in Indianapolis.

William T. Sherman (February 8, 1820–February 14, 1891) Born in Lancaster, Ohio, the son of an attorney. Graduated from West Point in 1840. Served in Florida and California, but did not see action in the U.S.-Mexican War. Married Ellen Ewing in 1850. Promoted to captain; resigned his commission in 1853. Managed bank branch in San Francisco, 1853–57. Moved in 1858 to Leavenworth, Kansas, where he worked in real estate and was admitted to the bar. Named first superintendent of the Louisiana State Seminary of Learning and Military Academy at Alexandria (now Louisiana State University) in 1859. Resigned position when Louisiana seceded in January 1861. Commissioned colonel, 13th U.S. Infantry, May 1861. Commanded brigade at First Bull Run, July 1861. Appointed brigadier general of volunteers, August 1861, and ordered to Kentucky. Assumed command of the Department of the Cumberland, October 1861, but was relieved in November at his own request. Returned to field in March 1862 and commanded division under Ulysses S. Grant at Shiloh. Promoted major general of volunteers, May 1862. Commanded corps under Grant during Vicksburg campaign, and succeeded him as commander of the Army of the Tennessee, October 1863, and as commander of the Military Division of the Mississippi, March 1864. Captured Atlanta, September 1864, and led march through Georgia, November–December 1864. Marched army through the Carolinas and accepted the surrender of Confederate General Joseph E. Johnston at Durham Station, North Carolina, April 26, 1865. Promoted to lieutenant general, 1866, and general, 1869, when he became commander of the army. Published controversial memoirs (1875, revised 1886). Retired from army in 1884 and moved to New York City. Rejected possible Republican presidential nomination, 1884. Died in New York City.

George W. Smalley (June 2, 1833–April 4, 1916) Born in Franklin, Massachusetts, the son of a minister. Graduated from Yale in 1853, attended Harvard Law School, and admitted to the bar in 1856. Practiced law in Boston, 1856–61. Reported on the Union capture of Port Royal, South Carolina, the Shenandoah Valley campaign, and the battle of Antietam as a war correspondent for the *New-York Daily Tribune*, November 1861–October 1862. Married Phoebe Garnaut, the adopted daughter of Wendell Phillips, in 1862. Worked in the New York office of the *Tribune*, 1863–65, and helped defend it against draft rioters in July 1863. Reported on the Austro-Prussian War in 1866. Headed London office of the *Tribune*, 1867–95, and directed its reporting of the Franco-Prussian War. American correspondent for *The Times* of London, 1895–1905. Published *London Letters* (1891), *Studies of Men* (1895), and *Anglo-American Memories* (1911). Returned to England in 1905. Died in London.

Asa D. Smith (1836–November 25, 1911) A shoemaker from Natick, Smith enlisted as a corporal in the 16th Massachusetts Infantry on May 7, 1861. Served in the Peninsula campaign with Hooker's Division, Third Corps, Army of the Potomac. Severely wounded at battle of Glendale, June 30, 1862. Hospitalized at the U.S. Naval Academy at Annapolis, Maryland, before being discharged for disability on July 25, 1862. Joined Natick fire department in 1863. Served as deputy state constable from 1865. Married Abbie Louise Newhall in 1866. Graduated from Boston University School of Medicine in 1877. Established medical practice in South Boston from 1878 and in Dorchester from 1901. Died in Dorchester, Massachusetts.

Ezra Stacy (May 31, 1807–December 9, 1878) A plantation owner in Liberty County, Georgia, where he was born and died. Deacon of Midway Church, 1838–66.

Lewis H. Steiner (May 4, 1827–February 18, 1892) Born in Frederick, Maryland, the son of a merchant. Graduated from Marshall College, Mercersburg, Pennsylvania, in 1846. Received M.D. from the University of Pennsylvania in 1849. Practiced in Frederick before moving to Baltimore in 1852. Taught chemistry, physics, natural history, and pharmacy at the Columbian College and the National Medical College in Washington, D.C., 1853–55; at the College of St. James in Hagerstown, Maryland, 1854–59; and at the Maryland College of Pharmacy in Baltimore, 1856–61. Published several pamphlets on medical and scientific subjects and was assistant editor of the *American Medical Monthly*, 1859–61. Returned to Frederick in 1861. Served as chief inspector of the U.S. Sanitary Commission with the Army of the Potomac throughout the war. Married Sarah Spencer Smyth, 1866. Served as a Republican in the Maryland senate, 1871–83. Chief librarian of the Enoch Pratt Free Library in Baltimore, 1884–92. Died in Baltimore.

George E. Stephens (1832–April 24, 1888) Born in Philadelphia, the son of free blacks who had fled from Virginia after the Nat Turner rebellion. Worked as upholsterer and cabinetmaker. An active abolitionist, he helped found the Banneker Institute, a literary society and library for blacks, in Philadelphia in 1853. Served on coastal survey ship *Walker* in 1857–58 and visited Charleston, South Carolina. Became cook and personal servant to Lieutenant Colonel Benjamin Tilghman of the 26th Pennsylvania Infantry in 1861 while serving as war correspondent for the New York *Weekly Anglo-African*, an influential black newspaper. Helped recruit in early 1863 for the 54th Massachusetts Infantry, the first black regiment raised by a northern state, then enlisted in the regiment as a sergeant. Served in siege of Charleston, South Carolina, and fought in the assault on Fort Wagner on July 18, 1863. Continued to write for the *Anglo-African* and protested the failure of black soldiers to receive equal pay. Commissioned as first lieutenant before being mustered out in July 1865. Worked for the Freedman's Bureau in Virginia educating freed slaves, 1866–70. Returned to Philadelphia before moving in 1873 to Brooklyn, where he worked as an upholsterer until his death.

Kate Stone (May 8, 1841–December 28, 1907) Born Sarah Katherine Stone in Hinds County, Mississippi, the daughter of a plantation owner. Family moved to plantation in Madison Parish, Louisiana, thirty miles northwest of Vicksburg. Educated at boarding school in Nashville. Two of her five brothers died while serving in the Confederate army in 1863. Family fled plantation in March 1863 during the Vicksburg campaign and went to eastern Texas. Returned to plantation in November 1865. Married Henry Bry Holmes in 1869. Founded local chapter of the United Daughters of the Confederacy. Died in Tallulah, Louisiana.

George Templeton Strong (January 26, 1820–July 21, 1875) Born in New York City, the son of an attorney. Graduated from Columbia College in 1838. Read law in his father's office and was admitted to the bar in 1841. Joined father's firm. Married Ellen Ruggles in 1848. Served on Columbia board of trustees and as vestryman of Trinity Episcopal Church. Helped found the U.S. Sanitary Commission, June 1861, and served as its treasurer through the end of the war; also helped found the Union League Club of New York in 1863. Died in New York City.

Charles Sumner (January 6, 1811–March 11, 1874) Born in Boston, Massachusetts, the son of a lawyer. Graduated from Harvard College in 1830 and from Harvard Law School in 1833. Practiced law in Boston and became active in social reform movements. Unsuccessful Free Soil candidate for Congress in 1848. Elected to the U.S. Senate as a Free Soiler in 1851. Badly beaten with a cane on the Senate floor by South Carolina congressman Preston Brooks on May 22, 1856, two days after delivering his antislavery speech "The Crime Against Kansas." Reelected as a Republican in 1857, but did not regularly return to his seat in the Senate until December 1859; reelected in 1863 and 1869. Chairman of the Senate Foreign Relations Committee, 1861–71. Supported Radical Reconstruction and the rights of blacks after the war. Married Alice Mason Hooper in 1866. Joined Liberal Republicans in opposing reelection of President Grant in 1872. Died in Washington, D.C.

Richard Taylor (January 27, 1826–April 12, 1879) Born near Louisville, Kentucky, the son of army officer and future president Zachary Taylor. Graduated from Yale College in 1845. Managed father's cotton plantation in Jefferson County, Mississippi, 1848–49. Inherited sugar plantation in St. Charles Parish, Louisiana, after President Taylor's death in 1850. Married Louise Marie Myrthé Bringier, 1851. Served in the Louisiana senate, 1856–61. Commissioned as colonel of the 9th Louisiana Infantry, July 1861. Promoted to brigadier general, October 1861. Commanded the Louisiana Brigade in the Shenandoah Valley campaign of 1862. Promoted to major general, July 1862, and assigned command of the District of Western Louisiana, August 1862. Defeated General Nathaniel P. Banks in the Red River campaign in Louisiana, March–May 1864. Promoted to lieutenant general, May 1864. Commanded the Department of Alabama, Mississippi, and Eastern Louisiana from September 1864 to May 4, 1865, when he surrendered at Citronelle, Alabama. Active in the postwar Democratic Party in Louisiana. *Destruction and Reconstruction: Personal Experiences of the Late War* published posthumously in 1879. Died in New York City.

David L. Thompson (August 28, 1837–March 13, 1926) Born in Windham, Ohio. Taught school before enlisting from Flushing, New York, as private in Company G, 9th New York Infantry, on August 13, 1862. Captured at battle of Antietam, September 17, 1862. Held at Richmond; paroled to Annapolis, Maryland, October 6, 1862, and released from parole, December 1862. After the 9th New York mustered out in May 1863, Thompson joined Company B, 3rd New York Infantry. Served in South Carolina in 1863, in the Bermuda Hundred and Petersburg campaigns in 1864, and in North Carolina, where he was discharged on June 17, 1865, as a lieutenant. Married Mary Ann Wray in 1868. Lived in North Plainfield, New Jersey. Worked as a cashier, then as treasurer of a hardware company. Died in Newark, New Jersey.

Charles S. Wainwright (December 31, 1826–September 13, 1907) Born in New York City, the son of a farmer from Dutchess County in the Hudson Valley. Helped manage family estate near Rhinebeck. Served in New York state militia. Commissioned as major in the 1st New York Artillery on October 17, 1861. Served as chief of artillery in Hooker's division, Army of the Potomac, from January 1862. Promoted to lieutenant colonel, April 1862, and colonel, May 1862. Fought at Williamsburg and Fair Oaks before falling ill in early June 1862. Returned from sick leave in August 1862 and became chief of artillery in the First Corps in September 1862; joined his command after the battle of Antietam. Served at Fredericksburg, Chancellorsville, and Gettysburg. Commanded artillery brigade in Fifth Corps, 1864–65, and served in the Overland campaign, the siege of Petersburg, and the Appomattox campaign. Returned to farming in Dutchess County before moving to Washington, D.C., around 1884. Died in Washington.

Henry Walke (December 24, 1808–March 8, 1896) Born in Princess Anne County, Virginia, the son of a plantation owner. Family moved to Chillicothe, Ohio, in 1811. Entered the U.S. Navy as a midshipman in 1827 and was promoted to lieutenant in 1839. Served on brig *Vesuvius* during the U.S.-Mexican War. Promoted to commander in 1855. Commanded gunboat *Tyler* in support of General Grant's attack on Belmont, Missouri, in November 1861. Assumed command of the ironclad *Carondolet* in January 1862. Saw action at Forts Henry and Donelson, Island No. 10, Plum Run Bend, Memphis, and in battle with the Confederate ironclad *Arkansas* on the Yazoo River, February–July 1862. Promoted to captain in July 1862. Commanded the ironclad ram *Lafayette* during the Vicksburg campaign, February–August 1863, and the steam sloop *Sacramento* on patrol for Confederate raiders in the Atlantic, January 1864–August 1865. Promoted to commodore, 1866, and rear admiral, 1870. Retired in 1871. Published *Naval Scenes and Reminiscences of the Civil War in the United States* (1877). Died in Brooklyn, New York.

Lewis Wallace (April 10, 1827–February 15, 1905) Born in Brookville, Indiana, the son of a lawyer and politician. Reported on Indiana legislature for the *Indianapolis Daily Journal*, 1844–45. Served as second lieutenant with the 1st Indiana Infantry in the U.S.-Mexican War. Admitted to the bar in 1849. Married Susan Arnold Elston in 1852. Served as Democrat in the Indiana state senate, 1856–60. Commissioned colonel of the 11th Indiana Infantry in April 1861. Promoted to brigadier general of volunteers, September 1861. Commanded a division at Forts Henry and Donelson. Promoted to major general in March 1862. Commanded division at Shiloh, where his delay in reaching the battlefield on the first day led to his relief in June 1862. Organized defense of Cincinnati during the Confederate invasion of Kentucky. Appointed commander of Union troops in Maryland in March 1864. Led Union forces in battle of the Monocacy on July 9, 1864, successfully delaying the Confederate advance on Washington, D.C. Served on the military commission that convicted the conspirators in the Lincoln assassination, and was president of the commission that convicted Henry Wirz, the commander of the Andersonville prison camp. Resumed law practice in Indiana. Published *The Fair God* (1873), a novel about the Spanish conquest of Mexico. Served as governor of New Mexico Territory, 1878–81. Published *Ben Hur: A Tale of the Christ* (1880). U.S. minister to the Ottoman Empire, 1881–85. Published *The Boyhood of Christ* (1888) and *The Prince of India* (1893); his autobiography appeared posthumously in 1906. Died in Crawfordsville, Indiana.

Samuel R. Watkins (June 26, 1839–July 20, 1901) Born near Columbia, Tennessee, the son of a farmer. Attended Jackson College in Columbia and worked as a store clerk. Enlisted as a private in Company H, 1st Tennessee Infantry, in May 1861. Fought at Shiloh, Perryville, Murfreesboro (Stones River), Chickamauga, Chattanooga, the Atlanta campaign, Franklin, and Nashville and was wounded three times. Surrendered in North Carolina on April 26, 1865, one of sixty-five men remaining in his regiment and seven in his company. Married Virginia Jane Mayes in 1865. Became farmer and merchant in Columbia, Tennessee. Published memoir *"Co. Aytch," Maury Grays, First Tennessee Regiment, or, A Side Show of the Big Show* (1882). Died near Columbia.

Gideon Welles (July 1, 1802–February 11, 1878) Born in Glastonbury, Connecticut, the son of a merchant. Educated in Vermont at the American Literary, Scientific, and Military Academy (now Norwich University). Editor of the *Hartford Times*, 1826–36. Served as a Democrat in the Connecticut house of representatives, 1827–35. Married Mary Hale in 1835. Postmaster of Hartford, 1836–41. Served as chief of the bureau of provisions and clothing in the navy department, 1846–49. Helped organize Republican Party in Connecticut. Wrote for the *Hartford Evening Press*, the *New York Evening Post*, and other Republican newspapers. Secretary of the navy in the Lincoln and Andrew Johnson administrations, 1861–69. Died in Hartford.

Garland H. White (c. 1829–c. 1894) Born in slavery in Hanover County, Virginia. Sold around 1845 to Robert Toombs of Georgia and became his personal servant. Lived in Washington, D.C., while Toombs served in Congress, 1845–53, and in the Senate, 1853–61. Escaped from the District of Columbia in 1859 and fled to London, Canada West (Ontario), where he became a minister in the African Methodist Episcopal Church. Married Georgiana, a woman from Mississippi, around 1861. Began preaching in Toledo, Ohio, in January 1863. Helped recruit black soldiers in Indiana for the 28th U.S. Colored Infantry. Enlisted in regiment as private in January 1864 and began acting as regimental chaplain. Served with regiment in the Petersburg campaign. Wrote letters describing army life and the war to the *Christian Recorder*, an A.M.E. newspaper. Commissioned as regimental chaplain in October 1864. Reunited with his mother when he entered Richmond with his regiment on April 3, 1865. Served in Texas, July–November 1865, before being mustered out in January 1866. Returned to church in Toledo. Served as minister in Halifax, North Carolina, 1872–82. Lived in Weldon, North Carolina, 1884–89, before moving to Washington, D.C., where he died.

L. A. Whitely (1823–July 20, 1869) Raised in Kentucky. Associate editor of the *Louisville Journal* and later owner of the *Baltimore Clipper*. Accepted offer in 1861 from James Gordon Bennett, publisher of the *New York Herald*, to head its Washington bureau. Worked as clerk in the treasury department from 1861 to June 1863, when he was dismissed by Secretary of the Treasury Chase. Left the *Herald* after the war to become editor of the *National Intelligencer*, a position he held until the newspaper closed in June 1869. Died in Washington, D.C.

Walt Whitman (May 31, 1819–March 26, 1892) Born in Huntington Township, New York, the son of a farmer and carpenter. Moved with family to Brooklyn in 1823. Learned printing trade at Brooklyn newspapers. Taught school on Long Island, 1836–38. Became freelance journalist and printer in New York and Brooklyn. Published first edition of *Leaves of Grass* in 1855 (revised editions appeared in 1856, 1860, 1867, 1870, 1881, and 1891). Traveled to northern Virginia in December 1862 after learning that his brother George had been wounded at Fredericksburg. Became volunteer nurse in Washington, D.C., army hospitals. Published *Drum-Taps* and *Sequel to Drum-Taps* in 1865. Worked as clerk at the interior department, 1865, and the office of the attorney general, 1865–73. Published prose recollections of his war experiences in *Memoranda During the War* (1875) and *Specimen Days and Collect* (1882). Died in Camden, New Jersey.

Alpheus S. Williams (September 20, 1810–December 21, 1878) Born in Deep River, Connecticut, the son of a manufacturer. Graduated from Yale College in 1831. Admitted to the bar in 1834. Moved to Detroit in 1836, where he practiced law and joined the local militia company. Married Jane Hereford Pierson in 1839; she died in 1848. Served as probate judge of Wayne County, 1840–44, and published the *Detroit Daily Advertiser*, 1843–48. Commissioned as brigadier general of volunteers in August 1861. Commanded brigade in the Army of the Potomac, October 1861–March 1862. Led a division in the Shenandoah Valley campaign and at Cedar Mountain and Second Bull Run. Assumed temporary command of Twelfth Corps at Antietam following the death of General Mansfield. Commanded division at Chancellorsville and was temporary commander of the Twelfth Corps at Gettysburg. Sent with his division in September 1863 to Tennessee, where they guarded railroads. Served in the Atlanta campaign and commanded the Twentieth Corps in the march through Georgia and the Carolinas. Mustered out on January 15, 1866. Served as U.S. minister to San Salvador, 1866–69. Returned to Detroit. Married Martha Ann Tillman in 1873. Elected to Congress as a Democrat and served from 1875 until his death in Washington, D.C.

J. Montgomery Wright (February 22, 1839–January 2, 1915) Born John Montgomery Wright in Sackets Harbor, New York, the son of an army officer. Entered West Point in 1859. Commissioned as captain and assistant adjutant general of volunteers, September 1861. Promoted to major in June 1862 and served on the staff of General Don Carlos Buell. Resigned commission in January 1864. Married Nelly Butler Ewing. Served as adjutant general of the Kentucky state militia, 1875–79. Marshal of the U.S. Supreme Court, 1888–1915. Died in Washington, D.C.

Lot D. Young (January 22, 1842–April 2, 1926) Born in Nicholas County, Kentucky. Enlisted in September 1861 in the Confederate 4th Kentucky Infantry. Fought at Shiloh. Promoted to second lieutenant, May 1862, and first lieutenant, March 1863. Fought at Murfreesboro (Stones River), Chickamauga, Missionary Ridge, and in the Atlanta campaign. Severely wounded at Jonesboro, Georgia, on August 31, 1864. Spent six months in hospitals and was unable to rejoin his regiment before the war ended. Published *Reminiscences of a Soldier in the Orphan Brigade* (1918). Died in Lexington, Kentucky.

Note on the Texts

This volume collects nineteenth- and early twentieth-century writing about the Civil War, bringing together public and private letters, newspaper and magazine articles, memoranda, speeches, narratives, journal and diary entries, proclamations, messages, legislative enactments, military orders, poems, songs, and excerpts from memoirs written by participants and observers and dealing with events in the period between January 1862 and January 1863. Most of these documents were not written for publication, and most of them existed only in manuscript form during the lifetimes of the persons who wrote them. With fourteen exceptions, the texts presented in this volume are taken from printed sources. In cases where there is only one printed source for a document, the text offered here comes from that source. Where there is more than one printed source for a document, the text printed in this volume is taken from the source that appears to contain the fewest editorial alterations in the spelling, capitalization, paragraphing, and punctuation of the original. In fourteen instances where no printed sources (or no complete printed sources) were available, the texts in this volume are printed from manuscripts.

This volume prints texts as they appear in the sources listed below, but with a few alterations in editorial procedure. The bracketed conjectural readings of editors, in cases where original manuscripts or printed texts were damaged or difficult to read, are accepted without brackets in this volume when those readings seem to be the only possible ones; but when they do not, or when the editor made no conjecture, the missing word or words are indicated by a bracketed two-em space, i.e., [   ]. In cases where a typographical error or obvious misspelling in manuscript was marked by earlier editors with "[*sic*]," the present volume omits the "[*sic*]" and corrects the typographical error or slip of the pen. In some cases, obvious errors were not marked by earlier editors with "[*sic*]" but were printed and then followed by a bracketed correction; in these instances, this volume removes the brackets and accepts the editorial emendation. Bracketed editorial insertions used in the source texts to identify persons or places, expand contractions and abbreviations, or clarify meaning have been deleted in this volume. In instances where canceled, but still legible, words were printed in the source texts with lines through the deleted material, or where canceled words were printed and indicated with an asterisk, this volume omits the canceled words.

The texts of the letter from George Hamilton Perkins to Susan G. Perkins and of the journal entry by Charles B. Labruzan were presented as quoted material in the sources used in this volume, with quotation marks placed at the beginning of each paragraph and at the end of the text; this volume omits the quotation marks.

In *The Papers of Jefferson Davis*, material that was written in interlined form in manuscript is printed within diagonal marks; this volume prints the interlined words and omits the diagonals. Similarly, interlined material that was presented in footnotes in *Ham Chamberlayne —Virginian: Letters and papers of an artillery officer in the War for Southern Independence 1861–1865* has been incorporated into the text in this volume.

Diary of a Southern Refugee was first published in New York in 1867, with its author identified as "A Lady of Virginia" and with initials substituted for the names of a number of persons referred to in the text. The book was reprinted in 1889 in Richmond by J. W. Randolph & English, with Judith W. McGuire identified as its author, and with an appended list of "Corrections" supplying the omitted names. In the selection from *Diary of a Southern Refugee* presented in this volume, the names supplied in the "Corrections" section of the 1889 printing have been incorporated into the text.

The selections from the diary of Gideon Welles, the secretary of the navy in the Lincoln administration, are taken from *Diary of Gideon Welles* (1960), edited by Howard K. Beale. Welles kept a diary during the Civil War that he extensively revised between 1869 and his death in 1878. The revised text was published in 1911 as *Diary of Gideon Welles*, edited by his son Edgar T. Welles with the assistance of John Morse Jr. and Frederick Bancroft. In the 1960 edition, Beale presented the text of the 1911 edition while printing deleted material from the original diary in the margins and using brackets, italics, strike-through lines, and other editorial markings to indicate the differences between the original version of the diary and the revised text. The texts of the selections from the Welles diary printed in this volume are taken from the 1960 edition and incorporate the changes indicated by Beale in order to present a clear text of the diary as originally written by Welles during the Civil War.

In *The Francis Preston Blair Family in Politics* (1933), William Ernest Smith printed an incomplete text of Francis Preston Blair's letter to Montgomery Blair of November 7, 1862. The text presented in this volume is taken from *The Francis Preston Blair Family in Politics*, with the exception of the first sentence and the closing, which are taken from an unpublished transcription (also incomplete) made by the historian E. B. Long around 1960.

Two errors made in the transcription of documents are corrected in this volume, even though they were not corrected in the printed source texts: at 326.2, "*July 10*" becomes "*July 20*," and at 430.18, "to the report he had" becomes "to the support he had." Five slips of the pen in documents printed from manuscript sources are also corrected: at 414.30–31, "divisions fell back throug" becomes "divisions fell back through"; at 538.21, "to be in in favor" becomes "to be in favor"; at 549.12, "course of the administration is shakin" becomes "course of the administration is shaking"; at 700.13, "supply there men & animals" becomes "supply their men & animals"; at 746.24–25, "to 'work and wait, trusting" becomes "to 'work and wait,' trusting."

The following is a list of the documents included in this volume, in the order of their appearance, giving the source of each text.

Frederick Douglass: What Shall Be Done with the Slaves If Emancipated?, January 1862. *The Life and Writings of Frederick Douglass*, ed. Philip S. Foner, volume 3 (New York: International Publishers Co. Inc., 1952), 188–91. Copyright © 1950. Reprinted from *The Life and Writings of Frederick Douglass*, published by International Publishers, copyright © 1950.

John Boston to Elizabeth Boston, January 12, 1862. *Free at Last: A Documentary History of Slavery, Freedom, and the Civil War*, ed. Ira Berlin, Barbara J. Fields, Steven F. Miller, Joseph P. Reidy, Leslie S. Rowland (New York: The New Press, 1992), 29–30. Copyright © 1992 by The New Press. Reprinted by permission of The New Press.

Salmon P. Chase: Journal, January 6, 1862. *The Salmon P. Chase Papers*: *Volume I, Journals, 1829–1872*, ed. John Niven (Kent, Ohio: The Kent State University Press, 1993), 321–22. Copyright © 1993 by The Kent State University Press.

Abraham Lincoln to Don Carlos Buell and Henry W. Halleck, January 13, 1862. *The Collected Works of Abraham Lincoln*, volume V, ed. Roy P. Basler (New Brunswick, N.J.: Rutgers University Press, 1953), 98–99. Copyright © 1953 by the Abraham Lincoln Association.

Abraham Lincoln: President's General War Order No. 1, January 27, 1862; President's Special War Order No. 1, January 31, 1862. *The Collected Works of Abraham Lincoln*, volume V, ed. Roy P. Basler (New Brunswick, N.J.: Rutgers University Press, 1953), 111–12, 115. Copyright © 1953 by the Abraham Lincoln Association.

George B. McClellan to Edwin M. Stanton, February 3, 1862. *The Civil War Papers of George B. McClellan: Selected Correspondence, 1860–1865*, ed. Stephen W. Sears (New York: Ticknor & Fields, 1989), 162–70. Copyright © 1989 by Stephen W. Sears. Reprinted with permission by Stephen W. Sears.

Julia Ward Howe: The Battle Hymn of the Republic; from *Reminiscences, 1819–1899*. *Atlantic Monthly*, February 1862; Julia Ward Howe,

Reminiscences, 1819–1899 (Boston: Houghton Mifflin Company, 1899), 273–76.

The New York Times: An Important Arrest; The Ball's Bluff Disaster—Gen. McClellan and Gen. Stone. *The New York Times*, February 11, 1862, April 12, 1863.

Lew Wallace: from *An Autobiography*. Lew Wallace, *An Autobiography*, vol. I (New York: Harper & Brothers, 1906), 410–24.

John Kennerly Farris to Mary Farris, October 31, 1862. "Letters to Mary: The Civil War Diary of John Kennerly Farris," ed. John Abernathy Smith, *Franklin County Historical Review*, volume XXV (1994), 46–52. Copyright © 1994 by The Franklin County Historical Society. Reprinted courtesy of The Franklin County Historical Review.

Henry Walke: The Western Flotilla at Fort Donelson, Island Number Ten, Fort Pillow and Memphis. *Battles and Leaders of the Civil War*, volume I, ed. Robert Underwood Johnson and Clarence Clough Buel (New York: The Century Co., 1887), 430–52.

Braxton Bragg to Judah P. Benjamin, February 15, 1862. *The War of the Rebellion: A Compilation of the Official Records of the Union and Confederate Armies*, series I, volume VI (Washington, D.C.: Government Printing Office, 1882), 826–27.

John B. Jones: Diary, February 8–28, 1862. J. B. Jones, *A Rebel War Clerk's Diary at the Confederate States Capital*, volume I (Philadelphia: J. B. Lippincott & Co., 1866), 109–12.

Jefferson Davis: Message to the Confederate Congress, February 25, 1862. *The Papers of Jefferson Davis*, volume VIII, ed. Lynda Lasswell Crist and Mary Seaton Dix (Baton Rouge: Louisiana State University Press, 1995), 58–62. Copyright © 1995 by Louisiana State University Press.

George E. Stephens to the *Weekly Anglo-African*, March 2, 1862. *A Voice of Thunder: The Civil War Letters of George E. Stephens*, ed. Donald Yacovone (Urbana: University of Illinois Press, 1997), 185–88. Copyright © 1997 by the Board of Trustees of the University of Illinois.

Orpheus C. Kerr: from *The Orpheus C. Kerr Papers*. *The Orpheus C. Kerr Papers* (New York: Blakemon & Mason, 1862), 219–27.

Dabney H. Maury: Recollections of the Elkhorn Campaign. *Southern Historical Society Papers*, volume II (Richmond, Virginia: Southern Historical Society, 1876), 180–92.

Abraham Lincoln: Message to Congress on Compensated Emancipation, March 6, 1862; To James A. McDougall, March 14, 1862. *The Collected Works of Abraham Lincoln*, volume V, ed. Roy P. Basler (New Brunswick, N.J.: Rutgers University Press, 1953), 144–46, 160–61. Copyright © 1953 by the Abraham Lincoln Association.

Catesby ap Roger Jones: from "Services of the 'Virginia' (Merrimac)." *Southern Historical Society Papers*, volume XI, no. 2 (February–March 1883), 67–73.

Nathaniel Hawthorne: from "Chiefly About War-Matters by a Peaceable Man." *The Centenary Edition of the Works of Nathaniel Hawthorne*, volume XXII, *Miscellaneous Prose and Verse*, ed. Thomas Woodson, Claude M. Simpson, and L. Neal Smith (Columbus: The Ohio State University Press, 1994), 410–25, 433–38. Copyright © 1994 by The Ohio State University Press. Reprinted by permission.

George B. McClellan to the Army of the Potomac, March 14, 1862, and to Samuel L. M. Barlow, March 16, 1862. *The Civil War Papers of George B. McClellan: Selected Correspondence, 1860–1865*, ed. Stephen W. Sears (New York: Ticknor & Fields, 1989), 211, 213. Copyright © 1989 by Stephen W. Sears. Reprinted with permission by Stephen W. Sears.

Charles Francis Adams to Charles Francis Adams Jr., April 4, 1862. *A Cycle of Adams Letters, 1861–1865*, volume I, ed. Worthington Chauncey Ford (Boston: Houghton Mifflin Company, 1920), 123–24.

Emily Dickinson to Louise and Frances Norcross, late March 1862. *The Letters of Emily Dickinson*, ed. Thomas H. Johnson (Cambridge: The Belknap Press of Harvard University Press, 1986), 397–98. Reprinted by permission of the publishers from *The Letters of Emily Dickinson*, Thomas H. Johnson, ed., L835, Cambridge, Mass: The Belknap Press of Harvard University Press, Copyright © 1958, 1986, The President and Fellows of Harvard College; 1914, 1924, 1942 by Martha Dickinson Bianchi; 1952 by Alfred Leete Hampson; 1960 by Mary L. Hampson.

Frederick Douglass: The War and How to End It, March 25, 1862. *The Frederick Douglass Papers, Series One: Speeches, Debates, and Interviews*, volume III, ed. John W. Blassingame (New Haven: Yale University Press, 1985), 508–21. Copyright © 1985 by Yale University. Reprinted by permission.

Abraham Lincoln to George B. McClellan, April 9, 1862. *The Collected Works of Abraham Lincoln*, volume V, ed. Roy P. Basler (New Brunswick, N.J.: Rutgers University Press, 1953), 184–85. Copyright © 1953 by the Abraham Lincoln Association.

Ulysses S. Grant to Commanding Officer, Advance Forces, April 6, 1862; to Julia Dent Grant, April 8, 1862; to Captain Nathaniel H. McLean, April 9, 1862; to Jesse Root Grant, April 26, 1862; and to Elihu B. Washburne, May 14, 1862. *The Papers of Ulysses S. Grant*, vol. V, ed. John Y. Simon (Carbondale: Southern Illinois University Press, 1973), 18, 27, 32–36, 78–79, 119–20. Copyright © 1973 by the Ulysses S. Grant Association.

William T. Sherman to Ellen Ewing Sherman, April 11, 1862. *Sherman's*

Civil War: Selected Correspondence of William T. Sherman, 1860–1865, ed. Brooks D. Simpson and Jean V. Berlin (Chapel Hill: The University of North Carolina Press, 1999), 201–2. Copyright © 1999 by The University of North Carolina Press. Used by permission of the publisher.

George W. Dawson to Laura Amanda Dawson, April 26, 1862. "One Year at War: Letters of Capt. Geo. W. Dawson, C.S.A.," ed. H. Riley Bock, *Missouri Historical Review*, volume 73, number 2 (January 1979), 192–95. Copyright © 1979 by The State Historical Society of Missouri. Reprinted with permission of The State Historical Society of Missouri.

Herman Melville: Shiloh: A Requiem. Herman Melville, *Battle-Pieces and Aspects of the War* (New York: Harper & Brothers, 1866), 63.

Confederate Conscription Acts, April 16 and 21, 1862. *Public Laws of the Confederate States of America, Passed at the First Session of the First Congress; 1862. Carefully Collated with the Originals at Richmond*, ed. James M. Matthews (Richmond: R. M. Smith, 1862), 29–32, 51–52.

Abraham Lincoln: Message to Congress, April 16, 1862. *The Collected Works of Abraham Lincoln*, volume V, ed. Roy P. Basler (New Brunswick, N.J.: Rutgers University Press, 1953), 192. Copyright © 1953 by the Abraham Lincoln Association.

John Russell Bartlett: The "Brooklyn" at the Passage of the Forts. *Battles and Leaders of the Civil War*, volume II, ed. Robert Underwood Johnson and Clarence Clough Buel (New York: The Century Co., 1887), 56–69.

George Hamilton Perkins to Susan G. Perkins, April 27, 1862. *Letters of Capt. Geo. Hamilton Perkins* (Concord, N.H.: Ira C. Evans, 1886), 67–72.

Charles S. Wainwright: Diary, May 5, 1862. *A Diary of Battle: The Personal Journals of Colonel Charles S. Wainwright, 1861–1865*, ed. Allan Nevins (New York: Harcourt, Brace & World, Inc., 1962), 47–57. Copyright © 1962 by Allan Nevins.

John B. Jones: Diary, May 14–19, 1862. J. B. Jones, *A Rebel War Clerk's Diary at the Confederate States Capital*, volume I (Philadelphia: J. B. Lippincott & Co., 1866), 125–27.

Garland H. White to Edwin M. Stanton, May 7, 1862. *Freedom: A Documentary History of Emancipation, 1861–1867. Series II: The Black Military Experience*, ed. Ira Berlin (Cambridge and New York: Cambridge University Press, 1982), 82–83. Copyright © 1982, 1995 by Cambridge University Press.

Abraham Lincoln: Proclamation Revoking General Hunter's Emancipation Order, May 19, 1862. *The Collected Works of Abraham Lincoln*, volume V, ed. Roy P. Basler (New Brunswick, N.J.: Rutgers

University Press, 1953), 222–23. Copyright © 1953 by the Abraham Lincoln Association.

Richard Taylor: from *Destruction and Reconstruction*. Richard Taylor, *Destruction and Reconstruction: Personal Experiences of the Late War* (New York: D. Appleton and Company, 1879), 48–53.

Elizabeth Blair Lee to Samuel Phillips Lee, May 26, 1862. *Wartime Washington: The Civil War Letters of Elizabeth Blair Lee*, ed. Virginia Jeans Laas (Urbana: University of Illinois Press, 1991), 151–53. Copyright © 1991 by the Board of Trustees of the University of Illinois. Reprinted from the Blair and Lee Family Papers, Manuscripts Division, Department of Rare Books and Special Collections, Princeton University Library.

Thomas O. Moore: To the People of Louisiana, May 24, 1862. *The War of the Rebellion: A Compilation of the Official Records of the Union and Confederate Armies*, series I, volume XV (Washington, D.C.: Government Printing Office, 1886), 743–44.

Lord Palmerston to Charles Francis Adams, June 11, 1862; Benjamin Moran: Journal, June 25, 1862. Brooks Adams, "The Seizure of the Laird Rams," *Proceedings of the Massachusetts Historical Society*, volume XLV, October 1911–June 1912, 257; *The Journal of Benjamin Moran, 1857–1865*, volume II, ed. Sarah Agnes Wallace and Frances Elma Gillespie (Chicago: The University of Chicago Press, 1949), 1027–29. Copyright © 1949 by The University of Chicago.

Henry Ropes to William Ropes, June 3–4, 1862. Manuscript, Henry Ropes Letters, Boston Public Library.

Robert E. Lee to Jefferson Davis, June 5, 1862. *The Papers of Jefferson Davis*, volume VIII, ed. Lynda Lasswell Crist and Mary Seaton Dix (Baton Rouge: Louisiana State University Press, 1995), 225–26. Copyright © 1995 by Louisiana State University Press.

David Hunter to Edwin M. Stanton, June 23, 1862. *Freedom: A Documentary History of Emancipation, 1861–1867. Series II: The Black Military Experience*, ed. Ira Berlin (Cambridge and New York: Cambridge University Press, 1982), 50–53. Copyright © 1982, 1995 by Cambridge University Press.

Kate Stone: Journal, June 29–July 5, 1862. *Brokenburn: The Journal of Kate Stone, 1861–1868*, ed. John Q. Anderson (Baton Rouge: Louisiana State University Press, 1955), 125–29. Copyright © 1989 by Louisiana State University Press.

Edward Porter Alexander: from *Fighting for the Confederacy*. *Fighting for the Confederacy: The Personal Recollections of General Edward Porter Alexander*, ed. Gary W. Gallagher (Chapel Hill: The University of North Carolina Press, 1989), 94–104. Copyright © 1989 by The University of North Carolina Press.

Charles A. Page: from *Letters of a War Correspondent.* Charles A. Page, *Letters of a War Correspondent*, ed. James R. Gilmore (Boston: L. C. Page, 1899), 3–11.

George B. McClellan to Edwin M. Stanton, June 28, 1862. *The Civil War Papers of George B. McClellan: Selected Correspondence, 1860–1865*, ed. Stephen W. Sears (New York: Ticknor & Fields, 1989), 322–23. Copyright © 1989 by Stephen W. Sears. Reprinted with permission by Stephen W. Sears.

Abraham Lincoln to William H. Seward, June 28, 1862. *The Collected Works of Abraham Lincoln*, volume V, ed. Roy P. Basler (New Brunswick, N.J.: Rutgers University Press, 1953), 291–92. Copyright © 1953 by the Abraham Lincoln Association.

Charles B. Haydon: Journal, June 25–July 1, 1862. *For Country, Cause & Leader: The Civil War Journal of Charles B. Haydon*, ed. Stephen W. Sears (New York: Ticknor & Fields, 1993), 254–62. Copyright © 1993 by Stephen W. Sears. Reprinted with permission by Stephen W. Sears.

Asa D. Smith: Narrative of the Seven Days' Battles. "Asa Smith Leaves the War," ed. Bruce Catton, *American Heritage*, Volume XXII, Number 2 (February 1971), 56–59, 103–4. Copyright © 1971 by American Heritage Publishing Co., Inc. Reprinted by permission of *American Heritage* Magazine.

Judith W. McGuire: Diary, June 27–30, 1862. Judith W. McGuire, *Diary of a Southern Refugee, During the War*, third edition (Richmond, Va.: J. W. Randolph & English, Publishers, 1889), 122–26.

Sallie Brock: from *Richmond During the War.* Sallie Brock Putnam, *Richmond During the War: Four Years of Personal Observation* (New York: G. W. Carleton & Co., 1867), 150–52.

Sara Agnes Pryor: from *Reminiscences of Peace and War.* Sara Agnes Pryor, *Reminiscences of Peace and War* (New York: The Macmillan Company, 1904), 181–88.

Whitelaw Reid: General Hunter's Negro Soldiers, July 6, 1862. *A Radical View: The "Agate" Dispatches of Whitelaw Reid 1861–1865*, volume II, ed. James G. Smart (Memphis, Tennessee: Memphis State University Press), 71–74. Copyright © 1976 Memphis State University Press.

George B. McClellan to Abraham Lincoln, July 7, 1862. *The Civil War Papers of George B. McClellan: Selected Correspondence, 1860–1865*, ed. Stephen W. Sears (New York: Ticknor & Fields, 1989), 344–45. Copyright © 1989 by Stephen W. Sears. Reprinted with permission by Stephen W. Sears.

Thomas H. Dudley and J. Price Edwards: An Exchange, July 9, 10, and 16, 1862. *Correspondence Concerning Claims Against Great Britain,*

Transmitted to the Senate of the United States in Answer to the Resolutions of December 4 and 10, 1867, and of May 27, 1868, volume III (Washington: Philp & Solomons, Booksellers, 1869), 17–19.

Abraham Lincoln: Appeal to Border-State Representatives for Compensated Emancipation, July 12, 1862. *The Collected Works of Abraham Lincoln*, volume V, ed. Roy P. Basler (New Brunswick, N.J.: Rutgers University Press, 1953), 317–19. Copyright © 1953 by the Abraham Lincoln Association.

Confiscation Act, July 17, 1862. *The War of the Rebellion: A Compilation of the Official Records of the Union and Confederate Armies*, series III, volume II (Washington, D.C.: Government Printing Office, 1899), 275–77.

John Pope: Address to the Army of Virginia, July 14, 1862. *The War of the Rebellion: A Compilation of the Official Records of the Union and Confederate Armies*, series I, volume XII, part III (Washington, D.C.: Government Printing Office, 1885), 473–74.

John Pope: General Orders Nos. 5, 7, 11, July 18, 20, and 23, 1862. *The War of the Rebellion: a Compilation of the Official Records of the Union and Confederate Armies*, series I, volume XII, part II (Washington, D.C.: Government Printing Office, 1885), 50–52.

Fitz John Porter to Joseph C. G. Kennedy, July 17, 1862. Manuscript, Fitz-John Porter Papers, Manuscript Division, Library of Congress.

August Belmont to Thurlow Weed, July 20, 1862. Abraham Lincoln Papers at the Library of Congress. Transcribed and annotated by the Lincoln Studies Center, Knox College, Galesburg, Illinois.

Salmon P. Chase to Richard C. Parsons, July 20, 1862. *The Salmon P. Chase Papers: Volume III, Correspondence, 1858–March 1863*, ed. John Niven (Kent, Ohio: The Kent State University Press, 1996), 229–31. Copyright © 1996 by The Kent State University Press.

Salmon P. Chase: Journal, July 22, 1862. *The Salmon P. Chase Papers: Volume I, Journals, 1829–1872*, ed. John Niven (Kent, Ohio: The Kent State University Press, 1993), 350–52. Copyright © 1993 by The Kent State University Press.

Abraham Lincoln: First Draft of the Emancipation Proclamation, July 22, 1862. *The Collected Works of Abraham Lincoln*, volume V, ed. Roy P. Basler (New Brunswick, N.J.: Rutgers University Press, 1953), 336–37. Copyright © 1953 by the Abraham Lincoln Association.

Francis B. Carpenter: from *Six Months at the White House with Abraham Lincoln*. F. B. Carpenter, *Six Months at the White House with Abraham Lincoln: The Story of a Picture* (New York: Hurd and Houghton, 1866), 20–22.

Abraham Lincoln to Cuthbert Bullitt, July 28, 1862. *The Collected Works of Abraham Lincoln*, volume V, ed. Roy P. Basler (New

Brunswick, N.J.: Rutgers University Press, 1953), 344–46. Copyright © 1953 by the Abraham Lincoln Association.

Charles Sumner to John Bright, August 5, 1862. *The Selected Letters of Charles Sumner*, Volume II, ed. Beverly Wilson Palmer (Boston: Northeastern University Press, 1990), 121–22. Copyright © 1990 by Beverly Wilson Palmer; copyright © 1990 by University Press of New England, Lebanon, N.H. Reprinted with permission.

Henry W. Halleck to George B. McClellan, August 6, 1862. *The War of the Rebellion: A Compilation of the Official Records of the Union and Confederate Armies*, series I, volume XI, part I (Washington, D.C.: Government Printing Office, 1884), 82–84.

Memorial of a Committee of Citizens of Liberty County, Georgia, August 5, 1862. *The War of the Rebellion: A Compilation of the Official Records of the Union and Confederate Armies*, series IV, volume II (Washington, D.C.: Government Printing Office, 1900), 35–38.

Confederate War Department: General Orders No. 60, August 21, 1862. *The War of the Rebellion: A Compilation of the Official Records of the Union and Confederate Armies*, series III, volume V (Washington, D.C.: Government Printing Office, 1900), 712.

Abraham Lincoln: Address on Colonization, August 14, 1862. *The Collected Works of Abraham Lincoln*, volume V, ed. Roy P. Basler (New Brunswick, N.J.: Rutgers University Press, 1953), 370–75. Copyright © 1953 by the Abraham Lincoln Association.

Abraham Lincoln to Horace Greeley, August 22, 1862. *The Collected Works of Abraham Lincoln*, volume V, ed. Roy P. Basler (New Brunswick, N.J.: Rutgers University Press, 1953), 388–89. Copyright © 1953 by the Abraham Lincoln Association.

William T. Sherman to Thomas Hunton, August 24, 1862. *Sherman's Civil War: Selected Correspondence of William T. Sherman, 1860–1865*, ed. Brooks D. Simpson and Jean V. Berlin (Chapel Hill: The University of North Carolina Press, 1999), 284–86. Copyright © 1999 by The University of North Carolina Press. Used by permission of the publisher.

John Lothrop Motley to William H. Seward, August 26, 1862. Manuscript, William Henry Seward Papers, University of Rochester.

Harriet Jacobs to William Lloyd Garrison, September 5, 1862. *The Harriet Jacobs Family Papers*, Volume II, ed. Jean Fagan Yellin (Chapel Hill: The University of North Carolina Press, 2008), 399–407. Copyright © 2008 by Jean Fagan Yellin. Used by permission of The University of North Carolina Press.

Edward Porter Alexander: from *Fighting for the Confederacy*. *Fighting for the Confederacy: The Personal Recollections of General Edward Porter Alexander*, ed. Gary W. Gallagher (Chapel Hill: The University of North Carolina Press, 1989), 127–34. Copyright © 1989 The University of North Carolina Press.

Charles Francis Adams Jr. to Charles Francis Adams, August 27, 1862. *A Cycle of Adams Letters, 1861–1865*, volume I, ed. Worthington Chauncey Ford (Boston: Houghton Mifflin Company, 1920), 176–80.

John Hampden Chamberlayne to Martha Burwell Chamberlayne, September 6, 1862. *Ham Chamberlayne—Virginian: Letters and Papers of an Artillery Officer in the War for Southern Independence 1861–1865*, ed. C. G. Chamberlayne (Richmond, Virginia: Dietz Printing Co., 1932), 98–103. Copyright 1932 by C. G. Chamberlayne.

John Pope to Henry W. Halleck, September 1, 1862. *The War of the Rebellion: A Compilation of the Official Records of the Union and Confederate Armies*, series I, volume XII, part II (Washington, D.C.: Government Printing Office, 1884), 82–83.

Clara Barton to John Shaver, September 4, 1862. Manuscript, Clara Barton Papers, Henry E. Huntington Library, San Marino, California.

Gideon Welles: Diary, August 31–September 1, 1862. *Diary of Gideon Welles*, volume I, ed. Howard K. Beale (New York: W. W. Norton & Company, Inc., 1960), 93–104. Copyright © 1960 by W. W. Norton & Company, Inc.

John Hay: Diary, September 1, 1862. *Inside Lincoln's White House: The Complete Civil War Diary of John Hay*, ed. Michael Burlingame and John R. Turner Ettlinger (Carbondale and Edwardsville: Southern Illinois University Press, 1997), 36–38. Copyright © 1997 by the Board of Trustees, Southern Illinois University.

Edward Bates: Remonstrance and Notes on Cabinet Meeting, September 2, 1862. Manuscript, Abraham Lincoln Papers, Library of Congress.

Salmon P. Chase: Journal, September 2, 1862. *The Salmon P. Chase Papers: Volume I, Journals, 1829–1872*, ed. John Niven (Kent, Ohio: The Kent State University Press, 1993), 368–69. Copyright © 1993 by The Kent State University Press.

George B. McClellan to Mary Ellen McClellan, September 2, 1862. *The Civil War Papers of George B. McClellan: Selected Correspondence, 1860–1865*, ed. Stephen W. Sears (New York: Ticknor & Fields, 1989), 428. Copyright © 1989 by Stephen W. Sears. Reprinted with permission by Stephen W. Sears.

Robert E. Lee to Jefferson Davis, September 3, 1862. *The Papers of Jefferson Davis*, volume VIII, ed. Lynda Lasswell Crist and Mary Seaton Dix (Baton Rouge: Louisiana State University Press, 1995), 373–74. Copyright © 1995 by Louisiana State University Press.

George Templeton Strong: Diary, September 3–4, 1862. George

Templeton Strong, *Diary of the Civil War, 1860–1865*, ed. Allan Nevins (New York: The Macmillan Company, 1962), 251–53. Reprinted with permission of Scribner, a Division of Simon & Schuster, Inc., from *The Diary of George Templeton Strong* by Allan Nevins and Milton Halsey Thomas.

William Thompson Lusk to Elizabeth Freeman Lusk, September 6, 1862. *War Letters of William Thompson Lusk*, ed. William C. Lusk (New York: [privately printed], 1911), 188–90.

Abraham Lincoln: Meditation on the Divine Will, c. early September 1862. *The Collected Works of Abraham Lincoln*, volume V, ed. Roy P. Basler (New Brunswick, N.J.: Rutgers University Press, 1953), 403–4. Copyright © 1953 by the Abraham Lincoln Association.

Lord Palmerston and Lord Russell: An Exchange, September 14, 17, and 23, 1862. Spencer Walpole, *The Life of Lord John Russell*, volume II (London: Longmans, Green, and Co., 1889), 349–50.

Robert E. Lee to Jefferson Davis, September 8, 1862. *The Wartime Papers of Robert E. Lee*, ed. Clifford Dowdey and Louis H. Manarin (Boston: Little, Brown, 1961), 301. Copyright © 1961 by Commonwealth of Virginia. Reprinted by permission of the National Archives.

Lewis H. Steiner: Diary, September 5–6, 1862. *Report of Lewis H. Steiner, M.D., Inspector of the Sanitary Commission, containing a diary kept during the rebel occupation of Frederick, Md., and an account of the operations of the U.S. Sanitary Commission during the campaign in Maryland, September 1862* (New York: Anson D. F. Randolph, 1862), 5–11.

James Richmond Boulware: Diary, September 4–14, 1862. Typed transcription, Library of Virginia, Richmond.

Alpheus S. Williams to George B. McClellan, September 13, 1862; Robert E. Lee: Special Orders No. 191, September 9, 1862. Manuscript, George B. McClellan Papers, Library of Congress.

George W. Smalley: Narrative of Antietam, September 17, 1862. *The Rebellion Record: A Diary of American Events, with Documents, Narratives, Illustrative Incidents, Poetry, etc.*, volume V, ed. Frank Moore (New York: G. P. Putnam, 1863), 466–72.

Rufus R. Dawes: from *Service with the Sixth Wisconsin Volunteers.* Rufus R. Dawes, *Service with the Sixth Wisconsin Volunteers* (Marietta, Ohio: E. R. Alderman & Sons, 1890), 87–92.

Alpheus S. Williams to Irene and Mary Williams, September 22, 1862. *From the Cannon's Mouth: The Civil War Letters of Alpheus S. Williams*, ed. Milo M. Quaife (Detroit: Wayne State University Press, 1959), 122–32.

David L. Thompson: With Burnside at Antietam. *Battles and Leaders of the Civil War*, volume II, ed. Robert Underwood Johnson and Clarence Clough Buel (New York: The Century Co., 1887), 660–62.

Samuel W. Fiske to the *Springfield Republican*, September 20, 1862. *Mr. Dunn Browne's Experiences in the Army: The Civil War Letters of Samuel W. Fiske*, ed. Stephen W. Sears (New York: Fordham University Press, 1998), 10–12. Copyright © 1998 by Stephen W. Sears. Reprinted with permission by Stephen W. Sears.

Clifton Johnson: from *Battleground Adventures.* Clifton Johnson, *Battleground Adventures: The Stories of Dwellers on the Scenes of Conflict in Some of the Most Notable Battles of the Civil War* (Boston: Houghton Mifflin Company, 1915), 118–24.

Mary Bedinger Mitchell: A Woman's Recollections of Antietam. *Battles and Leaders of the Civil War*, volume II, ed. Robert Underwood Johnson and Clarence Clough Buel (New York: The Century Co., 1887), 686–95.

George B. McClellan to Mary Ellen McClellan, September 20, 1862. *The Civil War Papers of George B. McClellan: Selected Correspondence, 1860–1865*, ed. Stephen W. Sears (New York: Ticknor & Fields, 1989), 473. Copyright © 1989 by Stephen W. Sears. Reprinted with permission by Stephen W. Sears.

Ephraim Anderson: from *Memoirs: Historical and Personal.* Ephraim McD. Anderson, *Memoirs: Historical and Personal; including the campaigns of the First Missouri Confederate Brigade* (St. Louis, Times Printing Co., 1868), 239–44.

Gideon Welles: Diary, September 22, 1862. *Diary of Gideon Welles*, volume I, ed. Howard K. Beale (New York: W. W. Norton & Company, Inc., 1960), 142–45. Copyright © 1960 by W. W. Norton & Company, Inc.

Abraham Lincoln: Preliminary Emancipation Proclamation, September 22, 1862; Proclamation Suspending the Writ of Habeas Corpus, September 24, 1862. *The Collected Works of Abraham Lincoln*, volume V, ed. Roy P. Basler (New Brunswick, N.J.: Rutgers University Press, 1953), 433–36, 436–37. Copyright © 1953 by the Abraham Lincoln Association.

L. A. Whitely to James Gordon Bennett, September 24, 1862. Manuscript, James Gordon Bennett Papers, Library of Congress.

George B. McClellan to William H. Aspinwall, September 26, 1862. *The Civil War Papers of George B. McClellan: Selected Correspondence, 1860–1865*, ed. Stephen W. Sears (New York: Ticknor & Fields, 1989), 482. Copyright © 1989 by Stephen W. Sears. Reprinted with permission by Stephen W. Sears.

Abraham Lincoln: Record of Dismissal of John J. Key, September 26–27, 1862. *The Collected Works of Abraham Lincoln*, volume V, ed. Roy P. Basler (New Brunswick, N.J.: Rutgers University Press, 1953), 442–43. Copyright © 1953 by the Abraham Lincoln Association.

Fitz John Porter to Manton Marble, September 30, 1862. Manuscript, Manton Marble Papers, Library of Congress.

Braxton Bragg: To the People of the Northwest, September 26, 1862. *The War of the Rebellion: A Compilation of the Official Records of the Union and Confederate Armies*, series I, volume LII, part II (Washington, D.C.: Government Printing Office, 1898), 363–65.

Ralph Waldo Emerson: The President's Proclamation, September 1862. *The Atlantic Monthly*, November 1862.

Frederick Douglass: Emancipation Proclaimed, October 1862. *The Life and Writings of Frederick Douglass*, ed. Philip S. Foner, volume III (New York: International Publishers Co. Inc., 1952), 273–77. Copyright © 1950. Reprinted from *The Life and Writings of Frederick Douglass*, published by International Publishers, copyright © 1950.

Appleton's Annual Cyclopedia: Debate in the Confederate Senate on Retaliation for the Emancipation Proclamation, September 29, October 1, 1862. *The American Annual Cyclopedia and Register of Important Events of the Year 1862*, volume II (New York: D. Appleton & Company, 1863), 268–70.

The Times of London: Editorial on the Emancipation Proclamation, October 7, 1862. *The Times*, October 7, 1862.

George B. McClellan to Abraham Lincoln, October 7, 1862. *The Civil War Papers of George B. McClellan: Selected Correspondence, 1860–1865*, ed. Stephen W. Sears (New York: Ticknor & Fields, 1989), 493–94. Copyright © 1989 by Stephen W. Sears. Reprinted with permission by Stephen W. Sears.

Oscar L. Jackson: from *The Colonel's Diary*. *The Colonel's Diary: Journals Kept Before and During the Civil War by the Late Colonel Oscar L. Jackson of New Castle, Pennsylvania, Sometime Commander of the 63rd O.V.I.*, ed. David P. Jackson (Sharon, Pennsylvania: 1922), 71–78.

Charles B. Labruzan: Journal, October 4, 1862. Marion Morrison, *A History of the Ninth Regiment Illinois Volunteer Infantry* (Monmouth, Illinois: John S. Clark, Printer, 1864), 40–43.

J. Montgomery Wright: Notes of a Staff-Officer at Perryville. *Battles and Leaders of the Civil War*, volume III, ed. Robert Underwood Johnson and Clarence Clough Buel (New York: The Century Co., 1888), 60–61.

Sam Watkins: from *"Co. Aytch," Maury Grays, First Tennessee Regiment*. Sam R. Watkins, *"Co. Aytch," Maury Grays, First Tennessee Regiment, or, A Side Show of the Big Show* (Nashville, Tennessee: Cumberland Presbyterian Publishing House, 1882), 50–57.

Abraham Lincoln to George B. McClellan, October 13, 1862. *The Collected Works of Abraham Lincoln*, volume V, ed. Roy P. Basler (New Brunswick, N.J.: Rutgers University Press, 1953), 460–61. Copyright © 1953 by the Abraham Lincoln Association.

Lord Palmerston to Lord Russell, October 2 and 22, 1862. *The Later Correspondence of Lord John Russell, 1840–1878*, ed. G. P. Gooch (London: Longmans, Green and Co., 1925), 326–28.

Charles Sumner to John Bright, October 28, 1862. *The Selected Letters of Charles Sumner*, volume II, ed. Beverly Wilson Palmer (Boston: Northeastern University Press, 1990), 127–28. Copyright © 1990 by Beverly Wilson Palmer; copyright 1990 © University Press of New England, Lebanon, N.H. Reprinted with permission.

Francis Preston Blair to Montgomery Blair, November 7, 1862. William Ernest Smith, *The Francis Preston Blair Family in Politics*, volume II (New York: The Macmillan Company, 1933), 144. Copyright © 1933 by The Macmillan Company.

George G. Meade to Margaret Meade, November 8, 1862. Manuscript, George Gordon Meade Papers, Historical Society of Pennsylvania, Philadelphia.

Orville H. Browning: Diary, November 29, 1862. *The Diary of Orville Hickman Browning*, volume I, ed. Theodore Calvin Pease and James G. Randall (Springfield: Illinois State Historical Library, 1925), 588–90. Copyright © 1927 by the Illinois State Historical Library.

Abraham Lincoln: Annual Message to Congress, December 1, 1862. *The Collected Works of Abraham Lincoln*, volume V, ed. Roy P. Basler (New Brunswick, N.J.: Rutgers University Press, 1953), 518–37. Copyright © 1953 by the Abraham Lincoln Association.

Edward Porter Alexander: from *Fighting for the Confederacy*. *Fighting for the Confederacy: The Personal Recollections of General Edward Porter Alexander*, ed. Gary W. Gallagher (Chapel Hill: The University of North Carolina Press, 1989), 166–79. Copyright © 1989 by The University of North Carolina Press.

Samuel W. Fiske to the *Springfield Republican*, December 15 and 17, 1862. *Mr. Dunn Browne's Experiences in the Army: The Civil War Letters of Samuel W. Fiske*, ed. Stephen W. Sears (New York: Fordham University Press, 1998), 49–51. Copyright © 1998 by Stephen W. Sears. Reprinted with permission by Stephen W. Sears.

Henry Livermore Abbott to Josiah Gardner Abbott, December 14, 1862, and to George Perry, December 17, 1862. Manuscripts, Abbott Family Civil War Letters (MS Am 800.26). Houghton Library, Harvard University, series III, folder 17. Reprinted by permission of the Houghton Library, Harvard University, MS Am 800.26.

Clifton Johnson: from *Battleground Adventures*. Clifton Johnson, *Battleground Adventures: The Stories of Dwellers on the Scenes of Con-*

flict in Some of the Most Notable Battles of the Civil War (Boston: Houghton Mifflin Company, 1915), 143–49.

Walt Whitman: from *Specimen Days. Walt Whitman: Complete Poetry and Collected Prose*, ed. Justin Kaplan (New York: The Library of America, 1982), 712–13.

Louisa May Alcott: from *Hospital Sketches.* L. M. Alcott, *Hospital Sketches* (Boston: James Redpath, 1863), 31–45.

Orville H. Browning: Diary, December 18, 1862. *The Diary of Orville Hickman Browning*, volume I, ed. Theodore Calvin Pease and James G. Randall (Springfield: Illinois State Historical Library, 1925), 599–601. Copyright © 1927 by the Illinois State Historical Library.

Gideon Welles: Diary, December 19–20, 1862. *Diary of Gideon Welles*, volume I, ed. Howard K. Beale (New York: W. W. Norton & Company, Inc., 1960), 194–202. Copyright © 1960 by W. W. Norton & Company, Inc.

Harper's Weekly: The Reverse at Fredericksburg, December 27, 1862. *Harper's Weekly*, December 27, 1862.

George Templeton Strong: Diary, December 27, 1862. George Templeton Strong, *Diary of the Civil War, 1860–1865*, ed. Allan Nevins (New York: The Macmillan Company, 1962), 282–84. Reprinted with permission of Scribner, a Division of Simon & Schuster, Inc., from *The Diary of George Templeton Strong* by Allan Nevins and Milton Halsey Thomas. Copyright © 1952 by Macmillan Publishing Company; copyright renewed © 1980 by Milton Halsey Thomas. All rights reserved.

Fitz John Porter to Samuel L. M. Barlow, December 29, 1862. Manuscript, Samuel L. M. Barlow Papers, Henry E. Huntington Library, San Marino, California.

Cyrus F. Boyd: Diary, December 22–25, 1862. *The Civil War Diary of Cyrus F. Boyd, Fifteenth Iowa Infantry 1861–1863*, ed. Mildred Throne (Baton Rouge: Louisiana State University Press, 1998), 96–99. Copyright © 1953 by the State Historical Society of Iowa.

Jefferson Davis: Address to the Mississippi Legislature, December 26, 1862. *The Papers of Jefferson Davis*, volume VIII, ed. Lynda Lasswell Crist and Mary Seaton Dix (Baton Rouge: Louisiana State University Press, 1995), 565–79. Copyright © 1995 by Louisiana State University Press.

William T. Sherman to John Sherman, January 6, 1863. *Sherman's Civil War: Selected Correspondence of William T. Sherman, 1860–1865*, ed. Brooks D. Simpson and Jean V. Berlin (Chapel Hill: The University of North Carolina Press, 1999), 351–53. Copyright © 1999 by The University of North Carolina Press. Used by permission of the publisher.

Samuel Sawyer et al. to Samuel R. Curtis, December 29, 1862. *Free at*

Last: A Documentary History of Slavery, Freedom, and the Civil War, ed. Ira Berlin, Barbara J. Fields, Steven F. Miller, Joseph P. Reidy, and Leslie S. Rowland (New York: The New Press, 1992), 180–82. Copyright © 1992 by The New Press. Reprinted by permission of The New Press.

Ira S. Owens: from *Greene County in the War*. Ira S. Owens, *Greene County in the War, Being a History of the Seventy Fourth regiment, with sketches of the Twelfth, Ninety Fourth, One Hundred and Tenth, Forty Fourth, and One Hundred and Fifty Fourth Regiments and the Tenth Ohio Battery, embracing anecdotes, incidents and narratives of the camp, march and battlefield, and the author's experiences while in the army* (Xenia, Ohio: Torchlight Job Rooms, 1872), 30–35.

Lot D. Young: from *Reminiscences of a Soldier of the Orphan Brigade*. L. D. Young, *Reminiscences of a Soldier of the Orphan Brigade* (Louisville, Kentucky: Courier-Journal Job Printing Company, 1918), 45–51.

Ambrose E. Burnside to Abraham Lincoln, January 1, 1863. *The War of the Rebellion: A Compilation of the Official Records of the Union and Confederate Armies*, series I, volume XXI (Washington, D.C.: Government Printing Office, 1888), 941–42.

Abraham Lincoln to Henry W. Halleck, January 1, 1863. *The Collected Works of Abraham Lincoln*, volume VI, ed. Roy P. Basler (New Brunswick, N.J.: Rutgers University Press, 1953), 31. Copyright © 1953 by the Abraham Lincoln Association.

Abraham Lincoln: Final Emancipation Proclamation, January 1, 1863. *The Collected Works of Abraham Lincoln*, volume VI, ed. Roy P. Basler (New Brunswick, N.J.: Rutgers University Press, 1953), 28–30. Copyright © 1953 by the Abraham Lincoln Association.

Benjamin Rush Plumly to Abraham Lincoln, January 1, 1863. Manuscript, Abraham Lincoln Papers, Library of Congress.

Abraham Lincoln to John A. McClernand, January 8, 1863. *The Collected Works of Abraham Lincoln*, volume VI, ed. Roy P. Basler (New Brunswick, N.J.: Rutgers University Press, 1953), 48–49. Copyright © 1953 by the Abraham Lincoln Association.

This volume presents the texts of the printings and manuscripts chosen as sources here but does not attempt to reproduce features of their typographic design or physical layout. The texts are printed without alteration except for the changes previously discussed and for the correction of typographical errors. Spelling, punctuation, and capitalization are often expressive features, and they are not altered, even when inconsistent or irregular. The following is a list of typographical errors corrected, cited by page and line number: 8.30–31, Chandler Wade,; 31.40, Mondy; 86.3, wants; 105.33, Seigel's; 115.5, silenced; 116.11, killed; 161.19, danger; 169.17, We are; 170.14, the the next; 286.20, the he; 303.22, heart.; 305.11, Steven's; 335.23, us.?; 359.19–20, Government from; 363.4, P. W.; 406.10, description; 426.25, holding"; 455.8, rick; 526.28, we we would; 567.27, warefare; 568.20, onthe; 584.32, Casey, and; 594.3, solder; 615.28, McLellan; 616.10, Hallack; 680.22, comfortable There; 684.2, replied Some; 684.17, said Why; 708.33, to even; 720.34, he he; 735.1, pointing; 735.2, and; 737.1, lay,.

Notes

In the notes below, the reference numbers denote page and line of this volume (the line count includes headings, but not rule lines). No note is made for material included in the eleventh edition of *Merriam-Webster's Collegiate Dictionary*. Biblical references are keyed to the King James Version. Quotations from Shakespeare are keyed to *The Riverside Shakespeare*, ed. G. Blakemore Evans (Boston: Houghton Mifflin, 1974). Footnotes and bracketed editorial notes within the text were in the originals. For further historical and biographical background, references to other studies, and more detailed maps, see James McPherson, *Battle Cry of Freedom: The Civil War Era* (New York: Oxford University Press, 1988); *Encyclopedia of the American Civil War: A Political, Social, and Military History*, edited by David S. Heidler and Jeanne T. Heidler (New York: W. W. Norton, 2002); and Aaron Sheehan-Dean, *Concise Historical Atlas of the U.S. Civil War* (New York: Oxford University Press, 2008).

5.35 *"O hasten it in mercy, gracious Heaven!"*] Cf. "Universal Emancipation," a poem by William Lloyd Garrison that appeared in the first number of his newspaper *The Liberator*, January 1, 1831: "Oh! hasten it, *in mercy*, righteous Heaven!"

8.21–24 the Road . . . Lander] During a raid on the Baltimore and Ohio Railroad, Confederate troops led by Major General Thomas J. (Stonewall) Jackson shelled Hancock, Maryland, on the upper Potomac River, January 5–6, 1862, before withdrawing. Brigadier General Frederick W. Lander (1821–1862) commanded the troops defending Hancock; Major General Nathaniel P. Banks (1816–1894) commanded a division in the Army of the Potomac.

8.30–31 Chandler Wade . . . Covode] Zachariah Chandler (1813–1879) was a Republican senator from Michigan, 1857–75, and secretary of the interior, 1875–77; Benjamin F. Wade (1800–1878) was a Whig and then a Republican senator from Ohio, 1851–69, and chairman of the Joint Committee on the Conduct of the War, 1861–65; Andrew Johnson (1808–1875) was a Democratic senator from Tennessee, 1857–62, military governor of Tennessee, 1862–64, vice president of the United States, 1864–65, and president, 1865–69; Moses Odell (1818–1866) was a Democratic congressman from New York, 1861–65; John Covode (1808–1871) was a Republican congressman from Pennsylvania, 1855–63 and 1867–71.

11.9 Patterson] Robert Patterson (1792–1881) commanded the Union forces in the Shenandoah Valley in July 1861. His failure to engage General Joseph E. Johnston (1807–1891) allowed Johnston to send most of his troops from Winchester to Manassas Junction, Virginia, in time for them to fight at First Bull Run.

20.16 Caudine Forks] A valley in southern Italy where the Samnites trapped a Roman army in 321 B.C.E. and forced it to surrender its arms and then march under a yoke of crossed spears.

20.28 Sherman] Brigadier General Thomas W. Sherman (1813–1879) commanded the Union troops that captured Port Royal, South Carolina, in November 1861.

25.24 Sanitary Commission] The United States Sanitary Commission, founded in June 1861, was a civilian organization dedicated to improving conditions in Union army camps and caring for sick and wounded soldiers. It was based on the British Sanitary Commission in the Crimean War.

26.9 My dear minister] James Freeman Clarke (1810–1888), Unitarian minister of the Church of the Disciples in Boston.

29.11 Fort Lafayette] The fortress, built on an island off Brooklyn at the entrance to New York harbor, was used as a military prison during the Civil War.

31.3 Gen. BANKS] See note 8.21–24.

32.24 veil of Isis] The Greek historian Plutarch wrote that the shrine of Isis at Sais in Egypt bore the inscription: "I am all that hath been, and is, and shall be; and my veil no mortal has hitherto raised."

36.10 General John A. McClernand] Brigadier General John A. McClernand (1812–1900) commanded one of the three Union divisions investing Fort Donelson. McClernand had served in Congress as a Democrat from Illinois, 1843–51 and 1859–61.

37.11–12 Colonel Morgan L. Smith] Smith (1822–1874) commanded a brigade in the division of Brigadier General Charles F. Smith.

37.22 Cruft's return] Colonel Charles Cruft (1826–1883) commanded a brigade in Wallace's division.

37.26 General Charles F. Smith] Brigadier General Charles F. Smith (1807–1862) commanded one of Grant's three divisions investing Fort Donelson.

37.32 Ross] Lieutenant James R. Ross (1841–1900).

38.2 Colonel Ross] Colonel Leonard F. Ross (1823–1901), who commanded one of the brigades in McClernand's division.

39.8–9 Colonel Morrison's misassault of the 14th] Colonel William R. Morrison (1824–1909), commanding a brigade in McClernand's division, was wounded in a failed attack on the Fort Donelson lines on February 14.

39.19 the Lindell] A large hotel in St. Louis, Missouri.

39.40 McGinnis] Colonel George F. McGinnis (1826–1910) commanded the 11th Indiana Infantry, Morgan L. Smith's brigade, Charles F. Smith's division.

42.22 Kneffler] Captain Fred Knefler (1833–1901), Wallace's assistant adjutant general.

42.31 Colonel Webster] Colonel Joseph D. Webster (1811–1876), Grant's chief of staff and chief engineer.

49.40 file closers] Soldiers assigned to prevent straggling or fleeing during an advance.

50.38 Gen. Floyd] Brigadier General John B. Floyd (1806–1863) commanded the Confederate garrison at Fort Donelson from February 13 until the early hours of February 16, 1862, when he escaped on a riverboat, leaving Brigadier General Simon Bolivar Buckner to surrender the fort to Grant.

54.15 Rawlins, and McPherson] Captain John A. Rawlins (1831–1869) and Lieutenant Colonel James B. McPherson (1828–1864) of Grant's staff.

55.15 *avant-courrier*] Herald, scout, advance guard.

60.35 Columbiad] A heavy smoothbore cannon.

65.9 Commander Stembel] Commander Roger N. Stembel (1810–1900), captain of the gunboat *Lexington*.

65.26 the renowned *Arkansas*] An ironclad ram laid down at Memphis in October 1861 and completed at Yazoo City, Mississippi, in July 1862. The *Carondelet* was badly damaged in a battle with the *Arkansas* on the Yazoo River on July 15, 1862. After running past the Union fleet at Vicksburg, the *Arkansas* went downriver to Baton Rouge, Louisiana, where it was scuttled on August 6, 1862, after its engines broke down.

68.28 "spliced the main brace."] Received a ration of liquor.

73.4 Colonel Ellet's] A civil engineer known for his work on canals, railroads, and suspension bridges, Charles Ellet (1810–1862) was authorized by Secretary of War Edwin M. Stanton in March 1862 to convert nine Ohio River steamboats into unarmed rams.

75.15–16 Colonel Ellet . . . in the leg] Ellet died from his wounds on June 21, 1862.

75.31 General Jeff. Thompson] Merriwether Jeff Thompson (1826–1876) led Confederate partisans in southeastern Missouri and northeastern Arkansas.

78.20 at Pensacola] The steam frigate U.S.S. *Niagara* and steam sloop U.S.S. *Richmond* bombarded Pensacola, November 22–23, 1861.

80.19 Gen. Huger] Major General Benjamin Huger (1805–1877), the Confederate commander at Norfolk, Virginia.

80.21 Gen. Wise] Brigadier General Henry A. Wise (1806–1876), a former governor of Virginia, 1856–60, and prominent advocate of secession in 1861.

80.29 Capt. O. Jennings Wise] Wise (1831–1862), son of Henry Wise and coeditor of the *Richmond Enquirer*, was mortally wounded at Roanoke Island on February 8, 1862.

80.30 A thousand of the enemy fell] Union casualties in the battle totaled 264 men killed, wounded, or missing.

81.12 President Tyler] John Tyler (1790–1862), president of the United States, 1841–1845, had died on January 18.

81.13 Mr. Hunter] Robert M. T. Hunter (1809–1887) served as the Confederate secretary of state, 1861–62, and in the Confederate Senate, 1862–65. Hunter had earlier been a congressman from Virginia, 1837–43 and 1845–47, and a U.S. senator, 1847–61.

82.6 Benjamin] Judah P. Benjamin (1811–1884) served as the Confederate secretary of war, September 1861–March 1862, and as secretary of state from March 1862 until the end of the war. Benjamin had earlier been a U.S. senator from Louisiana, 1853–61.

82.22 Mr. Hunter has resigned] Hunter resigned as secretary of state to serve in the Confederate Congress.

83.17 the old general in command] Brigadier General John H. Winder (1800–1865), the Confederate provost marshal.

89.25–26 Professor Lowe . . . usual daily balloon reconnaissance] Thaddeus Sobieski Constantine Lowe (1832–1913) was chief of the Union army balloon corps, October 1861–May 1863. His balloon *Constitution* was posted at Budd's Ferry, Maryland, on the lower Potomac.

90.12–13 Colonel Graham . . . inroad into Virginia.] A force of four hundred men led by Colonel Charles K. Graham (1824–1889) of the 74th New York Infantry crossed the Potomac from Maryland on November 9, 1861, and carried out a successful reconnaissance of Mathias Point in Virginia. The Union troops returned with between thirty and forty escaped slaves.

93.34–94.1 Bancroft's History . . . Hardee's Tactics] George Bancroft (1800–1891), *History of the United States* (10 vols., 1834–74; eight volumes had appeared by 1862); William J. Hardee (1815–1873), *Rifle and Light Infantry Tactics* (1855).

94.31 Secretary's order to the press] Secretary of War Edwin M. Stanton issued an order on February 26, 1862, forbidding newspapers that published unauthorized military news from using the telegraph or distributing their publications by railroad.

94.39 Mason, Slidell, Yancey] James M. Mason (1798–1871), Confederate envoy to Great Britain, 1861–1865; John Slidell (1793–1871), Confederate envoy to France, 1861–65; William Lowndes Yancey (1814–1863), Confederate diplomatic commissioner in Britain and France, 1861–62, and a prominent advocate of secession during the 1850s.

95.39 correspondent of the London Times] William Howard Russell (1820–1907) reported on the secession crisis and the Civil War from March 1861 to April 1862, when he returned to England. His description of "the disgraceful conduct" of the Union troops at First Bull Run was denounced in the Northern press.

98.1–2 cabbage . . . Minister to Russia immediately."] Secretary of War Simon Cameron (1799–1889) resigned in January 1862 amid charges of widespread corruption in the War Department and was appointed minister to Russia by President Lincoln.

100.8–10 General Price . . . Springfield, or Oakhill] Major General Sterling Price (1809–1867) led troops of the pro-secession Missouri State Guard in the Confederate victory at Wilson's Creek (also called Oak Hill) in Missouri on August 10, 1861.

100.12 General McCulloch] Brigadier General Benjamin McCulloch (1811–1862) was the Confederate commander at Wilson's Creek.

100.14 Generals Curtis and Siegel] Brigadier General Samuel R. Curtis (1805–1866) and Brigadier General Franz Sigel (1824–1902).

102.1–2 quake as . . . Cæsar did] See *Julius Caesar*, I.ii.119–28.

104.2 *chasse*] Chaser.

108.14 Pelham] John Pelham (1838–1863) was an artillery officer in the Army of Northern Virginia who became known as "the gallant Pelham" after he was praised by Robert E. Lee for his courage at the battle of Fredericksburg. He was killed in action at Kelly's Ford, Virginia, on March 17, 1863.

108.25 Colonel Rives] Colonel Benjamin A. Rives (1822–1862) commanded the 3rd Missouri Infantry in the 1st Brigade of the Missouri State Guard.

110.4 *James A. McDougall*] McDougall (1817–1867) was a Democratic senator from California, 1861–67.

114.30–31 torpedoes] Floating mines.

116.31–32 Flag-Officer . . . his brother] Franklin Buchanan (1800–1874), the senior officer on board the *Virginia*, was commander of the Chesapeake Bay Squadron. McKean Buchanan (1798–1871) served as paymaster of the U.S.S. *Congress*.

117.29 the Ericsson] The *Monitor* was designed and built by the Swedish-American engineer John Ericsson (1803–1889).

121.29–31 a deputation . . . splendid whip.] Lincoln met with the delegation on March 13, 1862.

121.33 Major Ben Perley Poore] Journalist and writer Benjamin Perley Poore (1820–1887), Washington correspondent of the *Boston Journal*, had served briefly as a major with the 6th Massachusetts Regiment in 1861.

122.17 in the passage-way; and in lounged] In the *Atlantic Monthly* this appeared as "in the passage-way, etc., etc.*" The text that follows from 122.17 ("and in lounged . . .") to 124.38 (". . . immaculate page of the Atlantic") was deleted, and the footnote that appears on 125.33–38 was moved forward to where the passage had been removed.

124.27 he accepted the whip . . . not punishment.] As reported in *The New York Times* on March 22, 1862, Lincoln told the delegation: "let us not think only of whipping rebels, or of those who seem to think only of whipping negroes, but of those pleasant days which it is to be hoped are in store for us, when, seated behind a good pair of horses, we can crack our whips and drive through a peaceful, happy, and prosperous land."

125.33–34 *We hesitated to . . . have been written] In the *Atlantic Monthly* this read: "We are compelled to omit two or three pages, in which the author describes the interview, and gives his idea of the personal appearance and deportment of the President. The sketch appears to have been written . . ."

127.3–4 tavern in which Colonel Ellsworth was killed] During the Union occupation of Alexandria on May 24, 1861, Colonel Elmer Ellsworth (1837–1861), the commander of the 11th New York Infantry, took down a Confederate flag that was flying from the roof of the Marshall House hotel. On his way down the stairs Ellsworth was confronted by James Jackson, the hotel's proprietor, who killed him with a shotgun. Jackson was then shot and bayoneted by a corporal in Ellsworth's regiment. The incident was widely publicized, and both Ellsworth and Jackson were considered martyrs by their respective sides in the conflict.

131.1 report of a Congressional committee] On April 30, 1862, the Joint Committee on the Conduct of the War issued a report on the Confederate treatment of the graves of Union soldiers killed at First Bull Run. It contained the widely reported allegation that a New Orleans artilleryman had taken the skull of a Union soldier for use as a drinking cup on his wedding day.

133.31–36 *Apparently with . . . out the passage.] This footnote was omitted in the *Atlantic Monthly*.

137.1 Commodore Smith] Commodore Joseph Smith (1790–1877), a veteran of the War of 1812, was the father of Lieutenant Joseph Bryant Smith (1826–1862), acting commander of the *Congress*, who was killed on March 8, 1862, during the battle with the *Virginia*.

137.5 the gallant Morris] Lieutenant George U. Morris (1830–1875), executive officer of *Cumberland*, commanded the ship in its fight with the *Virginia*; when called upon to surrender, he replied, "Never! I'll sink alongside!"

137.10 Old Ironsides] The frigate *Constitution*, famous for its service in the War of 1812.

137.27 the brave Worden] Lieutenant John L. Worden (1818–1875) commanded the *Monitor* during its battle with the *Virginia* until he was temporarily blinded by a shell burst.

141.25 In December] On November 8, 1861, Captain Charles Wilkes of the U.S.S. *San Jacinto* boarded the British mail packet *Trent* off Cuba and seized the Confederate envoys James M. Mason and John Slidell (see note 94.39). The incident caused a major diplomatic crisis that continued until the Lincoln administration decided on December 26 to release the envoys in order to avoid a possible war with Great Britain.

142.3–4 *Louise and Frances Norcross*] Louise (1842–1919) and Frances Norcross (1847–1896) were Emily Dickinson's cousins, the daughters of her mother's sister Lavinia Norcross (1812–1860).

142.5 Late March 1862] The funeral of Frazar Stearns (1840–1862) was held on March 22, 1862.

142.22 Professor Clark] Lieutenant Colonel William S. Clark (1826–1886) of the 21st Massachusetts Infantry was professor of chemistry, botany, and zoology at Amherst College, 1852–67, and president of Massachusetts Agricultural College (now University of Massachusetts, Amherst), 1867–79.

142.30 his father.] William A. Stearns (1805–1876), president of Amherst College, 1854–76.

143.9 Austin] William Austin Dickinson (1829–1895), Emily Dickinson's brother.

146.23 a shot at one of our ships] On January 9, 1861, South Carolina batteries opened fire on *Star of the West*, a chartered civilian steamer carrying reinforcements and supplies to Fort Sumter in Charleston Harbor. The ship withdrew without casualties, and the Fort Sumter garrison did not return fire.

146.39–40 blood thirsty mob . . . Baltimore treason.] A secessionist mob attacked the 6th Massachusetts Regiment as it changed trains in Baltimore on its way to Washington, D.C., on April 19, 1861. Four soldiers and a dozen Baltimore civilians were killed in the fighting, the first fatal casualties of the war.

147.30–31 marshalling the savage Indian . . . your sons] In 1861 the Confederacy formed alliances with the Cherokee, Creek, Choctaw, Chickasaw, and Seminole tribes living in Indian Territory (later Oklahoma), and about eight hundred Cherokees fought with the Confederate army at Elkhorn Tavern (Pea Ridge), Arkansas, March 7–8, 1862. After the battle the Northern press reported that "many of the Federal dead" at Pea Ridge had been scalped and mutilated.

148.2 Floyd . . . Cobb] John B. Floyd (1806–1863) served as governor of Virginia, 1848–52, before becoming secretary of war in the Buchanan administration in 1857. He resigned on December 29, 1860, after being implicated in a financial scandal, and later served as a Confederate general (see note 50.38). Floyd was accused of treason in the Northern press for transferring 115,000 muskets and rifles from Northern to Southern arsenals in the spring of 1860, and for ordering the shipment of 124 large cannon from Pittsburgh to Mississippi and Texas on December 20, 1860. (The order to transfer the artillery was canceled after his resignation.) Howell Cobb (1815–1868) was a congressman from Georgia, 1843–51 and 1855–57, and its governor, 1851–53. He served as secretary of the treasury in the Buchanan administration from 1857 until his resignation on December 10, 1860, and was subsequently accused of having deliberately undermined the national finances. Cobb supported secession in 1861 and served as a Confederate general, 1862–65.

148.5 the rod of Moses it swallowed all others] See the description of Aaron's rod in Exodus 7:10–12.

148.26 General McClellan in his recent address] See pp. 138–39 in this volume.

149.19–20 General Sherman . . . erring rebels] Following the occupation of Port Royal, Brigadier General Thomas W. Sherman issued a proclamation addressed to "the People of South Carolina" on November 8, 1861, in which he declared that the Union forces "have come amongst you with no feelings of personal animosity; no desire to harm your citizens, destroy your property, or interfere with any of your lawful rights or your social and local institutions, beyond what the causes herein briefly alluded to may render unavoidable."

151.4–5 Syracuse . . . rescue of Jerry] Jerry McHenry, a fugitive slave from Missouri, was arrested in Syracuse on October 1, 1851. A group of about thirty abolitionists who were attending a Liberty Party convention broke into the police station where he was being held and helped him flee to Canada.

151.7–8 Dr. Cheever . . . William Goodell] George B. Cheever (1807–1890), a Congregationalist minister who helped found the Church Anti-Slavery Society; Gerrit Smith (1797–1874), a philanthropist and social reformer who helped found the Liberty Party in 1840; William Goodell (1792–1878), a social reformer active in the Liberty Party.

151.15–16 slave catching . . . forbidden] A new article of war passed by Congress and signed by President Lincoln on March 13, 1862, prohibited Union officers from returning fugitive slaves.

151.32 that message] Lincoln's message to Congress of March 6, 1862; see pp. 110–12 in this volume.

152.8–9 appointment of John C. Frémont] On March 11, 1862, Major General John C. Frémont (1813–1880) was appointed commander of the Mountain Department, covering western Virginia and eastern Tennessee and Kentucky.

152.15–16 Frémont's proclamation . . . removed] Frémont issued a proclamation on August 30, 1861, declaring martial law in Missouri and emancipating the slaves of secessionists. Lincoln revoked the emancipation provision on September 11 and removed Frémont from command in Missouri on November 2.

152.18 Jessie] Jessie Benton Frémont (1824–1902).

155.18 Blencker's Division] In response to pressure from Radical Republican supporters of Frémont, Lincoln had transferred the division commanded by Brigadier General Louis Blenker (1812–1863) from McClellan's command to Frémont's Mountain Department on March 31, 1862.

155.24–25 Gen. Hooker's old position] The division commanded by Brigadier General Joseph Hooker (1814–1879) had been posted in southern Maryland along the lower Potomac.

156.18 Gen. Wool's command] Brigadier General John E. Wool (1789–1869) commanded the Department of Virginia with headquarters at Fort Monroe.

158.15 162 regiments] There were seventy-six Confederate regiments at Shiloh.

158.16–17 Beaurigard . . . Breckenridge] General Pierre G. T. Beauregard (1818–1893) assumed command of the Confederate army after General Albert Sidney Johnston (1803–1862) was killed on the afternoon of April 6. Major General Braxton Bragg (1817–1876) and Brigadier General John C. Breckinridge (1821–1875) each commanded a corps in the battle. Breckinridge had served as vice president of the United States, 1857–61, and was the Southern Democratic candidate for president in 1860.

158.19 Bragg wounded.] Bragg was not wounded at Shiloh.

159.4 A A GENL] Assistant adjutant general.

159.24 Parrott guns] Muzzle-loading rifled cannon, named after the New York ordnance manufacturer Robert R. Parrott (1804–1877).

161.4–5 Genl W H L Wallace . . . wounded.] Brigadier General W. H. L. Wallace (1821–1862) died on April 10, 1862.

162.9–10 Genl Beaurigard . . . Correspondence] Beauregard wrote to Grant on April 8, 1862, asking permission to send a mounted party to Shiloh to bury the Confederate dead. Grant replied on April 9 that the warm weather had caused him to have the dead of both sides buried immediately.

162.32 Savannah] Grant was at Savannah, Tennessee, nine miles downriver from Pittsburg Landing, when the Confederates attacked on April 6.

163.6 E. B. WASHBURN] Elihu B. Washburne (1816–1887) was a Whig, and then Republican, congressman from Illinois, 1853–69. He served as U.S. minister to France, 1869–77.

166.28 I had at Muldrough hill.] Sherman occupied Muldraugh Hill, about forty miles south of Louisville, in September 1861.

166.32 Johns Brigade] A brigade of Ohio troops recruited in the fall of 1861 by Sherman's brother, Ohio Republican senator John Sherman (1823–1900).

167.10 Gen. Greene] Major General Nathanael Greene (1742–1786), a commander in the Continental Army during the Revolutionary War.

169.14 C.] Canister.

178.34 femes-covert] Married women.

180.15 Thomas T. Craven] Craven (1808–1887) entered the U.S. Navy in 1822 and was promoted to captain in 1861.

181.10–11 Head of the Passes] The point where the main stem of the Mississippi River divides into three separate channels, or passes: Southwest Pass, South Pass, and Pass a l'Outre ("Pass Beyond").

182.28 Admiral Porter . . . in this work] David Dixon Porter (1813–1891) contributed "The Opening of the Lower Mississippi" to volume II of *Battles and Leaders of the Civil War* (1887). He was the son of naval officer David Porter (1780–1843), and David G. Farragut (1801–1870) was his adopted brother.

187.9 sponger] A member of a gun crew who cleaned out the bore of the cannon between firings with a pole-mounted sponge.

191.24 arrived at quarantine] The quarantine station upriver from Forts Jackson and St. Philip.

197.27 General Lovell] Major General Mansfield Lovell (1822–1884) commanded the Confederate troops defending New Orleans.

198.1 Pierre Soule] Pierre Soulé (1801–1870) was the Confederate provost marshal in New Orleans. He had previously served as a U.S. senator, 1849–53, and as U.S. minister to Spain, 1853–55.

199.11–13 Bramhall and Smith . . . Osborn and Webber] Captain Walter M. Bramhall of the 6th New York Artillery, Captain James E. Smith of the 4th New York Artillery, Captain Thomas W. Osborn of the 1st New York Artillery, and Captain Charles H. Webber of the 1st U.S. Artillery were Wainwright's battery commanders.

203.31 Sumner] Brigadier General Edwin V. Sumner (1797–1863) was the Union commander at Williamsburg.

203.39–40 Hancock's attack. . . . Smith's division] Brigadier General Winfield Scott Hancock (1824–1886) attacked on the right of the Union line. He commanded a brigade in the division led by Brigadier General William F. Smith (1824–1903).

204.5 our regiment] The 1st New York Light Artillery.

204.12 Taylor's brigade] Colonel Nelson Taylor (1821–1894) commanded the Second Brigade in Hooker's division.

204.15 Dwight] Colonel William Dwight (1831–1888) commanded the 70th New York Infantry in Taylor's brigade.

205.22–23 Colonel Starr . . . his regiment] Samuel H. Starr (1810–1891) commanded the 5th New Jersey Infantry.

205.37 Farnum] Lieutenant Colonel John E. Farnum (1824–1870) was second in command of the 70th New York Infantry.

206.1–2 General Heintzelman] Brigadier General Samuel P. Heintzelman (1805–1880) commanded the Third Corps of the Army of the Potomac, to which Hooker's division was assigned.

206.24 General Grover] Brigadier General Cuvier Grover (1828–1885) commanded the First Brigade in Hooker's division.

206.29 Kearny's column] Brigadier General Philip Kearny (1814–1862) commanded a division in the Third Corps.

210.29–30 *tobacco be burnt . . . law.*] The Confederate Congress passed a law on March 17, 1862, authorizing military commanders to destroy cotton and tobacco stockpiles in order to prevent them from falling into Union hands.

210.31 the Baltimore rabble] Former Baltimore policemen and detectives now working for Brigadier General John H. Winder, the Confederate provost marshal. Jones described them in his diary on August 8, 1861, as "petty larceny detectives . . . illiterate men, of low instincts and desperate characters."

211.18 Major Griswold] A provost marshal serving under General Winder.

212.10 Mr. Randolph] George W. Randolph (1818–1867) was the Confederate secretary of war, March–November 1862.

213.16 Wm H Seward] William H. Seward (1801–1872) served in the U.S. Senate, 1849–61, as a Whig and then as a Republican. He was secretary of state in the Lincoln and Andrew Johnson administrations, 1861–69.

218.17 Ewell] Major General Richard S. Ewell (1817–1872). His division was sent to reinforce Jackson in the Shenandoah Valley in early May 1862.

219.19 Colonel Alek Boteler] Alexander R. Boteler (1815–1892), a member of Jackson's staff, served in the U.S. Congress, 1859–61, and the Confederate Congress, 1862–64.

219.20 Governor of Virginia] John Letcher (1813–1884) was governor of Virginia, 1860–64.

219.21 At Kernstown] The battle was fought on March 23, 1862.

220.4–5 lived twelve miles . . . the witty Dean.] The essayist and Anglican clergyman Sydney Smith (1771–1845) described his rural parish in Yorkshire as being "so far out of the way that it was actually twelve miles from a lemon."

221.3 Belle Boyd.] Maria Isabella Boyd (1844–1900), the daughter of a Martinsburg, Virginia, shopkeeper, was living in Front Royal in the spring of 1862. She was subsequently imprisoned twice by the Union authorities for spying. In 1864 she went to England, where she published her memoir *Belle Boyd in Camp and Prison* (1865).

224.14 Capt Fox] Gustavus Vasa Fox (1821–1883) was assistant secretary of the navy, 1861–65.

224.15 Capt Davis . . . Minna] Charles Henry Davis (1807–1877), who had succeeded the ailing Andrew H. Foote as commander of the Union gunboat flotilla on the Upper Mississippi on May 9; Mary Elizabeth Woodbury Blair (1821–1887), the wife of Montgomery Blair and sister-in-law of Gustavus Fox.

225.6 Frémont . . . Franklin] Following their defeat by Jackson at McDowell on May 8, Frémont's troops retreated to Franklin, Virginia (now West Virginia).

225.14–15 when Rogers was repulsed at Fort Darling] Commander John Rodgers (1812–1882) led the Union flotilla in the attack on Fort Darling (Drewry's Bluff) on the James River on May 15, 1862.

225.15–16 Old Grey beard] Secretary of the Navy Gideon Welles.

225.24–25 P King . . . Doolittle] Preston King (1806–1865), Republican senator from New York, 1857–63; abolitionist Wendell Phillips (1811–1884); James R. Doolittle (1815–1897), Republican senator from Wisconsin, 1857–69.

225.28 Our fat friend] Preston King.

225.33 Blair] Francis Preston Blair Lee, born in 1857, the only child of Elizabeth Blair Lee and Samuel Philips Lee.

225.39 Johns] Captain John F. Lee (1813–1884), Elizabeth Blair Lee's brother-in-law, was judge advocate of the U.S. Army, 1849–62.

226.2 Nelly] Eleanor Anne Hill Lee (d. 1891), John Lee's wife.

226.6 Fanny] Frances Ann Lee Pettit (1816–1889), Elizabeth Blair Lee's sister-in-law.

226.7 Ship Island] An island in the Gulf of Mexico near Biloxi, Mississippi, that served as a Union naval and military base.

230.10 BROCKET] A country house in Hertfordshire.

233.25 Casey] Brigadier General Silas Casey (1807–1882) commanded the Second Division in the Fourth Corps. His division was overrun by the initial Confederate attack at Fair Oaks.

233.30 the Tammany] The 42nd New York Infantry, which had been organized by the Tammany Society in New York City.

235.19 Colonel] Colonel Raymond Lee (1807–1891), commander of the 20th Massachusetts Infantry.

236.26 the R. R.] The Richmond and York River Railroad.

237.8–11 Genl D. H. Hill . . . Featherston] The letter sent to Lee by Major General Daniel Harvey Hill (1821–1889), a division commander in the Army of Northern Virginia, has not been found. At the time, Brigadier General Gabriel J. Rains (1803–1881) and Brigadier General Winfield Scott Featherston (1820–1891) commanded brigades in D. H. Hill's division. Rains was soon relieved of field duty, and Featherston was transferred to James Longstreet's division.

237.15 Col Long] Colonel Armistead L. Long (1825–1891), one of Lee's staff officers.

238.17–18 Mr. Wickliffe of Kentucky] Charles A. Wickliffe (1788–1869) was a congressman, 1823–33 and 1861–63; governor of Kentucky, 1839–40; and postmaster general of the United States, 1841–45.

239.15 Brig. Gen. T. W. Sherman] Brigadier General Thomas W. Sherman commanded the Union forces at Port Royal from November 1861 to March 1862, when he was succeeded by Hunter.

241.10 Brother Walter . . . My Brother] Walter Stone (c. 1845–1863) enlisted in the Confederate army in September 1862 and died of fever at Clinton, Mississippi, in May 1863; William Stone (c. 1840–c. 1882) was a captain in the Confederate army who was wounded twice fighting in the eastern theater.

241.20–21 a ditch . . . opposite Vicksburg] Work on the canal began on June 27, 1862, and stopped shortly before Admiral Farragut withdrew his flotilla downriver on July 24.

242.2–3 Mr. Mumford . . . shot] William B. Mumford (1820–1862) was convicted of treason by a military commission and hanged in New Orleans on June 7, 1862.

243.6 Richmond] A town in Madison Parish, Louisiana.

246.18 give a little map] Alexander did not include a map in his manuscript.

247.7 at Strasburg on ______] Jackson defeated Major General Nathaniel P. Banks at Winchester on May 25, 1862.

248.3 A. P. & D. H. Hill] Major General Ambrose Powell Hill (1825–1865) and Major General Daniel Harvey Hill were division commanders in the Army of Northern Virginia (the two men were not related).

248.15 Fitzhugh Lee, in his life of Gen. Lee] Fitzhugh Lee, *General Lee* (1894). A nephew of Robert E. Lee, Fitzhugh Lee (1835–1905) served as a major general in the Confederate army.

249.25 Century War Book] D. H. Hill, "McClellan's Change of Base and Malvern Hill," in *Battles and Leaders of the Civil War*, volume II (1887).

250.6 Maj. Dabney in his life of Jackson] Robert Lewis Dabney, *Life and Campaigns of Lieut.-Gen. Thomas J. Jackson, (Stonewall Jackson)* (1866). Dabney (1820–1898), a Presbyterian minister, served as Jackson's adjutant during the Shenandoah Valley campaign and the Seven Days.

251.1–3 Gen. Franklin . . . Century War Book.] William B. Franklin, "Rear-Guard Fighting During the Change of Base," in *Battles and Leaders of the Civil War*, volume II (1887). Franklin (1823–1903) commanded the Sixth Corps during the Seven Days.

251.32 about ____ miles] In his book *Military Memoirs of a Confederate: A Critical Narrative* (1907) Alexander wrote that the distance was between fifteen and sixteen miles.

254.13 Fitz John Porter . . . War Book.] "Hanover Court House and Gaines's Mill," *Battles and Leaders of the Civil War*, volume II (1887).

254.34 Slocum . . . French & Meagher] Brigadier Henry W. Slocum (1826–1894) commanded the First Division in the Sixth Corps. Brigadier

General William H. French (1815–1881) and Brigadier General Thomas F. Meagher (1823–1867) commanded brigades in the First Division of the Second Corps.

258.29–30 McCall's Division . . . Morrell] Brigadier General George A. McCall (1802–1868) commanded the Third Division, known as the Pennsylvania Reserves, in the Fifth Corps. Brigadier General George W. Morell (1815–1883) commanded the First Division in the Fifth Corps.

259.12 Pennsylvania Bucktails] The 13th Pennsylvania Reserves.

261.32–33 Mr. Crountze of "The World,"] Lorenzo L. Crounse (1834–1909), a correspondent for the *New York World* who later joined *The New York Times.*

262.20 bridge of Lodi] At the battle of Lodi, fought in Lombardy on May 10, 1796, Napoleon Bonaparte's troops advanced under heavy fire across a bridge over the Adda River and defeated the rear guard of the retreating Austrian army.

263.4 ex-Governor Wood of Illinois] John Wood (1798–1880) served as lieutenant governor of Illinois, 1857–60, and as governor, 1860–61. In May 1861 he was appointed quartermaster-general of Illinois.

263.10–12 the old regicide . . . the savages] According to legend, William Goffe, one of the judges who signed the death warrant for Charles I in 1649, emerged from hiding in Hadley, Massachusetts, in 1675 to defend the town from an Indian attack.

264.13 the entire wounded . . . at 800.] Union losses in the battle of Gaines's Mill were recorded as 894 killed, 3,114 wounded, and 2,829 missing or captured.

265.13 the right bank] The southern bank of the Chickahominy.

271.10 Arthur] Arthur Haydon, Charles Haydon's younger brother.

271.22 Eliza] Eliza Haydon, Charles Haydon's stepmother.

275.12 Gen. Richardson] Brigadier General Israel B. Richardson (1815–1862) commanded the First Division in the Second Corps. Richardson had previously commanded the 2nd Michigan Infantry, Haydon's regiment, May–September 1861.

280.9 General Grover] Smith's brigade commander, Brigadier General Cuvier Grover.

281.34 The Colonel] Colonel Powell T. Wyman (c. 1828–1862), the commander of the 16th Massachusetts Infantry, was killed at Glendale on the afternoon of June 30.

290.19–20 my relative, Colonel J. M. Brockenbrough] John Mercer Brockenbrough (1830–1892) commanded the 40th Virginia Infantry.

291.12 Ballard House] A five-story hotel on Franklin Street in Richmond.

292.9 General C.] Thomas Jefferson Chambers (1802–1865), a lawyer and land speculator who was commissioned as a major general during the Texas Revolution.

292.29–30 "Potomac Rifles"] Company K of the 40th Virginia Infantry.

292.31 Edward Brockenbrough, dreadfully wounded] First Lieutenant Edward Brockenbrough (1835–1862) of the 40th Virginia Infantry died on July 2. John Mercer Brockenbrough (see note 290.19–20) was his older brother.

292.32 Our own boys] Judith McGuire's stepsons, James McGuire (1833–1903) and John P. McGuire Jr. (1836–1906).

292.37 "Praise the Lord, O my soul!"] Psalm 146:1.

292.39 Raleigh T. Colston] Lieutenant Colonel Colston (1834–1863) was the son of Judith McGuire's sister, Sarah Jane Brockenbrough Colston. He was mortally wounded at Mine Run, Virginia, on November 27, 1863.

293.1–2 Major Jones, . . . desperately wounded.] Francis Buckner Jones (1828–1862) died on July 9.

293.10–11 Lieutenant-Colonel Warwick, . . . wounded] Bradfute Warwick (1839–1862) died on July 6.

301.24–29 Colonel Coppens, . . . soon died] Lieutenant Colonel George Gaston Coppens (1836–1862) commanded the 1st Louisiana Zouave Battalion during the Seven Days. He was killed at Antietam on September 17, 1862.

302.3–13 "There everlasting spring . . . the shore,"] Cf. "There is a Land of Pure Delight" (1707), hymn by Isaac Watts (1674–1748).

302.14–15 crossed the river . . . the trees.] Cf. the last words of Lieutenant General Thomas J. (Stonewall) Jackson, May 10, 1863, as reported by his doctor, Hunter McGuire: "Let us cross over the river, and rest under the shade of the trees."

302.20 lively debate . . . Saturday] The debate took place on July 5, 1862.

303.22 Charles A. Wickliffe] See note 238.17–18.

303.33–34 Robert Mallory] Mallory (1815–1885) was a Unionist congressman from Kentucky, 1859–65.

304.5 Thaddeus Stevens] Stevens (1792–1868) served in Congress as an antislavery Whig from Pennsylvania, 1849–53, and as a Republican, 1859–68.

304.13 Owen Lovejoy] Lovejoy (1811–1864) was a Republican congressman from Illinois, 1857–64.

304.16 read Jackson's General Order] As recorded in the *Congressional Globe*, Lovejoy quoted from the address Jackson issued to his black troops on December 18, 1814. Thaddeus Stevens had previously read Jackson's proclamation of September 21, 1814, addressed to "the free colored inhabitants of Louisiana," in which he called upon free men of color to enlist in the war against Great Britain.

304.28 Charles B. Sedgewick] Sedgwick (1815–1883) was a Republican congressman from New York, 1859–63.

304.34 Alexander S. Diven] Diven (1809–1896) was a Republican congressman from New York, 1861–63.

307.35 the Act of Congress] The Confiscation Act of August 6, 1861.

309.16 Earl Russell] Lord Russell, the British foreign secretary, 1859–65; see Biographical Notes.

309.27–32 Oreto . . . privateer] After being commissioned as the C.S.S. *Florida*, the ship began raiding Northern commerce in 1863 and took thirty-three prizes before being captured by the sloop U.S.S. *Wachusett* at Bahia, Brazil, on October 7, 1864.

311.14–15 Captain Bullock . . . confederate navy] James D. Bulloch (1823–1901), a former lieutenant in the U.S. Navy, arrived in Liverpool in June 1861 and began purchasing arms and ships for the Confederacy. Bulloch was commissioned as a commander in the Confederate navy in March 1862.

312.5 General Burgoyne] General John Burgoyne (1782–1871), an officer of the Royal Engineers, had served in the Napoleonic Wars, the War of 1812, and the Crimea. He was the son of General John Burgoyne (1722–1792), who had surrendered his army to the Americans at Saratoga in 1777.

329.2 *Joseph C. G. Kennedy*] Kennedy (1813–1887) was superintendent of the Census, 1850–53 and 1860–65.

329.23 His address to his troops] See pp. 323–24 in this volume.

333.34 we stopped recruiting] On April 3, 1862, Secretary of War Stanton ordered the War Department recruiting service to close its offices.

335.10 Russia . . . Sebastopool.] Sebastopol fell to the British and French on September 9, 1855. Tsar Alexander II accepted peace terms proposed by Austria on January 16, 1856, and the treaty ending the Crimean War was signed in Paris on March 30, 1856.

337.3 Governor H. Seymour] Horatio Seymour (1810–1886) was the Democratic governor of New York, 1853–55 and 1863–65, and the Democratic nominee for president in 1868.

338.17 Nettie] Chase's daughter, Janet Ralston Chase (1847–1925).

339.14 the White House] White House Landing, where the Richmond and York Railroad crossed the Pamunkey River.

340.18 Today] July 21, 1862.

341.1 Katie] Chase's daughter, Catharine Jane Chase (1840–1899).

341.8 Gen. Webb] James Watson Webb (1802–1884) was the editor of the *Morning Courier and New-York Enquirer*, 1829–61, and U.S. minister to Brazil, 1861–69. His military title was honorific.

342.13 Col. Key] Colonel Thomas M. Key (1819–1869) of McClellan's staff.

342.35 5–20s] Bonds redeemable after five years and maturing in twenty years that carried 6 percent interest.

345.10 sixth section of the act of congress] See p. 319.11–28 in this volume.

347.31 Mr. Lovejoy] See note 304.13.

349.3 *Cuthbert Bullitt*] Lincoln later appointed Bullitt (1810–1906) as collector of customs for New Orleans and U.S. marshal for eastern Louisiana.

349.11–12 Mr. Thomas J. Durant] Durant (1817–1882) later served as attorney general of Louisiana, 1863–64.

352.16 Mr Atkinson] Edward Atkinson (1827–1905) was a Boston textile manufacturer.

352.25 Mr Johnson] Reverdy Johnson (1796–1876) served in the U.S. Senate as a Whig from Maryland, 1845–49, and as a Democrat, 1863–68. Secretary of State Seward sent Johnson to New Orleans in July 1862 to investigate complaints made by foreign consuls about the military occupation. In a letter to Johnson, Major General Benjamin F. Butler declared that the military would not confiscate cotton exports, while in another letter Johnson approved permitting an English merchant to export cotton from Confederate-held Mobile in exchange for non-contraband items.

353.9 *vis inertia*] Resistance to motion.

353.36 Yr Walcheren expedition] The British landed an expeditionary force of 39,000 men on the islands of Walcheren and South Beveland in the Scheldt estuary on July 30, 1809. By the time the force was withdrawn on December 9, 1809, nearly 4,000 men had died from malaria, typhus, typhoid, and dysentery, and more than 11,000 of the survivors were still listed as sick in February 1810.

368.31–32 Roberts] Joseph Jenkins Roberts (1809–1876), an immigrant from Virginia, was president of Liberia, 1848–56 and 1872–76.

374.18–19 Gaither . . . Stevens] Edgar B. Gaither (c. 1818–1855), James L. Rankin (c. 1817–1845), William Irvin (c. 1819–1852), Henry W. Halleck (see Biographical Notes), Edward O. C. Ord (1818–1883), and Isaac I. Stevens (1818–1862) had been in the class of 1839 at West Point with Sherman and Hunton.

377.14 F. Seward] Frederick W. Seward (1830–1915), William H. Seward's son, served as assistant secretary of state, 1861–69.

378.35 Qui nescit dissimulare neseit regnare] He who knows not how to dissemble knows not how to rule.

379.6–7 hostis humani generis] Enemy of the human race.

379.15 his Mexican villainy] Spanish, French, and British troops landed in Veracruz, December 1861–January 1862, in an intervention intended to force the Mexican government to pay its foreign debts. In April 1862 the British and Spanish withdrew from the expedition, while the French openly declared their intention to overthrow the government of Benito Juárez and make the Austrian archduke Maximilian (1832–1867) emperor of Mexico.

379.17–18 gigantic scheme . . . conquest of China] Britain and France had defeated the Manchus in the Second Opium War, 1857–60, and forced the Chinese to make a series of military, economic, and political concessions opening the country to European influence. The British and French then defended their interests in China by fighting a series of battles with the Taiping rebels in 1862.

380.28–29 Bright . . . unrepresented masses] A leading Radical member of Parliament, John Bright (1811–1889) advocated an enlarged electoral franchise and the redistribution of seats in the House of Commons in order to increase the representation of the urban population.

382.16–17 Progressive Friends at Longwood] An organization of liberal Quakers founded in Longwood, Pennsylvania, in 1853.

382.23–24 Duff Green's Row] A group of tenements on East Capitol Street.

383.18 Mr. Nichol] Danforth B. Nichols (1812–1907), a Methodist minister.

383.26 Rev. W. H. Channing] William Henry Channing (1810–1884), a Unitarian clergyman and reformer.

383.29 Gen. Wadsworth] Brigadier General James S. Wadsworth (1807–1864) was the military governor of the District of Columbia.

383.31–32 Miss Hannah Stevenson . . . Miss Kendall] Hannah Stevenson (1807–1887) and Julia C. Kendall (1815–1874) were volunteer nurses from Massachusetts at Washington military hospitals.

392.2–3 3rd, . . . 9th] The Third, Fifth, and Ninth Corps of the Army of the Potomac fought at Second Bull Run.

392.12 Gen. Winder killed] Brigadier General Charles H. Winder (1829–1862) had commanded a brigade in the Shenandoah Valley campaign and a division in the Seven Days.

394.5 Duane] James C. Duane (1824–1897) served as an engineering officer with the Army of the Potomac, 1861–62, and as its chief engineer, 1863–65.

399.5–6 Col. Stephen D. Lee] Lee (1833–1908) later commanded a corps in the Army of Tennessee, 1864–65. He was not related to Robert E. Lee.

401.18 Mr. Holt] Joseph Holt (1807–1894), a leading Kentucky unionist, had served as postmaster general, March 1859–December 1860, and as secretary of war from January 1861 until the end of the Buchanan administration. Holt was appointed judge advocate general of the U.S. Army by President Lincoln on September 3, 1862, and held the position until 1875.

402.4 battle of Hanover Court House] On May 27, 1862, McClellan sent 12,000 men to Hanover Court House, fourteen miles north of Richmond, to clear Confederate forces from his right flank. The Union troops defeated 4,000 Confederates and destroyed several railroad bridges before returning to the north bank of the Chickahominy River.

408.28 battlefield of Leesburg] The battle of Ball's Bluff was fought near Leesburg on October 21, 1861; see p. 28.7–12 in this volume.

409.32 Starke . . . his father] Brigadier General William E. Starke (1814–1862) commanded a brigade in Jackson's corps at Second Bull Run and Antietam, where he was killed.

413.17–18 Tuesday evening . . . Sunday morning] September 2 and August 31, 1862.

414.12 On Monday] September 1.

414.26 Reno's forces] Major General Jesse Reno (1823–1862) commanded a division in the Ninth Corps of the Army of the Potomac.

414.30 Kearney, Stephens & Webster] Major General Philip Kearny and Major General Isaac Stevens (1818–1862) were killed at Chantilly on September 1. Colonel Fletcher Webster (1813–1862), a son of Daniel Webster and commander of the 12th Massachusetts Infantry, was killed at Second Bull Run on August 30.

414.37 the Island] Name for area of southwest Washington bounded by the Potomac River, the Anacostia River, and the Washington Canal.

416.23 Wilkes] Commodore Charles Wilkes (1798–1877).

416.32 Smith] Caleb P. Smith (1808–1864) was secretary of the interior, 1861–62.

418.5–6 Baron Gerolt's.] Friedrich von Gerolt (1798–1879) was the Prussian minister to the United States, 1844–48 and 1849–71.

420.22 Watson] Peter H. Watson, a patent lawyer and former legal partner of Edwin M. Stanton, was assistant secretary of war, January 1862–July 1864.

420.37 Schenck] Brigadier General Robert C. Schenck (1809–1890) commanded a division in the First Corps of the Army of Virginia at Second Bull Run. Schenck served in Congress from Ohio as a Whig, 1843–51, and as a Republican, 1863–71.

421.17 my neighbor Corcoran's] William Wilson Corcoran (1798–1888) was a Washington banker, philanthropist, and art collector. A Southern sympathizer, Corcoran went to Europe in 1862 and remained abroad for the rest of the war. In his absence both his city home and country estate north of the city were used as military hospitals.

426.39 Haupt] Herman Haupt (1817–1905) served as chief of construction for the U.S. military railroads, April 1862–September 1863.

427.10 voltigeurs] Skirmishers, sharpshooters.

435.29 Loudon] Loudon County, Virginia.

436.24 Coxe's] Brigadier General Jacob D. Cox (1828–1900) commanded the Kanawha Division in western Virginia. During the Maryland campaign the division served with the Ninth Corps of the Army of the Potomac.

437.12 *Egomet Ipse*] I myself.

437.21 Queen City of the West] Cincinnati.

437.23 General Stahel] Brigadier General Julius Stahel (1825–1912) commanded a brigade in the First Corps of the Army of Virginia at Second Bull Run. He assumed command of his division on August 30 after Brigadier General Robert C. Schenck (see note 420.37) was wounded.

438.4 redans] A V-shaped earthwork fortification, with its point projecting toward the enemy.

438.7 Bellows] Henry Bellows (1814–1882), a Unitarian pastor from New York City, helped found the U.S. Sanitary Commission in 1861 and served as its president throughout the war.

438.12 Algeria, and Lombardy] Kearny had fought in Algeria in 1840 while studying French cavalry tactics. In 1859 he fought with the French army against the Austrians at Magenta and Solferino in northern Italy.

438.16 dark cloud six years ago] In 1855 Kearny began living openly on his New Jersey estate with Agnes Maxwell, a young woman he had met in Paris, after his wife Diana initially refused him a divorce. Kearny and Maxwell were eventually able to marry in April 1858.

439.34–440.1 Carl Schurz, . . . the army] Schurz (1829–1906) had campaigned for Lincoln in 1860 among German-American voters. He was commissioned as a brigadier general in April 1862 and commanded a division in the First Corps of the Army of Virginia at Second Bull Run.

440.18 Fort Lafayette] See note 29.11.

440.37–8 the mutiny of last year.] The 79th New York Infantry lost 198 men killed, wounded, or captured at First Bull Run, including its commander, Colonel James Cameron. Many in the regiment believed they should be permitted to return to New York to recruit replacements and elect new officers. On August 14, 1861, the regiment refused orders to strike camp at Washington and march into Virginia. The mutiny ended later in the day when the 79th New York was confronted by regular troops and addressed by their new commander Colonel Isaac Stevens (see note 414.30), a regular officer. Twenty-one suspected ringleaders were sent to Fort Jefferson in the Dry Tortugas, where they performed hard labor until February 1862.

443.27 Gotha] Lord Russell had accompanied Queen Victoria on her visit to the duchy of Saxe-Coburg-Gotha, the home of her consort Prince Albert, who had died on December 14, 1861.

444.14 Newcastle] Henry Pelham-Clinton, 5th Duke of Newcastle (1811–1864), was secretary of state for the colonies in the Palmerston government, 1859–64.

444.16–17 the new interest . . . for her.] Edward, the Prince of Wales, had become engaged to Princess Alexandra of Denmark (1844–1925) on September 9, 1862.

444.19 Broadlands] Palmerston's country estate near Romsey in Hampshire.

450.6 Bradley T. Johnson, *soi-disant* Colonel C.S.A.] Colonel Johnson (1829–1903) was, like Steiner, a native of Frederick, Maryland.

450.34 "My Maryland"] "Maryland, My Maryland," song (1861) with words by James Ryder Randall (1839–1908), sung to the German folk tune "Lauriger Horatius" (the same music as "O Tannenbaum!").

452.14 "If thine enemy hunger, feed him,"] Romans 12:20.

452.29 The coals . . . his head."] See Romans 12:20.

455.27 Col. Steedman] Lieutenant Colonel John M. Steedman (d. 1867), commander of the 6th South Carolina Infantry.

460.6 III] The first two paragraphs of Special Order No. 191 were not included in the copy that was sent to Major General D. H. Hill and subsequently discovered by the Union army. Paragraph I prohibited Confederate soldiers not on official business from visiting Frederick, Maryland, and paragraph II detailed arrangements for evacuating sick soldiers to Virginia.

462.23–24 two hundred thousand men] The Army of the Potomac had about 75,000 men at Antietam, and the Army of Northern Virginia about 35,000.

462.34 brilliant victory near Middletown] The battle of South Mountain, fought on September 14, 1862.

463.14–15 Hooker . . . his corps] Major General Joseph Hooker commanded the First Corps at Antietam.

463.20 Richardson] Major General Israel B. Richardson commanded a division in the Second Corps.

464.21–22 Sumner, Franklin, and Mansfield] Major General Edwin V. Sumner commanded the Second Corps, Major General William B. Franklin commanded the Sixth Corps, and Major General Joseph K. F. Mansfield (1803–1862) commanded the Twelfth Corps.

464.25–26 Porter . . . Burnside] Fitz John Porter commanded the Fifth Corps; Ambrose Burnside commanded the Ninth Corps.

464.29 Sykes] Brigadier General George Sykes (1822–1880) commanded a division in the Fifth Corps.

465.19–21 Ricketts's . . . Doubleday] Brigadier General James B. Ricketts (1817–1887), Brigadier General George G. Meade, and Brigadier General Abner Doubleday (1819–1893) commanded the three divisions in Hooker's First Corps.

466.28–29 McDowell . . . Manassas] Major General Irvin McDowell (1818–1885) had commanded the Third Corps of the Army of Virginia at Second Bull Run. When the Army of Virginia was merged into the Army of the Potomac in September 1862, the Third Corps's troops were assigned to the First Corps.

467.32 General Hartsuff] Brigadier General George Hartsuff (1830–1874) commanded a brigade in Rickett's division.

471.4–7 Major Sedgwick . . . not mortal.] William D. Sedgwick (1831–1862), a relative of Major General John Sedgwick (1813–1864), died of his wounds on September 29.

471.17–18 Lieut. Spurr . . . wounded.] Thomas J. Spurr (1838–1862) died on September 27.

471.21 Gen. Dana was wounded.] Brigadier General Napoleon J. T. Dana (1822–1905) commanded a brigade in Sedgwick's division.

471.26–27 Lieut.-Col. Revere . . . wounded severely,] Lieutenant Colonel Paul Joseph Revere (1832–1863) and Captain Joseph C. Audenried (1839–1880) survived their wounds at Antietam. Revere, the grandson of the Revolutionary War hero, was mortally wounded at Gettysburg on July 2, 1863, while commanding the 20th Massachusetts Infantry.

471.30–33 Richardson . . . his brigade.] Richardson died on November 3, 1862. Brigadier General Thomas F. Meagher (1823–1867) commanded a brigade in Richardson's division.

481.13–14 Lieutenant John Ticknor was badly wounded] Ticknor (c. 1836–1863) survived his wound, but was killed at Gettysburg on July 1, 1863.

481.16–18 Bragg . . . shot,"] Lieutenant Colonel Edward S. Bragg (1827–1912) returned to the regiment in November 1862.

482.12 Virginia rail fence.] A zigzagging rail fence.

483.38–484.1 reported to General Doubleday,] The 6th Wisconsin was assigned to Doubleday's division.

485.3–4 *Irene and Mary Williams*] Irene Williams (1843–1907) and Mary Williams (1846–1935) lived with their father's relatives in Connecticut. Their mother had died in 1849.

491.30 Pittman] Williams's aide, Lieutenant Samuel E. Pittman (1831–1922).

492.39 Napoleon gun] A smoothbore field artillery gun that fired a twelve-pound projectile with a maximum range of 1,600 yards. It was developed in France under the auspices of Napoleon III.

494.40 just been surrendered] The Confederates captured Maryland Heights on September 13, 1862.

495.14 third time up the valley.] Williams had served in the Shenandoah Valley in the winter and spring of 1862.

500.3–4 Lieutenant-Colonel Kimball] Edgar A. Kimball (1822–1863), commander of the 9th New York Infantry.

500.32–34 singular effect . . . Goethe on a similar occasion] In August 1792 Johann Wolfgang von Goethe accompanied his patron Karl August, Duke of Saxe-Weimar, in the Austrian-Prussian invasion of revolutionary France. At the battle of Valmy on September 20, Goethe rode out to witness the French artillery bombardment, and later wrote: "In the midst of these circumstances, I was soon able to remark that something unusual was taking place within me: I paid close attention to it, and still the sensation can be described only by similitude. It appeared as if you were in some extremely hot place, and at the same time quite penetrated by the heat of it, so that you feel yourself, as it were, quite one with the element in which you are. The eyes lose nothing of their strength or clearness; but it is as if the world had a kind of brown-red tint, which makes the situation, as well as the surrounding objects, more impressive." (Translation by Robert Farie, 1849.)

503.24 where the 14th . . . made their fight] The 14th Connecticut Infantry attacked the Sunken Road in the center of the Confederate line as part of French's division in Sumner's Second Corps.

505.13 the Sunday before the battle] September 14, 1862.

512.3 "Sheridan's ride."] On October 19, 1864, Confederate troops surprised Union forces at Cedar Creek, Virginia, and drove them from their positions. Major General Philip Henry Sheridan (1831–1888), who was returning to his command from a conference in Washington, learned of the attack in Winchester, Virginia, and rode to the front, rallying stragglers and directing a successful counterattack.

524.19–20 Rodman . . . Kingsbury died] Brigadier Isaac P. Rodman (1822–1862), the commander of a division in the Ninth Corps, died of his wounds on September 30. Colonel Henry W. Kingsbury (1836–1862), commander of the 11th Connecticut Infantry, was mortally wounded in an attack on the Rohrbach (Burnside's) Bridge.

526.22 OUR BRIGADE] The 1st Missouri Confederate Brigade.

531.28–29 when the President . . . funeral of Stanton's child] The funeral was held on July 13, 1862. Welles recorded in his diary Lincoln saying that "he had given it much thought and he had about come to the conclusion that we must free the slaves or be ourselves subdued."

539.1 Cassius M. Clay] Clay (1810–1903), an antislavery Whig from Kentucky who joined the Republican Party in 1856, served as U.S. minister to Russia, 1861–62 and 1863–69.

543.3 *Manton Marble*] Marble (1835–1917) was the editor and owner of the *New York World*, 1862–76.

543.17 the Clipper] The *Baltimore Clipper*, a newspaper published from 1847 to 1865.

543.24 Lafayette] See note 29.11.

547.1 Joe Johnston did on Patterson] See note 11.9.

547.38 Mitchell] Major General Ormsby M. Mitchel (1809–1862) led a division in the Army of the Ohio, December 1861–July 1862. As commander of Union occupation forces in northern Alabama, April–July 1862, Mitchel endorsed harsh reprisals against Confederate guerrilla attacks, and was criticized for the pillaging of Athens, Alabama, by one of his brigades. In September

1862 Mitchel was appointed to command the Department of the South; he died from yellow fever in South Carolina on October 30.

548.4 Dix & Banks] Major General John A. Dix (1798–1879) commanded the Department of Virginia with headquarters at Fort Monroe, June 1862–July 1863. Dix had served as a Democratic senator from New York, 1845–49, and as secretary of the treasury in the Buchanan administration, January–March 1861. Major General Nathaniel P. Banks commanded the defenses of Washington, September–October 1862. Banks had served in Congress, 1853–57, as a Democrat, an American (Know Nothing), and a Republican. He was governor of Massachusetts, 1858–61.

549.15 Curtis] Major General Samuel R. Curtis commanded the Department of the Missouri, September 1862–May 1863.

554.23 Confession of Augsburg] The primary confession of the Lutheran Church (1530), drafted by Philip Melanchthon (1497–1560) and endorsed by Martin Luther.

554.26 emancipation of slaves in the West Indies] The Abolition Act of 1833 resulted in the emancipation of all slaves in the British West Indies in 1838.

554.26–27 passage of the Reform Bill] The Reform Act of 1832 extended the electoral franchise and redistributed seats in the House of Commons.

554.27 repeal of the Corn-Laws] The Corn Laws imposing duties on grain imported into Great Britain were repealed in 1846.

554.27–28 Magnetic Ocean-Telegraph] The first trans-Atlantic telegraph cable was tested in August 1858. It failed the following month, and regular cable service was not established until 1866.

554.28–29 passage of the Homestead Bill] The Homestead Act of 1862 granted 160 acres of public land to settlers in return for making improvements to the claim and residing on it for five years.

557.7–9 "if that fail, . . . on stubble."] John Milton, *Comus* (1637), lines 597–99.

559.19–20 condition of Italy . . . French Algiers] The unification of Italy began with the defeat of Austria by Sardinia-Piedmont and France in 1859; Poland was partitioned among Austria, Prussia, and Russia in 1772, 1793, and 1795; France began its conquest of Algeria in 1830.

560.13–14 "Incertainties . . . endless age."] Shakespeare, Sonnet 107, lines 7–8.

565.36 the late Col. Miles] Colonel Dixon S. Miles (1804–1862), the Union commander at Harper's Ferry, Virginia, was mortally wounded by Confederate artillery fire shortly after he ordered his garrison to surrender on

September 15, 1862. Although a subsequent army inquiry condemned his "incapacity, amounting almost to imbecility," there is no evidence that he had Confederate sympathies.

567.18 Mr. Semmes] Thomas J. Semmes (1824–1899) was a Confederate senator from Louisiana, 1862–65.

567.33 Mr. Clark] John B. Clark (1802–1885) was a Confederate senator from Missouri, 1862–64, and a representative in the Confederate Congress, 1864–65. He served as a Democrat in the U.S. House of Representatives, 1857–61.

568.10 Mr. Henry] Gustavus A. Henry (1804–1880) was a Confederate senator from Tennessee, 1862–65.

568.15 Mr. Phelan] James Phelan (1821–1873) was a Confederate senator from Mississippi, 1862–64.

568.18 Mr. Burnett] Henry C. Burnett (1825–1866) was a Confederate senator from Kentucky, 1862–65. He served as a Democrat in the U.S. House of Representatives, 1855–61.

570.21 Mr. Hill] Benjamin Hill (1823–1882) represented Georgia in the Provisional Confederate Congress, 1861, and in the Confederate Senate, 1862–65.

570.22–23 *brutum fulmen*] Insensible thunderbolt; a futile threat.

573.10–11 "the efforts . . . actual freedom"] Cf. the Preliminary Emancipation Proclamation, p. 534.14–15 in this volume.

573.17 MAZZINI] Italian revolutionary Giuseppe Mazzini (1803–1872), who sought to unite Italy as a democratic republic.

580.14–15 General Rodgers of Texas] Colonel William P. Rogers (1819–1862) commanded the 2nd Texas Infantry.

580.29 Colonel Sprague] Colonel John W. Sprague (1817–1893) commanded the 63rd Ohio Infantry, January 1862–April 1864.

580.36 parrot guns] See note 159.24.

582.30 "with my back . . . to the foe."] From "Lochiel's Warning" (1802), poem by Thomas Campbell (1777–1844).

583.11–12 I sank . . . knew nothing more] David L. Jackson, Oscar L. Jackson's brother, wrote in *The Colonel's Diary* that after he lost consciousness, Jackson was placed among "the supposedly mortally wounded and dying" for several hours until Mose, his black servant, carried him to a field hospital and made the surgeons treat him.

585.25 Col. Sawier] Possibly Lieutenant Colonel Thomas C. Lanier, second in command of the 42nd Alabama Infantry.

589.32 His tragic death] Major General William Nelson (1824–1862) was shot to death by Union Brigadier General Jefferson C. Davis (1828–1879) in Louisville on September 29, 1862. The two men had quarreled previously, and when Davis angrily confronted Nelson in the grand hall of the Galt House hotel, Nelson called him a "damned puppy." Davis then flipped a crumpled visiting card into Nelson's face, and Nelson slapped Davis and called him a coward. After Davis borrowed a revolver from a friend in the hotel, he confronted Nelson at the bottom of a stairway and shot him. Davis returned to duty, and was never tried for the killing.

592.16–17 Jackson's . . . death] Union Brigadier General James S. Jackson (1823–1862), a Kentucky lawyer who had served in Congress as a Unionist in 1861 before joining the army.

592.23 Terrill . . . brigade] Brigadier General William R. Terrill (1834–1862) led a brigade in Jackson's division, part of the corps commanded by Major General Alexander McCook.

592.25–29 Parsons] Lieutenant Charles C. Parsons (1838–1878), an 1861 graduate of West Point, resigned from the army in 1870 to become an Episcopal clergyman.

593.34 "Bonnie Blue Flag,"] A popular Confederate marching song, written in 1861 by the variety performer Harry Macarthy (1834–1888) and sung to the tune of "The Irish Jaunting Car."

594.3–4 Mumfordsville] The Union garrison at Munfordville, Kentucky, surrendered on September 17, 1862.

594.6 Camp Dick Robinson] A Union recruiting and training camp established in August 1861 near Danville, Kentucky.

594.26 General Chalmers] Brigadier General James R. Chalmers (1831–1898) commanded a brigade in Bragg's army.

594.40 Cheatham's] Watkins's regiment, the 1st Tennessee Infantry, was assigned to the division commanded by Major General Benjamin F. Cheatham (1820–1886).

596.8–9 Field . . . Patterson] At Perryville, Colonel Hume R. Feild (1834–1921), the commander of the 1st Tennessee Infantry, acted as chief of staff to his brigade commander, Brigadier General George Maney (1826–1901), while Lieutenant Colonel John Patterson led the regiment.

597.14 Missionary Ridge] The ridge was captured by Union troops in the battle of Chattanooga, November 25, 1863.

598.14 Rock City Guards] A Nashville militia battalion whose members formed Companies A, B, and C of the 1st Tennessee Infantry in 1861.

599.1–5 Billy Webster . . . we shall meet again.] William H. Webster (1840–1863) was killed at Chickamauga on September 19, 1863.

603.16 Granville's letter] Granville George Leveson-Gower, 2nd Earl Granville (1815–1891), was the Liberal leader of the House of Lords, 1859–65. He wrote to Russell on September 27 that it was unlikely that both sides in the conflict would accept British mediation, and that if Britain recognized the South, Granville doubted "whether it will be possible for us to avoid drifting into" the war.

604.31–32 Memorandum on . . . Lewis's observations.] In a memorandum sent to the cabinet on October 13, Russell proposed that the Great Powers of Europe should ask both sides to agree to "a suspension of arms for the purpose of weighing calmly the advantages of peace." Sir George Cornewall Lewis (1806–1863), secretary for war, 1861–63, responded on October 17, arguing that an armistice proposal would anger the North and might lead to war with the United States.

606.15 Landudno] Llandudno, a seaside resort in northern Wales.

607.20 Sepoy Rebellion] The Indian rebellion of 1857–58, which began with a series of mutinies by soldiers of the East India Company.

609.25–26 the charges of late . . . the public mind] The text of Blair's letter is taken from *The Francis Preston Blair Family in Politics* (1933) by William Ernest Smith. In an unpublished and incomplete transcription made around 1960 by the historian E. B. Long, this passage reads: "the charges of the Democracy that gave it the late strength & confirmed hold on the public mind."

609.35–610.1 their conclusive policy] In the Long transcription, "their conservative policy."

610.15 supply strength] In the Long transcription, "supply thought."

611.3 *Margaret Meade*] Margaretta Sergeant Meade (1815–1886) was the daughter of a Pennsylvania congressman. She and Meade were married in 1840.

611.15 Seymour] Brigadier General Truman Seymour (1824–1891) commanded a brigade in Meade's division.

611.17 Reynolds] John F. Reynolds (1820–1863) assumed command of the First Corps of the Army of the Potomac in late September 1862 and led it until his death at Gettysburg on July 1, 1863.

611.18 Gibbons position] John Gibbon (1827–1896) had recently been advanced from brigade to division command within the First Corps.

611.19 Col. S. Meredith . . . old politician] Colonel Solomon Meredith (1810–1875) had commanded the 19th Indiana Infantry in Gibbon's brigade until October 1862, when he was promoted to brigadier general. Meredith had served as a county sheriff, state legislator, and U.S. marshal, and was active in Indiana Republican politics.

611.22–23 *you & I & Meade . . .* promoted.] Reynolds and Meade were promoted to major general effective November 29, 1862; Gibbon was promoted to major general in June 1864.

612.15 attempt to put down Taylor in Mexico] Zachary Taylor became a popular hero after defeating the Mexicans at Palo Alto and Resaca de la Palma, May 8–9, 1846. On September 24 he accepted the surrender of Monterrey under terms that allowed the Mexican garrison to depart peacefully and established an eight-week armistice. The Polk administration subsequently repudiated the armistice, transferred many of Taylor's troops to the Veracruz expedition commanded by Winfield Scott, and ordered Taylor to remain on the defensive. He disregarded his orders, advanced south, and defeated the Mexicans at Buena Vista, February 22–23, 1847. In 1848 Taylor won the Whig nomination and was elected president.

612.39 Gov. Curtin] Andrew G. Curtin (1817–1894) was the Republican governor of Pennsylvania, 1861–67.

613.1 Senator Cowan] Edgar Cowan (1815–1885) was a Republican senator from Pennsylvania, 1861–67.

614.12 Sheffield] William S. Sheffield (1820–1907), a Union congressman from Rhode Island, 1861–63.

615.3 battle of Friday] August 29, 1862.

616.2–3 Butler . . . Griffing] Browning recorded his conversation with William Butler (1797–1876), the Republican state treasurer of Illinois, 1859–63, in his diary on November 12, 1862. Brigadier General Charles Griffin (1825–1867) commanded a brigade in the Fifth Corps under Porter at Second Bull Run.

618.25–26 treaty with Great Britain . . . slave trade] The treaty was signed in Washington by Secretary of State Seward and Lord Lyons, the British minister to the United States, on April 7, 1862, and ratified by the Senate on April 25. Under its terms the Royal Navy was for the first time permitted to stop and search American ships suspected of engaging in the slave trade.

620.34–35 republic of New Granada] Colombia, which at the time included present-day Panama.

625.26 chief of the Cherokees] John Ross (1790–1866) was elected principal chief of the Cherokee in 1839.

626.28 Colonel Webster] See note 42.31.

626.34 The Commissioner] Isaac Newton (1800–1867), commissioner of agriculture, 1862–67. (The first secretary of agriculture with cabinet rank was appointed in 1889.)

627.22–23 "One generation . . . forever."] Ecclesiastes 1:4.

640.28 "Benny Havens's"] A tavern in Buttermilk Falls (now Highland Falls), New York, near West Point.

644.24–25 Gen. Longstreet says] In "The Battle of Fredericksburg," published in *Battles and Leaders of the Civil War*, volume III (1888).

645.29–30 Gen. Couch, in the *Century*] Darius N. Couch, "Sumner's 'Grand Right Division,'" *Battles and Leaders of the Civil War*, volume III (1888).

647.11–15 The one casualty . . . in the yard.] Alexander later crossed out this sentence in his manuscript and wrote: "PS I have come to doubt the truth of this incident which was told me at the time by Roy Mason, himself, but I never heard it mentioned again by *any one*. It is inherently exceedingly improbable. Some of the 7 would only have been wounded."

648.18 Whitworth rifle] A rifled artillery gun capable of firing a twelve-pound projectile over four miles.

653.29–33 Gen. T. R. R. Cobb, . . . before the war.] General Thomas R. R. Cobb (1823–1862) commanded a brigade in Longstreet's corps. A prominent lawyer in Georgia, Cobb became an influential advocate of immediate secession following Lincoln's election and served in the Provisional Confederate Congress. He was the younger brother of Howell Cobb (see note 148.2).

657.21 grand army corps of Sumner] In November 1862 Burnside organized the Army of the Potomac into three Grand Divisions: the Right, commanded by Edwin V. Sumner; the Center, commanded by Joseph Hooker and the Left, commanded by William B. Franklin. Each Grand Division was composed of two corps, and was assigned its own cavalry and artillery.

658.30–31 heavy firing of Thursday] December 11, 1862, when Union troops crossed the Rappahannock and captured Fredericksburg.

659.19 Fort Darling] Union name for the fortifications on Drewry's Bluff overlooking the James River eight miles below Richmond.

660.20–21 Howard, . . . poor general] Major General Oliver O. Howard (1830–1909) had commanded a brigade at Fair Oaks, South Mountain, and Antietam, where he assumed command of the Second Division of the Second Corps after Major General John Sedgwick was wounded.

660.24–25 the fight of the previous day] Hall's brigade had been heavily engaged in the street fighting in Fredericksburg on December 11, during which Abbott's company of the 20th Massachusetts had lost ten men killed and twenty-five wounded.

660.28 the 19th] The 19th Massachusetts Infantry.

661.19 hinc illae &c.] *Hinc illae lacrimae*: hence these tears. Terence, *Andria*, line 126.

661.23 Macy] Captain George N. Macy (1837–1875) was the acting commander of the 20th Massachusetts Infantry.

661.32 Alley] Leander F. Alley (c. 1834–1862), a whaler from Nantucket, enlisted in the 20th Massachusetts in July 1861 and was promoted to second lieutenant in August 1862.

661.35 our great loss.] Edward Abbott (1840–1862), a captain in the 2nd Massachusetts Infantry, was killed at Cedar Mountain, Virginia, on August 9, 1862.

662.1 Fletcher] Fletcher Abbott (1843–1925), a second lieutenant in the 2nd Massachusetts Infantry, was suffering from dysentery and on sick leave. He later served as a staff officer in Louisiana before being medically discharged in December 1863.

662.20 Holmes] Captain Oliver Wendell Holmes Jr. (1841–1935) was returning to duty after being wounded at Antietam. Holmes later served as an associate justice of the U.S. Supreme Court, 1902–32.

663.17 the governor] John A. Andrew (1818–1867) was the Republican governor of Massachusetts, 1861–66.

663.22 Johnny Sedgwick] Major General Sedgwick returned to duty on December 22, 1862, after being wounded at Antietam.

665.7 Colonel Lang] Captain David Lang (1838–1917) was the acting commander of the 8th Florida Infantry.

671.19–20 "To gird . . . ramparts die,"] Felicia Dorothea Hemans (1793–1835), "Marguerite of France" (1832).

673.1–2 Richard was *not* himself again] Cf. "Conscience, avaunt, Richard's himself again," line by Colley Cibber (1671–1757) in Act V of his popular adaptation (1700) of Shakespeare's *Richard III.*

674.1 "a hard road to travel"] Cf. "Jordan is a Hard Road to Travel," song (1853) by Daniel Decatur Emmett (1815–1904).

674.32 *vi et armis*] With force and arms.

677.13 Dr. Watts] Isaac Watts (1674–1748), English theologian, logician, and writer of hymns.

678.1–12 "Beds . . . wondered."] Cf. Alfred Tennyson (1809–1892), "The Charge of the Light Brigade" (1854).

678.23 Munchausenism] An exaggerated or untrue story, after Karl Friedrich von Münchhausen (1720–1797), a German soldier and traveler known for his tales of fantastic adventures.

681.23 Thackeray's "Ensign Spooney"] In his novel *Vanity Fair* (1848).

683.17–18 Mr D W Wise] Daniel W. Wise (1813–1898) was an antislavery Methodist clergyman from Massachusetts and editor of the Methodist newspaper *Zion's Herald.*

685.21 Nicolay] John G. Nicolay (1832–1901) was Lincoln's private secretary, 1860–61, and his principal secretary in the White House, 1861–65.

685.27 Preston King and F. W. Seward] For King, see note 225.24–25; for Seward, see note 377.14.

686.10–11 Judge Collamer] Jacob Collamer (1791–1865) served as a judge of the Vermont Superior Court, 1833–42; as a Whig congressman, 1843–49; and as a Republican senator, 1855–65.

687.21–23 Fessenden . . . Wade was absent.] William P. Fessenden (1806–1869), Republican senator from Maine, 1854–64 and 1865–69, and secretary of the treasury, 1864–65; Ira Harris (1802–1875), Republican senator from New York, 1861–67; Lyman Trumbull (1813–1896), Republican senator from Illinois, 1855–73; James W. Grimes (1816–1872), Republican senator from Iowa, 1859–69; Jacob M. Howard (1805–1871), Republican senator from Michigan, 1862–71; Charles Sumner (1811–1874), Free Soil and then Republican senator from Massachusetts, 1851–74; Samuel C. Pomeroy (1816–1891), Republican senator from Kansas, 1861–73. Benjamin F. Wade (see note 8.30–31) was at Burnside's headquarters in Virginia.

688.12 heard from J.Q. Adams . . . Congress] Fessenden had served in Congress as a Whig, 1841–43.

688.15 Mr. Clay] Henry Clay was secretary of state in the administration of John Quincy Adams, 1825–29.

689.12 confidential dispatch to Mr. Adams, was read.] In a dispatch of July 5, 1862, to Charles Francis Adams, the American minister to Great Britain, Seward wrote: "The extreme advocates of African slavery and its most vehement opponents were acting in concert together to precipitate a servile war—the former by making the most desperate attempt to overthrow the federal Union, the latter by demanding an edict of universal emancipation."

689.36–37 Governor Robertson of Kentucky] George Robertson (1790–1874) had served in Congress, 1817–21; in the Kentucky state legislature; and on the Kentucky court of appeals, 1828–43.

692.35 Stanton came staving along.] In the remainder of his diary entry for December 20, 1862 Welles recorded a conversation with Senator Preston King and speculated about Stanton's involvement in the attempt to oust Seward from the cabinet.

696.29–30 Peninsular War.] Campaign fought on the Iberian peninsula, 1808–14, by Britain and its Portuguese and Spanish allies against the French.

696.33 Bidwell] Marshall S. Bidwell (1799–1872), Strong's law partner.

697.3 Jefferson Davis's precious proclamation!!] Davis issued the proclamation on December 23, 1862.

697.21–22 *brutum fulmen*] See note 570.22–23.

700.21 Banks] Major General Nathaniel P. Banks had recently replaced Benjamin F. Butler as commander of the Department of the Gulf.

701.18 Seymour . . . Curtis] Horatio Seymour (1810–1886), Democratic governor of New York, 1863–65, and Joel Parker (1816–1888), Democratic governor of New Jersey, 1863–66, were both elected in November 1862. George Ticknor Curtis (1812–1894), a conservative Democrat, was a prominent lawyer, legal scholar, and historian; his brother, Benjamin R. Curtis (1809–1874), who served as an associate justice of the U.S. Supreme Court, 1851–57, had recently published *Executive Power*, a pamphlet attacking the constitutionality of the Emancipation Proclamation and the suspension of habeas corpus by the Lincoln administration.

703.39 Col Murphy] Colonel Robert C. Murphy was dismissed from the service on January 10, 1863, for his "cowardly and disgraceful conduct" in failing to defend Holly Springs.

704.28–30 Col Murphy . . . Iuka] Murphy failed to destroy the supply depot at Iuka, Mississippi, when he retreated from the town on September 14, 1862. He was court-martialed and acquitted in October 1862.

710.18–19 conscription act . . . exemption act.] See pp. 172–76 in this volume.

711.18 your Governor] John Pettus (1813–1867) was governor of Mississippi, 1859–63.

714.24 when I went to Grenada] Davis visited the Confederate army at Grenada, Mississippi, December 23–25, 1862.

716.27 "But vengeance is the Lord's,"] Cf. Romans 12:19.

717.5–8 Gen. A. Sidney Johnston . . . Bowling Green] Confederate troops under Johnston's command occupied Bowling Green, Kentucky, from September 18, 1861, to February 14, 1862.

717.20–21 field of Chalmette] Chalmette Plantation in Louisiana, the site of the battle of New Orleans, January 8, 1815.

718.3 "Hold, enough."] *Macbeth*, V.viii.34.

718.26 that gallant soldier] General Joseph E. Johnston.

718.38–39 "put not your trust in princes,"] Psalm 146:3.

719.5 remarkable book . . . Mr. Spence] *The American Union: its effect on national character and policy, with an inquiry into secession as a constitutional right, and the causes of the disruption*, published in London in September 1861 by James Spence (1816–1905), a Liverpool businessman who became a prominent English supporter of the Confederacy.

720.22 a general unknown] Lieutenant General John C. Pemberton (1814–1881), an artillery officer before the war, commanded the Department of South Carolina, Georgia, and Florida, March–September 1862. Davis appointed him to command the Department of Mississippi and Eastern Louisiana in October 1862.

720.33–34 one from the army of the Potomac] Brigadier General Stephen D. Lee (see note 399.5–6). The Confederate Army of Northern Virginia was known as the Army of the Potomac before June 1862.

721.12–14 stated by the enemy . . . handled without gloves] Major General Henry W. Halleck wrote to Ulysses S. Grant on August 2, 1862: "It is very desirable that you should clean out West Tennessee and North Mississippi of all organized enemies. If necessary, take up all active sympathizers, and either hold them as prisoners or put them beyond our lines. Handle that class without gloves, and take their property for public use."

724.34–35 Gen. McClernand] McClernand (see note 36.10), now a major general, had been authorized by Lincoln and Stanton to lead an expedition against Vicksburg.

725.3 Morgan of Cumberland Gap] Brigadier General George W. Morgan (1820–1893) occupied the Cumberland Gap from June 18 to September 17, 1862, when the Confederate invasion of Kentucky forced him to abandon his position and retreat to the Ohio River.

725.9–10 attack this Post of Arkansas] Sherman captured Arkansas Post (also known as Fort Hindman) on January 11, 1863.

726.7 Henry Sherman] Henry S. Sherman (1845–1893), a sergeant major in the 120th Ohio Infantry, was the son of Charles Taylor Sherman (1811–1879), the eldest of Sherman's siblings.

727.21 capt Richmond] The officer in charge of black military laborers at Helena.

729.34 Colonel Moody] Colonel Granville Moody (1812–1887), a Methodist minister, commanded the 74th Ohio Infantry, December 1861–May 1863.

731.19–20 "Rosecrans' Campaign . . . Army Corps."] *Rosecrans' Campaign with the Fourteenth Army Corps, or the Army of the Cumberland; a narrative of personal observations, with an appendix, consisting of official reports of the battle of Stone River* (1863) by William D. Bickham (1827–1894), a correspondent for the *Cincinnati Commercial* who served as a volunteer aide to Major General William S. Rosecrans (1819–1898) at Stones River.

733.16 THE BATTLE] The fighting on December 31, 1862.

733.23–25 The National cemetery . . . 6,000 Federal soldiers buried.] Established in 1864, the cemetery was used to rebury soldiers disinterred in 1865–66 from wartime graves at several locations in Tennessee. The task of moving and burying the remains was carried out by men of the 111th U.S. Colored Troops.

734.11 General Breckinridge] John C. Breckinridge (see note 158.16–17), now a major general, commanded a division in the Army of Tennessee.

737.5–6 Lieut. George Burnley] Burnley died from his wounds on January 3, 1863.

738.3 Hanson] Brigadier General Roger W. Hanson (1827–1863), commander of the Orphan Brigade, was wounded on January 2 and died on January 4.

740.5–6 single grand division commander] See note 657.21.

745.28 Genl Saxton's] Brigadier General Rufus Saxton (1824–1908), the Union military governor of South Carolina, issued a proclamation on or before December 24, 1862, under the heading "A Happy New-Year's Greeting to the Colored People in the Department of the South." As printed in *The New York Times* on January 9, 1863, it read:

"In accordance, as I believe, with the will of our Heavenly Father, and by direction of your great and good friend, whose name you are all familiar with, ABRAHAM LINCOLN, President of the United States, and Commander-in-Chief of the army and the navy, on the 1st day of January, 1863, you will be declared 'forever free.'

"When, in the course of human events, there comes a day which is destined to be an everlasting beacon-light, marking a joyful era in the progress of a nation and the hopes of a people, it seems to be fitting the occasion that it should not pass unnoticed by those whose hopes it comes to brighten and to bless. Such a day to you is January 1, 1863. I therefore call upon all the colored people in this department to assemble on that day at the headquarters of the First Regiment of South Carolina Volunteers, there to hear the President's proclamation read, and to indulge in such other manifestations of joy as may be called forth by the occasion. It is your duty to carry this good news to your brethren who are still in Slavery. Let all your voices, like merry bells, join loud and clear in the grand chorus of liberty—'We are free,' 'We are free,'—until listening, you hear its echoes coming back from every cabin in the land—'We are free,' 'We are free.' "

745.34 "The Year of Jubilee."] A slave spiritual.

Index

This book is set in 10 point Linotron Galliard, a face designed for photocomposition by Matthew Carter and based on the sixteenth-century face Granjon. The paper is acid-free lightweight opaque and meets the requirements for permanence of the American National Standards Institute. The binding material is Brillianta, a woven rayon cloth made by Van Heek-Scholco Textielfabrieken, Holland. Composition by Dedicated Business Services. Printing and binding by Edwards Brothers Malloy, Ann Arbor. Designed by Bruce Campbell.

THE LIBRARY OF AMERICA SERIES

The Library of America fosters appreciation and pride in America's literary heritage by publishing, and keeping permanently in print, authoritative editions of America's best and most significant writing. An independent nonprofit organization, it was founded in 1979 with seed funding from the National Endowment for the Humanities and the Ford Foundation.

1. Herman Melville: *Typee, Omoo, Mardi*
2. Nathaniel Hawthorne: *Tales and Sketches*
3. Walt Whitman: *Poetry and Prose*
4. Harriet Beecher Stowe: *Three Novels*
5. Mark Twain: *Mississippi Writings*
6. Jack London: *Novels and Stories*
7. Jack London: *Novels and Social Writings*
8. William Dean Howells: *Novels 1875–1886*
9. Herman Melville: *Redburn, White-Jacket, Moby-Dick*
10. Nathaniel Hawthorne: *Collected Novels*
11. Francis Parkman: *France and England in North America*, vol. I
12. Francis Parkman: *France and England in North America*, vol. II
13. Henry James: *Novels 1871–1880*
14. Henry Adams: *Novels, Mont Saint Michel, The Education*
15. Ralph Waldo Emerson: *Essays and Lectures*
16. Washington Irving: *History, Tales and Sketches*
17. Thomas Jefferson: *Writings*
18. Stephen Crane: *Prose and Poetry*
19. Edgar Allan Poe: *Poetry and Tales*
20. Edgar Allan Poe: *Essays and Reviews*
21. Mark Twain: *The Innocents Abroad, Roughing It*
22. Henry James: *Literary Criticism: Essays, American & English Writers*
23. Henry James: *Literary Criticism: European Writers & The Prefaces*
24. Herman Melville: *Pierre, Israel Potter, The Confidence-Man, Tales & Billy Budd*
25. William Faulkner: *Novels 1930–1935*
26. James Fenimore Cooper: *The Leatherstocking Tales*, vol. I
27. James Fenimore Cooper: *The Leatherstocking Tales*, vol. II
28. Henry David Thoreau: *A Week, Walden, The Maine Woods, Cape Cod*
29. Henry James: *Novels 1881–1886*
30. Edith Wharton: *Novels*
31. Henry Adams: *History of the U.S. during the Administrations of Jefferson*
32. Henry Adams: *History of the U.S. during the Administrations of Madison*
33. Frank Norris: *Novels and Essays*
34. W.E.B. Du Bois: *Writings*
35. Willa Cather: *Early Novels and Stories*
36. Theodore Dreiser: *Sister Carrie, Jennie Gerhardt, Twelve Men*

37a. Benjamin Franklin: *Silence Dogood, The Busy-Body, & Early Writings*

37b. Benjamin Franklin: *Autobiography, Poor Richard, & Later Writings*

38. William James: *Writings 1902–1910*
39. Flannery O'Connor: *Collected Works*
40. Eugene O'Neill: *Complete Plays 1913–1920*
41. Eugene O'Neill: *Complete Plays 1920–1931*
42. Eugene O'Neill: *Complete Plays 1932–1943*
43. Henry James: *Novels 1886–1890*
44. William Dean Howells: *Novels 1886–1888*
45. Abraham Lincoln: *Speeches and Writings 1832–1858*
46. Abraham Lincoln: *Speeches and Writings 1859–1865*
47. Edith Wharton: *Novellas and Other Writings*
48. William Faulkner: *Novels 1936–1940*
49. Willa Cather: *Later Novels*
50. Ulysses S. Grant: *Memoirs and Selected Letters*
51. William Tecumseh Sherman: *Memoirs*
52. Washington Irving: *Bracebridge Hall, Tales of a Traveller, The Alhambra*
53. Francis Parkman: *The Oregon Trail, The Conspiracy of Pontiac*
54. James Fenimore Cooper: *Sea Tales: The Pilot, The Red Rover*
55. Richard Wright: *Early Works*
56. Richard Wright: *Later Works*
57. Willa Cather: *Stories, Poems, and Other Writings*
58. William James: *Writings 1878–1899*
59. Sinclair Lewis: *Main Street & Babbitt*
60. Mark Twain: *Collected Tales, Sketches, Speeches, & Essays 1852–1890*
61. Mark Twain: *Collected Tales, Sketches, Speeches, & Essays 1891–1910*
62. *The Debate on the Constitution: Part One*
63. *The Debate on the Constitution: Part Two*
64. Henry James: *Collected Travel Writings: Great Britain & America*
65. Henry James: *Collected Travel Writings: The Continent*

66. *American Poetry: The Nineteenth Century*, Vol. 1
67. *American Poetry: The Nineteenth Century*, Vol. 2
68. Frederick Douglass: *Autobiographies*
69. Sarah Orne Jewett: *Novels and Stories*
70. Ralph Waldo Emerson: *Collected Poems and Translations*
71. Mark Twain: *Historical Romances*
72. John Steinbeck: *Novels and Stories 1932–1937*
73. William Faulkner: *Novels 1942–1954*
74. Zora Neale Hurston: *Novels and Stories*
75. Zora Neale Hurston: *Folklore, Memoirs, and Other Writings*
76. Thomas Paine: *Collected Writings*
77. *Reporting World War II: American Journalism 1938–1944*
78. *Reporting World War II: American Journalism 1944–1946*
79. Raymond Chandler: *Stories and Early Novels*
80. Raymond Chandler: *Later Novels and Other Writings*
81. Robert Frost: *Collected Poems, Prose, & Plays*
82. Henry James: *Complete Stories 1892–1898*
83. Henry James: *Complete Stories 1898–1910*
84. William Bartram: *Travels and Other Writings*
85. John Dos Passos: *U.S.A.*
86. John Steinbeck: *The Grapes of Wrath and Other Writings 1936–1941*
87. Vladimir Nabokov: *Novels and Memoirs 1941–1951*
88. Vladimir Nabokov: *Novels 1955–1962*
89. Vladimir Nabokov: *Novels 1969–1974*
90. James Thurber: *Writings and Drawings*
91. George Washington: *Writings*
92. John Muir: *Nature Writings*
93. Nathanael West: *Novels and Other Writings*
94. *Crime Novels: American Noir of the 1930s and 40s*
95. *Crime Novels: American Noir of the 1950s*
96. Wallace Stevens: *Collected Poetry and Prose*
97. James Baldwin: *Early Novels and Stories*
98. James Baldwin: *Collected Essays*
99. Gertrude Stein: *Writings 1903–1932*
100. Gertrude Stein: *Writings 1932–1946*
101. Eudora Welty: *Complete Novels*
102. Eudora Welty: *Stories, Essays, & Memoir*
103. Charles Brockden Brown: *Three Gothic Novels*
104. *Reporting Vietnam: American Journalism 1959–1969*
105. *Reporting Vietnam: American Journalism 1969–1975*
106. Henry James: *Complete Stories 1874–1884*
107. Henry James: *Complete Stories 1884–1891*
108. *American Sermons: The Pilgrims to Martin Luther King Jr.*
109. James Madison: *Writings*
110. Dashiell Hammett: *Complete Novels*
111. Henry James: *Complete Stories 1864–1874*
112. William Faulkner: *Novels 1957–1962*
113. John James Audubon: *Writings & Drawings*
114. *Slave Narratives*
115. *American Poetry: The Twentieth Century*, Vol. 1
116. *American Poetry: The Twentieth Century*, Vol. 2
117. F. Scott Fitzgerald: *Novels and Stories 1920–1922*
118. Henry Wadsworth Longfellow: *Poems and Other Writings*
119. Tennessee Williams: *Plays 1937–1955*
120. Tennessee Williams: *Plays 1957–1980*
121. Edith Wharton: *Collected Stories 1891–1910*
122. Edith Wharton: *Collected Stories 1911–1937*
123. *The American Revolution: Writings from the War of Independence*
124. Henry David Thoreau: *Collected Essays and Poems*
125. Dashiell Hammett: *Crime Stories and Other Writings*
126. Dawn Powell: *Novels 1930–1942*
127. Dawn Powell: *Novels 1944–1962*
128. Carson McCullers: *Complete Novels*
129. Alexander Hamilton: *Writings*
130. Mark Twain: *The Gilded Age and Later Novels*
131. Charles W. Chesnutt: *Stories, Novels, and Essays*
132. John Steinbeck: *Novels 1942–1952*
133. Sinclair Lewis: *Arrowsmith, Elmer Gantry, Dodsworth*
134. Paul Bowles: *The Sheltering Sky, Let It Come Down, The Spider's House*
135. Paul Bowles: *Collected Stories & Later Writings*
136. Kate Chopin: *Complete Novels & Stories*
137. *Reporting Civil Rights: American Journalism 1941–1963*
138. *Reporting Civil Rights: American Journalism 1963–1973*
139. Henry James: *Novels 1896–1899*
140. Theodore Dreiser: *An American Tragedy*
141. Saul Bellow: *Novels 1944–1953*
142. John Dos Passos: *Novels 1920–1925*

143. John Dos Passos: *Travel Books and Other Writings*
144. Ezra Pound: *Poems and Translations*
145. James Weldon Johnson: *Writings*
146. Washington Irving: *Three Western Narratives*
147. Alexis de Tocqueville: *Democracy in America*
148. James T. Farrell: *Studs Lonigan: A Trilogy*
149. Isaac Bashevis Singer: *Collected Stories I*
150. Isaac Bashevis Singer: *Collected Stories II*
151. Isaac Bashevis Singer: *Collected Stories III*
152. Kaufman & Co.: *Broadway Comedies*
153. Theodore Roosevelt: *The Rough Riders, An Autobiography*
154. Theodore Roosevelt: *Letters and Speeches*
155. H. P. Lovecraft: *Tales*
156. Louisa May Alcott: *Little Women, Little Men, Jo's Boys*
157. Philip Roth: *Novels & Stories 1959–1962*
158. Philip Roth: *Novels 1967–1972*
159. James Agee: *Let Us Now Praise Famous Men, A Death in the Family*
160. James Agee: *Film Writing & Selected Journalism*
161. Richard Henry Dana Jr.: *Two Years Before the Mast & Other Voyages*
162. Henry James: *Novels 1901–1902*
163. Arthur Miller: *Collected Plays 1944–1961*
164. William Faulkner: *Novels 1926–1929*
165. Philip Roth: *Novels 1973–1977*
166. *American Speeches: Part One*
167. *American Speeches: Part Two*
168. Hart Crane: *Complete Poems & Selected Letters*
169. Saul Bellow: *Novels 1956–1964*
170. John Steinbeck: *Travels with Charley and Later Novels*
171. Capt. John Smith: *Writings with Other Narratives*
172. Thornton Wilder: *Collected Plays & Writings on Theater*
173. Philip K. Dick: *Four Novels of the 1960s*
174. Jack Kerouac: *Road Novels 1957–1960*
175. Philip Roth: *Zuckerman Bound*
176. Edmund Wilson: *Literary Essays & Reviews of the 1920s & 30s*
177. Edmund Wilson: *Literary Essays & Reviews of the 1930s & 40s*
178. *American Poetry: The 17th & 18th Centuries*
179. William Maxwell: *Early Novels & Stories*
180. Elizabeth Bishop: *Poems, Prose, & Letters*
181. A. J. Liebling: *World War II Writings*
182s. *American Earth: Environmental Writing Since Thoreau*
183. Philip K. Dick: *Five Novels of the 1960s & 70s*
184. William Maxwell: *Later Novels & Stories*
185. Philip Roth: *Novels & Other Narratives 1986–1991*
186. Katherine Anne Porter: *Collected Stories & Other Writings*
187. John Ashbery: *Collected Poems 1956–1987*
188. John Cheever: *Collected Stories & Other Writings*
189. John Cheever: *Complete Novels*
190. Lafcadio Hearn: *American Writings*
191. A. J. Liebling: *The Sweet Science & Other Writings*
192s. *The Lincoln Anthology: Great Writers on His Life and Legacy from 1860 to Now*
193. Philip K. Dick: *VALIS & Later Novels*
194. Thornton Wilder: *The Bridge of San Luis Rey and Other Novels 1926–1948*
195. Raymond Carver: *Collected Stories*
196. *American Fantastic Tales: Terror and the Uncanny from Poe to the Pulps*
197. *American Fantastic Tales: Terror and the Uncanny from the 1940s to Now*
198. John Marshall: *Writings*
199s. *The Mark Twain Anthology: Great Writers on His Life and Works*
200. Mark Twain: *A Tramp Abroad, Following the Equator, Other Travels*
201. Ralph Waldo Emerson: *Selected Journals 1820–1842*
202. Ralph Waldo Emerson: *Selected Journals 1841–1877*
203. *The American Stage: Writing on Theater from Washington Irving to Tony Kushner*
204. Shirley Jackson: *Novels & Stories*
205. Philip Roth: *Novels 1993–1995*
206. H. L. Mencken: *Prejudices: First, Second, and Third Series*
207. H. L. Mencken: *Prejudices: Fourth, Fifth, and Sixth Series*
208. John Kenneth Galbraith: *The Affluent Society and Other Writings 1952–1967*
209. Saul Bellow: *Novels 1970–1982*
210. Lynd Ward: *Gods' Man, Madman's Drum, Wild Pilgrimage*
211. Lynd Ward: *Prelude to a Million Years, Song Without Words, Vertigo*
212. *The Civil War: The First Year Told by Those Who Lived It*
213. John Adams: *Revolutionary Writings 1755–1775*
214. John Adams: *Revolutionary Writings 1775–1783*
215. Henry James: *Novels 1903–1911*
216. Kurt Vonnegut: *Novels & Stories 1963–1973*

217. *Harlem Renaissance: Five Novels of the 1920s*
218. *Harlem Renaissance: Four Novels of the 1930s*
219. Ambrose Bierce: *The Devil's Dictionary, Tales, & Memoirs*
220. Philip Roth: *The American Trilogy 1997–2000*
221. *The Civil War: The Second Year Told by Those Who Lived It*
222. Barbara W. Tuchman: *The Guns of August & The Proud Tower*
223. Arthur Miller: *Collected Plays 1964–1982*
224. Thornton Wilder: *The Eighth Day, Theophilus North, Autobiographical Writings*
225. David Goodis: *Five Noir Novels of the 1940s & 50s*
226. Kurt Vonnegut: *Novels & Stories 1950–1962*
227. *American Science Fiction: Four Classic Novels 1953–1956*
228. *American Science Fiction: Five Classic Novels 1956–1958*
229. Laura Ingalls Wilder: *The Little House Books, Volume One*
230. Laura Ingalls Wilder: *The Little House Books, Volume Two*
231. Jack Kerouac: *Collected Poems*
232. *The War of 1812: Writings from America's Second War of Independence*
233. *American Antislavery Writings: Colonial Beginnings to Emancipation*
234. *The Civil War: The Third Year Told by Those Who Lived It*
235. Sherwood Anderson: *Collected Stories*
236. Philip Roth: *Novels 2001–2007*
237. Philip Roth: *Nemeses*
238. Aldo Leopold: *A Sand County Almanac & Other Writings on Ecology and Conservation*
239. May Swenson: *Collected Poems*
240. W. S. Merwin: *Collected Poems 1952–1993*
241. W. S. Merwin: *Collected Poems 1996–2011*
242. John Updike: *Collected Early Stories*
243. John Updike: *Collected Later Stories*
244. Ring Lardner: *Stories & Other Writings*
245. Jonathan Edwards: *Writings from the Great Awakening*
246. Susan Sontag: *Essays of the 1960s & 70s*
247. William Wells Brown: *Clotel & Other Writings*
248. Bernard Malamud: *Novels and Stories of the 1940s & 50s*
249. Bernard Malamud: *Novels and Stories of the 1960s*
250. *The Civil War: The Final Year Told by Those Who lived It*
251. *Shakespeare in America: An Anthology from the Revolution to Now*
252. Kurt Vonnegut: *Novels 1976–1985*
253. *American Musicals 1927–1949: The Complete Books & Lyrics of Eight Broadway Classics*
254. *American Musicals 1950–1969: The Complete Books & Lyrics of Eight Broadway Classics*
255. Elmore Leonard: *Four Novels of the 1970s*
256. Louisa May Alcott: *Work, Eight Cousins, Rose in Bloom, Stories & Other Writings*
257. H. L. Mencken: *The Days Trilogy, Expanded Edition*
258. Virgil Thomson: *Music Chronicles 1940–1954*
259. *Art in America 1945–1970: Writings from the Age of Abstract Expressionism, Pop Art, and Minimalism*